P9-DBI-269

N

0   200 Miles

0   300 Kilometers

The American Horticultural Society
GARDENING MANUAL

THE AMERICAN HORTICULTURAL SOCIETY
GARDENING MANUAL

A DORLING KINDERSLEY BOOK

A DORLING KINDERSLEY PUBLISHING BOOK
www.dk.com

Senior Editor Gillian Roberts
Senior Art Editor Alison Lotinga

Senior Managing Editor Mary-Clare Jerram
Senior Managing Art Editor Lee Griffiths

Principal Editors Annelise Evans, Simon Maughan, Lesley Riley
Principal Art Editors Roger Daniels, Martin Hendry,
Miranda Kennedy, Kevin Ryan, Ann Thompson

Media Resources Neale Chamberlain, Rachel Hilford, Charlotte Oster
Picture Research Sean Hunter

DTP Designers Louise Paddick, Louise Waller

Production Ruth Charlton, Julian Deeming

US Publishing Team
Senior Editor Ray Rogers
Editorial Director LaVonne Carlson
Publisher Sean Moore

First American Edition, 2000
2 4 6 8 10 9 7 5 3 1

Published in the United states by
Dorling Kindersley, Inc., 95 Madison Avenue, New York, New York 10016

First published in Great Britain in 2000 by
Dorling Kindersley Limited, 9 Henrietta Street, London WC2E 8PS

Dorling Kindersley Publishing offers special discounts for bulk purchases for sales promotions
or premiums. Specific, large-quantity needs can be met with special editions, including
personalized covers, excerpts of exisiting guides, and corporate imprints.
For more information, contact Special Markets Department,
Dorling Kindersley, Inc., 95 Madison Avenue, New York, NY 10016 Fax: 800-600-9098

Library of Congress Cataloging-in-Publication Data

The American Horticultural Society gardening manual.
   p.cm
   Published simultaneously under title: The Royal Horticultural Society gardening manual.
   ISBN 0-7894-5952-3
   1. Gardening I. Title: Gardening manual. II. American Horticultural Society.
SB453 .A67 2000
635--dc21

00-022644

CONTRIBUTORS

PART ONE: PLANNING YOUR GARDEN
David Joyce

PART TWO: MAKING AND LOOKING AFTER YOUR GARDEN

Patios and Paths
Lin Hawthorne

Lawns and Ground Cover
Alison Copland

Boundaries, Divisions, and Structures
Pamela Brown, Claire Calman, Joanna Chisholm

Beds and Borders
Alison Copland, Lin Hawthorne

Containers and Raised Beds
Claire Calman, Alison Copland

Ornamental Trees in the Garden
Claire Calman, Alison Copland

Water Gardening Lin Hawthorne

Herbs in the Garden and their Uses Claire Calman

The Edible Garden
Louise Abbott, Lin Hawthorne

Looking After the Garden
Alison Copland

Dealing with Weeds and Plant Problems
Louise Abbott, Lin Hawthorne

PART THREE: WHAT LOOKS GOOD WHEN
Louise Abbott, Fiona Wild

PART FOUR: WHAT TO DO WHEN
Annelise Evans

GLOSSARY
Joanna Chisholm, Lin Hawthorne

INDEX
Lynn Bresler

Text film output by Graphical Innovations, London
Reproduced by Colourscan, Singapore
Printed and bound by MOHN media and Mohndruck GmbH, Germany

See our complete catalog at
www.dk.com

CONTENTS

DEALING WITH WEEDS AND PLANT PROBLEMS

PART THREE

WHAT LOOKS GOOD WHEN

PART FOUR

WHAT TO DO WHEN

SEASONS

In this book, the gardening year is divided into twelve seasons that correspond to calendar months, as shown below.

Early spring: March
Midspring: April
Late spring: May
Early summer: June
Midsummer: July
Late summer: August
Early autumn: September
Midautumn: October
Late autumn: November
Early winter: December
Midwinter: January
Late winter: February

COLD HARDINESS

The cold hardiness of plants in Part Three is given as a range of zones as defined on the United States Department of Agriculture Plant Hardiness Zone Map (see the end papers), or as the minimum temperature the plants will tolerate before experiencing cold damage. This information is given as a guide and is not absolute. Your local soil and climate conditions, microclimates throughout your garden, varietal differences, and the cultural practices you follow ultimately determine which plants will survive for you.

Ultimate height is shown as ↕ and spread as ↔

PART ONE

PLANNING YOUR GARDEN

A GARDEN OF YOUR OWN: CHOICES AND CONSIDERATIONS

WHAT MAKES A GARDEN?

SO POWERFUL ARE THE impressions made by flowers and foliage, it is tempting to think of the garden as essentially a place in which plants grow. Gardens are, however, first and foremost for people, whose preferences and requirements can be very different. You might relish the idea of honing your gardening skills and making a special collection of plants. But creating a pleasant, low-maintenance setting for outdoor living is an equally legitimate ambition. At its most rewarding, a garden is a highly personal creation, one that happily reconciles your idea of what is best for you with the potential of the plot that is available.

WHAT YOU NEED TO THINK ABOUT

The way you want to use the garden area affects the way you organize the space within its boundaries. This will be reflected in the relative weight given to hard landscaping, such as paving and walls, and the planted areas, or soft landscaping. If, for example, you want the garden to be an outdoor room for entertaining, you will probably need a large area of paving or decking. If your passion is plants or you want to grow fruit or vegetables, you might make do with narrow paths criss-crossing planted areas. A pond might be high on your list if you wish to attract wildlife into your property.

Once you have thought through how you want to use your garden, and how best to exploit the site, you can start planning how you want it to look.

△ GOOD USE OF SPACE
This property combines several elements into a visually integrated and functional whole: uniform lawn, colorful borders, and a pleasant area for sitting and dining. Even though it is not a large space, it provides its owners with a variety of gardening experiences and attractive areas for their enjoyment.

◁ EASY AND BEAUTIFUL
A landscape does not require a wide variety of showy plants or large amounts of maintenance to be highly pleasing. This green garden brings grass, groundcovers, and trees together to create a restful and soothing haven that does not demand a great deal of time to ensure it looks good throughout the year.

◁ A Plant Lover's Garden

The mix of shapes, textures, and colors in this garden shows that it has been created by someone with a broad love of plants. Choosing plants with good shape and form adds interest to the garden well beyond the flowering season.

△ A Natural Approach

Allowing plants to naturalize as they might in the wild can bring great satisfaction. Here, snake's-head fritillaries (Fritillaria meleagris) grow and bloom naturally among grass and trees as they would in their native habitats in Europe.

△ A Means of Self-expression

There are many ways in which the garden can declare the taste and interests of its creator. The layout, the choice of built features, and the way they are decorated can all bear the gardener's personal stamp. So, too, can the choice and arrangement of foliage and flowering plants.

△ A Source of Produce

Some gardeners value above all the chance to grow vegetables, fruit, and herbs. Even if the operation is scaled down to a few containers, the output can be worthwhile. With imaginative planting and design, the productive garden can be ornamental as well as practical.

△ The Challenge of Scale

There is no need to think you need a vast amount of space to create a successful garden. Some designs do extend over broad landscapes, but rewarding gardens, such as this arrangement of container-grown plants, can be made on a tiny plot or even on a balcony or roof terrace.

FINDING YOUR OWN STYLE

As well as reflecting the uses you are going to make of your garden, the design should be developed in a style with which you feel comfortable. Your choice, even in a small garden, can range from severe order to jungle effect, while in between taking in ideas from gardens of different cultures and climatic regions.

A distinction is often made between formal and informal styles of gardening, but in effect the difference is not clear-cut. The cottage garden, the inspiration of many highly sophisticated 20th-century gardens, appeals because of its happy jumble of plants, many of them remarkable survivors of changing fashions. The plants obscure the fact that the traditional cottage garden often has a simple geometric layout, which also underpins classically formal designs.

You need to weigh up carefully the pros and cons of the style you think might suit your garden. You may be drawn by the austere beauty of a minimalist garden, but is it suitable for a growing family? The idea of a wild garden is seductive, but it cannot be achieved simply by throwing seeds of pretty plants on the lawn. The best solution may be a style that you find sympathetic but that is also labor-saving.

△ **MINIMALIST APPROACH**
Carefully chosen rocks set in gravel, a patch of moss, and a background of trees and shrubs of varying foliage qualities make a powerfully designed garden, despite its spare content. Modern gardens such as this have their origins in traditional Japanese designs.

◁ **NATURALISTIC PLANTING**
An informal planting style using herbaceous perennials suited to the growing conditions is an environmentally friendly approach to gardening that takes its inspiration from plant communities in the wild. The textures of plants such as grasses count for as much as flower color. In contrast to the more rigid herbaceous border, this makes for relatively low-maintenance gardening.

◁ **A WILDFLOWER GARDEN**
The loss of natural habitats and the wildflowers that make them beautiful has encouraged conservation-oriented gardening. A meadow effect can be created with wild flowers growing in turf on soil that is low in fertility. The mowing regime must allow the wildflowers to set seed before being cut.

COTTAGE-GARDEN INSPIRATION ▷
The bright flowers of poppies (Papaver) crowding in on a brick path convey the style of a traditional cottage garden. This relies on the use of familiar flowers tightly packed together, often in close company with herbs and vegetables, but it can be interpreted in many different ways.

THE FORMAL VOCABULARY

For its enduring appeal, the formal garden relies on calm order. This is usually expressed in a balanced treatment of space, with symmetry in the details. The most common symmetrical arrangement is simple pairing, for example of matching containers of plants flanking a doorway or seat. An avenue, often of trees, is an extension of pairing and gives a strong formal structure to a drive or path.

Clipped plants, as hedges or as topiary, reinforce the formal tone of a garden, as do trained plants of many kinds, including fruit trees in restricted shapes. A much gentler approach to formality can be created simply by establishing rhythms in the garden, with a conspicuous planting repeated at intervals.

FORMAL TONE ▷
The neat lawn and matching paved areas at either end, clipped bushes, and symmetrical arrangement of details give this garden a clean — but not forbidding — formal tone.

MOOD AND THEME

The character of the hard landscaping and the planting both influence the mood of the garden. Colorful containers and mosaics, for example, make a much bolder impact than simple shapes in terracotta or stone.

A garden filled with foliage in subtle shades of green will have a very different feeling from one in which strong colors dominate. Yet another effect, one of airy lightness, could be achieved using white and very pale shades in a narrowly defined color scheme.

The choice of plants can also convey the idea of a garden from another climate. An impression of Mediterranean heat or a jungle effect with bamboos and other leafy plants can be created even in cool temperate gardens.

△ **SCULPTURE IN THE GARDEN**
Sculpture and interesting objects, including pieces of driftwood, unusually shaped rocks, and items of scrap, can help to establish a mood or tone. They are usually placed prominently at focal points but can also be effective in a more discreet location.

◁ **STRONG COLORS**
The tulip season lasts from late winter to late spring, and the wide range of single and mixed colors makes these bulbs useful for bold effects. A fence, painted blue-green, intensifies a powerful color scheme contrasting orange and near-black tulips.

△ **A MEDITERRANEAN THEME**
In a tableau that suggests a Mediterranean garden, the trumpet creeper (Campsis), with tubular orange flowers, makes a canopy over a collection of foliage and flowering plants, most of which are in containers.

THE CONTAINED GARDEN

AN ENCLOSED SPACE, separated by walls from the surrounding landscape and made distinct inside by its planting and design, is one of the oldest types of garden. Its original appeal may have been as a well-watered, cool, and green retreat from a harsh natural world. Now the harsh world outside is much more likely to be urban, and the relief that is needed is from the bustle and noise of the city. The typical modern version of this garden is contained by the walls of neighboring properties, or lodged above ground on a balcony or rooftop. The scale is small, but this can be made into a virtue by plantings that create a sense of privacy and intimacy. At its most extreme, the contained garden has no open ground but is simply a space magically transformed by container-grown plants.

A COURTYARD GARDEN

Although walls hem in a courtyard, an ingenious layout and well-chosen plants can help create a sense of space. Here, exuberant planting disguises the proximity of the walls and makes a lush green setting for an intimate and pleasant retreat.

CORNER DETAIL ▽

Small corners that are not needed for access can be filled with plants requiring little maintenance. Another attractive solution is to use the corner as a setting for an ornament. Here, a pair of pleasingly shaped vessels, raised on a platform, is complemented by minimalist planting.
SEE ALSO: Focal Points, p.29

A WALLED GARDEN

An arched opening in a brightly colored, rendered wall gives a glimpse of a brick-paved garden with low, clipped hedges and generous planting. This is a variation on the traditional walled garden in mellow brick. The epitome of the warm and sheltered garden is often laid out formally, with fruit trees, wall shrubs, and climbers planted to take advantage of reflected heat.

CONSERVING WATER

In areas of low rainfall, or when growing lots of plants in containers, watering can be a major task. Many problems can be overcome by selecting plants that tolerate drought. Other steps should be taken to make the most of the available water.

• When watering, give priority to new plants and to plants in containers.

• Cover the surface of soil or soil mix with a mulch to slow water loss: gravel is an effective topping in containers.

• Add water-retaining crystals or granules to soil mix in containers.

• When it is impossible to water regularly by hand, install a trickle or drip-feed irrigation system that incorporates a timing device.

ORNAMENTAL FEATURES △

Two pieces of metal sculpture – a wall-mounted relief and a free-standing head – make arresting focal points in this courtyard, despite their sober coloring. In small gardens, ornaments such as masks and reliefs that can be mounted on walls have the advantage of leaving the limited ground surface uncluttered. Here, the almost two-dimensional giant profile, looming out of richly textured foliage, takes up surprisingly little space and adds a surreal touch.
SEE ALSO: Focal Points, p.29

OUTDOOR FURNITURE ▽

Even in this small and densely planted courtyard, there is space for a weatherproof circular table of generous size. It almost fills the seating area by the pool, but there is enough room to accommodate five or six people comfortably. Lightweight folding chairs can easily be stored away when not in use.

SEE ALSO: Leisure Elements, pp.34–35

PLANTING FOR PRIVACY ▽

Containers packed with colorful impatiens provide bright splashes of color, but the emphasis in this garden is on foliage. Wall-trained shrubs, bamboos, and palms, including a paddle-leaved banana (*Musa*), create the impression of an intimate and private zone carved out of lush greenery.

SEE ALSO: Plants for a Purpose, pp.38–41

HANGING BASKETS △

Hanging baskets suspended from wall-mounted brackets are a useful way of introducing colorful planting to courtyard gardens where there is little ground space for containers. Once the initial display is over, they can easily be replanted, providing interest through much of the year – even in winter in mild climates.

SEE ALSO: A Place for Plants, pp.42–43

◁ WATER FEATURE

To underline the tropical character of this courtyard, cooling water overflows from a raised pool to trickle over large stones in the lower basin. The water, circulated by a submersible electric pump, provides a constant and soothing murmur.

SEE ALSO: Water Features, pp.32–33

◁ HARD SURFACES

The clean, hard surfaces that cover a relatively small proportion of the garden's area give access from the house to the space furnished for outdoor entertaining. The seating area is defined by stone paving slabs, and the access route by lengths of wooden decking.

SEE ALSO: Surfaces, pp.24–27

A ROOFTOP GARDEN

An L-shaped arrangement of benches makes a pleasant corner that is lightly sheltered and screened by plants growing in containers attached to the balustrade. The informal planting sets a relaxed tone; wooden decking makes a neat and clean surface underfoot; and the benches are made more comfortable by padded cushions covered in weather-resistant fabric. The weight-bearing capacity of flat roofs and balconies may make it necessary to use lightweight materials such as plastic and fiberglass for standing containers. To prevent their being dislodged by wind, all containers must be well secured.

THE FAMILY GARDEN

A SUCCESSFUL FAMILY GARDEN is a happy compromise between the competing claims of adults and children. The ideal is a garden with secure boundaries where plants have their place, but where there is also room for children to be boisterously active and for adults to relax. Although practical and safety considerations may be paramount, the garden can be attractively laid out and imaginatively planted. Needs change as the family grows up. From the outset it is worth thinking about how you might develop the garden, perhaps with more ambitious planting, when children's interests have expanded beyond play equipment.

ONE GARDEN FOR ALL

A "borrowed" background of leafy trees makes an attractive setting for a garden designed to balance the interests of adults and children. A furnished paved area near the house leads to a utility lawn flanked by plant-filled borders with ornamental features and a set of swings. At the far end, the gazebo, sitting on the center line, emphasizes the garden's underlying symmetry and its unifying and bold color scheme.

ROBUST PLANTING ▷
Tough perennials, bulbs, shrubs, and climbers fill the borders either side of a hard-working lawn, which serves as a play area. A Chusan palm (*Trachycarpus fortunei*), with distinctive fan leaves, makes an off-center focus. The vibrancy of the container plantings on the patio stands up to the strong colors of both furniture and features.

SUNKEN SANDBOX △
This wood-framed sandbox has been positioned so that playing children can be easily observed from the house or from the outdoor seating area. The rim helps prevent sand from being scattered and also provides a safe seat. SEE ALSO: Leisure Elements, pp.34–35

◁ PLAY EQUIPMENT

Climbing equipment and play areas that offer children an enjoyable challenge must be solidly built and designed with safety in mind. The footings should be on well-drained ground. A thick topping of shredded bark gives a relatively soft landing, when needed.
SEE ALSO: Leisure Elements, pp.34–35

◁ SWINGS

Swings, here matching the garden's bright color theme, are a strong draw for young children. They can be removed later on, when they are no longer required, without leaving a serious gap in this garden's design.

◁ PATIO AREA

Quarry tiles, decorated and laid with two contrasting patterns, provide an easily cleaned and firm surface for family activities, including eating outdoors. Planted pots soften the effect of the large tiled expanse.
SEE ALSO: Surfaces, pp.24–27

PLAYING SAFE

Special precautions have to be taken to be sure a garden is safe for children.

• Make boundaries secure, to prevent youngsters from straying onto busy roads.

• Site play areas where they can be easily supervised from house windows.

• Avoid growing plants with sharp thorns and those known to be toxic.

• Be aware of the danger of open water, even when it is shallow.

• Store tools and garden chemicals securely out of reach of inquisitive hands.

◁ FLOWER PATCH

Children feel they have a stake in the garden when they are allocated a decent piece of ground to themselves. To sustain their delight they usually need some unobtrusive help in growing plants that give quick results. Phenomenal growth and large flower heads make sunflowers (*Helianthus annuus*) firm favorites for a child's patch. Easy vegetables, such as radishes and looseleaf lettuces, are also good choices.

A PLAYGROUND GARDEN

As children grow older, their play tends to become more exuberant, and it often pays to dedicate a part of the garden to them. This sheltered activity area consists of a broad expanse of durable grass. Brightly colored play equipment is arranged so that there is still plenty of room in which to run about without the risk of collisions. The structures are light enough to be moved to different positions should patches of grass wear thin. In time, when the equipment is no longer used, the area could revert to uncluttered lawn, or it could be transformed by beds planted with ornamentals.

THE LEISURE GARDEN

FOR MANY WHO lead busy lives, juggling all manner of demands on their free time, the ideal garden is one that provides a pleasant setting for the house without presenting too many challenges. It is a matter of finding the right balance between the time you spend enjoying the garden – whether relaxing in it or simply viewing it from inside – and the hours you take to maintain it. Hard surfaces are less effort to look after than beds and borders, but even these can be planted with resilient, ground-covering ornamentals needing little care and attention to keep them looking good.

A GARDEN FOR RELAXATION

A long, narrow garden has been divided lengthwise to create three distinct areas, needing varying degrees of attention. Nearest the house is a paved outdoor room. At a higher level, at the far end, is an area laid as lawn. The terraced section in the middle of the garden, with formal beds and containers, is the most labor intensive but is small enough to make it manageable.

SIMPLE PLANTING ▷

Trees, shrubs, and climbers soften the boundary walls, but most of the planting is concentrated in the terraced central section of the garden, some of it in containers. The matching lower beds are outlined in dwarf boxwood (*Buxus sempervirens* 'Suffruticosa'), reinforcing the garden's formal tone, but the low-maintenance planting at the next level is more naturalistic.

SEE ALSO: Plants for a Purpose, pp.38–41; A Place for Plants, pp.42–43

△ SWIMMING POOL

A terraced site has here been used to accommodate a boldly designed swimming pool of irregular outline that has shallow and deep areas. Above the white retaining wall is a terrace for sunbathing, which is surrounded by neat planting and dominated by a giant amphora. The pump house, painted blue, circulates the pool water via a waterfall.

SEE ALSO: Leisure Elements, pp.34–35

SEATING AREA △

Two benches are set at right angles to one another, making the most of sun throughout much of the day. The crisp white of the furniture and its neat arrangement help define the garden's formal style. A looser arrangement of tables and chairs would give a garden with this structure a quite different, more relaxed appearance.

SEE ALSO: Leisure Elements, pp.34–35

PROVIDING SHADE

To be enjoyed when the weather is hot, a garden needs areas of cool shade. It may take years for trees to grow large enough to cast useful shade, but structures can be quickly covered by climbers.

• Train climbers over pergolas and arbors to create shady walks and seats.

• Plant trees with light foliage, such as the thornless honeylocust (*Gleditsia triacanthos* varieties), to provide areas of dappled shade.

• Use sun umbrellas to shade furniture that is moved about.

◁ QUALITY LAWN

Here, the lawn will not be subjected to heavy wear but can be enjoyed for its soft, springy texture underfoot and, when viewed from the upper windows of the house, as a calm, green extension of the garden. Regular cutting, a task made simple by the rectangular shape, will help make sure the lawn stays in good condition.
SEE ALSO: Surfaces, pp.24–25

◁ STAGED CONTAINERS

Two flights of steps invite a leisurely walk to explore the different areas of the garden. They can also serve as a tiered stage for plant-filled containers, to give an unchanging display or one that reflects the seasons.
SEE ALSO: Surfaces, pp.26–27

BARBECUE ▽

Although its purpose is utilitarian, a built-in barbecue can be an attractive feature if constructed of materials that match other hard surfaces in the garden.
SEE ALSO: Leisure Elements, pp.34–35

△ THE PATIO AS THOROUGHFARE

As well as providing a clean, hard surface where tables and seating can be set out for relaxation and entertaining, a patio also usually serves as a thoroughfare from the house to other areas of the garden. Using the same flooring material – such as quarry tiles – throughout helps strengthen the link between indoor and outdoor areas.
SEE ALSO: Surfaces, pp.24–27

A SECLUDED GARDEN

The most important function of your garden may be to provide a haven, somewhere to escape from the outside world. A backdrop of dense foliage and crowded planting makes this garden seem a magically secluded place, especially when viewed from an inner compartment and framed by the uprights of a delicate pergola.

A GARDEN FOR ENTERTAINING

This paved area adjoining a house conveys the impression of an outdoor salon about to be filled by a bright and chattering crowd. The tone is set by the architectural framework, partly consisting of clipped hedges and trees, and the space for people to circulate with furniture thoughtfully arranged about it. Container-grown plants, as perfect as meticulous flower arrangements, add to the air of elegance.

THE EDIBLE GARDEN

A PRODUCTIVE GARDEN, providing seasonal supplies of vegetables, fruit, and herbs for the home, can take many forms. The traditional kitchen garden laid out on a generous scale, with beds separated by a grid of paths, can meet all your needs, but requires space and is labor intensive. An attractive solution where space is limited is a potager, a garden of edible plants – even fruit trees trained in restricted forms – arranged to make the most of their decorative qualities, perhaps with a few ornamentals to boost the color. Patches of vegetables can be set among the flowers in a mixed border, and many edible plants grow well in containers so that even a tiny garden, a patio, or a windowbox can be a source of fresh produce.

SUPPORTS FOR CLIMBERS ▽

Temporary supports are needed for climbing vegetables such as pole beans and for plants such as sweet peas (*Lathyrus odoratus*), grown to provide cut flowers for the house. Here, frames are made of paired bamboo stakes inserted into the ground at a steep angle and strengthened by horizontal stakes. Where space is at a premium, the supports can consist of a tepee of bamboo stakes or a tapered column of brushwood.

A KITCHEN GARDEN

Mown paths separate the large beds of a kitchen garden, in which vegetables are planted in regimented rows, with the ground between kept clear of weeds. Comparable quantities of food can be produced in a smaller area using narrower beds with more deeply cultivated soil, and access paths on each side. Crops are then close-planted in blocks, rather than in rows.

PLANTS IN ROWS ▷

In the traditional system of orderly planting, vegetables are grown in rectangular beds with wide spacing between rows, a method that allows easy access for cultivation. To make the best use of the space, fast-maturing salad crops can be sown between rows of slow-growing vegetables while these plants are still small.

△ PEAR ARCH

Most fruit trees are very decorative and some can be trained into compact shapes. Pears and apples are sometimes grown as espaliers, with several tiers of branches trained horizontally on either side of the trunk, or – as the pear trees here – grown over a series of metal arches.

A Decorative Edible Garden

Herbs, vegetables, and a compact apple tree are here grown together in a way that is as attractive as it is productive. The mauve globes of alliums, members of the onion family, appear over red chard – one of the most colorful vegetables – and yellow and orange pot marigolds (*Calendula officinalis*). Pot marigolds are herbs, now often grown as ornamentals; they self-seed freely. The traditional cottage garden, with its casual mixtures of decorative and edible plants, can be a useful source of ideas for your own plot.

◁ Mown Paths

Grass paths are an attractive way of dividing up the beds of a large kitchen garden, but they need regular cutting and can soon become reduced to mud in wet weather. Where paths get heavy use, particularly in a small garden, a hard surface, for example of brick, is a better choice.
See also: Surfaces, pp.24–27

◁ Aromatic Edging

Plants with aromatic leaves make a delightful edging to beds and borders, releasing their scent when brushed against; they are useful also for picking. Suitable herbs include hyssop, lavender, rosemary, and thyme. Here, rows of the purple-leaved sage (*Salvia officinalis* Purpurascens Group) run along each side of a grass path.
See also: Plants for a Purpose, pp.40–41

Herb Corner △

Herbs can be grown formally, in a bed of their own, or informally, among other plants. Many thrive in a sunny position with well-drained soil. They include garden thyme, seen above covered with purple flowers in early summer.

Good Management

Keeping a kitchen garden healthy and productive depends on good management.

• Maintain soil fertility, condition, and capacity to hold moisture by working in plenty of well-rotted organic matter, such as compost.

• In a dedicated vegetable garden, prevent the buildup of pests and diseases by rotating crops from one area to another each year.

• Destroy diseased plants, and compost fallen leaves and other soft plant material.

Vegetables in Containers

Climbing beans do well in deep containers, provided they have support, such as a tepee of stakes. For containers in exposed positions, for example on a balcony, salad leaves and early bush tomatoes are among the most suitable edible plants.

THE ENTHUSIAST'S GARDEN

THE ENTHUSIAST'S GARDEN has many interpretations, reflecting the interests and tastes of the individual gardener and the challenges of the site. What makes it stand out is almost invariably the quality of the planting. The gardener's enthusiasm is often shown by a passion for collecting rare, unusual, or even obvious kinds of plants (such as roses), but most imaginatively when it brings into the garden plants suitable for all its growing conditions. Plants are grouped according to their needs, in a way that is pleasing to the eye, the standard of cultivation is high, and there is a sense that the garden is not static, but ever evolving.

A HIGH-MAINTENANCE BORDER
The enthusiast's commitment, from ground preparation and planning to staking and deadheading, shows in this well-staged border, with a late-summer display of pink dahlias. A border in such a state of perfection is deeply satisfying, while for the dedicated gardener the work involved is also a source of pleasure.

◁ DUAL-PURPOSE GREENHOUSE
A greenhouse can be costly, but it is a considerable asset to – and excellent investment for – an avid gardener. Unheated greenhouses are mainly used to raise and grow on plants so that they are well advanced by the time you plant them out in the open garden. A heated greenhouse offers greater versatility, and its protected environment can be a permanent home for tender plants.
SEE ALSO: Garden Maintenance, pp.36–37

A GARDEN ON THE WILD SIDE
Labor-saving design and planting allows the avid gardener to make the best use of limited time. Naturalistic associations of plants requiring similar growing conditions – the sedums and grasses here are tolerant of drought – can make the most of foliage qualities as well as of flower color. Mulches of gravel or of well-rotted organic matter help to keep down weeds and retain moisture.

CONTRASTS OF FORM ▷
In a naturalistic association of plants, forms interlock as they do in wild plant communities. In this garden, a low skirt of silver-leaved plants, including *Senecio cineraria*, outlines clumps of grasses, mounds of sedums, and a spiky yucca.

EXTENDED SEASON ▷
The garnet and tawny colors of autumn, or the spare and graphic contrasts of winter, play just as important a part in the enthusiast's garden as the fresh and dazzling combinations of spring and summer.

FOLIAGE FOR TEXTURE ▷
A garden of rich and subtle effects relies on the interplay of different textures found among foliage, as well as on flower and foliage color. A stiffly jagged yucca framed by softly arching grasses stands out in this autumn garden against rigid vertical stems.
SEE ALSO: Plants for a Purpose, pp.38–39

STOCKING THE GARDEN

Filling a garden with plants bought from a nursery or garden center can be expensive, but raising them yourself – from seed or cuttings, for example – is a way of increasing stocks at very low cost.

• Join local and national horticultural societies to take advantage of exchange programs for seeds and plants and to participate in shows, where specialized nurseries usually sell interesting plants.

• Set aside a nursery area in which plants raised from seed or from cuttings can be grown on before being planted out into their final positions.

• Use cold frames as well as a greenhouse to increase the number of plants you can raise from cuttings or seeds.

A WATERSIDE GARDEN

Special sites such as the margins of still or moving water and areas of boggy ground provide scope for imaginative associations of plants that have similar needs. Well-chosen plants that are thriving in conditions to which they are suited create the impression of a natural plant community, and yet the constituent members will often come from areas that are geographically far apart. This waterside planting, in which foliage plays a major role, includes a maple (*Acer*) and hostas from Japan, Asiatic primroses, a large-leaved *Lysichiton* from North America, a hybrid of Himalayan rhododendrons, and a New Zealand tree fern.

SURFACES 1

SURFACES ARE KEY ELEMENTS in gardens, even in those that are almost covered by ornamental planting. The structure of a garden is commonly defined by hard surfaces such as gravel paths and paved courtyards, which are clean underfoot, even in wet weather. Their function is to provide routes through the garden and neat surfaces for utilities, as well as to floor outdoor rooms used for relaxation and entertaining. Color, texture, and pattern can make much hard landscaping an attractive component of the garden.

Most soft surfaces, for example a lawn, are planted. Some are suitable for areas that are used for play or recreation. Few stand up to heavy wear, particularly in wet weather, but their functional value is often less important than their appearance.

SOFT SURFACES SEE ALSO: LAWNS AND GROUND COVER, PP.74–89

FINE LAWN

Lawn grass grown principally for its appearance consists of a mixture of fine-leaved species, commonly bents and fescues.
Advantages The uniform green is restful to the eye; the velvet sward a luxury surface to walk on.
Disadvantages Suitable only for an open, scrupulously prepared site. Needs very frequent mowing (roller needed for fancy striped effect), and a high level of maintenance, including watering in dry weather. Expensive as sod; slow to become established if sown from seed.

UTILITY LAWN

Lawn grass that provides a durable surface consists of a mixture of resilient species, often including perennial ryegrass.
Advantages Pleasing appearance and yet tough enough for a family garden. Less demanding to maintain than a fine lawn.
Disadvantages Ground must be thoroughly prepared. Appearance always inferior to that of a fine lawn. Requires frequent mowing and, in dry weather, watering. Fairly expensive as sod and slow to become established if sown from seed.

GARDEN STEPS

Steps are an architectural and theatrical way of linking different levels in a sloping site. They invite movement, but are unsuitable for taking equipment such as wheelbarrows.

• Safe steps have firm foundations, generous treads that are level, with a nonslip surface, and risers of a manageable height.

• Cost depends on the nature of the site, the scale of the steps, and the choice of materials.

• Materials, which can be mixed as in the wood and brick steps below, are best matched to other built features.

HARD SURFACES SEE ALSO: PATIOS AND PATHS, PP.56–73

WOOD DECKING

Lengths of lumber – rot-resistant such as western red cedar, or pressure-treated with preservative – are supported on joists to make a level surface, even over sloping or uneven ground.
Advantages Wood readily available in panel form. Good for linking the garden to indoor living space. Versatile material. Design possibilities with color, texture, and pattern.
Disadvantages Construction and weight-bearing requirements may be governed by local regulations. Structure needs regular maintenance to prolong life.

GRAVEL

Gravel consists of stone fragments and pebbles, graded according to size, which make a crunching sound when walked on. Color varies, depending on the original stone. It is usually laid over plastic to discourage weeds.
Advantages Relatively cheap; easy to lay, even in irregular shapes. Suitable for informal and formal settings. Mixes well and unifies planted and open areas. Crunchy noise deters intruders.
Disadvantages Scatters unless restrained by a firm edging, and is frequently carried indoors on shoes. Weed control often necessary.

ROUGH GRASS

Grasses, particularly native species, often combined with flowers that grow naturally in grassland, are allowed to flower and seed. Paths and patterns can be created by mowing.

Advantages Few cuts needed annually. Suitable for awkward areas, including rough and sloping ground, and poor soils. Can help conserve wild-flowers. Sympathetic to wildlife.

Disadvantages Cut grass needs to be removed. Control of pernicious weeds necessary. Small areas of rough grass can look messy.

CHAMOMILE LAWN

Plants other than grass used to create lawns include aromatic perennials such as chamomile (*Chamaemelum nobile*). The low-growing and nonflowering 'Treneague' is especially suitable.

Advantages Provides a contrast of texture to other areas of the garden. When bruised by light treading, the leaves release a pleasant applelike scent. Needs only occasional trimming.

Disadvantages Tolerates only very light wear and is best limited to small areas where there is no regular traffic. Requires frequent renovation.

BARK CHIPS

Mechanically chipped or shredded bark, widely used as a mulch among plants, is also suitable as a surface for footpaths and around children's play equipment.

Advantages Relatively inexpensive and easily applied material. Soft underfoot and an appropriate surface in a woodland garden.

Disadvantages Effect can be overpowering when used over large areas. Needs replenishing every two to three years because chips break down and scatter unless retained by edging.

POURED CONCRETE

Concrete, prepared from cement, sand, and aggregate mixed with water, is laid over a foundation of crushed stone. To prevent cracking, large areas must have expansion joints.

Advantages Relatively cheap and durable material, versatile enough to be laid in almost any site, however oddly shaped. Provided access is adequate, often possible to have premixed concrete delivered. Can be colored, and there are various ways of texturing the surface.

Disadvantages Harsh appearance of large areas is difficult to disguise, even with color.

CONCRETE SLABS

Precast concrete slabs are readily available in a range of sizes, shapes, and colors. They can be smooth or textured, some simulating stone. They are usually laid on strips of mortar on sand over a crushed stone base or, for heavy-duty areas such as drives, on a concrete base.

Advantages Relatively inexpensive and easily laid. Both versatile and durable. Weathering improves appearance.

Disadvantages When first laid, slabs look raw. Some of the brighter colors never really blend with plants or other materials.

GRANITE PAVERS (SETTS)

These roughly rectangular blocks of granite need to be bedded in mortar or sand. They provide a more even surface than cobblestones or rounded stones selected for uniformity of size and laid in the same way.

Advantages Very durable and maintenance-free. Mix well with other materials and small unit size makes for flexibility. Pleasing color variations. Attractive in formal and informal areas.

Disadvantages Expensive both to buy and have laid. Surface is slightly uneven. Slippery when wet, but no more so than other hard surfaces.

SURFACES 2

MORE HARD SURFACES SEE ALSO: PATIOS AND PATHS, PP.56–73

STONE SLABS

Regular slabs of quarried stone are usually bedded in sand that has been spread over a crushed stone base. The slabs are leveled, and the gaps between them filled with mortar or sand.

Advantages Wide range of colors and textures available. Very durable and require little maintenance. Create impression of quality in formal areas.

Disadvantages Expensive to buy and have laid. Heavy work to lay and skill required to achieve a highly finished surface of interlocking shapes.

RANDOM PAVING

Irregularly shaped fragments of quarried stone, bedded in sand that is laid over stone, are fitted together to cover the available area. A mixture of different kinds of stone can be used, as here. The joints are usually filled with mortar.

Advantages Broken fragments of stone are cheaper than whole slabs. Usually lighter work to lay than whole stone slabs. Durable.

Disadvantages Time-consuming to fit pieces together. Over a large area, the effect of the irregular joints can be irritatingly eye-catching.

CONCRETE STEPPING-STONES

Precast concrete slabs that are spaced to match an average walking pace are bedded in sand to create an easy route through plants or gravel.

Advantages Relatively cheap, easy to lay, and durable. Versatile material that has many utilitarian applications, making paths that are easily modified and clean underfoot. Appearance may improve with weathering.

Disadvantages Harsh appearance when first laid and often never weather sufficiently to blend in with their surroundings.

MIXED PAVING SEE ALSO: PATIOS AND PATHS, PP.56–73

STONE, GRANITE, AND GRAVEL

An unusual feature, such as an old grinding stone, here composed of fitted elements, forms the centerpiece of a design incorporating granite pavers and gravel.

Advantages Impressive when laid out with style, as here. Mix of materials creates a strongly textured and patterned effect. Suitable for a formal area. Durable.

Disadvantages Expensive. Can be difficult to combine materials satisfactorily when more than two are used. Control of weeds in the gravel probably necessary.

CUT BRICKS AND TERRACOTTA

Bricks cut to fit and laid around a series of rings composed of terracotta flower pots, sitting one inside another, make an unusual circular design. The flower pots are bedded in sand and the bricks in mortar.

Advantages A distinctive and eye-catching feature made from relatively modest materials. Suitable for a focal point in a larger brick surface.

Disadvantages Even if the flower pots are frostproof, the terracotta centerpiece is less durable than the brick edging. Skill needed to cut the bricks to shape. Weed control necessary.

LARGE STONES AND PEBBLES

Large fragments of stone are bedded in sand and laid, surrounded by pebbles, so that the upper surface is approximately level.

Advantages Naturally occurring pieces of stone are cheaper than shaped stone and may even be available free on site. Pleasing contrasts of textures, shapes and, in some cases, color. Suitable in an informal setting. Durable.

Disadvantages Not suitable for formal parts of the garden and appropriate only for secondary paths. Uneven surface of stones a potential hazard. Weed control may be necessary.

BRICKS

Weather-resistant bricks of various colors and textures used for flat surfaces are usually laid on a bed of mortar and pointed. Clay pavers, which are thinner than bricks, are laid in a similar way.
Advantages Sympathetic materials, particularly near brick buildings. Mix well with most other forms of paving. The various bonding patterns can be highly decorative in formal areas. Small unit size makes them flexible paving materials.
Disadvantages Because time-consuming to lay, work done by contractors likely to be expensive.

TILES

Quarry tiles, which are of clay fired to a high temperature, and frostproof glazed ceramic tiles are laid on leveled concrete. Quarry tiles are usually bedded in mortar but ceramic tiles are fixed with a tile adhesive.
Advantages Scope for colorful and decorative effects. Useful for linking indoor and outdoor areas. Mosaics can be made from tile fragments.
Disadvantages Glazed tiles can be slippery when wet. Cutting tiles often proves difficult and wasteful. Not suitable for informal areas.

PATTERNS IN PAVING

Patterns made from paving materials are traditional elements in garden design but, as this illustration shows, there is still scope for using them in original ways. Here, the spirals are filled with contrasting light and dark pebbles set in cement.

• Many patterns, such as the various brick bonds, provide a simple and pleasing way of bringing order to small units of paving.

• Interlocking patterns strengthen surfaces.

• The use of contrasting materials heightens the effect of pattern.

BRICKS AND GRAVEL

Frostproof bricks bedded in mortar on a firm base form a strong design and act as an edging for gravel infill.
Advantages An economical way of creating a strongly patterned design that exploits contrasts of texture and color. Mix of materials is suitable for a formal part of the garden.
Disadvantages Gravel tends to scatter and needs replenishing from time to time. A buffer zone of brick between mixed paving and house is advisable to stop gravel from being tracked indoors on shoes. Weed control may be necessary.

STONE SLABS AND LAWN

Stones slabs of various sizes bedded on sand are laid as a surround to neatly trimmed turf.
Advantages Pleasing contrasts of texture, color, and shape. The stone slabs provide a surface that can be walked on in wet weather. Suitable for formal settings. Effect can be achieved with only small patches of grass, so can be successful in even a tiny garden.
Disadvantages For maximum effect, careful and regular mowing of the grass and trimming of the grass edge are essential. Control of weeds between paving stones necessary.

STONE SLABS AND PEBBLES

Loose pebbles of varying size surround regular or irregular stone slabs that are bedded in sand.
Advantages An economical way of using a relatively small quantity of paving stone, which provides an even surface for walking. Attractive contrasts of texture and, in some cases, color. Combination suitable for informal areas of the garden. The pebbles can be treated as a mulch, with plants growing through it.
Disadvantages Weed control of the area covered by pebbles may be necessary. Pebbles may scatter unless retained by an edging.

BOUNDARIES AND DIVISIONS 1

WALLS, FENCES, AND HEDGES form barriers and screens that mark out the boundaries of a garden and create divisions within it. They can also make an area secure, keeping in children and animals and, if the barriers are high enough, keeping out intruders. Even when the security is not total, they create the intimate atmosphere of a place apart by blocking views into the garden and controlling what is seen of the world beyond. Open structures such as arches and pergolas can also play some of these roles.

By providing shelter, trapping warmth, casting shade, creating dry spots, and filtering wind, barriers and screens influence growing conditions in different parts of the garden. They also help muffle noise and keep out traffic fumes.

FREESTANDING WALLS SEE ALSO: BOUNDARIES, DIVISIONS, STRUCTURES, PP. 90–121

BRICK WALL

Walls of brick are built on a footing of stone and concrete, with the bricks laid in a bonding pattern and topped by a protective coping.
Advantages Durable and requires little maintenance. Good for security and privacy. Bricks available in many colors and textures. Attractively patterned bonds. Heat retained by wall creates warm microclimate on sunny side.
Disadvantages Expensive to have built; needs some skill. Acts as a solid barrier to wind, creating turbulence on sheltered side.

RENDERED WALL

Rendering is a coat of plaster or mortar applied to walls that lack a good natural finish, such as those of concrete blocks. The rendered surface is usually painted.
Advantages Solid and durable wall with good finish possible using relatively cheap materials. Render can be textured in many ways, such as by brushing or combing or with pebbles.
Disadvantages Forms a solid barrier to wind, creating turbulence damaging to plants and unpleasant for people. Requires maintenance.

FENCES SEE ALSO: BOUNDARIES, DIVISIONS, STRUCTURES, PP. 90–121

WOODEN PICKET FENCE

Vertical stakes or posts set in the ground are connected by horizontal rails, to which upright pales are fixed at regular intervals. The fence may be left plain but is often painted or stained.
Advantages Attractive, light barrier. Can be given individual character by varying spacing and width of pales, shaping the tops of the pales, and by giving a color finish. Because of gaps between pales, the fence filters wind, lessening the risk of turbulence near it.
Disadvantages Requires maintenance. Offers limited security and privacy.

WOODEN PANEL FENCE

Wooden panels consisting of a frame and slats or boards are supported by wooden or concrete posts to make screens and fences.
Advantages Relatively inexpensive. Easy to erect. Good for creating privacy. Closeboard fencing, which consists of overlapping vertical boards, can also be built on site and is reasonably solid.
Disadvantages Basketweave panels, with interwoven slats, and wavy-edged panels, with overlapping horizontal planks, as illustrated here, are lightweight and not long-lived.

POST-AND-RAIL FENCE

Upright wooden posts spaced at regular intervals support usually two or three horizontal rails or poles. Cedar and pine, split lengthwise and treated with a preservative, are commonly used. A more finished effect can be achieved using sawn and painted wood.
Advantages Relatively inexpensive boundary marker. Allows the garden to be part of its landscape setting.
Disadvantages Does not provide shelter or security against intruders. Will not keep children or small animals in – or out.

RETAINING WALLS SEE ALSO: BOUNDARIES, DIVISIONS, STRUCTURES, PP.90–121

DRYSTONE WALL

Drystone walls are constructed from local stone, laid in courses or randomly, without the use of mortar. Planting pockets can be created by filling gaps with soil.

Advantages Where local stone freely available, a relatively cheap material. Durable. Attractive when colonized by desirable plants.

Disadvantages Requires skill to erect. Some maintenance eventually required. Can be difficult to control pernicious weeds once they have become established.

WALL WITH RAILROAD TIES

Old railroad ties are heavy and therefore stable when laid to make low walls or a series of tiers, as here. If there are more than two courses, the ties need to be held in position, for example with metal rods.

Advantages Durable material that provides a good backdrop to plants. Suitable for raised beds.

Disadvantages Ties, once cheap, no longer are. Suitable only for low retaining walls. Heavy to handle. Often leak tar and may have been treated with a preservative that is toxic to plants.

FOCAL POINTS

When carefully placed in the garden, built structures, furniture, ornaments, containers, and plants act as focal points of the design.

• They create an inviting goal beyond a division or boundary.

• They arrest the eye, drawing attention to a particular area of the garden.

• Framing, as here, intensifies the magnetism of focal points.

BAMBOO FENCE

Various bamboos, cut to length either as stakes or as brushwood, are lashed together vertically with wire or cord and supported by posts to form screening panels and fences. Thicker stakes may, as here, be used as horizontal rails.

Advantages Excellent screens. Variety of textures and colors, all of which are sympathetic to plants.

Disadvantages Skill required to construct, unless bamboo bought as premade panels. Relatively lightweight barrier. Requires regular maintenance and renewal.

WATTLE HURDLE

Strips of wood or stems are interwoven to form panels that are usually of slightly irregular shape. When erected, they are supported by stakes or posts.

Advantages As a short-term measure, excellent for creating shelter and privacy, for example while hedges develop. Colors and textures pleasing and associate well with plants. Rustic but versatile.

Disadvantages Difficult to make on site. Relatively short-lived. Premade panels may be difficult to locate.

IRONWORK FENCE

Fences of wrought and cast iron usually consist of vertical and horizontal railings set close enough to form a barrier against animals and, when high enough, against human intruders. They allow a view, decorated by their own tracery, in and out of the garden. A paint finish is necessary to prevent rust.

Advantages Durable. Good for security. Many highly ornamental designs possible.

Disadvantages Quality ironwork expensive. Does not provide privacy or shelter. Requires repainting from time to time.

BOUNDARIES AND DIVISIONS 2

HEDGES SEE ALSO: BOUNDARIES, DIVISIONS, STRUCTURES, PP.90–121

FORMAL EVERGREEN HEDGE

Evergreen shrubs and trees suitable for formal hedges, making dense surfaces when trimmed regularly, include boxwood (*Buxus*), shown above flanking the path, and yew (*Taxus*), either side of the opening.
Advantages Strongly architectural and long-lived. Uses range from low edging to tall and secure barriers. Sympathetic to other plants.
Disadvantages As with all hedges, takes time to reach required height. Needs clipping annually, fast-growing kinds several times a year.

FORMAL DECIDUOUS HEDGE

A number of deciduous shrubs and trees (which lose their leaves in winter) respond to regular trimming by forming a dense surface and are therefore suitable for formal hedges. With beech (*Fagus*) and hornbeam (*Carpinus*), the dead leaves, attractively russet, are retained until spring. This purple-leaved hedge is of *Prunus cerasifera* 'Nigra'.
Advantages Textures and colors different from those provided by evergreen hedges.
Disadvantages Most suitable plants are leafless in winter. (*See also left*, formal evergreen hedge.)

HEDGES AND TOPIARY

Topiary shapes, usually trimmed from evergreen hedging plants, are used to create accents and focal points, here in combination with hedges. They may be simple geometric figures or representations of animals or birds.
Advantages When mature, give the garden an apparently timeless and dramatic structure.
Disadvantages Limited range of plants, most of slow to moderate growth, suitable for long-lived topiary. Shapes take time to develop and require regular trimming with care and precision.

ARCHES AND PERGOLAS

PLEACHED TREES

Pleaching is a method of forming a raised screen by training trees so that their stems and foliage become intertwined. Lindens are most commonly used (especially *Tilia platyphyllos* 'Rubra'), but any tree that has flexible branches is suitable.
Advantages Creates unusual perspectives. Unlike a barrier to ground level, allows cold air to drain away. Can be underplanted or combined with a conventional hedge or wall.
Disadvantages Rigorous initial training required, for which a wire or wooden framework is needed. Annual maintenance necessary.

INFORMAL HEDGE

Shrubs that are naturally dense and bushy, including, as here, some roses, can be planted in rows to form effective barriers. When left unclipped or only lightly trimmed, so that they produce flowers and fruits, these hedges can be very ornamental.
Advantages Often highly colorful at certain seasons. Little trimming required, and it does not need to be precise.
Disadvantages Hedges tend to be thick and space-consuming. Any trimming needs to be timed to avoid loss of flowers or fruit.

METAL ARCH

Metal arches are frames, usually of ironwork, spanning paths and consisting of uprights and crosspieces, often hooped. They can be bought in kit form or made to order. Like other arches, such as wood, they are placed to create accents or to mark transitions in a garden, and they usually support climbers.
Advantages The material is strong and versatile, making elegant structures in many styles.
Disadvantages Relatively expensive to have made. Some in kit form are flimsy. Usually needs painting from time to time.

HEDGE WITH OPENING

Arched openings and windows in hedges are normally planned from the outset to relate to main pathways and views through the garden. Stems are initially trained on supports, in some cases an arch rising above the hedge.

Advantages Underlines the architectural character of boundaries and helps define the garden's structure. Guides the eye to vistas and focal points, sometimes introducing surprises.

Disadvantages Care needed to train and clip. Completion depends on growth rate of hedge.

TAPESTRY HEDGE

A tapestry hedge, composed of a mixture of plants, makes a virtue of contrasts in foliage. In a hedge of plain- and purple-leaved beech (*Fagus*), as here, it is color that counts, but using more than one species, with different leaf surfaces and sizes, can create additional contrasts of texture.

Advantages Striking effects, changing with the play of light.

Disadvantages Some mixtures create a restless effect. Tendency for uneven development because plants grow at different rates.

SEE ALSO: BOUNDARIES, DIVISIONS, STRUCTURES, PP.90–121

WOODEN ARCH

Sawn wood and rustic poles make arches that are more conspicuous than those of ironwork (*see left*, metal arch), but the structures, spanning paths and often framing vistas or focal points, fulfill the same function.

Advantages Versatile material, which can be painted or stained, making it possible to build arches that match other garden features. Wood treated with preservative widely available.

Disadvantages Decorative finish needs renewing from time to time, and all wood eventually need replacing.

RUSTIC PERGOLA

The structure, consisting of linked arches made of poles, spans a walkway, creating shade and supporting ornamental climbers. Other materials used to build pergolas are sawn wood, brick, masonry, and metal.

Advantages Relatively cheap pergola and not difficult for an amateur to construct. Is useful for providing shade in a new sunny garden while slow-growing trees and shrubs develop.

Disadvantages Even treated lumber needs replacing. Structure is less durable and sturdy than pergolas made of other materials.

A VARIETY OF EDGING

Edgings, usually functional and often decorative, define where a surface such as a lawn or paving meets a bed or border. The edging may be a low barrier of a hard material such as bricks or tiles; it can be little more than an outline, a wood edging for example, framing a paved surface; or it may consist of a row of low plants.

• A narrow band of paving edging a lawn and set just below its level (*see above* combined with tile edging) simplifies mowing.

• Loose surfaces such as gravel require a firm edge to hold them in place.

• Surfaces that are composed of small units such as bricks or granite pavers need an edging, often laid level with the main surface, to hold the bond together.

• Low trimmed hedges, for example of dwarf boxwood (*Buxus*), make neat enclosures for looser planting, including vegetables, as above.

• Informal low hedges, aromatic in the case of the lavender (*Lavandula*) illustrated below, soften the lines where paving and steps meet beds and borders.

WATER FEATURES

THERE WERE PONDS and streams in the earliest gardens, and water remains almost universally fascinating. Still water pleases with its brilliant or darkly reflective mirror surface. Moving water catches the eye with its lively play of light, accompanied by murmuring or rushing sound.

Thanks to modern materials and equipment, water can be a feature of virtually any garden, where it will play an important role in attracting wildlife. The ready availability of liners makes it easy to create ponds of any size, and a flow of water can be maintained with a submersible pump.

Two warnings are necessary. Unless properly installed, electrical equipment can make a lethal combination with water. Open water is also a potential attraction and danger to young children.

PONDS SEE ALSO: WATER GARDENING, PP.198–223

FORMAL POND
Ponds with a geometrically regular outline can be built of concrete or made with rigid or flexible liners. They may be sunken, or raised above ground level, as here. The pond can be a simple mirror, or its surface can be partly covered by plants or broken by water from a fountain.
Advantages Works well with a wide range of paving materials. Successful on any scale, so suitable even for a very small garden.
Disadvantages May be difficult to marry formal shape with informality of marginal planting.

INFORMAL POND
Ponds with an irregular outline are usually constructed with a flexible or rigid liner, but they can also be made in a traditional way using puddled clay. To look natural they need to be set in a low-lying part of the garden and made with shelving edges that provide homes for moisture-loving plants.
Advantages Easy to make with a liner. The most suitable kind of pool to attract wildlife.
Disadvantages On a small scale, particularly when made with a rigid liner, can look contrived.

FOUNTAINS SEE ALSO: WATER GARDENING, PP.198–223

FORMAL FOUNTAIN
The simplest formal fountain consists of a single jet sending up a short column of water in the center of a pool. It is usually powered by a submersible pump, which recycles the water, and the height of the fountain depends on the size of the pump. More elaborate effects can be created with multiple and angled jets, which may be incorporated in statues.
Advantages Gives an extra dimension to a formal pool. Simple to install and operate.
Disadvantages Need to camouflage cable to pump. Flow may have to be stopped in winter.

WALL FOUNTAIN
A conventional wall fountain consists of two parts. A small stream of water issues from a simple spout or ornamental feature such as a mask. Beneath it, a pool, usually in the form of a raised basin, catches the water and spray. The water is recycled by a submersible pump.
Advantages Relatively inexpensive; available in a range of different styles. Easily accommodated in a patio or courtyard.
Disadvantages Feeble dribbling can be more irritating than pleasing. Cable and pipes from basin to spout need to be concealed.

NOVELTY FOUNTAIN
The jets and spouts of fountains can be incorporated in a wide range of improvised items, such as this metal watering can, as well as in conventional sculptures. Fountain heads and extension tubes to create a variety of effects are often supplied as attachments to submersible pumps, or they can be bought separately.
Advantages An unusual fountain helps to give a garden individual character. Improvisation with inexpensive materials not difficult.
Disadvantages Needs to be chosen with care since the novelty may quickly lose its appeal.

FLOWING WATER SEE ALSO: WATER GARDENING, PP.198–223

CONTAINER POND

Small water features that are suitable for a patio or conservatory can be made from a variety of watertight containers, including half barrels, tubs, and old sinks. Wooden containers may have been impregnated with substances harmful to plants and fish and need to be lined.
Advantages Relatively inexpensive. Simple way of bringing water into even the smallest garden.
Disadvantages Water needs frequent filling up in hot weather. May have to be drained in winter since small volumes of water tend to freeze solid.

CHANNELED WATER

Channels for flowing water can have a soft edge, bordered by naturalistic planting, or their character can be strongly architectural, as here, where they flow at right angles in and out of a pond surrounded by granite pavers. The stream can be one that occurs naturally or an artificial one, with the water circulated by a pump.
Advantages Interesting effects of light and sound possible with a modest flow of water.
Disadvantages Requires skill to create; expensive to have built professionally.

WATER CASCADE

Waterfalls and cascades are natural or artificial steps made by water descending a slope. The flow itself can be natural or be driven by a pump. In the example illustrated, a series of simple channeled steps, each with a stone lip, makes an extended water staircase through a sloping meadow garden.
Advantages Lively effect of movement, light, and sound. Materials not necessarily expensive.
Disadvantages If there is no natural stream, a powerful surface pump needed to recycle water.

BRIDGES SEE ALSO: WATER GARDENING, PP.198–223

COBBLESTONE FOUNTAIN

A low jet of water flowing gently over a bed of cobblestones forms a simple but effective feature. Here, a large stone, with a hole drilled through the middle, is used as a centerpiece and conceals the sunken water tank and electric pump.
Advantages Safe for children and suitable for a small garden. Relatively inexpensive in kit form or easily constructed from cheap materials.
Disadvantages If the flow is stopped, as may be necessary in winter, the feature looks dull. Needs to be surrounded by sympathetic planting to remain attractive all year.

BOARD BRIDGE

A rudimentary bridge consisting of a board placed across a stream can be elaborated, as here, to make a stylish wooden walkway. Texturing the surface, by carving shallow grooves into the wood or roughening it with a wire brush, helps prevent the boards from becoming slippery.
Advantages Materials relatively inexpensive and construction not difficult. Well suited to an informal wildlife pond.
Disadvantages Unsuitable for a main route in the garden. Requires regular maintenance to prolong life and keep surface safe underfoot.

BRIDGE WITH HANDRAILS

Arched or level bridges with handrails and with firm footings on either bank can be built from treated lumber, as here, or from more expensive materials, such as brick or masonry. Small-scale wooden bridges are available in kit form.
Advantages Makes a safe and picturebook feature to span small or medium-sized streams. Can be used to support trained plants. Wooden bridges in kit form are not expensive.
Disadvantages Custom-made bridges relatively expensive. If made of wood, regular maintenance required.

LEISURE ELEMENTS

A RANGE OF FIXED and movable features helps make the most of the garden by transforming it into a place for outdoor living.

Playhouses and sandboxes keep young children happy and occupied but will eventually be outgrown and need to be replaced. A swimming pool, which appeals to older children and adults alike, is a lasting, if ambitious, feature.

Some form of seating is essential. A summerhouse with comfortable chairs is delectable, but a few folding chairs may be sufficient. Permanent furniture is certainly practical if there is regular dining al fresco and, to many people, a barbecue is essential for authentic outdoor meals.

Lighting makes the garden a friendly place at night and magically different from the garden in daylight.

BUILT FEATURES SEE ALSO: PATIOS AND PATHS, PP.56–73

BUILT-IN BARBECUE

A simple barbecue built from bricks, as here, concrete blocks, or stone incorporates a bed for the fire and a cooking grid. There should also be storage space for fuel and surfaces for stacking plates and assembling food.

Advantages A focus for family meals and entertaining. Relatively easy to build.

Disadvantages Location critical to get good draft and to keep smells and smoke from being a nuisance. Needs strict supervision because of fire risk, and use may be controlled in some areas.

SUMMERHOUSE

Small ornamental buildings, usually of wooden construction and often open on at least one side, provide a shaded area for seating away from the house. They need to be sited where they please the eye while giving a good view of the garden.

Advantages An opportunity for a modest, but characterful, architectural feature.

Disadvantages Custom-made or commercial model that is well designed is likely to be expensive. Wooden summerhouses need maintenance to prolong life.

SEATING SEE ALSO: PATIOS AND PATHS, PP.56–73

WOODEN BENCH

Wood is a classic material for garden benches and is suitable for a wide range of designs, from plain and functional to boldly decorative, as this example. The wood can be stained or painted to suit the overall design of the garden, or oiled to give a natural finish. With hardwood furniture, be sure that the wood is from a sustainable source.

Advantages Sturdy and eye-catching styles available. Can be long-lived.

Disadvantages Good-looking designs usually expensive. Comfort often secondary. Requires maintenance. Best stored under cover in winter.

SLATTED METAL BENCH

Some of the most elegant garden furniture is made of metal. The simple bench illustrated here is of wrought iron with galvanized slats. More ornate metal furniture, often based on 19th-century designs, is usually cast in iron or in aluminum alloy and given a painted or enameled finish.

Advantages Elegant designs available. Can have a long life.

Disadvantages Usually expensive. Can be uncomfortable and cold to the touch. Requires maintenance. Best stored under cover in winter.

WOODEN SWING SEAT

Informal garden furniture, designed for comfort and relaxation, comes in an infinite variety of forms. The swing seat shown above has a fixed frame but the seat itself can be taken down for storage in winter. Items that can be moved about and stored easily include hammocks, deckchairs, cushioned loungers, and collapsible swing seats.

Advantages Comfortable. Sets a relaxed tone.

Disadvantages Takes up more space than a comparable bench set on the ground. Cannot be moved to take advantage of sun and shade. Requires maintenance.

SWIMMING POOL

Various methods are used to construct swimming pools but the basic material is normally concrete, which is often lined and edged with tiles.

Advantages Can be glamorous and beautiful.

Disadvantages Space-consuming and visually dominating. Best installed with professional advice and this is costly. Structures needed for changing rooms and to house filtration equipment. Potential danger to unsupervised children. Maintenance required.

PLAYHOUSE

The traditional material for a child's playhouse, as in this highly individual example, is wood, although many commercially available models are made of plastic, in bright, cheerful colors. Any playhouse needs a sunny position, where children can be supervised.

Advantages A source of pleasure to children, encouraging creative play.

Disadvantages As children grow up, will probably become unused. A wooden playhouse requires maintenance.

SANDBOX

Young children are almost always pleased to play in a bed of clean sand. A site in view of the house is required, ideally in a sunny spot. The sand, contained here by a wooden frame, should be laid over a water-permeable membrane, which is itself laid on a base of crushed stone topped with gravel. A cover keeps out debris and pets.

Advantages A safe focus for the outdoor activities of young children. Inexpensive, easy to build, and can be converted later, say, to a pond.

Disadvantages Unused after a few years.

LIGHTING See also: Patios and Paths, pp.56–73

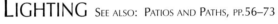

TABLE AND CHAIRS

For planned and impromptu entertaining and dining outdoors a table and chairs are indispensable. Garden furniture is made of wood, plastic, and metal, some lightweight and weatherproof, as this metal table and chairs. The furniture needs to be set on a level, hard surface, ideally with an umbrella for shade.

Advantages Practical and make the garden, or part of it, look like an outdoor room. Wide range of designs available.

Disadvantages Usually expensive. Space-consuming. Best stored under cover in winter.

ELECTRIC LIGHTING

Electric lighting in the garden can be used to illuminate paths and areas for entertaining, to create striking effects, particularly with spotlighting and uplighting, and to floodlight areas around the house to deter intruders. Soft lighting can be provided by low-wattage systems. Stronger lights need a house electricity supply, installed by a qualified electrician.

Advantages Easy to use. Makes walking in the garden safer when it is dark. Dramatic night-time transformations. Improved security.

Disadvantages Cost of installation can be high.

FLAME LIGHTS

The various light sources based on burning wax or kerosene include flares, lanterns, candles, and votive lights. In some cases, as with the votive lights illustrated here, the flame is partly sheltered by glass.

Advantages Inexpensive, and a flexible method of lighting that is easily rearranged according to need. Provides pleasant, soft light. Some forms include an insect repellent.

Disadvantages Weak source of light, more for decorative effect than practical use. Possible fire risk. Material burned needs to be renewed.

GARDEN MAINTENANCE

GOOD BACKUP FACILITIES help in the efficient running of a garden. A greenhouse makes it possible to keep frost-tender plants over winter and to start others growing early, giving flowers and produce over a longer period. Even without a greenhouse, much can be achieved using the modest equipment of cold frames and cloches.

With a good-sized compost bin, whether homemade or a commercial model, garden and kitchen waste can be recycled; once rotted down, it makes an excellent soil conditioner, improving both fertility and texture.

Neat storage of equipment under cover saves time and prolongs the life of tools. It must be borne in mind, however, that while locked sheds do offer some security, they also attract the attention of thieves.

GREENHOUSES SEE ALSO: LOOKING AFTER THE GARDEN, PP.274–287

FREESTANDING GREENHOUSE

One of the most widely used greenhouse designs consists of a framework of metal or, as here, wood, with vertical sides topped by a span roof, one that slopes evenly each side of a central ridge. The walls can be part solid or all glass.
Advantages Many models available in different price ranges. Allows economic use of space, with plenty of bench area. Headroom adequate. Many fixtures available.
Disadvantages May let in less light than greenhouses with all glass surfaces sloping.

LEAN-TO GREENHOUSE

The structure, with either a metal or a wooden frame, is set against the wall of a building and is often used as a garden room.
Advantages Many models available. Good solution where insufficient space for a free-standing greenhouse. Insulation provided by wall reduces heat loss. Cheaper to put in services, such as water supply and electricity, than to a freestanding greenhouse.
Disadvantages Solid wall reduces amount of light admitted. Ventilation often inadequate.

CLOCHES AND TUNNELS SEE ALSO: THE EDIBLE GARDEN, PP.234–273

GLASS CLOCHE

Traditional cloches consist of sheets of glass that are held in place with metal clips or a metal frame. They form a protective cover that can be lowered over plants or seed that is sown early. Rigid plastic cloches are increasingly common.
Advantages Easily moved about so a versatile means of protecting a single plant or a small group of plants. Glass allows better light penetration than does plastic.
Disadvantages Relatively expensive to use on a large scale. Glass easily shattered if not handled with care.

PLASTIC TUNNEL CLOCHE

A continuous tunnel of flexible plastic is supported by wire hoops over crops such as early carrots and salad vegetables grown in rows. The plastic should be heavy-duty and treated with an ultraviolet inhibitor. When not in use should be stored out of sunlight. Models made with rigid plastic are also available.
Advantages Relatively cheap way of protecting early crops.
Disadvantages In comparison with glass, plastic lets in less light and does not retain heat as well. Relatively short life.

COMPOST BINS SEE ALSO: LOOKING

WOODEN COMPOST BIN

Wooden bins provide a means of storing relatively large quantities of plant waste from the kitchen and garden in conditions that encourage it to break down. Removable front panels make emptying easy. If two bins are used, one pile can decompose while the other is assembled.
Advantages Materials fairly inexpensive and construction within the competence of many gardeners. Available in kit form.
Disadvantages Difficult to accommodate in a small garden. Unless covered, compost can dry out in summer and may need watering.

GARDEN MAINTENANCE • 37

COLD FRAMES SEE ALSO: LOOKING AFTER THE GARDEN, PP.274–287

ORNAMENTAL GREENHOUSE

Freestanding greenhouses designed as attractive garden features can have frames of plastic-covered steel, as here, plain aluminum, or wood. This model is essentially a traditional span greenhouse with part-solid walls of brick.
Advantages Can be as effective as other kinds of greenhouse in providing a protected environment for plants, but also makes a highly ornamental feature. Steel very strong.
Disadvantages Models of stylish design more expensive than utilitarian greenhouses.

HOMEMADE COLD FRAME

The traditional cold frame, a cabinet for protecting plants in cold weather, has wooden sides supporting sloping "lights" (the glass-paned tops), which are hinged or slide open. Commercial production of wooden frames has declined, but they are simple to make at home from railroad ties or other wood.
Advantages Wooden sides retain heat well.
Disadvantages When available, commercial models are expensive. Not easily moved about, as aluminum frames can be.

ALUMINUM ALLOY FRAME

Light frames of aluminum alloy and glass are available in a wide range of designs. The top panels, the "lights," normally slide open.
Advantages Readily available in kit form, easily assembled, and relatively inexpensive. Let in more light than brick or wooden frames. Can be moved to take advantage of changing conditions of light and shade.
Disadvantages Less sturdy than brick or wooden frame and in cold weather has greater need of additional insulation.

AFTER THE GARDEN, PP.274–287 # STORAGE UNITS SEE ALSO: LOOKING AFTER THE GARDEN, PP.274–287

PLASTIC COMPOST BIN

Many plastic models are available, most of which are designed for small and medium-sized gardens. Some have a mechanism for turning the compost, which speeds up decomposition.
Advantages More efficient than wooden bins at maintaining heat and moisture levels necessary to break down waste. Neat, compact, and of a subdued color. Generally sturdy.
Disadvantages Can be relatively expensive and price an unreliable guide to performance. The amount of compost produced, governed by bin size, often small.

WALK-IN SHED

Garden sheds are made of a variety of materials, including wood, concrete, metal, and fiberglass. Whether individually designed, assembled from a kit, or bought premade, a wooden shed is best built from naturally rot-resistant cedar or from pressure-treated lumber.
Advantages Moderate cost. Provides weather protection for tools, including large items such as lawnmowers. Provides all-weather protection for jobs such as potting.
Disadvantages Not for prominent position. Requires maintenance. Limited security.

ORNAMENTAL TOOL LOCKER

A tool locker can be custom-made, assembled from a kit, or bought commercially. In a small garden, it can be given a decorative finish and be treated as a design feature.
Advantages Relatively inexpensive and compact. Provides protection from weather. If sited carefully, can make a focal point.
Disadvantages Requires maintenance. Even with skillful arrangement of the interior, difficult to accommodate large items of equipment. Some commercially produced lockers of poor design. Limited security.

PLANTS FOR A PURPOSE 1

WHATEVER THE BALANCE between planting and hard landscape, it is plants that bring a garden to life through all seasons of the year. Color counts for much and the palette available in foliage and flowers is infinitely varied. The texture of foliage and all the other parts of plants that reflect light or create complex patterns of shadow adds another layer of interest to the garden. Of the many other plant qualities to exploit, one of the most valuable is scent, spicy and pungent as well as sweetly perfumed. Some plants come into their own when used for specific reasons, including those with which it is possible to create a low-maintenance garden, handsome specimens for accents and focal points, and those that are suitable for clothing vertical surfaces.

FOR SEASONAL EFFECT SEE ALSO: BEDS AND BORDERS, PP.122–165

SPRING
This is the high point in the year for colorful bulbs, which may be combined with annual or biennial bedding plants, as here, and set against a delicate background of burgeoning foliage. More subtle bulbs go well with leafy woodland plants and the numerous spring-flowering rock garden plants. Many trees and shrubs reach their flowering peak at this time, among them magnolias, *Prunus*, and rhododendrons. For house fronts and pergolas there are flowering climbers such as wisteria and several clematis.

SUMMER
The leafiest time of the year is also the main flowering season for many plants. In the first part of summer, roses that flower once produce a tremendous burst, but those that repeat will go right through to autumn. Lupines, delphiniums, and pinks (*Dianthus*), shown here, are just a few of the border plants that follow one another into bloom, running parallel with summer bulbs. For beds and containers there are long-flowering petunias and verbenas and numerous colorful but shorter-lived annuals.

FOR COLOR AND TEXTURE SEE ALSO: BEDS AND BORDERS, PP.122–165

THEMED COLOR
A color theme is one of the most reliable ways of giving a planting design coherence. It is a matter of choosing flowers that blend or contrast with one another and combining them with compatible foliage plants. Single-color themes are often more complex than they seem at first glance, as with this cool planting of white spring flowers with silver and cream-variegated foliage. Harmonies are based on closely related colors, but contrasts are just as important. The occasional shock, say of clashing purple and orange, wakes up the garden.

FLOWER COLOR
Although far from being the only ornamental feature of plants, flowers have a special value: choosing and combining their colors presents one of the most exciting challenges of gardening. The range extends from white and pastel shades to brilliant and saturated colors, some of fiery intensity, as in the Maltese cross (*Lychnis chalcedonica*) above, others of near-black depths. Flower color is rarely bland and uniform. Individual flowers or clusters are often a mixture of subtle shades, and sometimes a startling combination of base color and bold markings.

FOLIAGE COLOR
Except in autumn, the colors of foliage rarely match those of flowers in brilliance or variety, but leaves are long lasting – even those that are deciduous. We take for granted the green of foliage as the reassuring and restful background color of natural landscapes. In the garden there is the chance to exploit an infinite range of green shades and even more dramatic variations in color. Among the most conspicuous are variegations in white and yellow, golds, a range of silvers, grays, and blues, and weighty tones of bronze and purple, as in this barberry.

SEE ALSO: ORNAMENTAL TREES IN THE GARDEN, PP.184–197

AUTUMN

The illusion that summer continues is sustained by many long-flowering plants, among them roses, fuchsias, geraniums, and numerous small-flowered clematis. These overlap with plants that are more authentically autumnal, perennials such as asters, Japanese anemones, and heleniums, and bulbous plants ranging from delicate cyclamen and true autumn crocuses to colchicums. What gives the show away is the coloring foliage of deciduous trees and shrubs, bright berries, and, finally, leaf fall.

WINTER

Plant activity seems arrested in winter, when graphic qualities, dramatic when highlighted by frost or snow, count for more than flower color. Grasses as well as skeletal deciduous trees and shrubs have a subdued but often intricate beauty against the solid shapes of evergreens. Yet there are signs of movement, betrayed in the unexpectedly penetrating scent of several flowering shrubs, and in the flowers of precocious bulbs and perennials, such as snowdrops (*Galanthus*) and hellebores.

SEE ALSO: BOUNDARIES, DIVISIONS, STRUCTURES, PP.90–121

FOLIAGE TEXTURE

Foliage provides the major contrasts of texture in the garden. The richest textures rely on the interplay of several characteristics. One element is the quality of the leaf surface, which might be shiny or matte, waxy, or woolly. Crinkled and puckered leaves and those with wavy or serrated outlines contrast with those that are smooth and have a regular profile. Leaf shape and size are also important. Here the large leaves of a bergenia are set against deeply fretted fern fronds, but they would look equally effective paired with the slender blades of grasses.

MIXED TEXTURE

As well as foliage, many other parts of a plant bring texture to the garden. Flowers can be of markedly different textures, soft and velvety as in bearded irises, or bright and glistening, as in many tulips. Among the most striking effects are those produced by leaflike parts surrounding flowers. Here the jagged bracts encircling the flower heads of a sea holly (*Eryngium*) stand out from a background of love-in-a-mist (*Nigella*), whose flowers have a ruff of fine threads. Bark, twigs, seedheads, and fruit also add pleasing textures to the garden.

PLANT CATEGORIES

The following terms describing plants are those most commonly used by garden centers, nurseries, and plant catalogs.

• **ANNUALS AND BIENNIALS** Short-lived plants. Annuals complete their life span within one growing season, biennials within two.

• **BEDDING PLANTS** Plants, usually annuals, biennials, or tender perennials, used to create a temporary display.

• **BULBS** Strictly, bulbs are modified buds, usually underground, which store food during a rest period. Loosely, refers to plants growing from any kind of swollen underground storage organ, such as bulb, corm, rhizome, and tuber.

• **CLIMBERS** Plants with lax stems that grow upward by twining around supports or by attaching themselves with tendrils, specialized roots, or hooks.

• **CONIFERS** Usually evergreen trees or shrubs with needlelike, strap-shaped, or scaly leaves. Most bear woody cones, but yew (*Taxus*), for example, has fleshy fruits.

• **FERNS** Nonflowering plants that reproduce by means of spores that are borne in clusters on the leaflike fronds.

• **GRASSES** Plants with jointed stems, normally sheathed by long narrow leaves, and flower heads in plumes or spikes. Usually form tufts, clumps, or carpets. Bamboos are "woody" grasses.

• **GROUNDCOVER PLANTS** Mainly evergreen and low-growing plants with ornamental foliage that forms a dense cover over the soil.

• **PERENNIALS** Plants that live for more than two years. Usually refers to herbaceous perennials, nonwoody plants that die down in winter, but grow again in spring.

• **ROCK PLANTS** Low-growing shrubs, perennials, or bulbs (not necessarily alpines, which are natives of mountainous terrain) suitable for a rock garden or raised bed.

• **SHRUBS** Evergreen or deciduous woody-stemmed plants, smaller than trees and with main branches growing from near the base.

• **TREES** Evergreen or deciduous woody-stemmed plants, larger than shrubs, usually with a clear trunk supporting the branches.

• **WATER PLANTS** Very broad term used to describe plants that grow rooted, floating, or submerged in water; also plants that grow at the water's edge and in boggy conditions.

PLANTS FOR A PURPOSE 2

FOR FRAGRANCE SEE ALSO: ORNAMENTAL TREES, PP.184–197; HERBS IN THE GARDEN AND THEIR USES, PP.224–233

SCENTED TREES AND SHRUBS

Trees and larger shrubs with fragrant flowers create magical effects in the garden by perfuming the air over considerable distances. The scent, wafted by a breeze, often comes as a delicious surprise. This is particularly true of several fragrant but subdued winter-flowering shrubs, among them wintersweet (*Chimonanthus*). In summer, lindens (*Tilia*) can be a similarly mysterious source of fragrance. Spring-flowering azaleas (*Rhododendron*), seen here, are more showy, as are lilac (*Syringa*) and mock orange (*Philadelphus*).

FRAGRANT BORDER PLANTS

There is a wide range of smaller shrubs, perennials, and bulbs that can add a scented dimension to borders. Plants such as daphnes, pinks (*Dianthus*), and several lilies, like the Madonna lilies (*Lilium candidum*) shown here, have perfumes that carry well. Strongly scented annuals and biennials, such as stocks (*Matthiola*) and wallflowers (*Erysimum*), planted in blocks are an effective way of boosting the fragrance of borders. These plants are also suitable for bedding designs and containers.

AROMATIC PLANTS

Aromatic herbs have long been grown as flavorings for food and for medicinal use. As with other aromatic plants, a light bruising of the leaves is often all that is needed to release the volatile oils from which their fragrance comes. Whether grown in an herb garden or mingled with other plants, they need to be thoughtfully positioned: at the front of a border where they will be brushed against in passing, among paving where they get lightly trodden, or in containers close enough for the leaves to be gently pinched.

PLANNING PLANTING

Planting that defines and underlines the garden's structure and keeps it interesting throughout the year can be broken down into three broad categories.

• Plants for the framework of the garden come first. Trees and shrubs for windbreaks are not always necessary, but they belong here with hedging and large shrubs and trees that are meant to frame and divide the garden or to play key roles as focal points. Lawns are an almost two-dimensional component of the framework, while climbers are indispensable for disguising or decorating vertical surfaces such as walls and fences.

• The major plants filling in the framework are shrubs, perennials, and bulbs. Several specimens of the same plant can be used, best in odd numbers, to create informal groups or drifts. A more natural effect comes from mixed plantings that mimic the tapestries and tiered groupings of plants in the wild.

• Temporary planting offers a means of creating colorful displays or of filling a new garden. Annuals give almost instant results; fast-growing shrubs and perennials, close-planted as fillers, eventually need thinning.

FOCAL POINTS AND ACCENTS SEE ALSO: BOUNDARIES, PP.90–121

TOPIARY

Shrubs or trees clipped into formal geometric or representational shapes make a strong impact in the garden as a form of living sculpture. They can be used singly as focal points or accents or grouped, for example in avenues or walks. Evergreens are most often used. The relatively slow rate of growth of classic topiary plants such as bay (*Laurus nobilis*), boxwood (*Buxus*), and yew (*Taxus*), shown above, is initially frustrating but becomes a significant advantage when the shapes are complete, since a single annual trim is usually sufficient to maintain them.

DISTINCTIVE TREES AND SHRUBS

The combination of interesting natural shape and one or more other characteristic – it could be striking foliage, distinctive bark, or heavy crops of fruits – can make a tree or shrub a splendid eye-catcher. A specimen can be positioned to draw the eye to the end of a vista or to mark an important intersection in the garden. Good shapes include narrow columns and heads of weeping branches. The silver-leaved pear (*Pyrus salicifolia*) shown here makes a good focal point, and is also available in a weeping form that is equally suitable for this purpose.

For Easy Maintenance SEE ALSO: LAWNS AND GROUNDCOVER, PP.74–89; BEDS AND BORDERS, PP.122–165

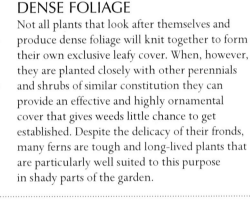

VIGOROUS GROUNDCOVER

Evergreen plants that are naturally dense can be planted to form a thatch of vegetation that gives weeds little opportunity to develop. Suitable plants require minimal care and are quick to spread and knit together with their neighbors to form an uninterrupted cover. To create a pleasing effect they must themselves be decorative. Ivies (*Hedera*) are popular for their leaf shapes and colors. Periwinkles (*Vinca*), as shown above, produce attractive flowers in spring and early summer.

DENSE FOLIAGE

Not all plants that look after themselves and produce dense foliage will knit together to form their own exclusive leafy cover. When, however, they are planted closely with other perennials and shrubs of similar constitution they can provide an effective and highly ornamental cover that gives weeds little chance to get established. Despite the delicacy of their fronds, many ferns are tough and long-lived plants that are particularly well suited to this purpose in shady parts of the garden.

SELF-SEEDERS

Plants that seed themselves provide a labor-saving way of filling gaps in a border, so discouraging weeds. Self-seeders give the garden an assured casualness, and any unwanted seedlings are easily removed. Careful selection of plants is needed, however, for some seed so freely they become weeds themselves. Good annuals and biennials include the poached egg plant (*Limnanthes*) and honesty (*Lunaria*). Welcome perennials include lady's mantle (*Alchemilla*) and aquilegias (the white flowers shown here).

For Clothing Boundaries and Divisions SEE ALSO: BOUNDARIES, DIVISIONS, STRUCTURES, PP.90–121

CLIMBING ROSES

Roses with ascending and sprawling stems are suitable for training on a wide range of supports. The most vigorous are ramblers, which usually bear small fragrant flowers in large clusters in early to midsummer. They are ideal for pergolas and for training into trees. The less vigorous climbers, many with large flowers in small clusters, can be tied to structures such as metal arches or a trellis, or to wires strung on walls. Some of the climbing roses are fragrant and many produce more than one flush of flowers between early summer and autumn.

SELF-CLINGING CLIMBERS

A number of highly ornamental climbers attach themselves to surfaces by aerial roots or suckers, and the most vigorous kinds are capable of covering very large areas. The ivies (*Hedera*) are outstanding evergreen examples, many of them small-leaved but some with large and handsomely variegated foliage, as in the example above. Virginia creeper and its close relatives (*Parthenocissus*) are deciduous, and the foliage colors brilliantly in autumn. Provided the supporting wall is sound, the roots of self-clinging climbers are unlikely to cause damage.

TWINING CLIMBERS

Many climbers, among them honeysuckles (*Lonicera*), pull themselves up by twining their stems around supports. Others, such as most clematis, including the large-flowered hybrid illustrated here, rely on twining leaf stalks to get a hold. Flowering climbers that twine are suitable for arches, and can be trained on walls that are fitted with strained wires or a trellis. If grown through trees or shrubs, twining climbers can produce happy coincidences of flowering — or a succession of blooms, when the supporting plant and the climber flower at different times.

A PLACE FOR PLANTS

THERE CAN BE two apparently very different approaches to organizing the planted areas of a garden. At one extreme, geometrically regular plots are allocated for planting, with the plants arranged in patterns that are precise and symmetrical. At the other extreme, the aim is to create a garden that seems to be a naturally occurring community of plants. In such a layout, a contrived grouping of plants is as out of place as straight lines and right angles.

The apparent distance between these two approaches is misleading. Whether plants are marshaled formally, arranged in casually organic groupings, or even displayed in containers, the underlying principle of successful planting is the same. Success comes by choosing plants to suit the growing conditions.

BEDS AND BORDERS SEE ALSO: BEDS AND BORDERS, PP.122–165

MIXED BORDER

The term "border" is sometimes used strictly for a plot of regular outline, planted ornamentally and running along the edge of a garden. A broad strip at the base of a wall or hedge fits in with this definition and with a notion of ordered space and methodical working of the soil. In reality borders can be much less regular in shape and lie in almost any part of a garden. A mixture of shrubs, bulbs, and perennials, including grasses, rather than a herbaceous border of perennials only, gives interest year-round.

SEASONAL BED

In its most general sense a bed is a plot of worked ground in a garden, but the term is often qualified. When used of an ornamental plot, it suggests an open area, often but not necessarily in the center of a garden, where the planting is temporary, changing with the season. The year might begin with winter-flowering pansies (*Viola*) and spring bulbs such as tulips, the bed then being filled with flowers, such as petunias and verbenas, that give a long-lasting summer display.

NATURALIZED PLANTINGS SEE ALSO: LAWNS AND GROUND COVER, PP.74–89; BEDS AND BORDERS, PP.122–165

PLANTING IN GRAVEL

This apparently casual and naturalistic method of planting is particularly suitable in a dry garden that is stocked with drought-tolerant plants. The topdressing of gravel improves surface drainage, allowing moisture to drain away quickly from the plants, but it also helps conserve moisture by slowing evaporation from the soil. The gravel acts as insulation and should not be laid over ground that is cold or frozen. Gravel discourages the growth of weeds, but perennial weeds must be eradicated before the gravel is spread.

PRAIRIE AND MEADOW

Ornamentals can be naturalized in grass to create the effects of wild plant communities in prairies, as above, and in meadows. Success depends on introducing plants that grow well together in the local conditions, either natives of the area or of areas with similar soil and climate. Establishing a stable and self-perpetuating community of naturalized plants may be slow. In the early stages it is necessary to control competitive weeds and, in the case of meadows, to reduce soil fertility to prevent the flowers from being swamped by vigorous grasses.

WOODLAND

Many plants thrive in the dappled light of deciduous woodland, although the main flowering season usually occurs in spring, before the foliage of the canopy unfurls. True woodland can be transformed into a naturalistic garden by large-scale planting, rhododendrons doing well under a canopy where the soil is acidic. An impression of woodland can be achieved with the remnants of an old orchard, even a solitary tree, underplanted with bulbs and shade-tolerant perennials such as hellebores, ferns, and perhaps a shrub or two.

SEE ALSO: CONTAINERS AND RAISED BEDS, PP.166–183; THE EDIBLE GARDEN, PP.234–273

HEDGED BEDS

Beds surrounded by low hedges were a characteristic feature of 16th- and 17th-century gardens and are familiar components in modern formal designs. The most widely used low hedging for beds, as in this garden, is the evergreen dwarf boxwood (*Buxus sempervirens* 'Suffruticosa'). The bed might be planted for seasonal displays or more permanently, for example, with roses. The loose growth in the bed often makes a pleasing contrast with the firm lines of the hedge.

RAISED BED

Beds raised above the level of surrounding paths are used in ornamental and kitchen gardens. A common reason for creating raised beds is to provide specific growing conditions, particularly for plants such as numerous bulbs and rock garden plants that do well only where the soil drains freely. The extra height also makes beds easier to work and helps to show off small plants that might be overlooked in a border. The walls of the beds can be made with a variety of materials, including bricks and railroad ties.

KITCHEN BED

The kitchen garden can be divided into several large beds, with the crops planted in long rows, as here. Crops are readily accessible in this arrangement, but the soil between rows is unproductive and becomes compacted by treading. As an alternative, a vegetable plot can be laid out in small permanent beds or strips and the ground worked only from paths running along each side. The soil is constantly improved, allowing plants to be grown much closer together, resulting in increased yields.

SEE ALSO: WATER GARDENING, PP.198–223

CONTAINERS SEE ALSO: CONTAINERS AND RAISED BEDS, PP.166–183

WATERSIDE

Few gardens have the advantage of a natural stream or pool where aquatic and marginal plants can be naturalized, but it is not difficult to create bodies of water and boggy areas using flexible liners. A bog garden can form a margin to a stream or pool or stand as a feature in its own right. To look convincing as an isolated feature, it must be set in a low-lying position. The liner for a bog area, unlike that for a pool, has some perforations in it, but the soil it contains holds enough moisture, kept filled in sunny weather, for waterside and bog plants.

POTS, TUBS, AND PLANTERS

Growing plants in containers increases the scope of any garden. Treated as either a permanent feature or a seasonal planting, used singly or in groups, containers can brighten a dull corner, provide a focus of attention, or bring color and greenery to a patio or terrace. The many different kinds of container include plastic and terracotta pots, wooden tubs and windowboxes, fiberglass planters, and metal urns. Almost any receptacle is suitable, however, providing it is stable and holes can be made in the base to allow excess moisture to drain away.

HANGING CONTAINERS

Containers that can be suspended increase the opportunities for displays in the garden and allow plants to be grown where there is neither ground nor the possibility of setting out pots and tubs. Like all other plant containers, those that are suspended must have drainage holes and be large enough to hold soil mix that will supply the plants with sufficient nutrients and moisture. Before containers are put in position it is necessary to work out how to water them. Fixtures for hanging baskets and brackets for pots must be securely fastened.

WORKING OUT WHAT YOU WANT

WHETHER YOU ARE PLANNING a garden from scratch or modifying something that already exists, created either by previous owners or by yourself, you need to have a clear idea of what you are aiming for. This does not mean that you have to work out all the details right from the start. What you must do, though, is bring into focus your own ideas about the style and mood the garden should have and the kind of features that really matter to you. It is expensive and time-consuming to make yet more changes later on, so it is worth taking the trouble to order your thoughts and work through what is involved in creating the garden that you really want.

FINDING OUT WHAT YOU LIKE

The information and ideas in books and magazines and on television are all useful when sorting out the way you would like your garden to develop. You can also get ideas from model gardens featured in garden shows, but remember that these have been specially staged and are unlikely to reflect the year-round practicalities of maintenance and plant care.

REAL-LIFE INSPIRATION Real gardens, those of friends and neighbors as well as those open to the public, are by far the best source of ideas. Even when a garden is on a grand scale, you can often find in it something that could be adapted to your own more modest plot. It might be the treatment of a slope, or a particular approach to planting, or the arrangement of features such as raised beds.

FLORAL DREAM ▷
For some, this is an idyllic garden — borders filled with flowers, a mown grass path, an old sundial, and a cast-iron gate giving a view of a distant landscape. But do you have the time and money to create and maintain this dream?

△ **LOW-MAINTENANCE PLANTING**
The green heads of Euphorbia characias *and a subtle combination of green and gray foliage make virtually care-free groundcover along the path to a wooden summerhouse.*

THINKING ABOUT WHAT YOU NEED

Whenever you are visiting gardens, it is worth carrying a notebook. Jotting down points on layout, style, and mood, as well as more specific information on features and planting, helps crystalize ideas that you might want to apply in your own garden. For this there needs to be a debate, whether it is simply in your own mind or with partner and family. The best way to sift through the options open to you is to draw up a list. The checklist (*opposite*) makes a useful starting point.

The difficult decisions often involve matching short-term needs with long-term ambitions. At an early stage, because of lack of time, you may have to rely on broad effects, using low-maintenance planting; but you might hope to provide conditions, later on, for a specialized group of plants — for example a raised bed in which to grow bulbs and rock garden plants. It is worth marking on your plan any future adaptations you would like to make.

You must also resolve conflicts between the style you are seeking and the features you want. A barbecue fits naturally on a patio that is laid out in a relaxed way as an outdoor room, but it may not sit so comfortably with the stark simplicity of a Japanese garden. These issues are matters of taste, and only you and those with whom you share the debate can resolve them.

PLANNING CHECKLIST

PRIORITIES

The point of this checklist is to help you rank the components of a garden according to the importance they have for you. Your priorities should reflect what is useful and desirable for you now and also, say, in 10 years' time, when you may have children to think of, or when you may have more time, but also may be less mobile.

▦ CHILDREN'S PLAY AREA ▦ FACILITIES FOR ENTERTAINING ▦ FRUIT ▦ HERBS ▦ LOW COST ▦ LOW MAINTENANCE ▦ PARKING ▦ PETS ▦ PRIVACY ▦ ORNAMENTAL PLANTS ▦ SPECIALIZED PLANTS ▦ SUITABLE FOR ELDERLY PEOPLE OR PEOPLE WITH DISABILITIES ▦ VEGETABLES

STYLE AND MOOD

Recognizing the style and mood you want to evoke will help you decide what elements to include in your garden. Structures such as arbors and gazebos help to create a romantic atmosphere, while obelisks and topiary can play important roles as accents in formal gardens. There are, however, many components that are perfectly at home in gardens of very different kinds.

▦ COTTAGE ▦ EXPANSIVE ▦ EXUBERANT ▦ FORMAL ▦ MEDITERRANEAN ▦ MINIMALIST ▦ NATURALISTIC ▦ PEACEFUL ▦ PRODUCTIVE ▦ ROMANTIC ▦ SECLUDED ▦ SUBTROPICAL

PLANTS

▦ BORDER PLANTS
- Colorful flowers
- Fragrance
- Good shape and texture
- Interesting foliage
- Long-term (perennials)
- Quick-growing (annuals)

▦ CLIMBERS
- Colorful flowers
- Decorative fruit
- Evergreen
- Interesting foliage

▦ FEATURE PLANTS
▦ FRUIT
- Soft fruit
- Tree fruit

▦ GROUNDCOVERS
▦ HERBS
▦ LOW-MAINTENANCE PLANTS
▦ NATURALIZED PLANTS
▦ PLANTS TO ENCOURAGE WILDLIFE
▦ PLANTS FOR ALL-YEAR INTEREST
▦ SHRUBS
- Colorful flowers
- Decorative fruit
- Evergreen
- Interesting foliage

▦ TREES
- Colorful flowers
- Decorative fruit
- Evergreen
- Interesting foliage

▦ VEGETABLES

SURFACES

▦ BARK CHIPS
▦ BRICKS AND PAVERS
▦ COBBLESTONES
▦ RANDOM PAVING
▦ GRANITE PAVERS
▦ GRAVEL
▦ LAWN
- Aromatic lawn
- Rough grass
- Traditional lawn

▦ PAVING SLABS
▦ PEBBLES
▦ POURED CONCRETE
▦ TILES
▦ WOODEN DECKING
▦ SURFACES FOR PLAY AREAS
- Bark chips
- Grass
- Rubber granules

LEISURE

▦ BARBECUE
▦ GARDEN FURNITURE
- Bench
- Hammock
- Loungers
- Swing seat
- Tables and chairs

▦ PLAY EQUIPMENT
- Basketball net
- Games area
- Play frame
- Sandbox
- Slide
- Swings
- Playhouse
- Treehouse

▦ SWIMMING POOL
▦ TENNIS COURT

BOUNDARIES AND DIVISIONS

▦ DIVIDERS
- Arch
- Pergola
- Trellis

▦ FENCES
- Bamboo
- Iron railings
- Chain link
- Picket
- Post and chain
- Post and rail
- Wattle hurdle
- Wire mesh
- Wooden panels

▦ HEDGES
- Breached
- Clipped
- Deciduous
- Evergreen
- Flowering
- Laid
- Mixed
- Pleached
- Topiary

▦ WALLS
- Brick
- Concrete block
- Dressed stone
- Drystone
- Glass brick
- Imitation stone
- Screen block
- Railroad ties

DECORATIVE FEATURES

▦ ARBOR
▦ BIRD BATH
▦ BIRD TABLE
▦ CONTAINERS
- Hanging baskets
- Pots and tubs
- Windowboxes

▦ GAZEBO
▦ RAISED BEDS
▦ ROCK OR GRAVEL GARDEN
▦ STATUES AND ORNAMENTS
▦ SUMMERHOUSE
▦ SUNDIAL
▦ VERTICAL ACCENT FEATURES
- Stake tepees
- Obelisks

▦ WATER FEATURES
- Bog garden
- Cobblestone fountain
- Container pond
- Flowing water
- Formal fountain
- Formal pond
- Informal pond
- Wall fountain

STORAGE AND UTILITIES

▦ COLD FRAME
▦ COMPOST BINS
▦ GREENHOUSE
▦ LIGHTS
- Electric
- Candles and flares

▦ POTTING SHED
▦ GARBAGE CANS
▦ STORAGE BENCH
▦ TOOL SHED
▦ WASHING LINE

ASSESSING WHAT YOU HAVE

BEFORE YOU CAN draw up a realistic plan for your garden, you need to make a proper assessment of your site. It is a good idea to spend some time over this. You need to get an impression of what the garden is like at different times of the day – which parts get the most sun; how much shade is cast and where. If at all possible, it is worth waiting to see it at different seasons of the year so that you discover its warmest and coldest corners, its wettest and windiest spots. Every plot has its good and bad points – yours may be very small, have impoverished soil, or be on steeply sloping ground – but a challenging site can be the making of an interesting and highly individual garden. In the light of what you discover, you may find yourself abandoning preconceived ideas of your ideal garden – or at least adapting them to suit the scale and conditions of your own particular plot.

MATTERS OF SIZE

There are various ways of making the best of the space in your garden, no matter how small or large the site.

LARGE SITES These are often best treated as a series of compartments, the partitions formed by hedges and other screening devices. Vistas, focal points, and the occasional surprise feature all help to give the garden coherence. There may be opportunities for planting trees and large shrubs (perhaps adding to specimens already on the site). Plants that need a lot of attention may have to be concentrated in a few small areas, with much of the garden planned for low maintenance.

SMALL SITES Many small gardens are rich in possibilities, despite the limitations of size. Concealing the boundaries by planting around the edges and "borrowing" the trees and shrubs of neighboring gardens helps to create a sense of space. A slight change of level and a few large plants lend dramatic touches, while the exclusive use of dwarf plants has a dull, miniaturizing effect.

◁ **GREEN COURTYARD GARDEN**
The intimate character of this tiny garden is emphasized by the curious tree-trunk barrier and the log sections making stepping stones across gravel to a small outdoor dining area. A cool, green atmosphere has been created using foliage plants.

△ **SMALL PATIO GARDEN WITH DECKING**
Although this garden is small, the decked area for outdoor entertaining, partially screened from the house, has given an impression of space. The depth of the garden is emphasized by the lengthwise run of the wood. The container-grown plants can be moved about to alter the shape of the garden room.

THINKING ABOUT SHAPE

The shape of the site is just as important as its area and has implications for the way the garden is designed.

NARROW GARDENS On a long and narrow site of the kind common in suburban areas, a straight path running from end to end is likely to draw the eye immediately to the far boundary, making the garden look smaller than it really is. To avoid revealing all at a single glance, it is worth introducing one or two screens that run partway across the garden, in effect subdividing it and forcing the path off a direct track.

WIDE GARDENS The broad spaciousness of a wide garden along the front of a house will often be welcome and might be designed with organic shapes and flowing lines. An interesting garden might also be made with a broad central path hedged on either side, with openings in the hedges giving access to separate compartments. Lighter barriers running from front to back, perhaps consisting of plants trained on ropes, offer a means of giving a short, wide plot more pleasing proportions.

AWKWARD SHAPES A design that masks the boundaries can overcome some of the disadvantages of an awkward site. In the case of a triangular garden, for example, the best solution may be to fill in the angled corners with planting, perhaps with a shed tucked behind, and to turn the rest into one or two spaces of regular shape, each surrounded by planting.

◁ **A PAUSE IN A LONG GARDEN**
In this long and lushly green garden, a place for pausing and resting to one side of the main pathway is a welcome diversion. The way the design opens out at this point creates a sense of space without contradicting the private character of the garden, resulting from the lavish use of foliage plants on the boundaries as well as in the beds.

DEALING WITH SLOPES

On a sloping site there are opportunities to make the most of different views and to create areas of distinctive character at different levels. Even a slight change of level can make a flat site more interesting.

TERRACING AND STEPS The most ambitious way to deal with a sloping site is to build a series of terraces supported by retaining walls and connected by steps. Terracing often involves having to move considerable quantities of soil, and retaining walls may need to be reinforced if they are to withstand the pressure of soil and moisture.

RAMPS Gentle slopes or ramps as alternatives to steps may take up more room in the garden, but they are easier for the elderly to negotiate and give access for equipment such as wheelbarrows and lawnmowers as well as wheelchairs. Slopes are more fun for children, too, allowing them an uninterrupted pathway for bikes, cars, and other wheeled toys.

◁ **TERRACING**
A short flight of steps connects two levels in a terraced garden. The structure of the retaining walls has been deliberately obscured by planting along the top and at the base. Enough of the upper terrace is hidden for it to retain an element of surprise.

LOCATION AND VIEW

If there is a good view from the site of the garden, it is worth taking it into account in the design. It is, however, much more common to have to block out unsightly views and to screen for privacy.

VIEWS To make the most of a good view, it needs to be framed. This principle applies to views beyond the garden and to those within it. Sight lines from windows and doors deserve special attention. Paired shrubs and trees, avenues, and arches are the most common framing devices.

PRIVACY If your garden is overlooked, you may want to consider increasing the height of walls and fences. Training climbers on trelliswork mounted on the top is one of the quickest ways to create an effective screen. Carefully chosen shrubs and trees planted on the boundary may give you enough privacy, but will take some time to reach the required height.

NOISE POLLUTION Traffic noise is a common problem in gardens near busy roads. A hedge or other thick barrier of foliage can help deaden the sound.

△ **SHELTER AND PRIVACY**
Hedges and open fences act as wind filters and can be used to create areas of the garden that are relatively calm and sheltered. Solid walls and close fences, though, tend to cause wind turbulence. Trees, large shrubs, and structures such as trellis screens clothed with climbers can block views into a garden and help make it private.

CLIMATE AND MICROCLIMATE

The range of plants you can grow and the way you can make use of your garden are greatly influenced by climatic factors such as rainfall, temperature, and wind.

CLIMATE You need to find out about the broad pattern of weather in the area where you are gardening, the effects of altitude and the proximity of the sea, and, in particular, when frost, cold winds, and low rainfall might be expected. Talking to local people is perhaps the easiest way of getting this information. Looking at other gardens in the locality will also give you a good idea of the kind of plants you can hope to grow well.

MICROCLIMATES Within any garden there may be several different microclimates, where conditions vary to some extent from those generally prevailing. Some parts of the site may be in a frost pocket, where cold air lingers longest, or may be particularly warm and sheltered, at the base of a sun-baked wall, for example. You can take advantage and make the most of a garden's patchwork of microclimates by matching plants to existing conditions.

△ **SUNNY SPOTS**
Many plants will retain their naturally compact shape and thrive only if they are given an open, sunny position. If grown in shade, almost all annuals, including Shirley poppies (Papaver rhoeas) and cornflowers (Centaurea cyanus), shown here, become drawn and straggly and produce few flowers.

◁ **SHADY CORNERS**
The understory of woodland provides a model for shady parts of the garden — not just areas under trees and shrubs, but also where there is shade from walls and buildings. Many spring bulbs that in their natural habitat flower before the tree canopy develops do well in these conditions. In summer, good foliage cover is provided by many perennials, including hostas.

SOIL AND DRAINAGE

The nature of the soil in your garden greatly affects what will thrive in it. There are five basic types — clay, silt, sand, chalk (alkaline), and peat (acidic) — and most plants grow better in one type than another.

SOIL STRUCTURE The ideal soil consists of a balanced mixture of clay, sand, and silt and is rich in organic matter (decaying remains of plants and animals). A well-structured soil, with plenty of air pockets but also retaining water well, is crumbly and moist. When you rub a small sample between your fingers, it will hold together, making a cylindrical shape, but without being sticky. The structure of any soil can be improved by digging, and by incorporating well-rotted organic matter.

ACID AND ALKALINE SOILS Soils vary in the degree to which they are acidic or alkaline, depending on how much lime they contain. This is known as the pH level and, since some plants prefer alkaline conditions and others acidic ones, it is worth testing your soil, using a simple kit.

DRAINAGE The rate at which water drains from the soil has a bearing on the plants you can grow. Some tolerate very dry soil; others survive in waterlogged ground. You can install irrigation or drainage systems, but it makes more sense to choose plants that like the natural conditions you have.

SEE ALSO: BEDS AND BORDERS, PP.122–165

◁ **ACIDIC SOIL**
The plants best known for needing lime-free, acidic soil are shrubs and trees belonging to the heath family. They include rhododendrons, azaleas, and heathers. There are in addition a number of perennials, many of them woodland plants, as illustrated here, that are really happy only on a neutral to acidic soil.

◁ **ALKALINE SOIL**
Many lovely gardens have been made on thin, alkaline soils over chalk. Unlike acid-loving plants, those that prefer alkaline soils generally tolerate conditions outside their ideal range. This is true for red valerian (Centranthus ruber), of which the white-flowered form is seen here. However, it often shows its preference by self-seeding freely over old walls.

WET PLANTING ▷
Rather than draining a low-lying wet area, it may be less expensive and more practical to transform it into a bog garden. Moisture-loving plants, such as the colorful marsh marigold (Caltha palustris) shown here, thrive in permanently boggy conditions at the margins of a pond.

◁ **DRY PLANTING**
Successful gardening in areas with low rainfall and where the soil is free-draining depends on choosing plants that tolerate drought. An attractive form of dry gardening is to plant in a gravel mulch, which helps reduce water loss, grouping plants in the manner of naturally occurring communities. In fact, the plants used may come from regions geographically far apart.

PLANNING CHANGES

IF YOU ARE TO DEVELOP your garden in a coherent way, you need to make a careful survey and prepare a plan, drawn to scale, of how you want it to be. Allowing the garden to develop in dribs and drabs, or haphazardly, tends to be less satisfactory than a planned approach, and in the long run usually proves more expensive.

◁ **WAITING TO BE TRANSFORMED**
Despite its neglected state, this walled site has great potential. The photographs on pp.52–53 show how clearing unwanted trees and shrubs and imaginative planning have transformed it into a beautiful and varied garden.

MAKING A SURVEY

The first impressions of a site, sometimes discouraging, can give a very false idea, particularly of scale. Gathering accurate information will help give the correct perspective, and form the basis of the plan that you eventually put into action.

SKETCH AND NOTES Making a rough ground plan (*see right*) is essential to get a grasp of the garden. Use this plan as the basis for notes, assembling information on anything that affects the way the garden grows: the site's exposure to prevailing wind, how much shade is cast throughout the day, the quality of the soil, and how well it drains. Note good views and those that need screening. Record the condition of built features, including walls, fences, and hard surfaces.

PHOTOGRAPHS A camera is a valuable tool when you are surveying your site, and the photographs you take will provide a fascinating record when the garden is mature. Take photographs from different angles, looking to and away from the house and from doorways and windows, including views from upstairs. The same shot taken at different times of the day and, if possible, at different seasons, will reveal a lot about the way shadows fall.

ESTIMATING SLOPES You need a clear idea of the levels and slopes on your plot, since they affect drainage and the position of features, as well as the moisture-proofing of the house. In a small garden it may be enough to know there is a slight slope away from the house. You need more precise information if the slope is more marked. Make the calculation over a fixed distance, say 6ft (2m). Lay a level board (testing with a spirit level) between two vertical pegs. The difference in height above ground of the two pegs gives the slope over the 6ft (2m) distance.

▽ **BEDS AND BORDERS**
The rigid pattern of the existing beds and borders, now overgrown with shrubs and weeds, could be reinstated, but there is no compelling logic to these vestiges of the garden's design and the best course is to make a fresh start.

▽ **OVERGROWN SHRUBS**
Hard pruning might make these shrubs vigorous and shapely again, but they are not well placed and it is better to take them out.

DRAWING A ROUGH PLAN

Draw a rough plan of your existing garden on site, pacing out distances to enable you to plot measurements approximately. Note the points of the compass and record all the built features, including paved areas, and the position of beds, borders, trees, and shrubs. Identify, if possible, any prominent plants. You may need to do additional research to establish the position of drains, the location of sewers, and the underground route of gas, electrical, and water services.

BEDS AND BORDERS

OVERGROWN SHRUBS

◁ **APPLE TREE**
A mature and healthy apple tree has character and is worth retaining as a major feature in the redesigned garden.

▽ **LARGE CONIFER**
The large and dark conifer seems to threaten the house. Removing it will let in light and air.

BEDS AND BORDERS

APPLE TREE

SKIMPY TREES

LARGE CONIFER

SHADED BED

ROUGH GRASS

△ **ROUGH GRASS**
There is no paving around the house, and the lawn has become rough, weedy grass.

△ **SKIMPY TREES**
The poorly shaped fruit trees dotted randomly about the garden are not worth keeping.

△ **SHADED BED**
A mysterious bed where little would thrive in the shade of the conifer is best abandoned.

WORKING OUT YOUR NEW DESIGN

You may have a good idea of the way you want to develop your garden, but it is still worth looking at the information you have gathered with an open mind. An accurate scale drawing recording the features you want to retain (*see below*), as well as the changes you want to make, allows you to review the options and to make realistic assessments of the materials and plants required.

TESTING IDEAS In the initial stages, you can treat your scale drawing as a base plan, and use overlays of tracing paper to test out different ideas.

VISUAL AIDS With your plan in hand, go back to the garden and try to visualize how your ideas would work. Marking the outlines of beds and borders and other features with a hose, with a garden line strung between stakes, or with a trickle of sand can help you assess the proportions. Stakes can be used to give an idea of the position of upright features such as trees.

PLANTING AND STRUCTURAL PLANS Once you have established the broad outlines of your garden, you may find it helpful to make detailed planting plans for particular areas, as well as to draw cross-sections of specific features, for example, a pond or a pergola.

MAKING A SCALE DRAWING

In the first instance, the scale drawing should record the position of the features of the garden, both old and new. Make the drawing accurately, on graph paper, basing it on the measurements you have taken on site (*see below*, Plotting Boundaries and Features). Use a scale relating to the size of the grid on the paper and one that allows the plan to fit comfortably on the sheet, ideally with space at the margins for notes or an explanation of any codes used.

ARBOR AND GRASS WALK ▽
The narrowing perspective of the grass walk leading to an arbor helps to make the garden seem larger than it is.

▽ **TREE WALK**
The avenue of trees is intended to create another vista and to provide a screen higher than the garden wall.

▽ **POND AND VEGETABLE PLOT**
Screening adds mystery to the pond area and sets the productive part of the garden apart.

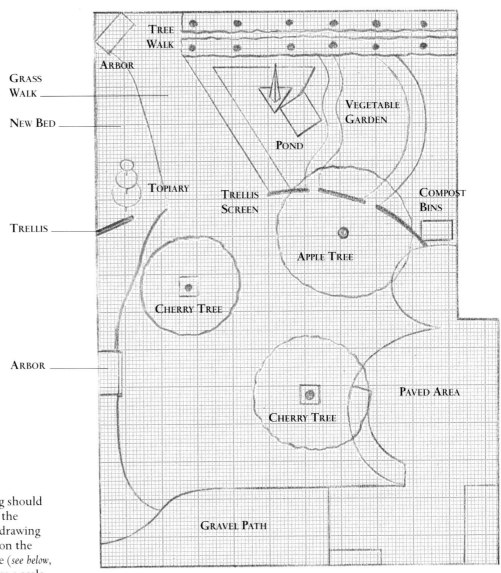

△ **HARD SURFACES**
Much of the garden is lawn and planting, but access areas around the house have hard surfaces.

△ **APPLE TREE AND TRELLIS**
The mature apple tree has been retained as a key feature and given extra weight by the trellis curve.

PLOTTING BOUNDARIES AND FEATURES

Work methodically, taking measurements of all buildings, trees, and planting areas and marking them on your rough plan.

• If the garden is a simple rectangle or square, take measurements, at right angles, from a base line such as a boundary.

• Triangulation is a useful way of pinpointing features or establishing the boundaries if the shape of the garden is irregular.

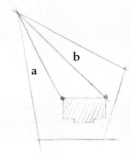

1 MEASURING
Measure to the junction of two boundaries from two fixed points, here two corners of the house. Note the measurements (a and b) on your rough plan. Take measurements in the same way for each of the other boundary corners.

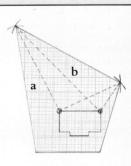

2 DRAW TO SCALE
On graph paper, draw the house to scale. Set a compass to the scaled-down measure (a) and draw an arc from the first fixed point. Repeat with (b) from the second fixed point. Where the arcs intersect marks the boundary corner.

PUTTING THE PLAN INTO PRACTICE

It is difficult not to be impatient when at last you have decided on the way ahead for your new garden. Before rushing in to order materials, it is worth shopping around, particularly for paving and for large quantities of plants. You may want to get most of the work done in autumn or spring, but it is wise to delay if the ground is sodden. The compaction caused by treading and machinery can result in serious drainage problems.

A GARDEN IN THE MAKING

The garden illustrated in the rough plan on p.50 provides a case study of garden making. The three-dimensional plan (*right*) of the new garden shows that the mature apple tree was retained, while the photographs record how new features were created on either side of the lawn's strong diagonal.

◁ **LAYING PAVED AREAS**
In an ideal sequence, the paving would have been laid first to avoid damaging the lawn. Fortunately, there was access from one side in this garden so that the paving operation had little effect on the established lawn, which otherwise would have needed to be protected with boards.

△ **SPRING BORDER**
Early in the garden's development, autumn-planted tulips were combined with forget-me-nots (Myosotis) to create a colorful effect in spring.

△ **SUMMER BORDER**
Blue-flowered perennials play an important role in this summer border, but late-flowering annuals such as cosmos are used to extend the season into early autumn.

△ **WINTER BORDER**
The stems of deciduous shrubs such as dogwood (Cornus) give texture and color in autumn and winter, but here the glowing focus is a cluster of ornamental cabbages.

△ **A Walk of Pleached Lindens**
Two rows of lindens (Tilia) along the far boundary have been pleached, the branches above a height of about 6ft (1.8m) trained horizontally to form an avenue on stilts. A pergola clothed with climbers would create a similar effect.

△ **Trellis Screens**
See-through trellis panels, which cast unusual shadows, help create separate but interrelated spaces within the garden and reinforce the barrier formed by the old apple tree. The screens have now been painted deep green.

△ **From the Kitchen Door**
The kitchen door provides the most frequently used access to the garden, and this corner serves as a gentle introduction to the whole. Colorful flowers and foliage plants are clustered close to the door before the paving opens out to a generous circular area.

ESTABLISHING PRIORITIES

You or your contractor may not be able to perform work on an ideal timetable, but you must order your priorities and think through the implications of the schedule you adopt.

■ **Boundaries** Build boundary walls and fences early to provide shelter and security and before the development of the garden makes access difficult.

■ **Services** Lay underground cables, pipes, and drains before putting down hard surfaces, creating lawns, or planting. Keep a plan of all underground services.

■ **Hard landscaping** Put down paving and other hard surfaces while it is still easy to move materials about and stack them. If you decide to lay quality paving little by little, as funds become available, work out how you will store materials and dispose of rubble.

■ **Lawns** Lawns sown from seed in spring or autumn take many months before they can withstand heavy wear, and even a sod lawn needs several months to settle down. Establish lawns when you know that the area can be left undisturbed.

■ **Renovation** The best time to carry out drastic pruning of overgrown and neglected trees and shrubs is between midautumn and early spring, but cutting back may be necessary at other times so that other work can be carried out.

■ **Planting** The main planting seasons are autumn and spring, but see PLANT PRACTICALITIES below.

LEGAL MATTERS

It is important to be aware of the legal dimension to every garden.

■ **Boundaries** Recognize that boundaries are the most sensitive areas, where there is the potential for conflicts of interests with neighbors, and where regulations and responsibilities may be laid down by local authorities.

■ **Building work** Familiarize yourself with building and planning regulations before undertaking any construction work, including putting up a greenhouse.

■ **Removal and demolition** Check planning regulations before felling trees, removing hedges, or demolishing structures such as walls or buildings.

PROFESSIONAL HELP

Even if you enjoy the practical side of gardening, use professionals for tasks that are potentially dangerous, require the use of specialized equipment, or are too heavy for you to undertake on your own. Use professionals, too, if you need legal advice and help on planning or engineering (for example, if building retaining walls). A personal recommendation counts for a lot, but in any case use a member of a trade or a professional organization.

■ **Electrical work** Use a qualified electrician for all electrical work.

■ **Tree work** Employ a qualified arborist to take down whole trees and remove large branches and for pruning where the work needs to be carried out above ground level.

PLANT PRACTICALITIES

Plants can be bought from a wide range of outlets, including specialized nurseries and garden centers, and also by mail order.

■ **Container-grown stock** This can be planted outside the traditional periods, which are autumn and spring, but attention to watering is essential until plants are well established.

TIPS FOR AN INSTANT GARDEN

Staged development of a garden, beginning with short-lived but colorful, fast-growing plants, is less expensive than trying to create an immediate mature effect using quality paving and well-grown trees and shrubs.

• For hard surfaces use gravel, combined with paving or decking for seating and access areas. Plant into the gravel.

• Screen, shelter, and compartmentalize the garden using trelliswork covered with fast-growing climbers such as Canary creeper (*Tropaeolum peregrinum*).

• Create vertical accents with arches, pergolas, and stake tepees, training climbers such as ornamental gourds and morning glories (*Ipomoea*).

• Fill beds and borders with bedding plants; placing taller annuals (e.g., cleomes) and fast-growing shrubs (e.g., buddleias and *Vitex*) at the back.

• Create height in the foreground with standard bushes of marguerites (*Argyranthemum*) and fuchsias in containers.

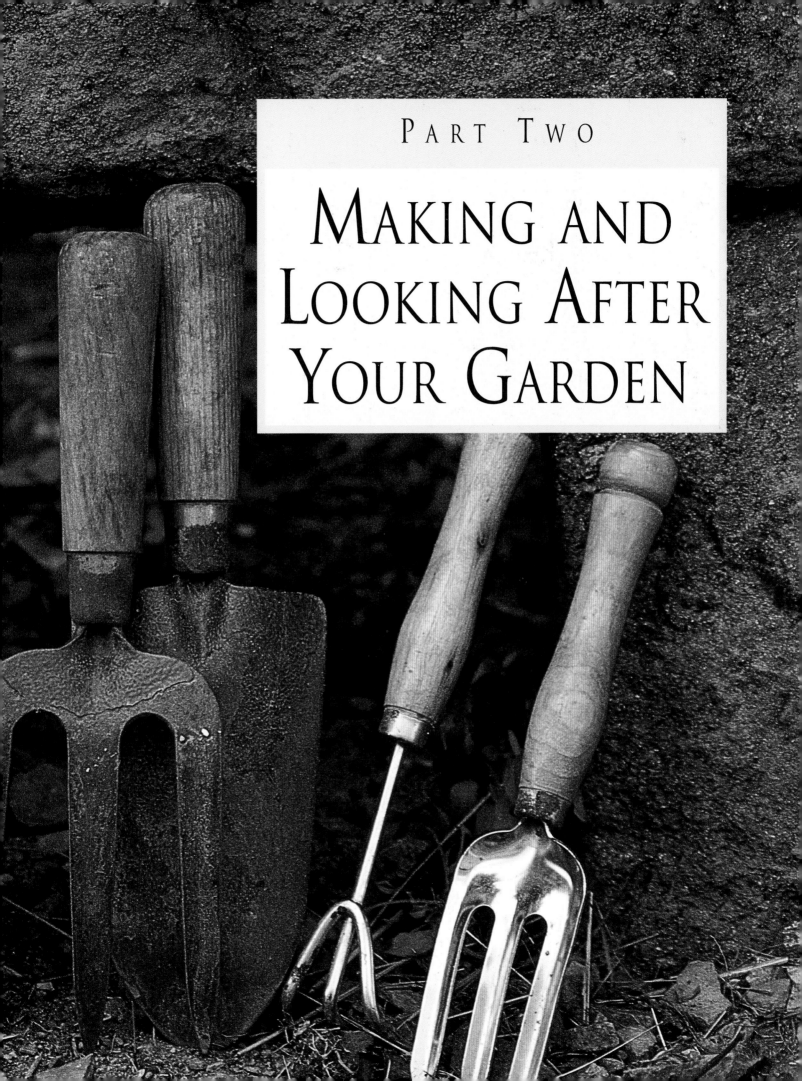

PART TWO

MAKING AND LOOKING AFTER YOUR GARDEN

PATIOS AND PATHS

SITING PATIOS

A PATIO THAT LINKS house and garden is both a practical and decorative means of enjoying outdoor living – a haven for simple relaxation or dining. Siting in the usual way, close to and foursquare with the house, is most convenient, with the advantage that a power source for lighting is readily accessible. If the site does not offer warmth and shelter or afford privacy, however, consider some alternatives. An angled or corner site, for example, might receive sun for much of the day, perhaps with views across the garden or to the landscape beyond, or two smaller areas could provide a choice of warmth or cool shade, a welcome retreat on a hot, sunny day.

SITING A PATIO AREA

A site that is warm and sheltered will be enjoyable both earlier and later in the year than one that is exposed to wind. Create wind shelter for comfort by using trellis screens or pergolas – both also provide planting opportunities for a range of fragrant plants to enhance the ambience.

Avoid sites too close to large trees; they may cast excessive shade, drip rain from their canopy, cause nuisance with falling leaves and insects, and may even dislodge paving with their questing roots.

GOOD IDEAS

• Size is important. Allow 4sq.yd (3.3sq.m) for each person likely to use the patio, and make room for seating and tables. Take into account the size of house and garden, too: the patio needs to be in proportion with both.

• Keep it simple. Furniture and plantings in ornamental pots usually look best against an unobtrusive surface. Simple materials are also easier to lay – important if you do it yourself.

△ SHOWING OFF
The neutral colors of paving do not detract from the clean lines of elegant patio furniture; textural interest is gained from the simple contrast of smooth flagstones and gravel.

◁ THE PERFECT SITE
A small patio sited away from the house receives maximum sunshine. High walls with trees behind lend shelter and privacy and the resulting still air is pervaded by perfumes from surrounding plantings.

MEASURING

The first task when building a patio is to measure the area in order to calculate quantities of materials needed. Given accurate measurements, a good home-supply store will be able to advise on the quantities you need.

Area is calculated simply by multiplying length by width. If the site is irregular, mark it out on graph paper, using one square per sq.yd (sq.m). Counting all full squares and any more than a third full gives a sufficiently accurate estimate of the area.

TAKING THE STRAIN

Patios and paving must be built with appropriate load-bearing paving laid on firm foundations if they are to be stable in use. Decide whether the surface will take only foot traffic or may occasionally need to bear vehicular weight. Consider also the climate; areas that suffer summer drought or severe winters usually need deeper foundations. Seek the advice of at least two reputable contractors.

| CAST SLAB | PRESSED SLAB |

CHOOSE THE RIGHT COURSE
Cast slabs are designed to bear light to medium-weight traffic, while pressed slabs, though lighter, are stronger. Cast slabs are ideal for patios that take only foot traffic, but if a patio is integrated with a driveway, for example, you must use a material that will take the strain.

SEE ALSO: Doing the Groundwork, pp.58–59; Using Lighting in the Garden, pp.70–71; Enhancing Patio Areas, pp.72–73; Garden Styles, pp.122–123

CHOOSING PAVING MATERIALS

While appearance is often a matter of taste, the best results are had by taking a cue from the color and materials used in the house and its setting, and by reflecting the mood and style of the garden.

The selection of pavers, with shapes, sizes, colors, and costs in bewildering variety, is daunting. Focus on structural factors first to narrow the possibilities. The finished surface must bear the expected load and be durable and weatherproof in the given climate, which may also include being nonslip when wet.

BELGIAN BLOCKS

RED BRICK PAVERS

CLAY PAVERS

△ SMALL UNIT FLEXIBLE PAVERS

Small units are ideal where a fine-textured or patterned surface is desired. In irregularly shaped areas, they can often be laid without wasteful cutting. Many are designed for easy laying on a compacted sand base without mortar.

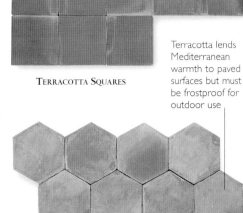

TERRACOTTA SQUARES

Terracotta lends Mediterranean warmth to paved surfaces but must be frostproof for outdoor use

TERRACOTTA TILES

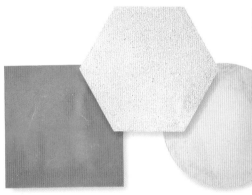

CONCRETE PAVING SLABS

Strong and durable, concrete is available in many attractive finishes, which belie its utilitarian image

Pointed slabs provide a fine-textured, non-slip surface that makes pattern work simple

POINTED SLABS

NATURAL STONE

ARTIFICIAL STONE

△ LARGE UNIT PAVERS

Large units are available in a wealth of shapes, sizes, and finishes, with a wide color range that allows selection to match local architecture and materials. They come in natural and reconstituted stone or cast concrete and are usually laid on mortar on a prepared sub-base.

EDGING MATERIALS

Edging serves practical functions as well as making a decorative finish to delineate and separate a path or patio from surrounding lawns and borders. Mortared in place, edging acts as a restraint for flexible surfaces, such as small unit pavers, and, if higher than a loose gravel surface, it is an effective means of keeping it in place. Suitable materials include pressure-treated wood, bricks, and clay tiles.

△ MODERN STYLE

Small unit pavers make a neat patio edge, and they make mowing easier set just below the level of the lawn.

TRADITIONAL STYLE ▷
Suitable for both informal or formal styles of garden, a rope edge is especially useful for keeping gravel off surrounding surfaces.

TERRACOTTA ROPE EDGING AND POST

PRE-CAST DIAGONAL BRICKS

◁ **COTTAGE STYLE**
A pretty edging that is simple to install as precast units; individual bricks on edge are difficult to lay level and true.

SEE ALSO: Doing the Groundwork, pp.58–59

DOING THE GROUNDWORK

THOROUGH PREPARATION of a firm foundation that takes into account the load-bearing requirements and existing soil conditions is essential if the finished surface is to be stable, durable, and long-lasting once in use. Accurate measurement and attention paid to making corners square and surfaces level are key to a professional finish.

Keep safe at work. Wear heavy gloves if using concrete and mortar; use goggles if dealing with loose materials; if using machinery, wear ear protectors and close-fitting clothing, and keep head, limbs, and shovels well clear of moving parts. Never overestimate your strength when lifting; share the load with a helper whenever you can.

PREPARING THE SUB-BASE FOR A PATH OR PATIO

Before excavating, locate all underground pipes, cables, and drains. Remove all plant material, including tree roots. Dig out the topsoil until you reach firm subsoil. For non-load-bearing areas, a 4in (10cm) layer of compacted stone covered with a 2in (5cm) layer of sand makes an adequate foundation. On heavy clay or peaty soils, which shrink when dry and expand when wet, use 6in (15cm) of stone and top with builder's sand. If the surface is to bear a car's weight, prepare a sub-base of at least 4in (10cm) of compacted stone, with a 4in (10cm) layer of concrete on top; increase the concrete layer to 6in (15cm) on peat or clay soil. Concrete may form the finished surface, or it may be used as a base for pavers bedded on mortar. In areas with severe winters or very dry summers, seek expert advice on foundations.

> ### GOOD IDEAS
>
> • Plate compactors can usually be rented by the half- or whole day; to reduce costs, prepare in advance so the machine can be used promptly.
>
> • Make sure you get clear instruction in the safe use of all rented machinery and that it works properly. Check on fuel type and have adequate supplies at hand. A good rental shop will advise you on these points.

PREPARING A SUB-BASE

1 MARK OUT THE AREA
Use pegs and string lines to mark out the area accurately, setting the strings at the desired level of the finished surface. Make right-angled corners, and use a builder's square to check that they are straight and true.

2 COMPACT THE BASE
Dig out the topsoil to firm subsoil. Level and compact the subsoil with a plate compactor. Allow for a 4in (10cm) depth of stone and a 2in (5cm) layer of sand (or deeper if appropriate), plus the thickness of the intended surface layer.

3 INSTALL LEVEL GUIDES
Drive in leveling pegs at 6ft (2m) spacings each way. For a patio, incorporate a slight slope for drainage (see below). Use a straightedge and level to make sure that the tops of the pegs are level with the strings. Adjust as necessary.

4 ADD CRUSHED STONE
Add a 4in (10cm) layer of stone to the entire area and level roughly. Compact until completely level, using pegs as a guide. Top with sand and compact again. The level, compacted surface is now ready to receive a surface layer of pavers.

DEALING WITH DRAINAGE

When building a patio, you must include a drainage slope – a fall of 1in (2.5cm) every 6ft (2m) usually suffices. If a wall borders the patio, it must slope so water runs away from the wall. Mark and dig out the patio area, and compact the base (*see above*). Work out the depth of the sub-base plus surface material, then mark this depth on several long pegs, measuring down from their tops. Next to the wall, drive in a row of these pegs, 6ft (2m) apart, so the marks are level with the bottom of the hole; the peg tops now indicate the final level of paving. Insert a second row of marked pegs 6ft (2m) away from the wall, with a 1in (2.5cm) thick scrap of wood on top of each one. Level the tops of the two rows of pegs. Remove the scrap and repeat the procedure down subsequent rows of pegs. Dig and rake soil so it is level with the marker lines on each row of pegs.

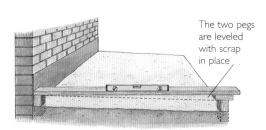

The two pegs are leveled with scrap in place

△ **BUILDING IN A FALL**
Use a level and straightedge to level adjacent rows of pegs, then remove the scrap and repeat the process for ensuing rows. The excavated base and the surface of the finished paving, as shown by the dotted line, should be parallel.

SEE ALSO: Marking out a Bed, p.145

LAYING PAVING SLABS

First establish a straight edge to start from, called a base line. A string line is best, even if you choose to start from a house wall, which may not be as straight as it looks. In this case, also consider whether the paving will be flush with the house, or if you want a planting gap between wall and paving. To save cost and reduce the need for cutting slabs, make the dimensions of the area divisible by the dimensions of whole slabs. Many standard slabs are 18 × 18in (45 × 45cm) or 18 × 24in (45 × 60cm). Prepare bedding mortar with a mix of 1 part cement to 5 parts sharp sand; the same mix can be used for jointing, but with less water to give a dry, crumbly texture. When the pavers have been laid, avoid walking on them until the mortar is dry. After jointing, brush surplus mortar off the slabs immediately and, to avoid staining, spray with water and sponge off excess mortar from the pavers.

HOW TO LAY PAVING SLABS

1 PREPARE MORTAR BASE
Mark out the area and prepare sub-base. Start at a corner of the base line (see above). Lay strips of mortar, 1½–2in (3–5cm) high, in a square just smaller than the slabs. Add cross strips for slabs 18in (45cm) square or larger.

2 MAKE IT LEVEL AND TRUE
Lower slabs into place. Tap gently with the handle of a club hammer to level. Check levels in both directions. Use ¼–½in (0.5–1cm) wide scraps of wood as spacers between the slabs. Check levels in each direction after every 3 or 4 slabs.

3 MORTAR THE JOINTS
Remove spacers before the mortar sets and without standing on the paving. After about 2 days, when the mortar is fully set, fill the joints with stiff mortar. Firm mortar down with a dowel or rounded piece of wood.

4 FINISH OFF USING A JIGGER
A jigger is a board of wood with a central slit, ¼–½in (0.5–1cm) wide. It allows joints to be mortared without staining the slabs. Simply align the slit above the joint and apply mortar through the slit; the mortar must be recessed by ⅟₁₆in (2mm).

LAYING FLEXIBLE PAVING

Small unit pavers are bedded onto sand of a total compacted depth of 2in (5cm) for normal garden use; on unstable soil or for heavy use, increase the sub-base to 8in (20cm) deep. Since they can be lifted and relaid if they sag in use, this type of paving is called flexible paving. It is laid with a firm edge restraint to prevent creepage of sand or blocks after laying. The top surface of the compacted sand layer should be 1¾in (4.5cm) below the level of finished paving if using 2⅜in (6cm) blocks, or 2in (5cm) for 2½in (6.5cm) blocks. Keep sand dry and do not walk on it while laying pavers; work from a kneeling board. Most manufacturers of flexible pavers offer telephone helplines or websites, which are good sources of expert advice.

HOW TO LAY FLEXIBLE PAVING

1 LAY THE EDGE RESTRAINT
Prepare a sub-base of 3in (8cm) of compacted crushed stone on firm subsoil. Lay edging strips around the entire area and bed them in concrete. Use a level and the handle of a club hammer to tap the edges level.

2 LAY THE SAND BASE
Divide area into 3ft (1m) wide strips, with 2in (5cm) thick boards. Fill to top of boards with sharp sand. Compact with a plate compactor. Add more sand to top of boards. Strike level with a piece of wood. Remove boards, and fill voids with sand.

3 LAY PAVERS
Begin at one corner, and lay blocks in required pattern. Proceed along the edge restraint and complete one course before laying the next. For a herringbone pattern, with blocks at 45°, lay whole blocks at this stage; cut blocks to fill any spaces last of all.

4 COMPACT AND FINISH
Vibrate pavers into place by running over the area 2 to 3 times with a plate compactor fitted with a rubber-faced vibrating plate. Brush fine, dry sand over the surface and make another 2 or 3 passes with the compactor to vibrate sand into the joints.

SEE ALSO: Laying Concrete, pp.60–61; Laying Gravel, pp.62–63

LAYING CONCRETE

CONCRETE IS ONE OF the least costly ways to make large areas of hard surface and is easy and quick to lay. Valued for its strength and durability, it is far more versatile than its utilitarian image suggests. Concrete forms an excellent base for a variety of inlaid decoration, or it can be brushed, pressed with patterning tools, or scored to produce a variety of surface textures. Avoid laying concrete if the temperature is above 90°F (32°C) or close to freezing, and never lay it onto frozen ground. Dry, windy days are also best avoided: they can create problems with surface drying. Wet concrete is caustic, so always cover up your skin when working.

HOW TO LAY CONCRETE

A standard mix for poured concrete is 1 part cement to 1½ parts sharp sand to 2½ parts ¾in (2cm) aggregate (by volume). Heap sand and aggregate onto a board or into a barrow and place dry cement on top. Mix well by turning with a spade. Make a hollow in the dry mix and almost fill it with water. Push dry mix into the hollow bit by bit, adding more water gradually until you have a firm mix that has absorbed all of the water. Smooth the surface and make a row of troughs with a spade; the concrete is ready to pour if it holds peaks without slumping.

When leveling, a film of water appears on the surface; let it evaporate before smoothing further. Do not overwork concrete once poured: this weakens it.

LAYING AN AREA OF CONCRETE

1 MARK OUT AND INSTALL LEVELING PEGS
Mark out the site with pegs and string, and excavate to about 8in (20cm) into firm subsoil. Drive in leveling pegs at 3ft (1m) intervals, using the string as a guide. Level pegs with a straightedge and level.

2 INSTALL THE FORMWORK
Remove the string lines and nail wooden boards to the inner side of the pegs, joining the boards at the corners end to face. This formwork holds the concrete in place until it is fully set ("cured").

3 LAY THE SUB-BASE
Divide large areas into sections, no more than 12ft (4m) long, using formwork. Spread a 4in (10cm) layer of crushed stone and compact it using a roller, or firm it down with a heavy wooden post.

4 POUR THE CONCRETE
Starting with the first section, pour in the concrete and spread it level so that it stands just above the formwork. Work the concrete well into the edges using a spade or shovel with a chopping motion.

5 LEVEL OFF THE CONCRETE
Use a wooden beam that spans the width of the formwork to compact the concrete with a downward chopping motion. Then slide the beam from side to side to level the surface at the height of the formwork.

6 FILL AND SMOOTH
Stroke the surface smooth with a builder's float. Fill any hollows with fresh concrete and level again. Protect concrete with plastic sheeting until set, which takes about 10 days. Remove the formwork only when concrete has set hard.

SEE ALSO: Doing the Groundwork, pp.58–59; Making Paths, pp.66–67

PREMIXED CONCRETE

Premixed concrete is a labor-saving solution for large areas, but you must prepare the sub-base and have the formwork in place on delivery. Give the supplier the dimensions and information about the intended use of the surface, so that the correct mix and quantities are delivered. The site must be accessible to a large vehicle, on firm ground, and with room to maneuver; the delivery chute needs to be repositioned several times as the formwork fills. Otherwise, recruit a team of helpers and several barrows to move, firm, and level the concrete quickly, before it sets.

ALWAYS REMEMBER

BE PREPARED!

Premixed concrete shoots rapidly down the chute and must be firmed and leveled before it hardens. If necessary, ask the delivery driver to slow down the delivery rate. Make sure you have enough helpers – equipped with gloves, goggles, sturdy boots, and tough clothes that cover all bare skin.

EXPOSING AGGREGATE

If you use an attractively colored aggregate in the concrete mix, it can be exposed to give a decorative finish, and different textures are created according to the size of aggregate used, ranging from coarse sand through different grades of gravel to water-worn pebbles. Choosing a locally sourced material will ensure that it blends well with its surroundings.

◁ **BRUSH AND CLEAN**
After pouring the mix, do not smooth with a float. Let dry for about six hours, then brush the surface with a stiff-bristled brush. After a further 36–48 hours, clean remaining cement residue from the aggregate with a high-pressure hose.

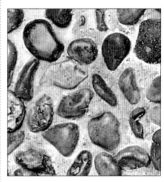

△ **WATER-WORN PEBBLES**
Pebbles give an attractive, subtly colored but rough-textured finish. It can be uncomfortable to walk on, so use it for edging or deterrent barriers.

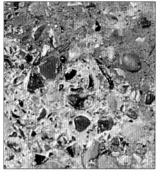

△ **PEA GRAVEL**
Choose ¼–⅜in (6–8mm) gravel or standard aggregates up to ¾in (2cm) in diameter for a comfortable, nonslip walking surface.

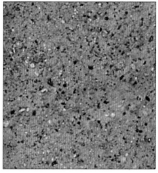

△ **FINE-GRADE GRAVEL**
The finest grades of gravel give a finely textured, natural-looking surface, which is especially useful where a nonslip surface is required.

APPLYING COLOR

Concrete can be colored during mixing with a mineral pigment or with powder pigment dry-sprinkled onto the wet surface after it has been smoothed with a float. Other types of color are applied when it has set fully, after about a month.

■ Patio sealants add color pigment and an extra protective layer.

■ Stains can be applied about six weeks after laying concrete.

■ Semitransparent wood stains take well on concrete.

■ Specially formulated concrete paints offer the widest choice of color. Water-based, latex ones are the most effective. Apply two or three coats.

◁ **APPLYING COLOR**
Apply paints, stains, or sealants – as shown here – with a clean, dry brush, and follow the manufacturer's instructions. Make the application on a clear and dry day when no rain is forecast and when winds are light.

DECORATIVE FINISHES

Concrete and mortar both make an ideal matrix in which to set more decorative materials. Provided the inlaid material is pushed in to at least two-thirds of its depth, they will be securely fixed once the matrix is dry. This method can be used for pebbles, stones, glass nuggets, or pottery shards to create intricate patterns. Bear in mind that large inclusions will be difficult to walk on.

If your ambition is to create a large-scale mosaic, plan ahead. Lay the sub-base first, graph out the design, and sort materials by size and color. Divide the area into square sections. Lay a topping of mortar or concrete onto one section, and push in the mosaic fragments. Complete each section before moving onto the next, or the concrete or mortar may be dry before you finish.

△ **PEBBLE MOSAIC**
Bed pebbles by pressing into bedding mortar to two-thirds of their depth. Level with a presser board.

MIXED MEDIA ▷
A broad band of cement with inlaid pebbles borders concrete slabs with finer-textured, exposed aggregate.

SEE ALSO: Making Steps, pp.68–69

LAYING GRAVEL

A SMOOTH SWEEP of raked gravel has everything to recommend it esthetically, especially if it is locally sourced. Few other materials blend so seamlessly with brick and stone while at the same time making a fine-textured foil for plants. Lay it around the house and its crisp crunch underfoot will also be a subtle deterrent to intruders. Gravel is also relatively inexpensive and easy to install. There are downsides, however: gravel needs regular replenishment and continuous attention to weed control, but if a modern landscape fabric (geotextile) is used as a weed-suppressing barrier, gravel replenishment becomes the only regular chore involved.

TYPES OF GRAVEL

Gravel comes in two main types: angular chips from parent rock, and water-worn, rounded pebbles that are obtained by dredging. The sizes vary from fine to fairly chunky chips ⅜in (2cm) or more in diameter. The smaller the size, the finer the finished surface texture.

In practical terms, finer grades are the easiest to walk on. Fine grades, however, are picked up readily on shoe soles and tracked into the house or onto the lawn. Coarse grades make for an uncomfortable walking surface but are hardwearing under regular use. Grades in the ¼–⅜in (6–10mm) range suit most garden uses.

△ **PEA GRAVEL**
Rounded stones give a fine-textured surface for comfort and suit formal and informal garden styles.

△ **GRANITE CHIPS**
Granite chips are available in a range of colors; use a local source to blend well with the surroundings.

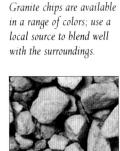

△ **LIMESTONE CHIPS**
Chips give a more formal effect than pebbles; a local source is nearly always the cheapest.

△ **COARSE GRAVEL**
Use coarse-gauge gravel as a deterrent barrier to foot traffic or as a durable surface for vehicles.

SITE CLEARANCE

To make the most of this versatile and practical medium, and to reduce later maintenance to a minimum, thorough preparation is essential.

■ The site must be level. Gravel will work its way down even the slightest of slopes.
■ The site must be cleared of all weeds and roots. Take off fertile topsoil to reduce regrowth and to remove the reservoir of weed seeds, or simply lay gravel over an impermeable landscape fabric.
■ The sub-base must be firm and well compacted. Gravel gradually but surely works down into loose surfaces. A landscape fabric helps prevent this.
■ Rake and roll laid gravel to provide a firm surface for walking and to make pushing barrows and other wheeled machinery easier.

GRAVEL PATIOS AND PATHS

Unlike harder, more solid materials that need cutting and shaping to conform to awkward shapes, the loose nature of the material means that gravel will flow easily into the most intricate corners and the tightest of curves. It is the easiest material to use to create winding or zigzag paths, patios of irregular organic forms, or experimental geometric outlines.

EDGING GRAVELED AREAS

Since gravel is a loose material, it needs some form of edge restraint to prevent the nuisance it can cause when scattered underfoot onto lawns and borders and to reduce the frequency of replenishment.

A wide range of materials can be used. Inexpensive but utilitarian wooden boards are simply nailed to pegs sunk into the ground; they are effectively disguised once the adjacent plantings grow. Reclaimed railroad ties are expensive but practically maintenance-free and last a lifetime if laid on a modest foundation of compacted crushed stone. Edgings of stone, clay, concrete, cobblestones, or bricks must be mortared in place in a shallow foundation trench on firm subsoil or crushed stone, deep enough to hold a laying base of 2in (5cm) of compacted sand.

△ **A PAVER RETAINER**
A broad band of pavers is complementary in color and texture and makes an effective retainer.

◁ **THE ROPE TRICK**
Rope edging reinforces the crisp lines of a formal knot garden and keeps gravel firmly in place.

SEE ALSO: Edging Materials, p.57; Preparing the Sub-base for a Path or Patio, p.58

LAYING A GRAVELED AREA

1 PREPARING THE GROUND
Clear the ground of weeds and remove a 4in (10cm) layer of topsoil from the entire area so that it is fairly level. Mortar edging bricks in place or install treated lumber edging to keep the gravel in place.

2 LAYING A SUB-BASE
Rake the surface level, then fill the excavated area with a layer of unprocessed gravel or crushed stone almost back up to the original soil level. Rake the surface completely flat.

3 COMPACT THE SUB-BASE
Use a rented plate compactor or heavy garden roller to compact the base and remove air pockets. This provides a stable base. Compress the base to at least ¾in (2cm) below the original ground level.

4 LAY THE GRAVEL
When the base is firm and compacted, add the surface layer of gravel. Start at one side and rake level as you go. If using landscape fabric, lay it before adding gravel and peg it in place with small wire hoops or staples.

5 RAKE AND ROLL
Rake over the entire surface to produce a level finish of uniform depth. The gravel depth will be about 1in (2.5cm) and the finished surface just below the edging material. Use a garden roller to bed the gravel down.

6 FINISHING OFF
The freshly laid gravel will be dusty, so wash it down by spraying with a hose fitted with a nozzle. Watering while rolling will further compact the ground. Alternatively, let rainfall do the work.

PLANTING IN GRAVEL

Gravel is an ideal substrate for a range of plants, but its free drainage and light- and warmth-reflecting qualities make it especially suited to robust alpines and natives of Mediterranean climates, both of which are vulnerable to wet winters.

Planting in gravel is essentially the same as in open ground; gravel is scraped away to dig out a planting hole and pushed back after planting up to the plant neck. If a landscape fabric is used, cut two crosswise slits wide enough to hold the root ball, fold back in place, and top off with gravel.

ALL THE ADVANTAGES ▷
Not only is gravel an elegant foil for architectural plants, but it is also a great way of ensuring excellent drainage at their necks in winter, which reduces the risk of rot. Structural plants, such as this verbascum, will also help to break up an expanse of gravel.

△ **A LIVING FOUNTAIN**
The feathery plumes of this grass, Stipa tenuissima, rise above a sea of gravel to lend summer-long textural contrast and dynamic movement as the delicate plumes shimmer in the slightest breeze.

SEE ALSO: Beds for Drought-tolerant Plants, pp.132–133; Establishing Plants in the Border, pp.148–149; Gravel Herb Garden, p.229

INSTALLING DECKING

WOODEN DECKING IS ONE of the most modern and practical of design elements and brings the natural beauty of wood into the garden in ways that appear perfectly at home in a diversity of garden styles. Whether used for dining and entertaining or for simple relaxation, decks can be a magnificent way of extending your living space.

Depending on climate, they may be sited to receive full sun or cool shade; you should also consider how their location might affect privacy and security. In some areas, building regulations apply, which stipulate load-bearing requirements and inspection of work; you may also need to obtain approval from the relevant authority.

WOOD FOR DECKING

Local lumber dealers give helpful advice when choosing lumber for decking, and custom deck companies may even send a representative to your home. Lumber is graded for its durability and suitability for outdoor use. Some wood is naturally rot-resistant, but most is pressure-treated with preservative. Treat all wood regularly with preservative after installation to extend its

life. Seek out decking lumber with a grooved surface for a nonslip finish, and use brass hardware where possible, because brass will not rust or stain the wood.

USING PREMADE LUMBER PANELS ▷
Premade panels, which are sometimes available with a nonslip finish, are the simplest way of achieving surface detail on a deck. The supporting joists (see below) must *be spaced to ensure that each panel is securely supported.*

CHECKERBOARD PANEL   HERRINGBONE PANEL   PARALLEL-SLATTED PANEL

LAYING A DECK

This simple, freestanding deck is 8ft (2.5m) square and uses elementary building methods and a design that is easily adjusted for size and shape.

All simple decks are constructed in a similar way, with a foundation at the base and a framework of bearers and joists to support the surface. To ensure structural strength, the joists must be joined on top of, and at right angles to, the bearers. Decking boards run parallel with the line of the bearers. Here, concrete blocks are used as bearers. For elevated decks, joist shoes (*see opposite, top*) make construction simple, and the bearers would be made of lumber in this case. The surface boards are laid with small gaps to allow room for the boards to swell when wet without warping.

GOOD IDEAS

• You can find specialty suppliers, plans, and specifications for decks on the Internet; many have details that are specific to a given region and climate.

• Use the construction method shown here to create a staggered series of decks or perhaps to frame a corner site. Joist shoes make it simple to build stepped decks by varying the height of the support posts.

HOW TO LAY A DECK

1 MARK OUT THE SITE
Lay out 4 boards in a square; check that corners are at right angles using a builder's square. Mark the outline with a spade on the outside of the boards. The final area will be 6in (15cm) larger than the 8ft (2.5m) square platform.

2 LOCATE THE JOIST FOUNDATIONS
Put 3 of the boards aside and align 4 joists at even spacings along the remaining board. Ensure the end joists lie flush with the ends of the board. Mark a 6in (15cm) wide border around the length of each joist.

5 BACKFILL THE TRENCH
Backfill each trench with sand, tamping it down firmly to compact it. Do this thoroughly; otherwise, the blocks will shift and the decking will warp. Level off the sand so that it is flush with the level of the soil.

6 LAY THE JOISTS
Lay and center the joists across the blocks; check that the first and last joists are exactly 8ft (2.5m) apart, using one of the boards. Check that all the ends are in line with each other.

SEE ALSO: Using Lighting in the Garden, pp.70–71

USING SHOE SUPPORTS

Steel joist shoes bolted on to concrete to make a firm underpinning for bearers and joists and are especially useful for elevated decks. Each needs a foundation, 12in (30cm) square, filled with at least 4in (10cm) of crushed stone topped off with a 4in (10cm) layer of concrete.

◁ **HOW IT WORKS**
Space joist shoes 4ft (1.2m) apart. Level lumber uprights and nail the bearers in place, flat side down. Fix joists at right angle to bearers, 18in (45cm) apart, with nails at an angle of 45°. Then fix slats or panels on top.

Shoe is bolted on to cured concrete with 2in (5cm) wall bolts in predrilled holes

JOINING LUMBER SUPPORTS

Ideally, a single length of joist lumber should be used to span the bearers, but where this is not possible two lengths can be joined safely and securely using a simple lap joint. The two lengths are nailed together with two vertical nails and to the bearer with skewed nails.

△ **MAKING A LAP JOINT**
A lap joint is a strong and simple way of joining joists. Make a 2in (5cm) horizontal cut and a 4in (10cm) vertical cut in the end of each joist. Half-lap them where they cross the bearer and nail in place as shown.

MAINTAINING DECKING

Check all lumber annually for splits or cracks and replace any that are damaged. If the chosen finish wears thin in areas of heavy foot traffic, clean the surface and reapply. Keep surfaces free of algae and moss. Sweep away fallen leaves and other plant debris regularly.

ALWAYS REMEMBER

KEEP DECKING SAFE

In damp climates, the inevitable algal and/or fungal growth on wood makes surfaces dangerously slippery. Make sure that any commercial cleaners are safe for use near plants and nontoxic to wildlife; if not, take steps to protect them, or choose the safer alternative – a stiff broom with a scrub of water and sharp sand or household bleach.

FINISHING LUMBER

Pressure-treated lumber needs only occasional preservative treatment. The range of finishes that protect wood is extensive, and many both color and preserve. Check with the supplier that the treatment you buy will give the desired effect and is suitable for outdoor use. Translucent wood stains penetrate wood and darken or color it while enhancing the grain; dyes offer more intense color. Nonpenetrating finishes should be microporous to allow wood to breathe and reduce risks of flaking or peeling.

3 DIG OUT FOUNDATION TRENCHES
Using the marker lines as a guide, dig out the trenches 4in (10cm) deeper than the depth of the concrete bearers. Line each trench with sand and compact it to produce a total compacted depth of 2in (5cm).

4 LAY CONCRETE BEARERS
Lay the concrete bearers, 3 to a trench, placing one at each end and one at the center of each trench. They should stand above the soil by ½in (1cm) so that the joists do not come into contact with the soil. Level and adjust.

7 SECURE JOISTS AND INSTALL BOARD PANELS
Secure joists in place using metal brackets on both ends of each joist; screw them to joist and block (see insert). Fix the first plank in place with its ends flush with the joists; use 2 countersunk screws per joist.

8 FINISH AND FIT FASCIA BOARDS
Position remaining boards, ¼in (5mm) apart, and screw in place. Fit 4 more 8ft (2.5m) boards as fascia boards by nailing them into joist ends; 2 of the fascia boards must be 1½in (4cm) longer, so they overlap neatly at the corners.

△ **NATURALLY STYLISH**
Most outdoor lumber is pressure-treated with a green-tinted preservative. For a more natural effect, as shown here, seek out naturally rot-resistant lumber or special landscaping lumber treated with colorless preservative. Use shoe supports.

SEE ALSO: Enhancing Patio Areas, pp.72–73; Containers, pp.166–179

MAKING PATHS

THE PRIMARY PRACTICAL reason that our gardens have paths is, of course, to get from A to B, taking the most convenient route on a clean, hard-wearing surface. But there are legions of other, less prosaic roles that paths play in the scheme of things. The wealth of available materials allow paths to enhance a garden design and can make beautiful features in their own right. A meandering route can ensure that all the garden's beauties are not seen at once, often lending the illusion of greater space, while intersecting linear paths lend possibilities of vistas in variety. Not least, paths form a vital element of unity that ties a design together.

ROUTING A PATH

When planning paths, identify the most travelled routes in the garden, from gate to door, from house to utility areas, or down to the compost pile, for example. These paths form the main framework. Take account of usage paths – usually the shortest distance between two points – since an inconvenient route is seldom used. To avoid trampled lawn or border edges, make corners curve across right-angled bends – they will also be much easier to negotiate with a wheelbarrow.

With a main framework defined, decide on secondary routes that might lead to a view or a secluded arbor, or simply meander among favorite plants.

DESIGN CONSIDERATIONS

In every well-designed garden, pathways form a major element in·the architectural skeleton that underpins, frames, and enhances the plantings that clothe it. When planning, easy access is obviously a high priority, so bear in mind the natural tendency to take the shortest route from point to point. But consider also the role paths make to dividing a garden into areas of different use, or how they might delineate and shape planting areas.

You could consider combining purely functional paths with secondary ones for other purposes. For example, a side branch that is hidden from view until you stumble upon it creates an exciting element of surprise. A narrow path that opens out before a view will invite a pause to stop and stare. Use a change of surface texture to proclaim a change of direction or define the boundaries of different garden rooms.

ALWAYS REMEMBER

FORM FOLLOWS FUNCTION

Access paths need to be level, smooth, and wide enough for walking and wheel-barrowing. A width of 4–5ft (1.2–1.5m) allows two people to walk side by side, even where plants spill over the edges. Secondary paths, intended to gently meander around the garden, can be narrower and less even.

PATH STYLES

Since the essence of formality is geometry and precision, and the converse sinuous irregularity lends informality, the line of a path and the materials used in its construction define its style. Natural materials, perhaps in the form of slabs of tree trunk set in bark chips or stone slabs used as random stepping-stones through gravel, are perfect in an informal setting. Formal gardens positively demand the use of elements with clean, straight edges laid out in strong, crisp lines; here, pavers or dressed stone might be the materials of first choice. Gravel is the obvious exception to the general rule, since this versatile material can be used in almost any style of garden.

BREAKING THE RULES ▷
It is satisfying to use reclaimed materials, not least in terms of cost. Old bricks can lend an aged charm, but usually flake during freeze-thaw cycles. If they disintegrate entirely, chisel out and replace them.

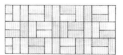

BASKETWEAVE

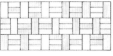

INTERLOCKING

HERRINGBONE

△ **PATTERNWORK**
Bricks or pavers can be laid in various formal patterns. Choose bricks that are suitable for exterior use and resistant to wetting and freezing. In a herringbone pattern, bricks are laid at an angle of 45°, and a great deal of cutting is required.

SEE ALSO: Surfaces, pp.24–27; Laying Paving Slabs, p.59; Laying Gravel, pp.62–63

A RANDOM-PAVING PATH

Random paving is a relatively inexpensive way of constructing an informal path. It can be laid on sand or, for a safer, firmer, and more durable surface, on mortar. To make bedding mortar, mix 1 part cement to 5 parts sharp sand and add water to give a dry, crumbly consistency.

Prepare the sub-base with a slight slope for drainage. Loose-lay the slabs, in areas about 3ft (1m) square, without mortar. Lay large slabs first, and fill in with smaller ones, fitting together like a puzzle. You may need to trim to size with a bolster chisel and hammer (wear goggles). Make gaps as small as possible. When satisfied with their placement, bed them in. Adjust the levels by lifting slabs and removing or adding more sand or mortar, as necessary.

GOOD IDEAS

• If using a dark-colored stone, like slate, add a concrete dye powder to the mortar mix to make the cracks less conspicuous.

• If you wish to grow plants in paving cracks, bed random paving on sand. For a firmer, more durable surface, bed the paving on mortar.

HOW TO LAY RANDOM PAVING

1 LAY EDGING PIECES
Use string lines and pegs to mark out the area and prepare a sub-base of compacted stone. Lay edging pieces first, on either side of the path, with straight edges outermost. Mortar edges in place to form a firm edge restraint, even if you bed the remaining pieces on sand.

2 FILL THE CENTER
Lay large slabs in the center and fill in with smaller ones. Lay them on sand or blobs of mortar, using a wood scrap and club hammer to bed them in. Check that central slabs are level with edge pieces using a straightedge and level. Lift and adjust as necessary.

3 FINISHING OFF
If bedding on sand, brush dry sand into the cracks. If using a mortar finish, fill the cracks with crumbly, almost dry mortar. Bevel the mortar with a pointing trowel so that surface water drains quickly away from the slabs (see inset).

◁ **GRAVEL PATHS**
Gravel paths are very simple to lay and, if laid on a landscape fabric, need little maintenance. Here, an edge restraint of boards is completely hidden by the billowing growth of lavender. A clear case of minimum effort, maximum effect.

△ **COBBLED PATH**
Visually pleasing, but seldom even, cobblestones are best reserved for informal secondary paths.

STEPPING-STONES ▷
Here, informality meets practicality; stepping-stones keep feet dry, lead the eye on, and invite exploration.

SEE ALSO: Doing the Groundwork, pp.58–59; Laying Gravel, pp.62–63; Herbs for Cracks and Crevices, p.229

MAKING STEPS

IF YOU GARDEN on a sloping site, steps are the obvious way of negotiating a change in level, but don't think of them simply as a utilitarian device – they can add an attractive element of interest, perhaps to replace a previously bland, grassy incline or to allow other focal points in the garden to be viewed from another angle. Wide, shallow steps invite a pause to enjoy a view, and they make plinths to display pots filled with plants. Narrow, steep steps move you faster to a different area of the garden. Safety is paramount, so where winters are icy and wet, use textured, nonslip surfaces for treads, and make sure that they are wide enough for safe use.

TREADS AND RISERS

The width of treads and the height of risers must be in the correct proportion to each other for safety and comfort. Treads must be a minimum of 12in (30cm) from front to back, and the height of risers will vary between 4–7in (10–18cm).

As a rule of thumb, the width of the tread plus double the height of the riser should equal about 26in (65cm). First, choose the height of the riser, double it, then subtract it from 26in (65cm) to give the width of the tread.

To calculate the number of steps, divide the slope height (*see step 1, right*) by the height of one riser. You may need to adjust the height of the riser to fit the slope.

If you want to check your math, plot the run and rise of the steps to scale on graph paper and sketch out risers and treads to fit comfortably with the given proportions.

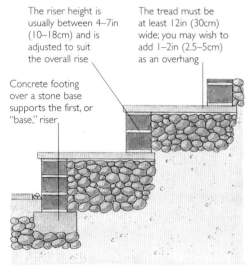

The riser height is usually between 4–7in (10–18cm) and is adjusted to suit the overall rise

The tread must be at least 12in (30cm) wide; you may wish to add 1–2in (2.5–5cm) as an overhang

Concrete footing over a stone base supports the first, or "base," riser

△ **HOW IT WORKS**
This construction detail illustrates principles that can be used for a wide range of materials in any number of combinations. You could substitute stone or concrete flags for the brick risers, for example. The dimensions can be adjusted to avoid having to cut bricks or stone.

BUILDING STEPS UP A BANKED SLOPE

Measure the height and run of the slope to calculate the number and proportions of the steps needed (*see left*). The height of each riser includes slab and mortar.

Mark out the width of the steps and the position of the risers with wooden pegs, and excavate soil to form a series of steps. Make a concrete footing using a mix of 1 part cement to 2½ parts sharp sand to 3½ parts ¾in (2cm) aggregate; or use 5 parts combined aggregate to 1 part cement. Construct risers using masonry mortar (1 part masonry cement to 3 parts soft sand). Check that bricks are level using a straightedge and level.

After laying the first tread, mark the position of the next riser on the tread, then mortar it into position.

HOW TO BUILD THE FOUNDATIONS

The run, or length, of the slope is the distance between the peg at the top of the slope and the post at the bottom

1 MEASURING UP
Measure the height and run of the slope to work out how many steps are needed. Drive a peg into the top of the slope and a post into the base. Tie a string between them and measure the height between ground level and the string (the height).

2 EXCAVATING THE TREADS
Mark out the width of the steps using pegs and string line, then run string lines to mark the front of each tread. Calculate the number of steps, the depth of the risers, and width of the treads. Dig out the steps and compact the soil at each tread position.

3 MAKE A FOOTING FOR THE RISER
Dig out a trench for the footing, 6in (15cm) deep and twice the width of the riser bricks. Pack the base with a 3in (8cm) layer of crushed stone and fill to the top with concrete. Allow it to set hard for a few days before laying the riser bricks.

ALWAYS REMEMBER

PROPORTIONS ARE VITAL FOR SAFETY

The technique shown here can be adapted to suit a range of materials, but it is vital when planning steps to keep safety and ease of use in mind. The most important factor is to ensure that the height of the risers are uniform – if shallower or deeper than expected they will, sooner or later, cause someone to trip or stumble. The treads must also be deep enough so that they can be stood on easily: they should be a minimum of 12in (30cm) from front to back, and the overhang should be no greater than 2in (5cm).

SEE ALSO: Doing the Groundwork, pp.58–59; Laying Concrete, pp.60–61

LAYING THE BRICKS AND SLABS

4 LAYING THE RISERS
Lay the first riser on the footing, using a single course of bricks, making sure that the joints between bricks are staggered in subsequent courses, as shown. Use a string line stretched between pegs to ensure that bricks are straight and level.

5 LAYING THE TREADS
Backfill behind the riser with stone and compact it well, using a post as a tamper. Set the paving slabs on a ½in (1cm) bed of mortar, leaving a small gap between the two slabs. The slabs should make an overhang of 1–2in (2.5–5cm), and have a slight forward slope for drainage.

6 LAYING THE SECOND STEP
Mark the position of the second riser on the slabs and mortar the bricks in place. Backfill the void with stone as before, compacting it well, and lay the second set of treads. Continue for the remaining steps, and then mortar the joints between each slab.

STYLES OF STEPS

Brick and slab steps are easy and practical because these materials come in standard sizes, making calculations relatively simple. The same basic methods of construction apply even if you choose railroad ties or concrete or stone flags as the risers, with a gravel infill or patterned bricks for the treads. Lay gravel over a compacted base of unprocessed gravel with a 2in (5cm) layer of firmed sand to fill any voids.

Long, shallow slopes might be better traversed by single risers separated by long landings, or pairs of equal-height steps and landings. Such arrangements are often more visually impressive and encourage a more leisurely ascent than a short run of steps. As long as the risers are uniform and no more than 4–7in (10–18cm) high, and the treads are a minimum of 12in (30cm) wide, the variations are infinite.

△ **HERRINGBONE**
In this case, the steps are constructed without an overhang. The bricks are laid lengthwise at the edge of each tread, with a double course of brick risers beneath. The treads are laid on a full mortar bed.

RAILROAD TIES ▷
Here, ties form a generously broad sweep of curving, shallow steps. The ties are bedded in a shallow trench onto firmed soil topped off with a 2in (5cm) layer of compacted sand.

◁ **NATURAL STONE**
A short flight of natural stone steps with a broad platform on top uses elevation to great effect. It almost demands that you pause to enjoy the sweeping view across the garden.

△ **DECKING PANELS**
Here, decking panels form a series of shallow landings with a rhythmic repetition of alternating diagonals. It is ideal for dry climates, where slippery algal growth is seldom a problem.

SEE ALSO: Choosing Paving Materials, p.57; Installing Decking, pp.64–65; Using Lighting in the Garden, pp.70–71

USING LIGHTING IN THE GARDEN

THE NEED for safe access and security often first prompts consideration of garden lighting, but this seriously under-estimates its potential for bringing the garden to life at night and creating striking features of interest after sun-down. Furthermore, lighting can be enjoyed from inside or outside the home. With a little applied imagination, a variety of functional and beautiful effects can be created. Detail lighting, used primarily to highlight a feature, also scatters light to illuminate its surroundings for safety, with incidental effects of providing a degree of security and deterrence to intruders. So why settle for utility only, when you can have beauty, too?

WHY USE LIGHTING?

One of the best reasons for installing garden lighting is to extend the use of the garden at night, especially if busy working days limit daytime enjoyment. Consider installation at the garden's planning stage, rather than as an afterthought, and it can be sited to achieve specific ends: to provide for atmospheric evening dining or to light a meandering path, perhaps fitted with movement-activated sensors, where you can wind down after work. Use lighting to set a mood, lend theatrical shadows to favorite features, or, most practically, to provide a safe route to the door on dark nights.

▽ **SUBTLE DIFFUSION**
Several light sources above ground level provide subtle illumination for evening dining. Diffusion through frosted glass shades eliminates glare, and strategic placement, at points where levels change, increases safety.

LOW-TECH SOLUTIONS

Low-tech solutions — hurricane lamps, flares, and candle lights — are a cheaper alternative to permanent systems, ideal if cool summers lend few opportunities to use the garden at night. They cast the most atmospheric light for a midsummer party; a string of candle lanterns among the trees can be enchanting. Use citronella candles in pretty, open jars to scent the air and keep biting insects at bay.

SHINE ON... ▷
Position lamps, naked flames, or other heat-producing sources well away from foliage to avoid damage. Attach hanging lights with wire, not string. Take sensible precautions with flamed lights and be sure to extinguish them at the end of the evening.

FIXTURES

All exterior light fixtures must be sturdy and specifically made for outdoor use. Exterior lighting units are sealed and specified as waterproof — never use internal fixtures outdoors. Site the lighting system so that it can be turned on from indoors and out. Make sure that power sockets have a screw-fit or lockable cap, and site them out of reach of children.

ELECTRICAL SAFETY

Outdoor lighting is powered by a house or low-voltage source. Low-voltage systems are safest; many are suitable for do-it-yourself installation. Ideal for small gardens, it uses only short wiring runs and small lighting units and may be run off the house power with a transformer. For higher intensities and long runs, use house electricity and have it installed professionally. Armored wiring must be buried at least 18in (45cm) deep, along a wall, path, or other marked site, safely out of harm's way when cultivating. All systems should include a circuit breaker.

◁ **ATTEND TO DETAIL**
There is a huge range of lighting styles available, so finding a style that fits with home and garden will not be difficult. They may be wall-mounted, as here, post-mounted, recessed into walls or floors, or set on fixed or adjustable spikes.

SEE ALSO: Enhancing Patio Areas, pp.72–73; Safety First, p.199; Always Remember box: Out of your depth?, p.209

LIGHTING EFFECTS

For security and safety, area lighting in the form of a downlighter, usually a high-output flood- or spotlight, is most often used. Crosslighting with two floodlights gives excellent coverage over a wide area, and installing below eye level helps reduce dazzle. For dining and entertaining, a softer glow is more comfortable, so choose a diffuse form of area lighting rather than a strongly directional beam. Detail lighting is closely focused and may be used for safety, close to steps for example, yet it is also the type to use to create the special effects shown below.

◁ **MOONLIGHTING**
A high-level, downward-pointing source provides soft-shadowed highlights for a focal point; at the same time, the scattered light provides a measure of safety and security.

SPREADLIGHTING ▷
A hooded light source casts its beam downward and outward, here creating safe and practical lighting for a flight of steps without the potential danger of blinding glare.

◁ **SHADOWING**
A light angled toward a flat surface creates impressive shadows when used with architectural plants. Effects vary with light intensity and the distance from the object.

SPOTLIGHTING ▷
Spotlighting uses a highly directional, low-level and full-frontal beam for the dramatic highlighting of important focal points or features, such as a piece of sculpture or fine tree.

◁ **UPLIGHTING**
Use a ground-level source that casts an upward beam to create plays of shadow and light. Angle it away from the viewer to avoid glare; remember it may be a source of light pollution.

SPECIAL LIGHTING EFFECTS

Lighting brings an added dimension to water features, perhaps intimating that a pool has hidden depths, or lending a vital spark to the sound and movement of cascades or spouts. Safety is paramount. It is important when lighting water features to make sure that the lighting units and all wiring and connectors are sealed, waterproof, and specified as suitable for submersion. Ordinary exterior lighting is waterproof, but it is not submersible and regulations stipulate that it should not be installed within 6ft (2m) of a pool or water source.

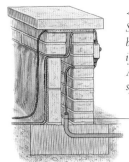

◁ **ELECTRICAL SUPPLY**
Supply is installed during building, by a professional if it uses house electricity. All equipment must be specified for submerged use.

Wiring runs through armored ducts, and lighting is plugged into a waterproof connector

▽ **SOUND AND LIGHT**
An underwater light source can lend a sense of magical enchantment, elevating an already beautiful feature to new heights. The spurting fountain spouts hit the light-suffused water beneath, making it gleam and sparkle.

HINTS AND TIPS

Bear in mind that thoughtlessly placed lighting may be irritating to neighbors and disturbing to wildlife, so site with care.
■ For safety and comfort, site and angle lighting to avoid direct glare at eye level.
■ Choose frosted or translucent glass shades for soft, diffused, glare-free effects.
■ Use white light, like that from a halogen source, to reveal true natural colors, of foliage for example; tungsten sources give a softer, yellow-tinted light.

GOOD IDEAS

• Use long-life, low-energy bulbs to reduce running costs and maintenance. Look for solar-powered units that conserve energy.

• Achieve different color tones by using lamps with tinted bulbs, and vary intensity with lamps of different wattage. Color filters may be used, but effects lack subtlety.

• The effects of detail lighting often work best if the source is concealed.

SEE ALSO: Enhancing Patio Areas, pp.72–73; Safety First, p.199; Always Remember box: Out of your depth?, p.209

ENHANCING PATIO AREAS

A NEWLY CONSTRUCTED PATIO is a blank sheet that, like an empty room, awaits decoration and furnishings to turn it into an inviting living space. The design principles that apply to interiors are equally applicable outdoors – thinking about the flooring, lighting, and how to arrange furniture for dining or relaxing is as essential in creating comfort and pleasure on the patio as it is in the home. And outdoors, you have the additional element of planting to consider. Plants not only play a vital role in creating shelter, shade, and privacy, but they also lend their fresh scents and heady perfumes to turn simple outdoor living into a sensory delight.

LINKING HOME INTERIOR AND GARDEN

The key to tying in the house and garden successfully lies in paying the same detailed attention to outdoor materials, furnishings, and their spatial arrangement as you do when considering interior decor. You might choose, for example, outdoor flooring to match indoor carpeting, or to echo a color theme of interior soft furnishings with those of outdoor upholstered seating and plantings. Time spent seeking out the right textures, colors, and furnishings – and the fun you have doing it by visiting shows, gardens, and websites, for example – pays off as well in the finished effect of outdoor rooms as it does in interior ones.

Glazed doors or French windows are an obvious and psychologically inviting way to link house and garden. They allow obvious physical access, and they act as a picture frame for the outdoor composition, whether the doors are open or closed. So when planning the planting, remember to take a view from indoors, too.

GOOD IDEAS

• Pots, containers, and lighting details made of natural materials such wood, wicker, metalwork, or terracotta look equally at home indoors and out. Use them as a unifying element between the two areas.

• Use awnings or pergolas to lend a room-like quality outdoors. If you wish, reinforce the sense of enclosure with screening plants, chosen and placed where their fragrance can waft indoors.

A PERFECT FRAME ▷
An open doorway, framing a long-flowering composition that includes fuchsias, Japanese anemones and crocosmias, provides an irresistible invitation onto the patio and into the garden beyond, while the garden's sweet scents and the sound of birds drift gently into the house.

COMBINING PATIO AREAS AND WATER FEATURES

The idea of enhancing an area for peaceful repose with water has long held special appeal for garden makers, whether used for the contemplative beauty of its still reflections or the somnolent murmur of a bubbling rill or splashing fountain. Even the smallest patio may have room to add a wall-mounted spout, a bubble fountain, or a container pool. Still more ambitious effects – incorporating a raised pool, or building out over a body of water with decking, for example – can be achieved if they are well thought out at the planning stage. And what better way of appreciating plantings or observing visiting wildlife at close quarters than from the comfort of a recliner, with a drink in hand?

◁ **GONE FISHING**
An overhanging deck is the perfect site from which to observe ornamental fish or wildlife, such as songbirds and darting dragonflies.

△ **CLASSICAL CANAL**
A simple canal lends cool humidity for comfort on hot days and is kept safe after dusk in the ethereal glow of submerged lighting.

SEE ALSO: Installing Decking, pp.64–65; Moving Water in Small Spaces, pp.212–213

COMPLEMENTING WITH PLANTING

With careful selection, patio plantings can perform a number of functions. Tall and climbing plants lend shade and shelter while enclosing the space and screening it off for privacy. Choose wisteria, jasmine, honeysuckle, and climbing roses for their sumptuous perfume, or a luxuriant grapevine for fruit and ornament. Grow smaller plants – selected for color and scent – in open soil or in containers. Try lilies (such as *Lilium regale*), nicotianas, or a scattering of night-scented stock (*Matthiola longipetala* subsp. *bicornis*) – all have scents that are delightfully pervasive in still evening air. And underfoot, use creeping thymes and chamomile to release a heady fragrance when brushed by passing feet. If you cook outdoors, consider having aromatic herbs, like rosemary, thyme, and sage, close at hand to add a stroke of culinary brilliance to barbecued food and scent the night air with fragrant smoke.

HOME COMFORTS ▷
A pergola, clothed with scented climbers and beautiful pots filled with aromatic plants, provides sensory delights as well as shelter, shade, and a feeling of seclusion.

△ **POCKET PLANTING**
Planting pockets can be built into the patio at the design stage, or flags may be lifted later and the space filled with good topsoil or soil mix to provide a home for low-growing, preferably fragrant plants.

PATIO FURNITURE

Taste, comfort, and expense aside, patio furniture must be tough enough to withstand the elements or, if upholstered, light enough to bring under cover. Wooden furniture is sympathetic to a wide range of settings, ages gracefully, and lasts for years if properly maintained, but if you choose tropical hardwoods, like teak or iroko, make sure that it comes from sustainably managed sources. Metal furniture is durable, strong, and often surprisingly comfortable. Plastics are widely available and inexpensive, and although resistant to wet, they often become dingy and sometimes brittle after prolonged exposure to sunlight.

△ **FUNCTIONAL ELEGANCE**
This lightweight furniture has a durable and weatherproof finish and folds flat for easy winter storage — the perfect combination of elegant appearance with practicality.

BARBECUE AREAS

Food undeniably tastes better when eaten outdoors, especially so if taste buds are primed by the delicious odors that arise from food cooked on a barbecue.

Whether you choose a built-in or a portable barbecue, plan the cooking area with easy access to the kitchen indoors – impromptu meals are infinitely more enjoyable if you don't need to ferry ingredients across the yard. Give the chef plenty of elbow room and a weather resistant, easy-clean work surface. Site with shelter from the prevailing winds so that diners are not engulfed in smoke.

ALWAYS REMEMBER

SAFE AND HAPPY COOKING!

Be sure to place the barbecue far enough away from wooden fences, trellises, and pergolas to avoid damage and risk of fire. Keep a fire blanket or extinguisher on hand. Be considerate of neighbors by siting, if possible, to avoid smoke drift into nearby gardens (or invite them to share the feast).

A MOVABLE FEAST ▷
Portable barbecues are ideal for small spaces, especially if unreliable summers do not justify a built-in one, and siting to account for wind direction is almost infinitely adjustable.

SEE ALSO: Lighting in the Garden, pp.70–71; Herbs in the Garden and their Uses, pp.224–233

LAWNS AND GROUNDCOVERS

A LIVING CARPET

MANY PROPERTIES HAVE at least one area, large or small, that is ideal for carpeting with low-growing plants to create a gentle, pleasing, and lasting surface for walking, sitting, or playing on. Grass is an obvious choice, but spreading plants, such as chamomile or thyme, offer an attractive alternative on a small scale. Grass lawns can vary from an exquisitely tended showpiece to a hard-wearing play area for children and may be planted with bulbs or wildflowers to provide fragrance and color. Where an area is unlikely to be walked upon, the choice widens to include groundcover plants such as prostrate conifers, heathers, or flowering shrubs and perennials.

WHY A LAWN?

Make absolutely sure that a grass lawn is the right option before embarking on seeding or sodding. If you have unlimited enthusiasm and time to spend in the garden, creating a beautifully manicured lawn fit for a golf green may be a challenge you will relish. If, on the other hand, you would prefer to keep the maintenance to a minimum, first think hard about the area you intend to surface:

■ Is it really suitable for grass? If there is not much sunlight, for example, which is essential if grass is to thrive, it might be better for you to choose either a hard surface, such as gravel or paving, or one or more of the groundcover plants that grow well in shade.

■ How easy will the lawn be to mow and maintain once established? If the area to be covered is on a steep slope, creeping plants may be far easier to look after.

△ **ATTRACTIVE INFORMALITY**
The sweeping curves of this informal grass lawn enhance the bold use of flowers and foliage in the adjoining borders. The curves are continued in the winding gravel path beyond, combining a delightful visual effect with hardwearing practicality.

△ **LARGE LAWN**
For a large area, grass often proves the cheapest option, and it can be easier to maintain than a network of paths and flower borders.

SMALL LAWN ▷
Where space is restricted, a formal grass lawn, edged with bricks and surrounded by a profusion of flowers and foliage, looks stunning.

TELL ME WHY

WHY IS GRASS SO POPULAR?

Grass has many advantages: it grows close to the ground and has tough, narrow leaves that are stimulated by regular cutting, making it resilient to a range of conditions and uses. It is also relatively cheap to create a lawn with sod or seed and increasingly easy to maintain an established lawn with the help of modern lawnmowers and other specialized equipment.

SEE ALSO: Patios and Paths, pp.56–73; Planning a Lawn, pp.76–77; Alternative Lawns, pp.88–89; Using Groundcovers in Shady Areas, p.131

CHOOSING THE RIGHT SURFACE

Think about the activities for which the area will be used – games, relaxing, entertaining, for example – and also assess the position and conditions of the site.

■ Grass needs sunlight and good drainage; some groundcover plants, however, are tolerant of shady and damp conditions.

■ There are several types of grass, from coarse "family lawn" mixtures, ideal for play areas, to high-quality fine grasses suited to formal, less-used lawns.

■ If you live in a warm climate, you will need a grass that is tolerant of drought and long periods of hot sunshine.

WEAR AND TEAR ▷
Children playing, especially on a small area like this one, make great demands on the grass, so choose coarse, creeping grasses that are able to withstand constant use. They are available as both sod and seed mixtures.

FINE GRASS   **COARSE GRASS**

WHAT WILL THRIVE?
High-quality fine grasses (see above) need good growing conditions, regular and careful maintenance, and little use. Coarse grasses (see above right) are less fussy in their requirements and extremely hardwearing. Groundcover plants that tolerate shade, such as deadnettle, (see right) need little attention once established.

SHADE-LOVING PLANTS

LAWNS WITH ADDED INTEREST

Grass lawns can occasionally be a little dull visually, but you can provide more interest by planting spring bulbs in the grass to cheer up the garden early in the season. Wildflowers, available as seed mixtures, can also add summer color to the grassed area and attract beneficial insects such as butterflies and bees, but these plants can be invasive and should be treated with care. Small areas can also be brought to life with low-growing herbs such as chamomile, creeping thymes, and mints, which produce delightful scents when they are walked on.

▽ **NATURALISTIC WILDFLOWER MEADOW**
If you have the right setting – such as a larger, more rural yard with an area that is not in constant use – creating a thoroughly informal meadow full of colorful wildflowers can be a joy. Remember to use plants and grasses that are native to your area and therefore more likely to put on a good show.

GROUNDCOVERS

Any plant with a low, quickly spreading habit can be used to cover patches of ground, suppressing the growth of weeds, and usually requiring little maintenance. Most will withstand the occasional tread but are not as likely as grass to survive if they are constantly being walked over. They are best for small, less-used areas and should be matched carefully to the conditions of the site. Combining ground-cover plants creates even more interest.

WOODLAND EFFECT ▷
Fill the shady area beneath the canopy of a tree with a combination of low-growing plants that will thrive there to create the impression of a natural woodland floor.

△ **CARPET OF PACHYSANDRA**
This plant has all the qualities of the perfect groundcover alternative to grass: it is low-growing, evergreen, neat, and easy to look after all year.

SEE ALSO: Choosing Seed Mixtures, p.77; Alternative Lawns, pp.88–89; Daffodils, p.137; Planting and Cultivating Herbs, pp.228–231

PLANNING A LAWN

YOU MAY THINK that it is simply a matter of buying some seed or sod and getting on with the job as quickly as possible, but your lawn will benefit greatly from careful planning before you embark on creating it. Only after considering all the relevant factors and options should you start to make important decisions about site, shape, paths, edges, type of grass, and whether to use seed or sod. Remember also that in warm climates, plugs and sprigs will establish better than either seed or sod. A little thought and effort put in at this planning stage will help avoid problems occurring later, when they may turn out to be very difficult and expensive to solve.

SITING AND SHAPING

There may not be any choice about where you put your lawn, especially if your yard is quite small, but it will pay you to analyze the site anyway. Is it sunny or shady? What is the soil like? Is the area well-drained or prone to retain moisture to any degree? If there is not likely to be enough sunlight or adequate drainage, consider whether there is a better site for the lawn than the one you first chose.

When it comes to shape, squares and rectangles may be practical but visually unstimulating. Resist the temptation, however, to make the shape of the lawn too fussy; this may cause you problems when mowing and trying to keep the edges neat. Ovals and circles can look very attractive in some settings. Narrow strips are better avoided, since they can quickly start to look messy.

When you have laid the lawn, you may wish to create "island" beds for shrubs and flowers, or plant specimen trees in the lawn. It is a good idea to take such features into consideration early in the planning stages so that you can make sure the siting and conditions will be suitable.

NARROW LAWN ▷
For plant enthusiasts, borders may take priority, greatly reducing the lawn area. This size and shape of lawn will need a lot of attention to look its best.

ALWAYS REMEMBER

The lowest branches of a tree cast a dark shadow and keep out rain, creating difficult conditions for grass. Such areas underneath established trees will be obvious and are best planted with shade-loving, drought-tolerant plants. If planting a young tree in a new lawn, it is worth thinking about how it might affect the lawn in the years to come.

△ **CHANGING VIEW**
With an interesting shape of lawn, you can view the garden from different angles by moving the seat.

GENTLE CURVES ▷
For easier mowing and edging, keep the shape of the lawn simple and the curves wide and sweeping.

SEE ALSO: Plugs and Sprigs, p.81; Using Groundcovers in Shady Areas, p.131; Marking out a Bed, p.145

A Variety of Lawn Shapes

The shape of your lawn should blend in with the style and formality of the rest of the garden or at least the area immediately surrounding it. In general, straight edges complement formal gardens, and curves create a more relaxed effect. Tight curves and complicated angular shapes will require more effort to keep neat.

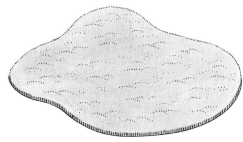

△ Wide Curves
Choose this type of shape if you are looking for informality, perhaps surrounding it with tumbling plants.

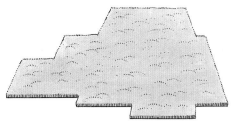

△ Classical Elegance
The right angles in this shape create an instant formality but will need regular attention to keep the edges crisp.

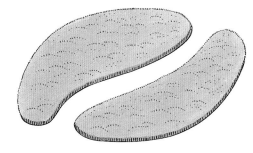

△ A Divided Lawn
A large area of grass, formal or informal, can be bisected by a path to give a greater degree of visual interest.

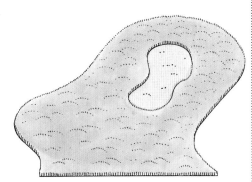

△ Island Beds
An island bed is an ideal way of breaking up a large lawn, but it should reflect the overall style of the area.

Seed or Sod?

Both methods of creating a general-purpose lawn have their advantages (*see below*), but for a specialized lawn requiring a particular species of grass, seed will probably be the only choice. Only you can make the final decision, because it depends on a large number of factors.

■ Are you fit and able to transport and lay sod, bearing in mind that it must be laid as soon as it is delivered or picked up?

■ Do you have friends or family members who can help you lay sod? If not, seed may be a better option.

■ Is the area to be grassed large or small? If small, sod may be more suitable.

Seed

The advantages of using seed are:

■ It is relatively economical.

■ It requires no heavy, physical work.

■ There is a choice of seed mixtures.

■ It is easy to transport.

■ It can be stored without harm.

■ You can resow bare patches with the same seed mixture.

Easy Sowing ▷
Scattering seed by hand can result in unevenness, so try using a pot that has several small holes in the base. When the pot is shaken, the seed is distributed evenly.

TELL ME WHEN

WHEN SHOULD I LAY OR SOW THE LAWN?

If you have opted for sod, it can be laid at any time except when the weather is very hot and dry, very cold, or if the ground is frozen. Autumn or early spring are preferable because the lawn will not be subject to much use before it has had a chance to establish as it might be in summer, when it is also difficult to keep it moist. For seed, the best times to sow are mid-spring or early autumn, when the soil is moist but not wet. Autumn is often the better option, because the new lawn will be advanced enough in the following summer to take light use; if sown in spring, the new lawn will need watering in dry weather and may not be ready before autumn.

CHOOSING SEED MIXTURES

Many seed mixtures are available; avoid unspecified ones. For quality lawns, you will need a fine-leaved mixture with fescues and bents, which can be very closely mown. Ryegrasses are coarser and resilient, but some also have attractive, fine leaves. Single species, suited to warm climates, include bents (*Agrostis*), carpet grass (*Axonopus*), and red fescue (*Festuca rubra*). Special mixes for light shade include meadow species that should not be closely cut.

▽ Buying Sod
Before you part with any money, inspect the sod closely for quality. Check that the grass is uniform in habit and has a good system of roots and leaves, that there are no bare or brown patches, and that all the pieces of sod are of similar quality. Buy more than enough, so that all the sod will be from the same batch.

The major disadvantage of seed is that it looks sparse for a time and cannot be used in the first season. Furthermore, diseases and weeds lurking in the soil, unless rigorously prepared, may stunt or choke the grass seedlings.

Sod

Sod can be inexpensive, but be sure to inspect it before buying in order to be satisfied that it is good-quality sod rather than cheap, poor-quality sod. Although it is cheap, lesser grades of sod may include a mix of coarse grasses and weeds that have the potential to cause many problems later on.

The advantages of using sod are:

■ It gives fast results – an instant lawn that can soon be used.

■ The edges are well defined.

■ No weeding is necessary while the lawn establishes.

■ It can be laid at almost any time of year;

■ You can fill in any bare patches with pieces of new sod.

SEE ALSO: Creating a Lawn, pp.78–79; Laying Sod, p.80; Repairing Damage, p.86

CREATING A LAWN

ONCE YOU HAVE decided exactly where and what shape your lawn should be, your next task is to level and prepare the ground thoroughly to remove any lumps, stones, or weeds. This will give the grass a good chance of establishing successfully without developing any bare or weedy patches. You may need to install drainage if the area is likely to become waterlogged. Then you are ready to sow the lawn seed or begin laying the sod. If you live in a warm climate, however, alternative methods of planting the grass, such as plugs and sprigs, may give far better results than either seed or sod. Your final task will be to finish off the edges of the lawn neatly.

PREPARING THE SOIL

Dig over the soil, removing all perennial weeds, and level if necessary (*see right*). Firm and rake the soil to clear it of unwanted matter such as leaves and large stones. The area may also require drainage (*see opposite*) or the addition of organic matter to improve the soil quality.

For seed, leave the prepared ground alone for two to three weeks; in this time any annual weed seeds that are still in the soil will have germinated, and you can then remove them by hoeing or spraying.

△ FIRMING THE SOIL
If the area for your lawn is already fairly level, begin preparation by firming the ground. This can be achieved by treading the soil carefully and evenly in a methodical manner over the whole area to be sown or sodded. Alternatively, you can use the back of a rake to firm down an area of soil. Repeat this process until the entire site has been consistently and well firmed.

◁ RAKING
Rake the soil very finely, removing any debris or weeds. For seed sowing, leave the area until annual weeds have appeared, then apply a weedkiller or hoe them off.

LEVELING THE GROUND

How level the ground needs to be depends on the type of lawn you are creating. If it is to be rough grass or a meadow area, exact leveling is not critical, but if you are looking for a more formal lawn or an area for ball games, you will need to be much more precise. Rough leveling by eye can be achieved by raking soil from mounds into hollows and then firming. More accurate leveling will require the use of marked pegs, a wooden board, a level, and a hammer. Insert the pegs to the desired level (*see below*) and then rake the soil to the marks on the pegs. This method can also be used to create smooth slopes with a gentle gradient (*see right*).

△ USING LEVELING TOOLS
Mark some pegs 2in (5cm) from the top. With a hammer, drive in a peg so that the mark sits at the desired ground level. Insert the rest so that the tops are level, using a board and level.

CREATING A LEVEL BASE

1 MARKER PEGS
Insert a row of pegs along the edge of the site. The marks on the pegs should sit at the desired final level of the ground.

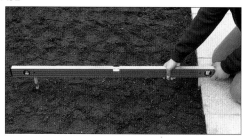

2 CHECKING THE LEVEL
Add a second row of pegs about 3ft (1m) from the first. Using leveling tools, adjust until the tops are level.

▽ MAKING A SLOPE
If you want to create a gentle slope, maybe leading away from a paved area, mark the pegs (see right) at increasing distances from the top, using standard increments. Drive the pegs into the soil at constant intervals across the area, and check with a board and level (see below) that the tops are level. Rake the soil to the marks to provide a gradient for the area to be grassed.

PEGS

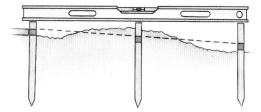

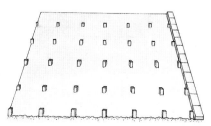

△ LEVELING METHOD
Drive in the pegs in a grid. Then use the board and level in every direction to make sure they align at the top, adjusting the pegs as necessary.

3 MOVING THE SOIL
Repeat to create a grid of pegs. Rake the soil to the level of the marks, filling in any hollows with topsoil. Remove the pegs.

SEE ALSO: Seed or Sod?, p.77; Plugs and Sprigs, p.81; Improving Soil Types, p.142

SOWING GRASS SEED

Having prepared the ground thoroughly, you are ready to sow. Calculate how much seed is needed, depending on the mixture:

- For **fine-leaved grasses**, use 1–1⅛oz (25–30g) per sq yd (sq m).
- For **coarser grasses**, use 1⅜–1⅝oz (35–40g) per sq yd (sq m).
- For **single species**, check the rate for the particular species you have selected when buying – rates vary from about ⅒oz (2g) per sq yd (sq m) for centipede grass (*Eremochloa ophiuroides*) to about 1⅛oz (30g) for perennial ryegrass (*Lolium perenne*).

Weigh out the correct amount of seed for the entire lawn, and sow evenly using either a hand-held pot or a spreader. Rake the soil lightly to cover the seed. Keep the soil moist, and you should witness the first signs of growth in one or two weeks. The lawn will need its first mow in spring when the grass is about 2in (5cm) tall; set the mower blades high.

GOOD IDEAS

- Choose a dry, still day for sowing so that the seed does not blow away.
- Do not sow seed too thickly – there is no advantage to be gained.
- Divide the area into sections, and measure and sow the seed for each section; this will help you to sow evenly.
- Keep birds off the seed once sown. To do this, use seed treated with a repellent, cover the area with fine chicken wire, suspend strips of foil from sticks or a line over the soil, or attract them to another part of the garden with food.

SEEDING A LAWN

△ **USING MARKERS**
When sowing grass seed over a small area, you can mark out measured squares with pots or sticks and scatter the correct quantity of seed evenly between them. Repeat the process until the whole area has been seeded consistently.

△ **MAKING A GRID**
For larger areas, it is better to mark out a grid system before sowing, using stakes to divide up the site into many equal squares. Weigh out each portion of seed, scattering half of it up and down and the other half side to side.

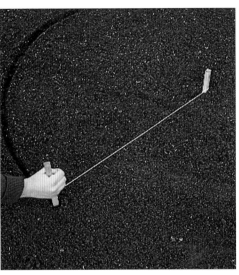

△ **CREATING A CURVE**
Attach a length of twine to two sticks; the length depends on the size of the desired curve. Insert one stick in the ground and use the other to mark the curved line.

◁ **USING A SPREADER**
To ensure that you get even distribution, you can use a seed spreader. Lay down a plastic sheet where you want the edge to be. Sow half the seed in one direction and the other half at right angles to the first.

◁ **FINAL TOUCHES**
Once you have finished sowing, lightly rake over the surface of the soil across the whole area to cover the seed. In the following days and weeks, if the weather is dry, water the site regularly to encourage germination of the grass seed.

MAKING A DRAIN

Depending on the site of your lawn, it may be a good idea to install a simple drain at the lowest point, before laying sod or seeding. This will counteract any potential problems caused by a buildup of moisture in wet periods. Make sure that the drain is sited well away from any house walls in order to prevent water from entering. If drainage is a real problem, grow plants better suited to moist conditions, or consider creating a bog garden.

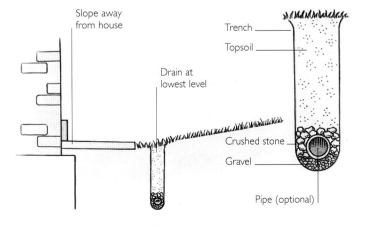

Slope away from house

Drain at lowest level

Trench

Topsoil

Crushed stone

Gravel

Pipe (optional)

◁ **LAYING A SIMPLE DRAIN**
Dig a trench and fill the base with stone and coarse gravel so that excess water can drain away. Cover this with topsoil to the level of the rest of the prepared area. The pipe or perforated tube is an optional feature, and it is necessary only if drainage is a serious problem.

SEE ALSO: Seed or Sod?, p.77; Mowing, p.82; Bog Gardens, pp.204–205; The Moisture-lovers, pp.218–219

LAYING SOD

The best aspect of using sod rather than seed is that it gives an instantly pleasing effect. You must resist the temptation to walk on it right away, however, since the grass roots must be given time to penetrate the soil and get a good foundation before the lawn is used. You must also keep the sod moist to prevent it from turning brown and curling up at the edges. Although you can lay sod at any time, it is advisable to avoid rainy or frosty conditions as well as hot, dry spells during which it will be hard to keep the new grass sufficiently watered.

Be sure to plan thoroughly before you start. Calculate how much sod will be needed, allowing extra for wastage, and make sure you have time to prepare and level the soil thoroughly before the sod is delivered. Also ensure that you have allowed enough time to lay it. If you cannot lay the sod as soon as it arrives, for example if it is raining or if there is a heavy frost, you can store it (*see right*) for up to three days; if kept any longer, the pieces may start to dry out and turn yellow.

If there are any pieces left over when you have completed the lawn, stack them upsidedown in a little-used place. After a while, they will break down into a fine soil that can be used for lawn topdressing.

△ **HOW TO KEEP SOD FRESH**
If you cannot use the sod as soon as it arrives, lay it out flat, but not touching or overlapping, on some plastic sheeting or soil, and water it well every day.

SODDING A LAWN

1 MAKING A START
Begin by laying the first row of pieces using a straight edge, such as a path or board, as a guide, making sure that each new piece of sod lies flush against the next one.

2 USING A BOARD
Once the first row is complete, place a board on top of it and kneel on it. Lay the second row of sod, remembering to stagger the joints against those of the previous row. Repeat this process until you have covered the entire area. Try not to walk on the bare soil at any time.

3 SETTLING IN
With the back of a rake, firm down the sod to get rid of any air pockets and to create good contact between the grass roots and the soil. Alternatively, use a light roller.

4 FINISHING OFF
First apply a light topdressing of sieved, sandy soil, then brush it into any gaps between the pieces. Soak the lawn, and continue to keep it moist if the weather is dry.

GOOD IDEAS

• Begin to lay the sod at the part of the lawn that is closest to where the pieces are being stored.

• To avoid compacting the sod, use a board to spread your weight as you work .

• If you have any small pieces of sod, lay them in the middle of the lawn rather than at the edges, where they may be prone to drying out and shrinking.

• In each new row of sod, stagger the joints with those in the previous row.

• Extend the sod beyond the final desired area and trim it afterward.

• When making the first cut in late spring, set the mower to its maximum height.

SEE ALSO: Seed or Sod?, p.77; Preparing the Soil, p.78; Leveling the Ground, p.78; Mowing, p.82

PLUGS AND SPRIGS

In warm, dry climates it can be difficult to establish a traditional lawn. In these areas, it is best to use warm-season, spreading grasses that are capable of tolerating extreme conditions, or cool-season bent grass. In order to prevent the lawn having a patchy appearance, use just one type of grass for the whole area.

Small pieces of these plants, known as plugs and sprigs, are used to get the lawn established. The best time to do this is spring or early summer. Plugs are small pieces or tufts of rhizomatous grass, and these should be planted in individual holes (*see right*). New shoots will grow outward from the joints and quickly mesh together. Sprigs are rooting stems or rhizomes that should be strewn evenly over the soil surface (*see right*), covered with a thin layer of soil, and then watered in well. With both of these methods, the grasses should have rooted after a couple of months and grown together to produce a smooth, even lawn.

ALWAYS REMEMBER

Lawns created from plugs or sprigs of tough, drought-tolerant grass species will never exactly resemble their cool-climate counterparts, but they are resilient, practical, and easy to maintain. As with all lawns, the soil must be well prepared in advance, because plugs and sprigs are living plant material that cannot be stored for long.

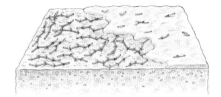

△ **SCATTERING SPRIGS**
Distribute the sprigs over the surface of the soil and then cover them with top-dressing of fine soil. Water well.

△ **PLANTING PLUGS**
Space the plugs evenly over the area, 6–12in (15–30cm) apart. Apply a top-dressing of soil and keep well watered.

FINISHING THE EDGES

Once the main task of creating the lawn has been completed, it is time to turn your attention to the edges. Far from being an afterthought, the way you edge your lawn is one of the most important aspects from both a practical and an esthetic point of view. Even if the grass in the main part is not absolutely perfect, well-kept edges give a fine impression of neatness and good care. Whether you choose hard or soft edging, remember that ease of mowing is a vital considera-tion. Mowing strips or raised edging with holding strips (*see below*) and hard edging (*see right*) reduce the need to trim the edges with shears or a lawn edger.

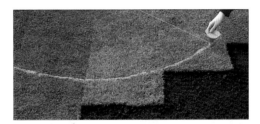

△ **CURVED EDGE**
After sodding, mark out a curve using string attached to a peg and a funnel of fine, dry sand. Then trim off the excess sod.

STRAIGHT EDGE ▷
Use a taut string, a board, and a lawn edger to create a true, straight edge.

△ **SOFT EDGING**
Plants in the border will need staking and the lawn edges regular trimming if you prefer this soft look.

△ **HARD EDGING**
Narrow stone pavers and terracotta edging tiles make a practical and attractive finish to the lawn.

RAISED EDGING ▷
The lawn may be raised above the level of the path and attractively edged with wood (see right) or plastic holding strips (see far right).

MOWING STRIP ▷
Separate the grass from the borders (see right) with a row of bricks on a layer of mortar (far right) to slightly below the level of the lawn for ease of mowing.

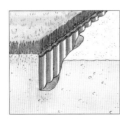

BRICK APRON ▷
To avoid the mowing problems that would arise if a step (or other raised feature) immediately adjoined the lawn, try surrounding it with an area of brick paving. This brick apron allows trouble-free mowing as well as providing a hardwearing surface just below the step.

SEE ALSO: Edging Materials, p.57; Making Steps, pp.68–69; Lawncare, pp.82–85

LAWNCARE

YOUR LAWN WILL look good and stand up to wear only if you spend a little time caring for it properly. Mowing and keeping the edges neat are the most obvious jobs to many people, but there are a few other important seasonal tasks. During much of the growing season (spring into summer) the grass will need feeding and watering in hot, dry spells, as well as mowing; in autumn, it will benefit from scarifying, aerating, top-dressing, and raking or sweeping up dead leaves that have fallen onto it. If these are left on the grass, they will shade it and slow its growth and may encourage disease. Doing these tasks will help prevent common problems.

MOWING

The act of mowing should stimulate the grass to produce more shoots and therefore a denser cover, inhibiting weeds. To achieve this, you should mow little and often (*see below*). For a formal look, work to a pattern (*see right*), but remember to vary the direction of the pattern each time so that ridges do not build up. If possible, always use a grass catcher to prevent a buildup of clippings at soil level.

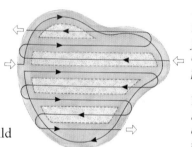

◁ IRREGULAR SHAPE
For an asymmetrical lawn, first mow around the edges and then work across in parallel lines.

REGULAR SHAPE ▷
Start by mowing down the edges of opposite sides, and then work across the lawn at right angles to them.

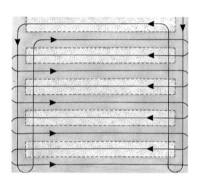

WHEN TO MOW

Begin mowing when the grass begins to grow again after a period of dormancy. During periods of moisture (usually spring and autumn in much of North America) mow more frequently than during dry periods, generally in summer.
■ For high-quality lawns, mow once or twice a week in spring and autumn; in summer, mow as needed, depending on how fast the grass is growing, if at all.
■ For coarser utility lawns, mow less frequently and higher than for a high-quality lawn.
Overcutting or "scalping" the lawn will result in unsightly bald patches, so set the mowing height appropriately and be careful when mowing high spots.

LAWNS WITH BULBS ▷
If you have planted some spring-flowering bulbs in your lawn, you can still cut the grass until late autumn, but do not start mowing again until at least 6 weeks after flowering has finished. This will enable the bulbs to build up food reserves for the following year's flowers.

CHOOSING A MOWER

There is a huge array of lawnmowers to choose from – so which is best for you? For small lawns, a manual reel mower may be sufficient; it is cheap, quiet, and needs no gas or electrical cords. It will, however, require some physical effort on your part. If you have a larger area, or prefer to expend less energy, you will need a mower powered by either gas or electricity. Electricity is cleaner and more efficient than gas but is not suitable for powerful engines (such as those found in riding mowers), but dealing with the power cord can be an annoyance.

Power mowers come in various types:
■ **Reel mowers** give the finest cut and produce an attractive stripe pattern, but they can tear the grass if incorrectly adjusted and can be quite difficult for some people to maneuver.
■ **Rotary mowers** are easier to handle, especially in longer grass, but will not produce stripes.
■ **Riding mowers** are extremely useful for mowing large areas of lawn.

For all types, check that the height of cut is adjustable, and choose a model with a grass catcher, if possible.

PUSH REEL MOWER ▽
This mower gives a very clean cut when the blades are kept sharp, and it is certainly the most environmentally friendly of all mowers. But remember that the power to operate this kind of mower comes from the person behind the handle, not from a gas- or electricity-powered engine.

SEE ALSO: Lawncare, pp.84–85; Planting Bulbs in Grass, p.89

TRIMMING EDGES

Keeping the edges of your lawn neat and sharp will greatly enhance the appearance of your entire yard. During the growing season, trim the edges regularly with shears (*see below*), using an angled cut that is hard against the grass edge, or with a nylon-line trimmer (*see below, right*). Gather the clippings so that they cannot root in adjoining beds or paths. Also make sure that border plants do not spill over onto the lawn, causing areas to brown and die. If you trim regularly in this way, you will need to recut the edges only once a year in early spring to retain the lawn's shape and create definition. This task involves removing a small strip of sod with a half-moon edger (*see below*) or with a power edger, which can be rented. Do not use a digging spade, because the concave blade will produce a scalloped effect.

△ **TRIMMING AN EDGE**
Trim edges with long-handled edging shears or a nylon-line trimmer.

△ **RECUTTING AN EDGE**
Use a sharp half-moon edger and a board to achieve a well-defined, straight edge.

◁ **NYLON-LINE TRIMMER**
Electric trimmers have a flexible nylon cutting line that rotates at high speed. Some have an adjustable head that may be turned into a vertical position for trimming edges. They are ideal for a large lawn.

△ **CUTTING GUIDE**
This keeps the line off the ground for an even trim.

ROTARY MOWER ▽
As opposed to the blade on a reel mower, the blade on a rotary mower cuts horizontally, so scalping turf is less likely. The whirlwind action of the rotating blade drives the cut grass into the grass catcher. As with all mowers, be sure to keep the blades sharp to prevent tearing the grass and leaving rough ends that will turn brown.

MULCHING ROTARY MOWER ▽
Instead of gathering up the cut grass into a bag, a mulching mower chops up the grass blades more finely than other mowers and returns them to the lawn. This provides an organic mulch but may contribute to the problem of thatch buildup.

RIDING MOWER ▷
This kind of mower is usually considered a necessity for managing a large area of lawn. It may be fitted with a large-capacity grass catcher or used without the catcher as a mulching mower. Riding mowers are very useful for picking up leaves in autumn as well as in early spring before the grass begins to grow again.

SEE ALSO: Finishing the Edges, p.81

WATERING A LAWN

New lawns should be kept moist by regular watering until they are well established. Thereafter, the grass will look after itself quite well, except during prolonged dry spells of weather when growth slows down and the grass turns brown. It is often wise to let a lawn go brown in summer if you are concerned about water conservation. The lawn should green up again in autumn.

To avoid wasteful evaporation, the best times to water are either early morning or evening. Make sure you give the lawn enough water (*see right*); if the soil is heavy, do not allow pools to form on the surface because this inhibits the intake of oxygen and minerals by the roots. To check if you have watered sufficiently, dig a small hole to the required depth, and see whether the soil is damp all the way down. Electric moisture meters are also available.

For small areas you can use a watering can, but for larger lawns you will probably need either a hose or a sprinkler. Before using either of the latter, check that there are no restrictions in force preventing their use in your area. Extensive grassed areas that are likely to need repeated watering will benefit from the installation of a built-in, pop-up, underground sprinkler system, but these are expensive. When the water supply is turned on, the pressure lifts the sprinkler heads above the surface and water is released.

△ LACK OF WATER
Shallow watering, where the soil is moistened only slightly below the surface, as shown in the dark-colored soil above, may make the lawn vulnerable to drought by encouraging the grass roots to remain near the surface of the soil.

△ SUFFICIENT WATER
After watering, remember to check that the soil has been moistened to a depth of about 4–6in (10–15cm), as shown above. This will encourage the roots to grow strongly and will help them to find water more easily during dry spells.

FERTILIZING A LAWN

To avoid problems of disease, patchiness, moss, and weeds, supply your lawn regularly with a special lawn fertilizer to stimulate dense, healthy, bright green growth. For most lawns, two applications a year are sufficient: one in early to midspring and the other in late summer or early autumn.

Most lawn fertilizers come in granular or powder form. Only small amounts are needed for lawns on heavy clay soils that are rich in nutrients; greater quantities will be required for those on light, sandy soils. Spread fertilizer evenly, either by hand for small areas or with the use of a spreader for large areas (*see right*).

TELL ME WHY

WHY USE LAWN FERTILIZER?

Lawns flourish when they have access to high levels of the essential nutrients that grass requires for good growth – nitrogen, phosphorus, potassium, and iron. Lawn fertilizers are formulated to provide these nutrients. The formulations vary at different times of year: in spring, more nitrogen is included to replace what has been lost over the winter; in autumn, there is more potassium to toughen the grass for winter. Some lawn fertilizers are combined with chemicals to control weeds.

SPREADER FOR LARGE AREAS

◁ APPLYING FERTILIZER WITH A SPREADER
The spreader's hopper releases fertilizer evenly. Apply half one way, then the other half at right angles.

△ SCORCH
This area of scorch, where the grass has died off, has been caused by an over-lapping, double application of fertilizer. Using the application methods shown on the left and below should help eliminate this.

△ FERTILIZING BY HAND
When doing a small area, divide the lawn into equal-sized squares and measure the fertilizer into portions. Scatter it evenly one way and then the other, using a pot.

SEE ALSO: Repairing Damage, p.86; Watering Equipment, p.280

AUTUMN MAINTENANCE

After summer, when the lawn has been well used and the soil may be compacted, it is beneficial to let air into the lawn by creating holes and channels. This alleviates compaction, which chokes the grass, and it encourages deep roots for healthy growth. Top-dressing helps further by improving drainage. These two tasks are best carried out in early autumn after vigorous scarifying to remove excess thatch (*see below*). Together, they give the lawn an excellent chance of coming through strongly the following spring.

There are several ways of aerating a lawn (*see right*). The simplest is spiking with a garden fork. You can also remove cores of soil with a hollow-tining tool or machine, or use a rotary aerator. After aerating, the lawn will benefit from top-dressing (*see below, right*) to fill the holes left by aerating, to keep the passages open, and to level small hollows in the lawn.

GOOD IDEAS

• Before aerating, mow the lawn to its normal summer height. After aerating, apply a low-nitrogen autumn fertilizer.

• Aerate when the soil is moist; it is easier and the lawn will be less vulnerable to drought.

• Apply topdressing on a dry day so that it does not get washed away.

• Use topdressing at a rate of about 7lb (3kg) per sq yd (sq m).

HOLLOW-TINING ▷
In order to improve surface drainage, use a specially designed tool to remove cores of grass and soil up to ¾in (2cm) wide. Work methodically over the area so that you do not step on the cores. Brush the cores away and compost them.

△ **SLITTING**
For large lawns, it may be a good idea to rent a rotary aerator, which will create deep slits in the turf.

SPIKING ▷
If you have only a small area of grass to aerate, you can do it with an ordinary garden fork. Insert the fork into the ground at 15cm (6in) intervals across the lawn, and then rock it back and forth gently to allow more air to enter the soil.

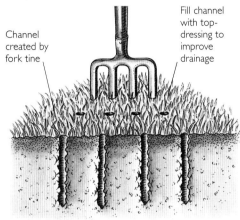

Channel created by fork tine

Fill channel with top-dressing to improve drainage

◁ **ADVANTAGES OF AERATION**
The channels created by aeration allow moisture, air, and fertilizer to reach the roots of the grass more easily, discouraging moss. The soil next to each channel expands slightly, reducing the chance of compaction. This, in turn, creates better drainage, especially if the channels are filled with top-dressing.

TOPDRESSING LAWNS

TOPDRESSING MIX ▽
You can create your own topdressing by mixing together 6 parts of medium-fine sand (top), 3 parts of garden soil (below right), and 1 part of either peat or peat substitute (below left) or leafmold. Pass the mixture through a ¼in (5mm) sieve to remove stones.

◁ **APPLYING A TOPDRESSING**
For small areas, you can use a shovel or spade to apply the topdressing; for larger areas, however, you may prefer to use a mechanical spreader. Apply evenly over the lawn, then use a brush to work it into the grass.

SCARIFYING

This is another job for early autumn. Scarifying serves to remove thatch (*see below, right*) and dead moss, and it lets air enter the surface of the lawn, thus allowing the grass to breathe. The lawn will look worse after you have finished than it did before, but you will reap the benefits in the following spring when plenty of new, healthy shoots appear.

Scarifying is best undertaken when the soil is just moist. It is advisable to kill off any moss before you start, or it may be spread to other parts. For small areas, you can use a rake to scarify the grass.

An ordinary wire or spring-tined rake will be effective, but a sharp-toothed scarifying rake is specially suited to the job. With large areas, you may find it easier to use a mechanical or powered scarifier. Work the machine back and forth across the lawn, just like using a lawnmower.

THATCH ▷
By autumn, there may be a buildup of dead material, known as thatch, in the lawn. If left, this will choke the grass and result in brown or bare patches.

◁ **USING A SPRING-TINED RAKE**
Pull the rake vigorously over the lawn, making sure that the tines are pushed well down into the surface.

◁ **SCARIFYING RAKE**
This rake has rigid metal tines that are designed to cut deeply into the thatch and even the grass itself.

SEE ALSO: Mowing, p.82; Repairing Damage, p.86; Hollows and Humps, p.87; Rakes, p.279

DEALING WITH PROBLEMS

UNLESS YOU ARE very lucky, your lawn will incur a few problems from time to time. These can include damage caused by wear and tear, the appearance of hollows or humps, moss, weeds, and even some pests and diseases. Most are fairly minor, and sometimes you may even choose to tolerate them. Repairing damage is fairly easy to do, as is rectifying a hollow or hump. For moss, weeds, pests, and diseases, always consider remedying the cause of the problem or employing organic methods of control before resorting to chemicals. For example, some diseases can be eradicated by improving drainage. Early treatment of problems is strongly recommended.

REPAIRING DAMAGE

Uneven wear can cause parts of the lawn to become damaged and unsightly. This is easily rectified by removing the affected piece and then resodding or reseeding. The best time to do this is in midspring or midautumn. It is essential to use the same type of seed or sod as was used originally for the rest of the lawn; if you do not know the sod or seed type used, swap a piece of sod from a little-used part of the garden with the damaged patch. If the lawn repeatedly becomes damaged, you could replace it with a more durable surface such as paving or gravel.

To repair a damaged edge, remove the affected piece and fill in the gap with new sod or with soil for reseeding (*see right*). Alternatively, cut out a section containing the damaged edge, and simply turn it so that the damaged edge now butts up to the lawn. Firm it into place, then add some sandy soil to bring the damaged edge up to the level of the rest of the lawn. Sow grass seed over the soil, and water in. To repair a patch, remove the affected grass, fork over the soil, fertilize it, and then resod or reseed as necessary (*see below*).

REPAIRING A DAMAGED EDGE

1 REMOVING A SECTION
Cut a square of sod including the damaged area. Undercut the sod with a spade and slide it forward.

2 TRIMMING THE EDGE
Using a board aligned along the lawn edge, trim the sod with a half-moon edger so that it is level.

3 FILLING THE GAP
Now cut a new piece of sod and ease it into the resulting hole. Trim it until it forms a perfect fit.

4 ADJUSTING THE LEVEL
Remove or add soil beneath the new piece of sod until it sits exactly level with the rest of the lawn.

5 FIRMING IN
Press the new sod firmly into place with the back of a rake, or use a medium-weight roller.

6 FINISHING
With a trowel, apply some sandy topdressing over the repaired area, especially on the seams. Water well.

REPAIRING A DAMAGED PATCH

1 REMOVING THE PATCH
Cut out a square around the damaged area using a half-moon edger, then undercut the grass with a spade and remove it.

2 PREPARING THE SOIL
Loosen the soil to encourage rooting by lightly forking or raking it over. Apply a dressing of a liquid or granular fertilizer.

3 FIRMING THE SOIL
Carefully tread over the prepared soil to consolidate it and firm the surface before inserting new sod.

4 RESODDING
Cut a new piece of sod to fit the space, trimming it with a half-moon edger to match the exact size and shape of the hole.

5 FINISHING
Check the sod is level with the rest of the lawn, adjusting the soil level if necessary. Firm in the sod and water it well.

SEE ALSO: Patios and Paths, pp.56–73; Seed or Sod?, p.77; Sowing Grass Seed, p.79; Laying Sod, p.80

HOLLOWS AND HUMPS

After a while, you may find that your lawn develops a few hollows or humps, or both. The grass in a hollow will become unevenly long, and the grass on a hump will be mown too closely, resulting in scalping. On a small scale, these problems may be quickly and easily rectified by cutting a cross in the affected grass, peeling back the corners, and leveling the soil underneath (*see right*).

Where a large area is affected, it may be better to remove entire sections of grass. Store them on one side, making sure they do not dry out. Then level the soil over the whole area, using a level (*see p.78*), before carefully relaying all the pieces of sod in their original positions.

LEVELING A HOLLOW OR HUMP

1 CUTTING A CROSS
Using a half-moon edger, cut a cross through the hump or hollow. The cuts should extend to a little beyond the problem area. Then undercut the resulting triangles of grass with a spade.

2 LIFTING THE SOD
Fold back the triangles of grass from the center of the cross. Take care not to pull them too vigorously or they may crack.

3 LEVELING
Fill in a hollow with good, sifted, sandy topsoil, firm it, and make sure it is level. For a hump, remove some of the soil and check that the rest is firm and perfectly level.

4 REPLACING THE GRASS
Fold back the triangles of sod. Lightly firm, and check that the level is correct. If necessary, readjust the soil level beneath the sod. Top-dress and water well.

CONTROLLING WEEDS

Some lawn weeds, such as daisies and clover, can look attractive and, unless you have a very high-quality lawn, you may wish to leave them alone. Others, however, if left, will cause the grass to suffer, and even on a utility lawn it is better to control them. Most lawn weeds are creeping or rosette-forming plants that are not affected by mowing, such as plantains and dandelions. Some of the most common examples are shown here. Others that may cause problems are quackgrass, ground ivy, crabgrass, goose-grass, annual bluegrass, and oxalis.

Regular mowing, feeding, and watering should discourage weeds. If they do appear, however, it is possible to cut out individual weeds by hand using either an asparagus knife or a kitchen knife. Remember that some weeds have long taproots that must be completely removed. On large lawns, you may need to use chemical weedkillers.

Weedkillers come in various forms:
- **Liquids** are diluted and watered onto the lawn with a nozzle or dribble bar.
- **Powders and granules** are applied to the lawn when the soil is moist, and they can be spread either by hand or with a wheeled spreader.
- **Spot weedkillers**, usually a gel, are applied to individual weeds.

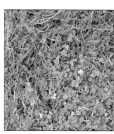

△ **FIELD BINDWEED**
Spreading by underground shoots, this can be quite a problem in poor soils.

△ **SLENDER SPEEDWELL**
On moist soil, this weed is very difficult to control. Mowing spreads it around.

△ **CREEPING BUTTERCUP**
This is a fairly common weed on moist, clay soils.

△ **BROAD-LEAVED PLANTAIN**
A weed that forms broad, grass-smothering rosettes.

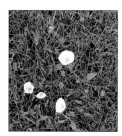

△ **YARROW**
This weed thrives on poor, dry soils. Small areas may be forked out.

△ **DANDELION**
These have long taproots, form rosettes that smother grass, and self-seed.

△ **LESSER YELLOW TREFOIL**
An annual weed that is spread in grass clippings.

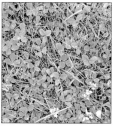

△ **COMMON WHITE CLOVER**
This plant will spread quickly in dry weather.

CONTROLLING MOSS

Moss can be a problem even in the best-kept lawns, but is commonly found in wet lawns in shade and in underfed lawns. Treat it with a chemical moss-killer or lawn sand, preferably in spring, and rake out the dead moss. If done in autumn, scarifying may spread the problem. If the soil is poor and acidic, try applying lime. Fertilize regularly to encourage strong grass growth. If the moss keeps reappearing, try to identify the cause and take steps to rectify the problem. This may involve improving soil aeration, drainage, and fertility. In dense shade where moss recurs repeatedly, it may be sensible to replace the grass with ground-cover plants or even to create a moss lawn.

SEE ALSO: Leveling the Ground, p.78; Alternative Lawns, pp.88–89; Dealing with Weeds, pp.290–291

ALTERNATIVE LAWNS

THERE ARE SEVERAL options open to you if you are not bent on a traditional grass lawn, such as using ground-cover plants or herbs, or brightening up grass with wild-flowers or bulbs. These are best suited to small areas that are not subject to heavy use, because not only are they more expensive than grass, but also the plants cannot withstand being walked on regularly. A lawn with flowers or bulbs in it is more likely to thrive if left alone during flowering. The occasional tread, however, on a herb lawn will release delicious scents. Mowing is not required for a nongrass lawn, but you will still need to care for it by watering, feeding, weeding, and trimming.

GROUNDCOVER PLANTS

Some choices for nongrass lawns include pachysandra (*see p.75*), non-flowering chamomile (*Chamaemelum nobile* 'Treneague', which cannot be grown from seed), and herbs like creeping Corsican mint (*Mentha requienii*), and low-growing, fragrant thymes, such as *Thymus serpyllum*. These can also be combined (*see below*).

Other groundcover plants useful for filling awkward places are:
■ Creeping plants, such as acaenas, cotulas, dichondras, or periwinkles.
■ Dwarf, spreading conifers, such as *Juniperus squamata* 'Blue Carpet'.
■ Low-growing shrubs or climbers, such as euonymus, heathers, and ivies.

CREATING A NONGRASS LAWN

A nongrass lawn can be costly to create, unless you raise your own plants to start it off. To do this, you will need room to care for seedlings and small plants. Most chamomiles and thymes may be grown from seed, and larger plants may also be divided into smaller sections and replanted. Cuttings may also be rooted from thymes and other herbs. Otherwise, you will need to buy enough plants for the area to be covered. Always choose plants that suit your soil and conditions.

Prepare the ground thoroughly as for a grass lawn, removing all perennial and annual weeds, and space the plants 8–12in (20–30cm) apart. Water regularly until established, and weed around the plants until they have begun to form a weed-smothering mat. Apply a general fertilizer in spring, and trim the plants in early spring or late summer. Remove any weeds that appear by hand. After a few years, the entire lawn may need to be replaced and the soil enriched.

△ **SCENTED LAWN**
Ideal for a little-used area, this mixture of chamomile and thyme has created an attractive carpet that looks good all through the year, suppresses weeds, and has the bonus of colorful flowers in summer. Walking lightly over the herb lawn every now and again will stimulate the release of a variety of delightful fragrances.

SINGLE-HANDED SHEARS

LONG-HANDLED SHEARS

△ **TRIMMING TOOLS**
Because you will need to trim your groundcover plants by hand, tools such as one-handed or long-handled shears have been designed to make the job easier.

◁ **MINIMUM MAINTENANCE**
It is best to keep the area of a nongrass lawn quite small, so that weeding and trimming by hand will not become too onerous. The lawn should then flourish.

SEE ALSO: Groundcovers, p.75; Creating a Lawn, p.78; Dividing Perennials, p.148; Increasing Border Plants, pp.162–163

NATURALISTIC EFFECTS

Grass never grows in isolation in nature; it mingles with meadow flowers or woodland-type plants. The simplest way to recreate a natural effect is to plant bulbs or corms in the grass (*see below*) and enjoy a colorful show of daffodils, snowdrops, or crocuses in spring. More effort is needed to create a wildflower meadow from seed, but the rewards can be exciting. Many wildflowers thrive on poor soil, so stop fertilizing and remove clippings for a season or two before sowing. Choose plants native to your area, or they may not survive. In general, cut a meadow in early spring and late autumn with a line trimmer.

△ **CROCUSES**
Spring flowers liven up the lawn before the grass begins to grow strongly.

◁ **MEADOW FLOWERS**
This meadow seed mixture includes poppies, corn-flowers, and corn cockles.

PLANTING BULBS IN GRASS

Bulbs and corms suitable for planting in grass include most spring-flowering ones, and some autumn-flowering crocuses and colchicums. Once you have taken the trouble to plant some bulbs in an area of grass, they will naturalize and multiply each year, providing even more color for no extra cost. It is vital to remember, however, not to cut their foliage down by mowing the grass too soon after flowering has finished, because this will inhibit the growth and flowering potential of the bulbs. Postpone the first mowing until at least six weeks after flowering, or until the foliage is turning yellow.

PLANTING LARGE BULBS IN GRASS

1 MAKE A HOLE
Clean the bulbs (here, daffodils) and scatter them on the grass. Make a hole 4–6in (10–15cm) deep for each one with a bulb planter or trowel.

2 PLANT THE BULB
Mix a pinch of bone meal with soil from the core of sod and place it in the hole. Put the bulb on top, with the growing point upward.

3 REPLACE THE CORE
Loosen the soil from the bottom of the core over the bulb, and replace the sod lid in the hole. Firm in gently, and fill in any gaps with soil.

PLANTING SMALL BULBS IN GRASS

1 CUTTING THE GRASS
Using a half-moon edger or spade, cut the shape of an "H" in the grass. Make sure the cut penetrates the soil.

2 FOLDING BACK
Carefully undercut the sod and fold back the 2 flaps to expose the bare soil beneath. Try not to tear the sod.

3 PREPARING THE SOIL
Loosen the soil with a hand fork to at least 3in (8cm) deep; mix in a small amount of slow-release fertilizer.

4 PLANTING THE BULBS
Place the bulbs (here, crocuses) on the soil, at least 1in (2.5cm) apart, with the growing points upward.

5 SCORING THE SOD
Score the back of the sod with a hand fork to allow the bulbs easily to grow through. Fold back the sod and firm.

GOOD IDEAS

• Plant bulbs randomly for a more natural effect by scattering them over the grass or soil and planting them where they land.
• Make sure that large bulbs are planted at least their own width apart.

SEE ALSO: Lawns with Added Interest, p.75; Daffodils, p.137; Planting Bulbs, p.149

BOUNDARIES, DIVISIONS, AND STRUCTURES

BOUNDARIES AND DIVISIONS

A BOUNDARY NOT ONLY establishes the edges of a legally defined area, it also creates an immediate visual impact, setting the atmosphere in a garden. Together with any internal divisions, boundaries form an integral part of the design, and, when coordinated with the surrounding planting designs, they provide a vital link through the entire garden and with the house, too. Different materials create different impressions: low walls and fences and open trellises allow for extensive views outward or across a garden, while dense hedges and high solid boundaries and screens provide intimacy and a sense of seclusion from the outside world.

DESIGNING WITH BOUNDARIES

When considering the suitability of a boundary, it is important to note what safety, security, and privacy it provides. Does it need to keep in small children? Will it deter intruders? Are you worried about neighbors looking into your garden? You may need to keep pets in and other animals out. To deter deer, a fence needs to be at least 6ft (2m) high. Chicken wire buried to 1ft (30cm) should prevent rabbits from burrowing underneath.

Open gardens, with low-key boundaries, often have a relaxed, informal ambience. Boundaries made from light, airy trellis-work look stunning covered in climbers such as honeysuckle (*Lonicera*). This lightweight material is also excellent on a

◁ **NATURAL BARRIER**
A homemade wooden fence such as this is reasonably easy to erect and makes a pleasing yet sturdy boundary. Suitable for rural areas, it is strong enough to keep out animals such as horses and cattle.

▽ **ORIENTAL TOUCH**
Bamboo fence panels provide privacy as well as an attractive background for this eye-catching mix of foliage plants.

rooftop garden, where greater privacy can be provided by canvas screening. The relative costs of different materials and their durability will inevitably influence your choice. A brick wall is extremely expensive but will last for decades. A much cheaper, more temporary option might be a mesh fence covered with climbers.

You should discuss any boundary changes with your neighbors and your local government because you may need zoning permission. As a rule, fences and walls should be no more than 6ft (2m) high, except when they adjoin a public area, when they may need to be lower.

◁ **MELLOW BACKGROUND**
A high brick wall provides complete privacy and makes an effective foil for a wide range of planting in this colorful herbaceous border.

SEE ALSO: Boundaries and Divisions, pp.28–31

DESIGNING DIVISIONS

Even in a modest-sized yard you may want to create different areas of interest using constructed or planted screens. Trellis panels will separate off a vegetable plot or a children's play area, or hide the trash cans or compost pile. A difficult long, narrow property can be split into a series of small, more easily designed areas, and an enclosing screen or trellis around a patio provides shelter and seclusion, especially if it is clothed in climbing plants. On a wooden screen, paint or wood preservative will introduce color, but it needs to blend with the planting designs as well as your garden furniture. In exposed sites, screens of trellis, bamboo, burlap, or mesh, can be positioned to protect small areas or vulnerable plants.

Pergolas can sometimes form a division when covered with leafy climbers, and arches can be incorporated into screens, drawing the gaze to the area beyond. A tantalizing glimpse of another part of the garden can also be highlighted by creating a "window" in a fence, wall, or even a hedge (*see p.116*). Much grander in scale, a pleached hedge creates a similar effect, but it will take skill and time to achieve – perhaps up to 15 years. The branches of young trees are trained by tying them in horizontally to a strong wooden framework. Then they are gradually woven together to form a hedge on stilts.

△ **FOLIAGE SCREEN**
Pleached lindens have here created a leafy arch over the meandering pathway. Such a raised division delineates different areas within the garden and enticingly frames the view beyond.

VARIED DIVISIONS ▷
Three different types of screening – a hedge, a trellis, and bamboos – have been effectively used together to create a gap in an enclosure, with the trellis allowing glimpses into another area.

USING ORNAMENTAL PLANTS ON BOUNDARIES AND SCREENS

Boundaries and divisional screens can be made all the more decorative by planting with colorful climbers and wall shrubs. In a small garden or courtyard, you can make the planting around the edges so luxuriant that the boundary gets lost and you instead create a feeling of space or restful seclusion (*see p.14 and p.19*). Use a mixture of evergreen and deciduous plants: ivies, grasses such as *Miscanthus*, ferns, and bamboos, for example, and architectural *Fatsia japonica* and cordylines.

◁ **INTEGRATED PLANTING**
This pink climbing rose successfully links the border planting of California tree poppy (Romneya coulteri) and variegated iris with the hard boundary wall behind.

Depending on the materials used, screens and boundaries can be formal and elegant or informal and rustic. To create an informal atmosphere, allow roses and clematis to mingle unrestrained. For a more formal effect, fan-train a peach or cherry tree against a wall. Easily grown pyracantha makes a good evergreen choice, with its white flowers followed by berries.

Pergolas and arches, sometimes used to form a screen, can usually be viewed from all sides, and this should be reflected in the choice of planting. All such structures must be strong and durable enough to carry the weight of the plants, which is often considerable.

SEE ALSO: Grasses, Bamboos, and Ferns, pp. 140–141

FENCES AND TRELLISES

FENCES AND TRELLISES provide one of the quickest and cheapest ways of marking boundaries or forming screens or windbreaks. They can supply instant privacy and security and make an excellent support or background for climbers or wall shrubs. When chosen well, they can also play their own decorative role in the garden. They do, however, need maintenance to prevent rot. Fences and trellises are available in an extensive and versatile range of designs and qualities, so choose according to your purposes. Although simple styles are relatively inexpensive, unusual or ornate designs inevitably cost more because of their complex construction.

TYPES OF FENCES

There are two main styles of fencing: solid or open, both of which may be stockproof. Solid or closely woven fences provide greater privacy than open styles but also have greater resistance to wind. Since they are therefore subjected to increased stress, the support posts need especially secure foundations. Open fencing allows light and rain onto nearby plants and protects them by filtering the wind. Interesting patterns can be created by placing boards on the diagonal or to create a chevron design. In an open fence, this can make a dramatic feature in winter when low sun casts long shadows on a lawn or patio.

All fencing and fence posts must be within your own garden if the fence acts as a boundary marker between two properties. Choose a style sympathetic to your garden (*see pp.28–29*). Types of fencing include:

- **Bamboo** (*solid*): Available as panels of canes woven or lashed together; filters wind well but may deteriorate quickly.
- **Chain-link** (*open*): Wire mesh, attached to concrete, wooden, or iron posts; cheap and quick to put up long lengths.
- **Picket** (*solid or open*): Wooden or plastic vertical boards (pales) on horizontal rails; good for fronting suburban yards.
- **Post-and-rail** (*open*): Two or more wooden horizontal rails between posts; a strong and inexpensive boundary.
- **Railings** (*open*): Usually cast or wrought iron; expensive and not usually an option unless available from a salvage yard; best suited to fronting small gardens.
- **Wattle hurdles** (*solid*): Panels of woody woven stems, often hazel or willow; offers interim protection for young shrubs and hedges; not long-lasting.
- **Wooden panel** (*solid*): Interwoven or overlapping boards or slats, usually fir or pine, are attached to a frame easily nailed to posts; boards may be arranged vertically or horizontally; available in a range of heights and qualities; affords privacy but is not especially strong.

△ **CHANGING ROLES**
While the hedge is growing, the post-and-rail fence behind it marks the boundary and provides a barrier that will keep out farm animals from the meadow beyond.

△ **DOUBLE DUTY**
An open picket fence allows views beyond the boundary as well as enabling plants to grow through and over it. White paint, used to preserve the wood, also complements the flower colors.

NATURAL SHADE ▷
The soft color of this vertical featherboard fence provides an excellent foil for the clematis flowers and foliage in front.

SEE ALSO: Boundaries and Divisions, pp.28–29

TYPES OF TRELLIS

A trellis can be used as a freestanding, light boundary marker or to delineate divisions within an area, or it can be mounted on a wall or fence or secured on top. It is available in a range of sizes, weights, and materials, including curved and more complex designs for arches and arbors. Some diamond-lattice trelliswork can be expanded to fit a space exactly but should be nailed to wooden supports first. Opt for a close-patterned design if the trellis is to act as a windbreak. A custom or homemade trellis of bamboo or willow gives a garden an individual air, but beware if you use willow, since the stems may take root. Then you will need to weave in and prune the sideshoots as they grow.

Check that the trellis is sufficiently sturdy to support the plants you have in mind, and choose a sturdy quality if it is to be freestanding. Planed hardwood is stronger and more expensive than sawn softwood but is much more durable and, if it is to play an important role in the garden's design, may be worth the extra cost. Wooden slats are more pleasing than a plastic and plastic-coated wire trellis but need more maintenance and should be treated regularly with a nontoxic wood preservative. Some of the eye-catching new shades have instant impact, but shades of brown or sage green merge satisfyingly into the background.

DESIGN IDEAS

- Create a decorative feature by mounting trellis panels to the top of a fence or wall.
- Conceal ugly buildings, unwanted vistas, or utility areas in the garden behind a trellis.
- Frame a special view by fitting a trellis "window" between solid-fencing panels.
- Surround a rooftop garden with a sturdy trellis to provide a degree of privacy as well as to help shelter plants from wind.

◁ **DIAMOND-SHAPED TRELLIS**
Nail a finished trellis such as this securely to a wall or fence.

TRIANGULAR TRELLIS ▷
This shape is best suited to support a single climbing plant.

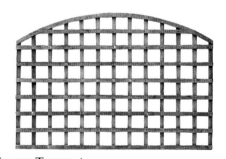

SHAPED TRELLIS △
A convex or concave trellis introduces an informal note to an otherwise formal boundary or screen.

▽ **TACKED TRELLIS**
Concertina-style trellis-work such as this is held together with tacks and is much less sturdy than a jointed trellis.

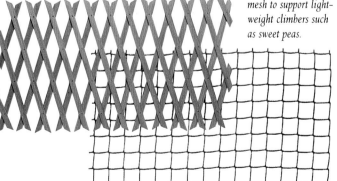

▽ **NETTING**
Use plastic-coated wire mesh to support light-weight climbers such as sweet peas.

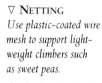

△ **HOMEMADE TRELLIS**
This charming screen of interwoven willow wands adds character to the garden as well as helping to shelter the plants in the vegetable patch.

GARDEN GATES

The style and condition of your garden gate or gates are important because they are likely to make an instant impression on visitors, and they set the tone for the garden and house within.

When choosing a new gate, consider the practicalities:
- How wide does it need to be, and will you hang it yourself? Any gate needs posts set securely in the ground, usually using concrete, and the wider the gate the more difficult it is to hang.
- Does it need to be kept shut, to keep in small children or pets? If so, choose a latch that is reasonably toddler-proof and remember that small animals can easily squeeze through a gap at the bottom.
- Do you want privacy? A tall, solid gate, of similar height to the surrounding boundary, may be the answer.

Most gates are in constant use. As well as choosing an appropriate style that blends well with the boundary on either side, make sure that the materials and construction will be able to withstand everyday wear and tear.

△ **WOODEN GATE**
The strong geometric lines of this square wooden gate echo the shape of the formal clipped hedges on either side. Although a rather heavy-looking, austere design, the way in which it offers glimpses of the garden within and the countryside beyond prevent it from seeming intimidating.

SEE ALSO: Ways of Supporting Plants, pp. 108–109

ERECTING A WOODEN FENCE

A wooden fence should be placed on your side of any boundary, with the better side facing outward. The easiest type to erect is panel fencing, which is widely available in a range of styles, often in ready-to-assemble kits complete with brackets.

Each panel is held in position by wooden or concrete posts. The latter are less attractive but last considerably longer than wooden posts, which need metal supports to prevent rot, or a footing of concrete with a base layer of stone to allow drainage. To prolong a fence's life further, use pressure-treated lumber and put protective coping on each post top. A replaceable wooden gravel board (also available in concrete), at the bottom of each panel, saves needing to replace a whole panel if damp soil causes rot. The panels should fit tightly against the posts, which must be checked with a level at all stages of construction.

◁ METAL POST SUPPORT
To prolong the life of wooden posts, insert them into metal post supports. These are driven into the soil by hitting a steel or wooden post-driving tool, inserted into the support, with a sledgehammer or mallet. Using this type of tool protects the metal edges of the support.

PUTTING UP PLAIN PANEL FENCING

TOOLS AND MATERIALS

- Metal post supports
- Fence panels
- Post-driving tool
- Sledgehammer
- Level
- Wooden posts
- Mallet
- Metal panel and trellis brackets

- White crayon
- Screwdriver
- Galvanized screws and nails
- Gravel boards
- Metal gravel-board brackets
- Trellis and coping
- Hammer

1 MEASURE POST POSITIONS
Insert the first metal post support into the ground (see above). Locate the position for the second post support by laying the panel against the base of the first one.

2 CHECK POST SUPPORT LEVELS
Drive in the second post support. Then check that it is level by laying a board and level over the top of both post supports. Put in other post supports in the same way.

3 SECURE POST
Set the first post in its metal support, driving it to the base with a mallet. Check that it is vertical on all sides, then secure in position by tightening the clamping bolt firmly.

4 PANEL BRACKET
Mark a central white line down the post and two or three evenly spaced horizontal lines for the tops of the metal panel brackets. Screw the panel brackets in position.

5 GRAVEL BOARD
Place one end of the gravel board centrally into a gravel-board bracket. Nail the bracket to the gravel board and the panel. Repeat at the other end of board and panel.

6 INSERT PANEL
Slide the panel into the brackets and hammer into place using a wood scrap and mallet. Screw brackets to one side of second post, put it into the ground, and fit panel into its brackets.

7 INSERT TRELLIS
Position metal brackets for the trellis on both posts and screw them into place. Slide the trellis into the brackets. Repeat these steps to complete the length of fence.

ALWAYS REMEMBER

TO KEEP FENCES IN GOOD CONDITION
- Clear soil and debris away from the base of posts and wooden gravel boards to prevent premature rot, or use concrete gravel boards.
- Every 3–4 years treat all exposed wood with a nontoxic wood preservative.
- Secure any loose panels or boards with nails, or replace with pieces in a matching style.

8 WOODEN COPING
Secure some flat wooden coping over each post top, using 2in (5cm) galvanized nails. Then screw on the decorative top, if required. Such a top sheds rainwater even more effectively than flat coping.

9 FINISH
Secure each panel and piece of trellis firmly in position by screwing into them through the holes on each metal bracket. Do this on both front and back surfaces of the panels and trellis.

SEE ALSO: Types of Trellis, p.93

PICKET FENCING

The easiest way to put up picket fencing is using preassembled panels supported by concrete or wooden posts. A wider range of styles is available if you style and attach the pales (vertical boards) yourself. Using a template, the top of each pale can be rounded or cut to a point so that it readily sheds rainwater, or you can create more distinctive outlines, using a jigsaw. The length of the pales can also be varied, for example by alternating long and short pales, as can the spacing between pales. For a decorative fence, pales are generally spaced at their own width apart, but for greater privacy put them closer together. If you want a rustic picket fence, make it from rough, unplaned wood, but if you prefer a more sophisticated style, or want to paint the fence, choose planed wood.

If you decide to make your own fence – perhaps because you want an individual style – determine the position of the posts and put in the post supports and the posts (see facing page, Steps 1–3). Then, to make your own panels of the appropriate size, lay the pales on the ground between the posts, with their bases aligned against a straight board. Place two horizontal crossrails across the pales at a suitable distance from the top and bottom, checking with a set square and using a spacer to give an even distance between pales. Secure the crossrails by driving two nails diagonally into each rail. Drill holes at the ends of the crossrails and screw them to the posts.

△ **VERSATILE PALETTE**
A fence stained or painted to complement the surrounding planting will not only look professional but will also help to keep the wood in good condition. A different preservative shade can be used if you change your planting design.

PUTTING UP TRELLIS PANELS

Freestanding trellis panels can be erected and mounted onto posts in the same way as wooden fence panels (see facing page), but often they are to be attached to a wall or fence to provide support for plants.

Any flat garden, house, or garage wall or fence in good condition should be suitable, but for safety reasons, if in doubt, seek professional advice, and have any necessary repairs done before you start work. To minimize the chances of causing damage to a wall, attach horizontal wood slats between it and the trellis panel. This also benefits plants trained onto the trellis, since it allows a little more air to circulate around the foliage, reducing the risk of disease, especially mildew. Trellis panels can be secured permanently in position, using galvanized nails, but it is often wise to attach them to the slats with hinges and hooks so that the panel, plus the plants it supports, can be lowered whenever you need to reach the surface for maintenance work.

ATTACHING A TRELLIS TO A WALL

TOOLS AND MATERIALS

• Trellis panel
• Pencil
• Drill with wood and masonry bits
• 2 pieces of 1½×1in (3.5×2.5cm) wood slats, as long as the trellis panel is wide
• Metal tape measure

• Awl
• Hammer
• 6 wall anchors
• Screwdriver
• 6 2in (50mm) galvanized screws
• 2 hinges, plus galvanized screws
• 2 hooks and eyes

1 MARK OUT
Hold the trellis panel in position against the wall and make a pencil line on the wall at the top and bottom of the trellis panel. Drill three evenly spaced holes in each slat. Aligning the slats against the wall marks, pencil in the position of the screw-holes on the wall. Drill the holes in the wall and tap in the wall anchors.

2 ATTACH THE UPPER SLAT
Screw the top slat to the wall, aligning its upper edge with the appropriate positional marks for the trellis. Screw the hinges to the lower slat.

3 ATTACH THE TRELLIS PANEL
Align the lower slat on the wall and screw in position. Then screw the hinges attached to the slat to the bottom edge of the trellis panel.

4 SECURE THE TRELLIS TOP
Carefully swing the trellis panel up against the wall, checking that it aligns correctly at the top. Then put a hook into each end of the upper slat (see inset) and an eye into an adjacent part of the trellis panel.

SEE ALSO: Designing with Climbers and Wall Shrubs, pp.102–103; Choosing Climbers and Walls Shrubs, pp.104–107

WALLS

THE HEIGHT, TEXTURE, AND COLOR of a permanent hard structure such as a garden wall must always harmonize with its surroundings. A retaining wall near a house, for example, should be built from the same or similar materials, so that it forms a satisfying visual link between house and garden. A well-built wall, although initially much more expensive than other types of boundary or screening, fortunately needs almost no maintenance and will last for decades. It may, however, require planning permission, because there may be local ordinances dictating its maximum height. Your property deed may similarly impose special conditions.

DESIGNING WITH WALLS

When building either a boundary or a retaining wall (to terrace a slope or create a raised bed), it is important to select appropriate materials. Since color and type of brick can vary from area to area, try to match new bricks to existing nearby buildings. The same goes for stone. Golden sandstone, for instance, will look completely out of place in an area where the local material is gray-white limestone. Even reconstituted stone is available in different shades. This can be a useful substitute for prohibitively expensive natural stone, but shop around for the best, because it varies greatly in quality.

Stone walls can be constructed with evenly laid courses or in a random style depending on how the stone is cut (*see facing page*). Drystone walls, often used as retaining walls, contain no mortar at all and need patience and skill to fit together. A solid retaining wall will need weepholes to provide drainage. All walls need a top

row of coping, or capping, bricks or stones. These can be decorative as well as functional and often have a sloping shape or are wider than the rest of the wall to shed water easily. Check that bricks are frostproof, or they may crumble when moisture inside freezes.

Any substantial length of walling, even of local materials, will create impact in a garden and needs choosing with care. A wall with a rendered surface can be useful for introducing unexpected color or decorative elements such as mosaic.

Pierced blocks can be used to build semi-permeable screens. In exposed areas, these will reduce wind speed and help protect plants on the leeward side. Solid barriers often tunnel wind and instead create turbulence. Glass blocks can make an interesting screen in a contemporary design but, if they become grimy, cleaning them may be a chore.

△ **MULTIPURPOSE MARKER**
This low stone wall cleverly defines the boundary between two areas of the garden while at the same time allowing extensive views. The broad coping doubles as a seat.

△ **STRONG CONTRAST**
The white coloring of this reconstituted-stone wall contrasts starkly with the black-metal built-in seat, but it nicely ties in with the white-flowered planting in the foreground.

▽ **CURVED WALL**
The possible monotony of a long, plain wall has been avoided here by giving it gentle curves, a brickwork base, and stylish coping. The neutral color prevents it from being obtrusive.

SEE ALSO: Planting against a Wall, p.110

WALLING MATERIALS

The materials for a garden wall need to be frostproof and capable of preventing moisture penetration from both sides. They also need to be strong enough for the purpose at hand. Low retaining walls do not require professional expertise, but remember that if they are of any length, the pressure exerted by damp soil behind can be considerable. Building regulations generally apply to retaining walls over 3ft (1m). All walls need firm foundations (*see right*). A wall can be built of single-brick thickness up to 26in (65cm). A wall higher than this requires much greater skill and should be of double-brick thickness or have supporting piers. Screens also need firm foundations.

Types and styles of walling include:
- **Adobe:** traditionally made from clay but now more likely to be concrete blocks covered with a clay rendering; moderately priced and fairly strong.
- **Brick:** color and weather resistance will depend on the source of the clay and firing – not all bricks are frostproof; expensive, strong, and long-lasting.
- **Cinder block:** lightweight and cheap; not very strong; can be faced with brick or stone or rendered and painted.
- **Concrete block:** available in a variety of finishes and styles but often utilitarian-looking; reasonably cheap, strong, and easy to use; can be faced with brick or rendered and painted.

- **Glass block:** made from reinforced glass; can form an unusual screen.
- **Natural stone:** can be cut into uniform blocks or left undressed; color varies with type; strong and extremely costly.
- **Reconstituted stone:** made from crushed rock and cement; it is much cheaper but not as strong as natural stone.

△ **PERFECT BACKDROP**
Weathered and attractively colonized by lichens, an old high brick wall retains and radiates warmth, encouraging a rose to thrive and bloom profusely.

◁ **COURSED BRICK**
The arrangement of bricks (bonds) within a wall, and the wall's thickness, define its strength. This wall is Flemish bonded; that is, the bricks are laid alternately lengthwise and sideways within each row.

◁ **COURSED STONE**
This limestone wall has been laid dry, in rows, without mortar jointing. Such a wall is often topped with a coping set in mortar. The crevices can be filled with soil and planted with rock plants.

◁ **RANDOM STONE**
Stones of many shapes and sizes are used in a random stone wall, so they need to be secured in place with mortar. Such a wall can be expensive, since fitting and matching the various shapes is time-consuming.

ALWAYS REMEMBER

SAFETY AND SECURITY

For a wall 18–26in (45–65cm) high, concrete footings should be 4–6in (10–15cm) deep and 8–12in (20–30cm) wide. Walls up to 3ft (1m) need footings 9–12in (23–30cm) deep and 18–24in (45–60cm) wide. For a wall any higher than this, you should almost certainly call in a professional builder.

MIXING WALLING MATERIALS

◁ **SYMPATHETIC MATERIALS**
Bricks provide a wall of native stones set in mortar with a secure, weatherproof edging, as well as softening the rather harsh texture of the stones.

Traditionally, materials are often mixed. An edging of brick makes a wall of soft local stone weather-resistant as well as adding to its esthetic appeal. Red brick enhances gray stone. Mixing modern materials can create some superb effects, too, and frequently helps reduce costs.

Concrete or cinder-block walls can be disguised by rendering with a mix of masonry cement and fine sand, finished with a coat of masonry paint. White and cream are effective in shade since they reflect light; earthy tones are warm and mellow and induce a feeling of relaxation; or in urban areas, you may be tempted to try a more vibrant color. While the cement is still drying, you could also score or stamp patterns into it, or embed pebbles, seashells, broken crockery, or tiles. Work on a small area at a time, embedding the pieces of decoration to at least two-thirds their depth. The same idea could be applied to an old brick or stone wall that needs renovating. Fill gaps or small crumbling areas with cement and sand and stud them with a suitable decoration.

SEE ALSO: Boundaries and Divisions, p.28; Laying Concrete, pp.60–61; Building a Raised Bed, p.181

ORNAMENTAL ARCHES

EVEN THE SMALLEST OF PROPERTIES may be enhanced by the careful positioning of an ornamental arch, which can be used in many ways: for example, over the gate to provide an appealing entrance or to outline a doorway; to make an opening through divisions within an area; or to partition your yard into separate areas without the solidity of a wall, hedge, or fence. An arch can be ornate or simple, to suit your style, and it can be bought in kit form in an extensive range of styles. It is also comparatively easy to build your own simple structure, or you could have one custom-made professionally, especially if you want an intricate design.

DESIGNING WITH ARCHES

Before you introduce an arch into your garden, decide on its purpose. It will not look right unless it has a function to serve, whether it is to guide you along a path or perhaps act as an inviting entrance to another part of the garden.

A freestanding arch is likely to be made of wood or metal. For a bold statement, select an eye-catching design and think carefully about what sorts of climbers to grow up it. Arch and plants need to complement one another. For a subtle effect, choose a style that will blend with the surrounding planting, for example a simple rustic arch that can be covered with traditional climbing roses.

Any arch will usefully add height. It can also act as a focal point, drawing the eye

◁ **MATCHING LOOK**
The style of this rustic-poled, homemade arch attractively complements its surroundings, but it would look totally out of character if set in a formal garden.

△ **ELEGANT SUPPORT**
An iron arch and a rose make ideal partners. The rose does not hide the arch's slender shape yet its profusion of flowers are displayed to perfection.

to a feature such as a pond, steps, or seat at the end of a path. It can also serve to distract the gaze from a less glamorous part of the garden. Skillful designers sometimes create a *trompe l'oeil* effect by placing an arch at the boundary and a mirror within it. The reflected view makes the garden appear larger, but arch and mirror need careful placing and the mirror should be angled downward slightly to avoid catching the sun.

SEE ALSO: *Covering Arches and Pergolas,* p.103

BUILDING A WOODEN ARCH

A homemade arch of unpeeled poles or pressure-treated lumber is generally cheaper to make than a kit. Treat any cut ends and areas where the bark has flaked with preservative before assembly. Insert the uprights securely into the ground using metal post supports or concrete and a base layer of crushed stone. Attach the top and crossrails with galvanized nails or screws. Allow a minimum height of 7ft (2.2m) to give adequate head clearance.

SIMPLE WOODEN ARCH

This plain arch is relatively easy to build from a kit. The crossrails on the roof add strength. For additional rigidity, secure diagonal struts on each side between the uprights.

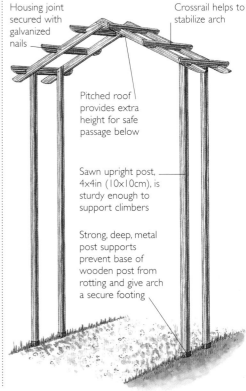

Housing joint secured with galvanized nails

Crossrail helps to stabilize arch

Pitched roof provides extra height for safe passage below

Sawn upright post, 4x4in (10x10cm), is sturdy enough to support climbers

Strong, deep, metal post supports prevent base of wooden post from rotting and give arch a secure footing

Erecting a Metal Arch

Metal arches are available in a wide variety of styles, some much sturdier than others, so ensure that you select one capable of taking the weight of your chosen plants when they are fully grown.

Fortunately the components of most kits readily slot together with the aid of only a few basic tools. Before you start to assemble the pieces, read the instructions thoroughly and check that you have all the pieces. Moisture seals slid over the joints keep out rain, while crossrails help prevent the structure from twisting. Accurately mark the arch's position on the ground and make the post holes. If the hole-maker in the kit is not pre-marked, make your own depth indicator on the tube 12in (30cm) from the base. Finally, the whole structure must be carefully checked with a level.

Always Remember

Structures must be secure

The slender but strong uprights of the arch below are easily inserted into the ground to a secure depth. Heavier wooden structures may need their posts setting into concrete, with a base layer of stone to prevent rot. Wooden kits often use metal post supports. Security is doubly important in windy sites.

Putting up a Metal Arch

Tools and Materials

- Metal arch kit
- PVC moisture seals, as supplied
- Nuts and bolts, as supplied
- Screwdriver
- Hole-maker, as supplied
- Club hammer
- Level

1 Join Uprights
Place a moisture seal along one upright section, then slot a second upright into the first section. Drag the moisture seal back over the join. Repeat to make all the other uprights.

2 Fix Crossrails
Starting 24in (60cm) from the base, evenly space three T-joints down two sets of joined uprights. Insert three crossrails into the T-joints and screw tight to form an arch side.

3 Erect Second Side of Arch
Repeat Step 2 for the other arch side. To ensure that the crossrails on the second side are similarly positioned to those on the first, lie the second side beside the completed one.

4 Assemble Top
Slot two curved pieces together and loosely secure with a T-joint. Repeat with the other two curved pieces. Insert and secure the crossrail between the two top sections. Then add the decorative finials.

5 Make Post Holes
To complete the arch, set the top section into the sides, then cover the joins with moisture seals. Make four holes where the arch is to stand by hammering the hole-maker into the ground to the marked depth.

6 Check Alignment
Set the completed arch in the holes and then check on all sides that it is vertical. Tighten all nuts and bolts.

Planting Against an Arch

To transform the arch, plant one or two climbers on either side that will grow up and eventually cover it. To help the plants reach the top, attach large-mesh plastic netting to the arch sides and fan out the young, pliant shoots. Most climbers will flower more readily if their stems are spiraled around the supports. When they reach the top of the arch, prune the stems as necessary so that the plants do not outgrow their position or become too heavy for the structure.

1 Netting Support
Using ratcheted plastic ties, secure large-mesh plastic netting to both sides of the arch.

2 Planting Angle
Plant the climber at an angle of 45° toward the arch. Tie the main stems to the crossrail.

3 Initial Training
As soon as the stems are long enough to reach the netting (and have all been untied from the stake) spread them out evenly across the side of the arch. Using figure-eight knots, loosely secure them to the crossrail and tie them in to the netting. Keep training and tying as the plant grows, until it starts to twine or cling.

See also: Annual Climbers, p.106

PERGOLAS AND ARBORS

COVERED IN CLEMATIS, WISTERIA, or other climber, a pergola provides shade and welcome refuge from hot, bright sun. It can make a refreshing place to eat and relax or a cool spot to linger on a path. Pergolas may be freestanding or attached to a building. Adjoining a house they may also shade the rooms inside. Arbors, usually smaller, enclosed on three sides, and sited near the garden's boundary, also offer retreat and a sense of seclusion. Both can be invaluable in a new garden for they will also provide an immediate focal point. In a more mature garden, a pergola can act as a link that binds the entire garden together year-round.

DESIGNING WITH PERGOLAS

If a pergola is to shade a sitting or eating area, its position is most likely to have already been decided, but if it is to cover a path, where it will immediately become the focus of attention, it needs very careful siting. It might, for instance, also be used to act as a screen between two distinct areas of the garden.

Thought must also be given to its design. It is essential that the style and materials used are in sympathy with the surroundings. A straight pergola, for example, would look out of place in a garden filled with gentle curves, and a formal, elegant pergola would not fit a rustic, country-style garden. Wood or metal would suit an informal setting, whereas brick, concrete, or stone columns conjure up a formal atmosphere.

◁ SHADE AND SECLUSION
A difficult corner, bounded by three walls, has been transformed into an interesting eating area by bolting the beams of a pergola on to the top of each wall. Its solid design is in keeping with the somewhat monumental look of the stone table.

Pergola proportions are notoriously difficult to get right, so you may decide to seek the services of a professional for all but the most simple designs. A pergola must itself be a balanced structure as well as being in scale with the rest of the garden. The spacing between the uprights should be roughly equal to the pergola's width. Its height will depend on whether it is over a path or sitting area.

◁ NATURAL SHADOW
Strong sunlight piercing this terrace balustrade produces a striking honeycomb pattern on the ground, similar to the pergola roof above. In summer the flowers of a wisteria hang gracefully through the beams.

△ SUMMER GLORY
This rose-covered wooden pergola forms an inviting tunnel for a fragrant, leisurely stroll. Not only does such a planting soften the outlines of the pergola, it also provides welcome shade during the summer months.

TELL ME WHY

WHAT SHOULD I TAKE INTO ACCOUNT WHEN CHOOSING AND SITING A PERGOLA?

- Simple designs are usually most satisfying; plants will add to the decorative quality.
- The size and scale must be appropriate to the size of your house and garden.
- Materials and construction must be sturdy enough for the plants you have in mind.
- If the pergola is to cover an eating area, make sure it is large enough to comfortably accommodate a table and chairs.
- A pergola might be useful if your garden is overlooked, because the canopy can offer privacy from neighboring windows.
- If it is to be attached to one side of the house, make sure the pergola and will not make the rooms inside too dark.
- A pergola will draw attention to a path. Check that the path is definitely in the right place, that it is wide enough, and that the pergola will frame a suitable view.

SEE ALSO: Autumn and Winter Interest, p.107; Fragrant Climbers and Wall Shrubs, p.107; Ways of Supporting Plants, pp.108–109

ARBORS

These climber-clad structures inject a feeling of intimacy and privacy into an otherwise open space. They generally house a seat from where you can enjoy views out across the garden.

Where an arbor should be sited depends on when it is most likely to be used. If it is to provide a leafy retreat on hot summer evenings, for example, it will need to be placed where it catches the sun's fading rays. It should be at least 7ft (2.2m) tall so that the seating area does not feel claustrophic, especially when screened by trailing plants.

The structure itself must be sturdy enough to support the ornamental plants trained over it, yet open enough to admit any fragrances they exude. Wrought iron and wood are the most popular materials, but how they are used depends on the style that fits your garden.

A simple wooden shelter, made from sawn or rustic poles with a trellis on three sides, would suit an informal setting, whereas extravagantly molded and carved wood would be more appropriate in a formal garden. Delicate wrought ironwork or wirework might suit a small garden, while an ornate Italianate style needs spacious surroundings to look right.

△ **CLASSIC SIMPLICITY**
The clean lines of this wrought iron arbor rise elegantly above the sea of colorful plants, and it provides a spectacular focal point enhanced by the evergreen backdrop.

BUILDING A PERGOLA

Pergolas are available in kit form, or you can build your own. A simple design of rustic poles nailed together will support lightweight climbers, although with untreated wood it will not be long-lasting. For heavier plants the pergola should be much sturdier and, unless you are confident of your skills, it is better to have one professionally designed and built.

A pergola is generally at least 8ft (2.5m) high, so that people can walk under it unhindered, even when it is covered with mature trailing plants. A pergola over a seating area may be slightly lower.

If you do decide to build your own wooden pergola from a kit, you should

WOODEN PERGOLA WITH TRELLIS TOP
An all-wood pergola with a trellis top, such as this, is quite cheap to buy and straightforward to construct from a kit. It would look pleasing painted with a soft green or blue preservative.

SECURING THE TOP
Rest the trellis on the top of the uprights and crossbeams. Then, using brass screws, attach the trellis framework firmly to the uprights.

find that the manufacturers have made its assembly reasonably simple. Kits come with lumber planed and prenotched, so that crossbeams can be gently hammered into place. Check that you have all the necessary nuts, bolts, and screws or nails. Metal post supports are generally supplied for securing the uprights in the ground. If you have any doubts about the structure's security, set the posts in a footing of concrete with a base layer of crushed stone to help prevent rot.

Put up the endposts first, then the remaining uprights, and finally fit the crossbeams and other supports. If one or more sides of the pergola is to be supported by a wall, use metal, L-shaped joist shoes or lumber plates to attach the crossbeams to the masonry.

ALWAYS REMEMBER

MAKE CONSTRUCTION EASY
Upon unpacking a kit, check that you have all the pieces, plus all the tools for the job. A level is essential to ensure the uprights are vertical. Follow the instructions carefully. It will help to have someone to assist. Do not fully tighten any nuts or bolts until satisfied that the pergola is complete.

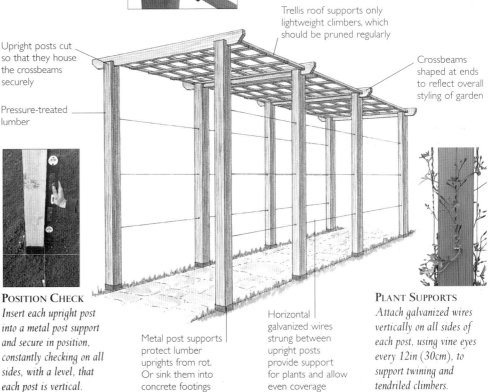

Upright posts cut so that they house the crossbeams securely

Pressure-treated lumber

Trellis roof supports only lightweight climbers, which should be pruned regularly

Crossbeams shaped at ends to reflect overall styling of garden

POSITION CHECK
Insert each upright post into a metal post support and secure in position, constantly checking on all sides, with a level, that each post is vertical.

Metal post supports protect lumber uprights from rot. Or sink them into concrete footings

Horizontal galvanized wires strung between upright posts provide support for plants and allow even coverage

PLANT SUPPORTS
Attach galvanized wires vertically on all sides of each post, using vine eyes every 12in (30cm), to support twining and tendriled climbers.

SEE ALSO: Covering Arches and Pergolas, p.103

DESIGNING WITH CLIMBERS AND WALL SHRUBS

MANY GARDENS CONTAIN VERTICAL SURFACES that would look much more attractive if they were decoratively clothed with climbers or wall shrubs. Such plants help soften hard structures such as walls, fences, and pergolas, integrating them into the garden as well as adding height to a planting design. More vigorous climbers, such as honeysuckles and *Clematis montana*, are also excellent at masking functional buildings or ugly expanses of wall. Many climbers and wall shrubs produce marvelously scented flowers or brightly colored berries, while some of the most spectacular results can be produced by training climbers into suitable trees.

COVERING WALLS AND FENCES

In order to make the most of the hard surfaces in your garden, it is important to understand how climbers and wall shrubs differ and why this affects the way they are used in a planting design.

Most climbers need other plants or a support to gain height while they grow. They have developed various means of anchoring themselves to their support, for instance by using adhesive pads, twining stems, tendrils, or hooked thorns (*see p.108*). Wall shrubs, however, have no such devices. They may simply look their best or benefit from being grown against a wall because of the protection it gives. For example, many less hardy shrubs such as flannel bush (*Fremontodendron*) will thrive against a sunny wall because they respond to its reflected warmth and shelter.

Climbers can be allowed to scramble attractively over a wall or fence, given a support system of a trellis or wires to which they can be loosely tied at strategic points. Use evergreens which provide year-round cover to camouflage eyesores.

△ CONCEALED FENCE
This crisp, architectural boundary marker has been created by training Muehlenbeckia complexa, *a tiny-leaved, vigorous climber over a stepped, wiremesh fence.*

The stems of some wall shrubs can be trained into a tiered or fan shape, so that flowers and fruit are displayed to full effect. Woody-stemmed wall shrubs are difficult to detach from their supports for maintenance and must be trained against supports secured only to sound walls or fences that do not need frequent attention.

△ FLORAL BEAUTY
The surface of this brick wall has been softened by a ceanothus that has been trained to display its glorious crop of spring flowers.

◁ GREEN CURTAIN
New fencing or other stark surfaces can be entirely clothed by interestingly textured evergreens, such as variegated ivy here, for year-round interest.

△ TRELLIS FENCE
One advantage of open fencing such as this is that the stems of climbing plants, such as roses, can be supported by weaving the young stems through the holes.

SEE ALSO: Ways of Supporting Plants, pp.108–109

COVERING ARCHES AND PERGOLAS

Arches and pergolas bring height to a design, especially if there are no mature trees, and can link or separate two areas of the garden. When covered in lush foliage, they create private, refreshingly shaded spaces. Choose climbers with fragrant flowers, and the stark lines of a large new pergola can be wonderfully transformed into a cool, scented tunnel, inviting you to explore the area that lies beyond.

△ **ABUNDANT CLIMBER**
This arch laden with hops (Humulus lupulus) charmingly frames the view beyond. Such a well-planned feature anchors the arch into the surrounding planting.

It is vital to select climbers and wall shrubs whose growth habits are appropriate to the site and their intended supports. A vigorous evergreen such as Persian ivy (*Hedera colchica*), for example, would soon swamp a fine wrought iron arch. Pergolas, on the other hand, often need a tall, strong-growing climber. A rose such as 'Seagull' or 'Albéric Barbier' will produce sufficient growth to cover the top generously with its cascading flowers.

Plants of different vigors may also be mixed and matched successfully. Fast-growing *Clematis montana* var. *rubens* will provide spring interest, while its pink tones could be picked up later in summer by C. 'Mrs N. Thompson' and C. 'Nelly Moser'. Think, too, about using foliage to introduce color and texture. The leaves of the golden hops (*Humulus lupulus* 'Aureus') are brighter than many a flower, while those of grapes such as *Vitis coignetiae* and *V.* 'Brandt' turn stunning red or purple in autumn. In summer they also cast particularly refreshing shade.

All wall shrubs and climbers naturally grow toward the light and so may bloom on only one side of the arch or pergola. It is worth trying to position them so that their flowers and fruits are displayed to maximum effect.

△ **LINKED DIVISIONS**
Two separate structures — a pergola and an arch — are connected by a planting of glorious white roses.

SUMMER SCREEN ▷
The trailing flowers of a wisteria create an alluring summer partition on a metal pergola. When mature, its woody twining stems can make maintenance of a wooden structure difficult.

OVER HEDGES AND TREES

Trees with only one season of glory can be made to work harder by growing climbers into them. In a small garden particularly, where space is limited, such double use of an area can produce displays of fragrant flowers or colorful leaves from spring to autumn. Or you might be able to train a herbaceous climber up a hedge. Neatly clipped yew dramatically sets off the scarlet flowers of flame creeper (*Tropaeolum speciosum*), although this can be a tricky plant to grow.

A climber or shrub and its host must be compatible not only in the type of soil each requires but also in their habit of growth. Plant vigorous climbers, such as the splendid honeysuckle *Lonicera* × *americana*, into large trees, and smaller, lighter-weight

◁ **FRAGRANT TREAT**
Rampant rambling roses such as 'Wedding Day' look marvelous trailing through a large tree.

HELPING HAND ▷
A stake may be needed to guide a newly planted clematis, such as 'Comtesse de Bouchard' here, up into a tree fork, from where it will naturally grow through the branches.

climbers such as annual morning glory (*Ipomoea*) over hedges or shrubs. Pruning regimes must also be complementary. Both plants should be accessible for maintenance, and the host must not need pruning while the climber is at its peak.

SEE ALSO: Ornamental Arches, pp.98–99; Hedges in the Garden, pp.116–119

CHOOSING CLIMBERS AND WALL SHRUBS

IF CLIMBERS AND WALL SHRUBS are to provide long-lasting pleasure, select those that suit the conditions in your garden. You will need to ascertain how much sun a particular wall or fence receives, and at what time of day. Avoid acid-loving plants if the soil is alkaline; if dry, choose those with some tolerance to drought. If the space will not allow plants to grow freely, find out their vigor first. Take account of climate and the risk of strong, possibly salt-laden, winds or harsh winters, although some plants that are not completely hardy may survive against a warm wall or fence. Some planting suggestions are given below and on the following pages.

PLANTS FOR A DRY SUNNY SPOT

The soil at the base of a sunny wall or fence is likely to be dry, because of the rainshadow, and is best suited to climbers like actinidia that tolerate such conditions. A clematis will grow well only if its roots are kept cool and moist by placing paving slabs or tiles over the surrounding soil.

Many wall shrubs positively need a sunny wall to thrive: the heat absorbed by the wall is reflected back, helping to mature their wood so that they are better able to withstand cold. Aromatic Mediterranean shrubs such as rosemary benefit from such a site, and some shrubs, ceanothus for example, may grow taller than when planted in open ground. Early morning sun, however, will damage frosted shoots and blooms of winter- and spring-flowering plants by thawing them too fast.

OTHER RECOMMENDATIONS

Abutilon megapotamicum. Evergreen or semievergreen shrub with bell-shaped yellow flowers in summer.
Actinidia kolomikta. Deciduous climber with variegated pink, white, and green leaves when mature.
Buddleia crispa. Deciduous shrub with mid- to gray-green leaves, white-woolly young shoots, and, from mid- to late summer, fragrant, lilac-pink flowers.
Clematis 'Bill MacKenzie'. Deciduous climber with bell-shaped, yellow flowers, from midsummer to late autumn, and large, fluffy seedheads.
Cytisus battandieri (pineapple broom). Vigorous, tree-like, Mediterranean shrub with silver leaves and yellow flowers smelling of pineapple.
Fremontodendron 'California Glory'. Evergreen wall shrub. Deep yellow blooms, late spring to autumn.
Lavatera maritima. Shrubby evergreen with saucer-shaped, lilac-pink to white flowers. Late summer.
Rosa banksiae Vigorous climbing rose with scented, double flowers in late spring.
Vitis vinifera 'Purpurea'. Deciduous climber. Gray-hairy leaves turn plum purple then dark purple in autumn. Bears purple unpalatable grapes.

◁ **PASSIONFLOWER**
Passiflora caerulea is the hardiest passionflower but still needs a sunny, sheltered site. It may climb to 30ft (10m) but often loses some or all of its topgrowth during winter.

△ **LEMON BOTTLEBRUSH**
Callistemon pallidus, a shrub that grows to 12ft (4m) tall, is prized for its gray-green leaves and, from late spring to mid-summer, its abundant spikes of flowers.

△ **SOLANUM CRISPUM 'GLASNEVIN'**
The Chilean potato vine (a relative of the more down-to-earth vegetable) needs a sheltered site, where it will quickly scramble to 20ft (6m) and produce its flowers in summer.

△ **VITIS COIGNETIAE**
This vigorous grape needs space to display its brilliant autumn colors. It can be pruned heavily in spring, but it rapidly makes new growth and can reach 50ft (15m).

IVIES

Evergreen climbers such as self-clinging ivy provide year-round cover in cool temperate areas. Ivies are easy to grow and, when mature, their green autumn flowers provide a late source of nectar for insects, while the black midwinter berries supply food for the birds. In heavy shade, an all-green ivy such as *Hedera colchica* 'Dentata' gives interesting texture. Some variegated ivies such as *H. helix* 'Goldheart' color best in reasonable light. Always match the mature size of an ivy to its planting site, because ivies vary greatly in their vigor.

△ **HEDERA HELIX 'EVA'**
One of the smaller-growing types, this pretty white-variegated ivy grows to only 4ft (1.2m) tall. It prefers a sunny position in the garden.

△ **HEDERA COLCHICA 'SULPHUR HEART'**
Growing to 30ft (10m) tall, this ivy's yellow-variegated foliage provides a welcoming wall of color in a dark corner, especially during long, bleak winters.

OTHER RECOMMENDED IVIES

H. colchica. Almost oval, leathery, dark green leaves, 3–5in (8–12cm) long; to 30ft (10m) tall.
H. helix 'Glymii'. All-green leaves take on purple or bronze tints in winter; 6ft (2m) tall.
H. helix 'Green Ripple'. Midgreen leaves with five jagged, veined lobes; 6ft (2m) tall.
H. helix f. *poetarum.* Shiny, midgreen leaves, 3in (8cm) long, and orange-yellow fruits; 10ft (3m) tall.
H. helix 'Pedata'. Dainty, midgreen leaves that resemble the shape of a bird's foot; 12ft (4m) tall.

SEE ALSO: Planting Climbers and Wall Shrubs, pp.110–111

PLANTS FOR SHADY WALLS

As long as a wall or fence receives some light, there are climbers and wall shrubs that will tolerate and often thrive in such cool conditions. In the wild, many such as jasmine grow naturally in woodland or similarly shaded places. Some plants, such as silk-tassel bush (*Garrya elliptica*), tolerate the dry soil in the shade of a tree or beside a moisture-absorbent brick wall, while others, such as hops (*Humulus lupulus*), prefer damp shaded areas, at the bottom of a slope for example. A few plants such as honeysuckles can be grown in shade or sun, although, like shrubby flowering quince (*Chaenomeles speciosa*), they may flower or fruit less reliably in shade. Chinese creeper (*Parthenocissus henryana*) also tolerates sun, but it tends to produce better-colored foliage in shade.

CHEERFUL PYRACANTHA ▷
Pyracantha berries – here orange but also yellow or, more commonly, red – are produced in great abundance. They bring vivid color to a dull wall for several months, persisting well beyond the middle of winter.

CHILEAN BELLFLOWER ▷
This climber, Lapageria rosea var. albiflora, *is a tender acid-lover needing a sheltered spot. It produces its showy white flowers from summer to autumn amid dark green leaves.*

OTHER RECOMMENDATIONS

Clematis. Large-flowered hybrids with pale flowers, 'Nelly Moser' and 'Bees' Jubilee' for example, are less inclined to fade in light shade.
Euonymus fortunei cultivars. Evergreen shrub. Foliage is often variegated white or gold.
Lathyrus latifolius. Climbing perennial sweet pea, but not scented. Bears pink to purple or white flowers in summer and early autumn.
Lonicera × tellmanniana. Deciduous twiner with bright copper-orange flowers that appear in late spring to midsummer. Not scented.
Mitraria coccinea. Evergreen shrub with tubular, scarlet flowers borne from spring to autumn.
Parthenocissus tricuspidata. Deciduous climber, potentially rampant, so keep out of gutters. Bright green leaves turn bright red and purple in autumn.
Rosa 'Mme Alfred Carrière'. Repeat-flowering climber with fragrant white flowers tinged pink.

◁ CLIMBING HYDRANGEA
*A deciduous climber (*H. petiolaris*) that bears its lacy flowers in late summer. During winter, the bare stems are attractively cinnamon-colored.*

FAST-GROWING CLIMBERS

To cover a large expanse of wall or quickly camouflage a boring shed you need vigorous climbers such as *Muehlenbeckia complexa* or *Clematis* 'Perle d'Azur'. Exceptionally rampant plants, however, such as mile-a-minute vine or Russian vine (*Fallopia baldschuanica*), should be avoided in confined areas, where they may smother plants as well as neighboring gardens. Always match a climber to its support. Many fast-growing climbers eventually grow very large. A huge rambling rose such as 'Kiftsgate', for example, needs a large garden and large forest tree for support. For lightweight structures that need fast cover, an annual climber such as morning glory (*Ipomoea tricolor*) is often a good choice (*see also p.106*). In sheltered sites, some tender perennials, often grown as annuals elsewhere, may survive and, even if cut to the ground in winter, will quickly reshoot to give good but lightweight cover. Try yellow- or red-flowered Chilean glory flower (*Eccremocarpus scaber*), for example.

◁ CLEMATIS MONTANA
This vigorous clematis can reach anything from 18 to 30ft (6 to 10m) depending on conditions. Some of the pink-flowered types are shorter-growing.

▽ AKEBIA QUINATA
The chocolate vine, so called because of its scent, is not as speedy as some but will reach 30ft (10m). It is a useful climber because it will grow in light shade as well as sun.

◁ AMPELOPSIS BREVIPEDUNCULATA
A tendriled climber that will quickly cover a wall or pergola or clamber into a tree. The small green flowers are insignificant but are followed by unusual berries that turn gradually from pink to blue.

OTHER RECOMMENDATIONS

Ampelopsis megalophylla. Deciduous. Dark green leaves, glaucous beneath, and black fruits in autumn.
Campsis × tagliabuana 'Madame Galen'. Deciduous. Orange-red flowers from late summer to autumn.
Clematis montana. Deciduous. Single flowers are borne in late spring and early summer.
Cobaea scandens. Evergreen perennial usually grown as an annual. Scented, bell-shaped, creamy green flowers mature to purple. Summer to autumn.
Jasminum polyanthum. Evergreen with very fragrant, pink-budded, white flowers in spring–summer.
Lonicera × americana. Deciduous. Has strongly scented, yellow flowers, flushed red-purple, in summer.
Rosa 'Paul's Himalayan Musk'. Deciduous. Bears masses of double, pale pink flowers in summer.
Vitis coignetiae. Grape with large sculptural leaves that turn shades of yellow and red in autumn.

SEE ALSO: Maintaining Climbers and Wall Shrubs, pp.112–115

COMBINING CLIMBERS AND WALL SHRUBS

To create a tapestry of different plants, grow wall shrubs and climbers together. Textures and colors should blend harmoniously. In autumn, the yellow flowers of *Clematis tibetana* look good winding through a yellow- or orange-berried pyracantha. Or team the white-margined leaves of the shrub *Euonymus fortunei* 'Silver Queen' with the plain green foliage and lacy white flowers of climbing hydrangea for a handsome partnership.

When combining plants in this way, you should ensure that a plant grown for its berries, such as cotoneaster, does not have these covered by the leaves of its partner.

Nor must the vigor of one plant dominate the other. Clematis and roses are a classic combination, because their cultivation and pruning needs are similar. They work particularly well up pergolas and tripods, where they are less likely to be affected by mildew (*see p.296*) than against a wall. Two clematis can also be planted together: try combining spring-flowering *Clematis alpina* with a later-blooming large-flowered hybrid for a long display. Or put a clematis with a grape. The mauve flowers of *Clematis* 'Jackmanii' look lovely intertwined with the dusky leaves of the purple grape, *Vitis vinifera* 'Purpurea'.

△ **TRIPLE BENEFIT**
Evergreens, such as long-flowering Japanese honeysuckle (Lonicera japonica), combine well with deciduous climbers, such as roses, to give year-round interest, greater variety of planting, and extended flowering season.

EFFECTIVE COVER ▷
Two walls of this tiny courtyard garden have been transformed by the imaginatively combined planting of a scarlet-flowered honeysuckle with a white-flowered climbing hydrangea (Hydrangea petiolaris) and deep red climbing roses.

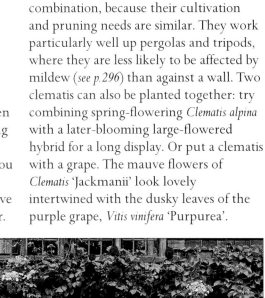

ALWAYS REMEMBER

PRUNING REGIMES

If two or more climbers are to grow harmoniously together their pruning needs must not conflict. Does only one of the climbers need cutting back hard each year? If so, is this at a time when its partner is past its best? If both plants need regular care, their pruning times should coincide.

ANNUAL CLIMBERS

These fast-growing plants are invaluable in a garden for giving quick, colorful cover, especially over new, bare arches or pergolas, and for training over tripods and obelisks in a border.

Because annual climbers are temporary, you can experiment with different colors and varieties and try out combinations, perhaps with perennial climbers. Sweet peas, climbing nasturtiums, and runner beans can all be grown against a trellis (they will need some tying in) and make effective screens in summer. Canary creeper (*Tropaeolum peregrinum*), black-eyed Susan vine (*Thunbergia alata*), Chilean glory

flower (*Eccremocarpus scaber*), and the cup-and-saucer plant (*Cobaea scandens*) are usually grown as annuals, although they are in fact perennials. Many, including sweet peas and nasturtiums, will also grow through shrubs, as long as they receive sufficient water and light. Some have rather fleeting blooms. Those of morning glory fade by afternoon and sweet peas need regular cutting to flower over a long period.

BLACK-EYED SUSAN VINE ▷
The eye-catching flowers of this twining climber (Thunbergia alata) are produced from summer to autumn. A perennial that is usually grown as an annual, it can be raised from seed on a warm windowsill.

SEE ALSO: Sowing Seed in Pots, p.162

AUTUMN AND WINTER INTEREST

For a garden to look good all year round, it must include plants that are peak performers in autumn and winter. Herbaceous borders, which will have died down, now need an interesting backdrop, especially if they can be seen from the house. The flowers, leaves, and fruits of many climbers and wall shrubs fill this role admirably.

In autumn, the vigorous trumpet vine (*Campsis*) produces a welcome display of showy, trumpet-shaped flowers in warming oranges and reds. In winter, wall shrubs such as fragrant wintersweet (*Chimonanthus praecox*) scent the air, while the drooping gray-green catkins of the silk-tassel bush (*Garrya elliptica*) look striking with a powdery dusting of frost.

Ivies provide a useful but unvarying year-round background for other plants, although a couple, 'Tricolor' and 'Glymii', turn deep pink and purple respectively in cold weather. Grapes offer some of the most spectacular autumn color, especially the huge, yellow and scarlet leaves of *Vitis coignetiae*. The fluffy seedheads of *Clematis tibetana* are delightful when they catch the fading autumn sun. They often appear while the yellow nodding flowers are still on the plant. The shrub *Berberis thunbergii* 'Dart's Red Lady' provides a double attraction in autumn with its orange and red leaves and glossy red fruits. For long-lasting winter color, plant yellow-, red-, or orange-berried forms of pyracantha.

△ **FIERY FOLIAGE**
The bright green leaves on this Boston ivy (Parthenocissus tricuspidata 'Veitchii') gradually change to dark red-purple in autumn before they finally drop.

◁ **WINTER CHEER**
Throughout winter and into early spring, the bright yellow flowers of winter jasmine (Jasminum nudiflorum) adorn many gardens, but regular tying back is needed.

FRAGRANT CLIMBERS AND WALL SHRUBS

Many climbers and wall shrubs bear such beautifully fragrant flowers that, to appreciate them fully, it is worth taking time to find the best position for them in the garden. Delicately scented ones such as *Clematis armandii* should be planted closer to a path or house than more heavily perfumed honeysuckles, whose heavy fragrance will carry farther.

Arches, pergolas, and gates can become doubly attractive to walk through when surrounded by richly scented roses such as thornless 'Zephirine Drouhin'. Plant wisteria or *Actinidia kolomikta* near a doorway or train it around a window, so that you can enjoy the fragrance indoors and out.

Some plants are at their most fragrant at a specific time of day, and this may affect where you site them. Those that release their scent during the day, for example chocolate vine (*Akebia quinata*), are best by arbors or arches, while patios – or other sitting areas that tend to be used later in the day – are excellent sites for common jasmine (*Jasminum officinale*), which is at its most fragrant in the evening. Shrubs with aromatic leaves, such as rosemary, help make a patio a more relaxing place.

△ **RICH FRAGRANCE**
The heady scent of the late Dutch honeysuckle (Lonicera periclymenum 'Serotina') travels a long way. It is especially strong in the evening.

◁ **PERFECT PERFUME**
Stiffly branched Rosa 'Gloire de Dijon' produces its glorious, fully double flowers repeatedly during summer and autumn, filling the air with its delightful fragrance.

GOOD PLANT CHOICES

CLIMBERS AND WALL SHRUBS RECOMMENDED FOR THEIR SCENTED FLOWERS

Actinidia kolomikta
Akebia quinata (chocolate vine)
Chimonanthus praecox (wintersweet)
Clematis armandii, C. montana 'Elizabeth', *C. rehderiana*
Cytisus battandieri (Moroccan broom)
Honeysuckles *Lonicera* × *brownii* 'Dropmore Scarlet', *L.* × *heckrottii*, *L. periclymenum* 'Serotina'
Itea illicifolia
Jasminum azoricum (jasmine), *J. officinale* (esp. 'Argenteovariegatum'), *J.* × *stephanense*
Prunus mume (Japanese apricot)
Roses 'Albertine', Bobbie James', 'Climbing Etoile de Hollande', 'Compassion', 'Gloire de Dijon', JACQUELINE DU PRÉ, LAVINIA, 'Mme Alfred Carrière', 'Meg', 'Wedding Day'
Schizophragma integrifolium
Solanum jasminoides 'Album' (potato vine)
Sweet pea *Lathyrus odoratus*, esp. 'Jayne Amanda', 'White Supreme', and old-fashioned types such as 'Painted Lady' and 'Matucana'
Trachelospermum asiaticum
Wisteria sinensis (Chinese wisteria)

SEE ALSO: Ivies, p.104; Planting Climbers and Wall Shrubs, pp.110–111

WAYS OF SUPPORTING PLANTS

CLIMBERS ARE BASICALLY plants with long, flexible stems, which, left to their own devices, trail over neighboring plants – at times smothering them. In a garden they generally benefit from artificial support so that they and the surrounding plants can all flourish and flower freely. The correct type of support depends on how the climber grows. A lightweight annual or herbaceous perennial, with stems that die down in winter, is unlikely to cause a problem, but a large climber that develops a woody framework may, when mature, prove too heavy a burden for an arch or trellis screen. For safety's sake, it is essential that such structures are sturdy and strong.

HOW CLIMBERS GROW

Climbers grow in one of three ways: clinging; twining or using tendrils; and scrambling. This influences the way they are trained but not how they are pruned. Some are self-supporting, while others may need initial assistance to reach a support but thereafter will climb by themselves. A few require frequent tying in to a permanent support.

■ **Clinging climbers** are all self-supporting. Some, such as ivy, use aerial roots to adhere to walls, fences, and tree trunks; they also make good ground-cover. Others, such as Boston ivy (*Parthenocissus*), develop touch-activated adhesive pads to stick to any hard surface. All clingers may need initial guidance toward a support.

■ **Twining and tendriled climbers** are all self-supporting once they have something to wrap their stems or tendrils around. Twiners grow upward in a spiraling motion – some, such as honeysuckle, twine in a clockwise direction while others, such as wisteria,

wrap their stems counterclockwise around any support. They can be grown into a strong host tree or shrub or tied to supporting wires, netting, or trellis against pillars, fences, and walls. Climbers such as vines and passionflower have true tendrils – modified shoots or leaves – which they use to twine around the stems of other plants or a suitable support. In others, such as clematis, it is the leaf stalks that act as twining tendrils.

■ **Scrambling climbers** all need full support when grown in a garden. Some, such as winter jasmine (*Jasminum nudiflorum*), produce a mass of arching stems that make good groundcover if left to sprawl informally over a bank. Against a wall or fence, however, they should be secured to wires or a trellis. Others, particularly brambles (*Rubus*) and climbing roses, have developed thorns to hook on to a host plant. When planted in a border, without the support of a tree or shrub, they too need tying to supporting wires or trellis at regular intervals.

SOME TYPES OF CLIMBER

△ **TRUE TENDRIL**
These modified shoots or leaves develop on plants such as passionflower (here). The climber uses them to coil tightly around any thin support.

△ **LEAF STALK**
The leaf stalks on plants such as clematis (here) act as twining tendrils, which curl tightly around a nearby support, for instance wire or plant stems.

△ **TWINING STEM**
Plants such as common jasmine and runner beans have stems that coil around their support. The direction in which they coil depends on the species.

△ **HOOKED THORN**
Some climbers use thorns as a kind of grappling hook to attach themselves to a support, even if it is not secure. Roses and brambles are typical examples.

△ **AERIAL ROOT**
These adhesive aerial roots form along the stems on plants such as ivy when the stem comes into contact with a fence, wall, or other rough surface.

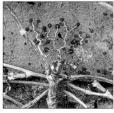

△ **ADHESIVE PAD**
Small adhesive suckers, or pads, develop on the tendrils of plants such as Virginia creeper (here) once they come into contact with a supporting surface.

△ **INITIAL TRAINING**
Support stems of tendriled and twining climbers (here a hop) by gently weaving them between crossed wires or mesh while they are still young and flexible.

TELL ME WHY

WILL CLIMBERS DAMAGE HOUSE WALLS?

If the mortar is sound, plants should not cause problems as long as you keep them clear of gutters, window frames, and roof tiles or slates. Avoid growing climbers against walls where their shoots may get under tiles or shingles and dislodge them. Plants with aerial roots and adhesive pads – ivies and Virginia creeper – are generally the only possible troublemakers. Usually the rewards outweigh the problems. Climbers can help to insulate house walls against extremes of temperature, and they offer food and roosting sites for birds.

SEE ALSO: Planting Climbers and Wall Shrubs, pp.110–111

ORNAMENTAL SUPPORTS

Introduce some ornamental supports into the garden to provide a focal point or to add a strong vertical element. Solitary pillars will form eye-catching features, but for a more formal effect, erect a row of single pillars linked by chain or thick rope (swags) and train climbers along them. Flexible-stemmed climbers such as 'New Dawn' rose or 'Etoile Violette' clematis, which produce glorious displays of cascading flowers, are ideal for training up the pillars and along the swags. For the best effect, select plants that are sufficiently vigorous to cover the support generously with their flowers and foliage.

Tripods, obelisks, and wigwams are among the easiest and cheapest ornamental structures to introduce into a garden. They instantly add height, can be used for any climber that is not too tall or vigorous, and encourage good plant health because they allow easy air circulation around the stems. Many are attractive in their own right. Plant them with annual or other herbaceous climbers, and their architectural outline will be a great asset in the winter garden.

◁ **ROSE PILLARS**
Training up pillars and along ropes is a traditional way of growing climbing and rambling roses. In this large kitchen garden, they also provide cut flowers.

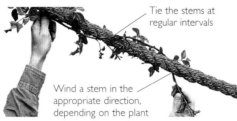

Tie the stems at regular intervals

Wind a stem in the appropriate direction, depending on the plant

◁ **SWAG TRAINING**
Carefully guide and secure the stems along a rope swag. Such horizontal training will encourage the formation of more abundant flowers than the same plant trained vertically.

△ **ORNAMENTAL BEAN**
Scarlet runner beans look attractive in a border (as here) or in a vegetable plot. 'Painted Lady' has pretty pink and white flowers. You can buy or make your own stake tepee.

HARDWARE

Most climbers can be trained against a trellis (*see p.93*), mesh netting, or taut lengths of galvanized wire. Use sheep or pig wire-netting for twining climbers; many with tendrils (sweet peas, for example) are light enough for plastic netting. Strands of heavy-duty wire are not too obvious and suit many climbers and wall shrubs. Soft garden twine can be used to tie in most stems. Hardware must be resistant to corrosion, and, in areas with high air pollution, use plastic or non-ferrous metal hardware.

Trellis and netting should preferably not be allowed to rest directly against a wall or fence, because air needs to circulate around a plant to prevent disease. Wooden 2in (5cm) slats can be attached to the surface, and the trellis or netting hooked, hinged, or screwed to the slats (*see p.95*). Wires are best held 2–3in (5–8cm) away from the supporting surface and secured between vine eyes or galvanized nails. Tighten them with pliers, or attach tensioners at 6ft (2m) intervals, to prevent sagging. Space wires 9–12in (23–30cm) apart, vertically and horizontally for maximum coverage, with the lowest wire 12in (30cm) above ground level.

△ **REGULAR MAINTENANCE**
To encourage healthy, attractive growth, climber stems should be trained to their supports regularly throughout the growing season. At the same time, cut out any dead or damaged shoots and check that old ties are not too tight.

HOW TO SECURE STEMS

◁ **FIGURE-EIGHTS**
Support stems against a trellis or strong wire using garden twine tied in figure-eights. This kind of knot will be loose enough to allow for expansion of the stems while the plant matures and to prevent their chafing against any hard surfaces on the supporting structure.

◁ **FENCE CLIPS**
Support thin stems against wooden surfaces with plastic fence clips. One end of the clip should be pushed into the fencing panel, and then the other end is looped over the plant stem and pressed firmly into the wood so that the stem is held securely in position.

SEE ALSO: Maintaining Climbers and Wall Shrubs, pp.112–115

PLANTING CLIMBERS AND WALL SHRUBS

MOST CLIMBERS AND WALL SHRUBS make long-lasting features in a garden, and, if they are to fulfill this role, must be carefully chosen to suit the intended site. Before planting, the ground must be thoroughly prepared (*see p.142*). The choice of support is important, too. If planting by a wall or fence, put any wires or trellis in place before you prepare to plant. Walls, fences, and whatever support you use all need to be in good condition, because they will be difficult to repair once the plant is growing well. After planting, the plants should be well watered until they are established, carefully trained to their supports, and regularly checked for pests and diseases.

PLANTING AGAINST A WALL

Autumn or spring is the best time to plant wall shrubs. Bare-rooted climbing and rambler roses should be planted in late autumn or in early spring, and other climbers in autumn and mid- to late spring. Have your trellis or other system of support ready in place (*see p.95 and pp.108–109*) and prepare the planting area well, digging in plenty of well-rotted organic matter (*see p.142, also p.147 and p.150*). To avoid the rainshadow, the dry area beside the foot of a wall or fence, make the planting hole at least 12in (30cm) away from the base. Such an area, sheltered from the prevailing wind, receives little or no rain, and the wall itself may absorb moisture from the soil.

The plant should be angled toward the wall, and, if grafted, as with many roses, the graft union should be set 2⅜in (6cm)

below soil level. This discourages the production of suckers from the rootstock. When refilling the planting hole, work the soil around the roots so that no air pockets remain. Any weak stems should be removed and, if only one main stem is desired, all but the most vigorous should be cut away. The addition of a thick, weed-suppressing mulch after watering well will speed the plant's development (*see p.152*).

All newly planted climbers and wall shrubs should be tied to their supports at once, to prevent wind damage to their young stems. If necessary, angle a bamboo stake between the stems and their support. Initially stems may require tying in but, once established, twining and tendriled climbers will attach themselves. Wall shrubs and scrambling climbers will always need securing to their support.

PLANTING NEAR A TREE

Rubber hose threaded on supporting wire protects host tree

INITIAL TRAINING
Carefully spiral the climber stems (here of a rose) around the supporting wire and up into the host tree and its lower branches. Secure the stems at intervals with twine tied in figure-eight knots.

A climber should be planted about 3–4ft (1–1.2m) away from the base of its host tree, beyond the edge of the tree canopy, to avoid competition for nutrients and moisture. This distance should be even greater if the host tree has a low crown or dense foliage that will restrict light. If planting in grass, clear a generous area around the planting site so that the climber is not competing with the grass.

To help a climber grow into a tree, its stems should be trained to a supporting wire or rope stretched between an angled peg in the ground and a low branch in the tree. When planting, angle the climber toward the tree, spreading out the roots (if bare-root) behind. Tie the stems to the guide. Winding the stems around the support will encourage flowering.

Never choose a climber that might swamp its host. *Clematis montana*, for example, needs a large tree. Small trees can support less vigorous large-flowered clematis or annuals such as morning glory.

PLANTING A CLIMBER AGAINST A WALL

1 CHECK LEVEL
Prepare a hole at least 12in (30cm) away from the wall. Insert the plant at a 45° angle, spreading the roots away from the wall. Use a horizontal stake to ensure the old soil marks on its stems are at ground level.

2 TRAIN STEMS
Fill in around the plant, firming the soil well. Then carefully untie the plant's original stake. With clips or soft twine, attach a stake to the base of each strong stem. Fan out and secure each stake top to the lowest wire.

3 INITIAL PRUNING
Using pruners, cut out any remaining, unsupported stems — those that were spindly, damaged, or even dead. If strong stems are sparse, pinch out the tip of each supported stem to encourage new growth.

4 MULCH WELL
Now that the initial framework of the plant has been established, water well, then cover the soil with an 3in (8cm) layer of well-rotted garden compost or manure to conserve moisture and discourage weeds.

SEE ALSO: Fences and Trellises, pp.92–93; Walls, pp.96–97; Hardware, p.109; Preparing the Ground, pp.142–143

PLANTING CLEMATIS

Clematis planted in spring or autumn, when the soil is warm and moist, are likely to establish the most successfully. Position them at least 12in (30cm) away from a wall or fence, to avoid dry soil. The planting hole should be deep, with the base of the stems buried well below soil level. This encourages plenty of new shoots to grow from the base, important if clematis wilt strikes and the stems need to be cut back. It may survive (*see p.301*).

Clematis prefer cool roots, so, after planting, shade the soil with stones, slabs, or roof tiles, or introduce low-growing plants in front. A deep mulch of well-rotted manure or garden compost will also help. Once established, clematis should flourish without extra water.

◁ A GOOD
BEGINNING
For fine flowers and foliage, give clematis (here C. montana 'Warwickshire Rose') a good start by adding plenty of organic matter, making a deep planting hole, and keeping the roots cool and moist.

PLANTING CLEMATIS BY A WALL
Most clematis need plenty of moisture, so at planting time bury a flower pot or piece of plastic pipe alongside the plant. This will channel the water down to the plant roots.

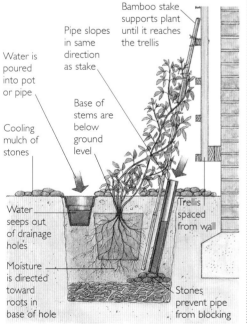

Bamboo stake supports plant until it reaches the trellis

Pipe slopes in same direction as stake

Water is poured into pot or pipe

Base of stems are below ground level

Cooling mulch of stones

Water seeps out of drainage holes

Moisture is directed toward roots in base of hole

Trellis spaced from wall

Stones prevent pipe from blocking

GETTING THE BEST FLOWERS

Climbers need good training in their first season or two. Start by tying in shoots after planting and keep tying in as they grow to form a well-spaced, attractive framework. Spreading out stems allows flowers to be produced over a larger area. The closer stems are to the horizontal, the more sideshoots are likely to develop, all of which may be capable of producing flowers. Train plants in this way to create a tunnel of blooms on a pergola. For the

best wisteria flowers, prune an established plant by cutting back long growths and shortening sideshoots in late summer to form spurs, and reducing these spurs again in midwinter to two or three buds.

Although many climbers prefer their roots to be shaded, they flower best at the top, in light and sun. Training shoots horizontally helps, but extra support such as a trellis is often needed at the top of a wall to prevent stems from flopping over and giving your neighbor the benefit. Wind climber stems around obelisks and tripods (*see below*), rather than letting them shoot straight up the supports.

MORE FLOWERS ▷
On a tripod, obelisk, or similar structure, wind the stems (here of a rose) around the supports, tying them at intervals to horizontal wires. Such training will induce flower buds to form at all levels.

◁ GOOD COVERAGE
The stems of a young climber should be fanned out across a wall or fence while they are still flexible. Any gaps at the base can be difficult to fill once the framework is set.

AVOIDING PROBLEMS

When grown by a wall or fence, plants are sometimes more likely to suffer from certain problems. Powdery mildew (*see p.296*), is usually the worst, striking where air circulation is poor, especially if the soil is also dry. Avoid roses that are susceptible to mildew, blackspot, and rust (*see pp.296–297*). Even if you are willing to use chemical control, climbers are difficult to spray once they have reached any height. Clear away affected leaves to prevent disease lingering from season to season.

The shelter of a warm wall may help pests to survive as well as plants. Keep a watch for aphids on young shoots from early spring, and nip out tips, if necessary. Clematis wilt (*see p.301*) may attack large-flowered hybrids, but the smaller-flowered clematis (*see box, right*) are resistant.

Keep plants growing well. Check ties, feed after pruning, and mulch regularly. Soil must be damp when a mulch is laid.

TELL ME WHY

WHY ARE CHOICE OF PLANT AND PLANTING METHOD IMPORTANT?

Choosing a disease-resistant variety and giving it the best possible start will produce a plant that is best able to withstand attacks from pests and diseases.

Some roses are more susceptible to disease than others. Avoid mildew-prone types such as 'American Pillar', 'Handel', and 'Dorothy Perkins'. 'Aloha' and 'Golden Showers' are reasonably disease-free.

Small-flowered clematis, such as spring- and early summer-flowering *Clematis alpina*, *C. macropetala*, and *C. montana*, plus late summer-flowering *C. tibetana* and *C. viticella* types, are resistant to clematis wilt.

Soil at the base of a wall is usually poor and dry and needs the addition of plenty of organic material before planting to help retain moisture and nutrients. Keep roots moist until a plant is well established (*see illustration, left*), and mulch regularly.

SEE ALSO: General Border Maintenance, pp.152–153; Dealing with Weeds and Plant Problems, pp.288–311

MAINTAINING CLIMBERS AND WALL SHRUBS

THE TIME SPENT LOOKING AFTER a climber or wall shrub will be amply rewarded by a healthy plant that puts on a handsome display of flowers, foliage, and possibly berries. Pruning and training is important for some, but not all. A climber such as ivy can largely be left to its own devices. Cut out dead or diseased stems or variegated shoots that have reverted to plain green whenever you see them, but time other pruning according to the type of plant and its flowering season. Tie in stems promptly (while still pliant) and check that ties are not too tight and that supports are sound and secure. Feed after pruning, and mulch to conserve moisture in the soil.

HOW AND WHEN TO PRUNE

Pruning helps keep a shrub to an attractive shape, but remember that the harder you cut a stem back, the more vigorously it will regrow, so prune strong-growing stems lightly and weak ones more vigorously to achieve a balanced shape. Many shrubs, especially those with a lax habit grown in an informal fashion, simply need neatening after flowering.

Pruning at the wrong time is unlikely to kill a plant, but it could result in losing a season's flowers or fruit if you cut away the stems that would have borne them.

WHAT TO PRUNE

Prune shrubs and climbers that flower on growth produced in the current season, such as abutilon, *Campsis*, and *Solanum crispum*, in late winter or early spring, and those that flower on the previous year's growth, such as actinidia, flowering quince, and evergreen ceanothus, from early to late summer, after flowering.

Prune grapes grown for their foliage in winter; *Prunus* in midsummer. Evergreens are best left until midspring. Pruning, combined with training, especially in the early years, is necessary for most climbers if you are to develop a good framework that will display flowers well and keep the plant to a suitable size. Vigorous climbers can ramble freely in a suitable site. A few climbers, such as clematis (*see p.114*) and wisteria (*see p.111*), have specific needs.

△ CROSSING BRANCHES
Cut any crossing or straggly stems back to their point of origin, to prevent their rubbing each other and eventually becoming damaged and diseased.

△ CROWDED STEMS
Thin areas of congested stems to open out the climber or wall shrub, so that light and air can circulate around it. Such pruning also prevents the plant from becoming heavy.

◁ PRUNING SIDESHOOTS
To fill a gap in the framework, shorten an adjacent sideshoot to encourage new growth. If possible, cut to an up- or downward-pointing bud, so that the new shoot does not grow away from the fence.

TELL ME WHY

WHY IS IT NECESSARY TO PRUNE WALL SHRUBS AND CLIMBERS?

Creates a pleasing shape: when combined with training, stems can be encouraged to grow in a desired direction so that they cover a surface evenly and the plant develops an attractive shape. Some wall shrubs can pruned and trained to form a specific shape such as a fan or tiered espalier, which can be useful where space is restricted.

Improves flowering: pruning stimulates new shoots to form that will in turn bear more flowers than old wood. Vigorous new stems often produce fewer but fatter buds that open into larger flowers.

Restricts size: climbers, such as grapes, roses, and honeysuckles, can be kept within the available space on an arch, wall, or pergola.

Promotes health: cutting out dead, diseased, or damaged stems removes potential entry points for infection and helps to prevent its spread to the plant.

WHERE TO PRUNE

Pruning cuts should be made as close to a bud or sideshoot as possible. Angle the cut where possible, so that moisture runs off, but avoid too steep an angle. A large wound that is slow to heal can easily become infected. Take care, too, not to leave a budless stub, which will die back and be vulnerable to disease.

Make clean cuts using sharp tools. Bruised or damaged wounds create a potential entry point for infection. Most pruning can be done with pruners, but thick branches are best tackled with loppers or a pruning saw. Use shears on a climber with a mass of twiggy stems.

△ ALTERNATE BUDS
Where the buds or shoots alternate on a stem, always cut just above and parallel to their angle of growth. Choose a bud that points in the same direction as the required new shoot.

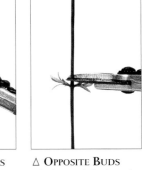

△ OPPOSITE BUDS
Climbers and shrubs with buds that grow opposite each other should be cut squarely across the stem just above a pair of plump, healthy buds or young, vigorous shoots.

◁ CUTTING TO REPLACEMENT SHOOT
When needing to shorten a stem, always assess the shape of the whole plant before making any pruning cuts and then, using pruners, cut just above a healthy stem pointing in the required direction.

SEE ALSO: Using Mulches to Suppress Weeds, p.145; Deadheading, p.155

SHAPING WALL SHRUBS

After planting, evergreen shrubs generally require little or no pruning, nor do those with a lax habit that are to be grown informally. Space out and tie in the stems to create an even, well-shaped framework, pruning out any ill-placed or weak shoots.

Shrubs that are to be kept flat to a wall, such as flowering quince (*Chaenomeles*) and pyracantha, or trained in a fan, for instance Japanese apricot (*Prunus mume*), need to have all outward-facing shoots removed, as well as any growing toward the wall. Space out the other shoots, gently pulling them down toward the horizontal, as appropriate, and tying them in.

◁ **ORNAMENTAL BUSH**
Pyracanthas can look particularly effective when the flexible young stems are trained in horizontal tiers against a wall. They can even be shaped around windows. A strong support is needed, as are gloves to protect against the thorns.

INITIAL STAGES

△ **TYING IN**
Using twine, secure all selected stems (here, of an evergreen ceanothus) to their support, spacing them out evenly.

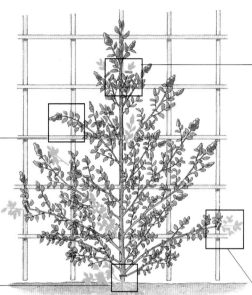

△ **PINCHING OUT**
Nip, or cut back with pruners, soft, young forward-pointing shoots, to encourage more branches to grow sideways.

△ **UNWANTED STEMS**
Remove at its point of origin any stem that is growing directly away from the support or toward it.

△ **CUTTING BACK**
Lightly prune back the longest stems by two or three buds in order to keep the shrub balanced and within its allotted area.

KEEPING IN SHAPE

Tie in new shoots to fill gaps in the framework while they are still young and flexible, and, at the same time, loosen old ties before they can begin to restrict stems. Prune out dead, dying, or diseased wood whenever you see it, but wait to cut out cold-damaged shoots until frosts are over. The time for pruning other stems depends largely on when the shrub flowers (*see facing page*). Do not remove shoots that have just flowered on a shrub grown for its berries. Continue to prune out shoots growing into or away from the wall.

Some shrubs need minimal pruning, for example the "rockspray" cotoneaster, *C. horizontalis*, and *Garrya*. It is possible to prune flowering quince twice a year to produce more flowering spurs: shorten long summer shoots in midsummer by two-thirds, then shorten these again in late winter to three or four buds. Avoid letting evergreen ceanothus get out of hand by pruning old flowering stems each season. Old wood will not reshoot.

PRUNING A DECIDUOUS CLIMBER

◁ **UNWANTED STEMS**
Remove weak stems, those that cross over another stem, and any growing directly toward or away from the support.

SPACING STEMS ▷
Tie in new growths, filling in any gaps in the main framework of the climber. If necessary, stimulate new growth by pruning.

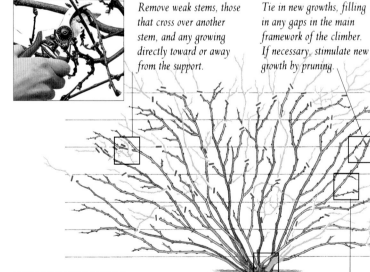

◁ **OLD WOOD**
Cut unproductive stems back to ground level. Then tie new growths into the resulting gap.

SPUR PRUNING ▷
Shorten long sideshoots to 3–6 buds to encourage the development of flowering shoots the following season.

SEE ALSO: Renovating Climbers, p.115

PRUNING CLEMATIS

The many types of clematis vary in their pruning requirements, depending on when they flower and age of wood they flower on. They can, however, be divided into three convenient pruning groups.

Group 1 clematis flower in spring and need minimal pruning, although occasional thinning will reinvigorate them. Most can be cut back hard if they need rejuvenating, but *Clematis montana* may not recover from pruning into old wood. If this gets too big, or the stems become heavy and tangled, cut away the old, dense growth but leave a few strong stems intact.

The clematis in Group 2, which start to flower in early summer, should be lightly pruned in late winter or early spring to thin the plant down to a framework of well-spaced one- or two-year-old stems.

Alternatively, these clematis can simply be cut back hard every three or four years, thus losing the first flush of flowers.

Late summer-flowering Group 3 types are pruned in late winter or early spring down to a pair of healthy buds within 12in (30cm) of the ground, but they can be cut back in autumn if the dead stems will mar a host tree, shrub, or other climber.

◁ **OLD GROWTH**
Remove old growth with a clean cut just above the point of origin. Tangled top-growth can also be sheared away, and the remaining stems unraveled, cut back to a healthy pair of buds, and spaced out against the support.

◁ **LIGHT PRUNE**
In late winter or early spring, shorten stems of Group 2 clematis back to strong growth or a pair of healthy buds, leaving a framework of one- or two-year-old stems to encourage flowering.

◁ **HARD PRUNE**
In late winter or early spring, once growth has just started, cut back all stems on Group 3 clematis to within 12in (30cm) of soil level. Remove any stems that are not shooting to stimulate new growth from below ground level.

CLEMATIS PRUNING GROUPS

Clematis in Pruning Group 1 include the evergreens that flower in winter, *Clematis alpina* types with nodding bells, dainty *C. macropetala*, and vigorous *C. montana*. The double-flowered clematis all belong to Group 2, as do the large-flowered hybrids that bloom in early summer, sometimes with a later second flush. The later summer large-flowered hybrids belong to Group 3, as do the easily grown smaller-flowered *C. viticella* types such as 'Alba Luxurians', plus *C. tibetana* and *C. tangutica*.

◁ **GROUP 1, FOR EXAMPLE *CLEMATIS MONTANA***
These clematis require only minimal pruning, because any cuts will remove potential flowering stems. They do, however, benefit from occasional thinning and shortening of some stems to healthy buds or shoots after flowering. Also remove dead, weak, and diseased stems.

THE THREE PRUNING GROUPS

Some of the most popular clematis and their groups:

GROUP 1
Clematis alpina, 'Frances Rivis', 'Pink Flamingo', 'Ruby', 'White Moth', *C. armandii*, *C. cirrhosa*, *C. macropetala*, 'Maidwell Hall', 'Markham's Pink', *C. montana*, 'Elizabeth', 'Marjorie', 'Picton's Variety'.

GROUP 2
'Arctic Queen', 'Beauty of Worcester', 'Bees' Jubilee', 'Dr Ruppel', 'Elsa Späth', 'Fireworks', 'Guernsey Cream', 'H.F. Young', 'Henryi', 'Lady Northcliffe', 'Lasurstern', 'Marie Boisselot', 'Miss Bateman', 'Moonlight', 'Mrs Cholmondeley', 'Multi Blue', 'Nelly Moser', 'Niobe', 'Royalty', 'Silver Moon', 'Sugar Candy', 'The President', 'The Vagabond', 'Vyvyan Pennell', 'Wada's Primrose', 'W.E. Gladstone', 'Vino'.

GROUP 3
Clematis rehderiana, *C. tangutica*, *C. terniflora*, *C. tibetana*, *C. viticella*, 'Alba Luxurians', 'Ascotiensis', 'Bill MacKenzie', 'Comtesse de Bouchaud', 'Ernest Markham', 'Etoile Rose', 'Etoile Violette', 'Gipsy Queen', 'Gravetye Beauty', 'Hagley Hybrid', 'Huldine', 'Jackmanii', 'Jackmanii Superba', 'Mme Edouard André', 'Mme Julia Correvon', 'Minuet', 'Pagoda', 'Perle d'Azur', 'Polish Spirit', 'Princess Diana', 'Rouge Cardinal', 'Royal Velours', 'Venosa Violacea', 'Ville de Lyon'.

△ **GROUP 2, FOR EXAMPLE 'VYVYAN PENNELL'**
In late winter or early spring, remove any weak laterals on these clematis to stimulate new shoots and more blooms. Prune congested or damaged growth back to a branching point or to the soil level. To prolong flowering, make your pruning cuts over a period of weeks.

△ **GROUP 3, FOR EXAMPLE 'GRAVETYE BEAUTY'**
In late winter or early spring, remove all dead, damaged, or diseased stems. Hard prune the remaining stems back to plump, healthy buds about 12in (30cm) above the soil level. To extend the flowering season, shorten some of the stems again in early summer.

SEE ALSO: Tools for Cutting and Pruning, p.279

CLIMBING AND RAMBLING ROSES

Deadhead roses to encourage more blooms on repeat-flowering types, and tie in new growths throughout the season. Fertilize plants immediately after pruning.

Ramblers and modern climbing roses differ in their growth and flowering habits and so are pruned in different ways. In fact, ramblers often flourish without pruning, but they look much better in a garden if cut back regularly and trained over a wall or to form a screen.

Rambling roses flower most prolifically on wood produced in the previous season. They are therefore pruned once their single flush of flowers is over in summer. Ramblers make more new growth from the base of the plant than climbers, and this should be encouraged by taking out old stems at ground level. Flowers develop on the same sideshoots for several years, so these need not be cut every year.

△ **SEASONAL CARE**
At the end of the growing season, in autumn, long, arching stems on climbing roses should be carefully tied in, cutting them back slightly if necessary.

Many modern climbing roses are repeat-flowering so are pruned in autumn, when leaves begin to fall. Long shoots should be tied in or shortened to avoid wind damage. Reduce flowered stems by two-thirds, and cut out less productive shoots.

PRUNING AND TYING IN RAMBLERS

1 MAIN STEMS
Cut back one in three old main stems down to the ground. This will stimulate fresh basal growth. Remove each long, thick stem in sections to prevent damage to adjacent stems.

2 EXCESS GROWTH
Thin some leading shoots and shorten others by 2–3in (5–8cm), and their sideshoots by two-thirds, to encourage branching and more flowers for the following season.

3 SECURING NEW SHOOTS
Throughout the growing season, tie in new shoots as they develop. Use commercial ties or soft garden twine in a figure-eight knot, and aim to maintain a well-balanced framework.

PRUNING AND TYING IN MODERN CLIMBERS

1 FLOWERED SHOOTS
Shorten stems that have produced flowers by two-thirds of their length. Tip-prune stems that have outgrown their allotted space.

2 UNPRODUCTIVE SHOOTS
Completely remove any leafless, weak, diseased, or damaged shoots back to a healthy stem. If necessary, cut main stems near ground level.

3 ADJUST TIES
Gradually loosen or replace ties, such as this ratcheted plastic one, as the stems expand. Prune or reposition and retie any stems that are rubbing.

RENOVATING CLIMBERS

A few climbers, such as passionflower and Chilean potato vine (*Solanum crispum*), are best replaced by new plants once they have become old and congested or outgrown their space. Many, however, can be saved by renovation, but some are better suited to hard pruning than others.

Evergreens are usually the least likely to respond well to severe pruning. Ivy will shoot readily from old wood: cut it back to within about 3ft (1m) of the base. Honeysuckle, grapes, *Campsis*, and Oriental bittersweet (*Celastrus orbiculatus*) usually reshoot well if pruned to about 24in (60cm) above soil level. All the renovation can be undertaken in one operation during winter while the plant is dormant, except for evergreens, which are best pruned in mid- to late spring.

Other climbers will recover best if renovation is staged over two or three seasons. This is the preferred method for climbing hydrangea. If in any doubt about a plant's ability to withstand hard pruning, renovate gradually in this way, taking out a few stems at a time. It may help to shear away tangled top growth, then sort out the main stems or detach the plant and lay it on the ground. Cut each stem back to a healthy bud. Keep most stems to a reasonable length, but prune one or two close to the ground. Rearrange the stems over their support and tie in. Mulch but do not fertilize heavily. Repeat this procedure over the next year or two, until all old stems have been removed.

△ **DRASTIC PRUNING**
Some climbers, such as this honeysuckle, quickly reshoot and flower well after cutting back to 24in (60cm) above ground level. Others such as wisteria and common jasmine (J. officinalis) may take several seasons to recover.

SEE ALSO: Applying Mulch, p.152; Maintaining Roses, p.160

HEDGES IN THE GARDEN

HEDGES COMBINE A PRACTICAL and an esthetic role within the garden, where they establish its basic style and framework. Although generally used to form a legal boundary, they also make excellent internal divisions as well as being architectural features in their own right. Because most hedges are permanent features, it is important to link such living boundaries with the landscape beyond. The right choice of hedging material is vital to success: it must suit the soil, site, exposure, and climate, and it must grow at a suitable rate. Hedges are cheaper and more environmentally friendly than walls and fences but are slower to create effective screens.

DESIGN CONSIDERATIONS

Choice and style of hedge are a matter of personal taste. Any hedge needs to suit the style of planting in a garden, but there are no rules. A dense, precision-clipped hedge of yew not only suits a formal design; it will also provide the perfect background to a naturalistic or cottage-garden style planting. In rural areas, native species blend attractively into the surrounding countryside. Informal hedges provide the opportunity to introduce flowers and berries, which in turn attract wildlife. Choosing the type of hedging plant goes hand in hand with deciding on the style. If you opt for a formal hedge, remember that the faster it grows the more frequently it will need trimming. No plant grows quickly to 6ft (2m) then stops. In the long term, a slow-growing hedge is a lot less work and much more rewarding. Informal hedges are easier to manage but will still need some pruning, and they often have a wider spread. Low aromatic hedges of lavender, boxwood, or santolina look marvelous within a garden, lining paths and edging beds.

Taller internal hedges can be used to screen one part of the garden from another. If you want to create an arch, let some stems on either side of the opening reach a length where you can tie them together in the center at an appropriate height. Prune out the tips regularly to encourage bushy growth, tying in more shoots whenever necessary. Once the arch is growing thickly, carefully cut it to shape. Although it is more difficult, you can also create a "window" in a similar way by cutting and tying and training stems, using stakes as a guideline if necessary to form the desired shape. A pleached hedge (*see p.91*) also offers glimpses to areas beyond.

Hedges are usually of a single species, but different plants can be combined for a tapestry effect. For formal hedges they need similar growth rates, but this is less important for informal styles. Given plenty of space, you could imitate rural hedges and plant a mixture including holly, hazel, hawthorn, or field maple.

△ **SQUARED EDGES**
The solid, geometric framework of this garden has been cleverly interrupted by use of some wooden screening and by the "window" trained in one of the boundary hedges.

▽ **RICH BACKDROP**
This solid, dark green conifer hedge makes an excellent foil for the pink sidalceas and poppies, the golden yellow Spanish broom, and the gray-leaved plants in the foreground.

◁ **FOLIAGE CONTRASTS**
The color and dense texture of this formal yew hedge is highlighted by the much lighter, looser, and longer leaves on the adjacent informal bamboo screen.

SEE ALSO: Boundaries and Divisions, pp.30–31

PRACTICAL CONSIDERATIONS

Before selecting which plant to grow, you need to consider the hedge's function. Some plants stand up well to wind (*see p.119*), and dense hedges muffle noise. Prickly plants such as hawthorn can form an almost impenetrable barrier (*see list, right*).

Take into account a shrub or tree's height when mature. If this is higher than you want, the hedge will need regular, time-consuming clipping, and if it is to form a garden boundary, it will need to be trimmed on your neighbor's side, too. You must keep fast-growing trees such as Leyland cypress under control and consider the effects on those around you. The conifer *Thuja plicata* is a good alternative; it is easily kept to 6ft (2m) or lower if clipped twice a year, in spring and early autumn. A wire-mesh or hurdle fence makes a useful short-term boundary until slow-growing plants reach a reasonable height.

Cost is likely to be all important. Bare-rooted hedging plants, especially of native species, cost much less than container-grown plants. Specialty suppliers often advertise in gardening magazines. You may have time to produce your own rooted cuttings (*see pp.164–165*), especially useful when planting long boxwood and lavender hedges, both of which root easily. The planting distances below will produce a good, thick hedge. A slightly wider spacing is acceptable for a tall hedge.

Avoid planting hedges in very dry soil or beside narrow borders, because they will take up nutrients and moisture to the detriment of surrounding plants.

◁ **SPIKY DETERRENT**
Sharp spiny hedges, such as this barberry, will help deter intruders and create an effective stockproof boundary. In autumn, the colorful leaves and berries vie with one another for attention in the garden.

△ **HEDGE FOR WILDLIFE**
The colorful fruits in this mixed informal hedge of red- and yellow-berried pyracanthas not only look good but also provide a source of food for birds.

GOOD CHOICES

RECOMMENDED PRICKLY HEDGES

Many plants that bear prickles or thorns on their stems or leaves make excellent hedges. Both evergreen and deciduous species are suitable – the choice depending on the style of hedge and whether it is to act as a uniform backdrop to the garden.

Barberries, especially *Berberis. julianae*
Flowering quince (*Chaenomeles*: lots to choose from)
Hawthorn (*Crataegus monogyna, C. laevigata*)
Five-leaf aralia (*Eleutherococcus sieboldianus*)
Holly (*Ilex aquifolium, I. × altaclerensis, I. opaca*)
Hardy, or trifoliate, orange (*Poncirus trifoliata*)
Pyracantha, many
Roses: especially 'Complicata', *Rosa eglanteria, R. rugosa*

PLANTING DISTANCES AND CLIPPING OR PRUNING FREQUENCY

FORMAL HEDGES

EVERGREEN	PLANTING DISTANCE	HEIGHT	CLIPPING TIMES
Boxwood (*Buxus*)	12in (30cm)	S	2 or 3 times in growing season
Escallonia	18in (45cm)	M–L	Once, immediately after flowering
Holly (*Ilex × altaclarensis, I. aquifolium, I. opaca*)	18in (45cm)	M–L	Once, in late summer
Lawson cypress (*Chamaecyparis lawsoniana*)	24in (60cm)	M–L	Twice, in spring and early autumn
Lavender	12in (30cm)	S	Twice, in spring and after flowering
Leyland cypress (X *Cupressocyparis leylandii*)	30in (75cm)	L	2 or 3 times in growing season
Lonicera nitida	12in (30cm)	S–M	3 or 4 times in growing season
Privet (*Ligustrum*)	45in (30cm)	M–L	3 or 4 times in growing season
Yew (*Taxus*)	24in (60cm)	M–L	Once or twice in growing season
DECIDUOUS			
Beech (*Fagus sylvatica*)	12–24in (30–60cm)	M–L	Once, in late summer
Berberis thunbergii	18in (45cm)	S–M	Once, in midsummer
Hawthorn (*Crataegus monogyna*)	12–18in (30–45cm)	M–L	Twice, in summer and autumn
Hornbeam (*Carpinus betulus*)	18–24in (45–60cm)	L	Once, in mid- to late summer

*S (small) 1–3ft (30cm–1m); M (medium) 3–6ft (1–2m); L (large) 6ft (2m) or taller

INFORMAL AND FLOWERING HEDGES

EVERGREEN	PLANTING DISTANCE	HEIGHT	WHEN TO PRUNE
Berberis	18in (45cm)	M–L	Immediately after flowering
Cotoneaster lacteus	18–24in (45–60cm)	M–L	After fruiting
Escallonia	18in (45cm)	M–L	Immediately after flowering
Garrya elliptica	18in (45cm)	M–L	Immediately after flowering
Holly (*Ilex × altaclarensis, I. aquifolium, I. opaca*)	18–24in (45–60cm)	M–L	In late summer
Lavender	12in (30cm)	S	After flowering
Pyracantha	24in (60cm)	L	In midspring
DECIDUOUS			
Forsythia × intermedia	18in (45cm)	M–L	After flowering, remove old stems
Fuchsia magellanica	12–18in (30–45cm)	S–M	In early spring, remove old stems
Hawthorn (*Crataegus monogyna*)	18–24in (45–60cm)	L	In winter, remove selected vigorous shoots
Hazel (*Corylus*)	18–24in (45–60cm)	L	After flowering, in midspring
Potentilla fruticosa	12–18in (30–45cm)	S–M	In midspring
Roses 'Roseraie de l'Haÿ', *Rosa rugosa*	18–24in (45–60cm)	M–L	In spring, remove thin twigs
Sloe/blackthorn (*Prunus spinosa*)	18–24in (45–60cm)	L	In winter, remove selected vigorous shoots

*S (small) 1–3ft (30cm–1m); M (medium) 3–6ft (1–2m); L (large) 6ft (2m) or taller

SEE ALSO: Planting and Maintaining Hedges, pp.120–121

FORMAL HEDGES

Plants used for formal hedges must produce dense growth and tolerate repeated close trimming. They are often small-leaved and slow-growing. Classic choices include yew, *Thuja plicata*, privet, holly, and, where there is sufficient space, large-leaved Portugal laurel (*Prunus lusitanica*). When frequently clipped, beech and hornbeam, although deciduous, attractively retain their dead, russet-colored leaves in winter.

Formal hedges usually contain a single species, but mixed hedging of contrasting foliage can provide variety throughout the year. The plants used, however, should have compatible growth rates if overly vigorous species are not to dominate. A favorite combination mixes green and copper beech (*see p.31*). Combining shrubs with different-sized leaves creates an

◁ **LARGE LEAVES**
Evergreens with handsome large leaves, such as Portugal laurel and this Elaeagnus × ebbingei 'Gilt Edge', should be trimmed using pruners. Leaves that are sheared in half turn brown at the edges, spoiling the appearance of the hedge.

interesting effect, for instance *Lonicera nitida* and privet. Add in their golden-leaved forms to make it all the more striking. A mosaic hedge of evergreen and deciduous species, such as hornbeam and holly, also looks attractive.

Boxwood, lavender, *Santolina*, and *Berberis thunbergii* all make good low hedges. As well as using them to line beds and paths, try them above low retaining walls.

PLANT LIST

RECOMMENDED EVERGREEN HEDGES
F = formal; I = informal; D = dwarf

Berberis × *stenophylla* F or I
Boxwood (*Buxus sempervirens*) F D
Cherry laurel (*Prunus laurocerasus*) F or I
Elaeagnus × *ebbingei* F or I
Escallonia: all, especially E. 'Donard Seedling' F or I
Holly (*Ilex*: use green or variegated types) F or I
Japanese laurel (*Aucuba japonica*) F or I
Lavender (*Lavandula angustifolia* 'Hidcote') F or I D
Lavender cotton (*Santolina*) F or I D
Lawson cypress (*Chamaecyparis lawsoniana*;
    'Chilworth Silver' is a good one to use) F
Lonicera nitida, L. nitida 'Baggesen's Gold' F
Portugal laurel (*Prunus lusitanica*) F or I
Privet (*Ligustrum ovalifolium, L. ovalifolium* 'Aureum') F
Pyracantha I
Western hemlock (*Tsuga heterophylla*) F
Western red cedar (*Thuja plicata*) F
Yew (*Taxus baccata, T.* × *media*) F

RECOMMENDED DECIDUOUS HEDGES

Although deciduous, beech and hornbeam retain their dead leaves over winter. Key as above.

Alder (*Alnus*: especially A. cordata) I
Beech (*Fagus sylvatica*; also copper beech: *F. sylvatica*
    f. *purpurea*) F
Berberis thunbergii: especially 'Atropurpurea Nana' F or I D
Cherry plum (*Prunus cerasifera* 'Nigra') I
Forsythia × *intermedia* I
Fuchsia magellanica I D
Hazel (*Corylus avellana*; try also filbert: *C. maxima,*
    C. maxima 'Purpurea') I
Hedge maple (*Acer campestre*) I
Hornbeam (*Carpinus betulus*) F
Potentilla fruticosa I D
Privet (*Ligustrum obtusifolium, L. quihoui*) F
Roses: *Rosa rugosa, R. glauca* I

◁ **ELEGANT BOUNDARIES**
Yew (Taxus) makes some of the best-looking, dense formal hedging, but it may take six to ten years to become fully established. During this time it needs precise, regular cutting to develop an even shape and density.

BAMBOOS

The woody, arching stems and ornamental foliage of these evergreens make them useful for hedges, screens, and windbreaks, if close-planted. They are good at muffling noise as well producing their own unique, soothing rustle.

Many bamboos have invasive root runs, so choose carefully. One of the most striking is slow-growing *Chusquea culeou*, which may eventually reach 20ft (6m). It bears graceful, olive-green stems. A slow-

spreading dwarf bamboo, with green-striped, golden yellow leaves, is *Pleioblastus auricomus*. It grows to 5ft (1.5m) tall. *Phyllostachys flexuosa* makes a good screen up to 9ft (3m) high, although its wavy green canes, sometimes noticeably zigzagged, will in time form large thickets.

YEAR-ROUND SCREEN ▷
The copious leaves on this Phyllostachys nigra var. henonis filter wind effectively, and this bamboo has the bonus of attractive, lustrous yellow stems when mature.

SEE ALSO: Bamboos, p.141

INFORMAL FLOWERING AND BERRYING HEDGES

Left unclipped, some foliage shrubs make delightful informal hedges (*see list, facing page*) but often part of the charm of an informal screen is its flowers or berries.

For spring and summer interest, plant hedges of flowering quince (*Chaenomeles*), hypericum, and species and hybrid shrub roses, for example. For the best value, select scented-flowered roses such as 'Roseraie de l'Haÿ'.

For reliable autumn color, introduce cotoneaster, for its cheerful, usually red berries, or snowberry (*Symphoricarpos*), for its dense clusters of white fruits that last well into winter. Among good informal hedging plants with fine flowers as well as fruits are thorny pyracanthas, which have white flowers and yellow, orange, or red berries, while the carmine red flowers of *Rosa rugosa* are followed by large red hips.

In gardens with young children, beware of planting a hedge that bears tempting but toxic berries. The berries of hawthorn, cotoneaster, barberry, and viburnum may cause stomach upsets if eaten.

PLANT LIST

HEDGES RECOMMENDED FOR THEIR FLOWERS

Some plants in this list of flowering hedge shrubs are also of interest for their berries, and vice versa.

Berberis darwinii, B. x stenophylla
Escallonia 'Apple Blossom, *E.* 'Langleyensis',
    E. 'Pride of Donard'
Forsythia x intermedia
Fuchsia magellanica, F. 'Phyllis', *F.* 'Riccartonii'
Garrya elliptica
Hypericum
Lavender: especially *Lavandula angustifolia* 'Hidcote'
Potentilla fruticosa
Ribes sanguineum
Tamarix ramosissima

HEDGES RECOMMENDED FOR THEIR BERRIES OR NUTS

Cherry plum (*Prunus cerasifera* 'Pissardii')
Cotoneaster horizontalis, C. lacteus, C. simonsii
Hawthorn (*Crataegus monogyna*)
Hazel (*Corylus avellana*)
Lonicera nitida 'Yunnan'
Myrtle (*Myrtus*: especially *M. communis* subsp. *tarentina*)
Pyracantha
Roses: *Rosa canina* (dog rose), *R. rugosa, R.* 'Schneezwerg'
Sloe/blackthorn (*Prunus spinosa*)
Snowberry (*Symphoricarpos x doorenbosii*)
Viburnum tinus 'Eve Price'

△ **FLORAL ASSET**
Flowering hedges such as potentilla will often be studded with a seemingly endless display of flowers from spring until autumn.

AUTUMNAL GLOW ▷
The orange-red berries on this Cotoneaster simonsii *are offset by the glossy, rich green leaves, creating an eye-catching combination.*

HEDGES IN EXPOSED AND COASTAL SITES

△ **WINDBREAK**
The arching stems of this graceful Tamarix ramosissima *flex readily and will not break in strong winds.*

◁ **TOUGH HEDGE**
Among the most tolerant plants of coastal exposure is spiny-stemmed sea buckthorn (Hippophae rhamnoides), *which has persistent, bright orange berries on female plants.*

Hedges can provide invaluable shelter for gardens in exposed sites, where wind may desiccate foliage or scorch shoot tips. Plants growing near the tops of hills are especially vulnerable to strong winds. By the coast, the wind may also carry damaging salt spray, causing leaves to

PLANT LIST

HEDGES RECOMMENDED FOR EXPOSED AND COASTAL GARDENS
c = hedges especially suitable for coastal sites

Although many hedges will tolerate coastal winds, few flourish in frequent salt-laden ones.

Daisy bush (*Olearia nummulariifolia*) c
Elaeagnus: all, for example *E. angustifolia* (oleaster) c
Escallonia (see list above) c
Griselinia littoralis c
Hawthorn (*Crataegus monogyna*)
Hornbeam (*Carpinus betulus*)
Holly (*Ilex x altaclerensis, I. aquifolium*)
Juniper (*Juniperus communis*) c
Sea buckthorn (*Hippophae rhamnoides*) c
Tamarix ramosissima c
Tree purslane (*Atriplex halimus*) c

turn brown. Any buildup of salt in the soil may harm roots as well.

Since hedging plants can suffer in just the same way, it is important to choose shrubs or trees able to withstand wind or salt spray (*see list, left*). Many of them share certain characterisitics: for instance, small, tough leaves, as on holly and hawthorn. Deciduous hedges can make the most effective wind filters. Thick evergreens may cause strong winds to "jump" the hedge and create turbulence.

In seaside gardens, the choice of hedging is greater. The temperature-moderating effects of the water enable you to choose plants that would not be hardy farther inland. For example, flowering shrubs such as hebes, the daisy bush (*Olearia*), and tree lupines (*Lupinus arboreus*) can be used to make attractive informal hedges.

To help a hedge to establish in a windy site, erect a temporary, semipermeable windbreak on the windward side, and perhaps support with wires (*see next page*).

SEE ALSO: Preparation and Planting, p.120

PLANTING AND MAINTAINING HEDGES

BECAUSE HEDGES ARE potentially long-lived, their site and soil must be thoroughly prepared before planting. The success of a newly planted hedge also depends on how it is pruned during its first two or three years – deciduous hedges, in particular, need formative pruning to ensure dense growth from the base to the top. Thereafter, the amount of trimming or pruning needed, or any other maintenance, depends on the type of hedge: evergreen or deciduous, formal or informal, flowering or berrying. All hedges, however, should be top-dressed with a balanced fertilizer each spring and then mulched, in order to maintain strong, even growth.

PREPARATION AND PLANTING

Container-grown plants are best planted in autumn or spring, and balled and bare-root plants in late autumn or early spring. Do not plant in frozen ground. If necessary, keep bare-roots moist until conditions are suitable by planting temporarily in a frost-free spot. Prepare the planting site well. It must be free from perennial weeds such as ground elder, brambles, and bindweed. These will be impossible to eradicate once the hedge has grown. Weed regularly while plants are getting established.

A couple of weeks before planting, mark the line of the hedge with a string guideline and dig a trench, deep and wide enough to accommodate the plants' roots comfortably. Add plenty of well-rotted manure or compost (see below), then allow the soil to settle.

■ **Water the plants well** the day before planting. Keep bare-roots wrapped until planting to prevent them from drying out.

PREPARING THE GROUND

1 DEEP DIGGING
Dig a trench 12–24in (30–60cm) deep, 24–36in (60–90cm) wide along the guideline, and remove the topsoil. On heavy, poorly drained ground, break up the subsoil.

2 FEEDING THE SOIL
Alternate 3in (8cm) layers of organic matter and topsoil in the trench. Finish with 4oz (110g) of general-purpose fertilizer such as blood, fish, and bone meal per yard/meter.

STRAIGHT PLANTING △
Most hedges are planted in a single row, with 12–24in (30–60cm) between plants (see also p.117). Tiny plants for dwarf hedges can be set 4–6in (10–15cm) apart.

STAGGERED PLANTING △
Only for a particularly thick barrier, 3ft (90cm) or more wide, alternate the plants between two rows 18in (45cm) apart. Space plants 36in (90cm) apart in the row.

■ **Lay the plants** along the string line, at the appropriate spacing, alternating any weak plants with stronger, healthier ones.
■ **Dig holes and plant** one by one, removing each plant from its pot or wrapping only when its hole is dug and you are ready to plant. Set the plant in the hole at the same level as it was in its container or in the open ground. There is usually a mark on the stem indicating the previous soil level. Lay a stake across the top of the hole to check alignment. Backfill with soil, firming in stages to prevent air pockets.
■ **Water well** once you have planted the whole row. Apply a 2–3in (5–8cm) layer of mulch over the entire trench.
■ **In very exposed sites** support plants with a couple of wires strung between posts on the windward side. Tie in plants loosely to the wires so that they do not rub against the wire, damaging the bark.

FORMATIVE PRUNING

Do not try to make the shoots on all plants an even length on planting. Most evergreens need minimal pruning, and shrubs in informal hedges are pruned as specimens (see p.158). Prune strong shoots on beech and hornbeam by one-third, weak shoots by two-thirds. Cut back hawthorn and privet to 6–12in (15–30cm) above ground level in late spring, then cut back side-shoots in late summer; the next winter, remove half the previous season's growth.

INITIAL STAGES

1 BEFORE PRUNING
Some vigorous evergreens, such as this Lonicera nitida, require formative pruning to encourage dense growth from the base.

2 AFTER PRUNING
The strong laterals have been pruned lightly and the weak ones hard. The leaders are trimmed lightly once the hedge is the desired height.

HEDGE SHAPES

ROUNDED TOP △
In heavy snowfall regions, shape a hedge so that it has a rounded or pointed top, which sheds snow more easily than a flat one.

SLOPED SIDES △
In areas prone to high winds, shape a hedge so that it is narrower at the top, to deflect the wind and reduce damage.

SEE ALSO: Preparing the Ground, pp.142–143; Planting Shrubs, p.150; Planting with Sheet or Mat Mulches, p.151; Perennial Weeds, pp.292–293

TRIMMING AND PRUNING

The aim of clipping a formal hedge is to ensure healthy, vigorous, dense growth from base to top and to maintain a neat outline. Diseased or damaged growth needs to be removed whenever it is seen; otherwise, trimming frequency depends on the rate at which a plant grows, plus the height it would normally reach when mature (*see p.117*). Aim to produce a shape with gently sloping sides that is narrower at the top than the base (*see facing page, below*). To keep the top level, use string stretched between stakes as a guide. Evergreens are trimmed from spring to early autumn; deciduous hedges are usually clipped after midsummer. Always avoid clipping while there are birds

nesting in a hedge. The shrubs in an informal hedge are pruned in the same way as freestanding specimens (*see pp.158–159*), usually after flowering or berrying, or in spring. At the same time, they can be given any additional pruning needed to maintain an attractive shape.

Use electric hedge trimmers or shears for formal hedges, and pruners, or a pruning saw if necessary, for an informal hedge. Prune or trim shrubs with large evergreen leaves with pruners (*see p.118*). After trimming, feed, water, and mulch.

▽ **USING SHEARS**
When trimming, hold the blades of shears parallel with the line of the hedge at all times. To get a straight, consistent shape, use a string line tied between stakes as a guide.

△ **USING ELECTRIC HEDGE TRIMMERS**
Most small-leaved formal hedges are cut with electric hedge trimmers, which should be worked with a wide, sweeping action, keeping the blade parallel to the hedge. Do not cut with the trimmer raised above shoulder height.

ALWAYS REMEMBER

GOLDEN SAFETY RULES

Never use an electric hedge trimmer in damp conditions. Always ensure that it is fitted with a ground fault circuit interrupter (GFCI or "circuit breaker"), and never allow the cord to trail dangerously. Protect yourself with goggles, ear protectors, and gloves, and make sure staging and ladders are stable.

TOPIARY

The tops of hedges, as well as freestanding shrubs, can be used for topiary. Spheres and cubes are the simplest shapes to create, while animals and birds allow scope for the imagination. Dense, slow-growing, small-leaved evergreens are the most suitable plants – yew and boxwood are ideal. Round shapes can be cut free-hand; stakes and wire make a good guide for straight-sided shapes. Complex designs generally require a wire frame to be secured in place as a permanent cutting guide. Take time clipping and shaping, standing back frequently to assess the effect, especially in the formative stages.

△ **TEMPORARY GUIDE**
After clipping roughly into shape, use stakes and wire to achieve an even, symmetrical cone.

△ **FINISHED CONE**
Clip regularly to keep in shape. Use whichever tools – shears or pruners – you feel most comfortable with.

RENOVATING HEDGES

Overgrown, straggly hedges can often be renovated by phased pruning, but success depends on the type of plant. Few conifers respond to severe pruning, apart from yew, which will readily resprout from old wood. Both height and width of a hedge can be drastically reduced, but separate the two operations by allowing at least a growing season in between. If only the sides are to be cut back, it is also best to cut them in alternate years (*see below*). Renovate deciduous hedges when dormant, in winter; evergreens respond best in midspring. To encourage vigorous regrowth, feed and mulch the hedge well the season before renovation is to start, and again after each pruning session.

△ **SECTION THROUGH A CONIFER HEDGE**
Even if trimmed regularly on the outside, conifer hedges eventually lose all their leaves inside, because most are unable to produce new shoots from old wood. Ultimately such a hedge usually needs replacing, although yew responds excellently to phased renovation.

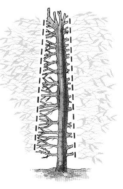

△ **YEAR ONE**
To reduce the width of a neglected or overgrown hedge, prune side growth almost to the main stem on one side only (here, the right side). Trim the other side less drastically. Then feed and mulch the hedge.

△ **YEAR TWO**
A year later, provided the hedge is growing vigorously, cut back the other side (here, the left side) almost to the main stem, to match the previous severe pruning. Lightly trim the opposite side; feed and mulch.

SEE ALSO: Pruning Established Shrubs, pp.158–159

BEDS AND BORDERS

GARDEN STYLES

OVER THE CENTURIES, the design of flower gardens has swung from artful formality to relaxed informality and back again, with a variety of styles in between. Each has its virtues, and gardeners today can either draw on aspects they like from former eras or throw away the instruction book to create their own individual, modern patterns. Beds and borders may be completely formal, with structured planting, or more natural-looking with intermingling plants; alternatively, you could try mixing the two. Height, shape, texture, and color of the plants are just as important as the site and shape of a bed or border and should be considered at the planning stage.

THE FORMAL LINE

Geometry, pattern, and symmetry, expressed in strong lines and bold shapes, are the essence of formality. The style relies heavily on hard landscaping in the shape of bricks and pavers, which form both a frame for plantings and a unifying element between house and garden.

Plantings, too, may follow a geometric template, as with close-clipped hedges or knot gardens. Symmetry, in which each planting has its echoing mirror image, can be relaxed for emphatic contrast or restrained to reinforce design unity.

AN INFORMAL APPROACH

The informal style tries to emulate nature by favoring irregular shapes. It uses sweeping curves and undulating forms as a framework for plantings of apparently undisciplined abundance and, if hard materials are used, they are usually of natural origin, such as stone or wood.

For the plant enthusiast, informality is the style of choice. If formality demands restraint and simplicity, informality has variety and exuberance at heart – new plant acquisitions can be added without fear of spoiling line or symmetry.

GOOD IDEAS

• Garden visiting is a prime source of ideas and inspiration; observe, borrow, and build on other gardeners' successful ideas.

• Look at books and magazines to identify appealing styles and features. Make a list of "wants" and "must haves" to help define the style and content of your own designs.

▽ **INFORMAL PROFUSION**
Drifts of plants that weave together to create a natural-looking tapestry are the essence of an informal flower bed, but this is the result of much planning and hard work.

△ **GEOMETRIC SHAPES**
Rectangles, triangles, and squares formed by low, clipped boxwood hedges create an instant impression of formality, but this can be softened by flowering plants contained within the pattern. Brick paving adds to the effect.

SEE ALSO: Border Types, pp.124–125; Raised Beds, pp.180–181

ON THE WILD SIDE

Wild gardening may be regarded as the ultimate expression of the informal style. Bringing native plants into the garden may stem from a desire to conserve plants threatened by habitat loss, or from simple appreciation of their natural charms. Some can be grown in traditional borders, but most do better in areas that imitate habitats like a sunny meadow or shady woodland. Such areas provide special conditions, influencing the range of plants that thrive. They are an ideal solution for exposed sites or those with poor, dry soils. Native plants can also provide food and refuge for local birds, animals, and insects.

TELL ME WHY

WHY GO WILD?

Wildflowers native to your region are a rich source of nectar for bees and butterflies, and food for insect- and seed-eating birds. Attracting wildlife brings its own fascinations and, since many of these creatures prey on garden pests, they can contribute to ecologically friendly forms of pest control.

A WILDFLOWER BORDER ▷
Wildflowers often grow well in poor soils and therefore can be used to give a spectacular display in an area of the garden where more demanding cultivated plants are likely to fail. Also, they should attract a variety of insects.

MAKING THE MOST OF SPACE

Beds and borders constitute one means of shaping and dividing up the garden in visually interesting ways that will provide privacy and enclosure as well as a setting for your favorite plants. The human eye perceives scale differently indoors and out because, in the open, scale is reduced by the comparison with broader horizons. Be bold when deciding on the size of beds and borders. Make them as large as possible, but aim for a balance of open space and planting mass, making the latter of sufficient substance to allow contrasts of form and graduation of height. Make lines clean and strong, to draw the eye into the distance, or form broad, sweeping curves to hide — and invite exploration of — what lies beyond.

◁ ISLAND BEDS
Seen from all sides, an island bed allows planting compositions that vary depending on the standpoint of the observer. This is an excellent way to maximize plant variety in a relatively small space.

△ NO WASTED SPACE
The tiniest space can be made to work hard for its living. This shady corner is enlivened by a range of foliage textures that gives interest through the growing season, forming a verdant backdrop for a seasonal succession of flowers.

△ LINEAR SPACES
Long, narrow borders let you play with perspective. They lead the eye onward and, punctuated with tall, architectural plants, reward the observer with a series of interesting focal points.

CURVING EDGES ▷
A curved line between two points is always longer than a straight one. This is a trick that designers often use to gain more space for planting in small and confined gardens.

SEE ALSO: Principles of Design, pp.126–127; Raised Beds, pp.180–181

BORDER TYPES

BORDERS MAY BE CLASSIFIED according to the plant groups they contain – herbaceous borders and shrub borders, for example. Each has different attributes, but all are designed to provide maximum interest through the year. This is especially true in small gardens, where every plant must work hard to justify inclusion. While favorites always deserve a place, however short their season, the best approach uses plants that give value over prolonged periods: ones that bloom long or often, or flower early, producing fruits later on. Try to exploit foliage to the full; it may offer glorious tints in spring or autumn, as well as forming a textural backdrop for other features.

SHRUB BORDERS

Woody-stemmed shrubs, both deciduous and evergreen, are valued for a wide range of ornamental virtues, and with careful selection their flowers, fruit, foliage, or stems can provide elements of interest in every season of the year. Shrub borders are particularly useful for creating a permanent and fairly low-maintenance framework for the garden.

GOOD IDEAS

• A shrub border can make a peep-proof, sound-muffling, and relatively labor-saving alternative to clipped hedging, with the added advantage of seasonal variety.

• Make use of the permanence of a shrub border. Create a barrier to divide the garden into spaces for different activities, form an intimate and sheltered enclosure, and screen off any unappealing features that may lie beyond the garden's perimeter.

△ **A FLOWER-COVERED BARRIER**
Shrub borders make ideal barriers, especially where formal hedging is out of keeping. Here, roses, hebes, and senecios combine long-lasting flowers with attractive foliage.

MIXED BORDERS

The mixed border is the most versatile of border types, since it exploits the virtues of all the plant groups. Shrubs lend height and structure, and they form an attractive backdrop for other plants. If chosen well, they add color and variety with their foliage, seasonal flowers, and fruit.

Spring bulbs enliven the early months, dying back to make way for summer-blooming perennials, with summer bulbs as highlights. Gaps are filled with annuals and biennials, while late blooms are staged against a backdrop of seedheads, dried flowerheads, and tinted autumn foliage.

▽ **COMBINING PLANT TYPES**
Here, long-blooming Geranium endressii *interacts with the late-summer blues of hydrangeas and towering plumes of giant reed grass* (Arundo donax).

SEE ALSO: Forming a Structure, p.126; Raised Beds, pp.180–181

HERBACEOUS BORDERS

The traditional herbaceous border is one of the highlights of the garden during the summer months, when most perennials are at their peak. Herbaceous perennials die back to a rootstock in winter and produce new growth and flowers each year. This is the main drawback of a perennial border, for dormant plants leave vacant areas of soil during the darkest months, when spirits are most in need of cheer. If the promise of the new season's regrowth and coming profusion does not satisfy you, extend interest with early-flowering spring bulbs, and into autumn with late bloomers and seedheads that lend sculptural beauties of their own.

▽ **PROLONGED PERFORMANCE**
Long-serving alchemillas and astrantias provide a foil for the more transient campanulas; the sword-shaped leaves of crocosmia hint at late summer and autumn glories to come.

USING ANNUALS AND BIENNIALS

Annuals and biennials are, by their very nature, short-term plants: annuals germinate, flower, set seed, and die within a single growing season; biennials produce leafy growth in their first year then flower, set seed, and die in the second.

Used alone, such short-lived but rapidly growing plants can provide instant color in new gardens, in anticipation of more permanent plantings. They are also useful as fillers of spaces left to accommodate the mature spread of longer-lived plants. Since many will self-sow if conditions suit, they can also add pleasingly unexpected associations to permanent designs.

ANNUAL EXPERIMENTS ▷
Short-lived plants are ideal for experiments in color and form. Here, a complementary theme of yellow lonas and blue ageratums proves a success that would bear repeating.

SEASONAL HIGHLIGHTS

For designing borders, the living palette of flowers, fruits, foliage, and stems has enormous potential for creating a year-long succession of ornamental highlights. Every border, however, has low points, so planning for additional features to cover seasonal gaps makes good sense, especially in small spaces where voids are especially noticeable. Bulbous plants offer a simple solution; their showy, highly seasonal flowering supplies vibrant color, while their disappearance during dormancy is rapidly masked by the burgeoning growth of their companion plants.

BULBS FOR SEASONAL INTEREST

WINTER
Snowdrops (*Galanthus*)
Winter aconite
  (*Eranthis hyemalis*)

SPRING
Anemone blanda
Chionodoxas (all)
Crocuses (most)
Daffodils (*Narcissus*)
Erythronium (most)
Fritillaria
Grape hyacinths
  (*Muscari*) (most)
Hyacinths (*Hyacinthus orientale*)
Iris histrioides, reticulata
Puschkinia
Spanish bluebells
  (*Hyacinthoides hispanica*)

Spring snowflake
  (*Leucojum vernum*)
Squills (*Scilla*) (some)
Tulips (most)

SUMMER
Agapanthus
Allium cristophii,
  A. giganteum
Cannas (most)
Galtonia candicans
Gladiolus (most)
Lilies (most)
Montbretia (*Crocosmia*)

AUTUMN
Crocuses (autumn flowering)
Colchicums (most)
Cyclamen hederifolium
Sternbergia lutea

△ **SPRING INTO SUMMER**
The backlit brilliance of 'Texas Gold' tulips illuminates this border in late spring; as they fade, golden-flowered daylilies (Hemerocallis) continue on into summer.

SEE ALSO: Natural-born Fillers, p.127; Raised Beds, pp.180–181

PRINCIPLES OF DESIGN

ORIGINAL, INNOVATIVE IDEAS serve to distinguish some of the best borders as the work of individual designers, but there are basic principles that underly all good design, whatever the scale or site. They are similar to those used by a painter when composing a picture, so that separate elements are united to create a harmonious whole.

Good compositions embrace a balance of mass and space, unity and contrast, with all elements in proportion to each other and in scale with the surroundings. Although decorative qualities are obviously important, designers choose plants primarily for their function – the part they play in forming a layered and cohesive composition.

FORMING A STRUCTURE

The structural elements in a garden may be likened to a skeleton that forms the bones beneath the flesh. In the broadest sense, these include the hard landscaping materials such as walls and paving, which define the garden's layout. Architectural plants, however, may also be used within the beds and borders to help in the creation of the garden's "skeleton."

Woody plants, chosen from a wealth of shrubs and trees, are key elements in building up planting designs. They serve to enclose, to give shelter, and to provide a backdrop for other plants. They constitute a permanent frame for a composition, but at the same time are part of it. While structure plants can be very attractive in their own right, garden designers usually choose them first and foremost for their functional contribution to a design.

TELL ME WHY

WHY TRY TO COPY NATURE?

Look at a woodland fringe and you will see distinct layers of plants. In sun, low grasses lie at the feet of taller perennials, some in dappled shade, which are themselves succeeded by a shrub layer and, finally, a tree canopy. This multilayered composition is not only functional for the plants but also very pleasing to the human eye, which commends its use to the garden designer.

FOCAL POINTS

A focal point acts as a visual "reward" as the eye moves along a planting design. Like a punctuation mark in a sentence, it tells the viewer where to pause, creating a striking contrast to the basic rhythm and flow of a design. Plants used as focal points must have distinctive presence by virtue of sheer size or strength of form. They may be used to terminate a vista, but gain greater value when viewed from more than one angle. One plant may form the focal point of adjacent compositions.

NATURAL LAYERS ▷
This layered planting, with Robinia pseudoacacia *'Frisia' as its golden focus, employs a framework of hollies, pittosporums, and olearias against a dark backdrop of cypress.*

△ **ARCHING ROSES**
Flexible-stemmed roses, like 'Mme Isaac Pereire', can form an enclosure just with arching branches. Other climbers or ramblers will do so more formally, if trained on a pillar, arch, or pergola.

△ **STAR PERFORMER**
The pale, metallic hue and strong, spiky form of Eryngium giganteum *demands full attention as it rises above a contrasting low carpet of dark leaves.*

STRONG LINES ▷
Providing height and distinct, vertical lines, Eremurus robustus *may be used to dramatic effect as a focal plant, especially against a plain, dark background.*

SEE ALSO: Shape and Form, p.128; Borders with Special Conditions, pp.130–131

PLANTING IN DRIFTS

The plants that form the most significant mass in a planting design should also be the most decorative. The designer relies on these, in contrast with the framework plants, to provide both flower and foliage interest throughout the growing season. When planning their arrangement, the aim is to link individual groups with an underlying rhythm that leads the eye on in a smooth visual flow in which nothing appears out of place. Planting in swaths, or drifts, is the technique used to achieve this. There are several methods, each lending a different feel and style, formal or informal, to the finished effect (*see below*).

△ **MASSED BLOCKS OF PLANTING**
For strongly architectural effects, structured masses of planting form a patterned collage providing contrasts in color, texture, and form. Here, white sedums and pink dahlias and mallows highlight a background of detail.

△ **INFORMAL DRIFTS**
Irregular, interlocking drifts, elongated and layered in height are punctuated with more upright groups to provide a more informal effect. Here, a drift of pale pink phloxes contrasts with the upright form of salvias.

△ **RANDOM DRIFTS**
Mimic the randomness seen in nature by setting large plants singly among groups of smaller ones, and allowing them to spread by seed or runner. Here, foxgloves and delphiniums are dotted around smaller pink poppies.

GRADUATING HEIGHTS

Using drifts of plants increasing gradually in height from the front of the border to the back, or along its axis, is traditional, but it is not an unbreakable rule. It gives a layered effect, meaning that no plant is obscured by its neighbors. The occasional use of taller plants of open, "see-through" habit, such as *Crambe*, at the border's edge simply emphasizes the graduated effect.

△ **LEADING THE EYE**
The tiered effect of graduated planting lends an illusion of depth to a border and generates a line that leads the eye smoothly onward and upward. If height increases along the border's length, it enhances perspective and the highest point obscures what lies beyond, thus inviting exploration.

USING GROUNDCOVERS

Most groundcover plants are dense, mat-forming or creeping plants that smother weeds by excluding light and thereby preventing seed germination. Their low-growing habit also makes them ideal plants for the first layer at the front or edge of the border. There, they form a strong horizontal line that provides a good foil for taller vertical plants and more rounded forms. As they grow, their spreading habit enables plants of similar vigor to weave together to form a carpet, which also helps to soften any harsh edges.

LOW-GROWING PLANTS

Alchemilla conjuncta. Lobed, blue-green leaves; sprays of lime green flowers all summer.

Anthemis punctata subsp. *cupiana.* Mat former; feathery, silver-gray leaves; white flowers in early summer.

Anthyllis montana. Silky, divided, gray-green leaves, and pink, red, or purple flowers in early summer.

Geranium renardii. Mounds of velvety, gray-green leaves; white or lavender flowers in early summer.

Heuchera micrantha. Gray-marbled leaves, and sprays of pink-tinted white flowers in early summer.

Nepeta × *faassenii.* Aromatic, silvery gray-green leaves, and spikes of lavender-blue flowers all summer.

Stachys byzantina. Mounds of densely silver-haired, gray-green leaves, and white-woolly spikes of pink-purple flowers throughout summer.

FILLERS AND BLENDERS

Annuals and biennials are perfect short-term gap fillers with the added benefit that they often self-seed to give naturally random effects in following years. If the results are not pleasing, the plants can be removed without great loss. If you choose colors initially to blend within a design, any seedlings will later produce flowers in the same range of complementary hues.

△ **UNEXPECTED EXCITEMENT**
Many annuals and biennials will self-seed with abandon where conditions suit them, but there is no telling where their offspring will arise. Here, poached egg plant (Limnanthes douglasii) sprawls across a path below sweet rocket (Hesperis matronalis).

SEE ALSO: Groundcovers, p.75; Color, Form, and Texture, pp.128–129; Using Groundcovers in Shady Areas, p.131

COLOR, FORM, AND TEXTURE

WHILE STRUCTURAL PLANTINGS and the creation of a layered composition form the bones of a design, it is the varied shapes and textures of the mass of plants that provide its finish and color. The form of plants provides potential for contrasts of line – verticals, horizontals, and dynamic diagonals – and between rounded, spiky, or arching shapes. Line and shape are linking elements, which can tie the whole design together, especially if repeated. Foliage texture may be used to form a verdant backdrop against which the more transient qualities of flowers will be highlighted, and the use of color dictates the mood of a planting perhaps more than any other factor.

VARIETY OR UNITY?

The degree of variety that is desirable in a design varies with the size of the site. Too much gives an impression of clutter and compromises the unity of a design; too little is simply boring. Contrasts are most telling if composed simply. Too many conflicting elements vie for attention – the eye darts restlessly about, unable to find a focus or follow a line.

Unity is the quality that ties a design together. It may be expressed in the use of patterns, shapes, or textures as repetitive motifs. A definite planting theme, perhaps in terms of color or type of plants used, is one of the best ways to create unity.

VARIATIONS ON A THEME ▷
Ornamental grasses provide the unifying theme for this unusual border, but it does not consist of grasses alone. Their architectural forms are both separated and highlighted by plants of contrasting shapes.

SHAPE AND FORM

Designers like to compose layouts so that the shapes and forms of the plants contrast and link together in a balanced and visually pleasing way. A successful composition might juxtapose, for example, two junipers: the vertical *Juniperus scopulorum* 'Skyrocket' with the horizontal form of *J. procumbens*, and join the two with a more rounded form, such as *Spiraea japonica*. Try playing with ideas at the planning stage by sketching shapes and outlines on paper, and rearrange them until satisfied with the overall balance.

STRENGTH IN UNITY ▷
The strong, spiky Yucca gloriosa 'Variegata' *forms a focus and sets the theme, which is echoed, but not overwhelmed, by the dark-needled pine,* P. mugo, *and metallic blue mounds of* Eryngium × oliverianum.

TEXTURAL ELEMENTS

Changes in texture form a subtle but vital element in a composition, especially in terms of foliage. Leaves form the greatest mass in a border and their textural qualities far outlive the more ephemeral delights of flowers. Texture depends on both leaf size and surface finish. Try contrasting the fine texture of small-leaved plants with large leaves of bold, simple outline, or offset matte and silky leaves with light-reflecting, glossy ones.

△ **FINE FRONDS**
Backlit by spring sun, the fronds of a soft shield fern unfurl. Their feathery texture is offset by foliage of simpler shape.

SOFT AND SMOOTH ▷
The downy, quilted feel of the large leaves of some hostas, such as this Hosta sieboldiana, *is a textural feast. Hostas form a good foil for finer-leaved plants.*

SEE ALSO: Perennials, pp.134–135; Grasses, Bamboos, and Ferns, pp.140–141

COLOR THEORY

The primary colors of red, yellow, and blue can be mixed, in pairs, to give the secondary colors of green, violet, and orange. With the exception of green, these intense hues can assault the eye if used in excess but lend brilliant and dramatic contrast in small masses if set against a backdrop of more subtle tones. Tertiary colors are formed by mixing secondaries and they *always* harmonize, since those next to each other on the color wheel share components. Conversely, colors opposite each other on the wheel form complementary contrasts.

TELL ME WHY

THE SUBJECTIVITY OF COLOR

Volumes have been written on color theory and its application in gardens, but color purists often overlook personal taste and the subjectivity of color perception. Some people adore hot, bright, and even clashing colors, while others find the cool restraint of pastels more appealing. The theory of harmonies and complementary contrasts has been used by artists for centuries and it *does* work in practice but, if rules don't give the effects you desire, don't feel bound by them – experiment freely instead.

COLOR IN PRACTICE

Light intensity affects color perception enormously, and it varies with latitude, season, and time of day. Pastels that appear washed out at midday acquire luminosity at twilight; a brilliant mass of magenta, as with bougainvilleas, achieves perfection in the bright subtropics but appears strident in the blue-tinted light of duller climes. Personal taste, tones of hard landscaping, and any views beyond the garden should also be considered in color associations.

Blue, indigo, violet, and their pastel tints provide cool sophistication; they appear to recede, so they can enhance the effects of perspective

Greens hold a design together and are used to separate strong or clashing colors

Colors next to each other on the color wheel form close harmonies, whether they are true hues or muted tints

Hot shades of yellow, orange, and red supply a mood of exuberant warmth and appear to advance, foreshortening perspective

Complementary colors (any pair directly opposite to each other) used together enhance each other's effects if used as contrasts

In general, the more intense the color, the smaller its mass needs to be within the design to give striking, but not overwhelming, effects

THE COLOR WHEEL ▷
Primaries in mixed pairs produce secondary hues; both have an intensity that is best used in small masses. Mixed secondaries produce tertiaries, which reflect the subdued colors of nature and can be used in greater masses.

△ **HARMONY**
An opulent harmony, here cerise and purple, is made from colors that lie near each other on the wheel.

△ **CONTRAST**
Grape hyacinths and tulips contrast primary blue with secondary orange, which are opposites on the wheel.

△ **HARMONIOUS SHADES**
This pastel palette uses mainly harmonizing colors from the same third of the color wheel; monotony is avoided by including stronger hues, such as the purple of salvias and the bright red of beebalm, to provide welcome contrast.

SEASONAL AND SUCCESSIONAL INTEREST

The advancing seasons bring a panoply of changing color and texture. The fresh greens of spring, often tinted with pinks and reds, revert to a darker, more uniform backdrop in summer before firing up in autumnal splendor. Short-lived flowers may give rise to ornamental seedheads or lustrous, often persistent fruit, which in many woody plants will decorate a stark and architectural winter outline. To gain maximum value throughout the seasons, try to choose reliable, long-flowering performers as well as plants that offer more than one season of interest.

△ **MELLOW FRUITS**
Crabapples with their plentiful blooms and fresh green foliage in spring assume renewed brilliance in autumn with foliage tints and fruits.

△ **RIPE SEEDHEADS**
Many poppies produce ornamental seedheads. The blue capsules of Papaver somniferum follow a succession of pink, mauve, or white flowers.

PLANTS FOR ALL SEASONS

Amelanchier laevis. Small tree or shrub with white spring flowers, blue fruits, and fine autumn color.

Cotinus 'Grace'. Purple-leaved shrub with clouds of tiny pink flowers and brilliant red autumn tints.

Honesty (*Lunaria annua*). Annual or biennial with white or purple spring flowers and silver seedpods.

Japanese maple (*Acer palmatum*). Small trees or shrubs renowned for autumn foliage.

Pyracantha. Evergreen shrubs with early summer flowers and persistent autumn fruits.

Rosa rugosa. Emerald green leaves, pink or white flowers in summer, and red hips in autumn.

Teasel (*Dipsacus fullonum*). Biennial with emerald leaves and thistlelike, winter-persistent seedheads.

SEE ALSO: Oriental Poppies, p.135; Shrubs for Foliage Color, p.139

BORDERS WITH SPECIAL CONDITIONS

MOST PLANTS ADAPT well to a range of soil conditions if their needs for sun, shade, and temperature are met. Some gardens, however, are located in sites with special conditions, and these are often considered less than ideal. The optimistic gardener, however, is not deterred, but sees them as an opportunity to grow a different range of plants. In all gardens, the key to success is to select plants to suit the prevailing conditions; if conditions are special, the plants must be, too. Throughout the world there are groups of plants adapted to various tough habitats, such as deserts, mountainous regions, waterlogged areas, and coastal sites — let these make up your planting palette.

DRY, SUNNY BORDERS

In dry, sunny sites, remember to make the soil more moisture-retentive (see p. 133) and to choose plants with an inherent tolerance of drought and heat. Plants native to sun-baked habitats, such as the Mediterranean maquis, or South African veldt, should fit the bill. Many of these have leathery leaves that reduce water loss, or leaves that have white hairs to reflect ultraviolet rays. Some, like tulips, have bulbs to store food and water and retreat below ground in the summer heat.

△ FRENCH LAVENDER
From dry, rocky maquis, this aromatic, gray-leaved perennial (Lavandula stoechas) needs hot, arid conditions to thrive.

PLANTS FOR DRY, SUNNY SITES

TREES AND SHRUBS
Ceanothus thyrsiflorus var. repens
Cistus ladanifer
Helianthemum
Juniperus communis
Lemon verbena (Aloysia triphylla)
Perovskia atriplicifolia
Vitex agnus-castus
Yucca

PERENNIALS
Acaena novae-zealandiae
Agastache mexicana
Anthemis cupiana subsp. punctata

Basket of gold (Aurinia saxatilis)
Dictamnus albus
Eremurus robustus
Erigeron karvinskianus
Ferula communis
Gypsophila repens
Hen and chicks (Sempervivum)
Osteospermum jucundum

HERBS
Lavender (Lavandula)
Oregano (Origanum vulgare)
Rosemary (Rosmarinus officinalis)

◁ HEAT-LOVING PLANTS
Helianthemums, verbascums, and sisyrinchiums are typical plants of hot and dry, stony habitats. Such plants dislike wet soil at their stem base in winter; apply a topdressing of gravel to aid rapid drainage and avoid waterlogging.

SEASIDE AND EXPOSED SITES

Coastal and exposed sites impose harsh conditions, owing mainly to strong winds. Wind can obviously cause mechanical damage to plants, but also scorches leaves; a rapid air flow makes them lose water more quickly than they can replenish it from the roots. In coastal zones, salt-laden winds worsen this effect.

Mountain, scrubland, and maritime native plants are the best choice here, and consider deep-rooting plants of creeping habit, such as *Dryas octopetala*, which are less affected by wind. Plants with leathery leaves, such as *Griselinia littoralis*, are often wind- and salt-resistant. The Latin epithets *montana* (of mountains), and *littoralis* and *maritima* (coastal natives) indicate likely survivors.

PLANTS FOR COASTAL SITES

TREES AND SHRUBS
Blue daisy (Felicia amelloides)
Brachyglottis
Cytisus × praecox
Genista hispanica
Griselinia littoralis
Nerium oleander
Nipponanthemum nipponicum
Pinus contorta, P. densiflora, P. mugo
Pyrus salicifolia 'Pendula'
Rosa rugosa
Sea buckthorn (Hippophae rhamnoides)

PERENNIALS
Anchusa azurea
Antennaria dioica
Arenaria balearica

Geranium sanguineum
Lavatera arborea
Lobularia maritima
Phlomis russeliana
Phormium
Red hot poker (Kniphofia)
Red Valerian (Centranthus ruber)
Sea holly (Eryngium maritimum)
Sea lavender (Limonium latifolium)
Sea kale (Crambe maritima)
Sea thrift (Armeria maritima)

SUCCULENT
Hottentot fig (Carpobrotus edulis)

△ SEA VIEW
Red hot pokers, blue daisies, and Hottentot figs feature among the thriving contributors to this exuberant planting, sited within reach of salt-laden winds that would be harmful to many common garden plants.

SEE ALSO: Beds for Drought-tolerant Plants, pp. 132–133; Preparing the Ground, pp. 142–143

SHADY SITES

Far from being a problem, the presence of some shade in the garden greatly increases the range of plants that can be grown; those native to woods and forests need shade to give their best. Flowers last longer and hold their color better out of the bleaching sun, and foliage stays fresh for longer periods. Slow to warm in spring, a shady site delays growth and provides a little shelter from frost. Shaded soil retains more moisture than that exposed to sun, reducing the need for watering, but this also means that some areas will be permanently damp. In the shade beneath the branches of large trees, however, the soil may be quite dry.

PLANTS FOR MOIST SHADE

TREES AND SHRUBS
Daphne laureola
Gaultheria mucronata
Japonica (*Chaenomeles*)
Mahonia (most)
Skimmia japonica
Witch hazel (*Hamamelis × intermedia, H. mollis*)

BULBS
Iris foetidissima
*Lilium chalcedonicum,
L. henryi, L. martagon*
Snowdrop (*Galanthus*)
Spanish bluebell (*Hyacinthoides non-scripta*)

FERNS (MOST)

PERENNIALS
Alchemilla mollis
Anemone × hybrida
Asarum
Cardamine pratensis
Chelidonium majus
Bleeding heart (*Dicentra*)
Hostas
Primrose (*Primula vulgaris*)
Solomon's seal (*Polygonatum × hybridum*)
Woodrush (*Luzula sylvatica* 'Marginata')

LUSH FOLIAGE ▷
This moist, marginal border in partial shade has been thoughtfully planted with Iris laevigata 'Variegata' at the front with hostas and heracleums behind.

ACIDIC SOIL

If you discover that your soil type is acidic, there are many attractive plants that you can grow. These include camellias, flowering in winter and early spring, rhododendrons, with blooms often succeeded by downy new leaves, such as in *R. yakushimanum*, and azaleas. Heathers offer year-round foliage interest: callunas with late summer or autumn flowers, and ericas with spring blooms. Shrubs noted for their autumn tints, such as fothergillas or witch hazels, color intensely on acidic soil.

PLANTS FOR ACIDIC SOIL

TREES AND SHRUBS
*Arbutus andrachne,
A. menziesii, A. unedo*
Arctostaphylos
Azaleas (*Rhododendron*)
Camellias
Dogwoods (*Cornus*) (some)
Embothrium coccineum
Fothergilla major
Gaultheria
Heathers (*Calluna, Daboecia, Erica*)
Japanese maples (*Acer japonicum, A. palmatum* and cultivars)
Spruce (*Picea*) (most)

Pieris
Rhododendrons
Stewartia pseudocamellia
Vaccinium
Witch hazel (*Hamamelis*)

FERNS (MANY)
Royal fern (*Osmunda regalis*)

PERENNIALS
Corydalis cashmeriana
Gentiana asclepiadea
Moltkia doerfleri
Sanguinaria canadense
Trillium

USING GROUNDCOVERS IN SHADY AREAS

Gardening in shade relies greatly on variations in foliage form and texture, since the majority of shade-lovers flower only in spring or early summer. Groundcover plants, often natural inhabitants of the forest floor, can be used to make a low-level backdrop for the short-lived, seasonal flowers. This not only extends visual interest, but also helps minimize the amount of maintenance required in the area by smothering weeds and reducing moisture loss from the soil surface.

△ **WALDSTEINIA TERNATA**
This creeping, semi-evergreen perennial, covered with flowers from late spring to early summer, is valued for its tolerance of dry shade.

△ **LIRIOPE MUSCARI**
Dense clumps of grasslike evergreen leaves make this drought-tolerant perennial a useful weed excluder. Its autumn flowers look good next to Cyclamen hederifolium.

GROUNDCOVERS FOR SHADE

SHRUBS/CLIMBERS
Cotoneaster horizontalis
Ivy (*Hedera helix*)
Sarcococca

PERENNIALS
Bergenia
Bugle (*Ajuga*)
Brunnera macrophylla
Cyclamen hederifolium
Deadnettles (*Lamium maculatum* cultivars)
Epimedium
Euphorbia amygdaloides var. robbiae
Galax urceolata

Heuchera cylindrica
Hostas (most)
Lily-of-the-valley (*Convallaria majalis*)
London pride (*Saxifraga × urbium*)
Maianthemum bifolium
Pachysandra terminalis
Periwinkle (*Vinca*)
Shortia galacifolia
Sweet woodruff (*Galium odoratum*)
Tiarella wherryi
Tolmeia menziesii
Vancouveria hexandra
Violets (*Viola odorata*)

△ **SPOILED FOR CHOICE**
The royal fern (Osmunda regalis) thrives in neutral to acidic soils. The rhododendron in the background, 'May Day', is spring-flowering, but there are hundreds to choose from that will give flowers from midwinter to late summer.

SEE ALSO: Clearing Weeds and Marking Out Beds, pp.144–145; Buying Good Plants, pp.146–147

BEDS FOR DROUGHT-TOLERANT PLANTS

MANY GARDEN SOILS are quite dry in summer and, if this is combined with hot, sunny weather, plants originating from Mediterranean regions and subtropical climes will flourish. This is why many aromatic herbs, silver-foliaged plants, and succulents can provide the answer for a sunny border. These plants are adapted to conserve moisture, however, so they cannot withstand the cold and wet of a temperate winter; if your garden is sunny and dry in summer, it is well worth producing special conditions so that such drought-tolerant plants can survive the winter. Improving drainage is the key, and this can be achieved in either a raised or gravel bed.

GROWING SUN-LOVING PLANTS

Drought-tolerant plants come from areas where soil moisture is hard to get – for example, semidesert regions, mountain sides, rocky scree, or cliff faces where rainwater drains away very rapidly. They develop long, penetrating root systems both for anchorage and to seek moisture and nutrients. Many are noted for their often white- or silver-haired foliage, and brilliant, gemlike blooms. Planting sun-lovers in gardens reflects the increasing need to conserve water. Many are cold-hardy, but excellent drainage is essential, since the combination of winter cold and wet can be fatal to them.

GOOD IDEAS

• Use field guides – or vacations in the sun – to help you spot plants that grow well in dry, hot places; these, and plants bred or selected from them, usually exhibit a good tolerance of dry conditions.

• Experiment with plants that show typical adaptations for conserving water – hairy, waxy, leathery, fleshy, silver, or narrow leaves and swollen stems or bulbs all give clues to likely tolerance of drought.

SOAKING UP THE SUN ▷
A sunny, gentle slope may easily be adapted to suit sun-loving plants that enjoy good drainage. Most are compact and flower freely – therefore ideal for small gardens.

GRAVEL BEDS

Drought-tolerant plants, including alpines or rock plants, are vulnerable to rots or freeze-thaw damage at their necks (the junction of stem and root) in cold, wet conditions. To avoid this occurring in winter, and killing off your prize plants, the best method is to create a gravel border or bed in your garden. This will provide much better drainage than a normal bed of moisture-retentive soil, and gives the plants a good chance of survival. Choose a gently sloping, open, sunny site, and cover it with loose, variably sized rubble, some inverted sod, light topsoil, and a deep layer of gravel or pebbles. If raised above ground level, the gravel bed will be a form of raised bed (*see pp.180–183*).

CREATING A GRAVEL BED

1 THE BASE LAYER
Remove the top layer of fertile soil and fork over the ground. Add coarse stones, to a depth of 6in (15cm), to form a low mound. This will ensure that drainage is excellent in the base layer.

2 RETAINING LAYER
Cap the stones with a layer of inverted sod, either removed from the area earlier or brought in specially. This will prevent the soil mix from being washed down to the layer of stones at the base.

3 ADDING SOIL
Cover the upturned sod with a layer of light soil mix (see opposite, top), 6–10in (15–25cm) deep. Rake the soil to an even depth, then firm it down by treading gently over the whole area.

4 TOPDRESSING
After firming, water the area to settle the soil, and add more to fill any voids. Prick over the surface with a hand fork. Topdress with 4in (10cm) of gravel or pebbles, and rake level.

SEE ALSO: Laying Gravel, pp.62–63; Plants for Dry, Sunny Sites, p.130; Establishing Plants in the Border, pp.148–149

THE SOIL MIX

If your topsoil is heavy or rich in clay, lighten it by mixing as given below:
- one part topsoil (removed from bed);
- one part compost or leafmold;
- 2 or 3 parts coarse grit or stone chips.

Sharp sand or gravel may also be added.

▽ MODIFYING THE RECIPE
The basic recipe can be altered to suit soil conditions or different plants. Poor soil will need enriching with organic matter in the form of rotted compost or rotted manure, for example. A more moisture-retentive mix would consist of 1 part loamy soil to 1 part leafmold or compost to 2 parts stone chips or coarse grit.

TOPSOIL   SHARP SAND   GRAVEL   COARSE GRIT   COMPOST

BUYING SUITABLE PLANTS

A healthy plant has compact growth and no discoloration or pest damage evident on foliage or flowers (if present). Avoid any with weak, yellowed growth or straggling stems; they may have been kept in poor light or watered poorly. Always check the eventual spread before you plant; vigorous plants can quickly overwhelm others.

Compact growth and clean, well-colored foliage, with no dead or dying leaves

A HEALTHY PLANT ▷
Check that the plant appears vigorous and healthy and the soil mix is weed-free, as for this saxifrage. Roots should almost fill the pot, without congestion.

HOW TO ESTABLISH PLANTS IN A GRAVEL BED

Plants in a gravel bed may need a little more care in the early stages, because the gravel, or pebbles (which have rounded rather than sharp pieces), dries out before the roots can penetrate the moist soil below.

Water regularly until the plants are established. One way of retaining soil moisture is to lay down a sheet of land-scape fabric (geotextile) and top it with gravel. Plant through slits in the fabric.

PLANTING IN GRAVEL OR PEBBLES

1 DIG A PLANTING HOLE
Scrape the gravel or pebbles surface to one side. Dig a planting hole slightly larger than the plant's root ball in the soil mix. Make sure the root ball is evenly moist; water it thoroughly and allow to drain.

2 LOOSEN THE ROOT BALL
Tease out the roots gently and put the plant in the hole with its neck level with the gravel surface. For alpines, shake the potting mix off the roots; they establish better and root more widely in a light soil mix.

3 FIRM IN AND FINISH
Backfill around the roots with more soil mix. Firm the root ball gently in place with your fingertips. Replace the gravel or pebbles, and water thoroughly. Keep well watered until new growth appears.

PLANTS FOR A GRAVEL BED

MAT-FORMING PLANTS	
Alpine pink (*Dianthus alpinus*)	Rock cress (*Arabis*)
Alyssum montanum	*Saxifraga burseriana*
Anacyclus pyrethrum var. *depressus*	*Silene acaulis*
Androsace sarmentosa	OTHERS
Antennaria dioica	*Aethionema*
Ballota pseudodictamnus	*Allium akaka,*
California poppy (*Eschscholzia*)	*A. neapolitanum*
Campanula cochleariifolia	Alpine toadflax (*Linaria alpina*)
Dianthus erinaceus	*Anemone coronaria*
Erinacea anthyllis	*Artemisia stelleriana* 'Boughton Silver'
Gypsophila aretioides	*Cistus creticus, C. × cyprius*
Jovibarba	*Convolvulus cneorum*
Oenothera acaulis	*Erinus alpinus*
Papaver burseri, P. rhaeticum	*Hypericum olympicum*
Petrorhagia saxifraga	*Narcissus cantabricus*
	Parahebe catarractae
	Viola cornuta 'Minor'

CARE AND MAINTENANCE OF A GRAVEL BED

Once established, a gravel bed will be essentially a low-maintenance feature. Gravel and pebbles both make a weed-suppressing mulch, and new weeds may be pulled easily from the loose surface if dealt with as soon as they are seen; they are difficult to extract if they gain a hold in the foliage mats of ornamentals.

Mat-forming or spreading plants will benefit from being lifted and divided (*see p.163*) every few years.

◁ RENEWING GRAVEL
Gravel or pebbles gradually wash away, especially on slopes. Refill bare patches as seen, and check again in midautumn and spring.

KEEPING NEAT ▷
In spring, when the danger of frost has passed, remove any dead or winter-damaged growth. Deadhead regularly throughout the season.

SEE ALSO: Laying Gravel, pp.62–63; Using Mulches to Suppress Weeds, p.145; Maintaining Border Plants, pp.154–155

PERENNIALS

HERBACEOUS, OR NONWOODY, PERENNIALS make up the most diverse of all plant groups. Trees and shrubs are technically perennials too, but the term normally refers to those nonwoody plants that live for two years or more and, once mature, produce topgrowth and flowers annually. Some are evergreen, with potential for winter interest, but most die back in autumn and overwinter beneath the soil. There are perennials to suit each and every garden, whether large or small, sunny or shady, sheltered or exposed, damp or dry. Over the years, plant breeders have developed varieties that extend the color palette and increase flower size and flowering period.

PERENNIALS FOR THE BORDER

Few other plant groups offer the gardener such a range of form and texture, or spectrum of color and fragrance, as the herbaceous perennials. They range in size from the lowest of groundcover plants to architectural giants. Many gardeners are happy to endure their absence during the winter, simply to experience the joy of their reemergence, heralding the return of spring. Others prefer to use them in mixed borders, which has greater potential for extending interest on either side of the perennials' midsummer peak.

While most perennials are valued for their flowers, many also offer value in terms of their foliage. All of the plants recommended here (*see right and below*) are chosen for a long season of interest and ease of cultivation; all they need to thrive is a sunny site and moderately fertile, well-drained soil. Such plants are the stalwarts that form the basic framework of a border. Remember there are uses, too, for plants whose beauty fades quickly, such as Oriental poppies. Their effects can be all the more intense for being brief.

Before you plant, analyze the site in terms of soil, light, moisture, exposure, and climate (*see pp.46–49*). To get the best results from your plants, select them to suit prevailing conditions; the aim is to establish a healthy, thriving population.

OTHER PERENNIALS

Cardoon (*Cynara cardunculus*). An architectural giant with silver gray, deeply cut leaves, and large thistle-like flowerheads from summer to autumn.

Daylilies (*Hemerocallis*). Narrow leaves and trumpet-shaped flowers from mid- to late summer.

Echinacea purpurea. Dusky, purplish red flowers with golden brown, cone-shaped centers, borne from midsummer to autumn.

Helenium. Sunny, golden daisy flowers produced from late summer to autumn.

Lavatera. Funnel-shaped, purple-pink flowers throughout summer.

Sedum spectabile. Gray-green leaves and flat heads of deep pink flowers in late summer and autumn.

Tradescantia. Grasslike leaves, and blue, purple, pink, or white flowers throughout summer.

△ **ACHILLEA 'MOONSHINE'**
Flat heads of pale yellow flowers are borne above divided, gray-green leaves from summer to autumn. At 24in (60cm) tall, ideal for midborder placement.

△ **DIANTHUS 'DORIS'**
Neat mounds of narrow, gray-green leaves, with several flushes of clove-scented blooms in summer. Grow at the border front, especially with roses. They are 12in (30cm) tall.

△ **LEUCANTHEMUM × SUPERBUM 'WIRRAL PRIDE'**
Pure white double daisies on 30in (75cm) stems are borne in mid- to late summer above low mounds of glossy, dark green leaves. Tough and reliable. The flowers are good for cutting for indoor displays.

△ **GERANIUM HIMA-LAYENSE 'GRAVETYE'**
Forming dense mats of foliage, 12in (30cm) tall, this plant bears several flushes of bright blue flowers in summer, and colors well in autumn.

△ **GEUM 'LADY STRATHEDEN'**
Semidouble, rich yellow flowers adorn clumps of divided leaves throughout summer. To 24in (60cm) tall, but with an airy habit that suits the border front.

◁ **LAMB'S EARS** (Stachys byzantina)
A tough, densely silver-haired perennial that, at 18in (45cm) tall, is ideal for the border front. Forms low, spreading masses, which bear white-woolly spikes of pink-purple flowers through summer.

◁ **SCABIOSA 'CLIVE GREAVES'**
Soft lavender blooms, which make good cut flowers, are borne from mid- to late summer above low mounds of gray-green leaves. It is 24in (60cm) in height, but its open habit looks fine at the border front.

◁ **ARTEMISIA LUDOVI-CIANA 'SILVER QUEEN'**
Clumps of jagged, silvery leaves, 30in (75cm) tall, produce few flowers but lend fine textural interest throughout the season and form a spreading foil for neighboring plants of more intense color.

SEE ALSO: Assessing What You Have, pp.46–49; Herbaceous Borders, p.125; Borders with Special Conditions, pp.130–131

△ **ANEMONE × HYBRIDA 'HONORINE JOBERT'**
A star performer, this anemone blooms from late summer into autumn, for two months or more. The pristine white flowers, on 5ft (1.5m) stems, appear luminous at dusk. It prefers to be in sun or light shade.

△ **ACANTHUS SPINOSUS**
Arching mounds of glossy, deeply cut leaves and spires of white and purple flowers in early summer make a lovely architectural specimen, 5ft (1.5m) tall, especially against the purple-leaved backdrop of Cotinus *'Grace'.*

ORIENTAL POPPIES

The many forms of *Papaver orientale* are the early summer mainstay of herbaceous borders. Clumps of divided leaves clothed in bristly hairs catch the light, especially if spotted with dew, and sumptuous flowers, crumpled at first, open to reveal satiny petals and a boss of dark, velvety stamens.

Their only fault is that the leaves die back after flowering to leave a gap in the border, but this is easily remedied; fill in with annuals or disguise with arching stems of plants like *Gypsophila paniculata*, with clouds of tiny white flowers. Grow in deep, fertile, well-drained soil in full sun. Divide in midspring, taking care not to damage the fleshy roots.

OTHER ORIENTAL POPPIES

P. 'Allegro'. Brilliant, glossy, orange-scarlet flowers marked boldly with black at the base.

P. 'Indian Chief'. Large, unmarked flowers of an unusual shade of rich mahogany red.

P. 'May Queen'. Double, orange-red, unmarked flowers with unusual, inrolled (quilled) petals.

P. 'Mrs. Perry'. Pale pink blooms with a black blotch.

P. 'Picotee'. Large white flowers with crinkled petals, which have frilled margins flushed with orange-pink.

P. 'BLACK AND WHITE' ▷
The satin-textured, pure white flowers have a dark crimson-black blotch at the center. This robust poppy, to 36in (90cm) tall, is an excellent choice for a monochromatic, gray- or white-themed border.

◁ **P. 'CEDRIC MORRIS'**
With gray, hairy leaves, and very large, soft pink flowers, this associates well with the rambling rose 'Albertine'. The poppy hides the often bare lower stems of the rose during its flowering time.

P. 'BEAUTY OF LIVERMERE' ▷
Large, glossy flowers, up to 8in (20cm) across, are a fabulously rich shade of crimson-scarlet with a black basal blotch. A vigorous plant that reaches a height of 4ft (1.2m).

HERBACEOUS PEONIES

Herbaceous border peonies are mostly cultivars of *Paeonia lactiflora* and variants of *P. officinalis*. Their saucer-, cup-, or bowl-shaped flowers are single, semidouble, or fully double, often globe-shaped at first. They come in reds and pastel colors and bloom in early summer. Grow in full sun or light shade in deep, fertile soil that is well-drained but organic and moisture-retentive. Propagate by division in early spring or early autumn, cutting the fleshy roots into pieces with a knife. They are long-lived and, contrary to popular belief, mature plants can be moved safely. Keep the root ball intact and keep the plants well watered until reestablished.

OTHER BORDER PEONIES

P. 'Bowl of Beauty'. Anemone-like, carmine-pink flowers with a central boss of creamy petals.

P. 'Festiva Maxima'. Very large, fragrant, double white flowers with frilled petals, the innermost flushed crimson at the base.

P. mlokosewitschii. Blue-green leaves and single, lemon yellow flowers in late spring to early summer.

◁ **P. 'SARAH BERNHARDT'**
A sturdy and reliable peony, about 36in (90cm) tall, with upright stems bearing very large, double flowers of soft rose pink, the inner petals ruffled and tinged with silver at the margins.

△ **P. 'DUCHESSE DE NEMOURS'**
The pristine white flowers, tinted green in bud, are large and fragrant and packed with many central petals that are flushed pale yellow at their base. To 32in (80cm) tall.

△ **P. OFFICINALIS 'RUBRA PLENA'**
In early and midsummer, bowl-shaped, fully double flowers of rich crimson with ruffled, satin-textured petals are borne. Quite compact in growth, to 30in (75cm) tall.

SEE ALSO: Borders with Special Conditions, pp.130–131; Establishing Plants in the Border, pp.148–149

ANNUALS, BIENNIALS, AND BULBOUS PLANTS

ANNUALS AND BIENNIALS are the group of plants that are most valuable for extending interest when used as fillers in a mixed border or for creating masses of color in bedding designs. Many have pretty seedheads that may scatter seed with abandon, resulting in informal and pleasingly unpredictable effects, where conditions suit.

Bulbous plants provide seasonal features that come and go, providing the added dimension of dynamic change in a planting. With careful selection, bulbs will kick-start the flowering season in late winter and early spring, illuminate the border throughout summer, and provide the season's glorious finale in autumn.

ANNUALS AND BIENNIALS

Annuals and biennials are short-term plants, although they may bloom for long periods. Annuals flower, set seed, and die in the space of one year, but the flowering period is prolonged if they are deadheaded regularly or harvested as cut flowers. Biennials make leafy growth in the first year and die after flowering in the second.

There are annuals and biennials to suit most conditions – sunny, moist, or dry – and seed packets give concise cultivation requirements. They can be used in borders devoted to them, which is a good idea for creating almost instant color in new gardens, giving you plenty of time for planning more permanent plantings. They are also invaluable when used as spot color or to prolong seasonal interest in mixed borders of shrubs and perennials.

OTHER ANNUALS & BIENNIALS

Begonia Semperflorens Group. Low-growing, with glossy leaves and a long succession of bright flowers.

Impatiens (*Impatiens*). Glossy foliage and masses of bright flowers all summer, in red, pink, or white.

Godetia (*Clarkia amoena*). Silky, funnel-shaped, fluted flowers in pastel colors all summer.

Larkspur (*Consolida ajacis*). Feathery foliage and spires of blue, pink, purple, or white flowers in summer.

Moluccella laevis. Shell-like green bracts. Summer.

Onopordon acanthium. Tall, architectural, gray-leaved, spiny biennial with purple thistles in summer.

Painted daisy (*Chrysanthemum carinatum*). Masses of daisy flowers zoned in red, yellow, white, or purple.

Papaver somniferum. Grayish leaves, white to purple flowers in summer, and blue-green seedpods.

Silybum marianum. Biennial with white-marbled, dark green leaves; thistlelike flowers in summer.

Sweet peas (*Lathyrus odoratus*). Climber with sweet-scented, brightly colored flowers.

BULBOUS PLANTS

The term bulbous plants includes true bulbs as well as plants with corms, tubers, or rhizomes. Most have highly seasonal blooms and look tired for only a short time, before they become dormant below ground. Allow the foliage to die down naturally, or leave it at least until yellow. Most demand only sun and well-drained soil; those of woodland habitats prefer moister soil and partial shade.

GALTONIA CANDICANS ▷
An elegant, summer-flowering bulb with spires of waxy white flowers in summer, and blue-green leaves. At 4ft (1.2m) tall, it is best placed in the middle of the border.

△ **COSMOS BIPINNATUS 'SEA SHELLS'**
This cosmos has quilled petals and a color range from white through pink to carmine-red, rising above feathery green leaves. At 36in (90cm) tall, this annual makes a colorful filler in mixed or herbaceous borders.

◁ **ALLIUM GIGANTEUM**
This ornamental onion reaches 5ft (1.5m) or more when flowering in summer, and it makes an excellent addition to a sunny border. It associates nicely with roses and is offset well by gray foliage.

△ **VERBASCUM OLYMPICUM**
White-woolly leaves and candelabra flower spikes all summer make this biennial useful as a focal point, growing to 6ft (2m) tall. It thrives in sun and tolerates poor, dry soils.

△ **DIGITALIS PURPUREA 'SUTTON'S APRICOT'**
Apricot flowers associate very well with many types of rose and all flowers of deep blue. This biennial reaches 5ft (1.5m) or more and prefers to grow in sun or light shade.

◁ **SUNFLOWER**
(Helianthus annuus)
All sunflowers are valued for their bright, sunny flowers; they range from rapidly growing giants, 15ft (5m) tall, to short ones at 24in (60cm). They make excellent cut flowers.

△ **CROCOSMIA 'LUCIFER'**
This extrovert, to 4ft (1.2m) tall, is valued for the brilliance of its flowers during mid- to late summer. The pleated, bright green leaves provide a strong vertical presence throughout the season, in sun or light shade.

SEE ALSO: Using Annuals and Biennials, p.125

DAFFODILS

With thousands to choose from, there are daffodils (*Narcissus*) to suit any border, and they can also be naturalized in grass. Careful selection will provide color from late winter to late spring. Plant bulbs at three to five times their own depth in autumn, in sun or partial shade, in moist, fertile, well-drained soil. Deadhead faded flowers, but after flowering leave the foliage in place for at least six weeks.

OTHER DAFFODILS

N. 'Cheerfulness'. Very fragrant, double, rounded white flowers in midspring. 16in (40cm) tall.

N. 'Hawera'. Diminutive, with slender, small-cupped, golden yellow flowers. 7in (18cm) tall.

N. × *odorus*. Strongly scented, golden, trumpet-shaped flowers in early spring. 10in (25cm) tall.

N. poeticus. Scented white flowers with tiny, yellow, red-rimmed cups in late spring. 20in (50cm) tall.

△ *N.* 'ACTAEA'
A late-spring delicacy with scented flowers that fill the air around them with fragrance. Pure white petals surround a flattened, yellow cup rimmed with red. 18in (45cm) tall.

N. 'ARKLE' ▷
A vigorous daffodil with very large golden trumpets in midspring. It is equally at home in borders or naturalized in grass, and it reaches 16in (40cm) in height.

TULIPS

Lending unrivaled brilliance to the spring border, there are several different groups of tulips that can provide color from late winter to late spring, either as annual bedding or as groups in borders. Grow in fertile, well-drained soil in sun with shelter from strong winds. Plant bulbs, 4–6in (10–15cm) deep, in late summer or autumn. Lift the bulbs as the foliage fades and ripen in a cool, dry place, or discard.

OTHER TULIPS

T. 'Artist'. Salmon-pink flowers, flushed green and purple, in late spring. 18in (45cm) tall.

T. 'Estella Rijnveld'. Fringed, white-flamed, red flowers in late spring. 22in (55cm) tall.

T. 'Plaisir'. Carmine-red and sulfur yellow flowers in early spring. 6in (15cm) tall.

T. 'White Triumphator'. Elegant tulip with pure white flowers in late spring. 18–24in (45–60cm) tall.

△ *T.* 'QUEEN OF NIGHT'
A robust tulip with velvety, deep maroon flowers. One of the deepest colored of all, it flowers very late in spring and is perfect among gray-leaved plants.

T. 'PEACH BLOSSOM' ▷
The double flowers are rich rose-pink, often flushed green at the base at first. This tulip blooms in late spring and associates well with blue forget-me-nots.

LILIES

Lilies (*Lilium*) are usually tall-growing and bear showy, often fragrant summer flowers, occasionally into autumn. The flowers are bowl-, trumpet-, funnel-shaped, or "turkscap" (where the petals curve back over themselves). Grow in well-drained soil enriched with organic matter; most prefer acidic to neutral soils and a sunny position. Plant bulbs in early autumn to a depth of two or three times their size on a bed of coarse sand to ensure good drainage.

OTHER LILIES

L. canadense. Nodding, trumpet-shaped yellow flowers in mid- to late summer. 5¼ft (1.6m) tall.

L. 'Fire King'. Bright orange-red flowers in midsummer. 4ft (1.2m) tall. Good in pots.

Madonna lily (*L. candidum*). Fragrant white trumpets. 6ft (1.8m) tall. Needs neutral to alkaline soil.

L. 'Sterling Star'. Upturned white, brown-speckled flowers in summer. 4ft (1.2m) tall.

△ *L. MARTAGON*
A woodland lily that bears turkscap flowers on stems to 6ft (2m) tall in early and midsummer. It is so versatile that it thrives in almost any well-drained soil in sun or partial shade.

L. REGALE ▷
Midsummer elegance and fragrance make the regal lily invaluable. It flowers best in sun but tolerates light shade. In favorable conditions it reaches 6ft (2m) in height.

IRISES

Most irises bloom for relatively short periods between spring and early summer, but their bold fans or clumps of foliage, variegated in some instances, last through the season. There are several different types. The bearded irises (the most familiar of irises) and bulbous irises need fertile, well-drained soil in full sun. The Siberian irises, more slender and delicate in appearance, prefer slightly moister soil and tolerate sun or light shade.

OTHER IRISES

There is a vast range of irises from which to choose, with many varieties introduced into commerce every year. Bearded irises grow from a few inches (centimeters) tall to giants that may exceed 4ft (1.2 m) in height. Beardless irises, for example the Siberians for moist soil and the spurias for drier soil and warmer climates, often have more delicate, "wilder-looking" flowers than the beardeds. Irises occur in a rainbow of colors.

△ *I. PALLIDA* 'VARIEGATA'
A bearded iris bearing blue-mauve flowers in early summer and creamy yellow, striped leaves through the growing season. It reaches 3ft (1m) tall.

I. 'ARNOLD SUNRISE' ▷
A beardless iris that, at 10in (25cm) tall, is ideal for front-border placement. The white petals have a crystalline texture, the lower ones blotched with pale yellow-orange.

SEE ALSO: Establishing Plants in the Border, pp.148–149; More Tulips, p.330; More Irises, p.336

SHRUBS AND ROSES

DECIDUOUS AND EVERGREEN SHRUBS are essential elements in providing a permanent framework for the garden, whatever its size or style. They range from low-growing groundcover plants to tall, almost treelike plants, although most are considerably smaller in stature. The choice available is huge, and, since they occur in all manner of situations throughout the world, there are shrubs to suit all exposures and soil types. They can offer architectural forms, often fragrant flowers, decorative fruits, and a great diversity of foliage in terms of size, shape, and color. Their woody stems, frequently with textures and tints of their own, also make a contribution.

SHRUBS FOR THE BORDER

By definition, shrubs are woody-stemmed plants that usually branch freely from the base, with many stems arising at or near ground level. Although distinguished by this feature from trees, which more often grow with a single stem, there is a degree of overlap between the two groups.

The shrubs described here are all easily grown, widely available, and most have an extended, or more than one, period of interest. These are vital aspects to consider as you begin to plant your garden. As your interest and experience grows, you will discover many more that fit the bill, but never discount the common ones – many shrubs are popular *because* they are robust and reliable. It is the associations that you can create with them that will lend your own individual and creative style.

Before buying, always research a plant's individual needs and take account of its size at maturity. Allow adequate space to develop its natural form, filling gaps in the meantime with temporary plantings.

OTHER SHRUBS

Burning bush (*Euonymus alatus*). Shrub with tiny flowers, red-purple fruits that split to reveal orange seed coats, and crimson autumn leaves.

Chaenomeles speciosa 'Moerloosii'. Vigorous, spiny shrub, with dark, glossy leaves, white, pink-flushed spring flowers, and yellow-green autumn fruits.

Cornus alba 'Sibirica'. Vigorous shrub with white flowers in late spring, red-orange autumn color; cut back every spring for bright red winter stems.

Exochorda macrantha 'The Bride'. Graceful, with white flowers in late spring and yellow autumn color.

Hibiscus syriacus 'Red Heart'. Upright shrub, with red-centered white flowers from summer to autumn.

Leycesteria formosa. Upright, suckering shrub, bearing white flowers and red-purple fruits in late summer.

Pyracantha 'Mohave'. Spiny evergreen with glossy, dark green leaves, white flowers in spring, and a mass of winter-persistent, bright orange berries.

Red chokeberry (*Aronia arbutifolia*). Small shrub with white spring flowers, red berries, and autumn tints.

KOLKWITZIA AMABILIS 'PINK CLOUD' ▷
Graceful, medium-sized shrub with arching branches smothered in early summer with yellow-throated, soft pink flowers. Lovely with Geranium macrorrhizum grown as groundcover beneath.

VIBURNUM OPULUS 'XANTHOCARPUM' ▷
Large, bushy deciduous shrub with creamy white, lacecap flowers in late spring and early summer, followed by persistent, glossy yellow fruits. The maplelike leaves blaze red in autumn.

△ **RIBES SANGUINEUM 'PULBOROUGH SCARLET'**
Vigorous, medium-sized deciduous flowering currant with dark red flowers in spring, blue-black fruit, and autumn tints of yellow and red.

△ **BUDDLEJA DAVIDII 'WHITE PROFUSION'**
Medium-sized deciduous shrub with very long sprays of tiny, yellow-eyed white flowers from summer to autumn. The fragrant flowers are attractive to bees and butterflies.

△ **FORSYTHIA × INTERMEDIA 'LYNWOOD'**
Medium-sized deciduous shrub bearing many rich yellow flowers in spring. Try underplanting it with sky blue grape hyacinths (Muscari).

△ **SYRINGA MEYERI 'PALIBIN'**
Neat, slow-growing lilac that is ideal for small gardens. It produces dense clusters of tiny, delightfully fragrant, lavender-pink flowers in late spring and early summer.

△ **PHILADELPHUS 'BOULE D'ARGENT'**
Compact, deciduous shrub that bears scented, creamy white flowers in early or midsummer. The color and fragrance make this, and other mock oranges, an ideal companion for roses.

△ **WEIGELA 'EVA RATHKE'**
Neat deciduous shrub of upright habit, reliably producing crimson flowers over long periods in late spring and early summer. Use it as a support for later-flowering clematis.

SEE ALSO: Plants for Acidic Soil, p.131; Buying Good Plants, pp.146–147; Maintaining Shrubs, pp.156–157; Pruning Established Shrubs, pp.158–159

SHRUBS FOR FOLIAGE COLOR

Colored foliage, beautiful in its own right, adds interest to a backdrop of framework planting. The color of gray or purple leaves often lasts a whole season. Many golden-leaved plants turn green by midsummer, so use companion plants to pick up the interest and carry it on.

◁ *BERBERIS THUNBERGII* '*ROSE GLOW*'
Red-purple, white-speckled leaves form a fine backdrop for gray or bright green foliage, and this spiny, medium-sized deciduous shrub makes an ideal host for Clematis 'Alba Luxurians'.

AMELANCHIER LAMARCKII ▷
This upright shrub has bronze leaves that turn dark green, then orange and red in autumn. It also has white spring flowers, followed by purple-black fruit.

◁ SOUTHERNWOOD
(Artemisia abrotanum)
This small, aromatic, semi-evergreen shrub with finely divided, gray-green leaves makes an eye-catching foil for flowers of intense color such as blue, crimson, and purple, and it associates well with old-fashioned roses.

OTHER FOLIAGE SHRUBS

Choisya ternata 'Sundance'. Medium-sized and evergreen, with bright yellow young foliage.

Cornus alba 'Aurea'. Medium-sized and deciduous, with persistently yellow foliage and red winter stems.

Cotinus coggygria 'Royal Purple'. Medium-sized, with deep purple leaves that turn red in autumn.

Elaeagnus × ebbingei 'Gilt Edge'. Evergreen and medium-sized, with yellow-margined, dark green leaves.

Pittosporum tenuifolium 'Tom Thumb'. Small evergreen, with glossy, bronze-purple, wavy-margined leaves.

Santolina chamaecyparissus 'Lemon Queen'. Compact evergreen, with finely divided gray leaves, and a profusion of soft lemon yellow flowers in summer.

Weigela florida 'Foliis Purpureis'. Compact and deciduous, with purple-flushed, bronze-green leaves, and funnel-shaped pink flowers in early summer.

ROSES

No other single group of plants offers such a profusion of flowers with such exquisite scents and colors. In many roses, flowering lasts right through summer until the first frosts. Roses vary from low groundcover plants to tall, arching shrubs and rampant scramblers. Use them in a border devoted to roses or exploit their versatility to the full in a mixed border. Ingredients for successful flowering are a sunny site, fertile, moist but well-drained soil, and appropriate pruning (*see p.161*). Add fertilizer in early spring and after the first flush of bloom. If possible, choose disease-resistant cultivars, and deal with pests and diseases as soon as they are seen.

△ *R.* '*HAMPSHIRE*'
A groundcover rose that, at 12in (30cm) high by 30in (75cm) across, is ideal for path or border edging, or for decorating a patio in pots. It bears masses of flat, single scarlet flowers from summer to autumn.

◁ *R.* '*WHITE PET*'
Polyantha rose with sprays of pompomlike white flowers that open from red buds from summer to autumn. A pretty border rose, or suitable for pots on the patio. 24in (60cm) tall and as much across.

R. '*QUEEN MOTHER*' ▷
A miniflora, 16in (40cm) tall, 24in (60cm) across, producing clusters of semi-double, clear soft pink flowers from summer to autumn. Very pretty with the deep purple flowers of Lavandula 'Hidcote'.

OTHER ROSES

R. 'Cornelia'. Arching shrub, with soft, coppery pink, rosette-form flowers throughout summer.

R. 'Graham Thomas'. Vigorous shrub, with fragrant, clear yellow flowers throughout summer.

R. 'Kent'. Low, groundcover shrub, with semi-double, creamy white flowers from summer to autumn.

R. moyesii. Tall, upright shrub, with waxy red flowers in early summer and flask-shaped, scarlet hips.

R. 'Rosy Cushion'. Spreading shrub, with scented, single, pale pink flowers from summer to autumn.

R. rugosa. Prickly shrub, with bright pink flowers all summer and red hips in late summer and autumn.

R. 'Swany'. Low, groundcover shrub, with double, creamy white flowers all summer.

R. 'White Wings'. Hybrid tea, with single white flowers with red stamens all summer.

△ *R.* '*BLESSINGS*'
Vigorous hybrid tea rose with dark green leaves and fully double, fragrant, salmon pink flowers from summer to autumn. It grows to 3ft (1m) tall and spreads to 30in (75cm) across.

△ *R.* '*JACQUELINE DU PRÉ*' ('*HARWANNA*')
Modern shrub rose with arching stems wreathed in musk-scented, ivory-white blooms with red stamens from early summer to autumn. 5ft (1.5m) tall by 4ft (1.2m) across.

△ *R.* '*MME ISAAC PEREIRE*'
Flexible-stemmed Bourbon rose with fragrant blooms in several flushes from summer to autumn. At 6ft (2m) tall, by as much across, it can also be trained as a climber.

△ *R.* '*AMBER QUEEN*'
Floribunda rose with shiny, dark green leaves and fragrant flowers from summer to autumn. It associates well with blue larkspur or Belladonna delphiniums. 20in (50cm) tall, 24in (60cm) across.

SEE ALSO: Establishing Shrubs and Roses, pp.150–151; Maintaining Roses, pp.160–161; More Roses, pp.334, 337, 339, 348, 362

GRASSES, BAMBOOS, AND FERNS

GRASSES, BAMBOOS, AND FERNS can bring an unrivaled sophistication to a planting design, for this group relies heavily on form and texture rather than on floral brilliance. The uninitiated often consider their color range limited, but this is not so — they offer a rich palette of greens, including tints of emerald and lime, as well as blue and gray, silver and gold. The flowerheads of grasses provide delicate textures, the whole plant often lending an extraordinary element of rippling movement in the slightest of breezes. Ferns offer no flowers at all, but their statuesque fronds provide eye-catching texture in shady areas of the garden where flowers may fail.

GRASSES

Grasses, including bamboos, are deciduous or evergreen perennials characterized by their narrow, usually linear leaves that come in a surprisingly wide range of colors, sometimes striped or variegated. Some are valued for their stately habit and delicate flowerheads that shimmer gracefully in the breeze. Use them as specimens, or in mixed borders, in gravel, or create dedicated grassy borders. Others, such as *Elymus* and *Festuca*, are low-growing and make good groundcovers.

Most thrive in full sun, in moist but well-drained soil that is not too fertile. They are best planted in spring. Once established, they need little maintenance other than cutting back to ground level in midautumn to early winter. Those with attractive winter seedheads or those that color well in autumn are lovely when rimed with frost or set off by snow; cut these and marginally hardy grasses back in spring as growth begins.

△ *ELYMUS MAGELLANICUS*
This low, mound-forming grass is 6in (15cm) tall with intensely blue leaves. It bears almost prostrate flower spikes throughout summer. Use it at the front of a mixed border, especially one based on a theme of gray leaves.

△ *CORTADERIA SELLOANA*
'SUNNINGDALE SILVER'
This pampas grass forms a majestic clump, 10ft (3m) or more tall, with silver plumes in late summer. The leaves are very sharp, so wear gloves when handling this plant.

OTHER GRASSES

Alopecurus pratensis 'Aureovariegatus'. Perennial foxtail grass with narrow, yellow and green-striped leaves. To 4ft (1.2m) tall.

Feathertop (*Pennisetum villosum*). Tufted annual or perennial, with green leaves, and plumelike flowerheads that are purplish when mature. 24in (60cm).

Festuca glauca 'Blaufuchs'. Evergreen perennial, with very narrow, bright blue leaves, and violet-flushed flowerheads in summer. 12in (30cm) tall.

Holcus mollis 'Albovariegatus'. Mat-forming and soft-textured, with flat, blue-green leaves with creamy white margins. 12in (30cm) tall.

Job's tears (*Coix lachryma-jobi*). Annual, to 36in (90cm) tall, with bright green leaves, and arching flowerheads bedecked with pearly gray seeds in autumn.

Stipa tenuissima. Upright and deciduous perennial feather grass, with threadlike, bright green leaves, and feathery, buff-colored flowerheads. To 24in (60cm) tall.

△ *HAKENOCHLOA MACRA* 'AUREOLA'
The bright yellow leaves of this deciduous clump-former are striped dark green and take on russet hues in autumn that persist into winter. It reaches 14in (35cm) in height.

△ *STIPA CALAMAGROSTIS*
A feather grass with clumps of arching, blue-green leaves, decorated in summer with clouds of purple-tinted, silver-buff flowerheads. Although 3ft (1m) tall, the open, airy habit is well suited toward the front of a border.

△ *ZEBRA GRASS*
(Miscanthus sinensis 'Zebrinus')
The fountainlike clump of broadly arching leaves with bands of creamy yellow looks good in mixed borders or by water. It reaches 4ft (1.2m) in height.

SEE ALSO: Establishing Plants in the Border, pp.148–149

SEDGES AND RUSHES

A large group of grasslike, usually evergreen perennials valued for their foliage – often a firmer, more leathery texture than true grasses – and for their flowerheads. They tolerate a range of conditions, but the majority thrive in damp or wet soils, in sun or shade. They provide strong verticals and dynamic diagonals within a planting design.

OTHER SEDGES AND RUSHES

Bowles' golden sedge (*Carex elata* 'Aurea'). Deciduous sedge with arching, bright golden yellow leaves finely margined with green.

Carex conica 'Snowline'. Low, tufted, evergreen sedge with dark green, white-margined leaves.

Luzula sylvatica 'Aurea'. Evergreen, tussock-forming woodrush with leaves that are yellow-green in summer and bright, golden yellow in winter.

BAMBOOS

Plants in this group form elegant screens or clumps in dappled shade, often rustling in the breeze. They thrive in damp soil rich in organic matter, with shelter from strong or drying winds. Some spread rapidly by rhizomes, even more so in warmer climates, but they can be planted in bottomless barrels to restrict their spread. Check before you buy.

OTHER BAMBOOS

Black bamboo (*Phyllostachys nigra*). Clump-forming, 10–15ft (3–5m) tall, with slender green canes that turn lustrous black in their second or third year.

Chusquea culeou. Elegant, to 20ft (6m) tall, with arching, glossy, yellow-green canes bearing clusters of narrow green leaves at each cane joint.

Pleioblastus variegatus. Compact, 30in (75cm) tall. Pale green canes and dark green, cream-striped leaves.

FERNS

If you have a damp, shady, and sheltered corner, you have the ideal conditions for most ferns — shade plants *par excellence*. Gain maximum textural contrast by associating them with bold-leaved shade lovers, like hostas. If the soil is rich in organic matter and reliably moist, most will tolerate a little sun early or late in the day, but not when it is at its hottest.

OTHER FERNS

Athyrium niponicum var. *pictum*. Creeping Japanese painted fern with silver-gray fronds flushed purple-red, and red-purple stalks. 12in (30cm) tall.

Ostrich fern (*Matteuccia struthiopteris*). Forms "shuttlecocks" of lance-shaped green fronds. 3ft (1m) tall.

Sensitive fern (*Onoclea sensibilis*). Creeping fern with almost triangular, pale green fronds, flushed pink in spring. 18in (45cm) tall.

△ **CAREX OSHIMENSIS** '**EVERGOLD**'
Low evergreen clumps of dark green leaves with a broad central band of gold. Brown flower spikes are borne in spring. It prefers any moist but well-drained soil, and it is suited to the front of a mixed border. 12in (30cm) tall.

△ **PLEIOBLASTUS AURICOMUS**
A textural feast of subtle color, the canes of this upright bamboo are purple-green, and the leaves are striped bright yellow and green. It is about 5ft (1.5m) tall and wide.

△ **PHYLLOSTACHYS BAMBUSOIDES** '**ALLGOLD**'
A spreading bamboo with golden yellow, sometimes green-striped canes; the leaves, usually green, may repeat the theme. It is 10ft (3m) or more tall.

△ **POLYSTICHUM SETIFERUM** **DIVISILOBUM** **GROUP**
An evergreen fern with arching, lance-shaped fronds that are very finely divided into narrow, leathery, mid- to dark green segments. It reaches 28in (70cm) tall and as much across and is invaluable for areas of light or deep shade.

△ **SNOWY WOODRUSH**
(Luzula nivea)
This rush flowers best in a sunny site in damp soil, although it will tolerate dappled shade. The early summer flowers are good for cutting. It forms loose clumps, 24in (60cm) tall.

△ **DROOPING SEDGE**
(Carex pendula)
A large, clump-forming sedge to 5ft (1.5m) tall that thrives in wet or moist soil in sun or partial shade. Catkinlike flowerheads appear in early summer and persist into winter.

△ **SASA VEITCHII**
Slender bamboo that is a suitable groundcover, with purple canes and rich green leaves margined with white. It needs good wind shelter to prevent scorched leaf margins. 4ft (1.2m) tall with a spreading habit.

△ **SHIBATAEA KUMASASA**
A compact evergreen bamboo with fresh green, elegantly tapered leaves. At 3ft (1m) tall, and spreading slowly to 30in (75cm) across, it can be clipped to shape.

△ **ASPLENIUM SCOLOPENDRIUM** **CRISPUM** **GROUP**
Smooth, leathery fronds, about 20in (50cm) long, have crisped, undulating margins; it contrasts well with more feathery ferns in a damp, shady border.

△ **ROYAL FERN**
(Osmunda regalis)
Deciduous fern that has bright green fronds and, in summer, brown tassels appear, which hold the spores. It tolerates sun if the soil remains moist. To 6ft (2m) tall.

SEE ALSO: Shady Sites, p.131; Establishing Plants in the Border, pp.148–149; More Ferns, p.320

PREPARING THE GROUND

THE SUCCESS OF ANY worthwhile activity depends on good preparation. In gardening the first and most important task is to understand the soil in your garden and to learn how to prepare and care for it. The soil is a living eco-system that provides plants with anchorage, air, water, and nutrients. Care taken to keep it healthy, fertile, and friable, replenishing the nutrients taken out by the plants, will be clearly reflected in the continuing health and productivity of plants that grow in it. Few gardens are naturally blessed with the perfect fertile, moist but well-drained loam, but most soils can be satisfactorily improved – some just take more work than others.

IMPROVING SOIL TYPES

All soils are improved by the addition of organic matter; this is broken down by soil organisms to provide nutrients and humus, which not only improves drainage, but also improves soil fertility and water retention. The ideal soil, known as loam, is a balanced mix of clay, silt, and sand particles.
■ Clay soils are heavy, sticky when wet, hard when dry, poorly aerated, and heavy to work. They are slow to drain and to warm in spring but are very highly fertile.
■ Silty soils are moisture-retentive and fairly fertile but can be easily compacted, becoming heavy, cold, and poorly drained.
■ Sandy soils are dry, light to work, and quick to warm in spring but drain rapidly, so nutrients are quickly washed out.
■ Alkaline soils generally drain freely and are often shallow and lack organic matter. They lose nutrients and water rapidly.
■ Peat soils occur where wet conditions prevent the breakdown of organic matter. Prone to waterlogging, they make a good growing medium if drained. You can reduce acidity by liming and remedy nutrient deficiencies with fertilizers.

This upper layer of topsoil includes organic matter and is fertile, unlike the poor subsoil beneath; never mix subsoil with topsoil

△ THE ANATOMY OF THE SOIL
Most soils are formed by weathering of rock, and they form distinct layers. Topsoil, from which roots extract nutrients and water, is made fertile by the presence of soil organisms and organic residues. The poorer subsoil layer lies below it.

FORKING THE SOIL

In well-established gardens, forking over is often all that is needed. Forks are good for rough digging, turning the soil, and for clearing deep-rooting weeds for new plantings, particularly in established beds. Ideal for relieving surface compaction, forks do less harm to soil structure than spades; they break clods up along natural fracture lines rather than slicing them.

HOW TO FORK OVER

1 BREAKING UP THE SOIL
At a time when the soil is moist, but not waterlogged, work methodically over the area, inserting the fork and then turning it over (see inset) to break up the compacted soil into a crumbly structure.

2 ADDING ORGANIC MATTER
After breaking up the surface, you can improve the structure and fertility of the soil by incorporating into it with the fork some organic matter, such as well-rotted compost, rotted manure, or spent mushroom compost.

CULTIVATING SOIL

The aim is to introduce plenty of organic matter, such as rotted compost, manure, or spent mushroom compost, to produce a crumbly structure that will allow air, water, and dissolved nutrients to reach the plant roots. The best time for digging is autumn, since winter cold helps break up clods; but, for light, sandy soils, spread organic matter over the bare soil in winter and fork over in spring. Never dig or walk on soil when it is very wet or frozen; this compacts it and damages its structure.

ALWAYS REMEMBER

TAKE IT EASY!

Digging can either be a back-breaking chore or, if you use common sense, healthy exercise. Use a spade or fork that is the correct size for you, and wear sturdy shoes. Take spadefuls of a size that you can lift comfortably. Take your time – if you have large areas to dig, plan ahead. Adopt a methodical approach and find your rhythm. Warm up gradually and use thigh muscles, not your lower back, to take the strain.

SEE ALSO: Nourishing your Crops, pp.238–239

SIMPLE DIGGING

This involves lifting a spadeful of soil, inverting it, and dropping it back in its original position, where clods are chopped up with the spade blade. It is useful for clearing the soil of debris and non-persistent weeds or for incorporating small amounts of fertilizer and organic matter or sharp sand. It is a good option when working in established borders or irregularly shaped beds.

ONE "SPIT" DEEP ▷
The instruction to cultivate the soil "one spit deep" refers to digging to the depth of the spade blade.

A "spit" is the depth of a spade blade, about 10in (25cm) long.

SIMPLE DIGGING TECHNIQUE

1 INSERTING THE SPADE
Drive the spade blade vertically into the ground to its full depth. Wearing sturdy shoes, exert pressure on the top of the blade with the ball or heel of the foot. Do not use the arch of the foot, since this will cause tension, which soon results in discomfort.

2 LIFTING THE SOIL
Pull back on the handle and lever soil onto the blade. Bend knees and elbows to lift the spade. Try to minimize bending at the waist since this strains the lower back. Do not try to lift too much soil at once, especially where the soil is heavy.

3 TURNING THE SOIL
Twist the blade to turn the soil over. This allows air and water to penetrate and is beneficial for soil organisms. Work methodically (along an imaginary line) to ensure that all soil is turned over. If sowing seeds, rake over to produce a fine tilth.

SINGLE DIGGING

Single digging is a methodical and labor-efficient approach that ensures that all of the soil is turned over to a uniform standard and depth. The technique can be adapted so that organic matter is forked in to the bottom of each trench, improving both quality and depth of topsoil.

HOW IT WORKS ▷
The bed is marked out into a series of trenches. The soil from the first trench is dug out and placed on one side, and then the soil from each subsequent trench is moved into the empty one. The last trench is filled with the set-aside soil.

The soil from the first trench is set aside and then used to fill the last trench

Work backward, so that you do not stand on, and so compact, soil that has been dug

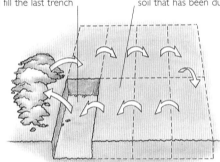

HOW TO SINGLE DIG

1 THE FIRST TRENCH
Dig out the first trench, 12in (30cm) wide and one spit deep. Lift soil onto the ground in front and keep it in reserve. If you need to incorporate organic matter, place it on the trench base and fork it in lightly.

2 SECOND AND SUBSEQUENT TRENCHES
Work backward, digging out soil from the second trench and turning it into the one in front. Invert it to bury annual weeds and weed seeds. Repeat for all subsequent trenches. Put the reserved soil into the last trench.

THE NO-DIG TECHNIQUE

Digging increases the breakdown of organic matter, reducing fertility unless replenished, and brings weed seeds to the surface, stimulating their germination. The no-dig technique relies on earthworms and microorganisms to aerate the soil and uses an organic mulch on the surface to preserve soil structure, conserve water and nutrients, and suppress weeds. It works best following one thorough, deep digging, when all perennial weeds must be removed. Before sowing, remove the mulch and hoe or rake the surface.

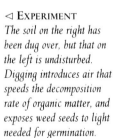

◁ EXPERIMENT
The soil on the right has been dug over, but that on the left is undisturbed. Digging introduces air that speeds the decomposition rate of organic matter, and exposes weed seeds to light needed for germination.

RESULT ▷
The uncultivated soil on the left shows little weed growth, but many more have germinated on the dug soil on the right. The no-dig method can reduce the amount of preparation needed for seed beds.

SEE ALSO: The Deep Bed Method, p.237; Dealing with Weeds, pp.290–291

CLEARING WEEDS AND MARKING OUT BEDS

THE NEXT STEP IN CREATING your new bed or border is to clear out all weeds and mark out the shape. Weeds are vigorous, opportunistic plants that will compete with ornamentals for light, air, and nutrients. Many are also alternative hosts to a range of pests and diseases that infest ornamental plants. Borders should be completely cleared of weeds, especially deep-rooting and perennial ones, before planting, so that new plants have the best possible chance of establishment. New borders look much better if accurately rather than roughly marked out, and extra care needs to be taken with ground clearance if creating beds in a lawn or neglected area.

CLEARING WEEDS ORGANICALLY

Nonchemical weeding methods remove weeds physically from the soil, and are ideal for organic gardeners. Hoes, hand forks, border forks, and digging forks are the main tools used. In most cases, the whole weed is removed, and this method causes little disturbance to existing plants. On very overgrown sites, you can use a line trimmer, scythe, or brushwood cutter to slash down topgrowth. Remove all debris and dig out roots by hand. Rotary cultivators, or rototillers, are useful for large areas, but they chop weed roots into pieces, each of which may develop into a new plant. After rototilling, therefore, remove weed fragments promptly by hand-digging, and rake all debris out of the soil to prevent rerooting.

DUTCH HOE

DRAW HOE

△ **THE RIGHT TOOL FOR THE TASK**
The Dutch hoe, easiest to use and most versatile, cuts surface weeds off at ground level. The draw hoe can be used for chopping weeds, but is more useful for hilling up or creating channels, known as drills, for seed sowing.

USING A DUTCH HOE ▷
A Dutch hoe can be used for weeding between border plants. It will destroy annual weeds, but deep-rooting ones need repeated hoeing. Keep the blade parallel with the soil surface and move forward on or just below the surface.

◁ **USING A FORK**
Use a hand fork or border fork to dig out weeds in a border; both create minimal disturbance to established ornamentals. Tease out the roots, tracing them back as far as you can. Remove as much root as possible; any left in place will resprout to form new plants. Use a digging fork for larger areas and for deep-rooted weeds.

USING WEEDKILLERS

Clearing weeds with a chemical weedkiller is the fastest and most effective method, because it also kills the roots. Once it has taken effect, either cultivate the soil by mixing in organic matter, such as rotted compost or manure, or plant directly into the treated soil. Remove and dispose of dead woody material. Tough weeds, like brambles, may need a second application.

ALWAYS REMEMBER

STRICTLY FOLLOW INSTRUCTIONS

Safe and effective use of chemicals demands that you follow the manufacturer's instructions to the letter. Weedkillers work best if applied on a warm and still, sunny day when the weeds are in active growth and with sufficient leaf area to absorb chemicals fully. If you time it correctly, only the toughest weeds are likely to need more than one application.

NEGLECTED SITES ▷
A neglected or weed-infested site must be cleared thoroughly before planting. Chemical weedkilling is the most effective method for such a job; if you prefer to use organic methods, it is a good idea to apply a sheet mulch after clearance to suppress further growth.

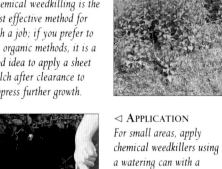

◁ **APPLICATION**
For small areas, apply chemical weedkillers using a watering can with a dribble bar. Keep a clearly marked can for the purpose, since residues may affect border plants if the can is later used for watering. For larger areas, use a backpack sprayer.

SEE ALSO: Dealing with Weeds, pp.290–291

SPOT WEEDING

In areas of established planting, it is not a good idea to apply weedkillers with a sprayer or a can and dribble bar. Most will kill a broad spectrum of plants — they are not specific to weeds — and any spray drift or splash on the foliage of border plants will be damaging or even fatal.

Where small numbers of weeds occur in an established border, it is a simple matter to spot-treat them with a weed wand or to apply a gel-based commercial weedkiller with a brush. This technique is also useful for weeds growing in gravel, in paving crevices, or in lawns. For organic gardeners, a nonchemical alternative is to use a flame-weeder, which directs a narrow flame onto the growing point. The drier the soil, the better the result. A few seconds of intense heat will kill small annual weeds; perennials need repeated treatments.

TREATING INDIVIDUAL WEEDS ▷
Spot-weeding chemicals are usually gel-based weedkillers that act on both the foliage and the roots. The gel gives good adherence, thereby minimizing the risk of drips or splashes. Brush it onto the leaves of the offending plant; wash your hands thoroughly after use.

USING MULCHES TO SUPPRESS WEEDS

Weed suppression by mulching is used for two main purposes: to clear weeds before planting, and to keep cleared areas free of weeds. It is a good method of clearance for organic gardeners. A light-excluding sheet mulch, such as black plastic or old carpet, kills most weeds if left in place for a season, or two seasons for tough weeds like horsetail. In reliably sunny areas, clear plastic sheeting is effective; temperatures rise rapidly beneath it and "cook" weeds to death.

Once the soil is completely clean of all weeds, sheet or loose mulches can be used to suppress further weed growth. Sheet mulches are effective but unattractive; they can be covered with a shallow layer of more presentable, loose materials.

GOOD IDEAS

• If you are averse to using chemicals, using sheet mulches is a good way to clear the ground, but you do need to plan well ahead.

• A combination of sheet and loose mulches is a cost-effective and attractive means of weed control. A 1–1¼in (2–3cm) deep layer of loose material is adequate to disguise the weed-suppressing sheet — half the depth (and cost) of using loose mulch alone.

• Local authorities or forestry enterprises often recycle and sell wood or bark chips; this is an ecologically sound and economical source of mulch material.

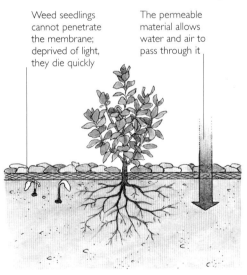

Weed seedlings cannot penetrate the membrane; deprived of light, they die quickly

The permeable material allows water and air to pass through it

△ LANDSCAPE FABRIC
For the mulch membrane, a material called landscape fabric is better than plastic; it is permeable to air and water, and fertilizers can be washed down by rain. The life of gravel or bark topdressing is extended, since it does not become incorporated into the soil. To plant through it, make two crosswise slits, and dig the planting hole beneath.

△ LOOSE MULCHES
A 2–3in (5–8cm) layer of loose material, such as ground bark, wood chips, coconut shells, or gravel, makes an effective weed suppressant. They can be laid on clean soil or over landscape fabric. Compost and manure are less efficient since they may contain weed seeds, but they still make valuable, soil-improving mulches.

MARKING OUT A BED

To mark out curved beds or borders, use a length of twine or hose laid on the ground, adjusted to the required shape. For best effect, make curves strong and sweeping. Wiggly lines are less pleasing to look at and harder to maintain. For formal beds, use pegs and twine to mark out straight lines. To make corners true, check with a builder's square. To make a circle, attach some string or twine to two pegs — the length of the string should equal the radius (not the diameter) of the desired finished circle. With the string taut, draw one peg around the other.

△ STRAIGHT LINES
A straight line can be created with a length of twine and two pegs. To achieve accurate right angles at the corners of a formal bed, use a builder's square as a guide.

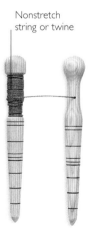

Nonstretch string or twine

CREATING CIRCLES ▷
Use two pegs, joined with string, to draw a circle on the ground. Drive one into the soil in the center and move the other around it.

SEE ALSO: Planting with Sheet or Mat Mulches, p.151; General Border Maintenance, pp.152–153

BUYING GOOD PLANTS

ONCE THE GROUND HAS BEEN CLEARED, get your plantings off to the best possible start with good, healthy, vigorous plants chosen to suit the soil, exposure, and climate of the position in which they will grow. It pays to be able to recognize, and therefore avoid buying, plants that have been produced in less than ideal conditions, since these are less likely to establish successfully. Poorly raised plants may also bring new pests and diseases into the garden. If you learn what to look for, however, and buy your plants only from a reputable supplier, the risks will be minimized, and you can look forward to a thriving garden that will give years of trouble-free pleasure.

PERENNIALS

Many perennials are sold as container-grown plants throughout the growing season, and they can be planted in full growth if kept well watered until established. It is best, however, to buy in spring; plants then have a whole growing season to establish before the onset of winter. If buying early, check that the plants have some healthy buds. In warmer areas, you can buy and plant perennials in autumn when the soil is still warm and less likely to dry out.

When buying, check that the soil mix is evenly moist and that its surface is free of weeds and mosses; these indicate that the soil mix may be poorly drained, or that the plant has been in its container too long and may have suffered nutrient starvation.

GOOD IDEAS

• When buying clump-forming perennials, choose large specimens that have several strong shoots; these can be divided before planting to yield two or three plants for the price of one (*see p.148*).

• With planning and forethought, you can raise many perennials from seed (*see p.162*). This yields many plants at a fraction of the cost, and you will have enough to give away or to swap with your gardening friends.

Strong growth and healthy green leaves with no evidence of pests or diseases

Strong, healthy stems, and plant is well clothed with foliage to the base

Soil mix surface is evenly moist and free of weeds, liverworts, and mosses

Well-established system of healthy roots retains soil mix to form a good root ball

△ **GOOD EXAMPLE**
The example above is a healthy, vigorous lupine with fresh green foliage that shows no signs of discoloration, which may indicate nutrient deficiency or virus infection. Check the foliage for obvious signs of pests or eaten leaves, and make sure that it exhibits no sign of wilting; this may indicate root pests, root damage, or lack of water. If possible, remove the plant from its pot to inspect the roots.

◁ **POTBOUND PLANT**
Plants that have been in their containers too long may be potbound; that is, the roots have filled the pot and begun to spiral around upon themselves, or they have rooted into the standing area beneath the pot. They may be starved of water and nutrients and suffered a severe check to growth.

Dry soil mix has resulted in a poorly developed root system

Topgrowth is weak and stunted by dry conditions

POOR EXAMPLE ▷
Plants with sparse, spindly, or woody topgrowth often have a poorly developed root system and do not establish well. As a result of erratic watering, the soil mix has dried out. Peat-based mixes are difficult to rewet, so growth is checked and the plant may not recover.

BULBS

Most bulbous plants are sold in a dry, dormant state and are best bought fresh, as soon as available – from late summer for spring bulbs; spring for summer bulbs; and from early summer for autumn ones. They deteriorate if kept dry for too long. Bulbs should be plump and firm, with strong growing points. Choose the largest ones you can find. Check that outer coverings and roots are entire and mold-free, with no damaged or diseased areas.

HYACINTH   TULIP

DAFFODIL   DAFFODIL
(SINGLE-NOSED)   (DOUBLE-NOSED)

ERYTHRONIUM   CYCLAMEN

SEE ALSO: Establishing Plants in the Border, pp.148–149

SHRUBS

Shrubs are usually sold in pots and are either container-grown or field-grown and containerized in the season before sale. Container-grown shrubs usually have a better-established root system and can be planted at any time, except in very wet, cold, or dry periods. Containerized shrubs are best planted in spring or autumn; they are slow to establish at other times unless their root system is particularly well developed.

Deciduous shrubs may be offered bare-rooted when dormant. Buy and plant these in late autumn to early spring; check that each fibrous root system is well developed and not dried out.

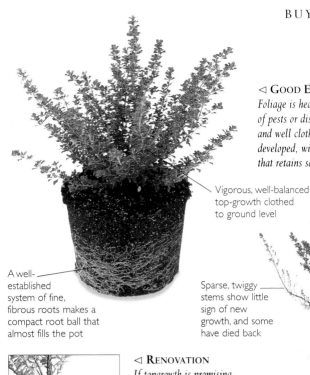

Vigorous, well-balanced top-growth clothed to ground level

A well-established system of fine, fibrous roots makes a compact root ball that almost fills the pot

◁ **GOOD EXAMPLE**
Foliage is healthy, of good color with no yellowing or signs of pests or diseases. Branch framework is evenly balanced and well clothed to the base. The root system is well developed, with healthy white tips, and forms a firm ball that retains soil mix when removed from the pot.

Sparse, twiggy stems show little sign of new growth, and some have died back

◁ **BALLED-AND-BURLAPPED**
These shrubs, sold in autumn and early spring, are grown in open ground, then lifted with a ball of roots and soil. They are wrapped in net or burlap. The root ball must be firm and the wrapping intact, or the roots may dry out.

◁ **RENOVATION**
If topgrowth is promising, with plenty of plump new buds to come, but roots are crowded, a little renovation will ensure recovery and good establishment. Tease out potbound roots, and cut any that are dead, very long, or damaged, back to clean, healthy growth.

Potbound roots spiral around pot and have used up nutrients in soil mix

△ **POOR EXAMPLE**
Avoid plants with dieback and sparse, leggy, uneven top-growth that has few or no visible new growth buds; they are likely to be potbound and will have suffered a severe growth check from lack of water and nutrients.

ROSES

Roses have long been sold bare-root for planting in the dormant season, in late autumn or early to midspring; if planted as soon as possible after buying, they will establish perfectly well. You may need to seek out old or uncommon roses from specialists who supply by mail order. These are often bare-root but will be packed well in plastic to avoid desiccation.

Container-grown roses can be planted at any time except when the soil is very wet, dry, or frozen. Unsold, bare-root plants that have been potted up at the end of their season may be satisfactory, but if they have dried out or been exposed to cold, they are not likely to establish well. Check before buying that the plant is well rooted by shaking the main stem gently.

Strong bud union and an evenly spaced framework of sturdy, healthy stems

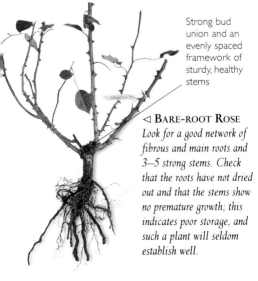

◁ **BARE-ROOT ROSE**
Look for a good network of fibrous and main roots and 3–5 strong stems. Check that the roots have not dried out and that the stems show no premature growth; this indicates poor storage, and such a plant will seldom establish well.

CONTAINER-GROWN ROSE ▷
A well-grown specimen has a well-balanced set of strong stems, clothed in an abundance of vigorous, healthy foliage of good, deep color. There is no evidence of pests or diseases, such as rust or blackspot. The soil mix is evenly moist and its surface is free of weeds and mosses.

Evenly moist soil mix with a system of plump and healthy roots

◁ **POOR EXAMPLE**
Avoid buying bare-root roses that have spindly shoots with evidence of dieback or fungal disease. A stunted, desiccated root system with few fibrous feeder roots will never sustain healthy growth and development.

POOR EXAMPLE ▷
Stems are sparse and spindly; leaves have black-spot, and some have fallen. A weedy soil mix surface suggests the plant has been in its container for too long.

SEE ALSO: Establishing Shrubs and Roses, pp.150–151

ESTABLISHING PLANTS IN THE BORDER

THE PERIOD BETWEEN planning and planting or sowing can seem unending, but, having prepared the soil and researched and chosen suitable plants, it is worth taking a little more time to establish your border plants – perennials, bulbs, and annuals or biennials – correctly. Planting and sowing techniques, and their timing, must be suited to individual plants and to the climate you are working in. Once in the soil, keep young plants watered and free of weeds until well established. Thereafter, they usually need watering only in prolonged dry spells. They will always need weeding, but a dense foliage canopy of well-grown plants will help discourage weed growth.

PLANTING PERENNIALS

Container-grown perennials may be planted out at any time of year when the soil is workable – not too wet, too dry, or frozen. The best seasons, however, are spring and autumn. In autumn, the soil is still warm and unlikely to dry out – ideal conditions for good root growth before the onset of winter. In cold areas, spring is better, especially for plants that need drier conditions or are not fully hardy. It gives them a full growing season to become established before their first winter. Spring or summer plantings are likely to need watering until they are established. Perennials always look better when planted in odd-numbered groups.

PLANTING A CONTAINER-GROWN PERENNIAL

1 MAKE A HOLE
Dig a planting hole with a border fork or hand trowel in a prepared bed. The hole should be 1½ times deeper and wider than the root ball of the plant.

2 REMOVE PLANT FROM POT
Water the pot thoroughly, let the excess drain away, and then gently slide the plant out, taking care not to damage either the roots or the growing points.

3 TEASE OUT ROOTS
Gently scrape off the top 1½in (3cm) of soil mix to remove weeds and their seeds. Tease out the roots gently with the fingers or a hand fork. This will speed up root establishment.

4 FIRM IN GENTLY
Put the plant in the hole at the correct depth (see below), and back-fill with soil. Firm in with your fingertips. Loosen the soil surface with a hand fork, and water in well.

DIVIDING PERENNIALS

Large, clump-forming, fibrous-rooted perennials, such as asters, phlox, and sedums, are easy to divide, instantly providing you with bonus plants. Remove the plant from its container, and gently pry the root ball apart, creating two or three sections of equal size. Plant out all the new divisions as soon as possible.

◁ **GOOD VALUE**
This aster is well grown, with a large number of healthy shoots that have not yet become so crowded as to weaken the plant's growth. It will consequently yield 2–3 good-sized divisions.

HOW TO DIVIDE ▷
Gently tease plant roots apart to form equal sections, each with a healthy root system. Keep plenty of soil around roots and plant out immediately.

PLANTING DEPTHS FOR PERENNIALS

As a general rule, most perennials are planted at exactly the same depth as they were in the pot, but a number will grow better if planted a little higher or deeper, depending on their individual preferences. Rhizomatous plants, like bearded irises, may rot if planted too deeply, and some variegated plants revert to green if planted at ground level. Tuberous and moisture-loving plants both enjoy the added protection of deeper planting.

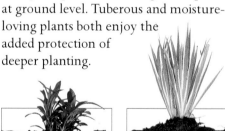

HOW DEEP TO PLANT PERENNIALS

△ **DEEP PLANTING**
Plant perennials with tuberous root systems (here, Solomon's seal) so that their crowns are about 4in (10cm) below the surface of the soil.

△ **SHALLOW DEPTH**
Perennials that need a moist environment (here, a hosta) should be planted with their crowns at about ¾–1in (2–2.5cm) below ground level.

△ **GROUND LEVEL**
The vast majority of perennials should be planted with their crowns at ground level, that is, at the same depth as they were when in the pot.

△ **RAISED UP**
Plants that are prone to rot, or variegated plants (here, Sisyrinchium 'Aunt May') that tend to revert, are planted with the crown just above ground.

SEE ALSO: Maintaining Border Plants, pp.154–155; Clearing Weeds and Marking Out Beds, pp.144–145; Increasing Border Plants, pp.162–163

PLANTING BULBS

As a rule, spring-flowering bulbs should be planted in late summer or in autumn, summer-flowering bulbs in spring, and autumn-flowering ones in early to mid-summer. Plant most bulbs their own width apart, at two or three times their own depth (four or five times in sandy soils and cold-winter areas). A few, such as nerines, need their tips to be at ground level.

PLANTING BULBS IN OPEN GROUND

1 MAKE A PLANTING HOLE
Excavate a hole in well-prepared soil to the appropriate depth. Place bulbs, growth points upward, on the base. Set bulbs that need good drainage on a layer of coarse sand.

2 COVER WITH SOIL
For a natural effect, space the bulbs randomly, at least their own width apart. Draw soil over them gently by hand to minimize any risk of displacing or damaging them.

3 FINISHING OFF
Firm the soil by tamping down with the back of a rake. Avoid treading on the soil surface, because this might damage the growing points. Mark the position of the bulbs.

◁ **SINGLY**
If you wish to produce a scattered effect, for example among other plants, plant singly in separate holes of the right depth. Dig holes with a trowel or bulb planter.

IN THE GREEN ▷
Some bulbs, like snowdrops, benefit from being planted or divided, when in growth, or "in the green." Make a hole wide enough to spread out the roots, and plant the bulb at the same depth as it was growing before.

◁ **NATURALIZING LARGE BULBS**
Scatter large bulbs (here, daffodils) and plant where they fall. Make individual holes with a bulb planter. Place the bulb in the hole, growth point upward, cover it with loose soil, replace the cap of sod, and firm gently in place.

◁ **NATURALIZING SMALL BULBS**
For small bulbs like crocus, make an H-shaped cut in the sod with a lawn edger or spade blade. Roll back the flaps and set the bulbs in place randomly. Score the sod flap to loosen the soil. Replace it carefully and pat gently to firm.

SOWING SEEDS OF ANNUALS AND BIENNIALS

True annuals and biennials are grown from seed. In spring, annuals can be sown direct or in pots for planting out later. Broadcast sowing gives natural effects when filling gaps in borders, but weeding must be done by hand. Biennials should be sown in pots or in nursery rows for bedding, from late spring to midsummer.

◁ **THINNING**
With broadcast sowing, when seedlings appear they are often growing too close together. Encourage the healthiest seedlings to flourish by thinning; press gently on either side, and pluck out the weaker ones.

◁ **TRANSPLANTING SEEDLING GROUPS**
A dense patch of seedlings seldom thrives. Carefully lift out small clumps, with plenty of soil around their roots, and transplant these to another area to grow on. Then thin as normal later.

BROADCASTING ANNUAL SEEDS

1 PREPARE AND SOW
Rake the soil into a fine tilth (fine, crumbly texture) and scatter, or broadcast, seeds thinly over the area, by hand or straight from the packet.

2 COVER OVER
To avoid disturbing the seeds, very lightly rake the area at right angles to cover them. Water them in using a fine-nozzled watering can, then label.

RAISING BIENNIALS

1 LIFT SEEDLINGS
To raise sufficient biennials for a bedding design (here, wallflowers), sow seeds in rows in a prepared seed bed in late spring to midsummer. Lift the seedlings when they reach 2–3in (5–8cm) tall and place on a tray.

2 TRANSFER TO NURSERY
Plant out the seedlings in a nursery bed, 6–8in (15–20cm) apart, in rows that are 8–12in (20–30cm) apart. If using biennials less formally, plant directly into their flowering site and grow on there.

3 PLANT OUT
In autumn, when the new plants are established and growing well, give them a thorough watering if dry. Lift each one carefully to avoid damaging the roots. Plant out in well-prepared soil in the final flowering site.

SEE ALSO: Clearing Weeds and Marking Out Beds, pp.144–145; Increasing Border Plants, pp.162–163

ESTABLISHING SHRUBS AND ROSES

SHRUBS AND ROSES ARE POTENTIALLY long-lived plants, so thorough preparation of the soil before planting is essential. Autumn and spring are the best times to plant shrubs. In autumn, residual soil warmth allows good root growth before the onset of winter, so that the shrub is well established before the following summer's dry weather occurs. Spring planting avoids winter exposure, but extra watering may be needed if the topgrowth emerges before the roots have developed properly. Roses should be planted late in the season and pruned carefully to stimulate new growth. Mulching will help new plants establish by suppressing weeds and conserving moisture.

PLANTING SHRUBS

Container-grown shrubs may be planted at any time the soil is workable, but they need careful watering in the early stages if planted in full growth. The best times, however, as for all shrubs, are autumn or spring. Clear the ground of weeds, and work well-rotted organic matter into the top 12–18in (30–45cm) of soil. Cultivate the entire bed, if possible; otherwise, prepare an area larger than the planting site. For bare-root shrubs, make the planting hole wide enough to spread the roots out fully. For balled-and-burlapped and container-grown shrubs, make it at least twice the width of the root mass. Plant the shrub at the same level as it was in its pot or in the ground.

HOW TO PLANT A CONTAINER-GROWN SHRUB

1 DIG OUT THE HOLE
Water the plant well, and set aside to drain. Dig a planting hole, twice the width of the root mass, or wider on heavy clay soils, and the same depth as the pot.

2 PREPARE THE SOIL
Use a fork to loosen the soil at the bottom and sides of the hole to relieve compaction and aid good root penetration. On one side, mix the excavated soil with organic matter.

3 REMOVE THE PLANT
Place a hand over the top of the soil and around the stem base to support it; slide the plant carefully out of its container. Place the root ball in the prepared hole.

4 ADJUST THE DEPTH
Lay a stake across the top of the hole to check that the soil level is the same as before. Adjust level, if necessary, by adding or excavating more topsoil beneath the shrub.

5 BACKFILL WITH SOIL
Use the mixed soil to backfill around the plant. Firm gently with your fingers or a trowel handle to remove air pockets and ensure close contact between roots and soil.

6 WATER AND MULCH
Firm the soil gently with your foot, and water in. On light soils, mound up soil to form a watering basin (see inset). Apply a loose mulch, leaving the stem clear.

TELL ME WHY

WHY PLANT EVERGREENS IN SPRING?

Broadleaved evergreens and conifers retain their leaves in winter, so they are especially vulnerable to desiccation in cold, dry, winter winds; the effect is worsened if they do not have a well-established root system. Spring planting allows them a full growing season to develop a good root system before the onset of winter.

STAKING SHRUBS

Shrubs do not normally need to be staked, except for large, root-bound specimens and standards. The former, which ideally should not have been bought in the first place, will need some support in their first year or two at least, until their roots begin to spread out and they become stable.

The best method for any shrub that branches from near ground level is to secure it with ties attached to 3 stakes spaced evenly around the shrub. To prevent bark damage, cover the ties where they touch the branches with rubber or padding.

For standards, insert the stake in the planting hole before planting to avoid damaging the root system. The top of the stake should be just below the first branches. Secure the stem to the stake, using a tie with a spacer or a homemade figure-eight tie to prevent chafing.

ALWAYS REMEMBER

PROTECT NEWLY PLANTED SHRUBS

Newly planted shrubs, especially broad-leaved evergreens and conifers, may suffer from desiccation or cold if not protected. A screen of burlap or mesh greatly reduces water loss from the foliage. To protect the roots from frost, spread a thick layer of mulch (see p.153) around the shrub.

SEE ALSO: General Border Maintenance, pp.152–153; Mulching Materials, p.153; Maintaining Shrubs, pp.156–157; Planting in Containers, pp.176–177

PLANTING ROSES

Plant bare-root roses in late autumn or early winter at the beginning of, or just before, their dormant period. In areas with severe winters, plant in early spring. If soil is too wet, dry, or frozen, delay planting until conditions improve; keep the roots moist in the meantime. If the delay is prolonged, heel plants in by burying roots in a shallow trench on spare ground. Container-grown roses may be planted at any time. Roses need good, fertile soil to flower well, especially those that repeat throughout summer. Prepare the soil well and add extra fertilizer before planting.

HOW TO PLANT A BARE-ROOT ROSE

1 PREPARE THE ROSE
Soak the roots in water for an hour or so, until moist. Cut out diseased, damaged growth, and remove crossing and straggly stems at their base, aiming for a balanced framework. Trim thick roots by a third of their length.

2 DIG THE PLANTING HOLE
Dig a hole that is wide enough to hold the roots and deep enough for the bud union (a bulge at the stem base where the rose to flower has been grafted onto a more vigorous rootstock) to be 1in (2.5cm) below ground level.

3 CHECK PLANTING LEVEL
Fork half a bucketful of compost and a small handful of balanced fertilizer into the base. Set the rose centrally in the hole and spread the roots evenly. Use a stake to check that the bud union is at the correct depth.

4 BACKFILL AND FIRM IN
Refill the planting hole with soil, in stages. Firm first by hand to remove air pockets and then gently with your toes. Rake over the soil and water the plant in well. Apply a layer of mulch in the following spring.

PRUNING AFTER PLANTING

A compact and healthy shrub needs no, or minimal, pruning on planting, but minor defects are easily remedied when plants are young (*see below*). Most roses are also pruned immediately after planting to remove weak, damaged, or dead growth and any overlong shoots that spoil the general shape of the bush. In the case of container-grown roses that have been planted when in full growth, carry out initial pruning to shape in the first spring after planting.

△ **PRUNING A SHRUB ON PLANTING**
Prune any dead, diseased, or damaged branches back to a healthy bud, and cut back any crossing or inward-growing shoots to an outward-facing bud. Remove weak or straggly stems, and shorten any very long shoots and those that spoil the overall balance of the branch framework.

SPRING PRUNING ▷
For container-grown roses, in the first spring following planting, remove any frost-damaged, weak, or dead shoots. Cut remaining stems back to an outward-facing bud, about 3in (8cm) above ground. For climbers, just remove weak, dead, or damaged growth.

PLANTING WITH SHEET OR MAT MULCHES

Using a sheet mulch (*see p.145*) can help newly planted shrubs establish. Lay the sheet over the soil and secure it at the sides with metal pegs. Make a slit in the sheet with a knife or spade and plant through the hole. Alternatively, you can use a circular mulch mat; this has a premade planting hole and it is slit from center to edge so it is easily laid on the ground around the newly planted shrub.

GOOD IDEAS

- Thoroughly water dry soil before applying a sheet mulch or mulch mat, or wait for waterlogged soil to drain; once in place, the mulch is impermeable to water.

- If necessary, incorporate organic matter or fertilizer in the soil before laying the mulch.

- Add fertilizer to the soil, as required, through small holes or slits in the mulch.

The mulch will help create better conditions for growth while the plant establishes

◁ **PLANTING THROUGH SHEET MULCH**
Lay the sheet of plastic mulch over the soil and secure it. Make a cross-shaped slit in the sheet, dig a hole beneath, and plant the shrub as normal.

SEE ALSO: Maintaining Shrubs, pp.156–157; Pruning Established Shrubs, p.158–159; Maintaining Roses, pp.160–161

GENERAL BORDER MAINTENANCE

WHILE GOOD PREPARATION reduces the amount of aftercare required, beds and borders need a degree of maintenance if they are continue to look their best. Weeds will appear, but their numbers will fall over the years if always removed before they produce any seeds. In well-prepared soils, established plants seldom need watering, except in prolonged dry spells, but new plantings may need watering until established. In fertile soils, if plants are growing and flowering well, they will need little in the way of fertilizers, although they should be mulched annually with organic matter. If pruned regularly or heavily, they will need an annual dose of nutrients.

WEEDING ESTABLISHED BEDS

• Always remove weeds as soon as they are seen. Weed little and often, rather than blitzing periodically. Hand pulling or forking are the safest methods around ornamental plants. Hoe carefully and not too deeply between the plants to avoid damaging nearby roots or stems.

ROUTINE WEEDING ▷
To remove weeds from borders, hoe carefully and not too deeply between the ornamental plants in order to avoid damaging their roots or stems. Any stubborn weeds not removed by hoeing should be lifted out with a hand fork.

WATERING TECHNIQUES

It is vital to water thoroughly if moisture is to percolate deeply enough to reach the roots. Watering little and often is wasteful and potentially damaging; if only the surface layers of soil are moistened, plant roots tend to stay near the surface and are then more vulnerable to heat, cold, and drought. Hand watering by can or hose, fitted with a fine nozzle for seedlings or a coarse one for established plants, is practical for small gardens and individual plants. For larger areas, sprinklers or drip-feed systems, which deliver a gentle trickle to the plant base from a perforated pipe or seep hose, are useful, but both should be fitted with a timing device to avoid waste.

△ **BASIN WATERING**
On light, sandy soils and sloping sites, make a ridge of soil around the root zone to create a basin and fill it slowly with water. This technique prevents water runoff and ensures that it seeps directly downward to the plant roots.

◁ **AVOID PUDDLING**
Applying water at too fast a rate, or under pressure, causes puddling at the soil surface and may wash soil away, exposing roots and damaging the soil structure. If using a hose, keep the pressure low, fit a fine nozzle, and move the spray gently back and forth.

◁ **POT WATERING**
On silty or clay soils, which are prone to capping (compaction of the soil surface by wetting), sink a large pot into the soil near to the plant roots and fill it with water. Water seeps down to the roots through the drainage holes without damaging the soil structure.

APPLYING MULCH

Mulches are multifunctional; they help prevent germination of weed seeds, keep roots cooler in summer and protected in winter, reduce evaporation of water from the soil surface, and prevent erosion by improving soil structure and fertility. Apply a mulch in autumn or spring, each or every other year, when the soil is moist. Never mulch dry, waterlogged, cold, or frozen soil. A 2–3in (5–8cm) layer helps control weeds; a 4–6in (10–15cm) layer provides winter insulation in cold areas.

△ **MULCHING SHRUBS**
For woody plants, apply a mulch to cover the entire root zone; this usually equates to the full extent of the foliage canopy. Leave a 4–6in (10–15cm) gap around the stem base; mounding mulch onto woody stems may cause rot.

△ **MULCHING PERENNIALS**
Perennials, like peonies, that prefer rich, moist but well-drained soil, benefit from a 2in (5cm) mulch of loose organic matter. Apply in autumn, or in spring before new shoots emerge, so they are not damaged in the process.

SEE ALSO: Clearing Weeds and Marking Out Beds, pp.144–145; Making Compost, p.236

MULCHING MATERIALS

As well as helping with weed control, soil temperature regulation, and water retention, organic mulches improve soil structure and fertility as they are broken down or incorporated by soil organisms. There is a wide range of suitable materials available. Coconut shells and shredded or ground bark have ideal characteristics and are free of weed seeds. Bark products are best if composted, since they may contain natural chemicals that can cause damage to susceptible plants. Compost, leafmold, and well-rotted manure add low levels of nutrients and are good soil improvers, but they often contain weed seeds. Spent mushroom compost improves soil and supplies nutrients, but it can be rather alkaline, making it unsuitable for acidic soils where lime-hating plants such as rhododendrons grow.

TELL ME WHY

WHY ARE ORGANIC MULCHES USEFUL?

Organic mulches protect the soil surface from drying out and from damage. Their loose structure allows nutrients, water, and air to penetrate down into the soil around the plant's roots, as well as easing the removal of any weed seedlings that germinate in the mulch.

ORGANIC MULCHES ▷
Material suitable for use as organic mulches range from well-rotted compost or spent mushroom compost to shredded or ground bark and pieces of coconut shell. All may be used to form a protective layer around border plants.

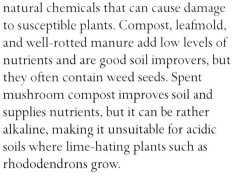

COMPOST

SHREDDED BARK

COCONUT SHELLS

SPENT MUSHROOM COMPOST

GROUND BARK

DECORATIVE MULCHES

Some mulches, such as gravel, pebbles, or bark chips, provide an attractive finish to the surface of a bed as well as performing the soil-protecting functions of a mulch. Lay the mulch on its own, 2–3in (5–8cm) deep, or at half that depth on top of a sheet of landscaping fabric. Such mulches are particularly useful in protecting the surface of clay or silty soils from problems caused by overwatering or heavy rain.

COMBINING LOOKS AND PRACTICALITY ▷
This gravel mulch serves to protects the flowers and leaves of plants (here, hellebores) from soil splash. It also ensures good drainage around plant stems, and it looks attractive.

△ **USING PEBBLES AS A DECORATIVE MULCH**
Golden creeping Jenny (Lysimachia nummularia 'Aurea') and bugle (Ajuga) growing through a pebble mulch. This looks particularly nice next to a stream or pool.

USING FERTILIZERS

An annual application of a balanced fertilizer gives plants an adequate supply of nitrogen, phosphorus, and potassium. Fertilizers come in different formulations, but all should be applied to moist soil; if conditions are dry, water the soil first. Apply slow-release fertilizers in spring as, or just before, growth begins. If needed, use quick-release powders to provide a boost to growth in late spring or early summer. Liquid formulas, some of which are foliar feeds, act rapidly and are best used as an aid to ailing plants in full leaf.

ALWAYS REMEMBER

Apply fertilizers at the recommended rate; too much is wasteful and carries risks of scorching or toxicity. Work solid formulations lightly into the soil with a hand fork, taking care not to damage any plant roots. Use a general, balanced fertilizer if growth is poor, and a specific one if plants show signs of particular nutrient deficiencies. Avoid applying a high-nitrogen fertilizer much later than late summer; it will promote soft growth that is more susceptible to cold damage.

△ **APPLYING FERTILIZER**
Sprinkle fertilizer around the plant at the recommended rate, then lightly fork it in. Solid fertilizers should not touch leaves or stems, since they may cause scorch damage.

SEE ALSO: Clearing Weeds and Marking out Beds, pp.144–145; Nourishing your Crops, pp.238–239; Dealing with Weeds and Plant Problems, pp.288–311

MAINTAINING BORDER PLANTS

TO GIVE A GOOD SHOW, most perennials need only a top-dressing of general fertilizer in spring, but a little extra attention will produce even better results. Thinning, stopping, and deadheading will all increase flower production. Taller perennials, annuals, and biennials, or those of arching growth, may need support to display their flowers to best advantage or to prevent them from flopping over. As perennials grow older, they should be rejuvenated by dividing and replanting to give them a new lease on life. At the end of each season, try saving seeds of annuals and biennials, and in autumn clear up any dead material that may harbor pests or diseases.

THINNING AND STOPPING PERENNIALS

These two techniques are used to increase both the quality and quantity of flowers. Perennials that form clumps, such as delphiniums, phloxes, and asters, make a mass of stems in spring, some of which are weak and spindly. If these are removed at an early stage, the remaining shoots grow more strongly and produce larger flowers. Some perennials, like New England asters, heleniums, and rudbeckias, often produce flowering sideshoots. If the growing tip is pinched out, or "stopped," plants branch more readily. If plants in a group are stopped a few days apart, this has the effect of prolonging the overall flowering display.

◁ **THINNING**
In mid- to late spring, when plants reach a quarter to a third of their final height, trace weak shoots back to their base and pinch or cut them out. Remove no more than 1 shoot in 3. The sturdier shoots will produce larger flowers and are also less likely to need staking.

STOPPING ▷
When shoots reach a third of their final height, pinch out the top 1–2in (2.5–5cm) of the growing tip. This encourages buds in the lower leaf axils to grow out and bloom, and it promotes bushier growth.

SUPPORTING AND STAKING

Perennials, annuals, and biennials that are tall and fragile, and those that tend to flop, may need supporting, especially in exposed and windy areas. It is best to put supports in place early in the season; then the plants are more likely to disguise the support completely as they grow. Take care when inserting stakes not to damage the root system of the plant. For stability, stakes should be inserted to about one-third of their height. Commercial supports are costly but can often be reused. It is also possible to improvise, using large-gauge wire mesh either attached to stakes, for supporting taller plants, or formed into a dome or cone for shorter ones.

GOOD IDEAS

• Twiggy pea sticks are unobtrusive and cheap. Push several in around a clump, arch over the center, and secure.

• Insert one sturdy stake at the center of a small group of plants or stems, with ties radiating out to loop around each stem.

◁ **STAKE AND TWINE**
For tall, single-stemmed plants, insert a stake to two-thirds of the stem's final height when the plant is 10in (25cm) tall. Tie twine loosely in figure-eight loops as the plant grows.

RING OF STAKES ▷
For low, weak-stemmed plants, place a ring of split stakes around the margins of the plant, and circle the stakes and plant with soft twine. Loop it around each stake to secure it in place.

△ **LINK STAKES**
For tall clump-formers, like New England asters and some campanulas, push link stakes deep into the soil and gradually raise them as the plant grows.

△ **GROW-THROUGH SUPPORTS**
These are ideal for tall, floppy plants. Set in place early in the season. As the stems grow through the mesh, they will hide it.

SEE ALSO: Using Fertilizers, p.153; Dividing Perennials, p.163

DEADHEADING

Unless ornamental seedheads are wanted, or you wish to gather your own seed, plants should be deadheaded as soon as flowers fade. This diverts energy from seed production into new growth and helps prolong the flowering season. With plants that produce sideshoots on their flowering stems, such as *Phlox paniculata*, removing the central flower encourages the sideshoots to bloom. In those that flower on a single stem, like delphiniums and lupines, removing the flowered stem at the base may encourage a second, though less profuse, blooming later in the season. Remove dead flowers with sharp pruners to make a clean cut.

△ **PHLOX**
Trace back the stem below the central flowerhead, and remove the faded cluster with a straight cut just above a pair of sideshoots. This induces new sideshoots to break into growth and flower later in the season.

△ **DELPHINIUM**
Tall delphiniums produce a main flower spike with a few small sideshoots in early and midsummer. Cut the entire spike back to the base as it fades; then, the plant may flower again in autumn as a result.

△ **LAVENDER**
Trimming back the midsummer flowers of lavender seldom induces a second flush, but by preventing seed production, energy is diverted into producing compact and bushy growth. The cut flowers can be dried for use in potpourri.

AUTUMN CLEARANCE

Some perennials, such as grasses, have attractive winter flowerheads; others gain a little protection from cold if topgrowth is left in place. Most perennials, however, are best cut back in autumn; remove dead leaves and stems at the base. Also take out any annuals or biennials that have finished flowering, and weed and mulch the bed.

CUTTING BACK PERENNIALS ▷
Use pruners or a pair of hand shears to remove all dead and faded growth at the base of the stem. With most perennials, all topgrowth should be removed to avoid the risk of diseases being harbored over winter.

RENOVATING PERENNIALS

Most perennials benefit from division every three to five years, or every other year for vigorous mat-formers such as *Stachys* and *Ajuga*. If allowed to become woody and congested, they will grow and flower less freely. Lifting and dividing (*see p.163*) rejuvenates the plant and allows the soil in the planting site to be dug over, improved, fertilized, and weeded.

Old, woody, and congested stems produce few new leaves or flowers

Topgrowth becomes sparse and stunted

△ **RIPE FOR DIVISION**
This woody, congested Heuchera has deteriorated in vigor and appearance and has produced few, sparse flowers. Lifting, dividing, and replanting in fresh soil restores health and vigor.

▽ **LIFT AND STORE**
Plants that are ripe for division can be lifted and put into temporary storage while their planting site is dug over and organic matter is incorporated to improve the quality of the soil.

Moist bark or soil mix over roots prevents drying out

New, divided plants are ready for transplanting

SAVING SEED

Saving seed of annuals and biennials, and occasionally perennials, is a simple and economical way of increasing your stock. The seeds of most species produce offspring almost exactly like the parent plant, but not all cultivars come true from seed. Gather seed from plants with good characteristics of their type, in dry conditions, since damp seeds may rot.

◁ **GATHERING SEED**
Seed should be gathered when dry and just ripe. Keep a close eye on ripening seedheads (here, a hollyhock); the aim is to gather seeds just before they start to disperse.

Unripe seedhead is still green and tightly closed

Seedhead splits open when ripe; gather the seed now before it is shed naturally

SAVING CAPSULES ▷
Some plants, like this Jacob's ladder (Polemonium), have seed capsules that explode at the moment they ripen; remove these seedheads on their stems as they turn brown. Place in a labeled paper bag; the seeds will then be shed into the bag when the capsule explodes.

SEE ALSO: Increasing Border Plants, pp.162–163

MAINTAINING SHRUBS

IF LEFT UNATTENDED, most shrubs will become straggly and overgrown, and they will not flower as profusely as you might like. To prevent this from happening, you will need to care for a shrub by watering, feeding, and mulching as appropriate, and also keep it healthy, neat in shape, and flowering well by means of pruning. The main aims of pruning are to remove any dead, diseased, or damaged shoots, to keep the size and shape of the plant in check, and to stimulate vigorous new growth, especially if the shrub is a flowering one. If carried out correctly at the appropriate time, pruning should enable the shrub to provide you with many years of enjoyment.

MAKING PRUNING CUTS

Use pruners correctly (*see below*) for all soft stems and on woody material up to about ⅓in (1cm) in diameter. The aim is to make a quick, clean cut, and never to crush or tear the stem. Use a lopper for stems up to 1in (2.5cm) in diameter and a pruning saw for anything larger. Always keep cutting blades clean and sharp.

△ INCORRECT METHOD
Here, the pruners are held in the "normal" position, but because the thicker blade lies next to the stem it determines the position of the cut, in this case too far from the main stem.

△ UNHEALTHY STUB
Making the cut too far from the main stem leaves behind a stub that is susceptible to infection and may become diseased or die back, causing problems for the entire plant.

△ CORRECT METHOD
Place the pruners so that the narrow blade is next to the main stem; the cut can then be positioned exactly where required. It will heal rapidly to keep the natural defense barrier intact.

HOW SHRUBS BRANCH

The branches of shrubs are arranged in one of two main patterns – alternate or opposite – and this affects how and where pruning cuts should be made. Alternate branches arise from buds on opposite sides of a stem at staggered intervals. Opposite branches arise in pairs from the same stem joint on opposite sides of the stem.

△ PRUNING SHRUBS WITH OPPOSITE BUDS
Cut squarely across the shoot, ¼in (5mm) above a stem joint with a healthy pair of buds. Two strong shoots should then develop from the buds. Although a sloping cut is normally preferable, in this case it would damage one or both of the buds, so a neat, straight cut is the only option.

GOOD AND BAD CUTS

Many shrubs have defense systems that respond to any kind of wound. Natural chemicals form a barrier to prevent the entry of disease and to form callus, to seal and protect a wound, or scar tissue. When pruning, try to aid this process by making your cuts as small and clean as possible, and in places where the plant's defenses are strong, like the point on a stem where a bud or leaf arises (*see below*). Choose a clear, dry day for pruning, since moisture may inhibit the healing of wounds.

GOOD PRUNING ▷
Use correctly oriented, sharp pruners to make a small, neat cut that does not breach the plant's defenses, so that the wound can heal easily. Prune in clear, dry weather to avoid infection by fungal spores transmitted through raindrops or in the air.

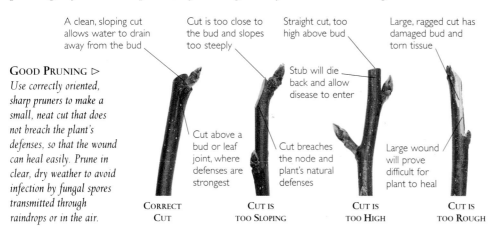

A clean, sloping cut allows water to drain away from the bud

Cut is too close to the bud and slopes too steeply

Straight cut, too high above bud

Large, ragged cut has damaged bud and torn tissue

Stub will die back and allow disease to enter

Cut above a bud or leaf joint, where defenses are strongest

Cut breaches the node and plant's natural defenses

Large wound will prove difficult for plant to heal

| CORRECT CUT | CUT IS TOO SLOPING | CUT IS TOO HIGH | CUT IS TOO ROUGH |

The cutting blade of the pruners is positioned nearest to the bud

△ PRUNING SHRUBS WITH ALTERNATE BUDS
Make a slanting cut, about ¼in (5mm) above the bud and sloping away from it; the lowest point of the cut should be opposite the base of the bud. The slope ensures that any rainwater drains away from the bud, and this reduces the risk of infection from fungal spores.

SEE ALSO: Pruning Established Shrubs, p.158–159; Maintaining Roses, pp.160–161

WHY PRUNE?

Good reasons to prune include removing dead, diseased, or damaged growth to ensure continued good health, improving flower or foliage quality, shaping young plants, and rejuvenating old ones. Pruning to restrict size may be unavoidable, but it is a poor reason to prune; you should always choose plants to fit the space available.

△ WEAK SHOOTS
Cut out at their point of origin weak, straggly, or misshapen shoots, and any growing in the wrong direction. All spoil the appearance of a shrub.

△ CROSSING SHOOTS
Shoots that cross over each other will rub and cause congestion; this damages bark and increases risk of infection. Cut them out or back to a well-placed bud.

△ DEAD SHOOTS
Cut back to living wood unless a clear demarcation between dead and live wood is seen, which indicates a natural barrier. In this case, cut just above it.

△ OLD SHOOTS
Cut out at the base old shoots that have ceased to flower. This rejuvenates the plant by encouraging the production of strong new shoots to replace them.

△ FROST DAMAGE
Wait until all danger of frost has passed, and cut damaged tissue well back to a leaf, bud, or shoot on completely healthy tissue. Further frosts could damage buds or any new growth.

Soft young growth is damaged, but there is no clear demarcation between damaged and healthy tissue

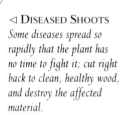

△ REMOVING REVERTED SHOOTS
In variegated shrubs, all-green, or reverted, shoots are more vigorous than their variegated counterparts, and will eventually dominate the whole plant. Remove them as soon as you see them, cutting them out at their point of origin.

Tissue in upper stems is dying; if pustules are visible, the wood is dead

Disease is working its way down the stem; there is no evidence of a natural barrier being formed

◁ DISEASED SHOOTS
Some diseases spread so rapidly that the plant has no time to fight it; cut right back to clean, healthy wood, and destroy the affected material.

△ DAMAGED SHOOTS
A damaged shoot can be cut out at its base or, if a replacement shoot in the same position is wanted, cut back to a bud well below the damage.

SHAPING A SHRUB

Evergreen shrubs usually grow naturally in a compact, even shape. Prune them in mid- to late spring, but only to remove dead, weak, straggly, or frost-damaged growth, and to shorten overlong stems.

Initial shaping of deciduous shrubs should be carried out when they have had one growing season to establish and when the leaves are shed. The aim of this exercise is to keep the center open to allow light penetration and air circulation, and to develop a strong framework of branches for the future.

SHAPING DECIDUOUS SHRUBS THAT FLOWER ON OLD GROWTH

Some shrubs flower on shoots produced in the previous year. With these, initial shaping aims to create a strong, open framework of branches that will promote good, healthy growth and flowering in later years. Removing unwanted branches when the shrub is young ensures rapid healing and less stress for the plant.

SHAPING DECIDUOUS SHRUBS THAT FLOWER ON NEW GROWTH

Shrubs that flower on the current year's growth should be pruned hard each spring back to a permanent framework. Establish this framework in the first spring by removing any weak or badly placed stems, retaining a few that are strong and well spaced.

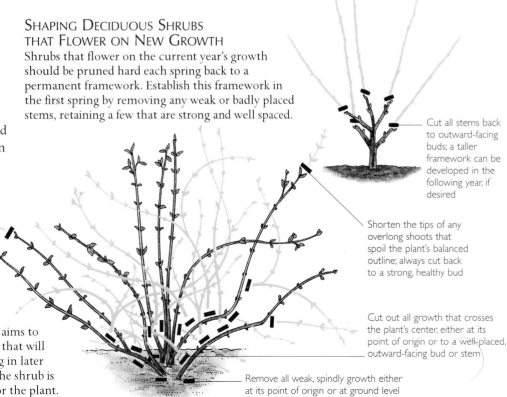

Cut all stems back to outward-facing buds; a taller framework can be developed in the following year, if desired

Shorten the tips of any overlong shoots that spoil the plant's balanced outline; always cut back to a strong, healthy bud

Cut out all growth that crosses the plant's center, either at its point of origin or to a well-placed, outward-facing bud or stem

Remove all weak, spindly growth either at its point of origin or at ground level

SEE ALSO: Maintaining Roses, pp.160–161; Pruning Established Shrubs, pp.158–159; Pruning Fruit Trees, pp.262–263

PRUNING ESTABLISHED SHRUBS

PERHAPS THE SINGLE most important thing you should know before pruning an established shrub is the age of the wood on which it flowers. If pruned at the wrong time, you might remove flowering stems. As a rule, plants that flower on the current season's growth bloom at or after midsummer; they are pruned in late winter or early spring. Those flowering on the previous season's growth bloom between late winter and early summer, and they are pruned after flowering. There are a number of pruning techniques to suit plants of different growth habits. All shrubs need to have dead, diseased, or damaged growth removed as soon as it is seen.

PRUNING DECIDUOUS SHRUBS

If left unpruned, most shrubs degenerate over the years; congested growth builds up and wayward shoots spoil the balance. Regular pruning aims to keep an open, balanced framework of productive stems. A few (usually slow-growing) shrubs like *Acer palmatum*, *Magnolia stellata*, or witch hazel (*Hamamelis*), do not need and cannot tolerate more than minimal pruning. Check with your supplier or research plants' needs before you start pruning.

ALWAYS REMEMBER

The way you position your pruning cuts determines the future direction and vigor of any new growth. New shoots will grow out from a bud in the same direction as that in which the bud is pointing. Provided a shrub tolerates hard pruning, the harder you prune the more vigorous the regrowth will be.

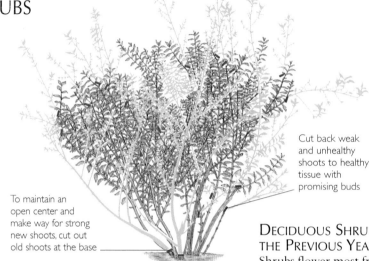

To maintain an open center and make way for strong new shoots, cut out old shoots at the base

Cut back weak and unhealthy shoots to healthy tissue with promising buds

△ FLOWERED WOOD
Cut flowered shoots back to nonflowered ones or to a healthy bud that is pointing in the desired direction.

◁ OLD STEMS
Cut back a third to a quarter of the oldest stems to within 2–3in (5–8cm) of the ground right after flowering. New shoots will flower the following year.

DECIDUOUS SHRUBS THAT FLOWER ON THE PREVIOUS YEAR'S GROWTH

Shrubs flower most freely on young, vigorous, matured (hardened) wood. Those that flower early in the year on shoots made the previous season are pruned immediately after flowering, so that the new growth that emerges has a whole season to mature. As wood gets older, its flowering potential decreases, and it is best removed to make way for younger, stronger, free-flowering growth.

PRUNING EVERGREEN SHRUBS

The majority of evergreens need minimal pruning, apart from the routine removal of dead, diseased, or damaged growth. Overlong or badly placed shoots that spoil the plant's symmetry may be trimmed back and congested growth thinned out. Flowering evergreens benefit from regular deadheading, especially when young. Shrubs grown mainly for their foliage, such as Japanese laurel (*Aucuba japonica*), usually tolerate hard pruning, if necessary; if grown as a screen, hedge, or clipped specimen, for example. Regardless of flowering time, main pruning is best done in mid- to late spring, when danger of frost has passed, to minimize cold damage.

Trim back any overlong or wayward shoots that spoil the shrub's symmetry

Remove flowerheads as they fade, taking care not to damage any growth buds beneath

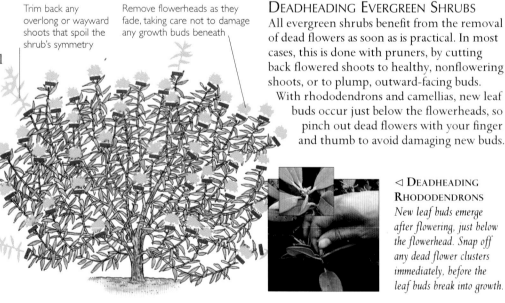

DEADHEADING EVERGREEN SHRUBS

All evergreen shrubs benefit from the removal of dead flowers as soon as is practical. In most cases, this is done with pruners, by cutting back flowered shoots to healthy, nonflowering shoots, or to plump, outward-facing buds.
With rhododendrons and camellias, new leaf buds occur just below the flowerheads, so pinch out dead flowers with your finger and thumb to avoid damaging new buds.

◁ DEADHEADING RHODODENDRONS
New leaf buds emerge after flowering, just below the flowerhead. Snap off any dead flower clusters immediately, before the leaf buds break into growth.

SEE ALSO: Maintaining Shrubs, pp.156–157; Maintaining Roses, pp.160–161

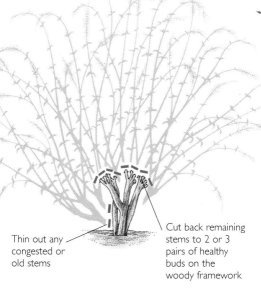

Thin out any congested or old stems

Cut back remaining stems to 2 or 3 pairs of healthy buds on the woody framework

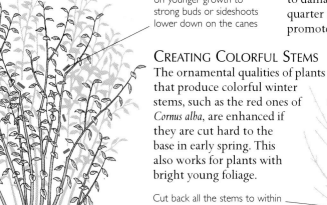

◁ **DEADHEAD**
Cut flowered shoots (here, buddleia) back to buds or sideshoots to concentrate the plant's energy into further flowering.

SHRUBS THAT FLOWER ON THE CURRENT YEAR'S GROWTH

These include buddleia and are pruned in late winter or early spring, just as the buds begin to swell, so that it is easy to tell healthy from unhealthy buds. The aim is to produce a well-balanced head of sturdy new shoots arising annually from a low, permanent, woody framework. If extra height is needed, cut back the basic framework less rigorously.

SHRUBS THAT PRODUCE NEW STEMS FROM THE BASE

Some shrubs bear canelike stems annually from the base and flower at, or near, their tips. Some, such as *Kerria japonica*, flower in spring on the previous season's wood, and they are pruned after flowering; others, like *Leycesteria formosa*, flower in late summer and are pruned in spring. In both, some old canes are removed every year.

Cut back a third to a quarter of the oldest flowered shoots to the base, to promote vigorous replacement growth

Cut back flowered shoots on younger growth to strong buds or sideshoots lower down on the canes

PRUNING HYDRANGEA HYBRIDS

Each year, in early to midspring, trim off the previous year's flowerheads to the first pair of buds beneath the flowerhead, taking care not to damage them. Cut back one-third to a quarter of the oldest shoots to the base to promote vigorous replacement shoots.

CREATING COLORFUL STEMS

The ornamental qualities of plants that produce colorful winter stems, such as the red ones of *Cornus alba*, are enhanced if they are cut hard to the base in early spring. This also works for plants with bright young foliage.

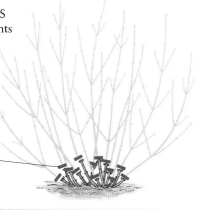

Cut back all the stems to within 2 or 3 buds of the base; fertilize and mulch well to compensate for loss of topgrowth

REJUVENATING OLD SHRUBS

If you inherit neglected or overgrown shrubs, hard pruning can give them a new lease on life, provided that they are healthy. In most cases, even for plants that respond well to hard pruning, it is better to renovate in stages, over two or three seasons. This causes less shock to the plant, and the garden still looks well furnished. A season's flowers may be lost, but strong new growth is ample compensation.

RESTORING A NEGLECTED SHRUB

Renovate deciduous shrubs in mid-autumn to mid-spring, and evergreens in mid- to late spring. At the initial stage, prune out up to half of the oldest stems, and shorten the others. Feed and mulch after pruning. In the second and third seasons, cut back remaining old stems and thin out any weak new shoots around the old cuts.

Either remove or shorten to a bud any sideshoots from main stems that grow across the center of the shrub, or that cross and rub against other stems

Remove dead, diseased, and damaged stems, and take out up to half of the oldest stems at the base; remaining healthy shoots are then trimmed to about half their length

◁ **HEALTHY SHOOTS**
After removing some of the oldest shoots, shorten any remaining, healthy stems by half, cutting back to a bud or sideshoot.

△ **OLD SHOOTS**
Trace back up to half of the oldest, least productive shoots, and cut them back to within 2–3in (5–8cm) of ground level, using loppers or pruners.

SEE ALSO: General Border Maintenance, pp.152–153; Maintaining Roses, pp.160–161

MAINTAINING ROSES

TO KEEP ROSES LOOKING GOOD, you will need to feed and mulch them after pruning. Bush roses benefit from extra fertilizer after the first flush of flower. Remove dead flowers and the unwanted basal growths known as suckers, and undertake some careful pruning. Different rose types require different pruning methods to give off their best. Roses are prone to a variety of ailments (*see pp.294–311*), especially if planted in numbers. To avoid this, control pests and diseases and prune in clear, dry, frost-free conditions. The main aims of rose pruning are to maintain the plant's health and vigor and to maximize its flowering potential throughout the season.

AUTUMN TRIM

Most roses will benefit from an initial shaping or trimming in autumn to help them survive winter and produce strong new growth in spring. To maintain an open center, cut to outward-facing buds. On arching shoots, or if new shoots are needed to fill out the center, cut to an upward- or inward-facing bud.

Plump, healthy bud will develop new growth in the required direction

Correctly angled cut directs water away from the emerging new bud

Healthy stem with no signs of disease or discoloration

◁ **A PERFECT CUT**
Make an angled cut, just above a bud, and sloping away from it. The bottom of the cut should align with the base of the bud.

Long stems, if whipped by strong winds, may cause rocking and disturbance of the roots

△ **BEFORE TRIMMING**
In exposed sites and in cold climates, growth may be damaged and roots loosened in strong winds. A trim in autumn reduces these risks.

△ **AFTER TRIMMING**
Stems have been shortened by a half to a third of their height. If the roots are loosened, carefully firm the soil at the plant's base.

DEADHEADING

With roses that bear flowers in more than one flush, known as repeat-flowering roses, deadheading diverts energy from seed production into further flowering. With roses that flower only once, it stimulates strong new growth. Avoid deadheading roses that have decorative hips in late summer or autumn.

△ **A SINGLE BLOOM**
Cut back faded, single blooms to a strong, outward-facing bud or shoot to encourage the production of a new flowering shoot.

FLOWER CLUSTERS ▷
In cluster-flowered roses, the central bloom fades first. Pinch or snip it out to display the remaining flowers to best effect.

REMOVING SUCKERS

Suckers are unwanted growths that usually emerge during the growing season from the base of the plant or sometimes a short distance away. Their leaves are frequently smaller, a different shape, or a different shade of green from those of the rest of the plant. They should always be removed as soon as they appear.

TELL ME WHY

WHY REMOVE SUCKERS?

Most roses consist of one plant grafted onto the root system, or rootstock, of another; this is done to increase the vigor or longevity of the desired flowering plant. The rootstock is often more vigorous than the grafted plant and, if allowed to grow, its suckers will eventually overwhelm the grafted plant. Removing suckers will ensure that the vigor of the roots passes into the grafted plant.

△ **HOW TO DESTROY SUCKERS**
Gently scrape away the soil and trace the sucker back to its origin; this will be on the stem or root below the point where the graft was made. Wearing thick gloves, grip the sucker firmly and pull it away sharply. This may not be easy, but the sucker is less likely to regrow if pulled rather than cut, because pulling also removes any dormant buds.

◁ **FADED CLUSTER**
When all flowers in the cluster have faded, remove the entire cluster, cutting back to an emerging bud or fully formed shoot. If no buds are apparent, cut back to the desired height, which should stimulate a dormant bud into growth. If a stub is left above this new shoot, cut it away later.

SEE ALSO: Initial Rose Pruning, p.151; General Border Maintenance, pp.152–153; Maintaining Shrubs, pp.156–157; Pruning Established Shrubs, pp.158–159

PRUNING ESTABLISHED ROSES

For all roses, whatever their type, the first step when pruning is to remove dead, diseased, damaged, or weak growth. Patio, polyantha, and miniature roses are treated like floribunda roses, only less so; their stems and sideshoots are shortened by one-third to a half. Prune groundcover roses when not in growth; cut back long stems to outward-facing buds. To confine to an allotted space, shorten sideshoots if crowded and, to renew, remove one in four old stems.

To keep compact and encourage free flowering, cut back the tips of a proportion of the sideshoots at the edges of the plant

As growth becomes crowded and old stems less productive, cut 1 or 2 of the oldest stems out at the base, to an outward-facing bud

After removing weak stems, shorten remainder to within 10–12in (25–30cm) of ground level and sideshoots to within 2 or 3 buds of the main stems

MODERN SHRUB ROSE

Most modern shrub roses, as well as hybrid musks and rugosas, are repeat-flowering. Prune when not in growth, preferably in early spring. Most need only light pruning to maintain shape. Shorten main stems by no more than one-third; sideshoots by a half to two-thirds; remove one in three old stems.

FLORIBUNDA ROSE

The beauty of these roses lies in their massed flower clusters. In principle, they are pruned as for hybrid tea roses but, in order to retain more potential in the flowering shoots, the stems are not shortened so drastically; any sideshoots are shortened to two or three buds.

Make all cuts to outward-facing buds to maintain an open center

HYBRID TEA ROSE

These bushes flower throughout the summer and should be pruned hard while dormant, preferably in early spring. Retain three to five strong, healthy shoots; cut back to 8–9in (20–22cm) above ground level. Remove all spindly shoots that are of less than average thickness.

ALWAYS REMEMBER

GET TO KNOW YOUR ROSES

Roses are classified into different groups; the major ones being species, modern, and old garden roses, the last two also with several subgroups. They have different pruning needs, depending on growth and flowering habit and whether they bloom once or repeatedly. Check the label when buying; it will include the rose's group and so gives vital information on pruning needs.

PRUNING OLD ROSES

Old Garden roses are noted for their grace and stature, and pruning aims to maintain these features. Most flower once a year only, in summer, and are pruned immediately after flowering in one of two ways, depending on their habit of growth. A few old garden roses – the chinas, bourbons, and portlands – flower in repeated flushes throughout summer; prune these as for modern shrub roses, when dormant, preferably in early spring.

△ ALBA, DAMASK, CENTIFOLIA, AND MOSS ROSES
Open, free-branching, often gracefully arching shrubs. After flowering, reduce main stems and sideshoots by a third of their length, cutting back to a healthy, outward-facing shoot or bud. When mature, remove 1 in 4 of the oldest stems to encourage replacement growth. Shorten any long, whippy shoots in autumn to reduce wind damage.

△ GALLICA ROSES
Characteristically, gallicas are dense, twiggy, free-branching roses with thorny stems. After flowering, thin growth by cutting back sideshoots by up to two-thirds of their length. Shorten any overlong shoots by up to a third. When mature, take out 1 or 2 of the oldest stems close to ground level, every 1–3 years.

SEE ALSO: Roses, p.139; Roses, p.147; Maintaining Shrubs, pp.156–157

INCREASING BORDER PLANTS

SOWING SEED AND DIVIDING mature plants are simple, inexpensive ways of increasing your stock of border plants. A few seeds need pretreatment before they will germinate: for hard-coated seeds, like lupines, rub gently between two sheets of sandpaper; for those with chemical inhibitors, like cyclamen, soak in clean water; and, for seeds that need chilling, sow outdoors in autumn or sow in spring after placing them in a refrigerator for a few months. Remember to always read the instructions on the seed packet and follow them closely. Division is a quick and easy method of increasing clump-forming perennials.

SOWING SEED IN POTS

Most seeds are sown between late winter and early spring. Garden-gathered seed of early to midsummer-flowering plants can be sown right away. A 3½–5in (9–13cm) pot or half-pot holds sufficient seedlings for most purposes. Cover seeds that need light for germination with a ¼in (5mm) layer of fine-grade vermiculite instead of soil mix. For most seeds, a temperature of 60°F (15°C) is ideal for germination. Hardy plants are best at about 50°F (10°C); marginal and frost-tender plants need a minimum of 60–70°F (15–21°C). Seedlings need bright light but not direct sun, which may scorch and kill them. When transplanting, handle seedlings only by their leaves; the vulnerable stems will rot if damaged.

RAISING PLANTS FROM SEED

1 PREPARE THE POT
Fill a container, here a 5in (13cm) pot, with moist soil mix and firm it gently with a presser board to remove any air pockets. The finished surface should be no more than ½in (1cm) below the pot rim.

2 SOW THE SEED
Sow seed as thinly and evenly as possible on the surface of the mix by tapping it carefully from a folded piece of clean, smooth paper, or directly from the seed packet in which it came.

3 COVER WITH SOIL MIX
Cover the seed to its own depth with a layer of finely sieved mix or vermiculite. Label the pot, and water with a fine nozzle or by standing in a tray of water until the surface glistens. Allow to drain.

4 COVER THE CONTAINER
Place a sheet of glass or plastic wrap over the pot to minimize moisture loss. Place in good light, but out of direct sun, in a greenhouse, cold frame, or closed case. Remove the cover when germination occurs.

5 TRANSPLANT SEEDLINGS
When the seedlings have developed 2 seed leaves, transplant the seedlings into individual pots. It is best to use biodegradable pots (see inset) for plants that dislike root disturbance.

6 HARDEN OFF AND PLANT
When the young plants have a good root system that almost fills the pot, first harden them off by placing the pot outside for increasing periods to accustom them to cooler conditions. Then plant them out in the border.

ALWAYS REMEMBER

One of the most common causes of failure when propagating from seed is when seedlings fall over, often with a brown ring at the stem base. This is known as damping off. It is caused by fungi that thrive in wet soil mix, poor light, and warm humidity. Crowded seedlings provide ideal conditions for their spread. To prevent damping off, use fresh soil mix, sow thinly, ventilate well, and provide good light.

FINE SEEDS

Some plants, like begonias, produce dust-fine seed that is difficult to sow thinly, increasing the risk of damping off. Mixing with fine sand allows them to be sown thinly. To prevent seed from being washed to one side, water from beneath by standing the pot in clean water until the top of the soil mix is uniformly moist.

SOWING FINE SEEDS

1 MIX WITH SAND
Place a small quantity of fine, dry sand in a small plastic bag. Add the seeds and shake well. Using a folded piece of paper as a funnel helps direct seed into the bag.

2 SURFACE SOW
Using a clean piece of folded paper as a funnel, place the mix of seed and sand in the crease, and sow onto the surface by tapping gently. Water the pot from beneath.

SEE ALSO: Establishing Plants in the Border, pp.148–149; Renovating Perennials, p.155; Saving Seed, p.155

SOWING ANNUALS AND BIENNIALS

Sowing times for annuals and biennials differ, depending on hardiness. Outdoor sowing means in a seed bed or where the plants are to flower; indoors means in a greenhouse, cold frame, or closed case.

■ Sow hardy annuals outdoors in spring, when the soil has warmed up to at least 45°F (7°C), or in autumn.

■ Sow marginal or tender annuals outdoors after frosts have ended, usually in late spring or early summer. Indoors, sow in late winter or early spring, at 59–70°F (15–21°C) and plant out seedlings after the frosts have ended.

■ Sow biennials outdoors or in pots from late spring to midsummer. If sown in a seed bed, transfer to a nursery bed before planting out in autumn.

SOWING SEEDS IN A BORDER

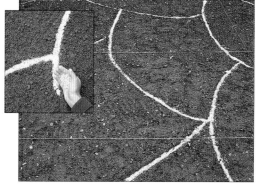

1 PREPARE THE GROUND FOR SOWING
Rake the soil to a fine tilth. Sprinkle grit or sand onto the surface or score with a stick, to mark out areas or drifts for blocks of different plants. Sow seed thinly in shallow rows within each drift. For a natural effect, orient the rows in different directions in adjacent drifts. Seedlings sown in rows are easier to identify and weed.

2 THINNING AND WEEDING
Label each drift and keep seedlings free of weeds. At this stage, they look regimented, but once thinned will form dense, informal drifts. Thin seedlings to recommended spacings when the soil is moist and the weather mild, in stages if necessary. Use any strong, thinned-out seedlings to fill gaps caused by poor or erratic germination.

DIVIDING PERENNIALS

Most perennials form clumps of shoots from growing points on spreading roots or rhizomes, making division an easy means of increasing stock. Plants are best divided when they are not in active growth, in autumn or spring, and when conditions are neither dry nor freezing. In climates with cold winters, division is safer if delayed until spring. Spring or early-summer bloomers, such as epimediums, pulmonarias, and bearded irises, fare best if divided soon after flowering, and kept moist until well established.

△ **DIVIDING FIBROUS-ROOTED PERENNIALS**
When dividing fibrous or fleshy-rooted plants, wash as much soil as possible off the roots and crown, so growth buds are visible and less susceptible to inadvertent damage. Insert two forks in the center of the clump, back to back with tines close together and handles apart. Lever the handles gently back and forth to separate into sections.

HOW TO DIVIDE MATURE PERENNIALS

1 LIFT THE CLUMP
Lift the entire clump with a fork, inserting it well away from the crown to avoid damaging roots. Shake off as much soil as possible and remove dead leaves and stems so that you can see the best places for division.

3 TEASE OUT SMALL SECTIONS
Divide the sections into even smaller pieces, teasing them out by hand. This causes less damage to roots than cutting. Each piece should have a good root system and several shoots. Remove and discard old and woody growth.

2 CHOP THE CLUMP
Many clump-formers develop new growth around the margins of the clump, with old, woody, and less productive growth at the center. Chop the clump into sections, using a sharp knife or spade to sever woody portions of the clump.

Avoid damaging the roots of vigorous young growth with the spade when dividing the clump

4 REPLANT DIVISIONS
New divisions should be planted as soon as possible, at the same depth as they were before, in prepared soil. Firm in gently and water thoroughly. If there is any delay before replanting, keep roots moist and plants cool.

SEE ALSO: Establishing Plants in the Border, pp.148–149; Renovating Perennials, p.155; Saving Seed, p.155.

INCREASING SHRUBS

SMALL PIECES OF PLANT MATERIAL, known as cuttings, can be induced to form roots, and this is one of the best ways of propagating shrubs. Take stem cuttings from any current season's growth that is free of pests, diseases, and damage. Cuttings from vigorous young plants root most easily. Avoid thin, weak, or over-vigorous growth; choose stems of medium thickness for an individual shrub, with only a short distance between two sets of leaves. To prevent any fungal infection killing the cuttings, you should sterilize all your equipment. Hormone rooting compounds may also be used to encourage rooting. Simple layering is another reliable method of raising your own shrubs.

HARDWOOD CUTTINGS

These are suitable for deciduous shrubs such as dogwoods and willows, as well as evergreens like firethorn. They should be taken from late autumn to midwinter, when the current season's wood is mature and hard. Keep the cuttings weed-free and watered; refirm the soil if necessary. By the next autumn, they will be well rooted and can be planted out.

△ **DECIDUOUS HARDWOOD CUTTINGS**
Trim off tips and cut stems into 8in (20cm) lengths. Make a horizontal cut just below a stem joint at the base and a sloping cut above, and angled away from, a bud at the top. Dip the base in hormone rooting compound. Insert them, 2in (5cm) apart, 6in (5cm) deep, in soil-based cuttings mix in pots either in a cold frame or outdoors.

Strip leaves and sideshoots from bottom half of cutting

△ **EVERGREEN HARDWOOD CUTTINGS**
Cut shoots into sections, 8–10in (20–25cm) long. Trim just above a leaf base at the top and below another at the base. Strip leaves from bottom half of cutting. Insert 5–8 cuttings in a 6in (15cm) pot, so the foliage sits just above the surface. Label, and place in a closed case with bottom heat, or in a clear plastic bag. Rooting occurs in 6–10 weeks.

SEMIRIPE CUTTINGS

A wide range of deciduous and evergreen shrubs may be increased from semiripe cuttings, from cotoneasters and mahonias to some lavenders. Take semiripe cuttings early in the day, when water reserves are at a maximum, in mid- to late summer, or early autumn. Most semiripe cuttings need a full growing season to root well. Harden them off gradually during the next spring and summer; apply a slow-release fertilizer in early summer. Pot up in autumn and grow on in a sheltered site.

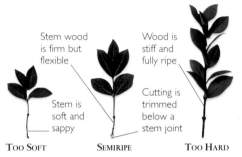

Stem wood is firm but flexible

Wood is stiff and fully ripe

Stem is soft and sappy

Cutting is trimmed below a stem joint

TOO SOFT   SEMIRIPE   TOO HARD

△ **DISTINGUISHING SEMIRIPE WOOD**
The ideal semiripe cutting is taken from current season's growth that has begun to firm up; the base is quite hard, while the tip is soft and still actively growing. Such stems will offer some resistance when bent.

PROPAGATING A SHRUB BY SEMIRIPE CUTTINGS

1 TAKE A CUTTING
In mid- to late summer, select a healthy, semiripe shoot of current season's growth (here, Aucuba) and sever the cutting just above a stem joint with clean, sharp pruners.

2 KEEP CUTTING MOIST
If the cutting is not to be used right away, place it in a clean plastic bag and label. Keep cool, out of direct sun for a couple of hours, or in a refrigerator for a few days.

3 TRIM THE CUTTING
Remove sideshoots from the stem with a sharp knife. Trim the stem to 4–6in (10–15cm), cutting just below a stem joint. Remove the soft tip and the lowest pair of leaves.

4 WOUND THE BASE
To stimulate rooting, cut a shallow sliver of bark, ½–¾in (1–2cm) long, from the base of the stem; do not expose the pith. This process is known as wounding.

5 ROOTING HORMONE
Dip the base of the cutting in hormone rooting compound. Make sure that the entire wound receives the thinnest possible, but even, coating, and shake off the excess.

6 INSERT CUTTINGS
Place cuttings 2–3in (5–8cm) apart in standard cuttings mix in a nursery bed outdoors (or in pots in a closed case). Label with name and date. Water and cover.

SEE ALSO: Tools for Cutting and Pruning, p.279; Other Useful Items, p.281; Cold Frames and Greenhouses, pp.284–287

SOFTWOOD CUTTINGS

Softwood cuttings can root in as little as two or three weeks and are suitable for most deciduous shrubs. Such soft tissue is prone to wilt and rot, however. Use sharp, clean tools and good hygiene; prevent wilting by taking the cuttings early in the morning and placing them right into a plastic bag. In dry weather, water the parent plant the night before. Handle cuttings gently; once rooted, harden them off, pot up, and grow on in a sheltered site.

◁ **SOFTWOOD CUTTINGS**
Take softwood cuttings in spring and early summer from the new season's growth before it has begun to firm up. Choose vigorous, nonflowering shoots with 2 or 3 pairs of leaves, cutting just below a stem joint.

GREENWOOD CUTTINGS ▷
Take greenwood cuttings in late spring to midsummer, just as new stems begin to firm up. They are less prone to wilt and easier to handle than softwood and root as readily. Treat them exactly as for softwood cuttings.

PROPAGATING A SHRUB BY SOFTWOOD CUTTINGS

Remove the soft tip because it is vulnerable to rot and scorch

Vent of closed case will be opened gradually to harden off rooted cuttings

1 TRIM THE CUTTING
Remove the soft tip just above a leaf joint, as well as the lowest pair of leaves. Cut large leaves in half to reduce moisture loss. Trim the base just below a leaf joint; the stem should be 1½–2in (4–5cm) long.

2 INSERT THE CUTTING
Fill a 5in (13cm) pot with cuttings mix. Make 2 or 3 holes around the edge and insert the cuttings so that the lowest leaves lie just above the surface and are not touching each other.

3 PLACE IN CLOSED CASE
After watering thoroughly with a commercial fungicidal solution, label, and place pots in a closed case heated, if possible, at the base to 59°F (15°C). Keep in a shaded place, out of direct sun.

4 POT ON ROOTED CUTTINGS
Once cuttings have rooted, admit more air to harden them off. Knock out of the pot, tease apart, and pot up singly into 3½in (9cm) pots of potting mix. Pinch out growing tips to encourage bushy growth.

SIMPLE LAYERING

For climbers and shrubs that have flexible stems, such as clematis, honeysuckle, and rhododendrons, simple layering is a good method of producing a few new plants. It has the advantage that the layer remains attached to and is sustained by its parent until it has rooted. Do layering at almost any time, but autumn or spring are best.

Find a low-growing, pliable stem that can be easily pegged down. Roots will form most readily at the point where one-year-old wood joins the older wood.

PROPAGATING A SHRUB BY SIMPLE LAYERING

1 SELECT A STEM
In autumn or spring, prepare the soil to make it friable. Choose a young, flexible stem from low down on the plant. Bend it to the ground and mark a position in the soil with a split stake, 9–12in (22–30cm) behind the stem tip.

2 PREPARE THE HOLE
Dig a hole, about 3in (8cm) deep in prepared soil, with a shallowly sloping side next to the parent plant and a near-vertical slope on the far side. Mix a little sand and organic matter into the bottom of the hole if soil is heavy.

3 WOUND THE STEM
Trim off sideshoots and leaves. At the point where the underside of the stem touches the soil, make a slanting cut through to the middle of the stem to make a "tongue" of bark, or remove a 1in (2.5cm) sliver of bark.

4 PEG THE LAYER DOWN
Dust the wound with some hormone rooting compound. Peg the stem down securely into the bottom of the hole using several U-shaped, galvanized wire pins or staples, placing them on either side of the wound.

5 FINISHING TOUCHES
Bend the stem tip up against the vertical side of the hole and secure with a stake. Backfill, firm, and water in. Keep weed-free and moist. A layer should be well rooted within a year, then sever it and plant out or pot up.

SEE ALSO: Tools for Cutting and Pruning, p.279; Other Useful Items, p.281; Cold Frames and Greenhouses, pp.284–287

CONTAINERS AND RAISED BEDS

DESIGN AND POSITIONING

WHETHER YOU HAVE A GRAND GARDEN to rival that of an estate or no more than a pocket-handkerchief backyard, containers can add another dimension to your outdoor space. Containers are tremendously versatile, allowing you to compose groups and rearrange plantings with relative ease. In a small garden, use them as linchpins of the design, to form focal points, flank a path or gateway, or accentuate an axis to enhance the garden's proportions. They can form a link between house and garden, combining hard materials with softer planting; stand them on the terrace or gathered by the door both to define and ease the transition from indoor to outdoor.

CONTAINERS IN THE GARDEN

If you have only a patio or courtyard, roof terrace or balcony, you may need to garden exclusively in containers. But don't let this limit the planting – or your imagination: there is an enormous choice of plants, up to and including small trees, that will grow happily in a container. There are so many advantages to gardening in containers. You can create a flexible design with elements easily shifted or replanted. Containers provide instant impact even while you wait for plants to grow and spread out. They also add sculptural interest and – carefully sited – provide a framework by repeating the same containers to help the overall design cohere.

Containers are useful in beds and borders too. Use them to fill gaps where herbaceous plants have died back or finished flowering. Use a dark pot if you want to minimize the impact of the container itself.

■ **Make a welcoming entrance** with pots by the front door, in either an informal cluster or formal pair. Include evergreens for year-round interest and bulbs to brighten the early days of spring.

■ **If you don't have wide windowsills,** affix sturdy metal brackets to the wall to support boxes; if you use plastic boxes, set the brackets low enough so that only the plants are in view when you look out. This also lets in more light.

◁ **A SHADY CORNER**
Pots filled with ferns and other shade-tolerant plants, like impatiens and begonias, turn this awkward patio corner beside a pond into a lush haven.

POTS OF IDEAS

• Conceal an eyesore such as a garbage can, drain cover, or compost pile with a tiered display of shrubs and trailing plants.

• Suspend a hanging basket at eye level or lower instead of overhead; you can see the flowers better and watering is easier.

• Improve a dull wall with plain clay pots filled with flowering and trailing plants. Circle pots with wire and suspend them from vine eyes driven into the wall.

SEE ALSO: Container Planting Design, pp.172–175; Raised Beds, pp.180–181

CREATING FOCAL POINTS

In any garden, having one or more focal points helps give the garden definition and shape, setting up a series of views to be appreciated from different standpoints. This holds true for even the tiniest plot, but you may need no more than a single strongly planted urn or barrel. Containers are invaluable in establishing key features in the garden or acting as focal points themselves – especially in a new garden, where plants that may later become more prominent are not yet established.

■ **Frame a view** out of the garden with containers on either side it or – more informally – to one side only. For a formal look, use a matching pair with a single, well-shaped specimen in each, such as clipped boxwood or a cordyline.

■ **In a long, narrow garden,** beware of accentuating the long axis by siting an ornamental container in the center at the far end. Instead, site a group of pots of different heights and sizes about one-third of the way along and off-center, which will improve the apparent proportions.

■ **Tiny garden or balcony?** Include one or two larger plants in generous pots to avoid an over-fussy effect. Check the sight-line to your focal point container from the windows if you enjoy looking out onto the garden as much as being in it.

△ **ON A LEDGE**
If your garden is limited in size, it is important to make the most of the space available. These pots bring color to a narrow ledge, which would be bare if it were not for the versatility of container plantings.

◁ **TRICK OF THE EYE**
This colorfully planted box has been cleverly placed on a windowsill on the sight line. Elevated to this level, the box forms a link between the house and garden.

CUSTOMIZED CONDITIONS

One of the benefits of container gardening is that you have a greater control over the growing conditions, so you can expand the range of plants you are able to grow. For example, if you have an alkaline soil in the open ground but yearn to grow lime-hating plants such as camellias or azaleas, cultivate them in containers using an ericaceous (lime-free) potting mix. Similarly, some plants, like many herbs and alpines, require good drainage; if the soil in your garden is heavy clay or boggy, you can improve its structure, but it is easier and more successful to grow such plants in pots or troughs, adding some sharp sand to the soil mix and raising the containers on bricks so that excess water can drain away freely.

The portability of containers makes them an ideal home for tender plants that won't survive winter outdoors. Grow palms, cordylines, daturas (*Brugmansia*), cacti, and lemon trees in pots to bring an exotic feel to the garden in summer, then transfer the plants to a greenhouse, conservatory, or sunporch before the first frosts. Potted houseplants usually benefit from a summer break outside, too.

■ **Provide alpine and rock plants** with a gritty soil mix and grow in an old sink or shallow trough. Topdress around the plants with a layer of coarse sand.

■ **Trees and shrubs** generally prefer a soil-based mix, which is heavier and contains more nutrients than soilless (usually peat-based) potting mixes.

A CUSTOM-MADE "DESERT" △
To grow plants with special requirements or ones that don't suit your garden soil, recruit the services of a handy pot. This china bowl is now a miniature garden. Filled with very free-draining soil mix, it suits the needs of its resident succulents. Remember to provide drainage holes.

SEE ALSO: Garden Styles, pp.122–123; Container Planting Design, pp.172–175; Planting in Containers, pp.176–177

CHOOSING AND CUSTOMIZING CONTAINERS

THERE ARE CONTAINERS AVAILABLE in every style imaginable, so take the time to find those that will look right in your garden. Some would not look out of place beside a palace, while others seem more at home outside a rural cottage or a simple wooden shanty by the sea. As well as the vast range of containers available to buy, you can make your own or decorate bought ones to make them unique – with paint, stencils, shells, or mosaics, for example. If you like something a little unconventional, keep an eye out for other vessels and objects that could be adapted for use as garden containers, such as fruit crates, chimney pots, or even old bathtubs or water tanks.

FITTING IN WITH THE GARDEN STYLE

Containers can have a strong impact on the design of a garden; you can use them to set the tone and atmosphere or to enhance the existing style. There are several factors to take into account, including style, color, texture, and material. A container's style includes the level of formality it suggests as well as its shape and any decoration.

Think about whether you want a formal or informal effect, modern or traditional, urban or rural. For example, very grand or fancy containers tend to look out of place in an informal or cottage-style garden, while wooden barrels might seem too simple and rustic in a geometrically laid out formal space or contemporary town garden. These guidelines, however, are often broken with great success; in a semi-wild garden, for example, the occasional formal urn could suggest past grandeur gracefully slipping away.

A shapely container is also a sculptural object. If you have a single large pot that is especially attractive, you might even leave it empty with no planting to distract the eye with its form. For a unique piece, you could commission a potter or carpenter to design and make one. In a small garden, use pots that are all the same color for a well-planned look, but for a more relaxed feel, include a variety of colors and textures.

■ **Terracotta pots and boxes** work well in a wide range of gardens, but they don't suit absolutely everywhere. If you live in a stone house or in a cold, rainy region, their Mediterranean style may look out of place. Local stone or glazed ceramic may be a more appropriate choice.

■ **Containers in seaside gardens** may be best kept simple. Note which materials are used locally and draw inspiration from the surrounding area, such as boats, barrels, driftwood, and ropework. Wooden or painted pots are often more in keeping than swanky urns or terracotta.

△ **AN INFORMAL STYLE**
A large metal urn densely laden with informal plants like petunias and Helichrysum petiolare *is not just informal but distinctive and individual, too.*

SELECTION AND RANGE

More and more people are turning to container gardening, with the result that there is a huge choice of pots, planters, barrels, and boxes. Before you buy, have in mind some idea of the style you want (*see above*), and the sizes you need. The pot size should balance with the planting visually and also be large enough to suit the plants' needs. Think about the materials that will suit your garden best (*see opposite, top*) and any practical considerations, such as weight if you will need to move the pots. If you might want to add more matching pots later, check that the store is planning to stock them in the future.

FORMAL CONTAINERS
These classic containers usually have gently sloping sides. Square containers are useful for plants with extensive root systems.

Glazed earthenware

Unglazed ceramic

Wooden Versailles planter

Painted Versailles planter

New Zealand flax (*Phormium tenax*)

Terracotta urn

Molded concrete urn

Period-style reconstituted stone urn

Terracotta trough

SEE ALSO: Easy Decorative Effects, p.170; Adapting Existing Containers, p.170

WHICH MATERIAL?

As well as styles, shapes, and sizes, think about which materials will best suit your garden. They should tie in with the other key elements and with the materials used in the house and any other structures, such as a path or patio. For example, terracotta pots look good with red brick, and painted or wooden tubs with wooden houses.

■ **Terracotta:** available in a huge range of styles and sizes, and it suits many garden styles. It ages well but may be damaged by cold and is heavy to move. It is porous, so the soil dries out quite quickly.

■ **Glazed ceramic:** often good value and available in a range of colors to tie in with your planting designs. The glaze reduces moisture loss, and pots are more likely to withstand cold, but the surface doesn't acquire a patina with age.

■ **Wood:** suits many styles of garden and may be painted to complement a planting design. You may be able to have items made to order. Weathers nicely with age,

but eventually disintegrates and should be treated with preservative to extend its life.

■ **Metal:** in keeping with modernist and minimalist garden designs. Best used with a plastic insulating liner to prevent temperature extremes damaging roots.

■ **Stone:** usually very expensive, but adds a feeling of grace and antiquity to a garden. Weathers well with age and should last for centuries. Heavy to move.

◁ **A GLAZED URN**
The grandiose appearance of this urn among the tentacles of vigorous climbers suggests formality surrendering to the grip of nature.

△ **NEW-AGE TULIPS**
White, silver, and darkest reds are a superbly modern complement to the clean lines and sheen of this galvanized metal bucket.

■ **Reconstituted stone:** cheaper than real stone but feels solid and often found in similar designs. Tends to look too perfect, so brush with live yogurt to speed aging.

■ **Plastic:** usually the lightest and cheapest material. Pots with a matte finish and dark color are less obtrusive if you don't like the look of plastic. Can also be painted if you rub the surface first with sandpaper.

■ **Basketware:** very light, relatively cheap, and complements plants well. Line baskets with plastic to retain moisture, and use a tough exterior varnish to extend their life.

ALWAYS REMEMBER

WATCH YOUR WEIGHT

If you garden on a roof terrace or balcony, don't forget that the prime consideration with containers may be that of weight; have the structure checked to be safe. Lightweight plastic pots may be painted for a variety of looks, and plastic pots disguised with a wooden casing (with no base).

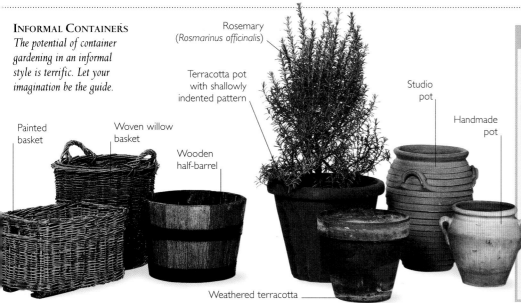

INFORMAL CONTAINERS
The potential of container gardening in an informal style is terrific. Let your imagination be the guide.

Rosemary
(*Rosmarinus officinalis*)

Terracotta pot with shallowly indented pattern

Painted basket

Woven willow basket

Wooden half-barrel

Studio pot

Handmade pot

Weathered terracotta

PRACTICAL MATTERS

• Unless you live in a very mild area, look for terracotta pots that are guaranteed frost-proof; otherwise, they may flake or even crack in cold weather. Raising them on bricks helps water drain away, which might otherwise freeze and cause cracking.

• Look for old urns, troughs, and planters in junk shops and architectural salvage yards. You may find cracked or chipped containers available cheaply, but mend cracks, if possible, before planting.

• You may find Versailles planters made of heavy-duty plastic that resembles painted wood. Unlike wood, these require no maintenance and won't deteriorate.

SEE ALSO: Aging Pots, p.171; Making a Wooden Trough, p.171; Winter Protection, p.179

EASY DECORATIVE EFFECTS

If you want containers that are unique but not too expensive, it is simple enough to decorate cheap, plain pots and boxes yourself. You don't need special artistic talents to create attractive and impressive effects, just some time and basic materials.

■ **Paint:** prepare plastic pots and boxes by rubbing the surface first with sandpaper before painting. Look out for small sample cans of paint if you want to use several different colors, such as milky pastels in blue, mauve, and green, or rich, dark tones like deep green, burgundy, and navy. Finish off with a waterproof varnish.

■ **Stencils:** buy premade or design your own, cut out from thin cardboard. Keep your motif simple and stylized for greatest impact. Repeat the stencil to make a decorative border. Apply the paint by sponging it on, then varnish to protect.

■ **Stain:** show off wooden barrels and planters with a natural or colored stain that lets the wood grain show through.

■ **Beadings and moldings:** add beading to a plain box to create a paneled effect, or glue on simple moldings such as fruits or leaves.

■ **Mosaic and shells:** cover a plain container with small mosaic tiles or pieces of broken crockery laid like random paving. Attach with tile cement and grout or tile adhesive, depending on your materials.

◁ **HOT POTS**
Brightly painting terracotta pots is a fun way to cheer up an area of the garden. Hot colors are ideal for cacti and succulents, with their bold shapes and outlines. These pots have boldly stenciled motifs around their sides.

△ **MELLOW YELLOW**
This painted yellow box has been thoughtfully planted with toning colors. It holds golden marjoram (Origanum vulgare 'Aureum'), zinnias, and feverfew (Tanacetum parthenium).

You can buy colored grout or pigment it yourself with a little latex paint. Instead of mosaic, you could use small seashells. If possible, work on the container in its final position since it will be heavy to move.

ADAPTING EXISTING CONTAINERS

When looking for containers for the garden, there's no need to limit yourself to what the garden center can offer. Keep an open mind and look for other containers that could be recycled for garden use. These might be as basic as wooden fruit crates that you could paint or stain, or old galvanized metal buckets. Some people adapt metal wheelbarrows that are past their useful life or battered bathtubs, water tanks, or feed troughs from farms. Let your imagination be your guide.

Whichever kind of containers you find, remember that you will need to make holes to allow for drainage, and ensure that there will be enough depth of soil for the kind of plants you plan to grow. With degradable materials, such as basketware and wood, treat with an exterior waterproof varnish and line the container with plastic to extend its life outdoors.

◁ **CROCK OF ROSES**
Miniature roses fill this old bread crock. For drainage, holes have been drilled through the base.

▽ **A STAINED CRATE**
An old, green-stained produce crate makes an effective windowbox for these white cyclamen. Preservative was mixed with green wood stain and then painted on.

Tall crock lifts this low-growing rose

Wood stain mixed with preservative extends life of crate

SEE ALSO: Fitting in with the Garden Style, p.168

AGING POTS

If you like your garden to have a settled, established look, you may find the raw brightness of new containers obtrusive. This is often especially true of terracotta, which may look very orange, and reconstituted stone or concrete, which may be almost white. One way of dulling down new terracotta is to sponge it with a light green wash (diluted paint). By the time this wears off, natural moss may be starting to take hold. Another method is to apply two colors of paint, then rub patches of the top layer away with steel wool. On concrete or terracotta molded urns and boxes, replicate the effect of moss or algae by applying a little dryish green paint in the crevices of the moldings – the areas where it would naturally tend to appear first.

If you want a more permanent solution, an alternative is to hasten the natural aging process yourself. Simply brush containers with live yogurt, sour milk, or chicken stock – anything that will encourage the growth of tiny plants. Repeat after heavy rain.

SPEEDING THE AGING PROCESS

1 PAINT ON YOGURT
Use live cultured yogurt to paint the surface of a terracotta or stone pot. Some pots may take a few days to dry.

2 MOVE POT INTO LIGHT SHADE
Place the container in a lightly shaded position. Plant with impatiens and geraniums, which suit the conditions, and allow a month for the surface to age.

MAKING A WOODEN BOX

Simple boxes made of weatherproofed wood can be directly planted up or used to hold pots or a plastic windowbox. This basic wooden box is reasonably easy to make. You don't need to be an expert, although you will need to be able to use an electric drill. The measurements here are for an average-sized windowbox, but of course you can adapt them to suit any windowledge or site; just make sure you have two matching end panels, two matching side panels, and a base panel that is the same length as the sides and the same width as the ends.

For this box, you will need planed lumber of about ¾in (2cm) thickness. Ask your lumber supplier to cut it to size or saw it yourself. Use either metric or imperial measurements, but don't mix the two. Sand rough edges before you start.

The finished box can be treated with a wood stain, painted, stenciled, or decorated in any way you like. If it is to be used on a windowsill, make sure it is securely fixed in place so that it does not pose a danger to passersby below. Stand the box on shallow wedges or feet to allow drainage, and slip a tray beneath it to catch surplus water if the windowsill is above a street. Boxes also look attractive simply raised on bricks or blocks on the ground, especially if filled with plants like hens and chicks (*Sempervivum*), which look good viewed from above.

HOW TO MAKE A WINDOWBOX

TOOLS AND MATERIALS

- 1 base panel (3ft×7in/1m×17cm)
- 2 identical end panels (7×8in/17×20cm)
- 2 identical side panels (3ft×8in/1m×20cm)
- Electric drill with 4mm (⅛in) drill bit
- Countersink
- ½in (13mm) drill bit
- Screwdriver
- Screws (2in/5cm long)
- Wood filler and sandpaper (*optional*)
- Exterior paint or stain and varnish

1 MARK THE ENDS
Lay the base flat on a table or workbench. Hold an end panel in position on the base panel, and mark along its inside edge on the base. Repeat for the other end panel. Now mark 3 spaced holes for screws at each end of the base within the marked-off areas.

2 DRILL THE BASE
Using the ⅛in (4mm) bit, drill the marked holes in the base. Rest the base on spare scraps of wood to keep it level and protect the work surface from the drill. Use a countersink to make a shallow depression so that the screw head will lie below the surface.

3 ASSEMBLE BOX
Screw the end panels in place on the base, using the predrilled holes. Lay a side panel down flat and place the ends-and-base assembly on top to mark its position as you did with the ends. Mark holes around 3 edges of the side panels, keeping clear of the corners. Drill the holes.

4 DRAINAGE HOLES
Turn the box upside down and drill holes in the base for drainage, using the ½in (13mm) bit.

5 LINE AND PROTECT
Use wood filler to fill in the screw holes and cover the heads, if you like. Allow to dry; sand smooth. Paint or stain the box, then protect with exterior varnish. If it is to be filled directly with soil, line with plastic punctured for drainage.

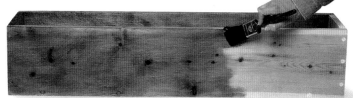

SEE ALSO: Fitting in with the Garden Style, p.168; Which Material?, p.169

CONTAINER PLANTING DESIGN

WHEN PLANNING PLANTING DESIGNS for containers, some of the same considerations apply as when designing beds and borders. Qualities such as shape and form, color, texture, and scent may all be relevant, as well as the style and level of formality. Another important factor is position; a pot on a patio that will be enjoyed at close quarters might contain fragrant plants, like myrtle, and those with subtle textures, such as hostas. A pot sited at the far end of a path needs a plant of striking form or color, perhaps a spiky yucca. Containers provide you with great flexibility; you can design a planting in one pot, and it can stand alone or as part of a group.

COMPOSING GROUPS

The relative portability of containers and the fact that they are self-contained means they can be moved to create different groups, changing the look of your garden as often as you like. Whether you want a formal or informal feel, your composition should have a sense of structure, both in the planting and in the arrangement of the containers. For example, for a strong centerpiece use a plant with a strong form, such as a New Zealand flax (*Phormium*) with fountainlike sprays of strappy leaves; then set smaller pots on bricks as tiers around it. Include trailing plants to spill over and soften the rigid lines of the containers and contrast with the sculptural silhouette of the architectural plant.

■ **Formal groups:** use containers that are identical or at least made of the same material. Keep planting simple, with just one type of plant per container. Try a row of pots filled with lilies to edge a pathway, or boxes, planted with primroses, set on bricks in a stepped formation.

■ **Informal groups:** containers may be loosely clustered as if randomly grouped, but you still need to lay them out with care for a satisfying composition. Include plants of sprawling habit to fill the composition

△ IN THE FRAME
The bold forms of these two agaves are used to frame an informal display of flowering container plants, which includes white lilies and geraniums.

A BRIGHT IDEA ▷
Pink petunias and silver senecio foliage in the same shimmering hues bring light to these steps, which would otherwise be dark and featureless.

and soften the hard edges of pots. Perhaps add one or two strongly shaped specimens to bring definition and structure.

■ **Color:** arrange a group of containers with plants in different hues of the same color – blowsy pinks, fiery reds, or cool whites and creams. Or combine plants with a restricted range of colors; silver-gray foliage with white and pale pink blooms; lime green with soft yellow and pure blue; bronze with purple and dark red. If you like a blast of clashing colors, fine, but still limit the range for maximum impact. If you include every color in the rainbow, the effect may look spotty and chaotic.

TELL ME WHY

CAN I GROUP PLANTS THAT NEED DIFFERENT GROWING CONDITIONS?

Within any single container, you should combine only plants that have the same basic needs in terms of soil mix, water, and fertilizer. It is easier to grow one type of plant per pot. In a mixed group, plants need the same sort of environment (sun or shade). You can use large plants to provide shade for smaller plants beneath, if necessary.

SEE ALSO: Garden Styles, pp.122–123; Design and Positioning, pp.166–167; Planting in Containers, pp.176–177

TOPIARY AND STANDARDS

△ **STYLE AND SYMMETRY**
This entrance is ideal for framing with standards in pots. Pictured here is a formal arrangement of two standard privets underplanted with geraniums and ivy.

Plants clipped into simple topiary shapes or trained as standards, with a clear stem like a miniature tree, are useful in containers to add height to any design or act as visual punctuation points. For a formal look, site a pair of standards on either side of a doorway, to mark the start of a path or drive or to flank a statue. They are not out of place in an informal setting either; use a clipped cone of boxwood or a holly to contrast with barrels filled with casually sprawling lavender and daisylike osteospermums.

To form a standard, choose a specimen with a strong central stem. Stake it, and gradually remove lower sideshoots over time. Cut the top off the main stem once at the required height to encourage growth of sideshoots and create a bushy head: pinch off the sideshoot tips each year.

PLANTS AS STANDARDS

Many trees and shrubs may be trained as standards with a length of clear stem. They should be staked during their initial training, at the very least.

Bay (*Laurus nobilis*)
Boxwood (*Buxus sempervirens*) **T**
Cherry laurel (*Prunus laurocerasus*)
Euonymus (such as *Euonymus fortunei* 'Silver Queen')
Fuchsia (such as 'Celia Smedley', 'Citation')
Geranium (*Pealrgonium*, many)
Hibiscus (such as *Hibiscus syriacus* 'Blue Bird')
Holly (*Ilex aquifolium*) **T**
Hydrangea (such as *Hydrangea macrophylla* 'Hamburg')
Laurustinus (*Viburnum tinus*)
Lemon verbena (*Aloysia triphylla*)
Myrtle (*Myrtus communis*)
Oleaster (such as *Elaeagnus* 'Quicksilver')
Privet (such as *Ligustrum ovalifolium* 'Aureum') **T**
Yew (*Taxus*) **T**

T = plant may also be trained and clipped into dense topiary shapes, such as spheres or cones.

DISPLAYING SINGLE SPECIMENS

If you possess a star plant that you really want to show off, grow it as a single specimen in a container. The plant might be a particularly well-shaped shrub or small tree or have especially fine flowers or foliage. Give it a prominent spot of its own to do it justice, in the natural line of sight from the house, for example, beside an ornamental garden bench, or raised on a small plinth, wall, or at the head of garden steps. Make sure its background forms a good foil; a plain wall, fence, or hedge is better than a confused mass of different-colored plants.

Choose a container that complements the plant's good looks rather than over-competing with it for attention. You may like to opt for a container that has a similar style or mood to the plant, or prefer a distinct contrast between the two. For example, a succulent agave with spiky, sculptural stems would look at home in a plain terracotta pot, but growing it in a formal pedestal urn creates an element of surprise, which adds a touch of vitality to a garden. The container should also be in proportion to the plant in terms of height and width. Set the plant, still in its original pot, in the container to check the effect and balance before planting.

◁ **A FORMAL FAVORITE**
This white hydrangea looks simple, cool, and elegant in its nicely proportioned formal container. To make it into a prominent feature, the hydrangea is positioned against an arborvitae hedge at the end of a gravel path edged with clipped boxwood.

SEE ALSO: Garden Styles, pp.122–123; Maintaining Shrubs, pp.156–157; Design and Positioning, pp.166–167; Routine Care and Maintenance, pp.178–179

PLANTING IN A SHADY SPOT

A shady area of the garden need not look dull or gloomy, and container plantings are a good way of turning an underused, dingy spot into a lush haven. One distinct advantage of using containers in shade is that the containers themselves add interest and color. The gleam of glazed pots or the light tone of real or artificial stone can be especially welcome here. In a site in full sun, containers are often quick to dry out, whereas in shade they will be less thirsty.

Although few plants flower as prolifically in shade as they do in sun, there are some honorable exceptions, such as impatiens and begonias (Semperflorens group – the small, fibrous-rooted type, not the more flamboyant, tuberous kinds), both of which will bloom tirelessly until the first frosts.

Add impact with bold foliage plants like ferns, hostas, fatshederas, arums, and the immensely tolerant Japanese laurel (*Aucuba japonica* 'Crotonifolia' has leaves densely flecked with golden yellow). Inclusion of variegated aucubas and ivies attractively splashed or margined with cream or yellow adds sparkle to a palette of mixed greens. To create a changing display and provide spots of light and color, plant woodland bulbs, such as dog's-tooth violets and *Anemone blanda*, to flower in spring.

◁ **A GREEN CURTAIN**
Pots and bowls of pastel-colored impatiens and begonias, mixed ferns, and ivy all grow well in this partly shaded spot against a dense, living curtain of evergreen shrubs.

▽ **SIMPLE BEAUTY**
This white, fibrous-rooted begonia in a small trough enjoys both the shade and the humidity of a watery location. The large, glossy waterlily leaves form a splendid backdrop.

■ **Assess the amount of shade:** check if the area receives some sun in the morning or evening. Many plants will prosper with only an hour or two of sunlight each day.
■ **Dense shade** cast by trees or high walls is more restrictive, but painting a wall white reflects light. Try mahonias, hollies, ivies, bergenias, fatsias, and osmanthus.
■ **Dappled shade:** a wider range of plants thrive in partial shade. Many golden-leaved or variegated plants scorch in full sun, so they prefer a slightly shaded position.

CONTAINERS IN EXPOSED SITES

In exposed sites, such as roof terraces and balconies, your entire garden may consist of containers, while in hilltop and coastal gardens, barrels and troughs may be a key element of the planting design. There are two typical problems: temperature extremes and wind. The soil mix in containers tends to dry out more quickly in any case, so drying winds may make plants even more vulnerable.

In windy gardens, choose low-growing plants and those with small leaves, which are usually more tolerant of wind. If you want to include tall plants, opt for those

◁ **GRACEFUL GRASSES**
Turn a problem into an opportunity by using a windy spot to grow grasses. They are more resistant to drying winds than broad-leaved plants and ripple gracefully in a breeze.

with soft, pliable growth such as bamboos and phormiums rather than those with brittle stems. Alpines, rock plants, and dwarf bulbs – any plants that grow in exposed situations in the wild – are a good choice for windswept gardens. Minimize evaporation from the surface of the soil mix by mulching with stones or coarse sand, and line clay pots and boxes with plastic to reduce moisture loss.

In coastal regions, choose plants that will tolerate salt-laden winds. Many shrubs will grow well in containers in these conditions and you can underplant them with low rock plants. Try prostrate and low-growing shrubs such as rosemary (*Rosmarinus officinalis* 'Benenden Blue') and tough-leaved seaside favorites like pines and oleander.

SEE ALSO: Mulching Materials, p.153; Design and Positioning, pp.166–167; Planting in Containers, pp.176–177; Routine Care and Maintenance, pp.178–179

CONTAINER DISPLAYS FOR WINTER

In winter, when there is no competition from showy summer borders, container designs come into their own. Planting is best done early to midautumn. Include conifers or broadleaved evergreen shrubs to form the core of a display, giving year-round interest and providing a strong framework around which to vary more transient elements such as spring bulbs and summer bedding for variety.

When choosing conifers, look for dwarf types so they don't outgrow their pot too quickly. Consider shape as well as color; there are upright types shaped like a rocket or flame (such as *Juniperus communis* 'Hibernica'), rounded, cushionlike forms (*Pinus sylvestris* 'Nana'), as well as numerous conical and ground-hugging types. Foliage colors include gold, silvery blue, bright green, and soft blue-green.

With broadleaved evergreens, seek out specimens with a good, well-balanced shape and handsome foliage. If you want winter berries, try cotoneasters, skimmias,

BEAUTIFUL BERGENIAS △
Bergenias are handsome and hardy evergreen perennials with large leaves that look attractive in the depths of winter. They flower from midwinter to early spring.

and hollies (with these last two, use female plants, but you also usually need a male pollinating plant nearby to ensure fruiting). Soften the slightly static look of many shrubs and conifers with ivies trailing over the sides of the container.

PERFECT PARTNERS

Each pair of plants listed below includes a shrub or permanent plant plus another plant to grow beneath, around, or even through it. Each pairing will form a good display for winter although you can change the effect in other seasons by including spring bulbs or summer bedding plants, for example. There is a recommended particular species or cultivar in each case, just to inspire you, but a substitute of similar type will often work just as well. For example, almost any trailing ivy will look good as an underplanting.

Viburnum with snowdrops: *Viburnum farreri* + *Galanthus* 'Atkinsii'

Blue juniper with cyclamen: *Juniperus squamata* 'Blue Star' + *Cyclamen coum*

Hebe with winter pansies: *Hebe pimeleoides* 'Quicksilver' + *Viola* Floral Dance Series

Variegated euonymus with winter aconites: *Euonymus fortunei* 'Emerald 'n' Gold' + *Eranthis hyemalis*

Hellebore with variegated ivies: *Helleborus argutifolius* + *Hedera helix* 'Eva'

Elaeagnus with saxifrages: *Elaeagnus* × *ebbingei* 'Limelight' + *Saxifraga* × *urbium*

Bronze bergenia with purple-leaved ivies: *Bergenia cordifolia* 'Purpurea' + *Hedera helix* 'Glymii'

New Zealand flax with stonecrop: *Phormium* 'Dazzler' + *Sedum obtusatum*

USING TRAILING PLANTS

When composing displays for containers, don't forget about plants that trail down as well as those that grow up. Deservedly popular for hanging baskets, where their pendent strands can move freely, trailing plants are also an asset for earth-bound pots and urns, and wall planters. They break the rigid geometric outline of a pot or box and add lightness and movement to a planting that is dense or architectural.

Use trailing plants to link a planted container with its immediate context. For example, a box sited on a low wall or a pot at the top of garden steps can be visually anchored with trailers that blur the distinction between the container and its platform. There is no shortage of choice. As well as evergreens, such as ivies and periwinkle (*Vinca minor*), try the felted, silver-gray *Helichrysum petiolare* or its golden form 'Limelight' (best grown in dappled shade to prevent scorching) in the warmer months. Remember that many climbers, such as clematis, make attractive trailers if allowed to grow without a support.

△ **HANGING SPIDER**
A spider plant cascades over Pogonatherum saccharoideum (*left*) *and* Tolmeia menziesii, *lending quiet color to this shady doorway in summer.*

GOLDEN BASKET ▷
Combine the trailing foliage of lysimachia and tradescantia with bright yellow oxalis and cosmos flowers to create this fresh green and yellow basket.

SEE ALSO: Design and Positioning, pp.166–167; Planting in Containers, pp.176–177; Routine Care and Maintenance, pp.178–179

PLANTING IN CONTAINERS

CONTAINER GARDENING allows you to grow a wider choice of plants than may be possible in open ground because you can provide them with the conditions that suit their needs. Get them off to a good start and help create a wonderful display by planting them – between spring and autumn – in a suitable soil mix and container.

Consider the plants' specific growing requirements, for example whether they need especially good drainage or an acidic soil mix. For a good-looking arrangement, it is usual to plant more densely than in a border. This still allows room for growth, but it does mean that container plantings demand more intensive maintenance.

BASIC PRINCIPLES

The first step before you plant is to prepare the container correctly. Make sure it has enough drainage holes, and add more if necessary. Use an electric drill with an appropriate bit (a masonry bit for stone or concrete); with plastic pots, you may find it easiest to melt a hole with a heated poker or screwdriver. Put a piece of window screening over the holes to prevent soil mix from washing out each time you water and clogging the drainage holes. Soak terracotta pots before planting so they won't draw moisture out of the soil mix.

A HAPPY COMBINATION ▷
Combine plants in containers that enjoy each other's company. Colors, shapes, and scents are all fun to experiment with. Here, ivy geraniums, dahlias, and malvastrums make a hot summer display.

TELL ME WHY

MY POTS DRY OUT SO QUICKLY: HOW CAN I REDUCE THE NEED TO WATER THEM?

Some types of container definitely dry out more quickly than others. Clay and terracotta need more frequent watering than plastic or glazed pots. Reduce the need to water by planting in plastic pots small enough to slip inside the terracotta ones. Add soil mix to conceal the plastic rim if necessary. Alternatively, use plastic as a liner, and make holes for drainage.
• **Improve** the moisture retention of the soil mix by mixing in perlite or water-retaining gel. Reduce evaporation with a surface mulch such as bark or gravel.
• **In hanging baskets,** place a saucer or shallow dish in the bottom of the basket between the liner and the soil mix to act as a small reservoir. Some plastic hanging containers incorporate a built-in reservoir.
• **Automatic watering systems** are essential if containers are regularly left unattended.

Use a soil mix that is appropriate for the plants: a soil-based one for trees, shrubs, and long-lived perennials; multipurpose soil mix for annuals and summer or short-term displays; acidic soil mix for rhododendrons and other lime-hating plants; and alpine soil mix (which includes plenty of coarse material) for rock plants. Garden soil is not normally recommended because it tends to become compacted in containers with regular watering and may include pests, diseases, or weed seeds.
■ **If using water-retentive crystals,** mix them thoroughly with the soil mix before planting and use only the recommended amount. Remember that they do not eliminate the need for regular watering.
■ **Raise pots off the ground** on "feet" or bricks to allow free drainage. It also prevents water from sitting around the roots, which could promote disease, and reduces cold damage to terracotta pots.

◁ **A CLEAN START**
If reusing an old pot, you can reduce the risk of possible disease problems or pests by scrubbing it with a dilute solution of water and disinfectant.

△ **MAGNIFICENT MULCHES**
As well as reducing water loss and keeping down weeds, a mulch can be attractive in its own right and provide a good foil to enhance planting. Try washed stones or seashells, glass nuggets or marbles, bark chips or cocoa shell mulch.

SEE ALSO: Mulching Materials, p.153; Composing Groups, p.172; Routine Care and Maintenance, pp.178–179

MAKING A WINDOWBOX DISPLAY

With a windowbox, the first priority is safety. Make sure the sill or brackets will be strong enough to support its weight when full (remember it will be much heavier once watered). As a precaution, screw it to retaining brackets or use mirror plates on a wooden box to secure to hooks fixed into the wall. If using brackets to support a trough, bear in mind that the established plants will be taller. A good idea is to position brackets so that the box itself will be just below the window: it won't reduce levels of natural light, and only the plants themselves will be visible. Ideally, plant up the box in its final position to save having to move it once full. Follow the same principles regarding drainage and suitable soil mixes as for other container plantings (*see opposite*). If the trough is to sit above a thoroughfare, add a long tray underneath so that excess water doesn't drain onto passersby. To keep a box level on a sloping sill, add wooden wedges beneath it at the front.

Plant up the box as shown, using a soil-based mix if including shrubs and if weight is not a problem. Pack the plants in for abundance, but avoid tall plants, which tend to look out of proportion and, in a windy site, may make the box unstable.

PLANTING UP A BOX

1 PREPARE THE BOX AND FILL WITH SOIL
Make sure the box has enough drainage holes. Place the box in position; once full, it will be heavy to move. Half-fill the box with moistened multipurpose soil mix, then firm lightly.

2 ARRANGING AND PLANTING
Remove each plant from its pot and loosen the root ball, without damaging the roots, before planting. Plant fairly closely, but allow space for growth. Leave at least ½in (1cm) between the necks of the plants and the box rim.

3 FINISHING AND WATERING
Continue to plant, firming in gently and adding soil mix between plants. Don't add soil mix right up to the rim; leave a gap for watering. Water well and allow excess to drain away. Add extra mix if needed to fill any sunken areas.

4 ROUTINE CARE
Water and fertilize plants regularly and deadhead frequently so they continue to flower. Here, only a couple of months after planting, the begonias, impatiens, and lobelias have all filled out to create an established display.

HANGING BASKETS

As with a windowbox, decide where to site a hanging basket before planting. Be sure the bracket or support is sufficiently strong. As an alternative to a house or garden wall, try suspending a basket from a tree (protect the bark with rubber), pergola, or archway.

Plastic-coated wire baskets are light, easy to use, and widely available but need to be lined before planting. Sphagnum moss, the traditional choice, is less in favor now because its commercial use, along with garden peat, has damaged some natural peat-bog habitats. Coir liners may be used instead; these are light and may be reused the following year. Foam liners are also available, or you can cut plastic to fit; it will be concealed once the planting display is well established. Use a suitable multi-purpose soil mix, and – if you wish – incorporate water-retentive crystals into the mix before planting.

PLANTING IN A BASKET

1 LINE THE BASKET
Balance the basket on a bucket or large pot, and fit it with a liner, trimming overlapping pieces inside as necessary. Add a saucer in the bottom as a reservoir, if desired.

2 PLANT THE SIDES
Cut slits around the liner at different levels for the plants. Add soil mix to just below the level of the lowest slit. Moisten the root ball of a plant before easing it through a slit.

3 PLANT THE TOP
Continue planting into the side slits, covering each root ball with soil mix as you go. Arrange the rest of the plants on the top to your liking. Remove each from its pot, then plant.

4 TRIM AND WATER
Fill in between the plants with more soil mix, firming well. Trim the top of the liner, leaving about ¾in (2cm) above the rim to prevent water from overflowing. Water well.

SEE ALSO: Design and Positioning, pp.166–167; Routine Care and Maintenance, pp.178–179

ROUTINE CARE AND MAINTENANCE

WHILE PLANTS IN THE OPEN GROUND can sometimes survive a degree of neglect or unsuitable conditions, those confined in containers are much more at your mercy and may well suffer or even die if you don't meet their individual needs. For this reason, it is definitely worth establishing a basic maintenance routine, including watering, feeding, deadheading, and clipping, as well as less frequent tasks such as repotting. Try to get into the habit of making a daily tour of your containers, especially if you have a balcony or courtyard and garden exclusively in pots, so that you keep your displays looking their best and any problems are picked up early and resolved.

WATERING AND FEEDING

Even in wet weather, plants in pots may stay drier than you think; dense foliage may mean little rain reaches the soil mix. Don't leave pots sitting in water, however; this impedes drainage and may lead to rotting of the roots. Flagging leaves or a suspiciously light pot usually indicates a need to water, but set up a routine rather than waiting until plants are in dire need. Periodically add a liquid fertilizer when watering or use a controlled-release fertilizer during the growing season.

Consider irrigation systems, which also solve watering problems while you're away. These basically consist of a hose with holes that trickle water into each pot. Set the timer for evening or night-time to minimize water loss caused by evaporation during the day.

△ **THIRSTY PLANTS**
A good-looking arrangement will need to be densely planted, but this necessitates frequent watering, occasionally with a dilute liquid fertilizer.

PULLEY SYSTEM ▷
Watering is simple for hanging baskets attached to a pulley system.

MAINTAINING CONTAINER DISPLAYS

Provided that you water and feed your container plants appropriately, they should thrive, but to keep them looking their best you may also want to carry out a few other minor tasks.

With flowering plants, it is a good idea to deadhead them regularly; as well as looking neater, this also encourages more flowers and so prolongs the display. Keep plants well shaped by pruning or pinching them out as necessary to encourage bushy growth. With topiaries or formally shaped specimens, you may need to clip them every few weeks during the growing season to maintain a well-defined outline. Climbing plants in pots should be regularly tied in, and the stems trained onto the support. To liven up a display that is starting to flag at the end of the season, replace two or three of the tired specimens with late-season plants; these will provide extra color and interest.

▽ **SHAPELY PLANTS**
These decorative container plants have been encouraged to grow into formal shapes by continual pruning and pinching out. It is simply a matter of confining all growth within the final shape; remove all leaves and stems that try to grow outside of these confines.

△ **DEADHEADING**
Cut off dead blooms at the stem joint to prolong the flowering season; leave them on the plant if you want berries or seedheads.

Strongly upright growth does not need to be supported by wire or stakes

BOXWOOD
Buxus sempervirens

CANARY ISLAND IVY
Hedera canariensis 'Gloire de Marengo'

Climbing evergreen growth must be tied in and trained over a frame

Growth should be trimmed with scissors if it becomes straggly

IMPATIENS
Impatiens 'Super Elfin Red'

SEE ALSO: Ways of Supporting Plants, pp.108–109; Maintaining Shrubs, pp.156–157; Topiary and Standards, p.173

REPOTTING AND TOPDRESSING

Thriving plants may soon outgrow their containers, so keep an eye out for tell-tale roots poking through drainage holes. Other indicators are loss of vigor or yellowing leaves. To check, lift the plant with its root ball from its pot. If the roots are crowded, or wound tightly around and around, it is time to repot. Very slow-growing plants also benefit from a change of soil mix, even if they don't need more root room. Lift the plant and remove as much of the old mix as possible. Prune any damaged or diseased roots before repotting it back into the same pot using fresh mix.

For the first year or two, in spring repot long-term plants into a pot the next size up. With large or mature plants, you can topdress them instead at the start of the growing season. Simply replace the top 2–3 in (5–8 cm) of the old soil mix with fresh mix of the same type, enriched with a balanced fertilizer. Topdressing is preferable to repotting for plants that dislike root disturbance or those that like their roots to be confined. In the case of surface-rooting shrubs, it is wiser to lift the plant and replace some of the soil mix beneath it instead.

HOW TO REPOT A CONTAINER PLANT

1 CHECK POT SIZE
To check the new pot is the correct size, slip the plant (here, Aucuba), still in its old pot, inside it. There should be a gap all around between the pots of about 1in (2.5cm).

2 SOAK ROOT BALL
An hour or so before repotting, and keeping the plant in its original pot, soak in water. This reduces the impact of the move and helps establish the roots in the new soil mix.

3 LOOSEN ROOTS
Encourage the roots to grow into the new soil mix by gently teasing out congested roots with your hands. Trim off damaged or dead roots with a sharp knife. Check for pests.

4 REPOT
Add some soil mix, firm lightly, and position the plant. Check that it is at the right level, with room to allow for watering. Fill around it with more soil mix, firming as you go.

Use scissors or pruners to remove dead or damaged growth

Fill pot with soil mix to within 1in (2.5cm) of the rim

5 TRIM AND WATER
Trim off any dead leaves and straggly or damaged stems, add a controlled-release fertilizer plug, and water soil mix well. Add more mix if needed in any sunken spots.

TELL ME WHY

WHY DO I NEED TO REPOT MY LARGE, UNWIELDY PLANTS EVERY YEAR?

Although annual topdressing (*see above*) may be sufficient, since it provides the soil mix with fresh nutrients, root pruning is most advisable, so it will still be necessary to lift the plant from its pot. Prune back about a quarter of the nonfibrous roots by up to two-thirds. Also prune the topgrowth proportionally to reduce transpiration from the leaves, which could overstress the plant. Replace the plant into its pot, or a new one of the same size, and add fresh soil mix to fill the space taken up by the pruned roots, making sure the soil level is the same as it was before.

WINTER PROTECTION

One of the great benefits of container gardening is that you can grow tender plants outdoors in summer, then move them under cover for winter. Container plants are more vulnerable to freezing than those in open ground because the roots and soil mix are insulated only by the container. Some plants may need no more than moving to the shelter of a warm house wall, while some will survive in a cool greenhouse; others require a warmer spot, such as a well-lit room indoors or a heated conservatory. Before the onset of cool nights, make sure you know each plant's level of tolerance.

Containers that are too heavy to move must be protected outdoors; the level of protection depends on a plant's hardiness. In general, insulate the roots by wrapping the pot in plastic bubble wrap or burlap packed with straw. Tie up strappy-leaved plants, like cordylines, to help protect the central growing point, and surround the topgrowth in row cover. Group plants together for mutual protection.

Tie in foliage of strappy-leaved plants before you move them

△ **DRAG ACT**
To move a heavy pot, first tilt it so you can put a burlap or heavy-duty plastic bag beneath it, then drag it toward you.

FAKING IT ▷
Avoid needing to bring heavy pots indoors by planting tender specimens in plastic pots to sit inside larger clay or stone pots. Then bring in just the plant.

SEE ALSO: Cold Frames and Greenhouses, pp.284–285; Dealing with Weeds and Plant Problems, pp.288–311

RAISED BEDS

LIKE CONTAINERS, RAISED BEDS allow you to grow plants, such as acid-lovers, or herbs and rock plants, which both require very free drainage, in conditions different from those in the open garden. They are often easier to maintain than beds and borders at ground level, which makes them especially useful for elderly, disabled, or partially sighted people, and when filled with fragrant, colorful, or trailing plants, they can form a striking feature in their own right. Unlike a pot or box, however, a raised bed is a permanent fixture, and therefore thought should be given to size, position, design, and style before construction begins. If you have room, link a series of raised beds to act as dividers.

DESIGN AND STYLE CONSIDERATIONS

A raised bed should blend in naturally with the rest of the garden and not be an eyesore. To achieve this, consider site and shape, proportions, materials, and ease of access. The type of plants you wish to grow in the bed will also be important. For better appreciation of scented plants, for example, you may wish to include a built-in seat in the design of the raised bed.

■ **Site and shape:** if you are planning just a small bed for growing one type of plant, for example, or for displaying small alpines, a modest-sized raised bed on a patio near the house may be sufficient. Remember to allow plenty of room around it for movement of people and garden implements, especially a wheelbarrow. In this case, a circular bed may be a more practical proposition than a square or rectangular one that has a number of awkward corners to negotiate; you must be able to reach the center easily. If you have a larger area available for a series of raised beds, try to plan out the design carefully on paper

△ USING SAWN LOGS
For an informal raised bed where plants intermingle seemingly at random, place upright sawn logs as close to each other as possible so that the soil does not spill out.

beforehand. Make sure that there will be easy access to all of the beds, and that they are linked by wide garden paths.

■ **Proportions:** the height and width of a raised bed should be tailored individually to the gardener who will be looking after it. If you are in a wheelchair, for example, make sure that you can reach into the center of the bed with no problems, and that the plants will eventually be at eye level. In a series of beds, heights may differ slightly to give variety. Raised beds should always be narrow enough to reach into the middle with ease.

■ **Materials** range from brick, stone, and concrete to railroad ties and sawn logs.

■ **Plants** that are suitable for raised beds include striking specimen trees such as Japanese maples, fragrant herbs, alpines, rock plants, and acid-lovers like azaleas.

TELL ME WHY

HOW DO I PREPARE A RAISED BED FOR PLANTING AND CARE FOR IT AFTERWARD?

Fill the bottom third with a layer of loose material, such as stones, to aid drainage. Cover with compost and inverted sod, then fill to the top with topsoil or a special mixture if you want to grow a specific type of plant. Water thoroughly before you plant. After planting, cover the soil or soil mix with a topdressing of stone or bark chips, or coarse sand, to suppress weeds and conserve moisture. Water regularly, and add more organic matter as necessary.

△ USING CONTAINERS FOR EXTRA INTEREST
These circular raised beds of brick topped with pavers are enhanced by plants growing in pots. The containers can be moved or changed as desired as the season progresses.

△ SOFTENING HARD FEATURES
The top of this stone wall has been brightened with vibrant flowers. The sides of raised beds can be planted in a similar way with trailing plants to soften the hard edges.

SEE ALSO: Beds and Borders, pp.122–165; Raised Beds: Planting and Maintenance, pp.182–183

CHOOSING MATERIALS

The material you choose for your raised bed will be dictated to some degree by the style of the rest of your garden. If it is a cottage-style design, then wood in the form of old railroad ties or rustic sawn logs will probably fit in well. If the garden is more formal, bricks or concrete blocks may look better. The shape of the bed is relevant – a straight-sided bed suits logs or railroad ties, but to create a curved or circular bed you will probably have to use either natural stone or bricks.

■ **Concrete walling blocks** are ideal for large, deep, rectangular beds, especially if this material has been used elsewhere in the garden. If the bed is for acid-lovers, however, the sides must be lined with a butyl rubber liner, or several coats of a waterproof paint, to prevent lime from leaching into the bed.

■ **Bricks** may be used for either curved or straight-sided beds. Use frostproof bricks rather than ordinary house bricks. For growing acid-loving plants, line the bed as for concrete walling blocks (*see above*).

■ **Natural stone** should be laid dry as for drystone walls. It is used for curves or straight sides. Stone beds are best kept low and small; if higher than about 24in (60cm), use mortar to set the stones in place.

■ **Railroad ties** are a good choice for large, low, rectangular beds, but they are heavy and expensive; treated wood is a less expensive option. If necessary, cut them to length with a chainsaw. Some ties may have been treated with a preservative that is toxic to plants; ask your supplier for untreated ones.

■ **Sawn logs** are perfect for woodland-style gardens and very low, informal beds.

△ **SERIES OF BEDS**
If you have room, a series of formal raised beds at different heights makes a striking feature, especially if planted with a variety of upright and trailing plants.

▽ **LOW TIES**
Railroad ties make excellent low beds, and these may be staggered, as here, to give a step effect. Boulders and varied plants complete the feature.

△ **COMBINING STONES AND BRICK**
The basic structure of this raised bed has been built with stones and mortar, and then the walls have been finished off with a decorative layer of bricks.

BUILDING A RAISED BED

Both concrete-block and brick beds need foundations, consisting of a stone sub-base and a concrete footing, for stability. Dig a trench about 9in (22cm) deep and a bit wider than the finished walls will be, soak it, and allow it to drain. For the sub-base, put at least a 5in (13cm) layer of stone in the bottom, and firm down well. For the footing, pour in concrete to a depth of at least 1in (2.5cm). Level it with a straight piece of lumber, but leave the surface rough for the mortar for the bricks.

You can also use full bricks to make a loosely curved bed. Lay them touching each other on the inside of the wall, and fill the outer gaps with wedges of mortar.

USING BRICKS

Make the foundation (*see above*) and lay the first course of bricks below soil level. Stagger the courses to create a strong bond. You may wish to leave gaps in the bricks for planting.

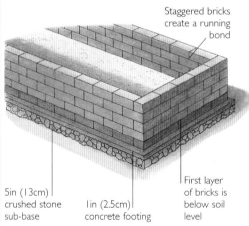

Staggered bricks create a running bond

First layer of bricks is below soil level

5in (13cm) crushed stone sub-base

1in (2.5cm) concrete footing

USING WOODEN TIES

A foundation is not required, since the length and weight of the ties makes them stable. Lay them, staggered like bricks, on a gravel base. If they are more than two courses high, use metal rods to secure them in place.

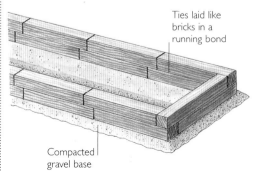

Ties laid like bricks in a running bond

Compacted gravel base

SEE ALSO: How to Lay Concrete, p.60; Beds and Borders, pp.122–165; Fitting in with the Garden Style, p.168; Planting in Walls and Crevices, p.183

RAISED BEDS: PLANTING AND MAINTENANCE

IF YOU HAVE BUILT a raised bed to create special conditions for growing certain kinds of plants, for example alpines or acid-lovers such as heathers and azaleas, it will probably be quite simple to formulate a planting design. For an all purpose raised bed, however, you may wish to base your planting design on a theme, such as evening fragrances or a striking mix of summer colors. Trailing plants can be used to good effect around the edges, some even planted in wall crevices. Routine maintenance of raised beds – weeding, feeding, pruning, watering, and so on – is less arduous than with a normal border, since the soil and plants are within easy reach.

COMPOSING PLANTING DESIGNS

Ask yourself about the primary function of your raised bed. Is it intended to provide architectural interest with a specimen plant? Do you want to create a scented garden for the visually impaired to enjoy? Would you like an oasis of color in a place that otherwise would be drab in summer? Does a feature of vibrant evergreens to brighten up midwinter days appeal to you? Unless you have opted to create special conditions for certain plants (*see opposite, top*), it is also possible to combine some or all of the above elements.

When you have decided on a theme or combination of themes, you can start to look at the different plants that might be suitable. These range from trees and shrubs to rock plants, bulbs, and herbs.

■ **A specimen tree or shrub** might be used as a focal point in the center of the bed, surrounded by low-growing plants. Miniature roses are ideal for small beds.

■ **Scented plants** include stocks, lavender, and herbs.

■ **Evergreens** for winter include evergreen cotoneasters, boxwood, and dwarf conifers.

■ **Trailing plants,** useful for softening the hard outline of the bed, include alyssums, aubrietas, some clematis, and nasturtiums.

■ **Acid-loving plants** needing acidic soil mix range from azaleas and dwarf rhododendrons to heathers and camellias.

■ **Alpine and fleshy-leaved plants** that relish the very good drainage of a raised bed include androsaces, cushion-forming saxifrages, sedums, and sempervivums.

PERFECT PARTNERS

The following alpine plants are just some of the many that are ideal for growing in a raised bed.

Androsace (most species and hybrids)
Antirrhinum molle, A. sempervirens
Campanula portenschlagiana, C. raineri
Daphne arbuscula, D. cneorum, D. petraea 'Grandiflora'
Gentiana acaulis, G. saxosa, G. verna
Papaver alpinum, P. miyabeanum
Phlox bifida, P. stolonifera
Sempervivum (most species and hybrids)
Saxifraga (most species and hybrids)

△ **A THEMED BED**
This formal bed features a horse chestnut as a central specimen tree, surrounded by clumps of lavender that provide scent in summer and foliage interest all year round.

◁ **LEVELING A SLOPE**
One solution to the many problems associated with gardening on a slope is to create a series of level, raised beds for planting. The retaining walls help keep the soil in place and prevent essential nutrients from being washed away.

△ **SEASONAL PLANTS**
Perennials such as lily-of-the-valley (Convallaria majalis) brighten up a raised bed in late spring or summer, but they will die down during winter.

SEE ALSO: Beds and Borders, pp.122–165; Establishing Plants in the Border, pp.148–151; Siting, Buying, and Planting Trees, pp.192–195

CUSTOMIZED CONDITIONS

Alpines and succulent plants with fleshy leaves – both used to cold but not wet weather – and desert plants, which are especially adapted to exist in an arid environment, thrive only in very well-drained conditions. A raised bed is the ideal opportunity to create them.

For the best possible drainage, build the raised bed at least 10in (25cm) above ground level. Do not site it on a base of concrete or other impermeable material. Fill it with stones to at least one-third of the total height of the bed. For alpines

and succulents, it should be in bright sun and slightly sloping for better drainage. A free-draining soil mix is vital: add 1 part coarse sand to 3 parts mix.

If your garden soil is neutral or alkaline (*see p.49*), a raised bed can also provide a home for acid-loving plants. It may be necessary to line the bed (*see p.181*) before filling it with acidic soil mix.

CONTENTED CACTI ▷
Cacti hailing from desert habitats are commonly perceived as dull, dusty plants, but given appropriate conditions and care, they can look lush and spectacularly colorful.

PLANTING IN WALLS AND CREVICES

Small plants may be grown in the gaps between stones or bricks in garden walls or in the sides of a raised bed. This will help soften the rigid appearance and break up the monotony of the wall. It is very effective with some alpine plants, such as sempervivums and saxifrages, which have

evolved to exploit natural crevices that occur in rocks, and they require little attention once established. Some trailing plants are also ideal for this purpose.

Fill the planting gaps or crevices with the appropriate soil or soil mix for the plant. Seedlings or small rooted cuttings are more likely to establish than large, mature plants. Ease the roots into the crevice, and firm the plant in, adding more soil mix if necessary. Water carefully, either through the top of the wall or with a mist spray.

△ **CLOTHING A DRYSTONE WALL**
For a gloriously informal, country-style look, try planting between the stones in a drystone wall. When established, colorful trailing plants will cascade down the side.

GOOD IDEAS

• If possible, plan for any planting in walls before they are constructed, leaving niches at desired intervals in the top and sides.

• Choose plants that will thrive in the growing conditions provided by the wall.

• For alpines, use 3 parts soil to 2 parts coarse fibrous peat substitute or peat, to 1 or 2 parts sharp sand, as the mixture.

• Wedge small stones around the plants to hold them and the soil mix in place.

HOW TO PLANT IN A CREVICE

1 ADD SOIL MIX
Crevices in drystone walls or under steps (as here) and holes between bricks in raised beds can be planted. Fill the crevice with soil mix, and firm it in as much as possible.

2 INSERT THE PLANT
Make a small hole in the soil mix. With extreme care, place the plant in the hole, position it as required, and firm it in gently but securely.

3 FINISH
Use more soil mix to backfill beneath and around the plant until you are happy that it is not likely to become dislodged. Water, then keep an eye on the plant until established.

ROUTINE MAINTENANCE

A properly constructed raised bed should not demand too much work to keep it looking attractive. Because of the good drainage, you will need to check regularly whether the soil or soil mix needs watering, especially around the edges where it may dry out and shrink away from the sides. If left, this could cause problems for the plants in cold periods. Large beds may warrant the installation of an irrigation system. Before filling the raised bed with soil mix, lay a series of drip or trickle pipes and an inlet pipe.

Other routine care consists of weeding, feeding, pruning, replacing old or diseased plants, and renewing the topdressing or mulch. Feeding should not be required for some years if the original soil mix was correctly prepared. Thereafter, fork in a little bone meal mixed with a slow-release fertilizer around the plants in midspring, or remove the topdressing and a layer of soil mix, replacing it with fresh mix and a new topdressing of coarse sand.

GOOD IDEAS

• Trim vigorous or invasive plants in early spring to keep the planting design balanced.

• Use gravel to generously mulch plants that are vulnerable to winter moisture.

• Protect vulnerable alpines from winter moisture with cloches or sheets of glass or plastic; support these with a brick or wire frame fastened down to prevent them from being blown away. Make sure air can still circulate around the plants.

SEE ALSO: Soil and Drainage, p.49; Beds and Borders, pp.122–165; Raised Beds, pp.180–181

ORNAMENTAL TREES IN THE GARDEN

USING TREES AS DESIGN ELEMENTS

TREES ARE BREATHTAKING IN THEIR DIVERSITY, varying not only in height, shape, and form, but also in ornamental qualities, with a wonderful range of foliage, flowers, fruits, and even bark to suit any setting. The passing of the seasons provides ever-changing interest, as deciduous trees come into bright new leaf, flower, fruit, and finally shed their colorful foliage. Evergreens, however, keep up their show throughout the year. Even a single tree will add height and structural interest to a garden, however small; it acts as a living sculpture at the same time as introducing a sense of permanence. Trees also need little or no maintenance once established.

TREES AS PART OF THE GARDEN DESIGN

Together with other long-term features, such as walls and paths, trees form part of the bones of a garden design, contributing greatly to its overall style and structure. In most gardens, small ornamental trees play a more important role than forest trees, which are really suited only to large gardens. It is vital to select and site a tree carefully so that it will become an asset rather than a problem – an ill-chosen or badly placed tree could obscure light and even annoy your neighbors. In some small gardens, coppiced or pollarded trees may be appropriate, and you can also train shrubs as single-stemmed standards (*see p.173*) to resemble small trees.

To decide on the right tree, picture its silhouette against the skyline, wall, or hedge. Bear in mind its increasing height and spread and how it will look at different times of year. Think about whether you want a single- or multistemmed tree in your design. Deciduous trees have a mass of foliage from spring to autumn, but bare branches in winter. Are you prepared to gather all the fallen blossoms, fruit, and leaves they will produce? Evergreen trees and conifers add welcome blocks of year-round texture and color. If you have room for a number of trees, consider how they will work together as a composition, taking into account the shape and density of each, as well as leaves, flowers, or fruits.

◁ **ADDING HEIGHT**
*A white birch (*Betula utilis*) adds height and balances the informal mixed border on the opposite side of the path. The birch's autumn colors complement those of the fiery burning bush; as the leaves fall, its striking white trunk will come to the fore.*

△ **FITTING THE BILL**
Here an upright, slow-growing juniper forms the focal point in a bed of low, mounded heathers, which provide winter color to offset the tree's evergreen foliage. The tree is in good proportion to the design and will not outgrow its space for a considerable time.

SEE ALSO: Seasonal Interest, pp.186–187; Features of Interest, pp.188–189; Coppicing and Pollarding, p.197

GROUPING TREES AND SINGLE SPECIMENS

◁ **SCULPTURAL FORMS**
This island bed of conifers, including cypress, juniper, thuja, and spruce, creates a harmony of repeated columnar and conical shapes. Subtle shifts in color are achieved by juxtaposing gray-blue foliage with greens that range from light to dark.

▽ **SPECIMEN MAPLE**
A specimen tree does not have to look formal or be isolated in the middle of a lawn. This beautiful Japanese maple (Acer palmatum) rises from a sea of bluebells and long grass and is sited so that its leaves are lit up by the sun.

Planting trees in groups can be highly effective visually. In an informal setting, try a relaxed grouping, designed to look like a natural copse, or a cluster of even just three or five trees such as maples (*Acer*) or birches (*Betula*). Odd numbers are always more pleasing to the eye than even numbers. If combining trees of different species, make sure that none will dominate by checking their growing requirements and their potential height and spread before you buy, and that the differing forms complement each other. You could plant a pair of trees to support a hammock in later years.

If you have a small garden, with space for only one tree, think about its large-scale qualities first – eventual height and spread, silhouette, form, color, mass – then consider its small-scale features such as flowers or fruits. Choose a tree to be in scale with its surroundings. To grow healthily and with a natural shape, all trees need adequate room, so check individual requirements before you buy. In larger gardens, growing a tree as a single specimen can create a dramatic effect. Select a tree with a strong shape or especially handsome foliage – beware the pitfall of choosing a tree for a brief display of spring blossoms only to find it does little the rest of the year – and site it on its own where it can be enjoyed from a variety of viewpoints.

■ **For a small specimen tree**, try crabapples (*Malus*), mountain ashes (*Sorbus*), Japanese maples (*Acer palmatum*), or trees with colorful foliage such as the yellow-green black locust (*Robinia pseudoacacia* 'Frisia').
■ **To edge a boundary**, choose trees that look good from a distance, such as white poplars (*Populus alba*), Leyland cypress (X *Cupressocyparis*), or lofty Italian cypresses (*Cupressus sempervirens*).

SHAPE AND FORM

A tree's shape and form dictate the effect of its initial impact – a columnar cypress forms a green pillar, while a hawthorn tree in bloom resembles a lollipop. In general, trees with an upright habit and dense growth look more formal than those with an open-branched framework. Spreading trees, especially evergreens and conifers, create a wide area of shade, allowing less underplanting, but provide a cool retreat on hot days. As well as the tree's overall silhouette, think of the shape and growth pattern of its branches – which visually come to the fore in winter, especially in deciduous trees. Birches and Japanese maples, for example, have delicate, narrow branches, while ornamental fruit trees often have a more solid framework.

BASIC TREE SHAPES

SPREADING

COLUMNAR

WEEPING

CONICAL

ROUND-HEADED

MULTISTEMMED

GOOD IDEAS

• To restrict the height of a tree in a small garden, change its natural single-stemmed shape by cutting it back hard (coppicing) or pruning to create a multistemmed tree.
• In a formal garden, try topiary – the art of clipping evergreen trees to create interesting shapes, such as birds, cones, or globes.

SEE ALSO: Topiary and Standards, p.173; Pruning to Form a Multistemmed Tree, p.196; Coppicing and Pollarding, p.197

SEASONAL INTEREST

ONE OF THE PLEASURES of gardening is to observe how your living creation ebbs and flows throughout the year. Many trees have a marked seasonal cycle: in spring, the first signs of fresh growth emerge; in high summer, there is an abundance of foliage and flowers; autumn brings ripe fruits and dramatic leaf colors; and in winter skeletal branches may be iced with frost or displaying attractive textured bark. Many have more than one peak period, with spring blossoms and autumn berries, for example. These changing effects can be set against a constant backdrop, such as the even color and texture of an evergreen hedge, surrounding buildings, or the sky.

SPRING

After a long winter, signs of spring as the first new leaves and flower buds appear are especially welcome. For a spectacular show of spring blossoms, try flowering cherries and almonds (*Prunus*). Have a look, too, at hawthorns (*Crataegus*), crabapples (*Malus*), and mountain ashes (*Sorbus*), many of which also bear attractive fruits in autumn.

Some of the earliest blossoms appear on bare branches, for example *Prunus* 'Pandora', with clusters of pale pink flowers in early spring, or the weeping *Prunus* × *subhirtella* 'Pendula Rubra', which has deep pink blossoms opening from ruby red buds that grace the tree all winter. If the tree is to be sited near the house or by a path, look for one with fragrant flowers to enjoy as you walk beneath or past it. Do not forget foliage: the leaves of many trees are at their best and brightest in spring when young.

- **Spring flowers:** *Prunus* 'Shirofugen', *Prunus avium* 'Plena', *Malus* 'Lemoinei', *Cornus nuttallii*, *Pyrus calleryana* 'Chanticleer'.
- **Scent:** *Magnolia kobus, M. salicifolia, Prunus* 'Taihaku'.
- **Emerging leaf buds:** Whitebeam (*Sorbus aria* 'Lutescens') – pale green leaves, gleaming silver beneath, are spectacular as they emerge. Site it against a dark background for best effect. Golden honeylocust (*Gleditsia triacanthos* 'Sunburst') – the emerging leaves are bright yellow, later turning to green. *Acer pesudoplatanus* 'Brilliantissimum' – the yellow-green leaves of this maple are a striking shrimp pink when they first appear.

SUMMER

As late spring merges into early summer, the trees are fully in leaf and take on their characteristic shapes. Their foliage forms large blocks of uniform texture and color, providing a backdrop or relief to bright summer flowers elsewhere in the garden. Many trees bloom during early summer, creating a smooth transition from spring; magnolias, laburnums, and – for large gardens – horse chestnuts (*Aesculus*) are all deservedly popular.

As the season progresses into mid- and late summer, some spring-flowering trees, such as mountain ashes and crabapples, come into fruit, their colorful berries anticipating the delights of autumn.

- **Summer blooms:** *Koelreuteria* – yellow flowers, light canopy. For large gardens, the tulip tree (*Liriodendron tulipifera*) – green and yellow, tulip-shaped flowers.
- **Fragrance:** *Eucryphia glutinosa* – scented, white flowers; site a garden seat nearby.

△ **SPRING SPLASH**
The English hawthorn (Crataegus laevigata) *'Paul's Scarlet' is covered with vibrant pinkish red blossoms – not scarlet – in late spring to early summer.*

BURST OF BLOSSOM ▷
Few sights in spring are as instantly breathtaking as a flowering cherry (Prunus) *in full bloom. Here, the profuse white blossoms are offset by low-growing evergreens.*

△ **SUMMER SPLENDOR**
This Cornus controversa 'Variegata' produces large, flattish heads of white flowers, in early summer, to complement its handsome, cream-variegated foliage.

SEE ALSO: Plants for a Purpose, pp.38–41

AUTUMN

This is the season when many deciduous trees are at their glorious, most colorful best, brightening up the garden when many border plants are past their peak. Most famous, perhaps, are the maples, especially the many types of Japanese maple (*Acer palmatum, A. japonicum*), with the brilliant tints of their reddening foliage lit up by autumn sunlight. The staghorn sumac (*Rhus typhina*) is one of the first to turn color, with dazzling shades of yellow, orange, and red, but its display is brief and it is prone to suckering.

■ **Foliage color:** Try the Japanese maple *Acer japonicum* 'Vitifolium', a beautiful specimen tree that thrives in dappled shade. Leaves turn rich crimson, orange, and purple in autumn. The Chinese tupelo (*Nyssa sylvatica*) has fiery red, orange, and yellow leaf colors in autumn.

■ **Autumn fruits:** For berries and fruits, look at the hawthorns (*Crataegus*), mountain ashes, and crabapples. Many also have good autumn leaf tints. Do not forget edible fruits, either, especially apple, pear, plum, and quince trees.

◁ **AUTUMN FIRE**
For large gardens only, scarlet oak (here Quercus coccinea 'Splendens') has sculptural leaves that turn deep red in autumn, bringing a blaze of color to the garden.

△ **BACKLIGHTING**
Plant a tree chosen for its autumn foliage – this is a Japanese maple (Acer palmatum) – where you can view it with the sun behind so that the colors are at their most vibrant.

CONTINUITY OF INTEREST

If you have space for only one tree, choose one that has something to offer all year – maybe an evergreen, or a deciduous tree with a graceful framework of branches. For continuous interest, look at slow-growing conifers as well as broadleaved evergreens.

■ **Evergreen:** Strawberry tree (*Arbutus unedo*); hollies (try *Ilex aquifolium* or *Ilex opaca*).

■ **Deciduous:** Try crabapples (*Malus*), hawthorns (*Crataegus*), or mountain ashes (*Sorbus*).

■ **Conifers:** Lacebark pine (*Pinus bungeana*); Monterey cypress (*Cupressus macrocarpa* 'Goldcrest'); the cedar *Cedrus deodara* 'Aurea'.

CRABAPPLE
Malus 'Butterball'

FLOWERS AND FRUITS ▷
Many of the crabapples (Malus) will provide at least 2 seasons of interest, with a fine show of white, pink, or red blossoms in spring, followed by numerous brightly colored fruits that may last into winter.

WINTER

Unlike the more transient attractions of many herbaceous plants, trees provide interest through winter, whether from the pattern of their branches against the sky, from their evergreen foliage, or from precious flowers or bright persistent berries. Trees with attractive bark or stems are often now seen at their best, too. At this time of year, many conifers come to the fore; as well as every shade of green, there are types with blue-gray foliage, cheerful yellow-green, or gold. Always check their eventual height and spread; some will soon outgrow their space.

■ **Flowers:** *Prunus* × *subhirtella* 'Autumnalis'.

■ **Fruits:** Arbutus; *Photinia davidiana*; hollies (*Ilex*) – easy to grow, bright red berries, especially *I.* × *altaclerensis* 'Camelliifolia', and others have variegated foliage; many mountain ashes (*Sorbus*).

△ **WINTER SHAPE**
The graceful form against the sky and white bark of Himalayan birch (Betula utilis *var.* jacquemontii) are unequaled in winter.

◁ **FROSTED ICING**
The winter stems and bright red berries of this hawthorn (Crataegus laevigata) are decorated with a crisp layer of frost.

SEE ALSO: Using Trees as Design Elements, pp.184–185; Features of Interest, pp.188–189

FEATURES OF INTEREST

TREES ARE OFTEN RIGHTLY PRIZED for the sense of scale they bring to a garden and for their architectural qualities of mass, silhouette, and form. Just like border plants, however, they also have individual ornamental features that make them worth growing. Many have especially good foliage, valued for its shape, color, texture, or even the way it moves. Others may be grown for their flowers or for their decorative or edible fruits, nuts, or cones. A lesser known, but no less desirable, quality is that of ornamental bark or stems, a distinctive feature of certain trees. Some trees may even have two or more special attractions that earn them a prime spot.

FOLIAGE

Leaves provide color and texture and help determine the shape and mass of the tree canopy. Foliage also helps set the tone and style of the garden – from the exotic effect of the large, deeply lobed leaves of the fig tree, *Ficus carica*, to the airy feel of the aspen, *Populus tremula*, with its small leaves trembling on long leaf stalks. Evergreens, such as hollies, provide rich background color all year round, and the leaves of some trees, both deciduous and evergreen, are brightly variegated with cream, white, or yellow. Conifers have needle- or scale-like leaves, each creating different textures, and some of the most colorful foliage, ranging from yellow-green to blue-gray.

When choosing trees for foliage, think about the overall effect. Look at the leaves' shape and size, which will influence the appearance of the canopy, and also their undersides – if felty or silvery, leaves shimmering in the breeze will provide a delightful color contrast. Consider the site of a tree in relation to its foliage: trees with purple or bronze leaves may be over-powering in a small garden. Show off trees with silvery or glaucous blue foliage by siting them against a dark background.

EXOTIC MOOD ▷
The narrow profile and dramatic, fan-shaped leaves of the Chusan palm (Trachycarpus fortunei) *can bring a touch of the subtropics to temperate seaside and city gardens. This is the hardiest of the palms.*

◁ GREEN AND GOLD
The large, golden, heart-shaped leaves of the Indian bean tree (Catalpa bignonioides 'Aurea'), *which is deciduous, form an impressive and wide-spreading canopy. This tree grows more slowly than the green-leaved species.*

△ COLOR MASS
The dense foliage of many conifers can make a good backdrop for other plants. The color range includes greens, golds, and glaucous blue such as in this spruce, Picea glauca 'Caerulea'.

FLOWERS

A tree in full bloom is a spectacular sight. Flowers vary hugely in shape and color: they may be sculptural, such as the goblets of many magnolias; pendulous, such as the swaying yellow chains of laburnums; or borne in dense clusters like cherry blossoms. Some, such as those of *Tilia* (linden) are also fragrant. Good deciduous choices for small or medium-sized gardens are dogwoods (*Cornus*), hawthorns (*Crataegus*), crabapples (*Malus*), mountain ashes (*Sorbus*), and flowering cherries (*Prunus*). Alternatively, try the glorious evergreen Southern magnolia (*Magnolia grandiflora*), which produces huge, cup-shaped, fragrant blooms throughout much of summer.

△ WINE GOBLETS
Some magnolias, like this Magnolia liliflora 'Nigra', *produce upright, goblet-shaped flowers.*

◁ BARE BEAUTY
Redbuds (Cercis) *bear their flowers before the leaves appear.*

SEE ALSO: Plants for a Purpose, pp.38–41

FRUITS, NUTS, AND CONES

Trees exhibit an enormous range of fruits, which contain the seeds: there are berries and other fleshy fruits, including plums, mulberries, and other edible types, nuts, pods and winged seeds, catkins, and cones. Trees that bear berries or other bright fruits are ideal for encouraging wildlife: they provide food for birds, and windfalls are often picked up by small mammals, as are nuts and acorns.

For colorful fruits, consider hollies (*Ilex*), mountain ashes (*Sorbus*), hawthorns (*Crataegus*), and crabapples (*Malus*). If you want berries that last through winter, choose a type with fruits that are persistent or less tempting to birds, such as the berries of *Sorbus cashmiriana*, which are pink ripening to white. Color does not need to come from berries – many maples (*Acer*) have winged seeds that may be tinged red in summer and autumn.

Certain conifers have very fine cones, such as the violet-blue, cylindrical fruits of the Korean fir (*Abies koreana*), which are borne even on young trees. Many have

cones that stay on the trees even after they have opened to disperse their seeds.

Bear in mind that some trees need to cross-pollinate if they are to bear fruit, while others are self-fertile, so check when buying. In hollies, for example, only female trees have berries, but a male holly must be in proximity for it to fruit. With apple trees, or any others where you plan to harvest the fruits, successful pollination affects the resulting yield, and it is often best to grow more than one tree.

◁ **BRILLIANT HARVEST**
Many hawthorns become covered with copious clusters of fruits that resemble bright beads. The small, spreading trees on average reach a height of 20–26ft (6–8m), making them a good choice for a small garden.

◁ **HOT COLORS**
Euonymus europaeus 'Red Cascade', has bright orange, fleshy seeds in bright reddish pink capsules. It is toxic, however, so is unsuitable for gardens where children play.

EDIBLE HARVEST ▷
The sweet chestnut (Castanea sativa) has edible nuts that also appeal to foraging animals.

BARK AND STEMS

Colored, patterned, or peeling bark and the bright growth of young stems are subtle attractions that are often overlooked. They are usually most noticeable in winter, when the tree's branches are bare of leaves. Some, such as white birches (*Betula pendula* and others) with their ghostly white bark, are impressive even from a distance, while others, such as snakebark maples (*Acer*) with their vertical stripes, are best enjoyed at close hand. The bark of the paperbark maple (*Acer griseum*) peels off in strips, revealing fresh new, cinnamon-colored bark beneath. Trees that have brightly colored juvenile shoots, such as some forms of *Salix alba*, are sometimes cut back at regular intervals (coppiced), to stimulate this attractive new growth.

APPEALING PEELING ▷
The glossy red-brown bark of paperbark cherry (Prunus serrula) continually peels off and renews itself. Position trees with attractive bark by a path where you can touch and enjoy the bark, but don't be tempted to peel it away.

BARK SELECTION

Acer griseum
Paperbark maple

Betula utilis var *jacquemontii*
Himalayan birch

Acer pensylvanicum
Moosewood

Acer capillipes
A snakebark maple

Eucalyptus pauciflora subsp. *niphophila*
Snow gum

SEE ALSO: Coppicing and Pollarding, p.197

TREES TO SUIT YOUR SITE

BY FAR THE EASIEST APPROACH to gardening is to choose plants primarily on the basis of the growing conditions in your garden – that is, the climate, including temperature range and rainfall, and the soil type. If you try to grow certain plants regardless of their preferred conditions, gardening will rapidly become an uphill task. With trees, this is a particularly important consideration, because they are long-term plants. Whatever your site, you will still have plenty of choice, however. Whether you have a garden by the coast, on a windswept hillside, by a busy road, or in an inner-city oasis overshadowed by neighboring buildings, there are trees that will thrive.

CLIMATE AND LOCATION

The better you know your own garden and the conditions it has to offer, the easier it will be to choose plants that will thrive in it. First think about your local climate, including the temperature range and extremes and the average rainfall. Is there ice every winter or drought every summer, or any other problem such as extended snow cover or strong seasonal winds? With regard to the site, are you near the sea, for example, or at a high altitude? Is your garden in a built-up area, or exposed to winds on a hillside? It is important to identify key factors such as these that will affect your choice of tree.

To identify trees suited to your local conditions, observe what grows well nearby in woods, neighboring gardens, and local parks and gardens open to the public. To blend well into the surrounding area, take into account any trees growing around or near your garden when you make your choice.

Remember that the garden itself may have sheltered areas and dry spots, as well as different aspects; bear in mind that what may grow vigorously in one part of the garden may do less well in another.

■ **Contact a local gardening club** if there is one and ask other members for advice.
■ **Be considerate:** if you plant a tree near a boundary, take care to choose one that will not restrict your neighbor's light, especially if the tree is dense or fast-growing. Think about your own light at the same time. Near boundaries, avoid trees such as sumacs (*Rhus typhina*) that produce suckers.
■ **Avoid root damage to house walls:** site trees with roots that vigorously seek out water, such as willows (*Salix*) and poplars (*Populus*), well away from houses.

◁ **SILVER BY THE SEA**
Trees that withstand salty breezes are good for coastal gardens, or even inland ones where salt can be carried. The undersides of white poplar leaves show up well in the wind.

◁ **SPLENDOR IN THE CITY**
*Not all trees respond well to an urban environment, but golden honeylocust (*Gleditsia triacanthos* 'Sunburst') is especially tolerant of air pollution. This pretty tree has an open, airy habit and leaves that emerge golden yellow.*

PLANT LIST

TREES FOR COASTAL GARDENS

While these trees will tolerate coastal winds, they will not stand up to being hit with salt spray.

Acer pseudoplatanus 'Brilliantissimum'
Hawthorn (*Crataegus monogyna*)
Highclere holly (*Ilex × altaclerensis*)
Mountain ash (*Sorbus aucuparia*)
Mount Etna broom (*Genista aetnensis*)
Strawberry tree (*Arbutus unedo*)
Whitebeams (*Sorbus aria*)

TREES FOR GARDENS IN EXPOSED OR WINDY SITES

Hawthorn (*Crataegus monogyna*)
Laburnums
Mountain ash (*Sorbus aucuparia*)
Silver birch (*Betula pendula*)
White birch, downy birch (*Betula pubescens*)
Whitebeams (*Sorbus aria*)

POLLUTION-TOLERANT TREES FOR URBAN GARDENS

Chinese privet (*Ligustrum lucidum*)
Common alder (*Alnus glutinosa*)
Dawn redwood (*Metasequoia glyptostroboides*)
English yew (*Taxus baccata*)
Hawthorns (*Crataegus*)
Highclere holly (*Ilex × altaclerensis*)
Honeylocust (*Gleditsia triacanthos*)
Indian bean trees (*Catalpa bignonioides* and 'Aurea')
Magnolia grandiflora
Mountain ash (*Sorbus aucuparia*)
Pyrus salicifolia 'Pendula'

TREES THAT WILL TOLERATE DAMP SOILS

Alders (*Alnus glutinosa, A. incana*)
Black gum (*Nyssa sylvatica*)
River birch (*Betula nigra*)
Salix alba 'Britzensis', *S. alba* subsp. *vitellina* (both should be coppiced for colorful stems)
Salix babylonica 'Tortuosa'
Kilmarnock Willow (*Salix × caprea* 'Kilmarnock')

SEE ALSO: Siting, Buying, and Planting Trees, pp.192–195; Coppicing and Pollarding, p.197

SOIL TYPE AND CONDITIONS

The soil is the foundation of the garden and, as with climate, it is easier to work with its basic conditions rather than try to fight against them. The good news is that you do not need "perfect" soil in order to grow trees. What you do need is to choose your trees according to the soil you have, although you can also improve the soil to create better conditions.

Many soils fall between the extremes of clay and sandy, and may be silty or loamy (*see p.238 for how to assess your soil type*). Some soils may also be very stony. The addition of well-rotted organic matter, such as homemade compost or rotted manure, will improve the structure of most soils. Incorporate it carefully into the topsoil. The ideal soil in any garden is loam (*see p.142*), and most trees will grow happily in this.

Trees that are tolerant of heavy, clay soils include alders (*Alnus*), magnolias, and poplars (*Populus*). For sandy soils, try birches (*Betula*), *Robinia pseudoacacia* 'Frisia', or conifers such as junipers. The Mount Etna broom (*Genista aetnensis*) will grow well in either sandy or silty soil.

Remember that other factors can also affect a tree's rate of growth; for example, hot, dry conditions frequently keep trees such as the dawn redwood (*Metasequoia glyptostroboides*) smaller than they would be if they were growing in rich, moist soil.

△ **GOOD FOR MOIST SOIL**
An excess of water in the soil can be just as damaging to some plants as a lack of soil water. Alnus glutinosa grows naturally on river banks, however, so it is perfectly suited to such conditions; it also tolerates heavy clay.

△ **GOOD FOR CLAY**
Clay soils are usually fertile, but their heavy texture provides poor drainage, which does not suit all trees. Magnolia × soulangeana is a magnificent specimen tree for clay soils, however.

AT-A-GLANCE GUIDE

Are you ready to make a shortlist of suitable trees for your garden? Use these quick reminders as a handy guide.
- **Climate:** Do you live in a temperate zone? Is there severe cold? Periods of drought?
- **Local factors:** Do you live near the sea? In a city? At high altitude? Are there any other special factors specific to your garden?
- **Soil type:** Is your soil sandy or clay-based, silty, loamy, or stony? Does it drain freely?
- **Soil pH:** Is your soil acidic or alkaline?

SOIL pH

As well as knowing the type and structure of the soil in your garden, you should also know its approximate pH, or degree of acidity or alkalinity (*see below and p.238 for how to test soil pH*). This will affect which plants can flourish in your garden, and which are likely to struggle or fail.
- **Look for indicator plants:** certain plants can provide a rough idea of the soil's pH. For example, heathers, foxgloves, and rhododendrons usually indicate acidic soil, while rosemary, barberries, ash, and beech grow well in alkaline conditions.
- **Test your soil:** you can buy soil-testing kits from most garden centers. Remember to take readings from more than one area of the garden, as conditions may vary.
- **Trees and conifers for neutral/acidic soil:** stewartias, firs (*Abies*), strawberry tree (*Arbutus unedo*), and spruces (*Picea*).
- **Trees and conifers for alkaline soil (chalky limestone):** Redbuds (*Cercis*), cherries (*Prunus*), *Robinia pseudoacacia* 'Frisia', hawthorns (*Crataegus*), junipers, and thujas.

△ **ALKALINE CHOICE**
Many trees are happy in free-draining alkaline soils, which warm up quickly in spring. The Yoshino cherry (Prunus × yedoensis) has almond-scented blossoms and is one of the earliest-blooming, most reliable of the flowering cherries.

ACID LOVER ▷
Like many other conifers, this white fir (Abies concolor 'Argentea') should grow well on acidic soils, preferring moist but well-drained conditions.

SEE ALSO: Preparing the Ground, pp.142–143; Get to Know your Soil, p.238; Soil Acidity and Alkalinity, p.238

SITING, BUYING, AND PLANTING TREES

ONCE YOU HAVE ACCURATELY ASSESSED which trees are suitable for growing in a garden of your size and particular conditions, you can proceed to the next stage of the process. First select the most suitable site in the garden, and then prepare the ground thoroughly. When this has been done, you can finally buy and plant a healthy, strong young tree that will give you pleasure for a long time to come. Since trees are so long-lived, meticulous preparation and good initial aftercare are essential in order to give them the best possible start.

PREPARING THE SITE

Within a garden, there may be a range of conditions, including frost pockets and damp areas, so consider the specific site for your tree carefully. One part of the garden may be much more exposed than another, which will suit some trees but not others. If your garden is steeply sloping, bear in mind that a spot halfway down a slope tends to be warmer and more sheltered than either the top or the bottom.

Do not plant trees very close to walls or buildings where they will suffer from lack of moisture and light. Also some, such as willows (*Salix*) and poplars (*Populus*), have strong, moisture-seeking roots, which can damage foundations and drainage systems; these trees are best avoided unless sited well away. Never plant a tree in a place where it may interfere with overhead power lines as it grows.

◁ THE RIGHT SITE
Take care to select trees that will thrive in the specific conditions and microclimate of the planned planting site.

△ BLENDING IN
Trees can be used to link the artificial setting of the garden to its natural surroundings. This may influence your choice.

It is advisable to prepare the planting site before buying the tree, because this will allow the soil to settle and means you can plant without delay after purchase.
■ **Choose a well-drained site**, unless the tree is a species that definitely tolerates wet conditions.
■ **Remove all vegetation** (sod, weeds, or ornamentals) in the immediate area that would compete for water and nutrients.
■ **Thoroughly dig the soil** throughout the chosen site, incorporating plenty of well-rotted organic matter.
■ **On an exposed, windy site**, protect a young tree until it establishes with some sort of windbreak.

SEE ALSO: Preparing the Ground, pp.142–143

TELL ME WHY

WHEN IS THE BEST TIME OF YEAR TO PLANT A TREE?

In general, it is best to plant trees in autumn or spring, depending on the type of tree, how it is sold, and the weather conditions. Autumn planting allows the roots to make some growth before winter, which helps the tree withstand dry spells in the following summer. In cold areas, planting in spring may be wiser, because this gives the tree more time to establish before the onset of winter. In all cases, do not plant during periods of severe cold or drought.
Container-grown trees: plant out at any time, except during drought or cold.
Bare-root deciduous trees: plant in the dormant season in autumn or spring.
Balled-and-burlapped trees: plant evergreens and conifers in midautumn or mid- to late spring; deciduous trees in spring or autumn .

SELECTING A HEALTHY TREE

Garden centers usually stock a range of popular trees, but if you want something more unusual, need several trees, or want bare-root trees, try mail-order; this may also be cheaper. Many trees for sale are grown in containers. Although usually quite expensive, they may be planted out at almost any time, and there will be less disturbance to the roots when planting – good for trees such as magnolias that dislike being transplanted. Bare-root trees, usually deciduous, are grown in open ground and are available only when leafless. A good nursery will advise when a bare-root tree is ready.

Bear in mind that, although a semi-mature tree has more instant impact than a juvenile tree, young trees are much cheaper and are more likely to transplant well and establish quickly.

BUYING BARE-ROOT TREES

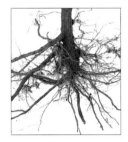

◁ **GOOD ROOTS**
Look for well-developed roots that spread out evenly. Plenty of small, fine roots are a good sign and suggest that the tree should grow well. Check that the roots do not look dried out, which indicates exposure to wind.

◁ **POOR ROOTS**
Avoid trees where the roots are wound in on themselves or with "hockey stick" roots, where all the growth is on one side; they will not establish well. Also make sure that the roots are free from damage or disease.

Check that the tree has a firm, straight trunk and a strongly growing central shoot

Look for a good, symmetrical shape with an even spread of branches

Check stems for dieback and foliage for browning or signs of disease

◁ **ASSESS THE TREE**
Choose a tree that has a good root system but is not pot-bound. Stand back to assess the tree's overall shape, then check closely for damage or disease.

A good nursery will let you check the roots: lift the tree and the soil mix should mostly stay intact

◁ **POTBOUND ROOTS**
Never buy a potbound tree with a mass of tightly wound, congested roots, or one with thick roots poking through the drainage holes.

BALLED-AND-BURLAPPED

Some trees for sale are described as "balled-and-burlapped" (b&b): these have been grown in open ground but are lifted with soil around the roots and then wrapped in burlap or other material. Evergreens, especially conifers, are often available as b&b trees, and deciduous trees over 12ft (4m) tall may also be sold this way. Balled-and-burlapped trees have an advantage over bare-root ones in that the roots are less likely to dry out in the time between the tree being lifted and subsequently replanted.

Because of the large volume of soil carried with a balled-and-burlapped tree, they are heavy and can be difficult to transport and maneuver into a planting hole. Be sure you are in good physical condition (or can rely on those with strong backs) before buying b&b trees.

CHECKING THE ROOT BALL △
When buying a b&b tree, check that the root ball is firm – the soil should be clinging to the roots – and the wrapping intact. Watch out for any signs of damage or drying out of the roots, since these give an indication that the tree is less likely to establish successfully.

TREE STAKES AND TIES

If you are planting a tree in an exposed or very windy site, it is advisable to stake it, with the stake positioned on the side of the prevailing wind. This helps support the tree until a strong root system has been developed. For "whippy" trees with flexible stems use a tall stake, reaching to just below the crown. In the second year after planting, cut down the stake to about 20in (50cm) in height, and finally remove it altogether in the following year.

STAKES AND GUYS
Newly planted trees should be supported with three evenly spaced stakes and guy wires. Protect the tree by wrapping a piece of hose around each contact point.

△ **ANGLED STAKE**
A low stake may be driven in clear of the tree's roots after planting. Drive it in firmly at an angle of 45° into the prevailing wind.

SEE ALSO: Other Maintenance, p.197

PLANTING A TREE

Once you have chosen an appropriate spot for your tree and prepared the site, you are ready to buy and plant. You can dig the planting hole in advance to minimize the delay before planting once you have bought the tree – worth it for bare-root trees, which are vulnerable to drying out.

In order to give a tree a good start, mix the soil you dig out of the hole with some well-rotted organic matter such as compost. This improves the structure of the soil and provides an ideal medium for the tree's roots to spread and grow strong.

Forking over the sides and base of the hole, particularly in areas with heavy, clay soil, will also make it easier for the roots to spread out and anchor the tree well. If planting in spring, add a little slow-release fertilizer (about 4oz/110g) to the topsoil mixture to encourage good growth.

When planting a container-grown tree, follow the basic procedure shown below. With a bare-root tree, prepare the site in the same way, but the hole must be large enough to take the tree's roots when fully spread out. Trim any damaged roots with pruners, but take care not to damage the delicate-looking, fibrous roots through which the tree absorbs nutrients.

■ **If preparing the hole** in advance, backfill it loosely until you are ready to plant so that the soil remains warm, and cover with a tarpaulin or plastic.

■ **When using a stake,** drive it in either before or during planting (*see below*), or it may damage the roots of the tree.

A FAITHFUL FRIEND ▷
Given a good start with careful planting and aftercare, a tree (here, a crabapple, Malus tschonoskii) *should live to grace the garden for decades or even centuries.*

HOW TO PLANT A CONTAINER-GROWN TREE

1 DIG THE HOLE
Roughly mark out the area of the hole: about 3–4 times the diameter of the tree's root ball. Dig a hole to about 1½ times the depth of the root ball.

2 PREPARE THE HOLE
Fork over the base and sides of the hole. Mix the removed soil with organic matter, such as compost, and add some of it to the base of the hole.

3 CHECK THE PLANTING DEPTH
Set the tree – here a beech – in the hole and use a stake to check its depth (see box, facing page). The top of the root ball should be level with the soil surface: fill or dig out soil until it is level.

4 DRIVE IN THE STAKE
Taking care not to damage the root ball, insert a stake into the hole next to the tree, and drive it firmly into place with a mallet. The stake should be just off-center on the side of the prevailing wind.

5 FILL WITH SOIL
Fill in around the root ball and the stake with the rest of the removed topsoil. Firm the soil gently as you go, with your hand or foot.

6 FIRM THE SOIL
Check that the tree is still upright, then finish by treading the soil gently until the surface is level, which also removes air pockets.

7 TIE THE STAKE
Attach the stake to the tree's young trunk with a plastic tree tie, taking care not to overtighten it – this would damage the stem.

8 WATER IN
Give your new tree a good drink of water to help it recover from planting. In the early stages, do not allow the roots to dry out.

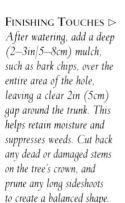

FINISHING TOUCHES ▷
After watering, add a deep (2–3in/5–8cm) mulch, such as bark chips, over the entire area of the hole, leaving a clear 2in (5cm) gap around the trunk. This helps retain moisture and suppresses weeds. Cut back any dead or damaged stems on the tree's crown, and prune any long sideshoots to create a balanced shape.

SEE ALSO: Preparing the Ground, pp.142–143; Applying Mulch, p.152; Tree Stakes and Ties, p.193

Planting a Balled-and-burlapped Tree

The basic method is as for a container-grown tree (*see facing page*), although the hole can be only two or three times the width of the root ball. If staking the tree, use an angled stake, driven in clear of the root ball, or three guy ropes secured to low stakes. In heavy, clay soil, plant the tree so that the root ball is slightly above the soil level, to assist drainage. Cover this exposed part with 2–3in (5–8cm) of a free-draining soil (such as topsoil mixed with organic matter), but leave a gap of about 2in (5cm) all around the stem.

1 Dig the Hole and Position the Tree
Dig a hole 2 or 3 times the width of the root ball. Mix the soil with well-rotted organic matter. Set the tree in the hole — easier with two people — and untie the root ball.

2 Remove the Wrapping
Tilt the tree over to one side and roll the wrapping up under the root ball; then lean it the other way and tug the material out. Backfill, firm, and water well.

Growing Trees in Containers

You do not need a great expanse of open ground to grow a tree: there are many small and medium trees suitable for large tubs, pots, and planters placed on patios, balconies, or roof terraces. If you have space for only one tree in a container, choose one with more than one season of interest and a good silhouette. Using containers lets you cultivate trees that prefer a different soil type from that in your garden, and tender ones that can be placed under cover for the winter.

Make sure any container you use has enough drainage holes to allow the soil to drain adequately. Use a good soil-based mix and incorporate a slow-release fertilizer. Water well in summer, and at other times as necessary, and keep an eye on it in winter. Mulch to minimize evaporation.

Tell Me Why

WHY IS IT IMPORTANT TO PLANT A TREE SO THAT THE SOIL LEVEL IS THE SAME AS WHEN THE TREE WAS FIRST RAISED IN THE NURSERY?

If a tree is planted too deeply, its roots may be deprived of oxygen, which may halt their growth or even kill them. On the other hand, if a tree is planted too shallowly, the roots may dry out. Always check the level carefully when planting: with a bare-root tree, look for the darker soil mark on the stem and lay a stake alongside the mark to ensure that the soil surface is at the same level as this, or is level with the top of the root ball for a container-grown tree.

△ **WINTER WILLOW**
The weeping branches and fat, furry catkins of the Kilmarnock willow (Salix caprea 'Kilmarnock') are set off against the evergreen foliage of Helleborus argutifolius to make a charming feature in late winter.

Tree Guards

In many gardens, especially rural ones, you may need to protect newly planted trees from rabbits, deer, and rodents. You can buy commercial tree guards from garden centers or tree nurseries or make your own using wire mesh; whatever the type, make sure it will protect the entire height of the trunk. Fit guards at the time of planting, and check them regularly to be sure they are still in place. As a tree grows, the bark becomes tougher, so the guard may eventually be removed. In areas with deer, however, you may need to provide permanent protection.

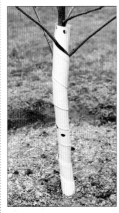

△ **EXPANDABLE PLASTIC GUARD**
This type of spiral, wrap-around plastic guard can expand as the tree grows. It is quick to use so is particularly suitable if you are planting a large number of trees. It should protect the bark from small animals such as rabbits.

△ **WIRE GUARD**
A barrier made from wire mesh or chicken wire is less intrusive visually than a commercial tree guard but more time-consuming to put in place. Make sure the supporting stakes are pushed well down into the ground so that the barrier cannot be easily displaced.

SEE ALSO: Routine Care and Maintenance, pp.178–179; Rabbits, p.298; Deer, p.301

ROUTINE CARE

MOST ESTABLISHED TREES need little maintenance to keep them healthy and attractive. Routine tasks that will benefit your trees include replacing mulches, checking ties, harvesting fruit, removing fallen fruit and leaves, and watering in dry periods. Light pruning can sometimes be used to enhance the ornamental qualities of many trees, leading to more flowers or larger leaves, for example. Coppicing and pollarding are two types of hard pruning that may be used specifically to achieve special effects such as brilliantly colored young stems or handsome foliage. Pruning can also help restore neglected trees or create elegant, multistemmed shapes.

LIGHT PRUNING

Most trees need very little pruning apart from removing any crossing, dead, or damaged branches. Overpruning may affect the growth and even health of the tree. If you do feel the need to prune, remember these simple principles: prune in the season appropriate for the type of tree; respect the habit of the tree and aim for a good all-around balance; remove any dead, damaged, or diseased branches, cutting back to healthy growth, or remove the entire branch if that makes for a well-balanced framework; take out weak or straggly growth and any crossing or congested stems – rubbing stems could encourage disease. Make pruning cuts just above a bud or pair of buds (*see below and pp.156–157*). If you are cutting back a mature branch, be sure to leave the branch collar, that is the slightly wider part close to the trunk, completely untouched.

△ **PRUNING FOR FOLIAGE EFFECTS**
This Acer negundo 'Flamingo' has been cut back to produce larger leaves and brighter variegation. Regular pruning of some trees will create strong, healthy foliage.

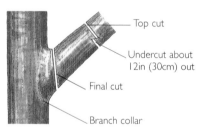

Top cut

Undercut about 12in (30cm) out

Final cut

Branch collar

△ **REMOVING A MATURE BRANCH**
To avoid a branch over 1in (2.5cm) thick tearing away from the trunk, remove it in two stages. When making the final cut to remove the stub, do not touch the branch collar.

CUTTING BACK A STEM

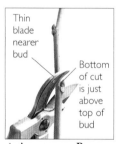

Thin blade nearer bud

Bottom of cut is just above top of bud

△ **ALTERNATE BUDS**
Make a slanting cut about ¼in (5mm) above a bud. The sloping cut allows water, which might encourage rot or disease, to drain away from the bud.

Keep blade clear of tops of buds

△ **OPPOSITE BUDS**
Cut straight across above a pair of strong, healthy buds, keeping the pruners as close above them as you can without grazing or damaging the buds.

FORMATIVE PRUNING

When you buy a new, young tree, it may occasionally be necessary to carry out some formative pruning to encourage the tree to develop a well-balanced crown. Some trees, such as alders (*Alnus*), are naturally multistemmed; you can also create this effect on certain other species (not grafted cultivars), such as snakebark maples (*Acer davidii*), birches (*Betula*), or black gum (*Nyssa sylvatica*), by cutting the main stem back hard (*see right*) so that several new stems develop. The resulting multiple trunks can be left clothed with foliage or the lower parts cleared to show off attractive bark.

PRUNING TO FORM A MULTISTEMMED TREE

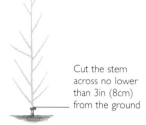

Cut the stem across no lower than 3in (8cm) from the ground

YEAR 1, WINTER △
Cut the main stem of a 2-year-old tree across at the desired height. Trim the wound so that there are no rough edges. The cut should stimulate low buds to shoot the following year.

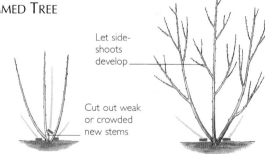

Let side-shoots develop

Cut out weak or crowded new stems

YEAR 2, WINTER △
Select 3 or 4 strong, well-spaced shoots – preferably ones that are equally vigorous so that they develop evenly. Remove all other shoots, cutting them back to the base.

YEAR 3, WINTER △
Let sideshoots develop, only removing the lower ones if you want to have clear stems. Remove any new suckers that occur from the base; these may regrow later and should be cut out.

SEE ALSO: Making Pruning Cuts, p.156; Why Prune?, p.157; Tools for Cutting and Pruning, p.279

COPPICING AND POLLARDING

Traditionally, these techniques were used to produce regular supplies of new straight growth for firewood or charcoal and fence- and basketmaking. Coppicing and pollarding are now ways to grow trees in small gardens that would otherwise lack the required space. They are also used to enhance leaf color or size or to stimulate bright young shoots. Pollarding of large trees is a job for a professional, since big branches must be removed, but pollarding of a young tree (*see below*) is not difficult. The new stems that appear are pliable and can be made into rustic plant supports, arches, or even garden sculptures.

■ **Coppicing:** in late winter or early spring, select a suitable tree, such as eucalyptus, paulownia, or willow, and cut it back almost to ground level, leaving the basal wood untouched.

■ **Pollarding:** a young standard tree is cut back to a clear stem of 3–6ft (1–1.8m) in late winter or early spring. Every second or third year, the young shoots are pruned back to the base. In the meantime, thin out excess stems if you wish.

△ **BRIGHT YOUNG GROWTH**
Some of the willows (Salix) that are known to produce colorful young growth make excellent candidates for pollarding. This is done on a main stem, about 5ft (1.5m) in height, to create an attractive crown of fresh and eye-catching new shoots at a manageable height.

OTHER MAINTENANCE

For most trees to establish well, they need watering, feeding, and weeding during the first few years. Trees grown in containers need regular topdressing and occasional repotting; they will also need to be watered and fed more frequently.

■ **Watering:** young or newly planted trees need a regular and plentiful supply of water throughout the growing season, especially if they are in light, sandy soil.

■ **Feeding:** most trees, especially newly planted ones and those that have been coppiced or pollarded, benefit from feeding. Apply fertilizer in midspring, according to manufacturer's instructions appearing on the bag, or an organic mulch such as well-rotted manure or compost in midautumn.

■ **Weeding:** keep the area beneath the tree canopy free of weeds (try mulching).

■ **Renewing mulches:** mulches, such as bark, laid to suppress weeds and conserve moisture should be renewed in late spring.

■ **Checking ties:** at the beginning and end of the growing season, check that the ties on staked trees have not become too tight around the trunk, restricting growth.

■ **Removing stakes:** when trees are established, remove all stakes and ties.

■ **Harvesting:** do not forget to pick any edible nuts or fruits, such as apples, when ripe and before they fall off the tree.

■ **Clearing up leaves and other debris:** rake up leaves and dead material as soon as you can, since they may harbor disease.

TREE SURGERY

All major tasks, such as removing large branches, crown thinning, and high-heading (having lower branches cut out to raise the canopy and so reduce shade), are best left to professional arborists. These procedures could be dangerous if tackled yourself and need experience to produce an esthetically satisfying result. Seek professional advice, also, if you wish to fell a tree completely; there may be both safety and legal considerations.

SEE ALSO: Applying Mulch, p.152; Repotting and Topdressing, p.179; Tree Stakes and Ties, p.193; Dealing with Weeds, pp.290–291

WATER GARDENING

WHY CHOOSE A WATER FEATURE?

THE USE OF WATER has long been valued for the added dimension it lends to a garden design; indeed, water is often considered the living soul of a garden. Water brings the ever-changing scintillation of reflected light and introduces the vitality of movement and sound to a garden in ways that no other single element can.

A water feature greatly extends the range of plants that you can grow, from simple moisture lovers and bog plants to true deep-water aquatics. Such plant diversity not only adds to the gardener's pleasure, but it also contributes to an inviting habitat for wildlife that will bring interest and benefits to the garden as a whole.

THE RIGHT STYLE

As with any component of garden design, you shouldn't be afraid to make your water garden express your individual taste, but remember that designs generally work best if they have a unified style that fits well with the immediate surroundings.

The first, most important, decision is whether you prefer a formal or informal style. This may also influence the possible choices of construction method, the types of plants you may grow, and the potential value of the finished feature for wildlife.

Formal features are characterized by crisp, geometric symmetry and strong, straight lines, framed with materials like stone or brick. Such hard edges often make access difficult for wildlife and may reduce potential for marginal plantings.

The informal style is expressed in natural irregularity, with soft outlines and sinuous curves. Informal pools are easier to meld into their surroundings with marginal planting, which incidentally provides cover for waterfowl and amphibians alike.

GOOD IDEAS

• Formal ponds sit best in their surroundings if the hard materials used blend with those of the house and existing patios or paving.

• An informal feature looks best if placed in a low-lying area that might fill with water naturally.

• Make a "wish list" to help you decide on a suitable style. If ease of installation, wildlife habitats, and maximum planting potential are priorities, an informal pond is best.

△ **CRISP GEOMETRY**
The firm lines of this small formal pond echo the fence line beyond and are thrown into high relief by strong verticals provided by the upright leaves of basket-planted marginals. Softer plantings contrast and so emphasize the strength of the geometry.

SINUOUS IRREGULARITY ▷
An artfully random arrangement of stones enhances the sinuous outline of an informal pond. The margins are masked by a soft, naturalistic planting that extends into the shallows to provide safe shelter for fish fry, amphibians, and bathing or drinking birds.

SEE ALSO: Water Features, pp.32–33, The Aquatic Environment, pp.214–215; The Transitional Zone, pp.216–217; The Moisture-Lovers, pp.218–219

SOUND AND MOVEMENT

Moving water in a design brings the visual excitement of glittering light and the soothing murmur of splashing water. Less obviously, it improves water quality by oxygenation to benefit plants and other living creatures, and it lends cool humidity to the surrounding air to refresh both gardener and moisture-loving plants alike.

Provide electricity to drive a circulating pump, and you could create sparkling cascades, smooth, gleaming sheets over spill stones, or a gurgling fountain from a simple or ornate spout.

△ SPLASHING LIGHT
A simple but elegant fountainhead, powered by a low-voltage circulating pump, forms the focal point in this naturalistic pool. Dispersed jets of water catch the light as they fall, creating the sound of splashing raindrops while maintaining oxygen levels in the water.

△ A ROCKY CASCADE
Constructed on a gentle slope to provide the necessary fall, this cascade is lined with a waterproof membrane, which is disguised by thoughtfully sited planting and naturally disposed rocks and gravel. Such rapidly moving water is amply refreshed with oxygen as it traverses the cascade.

QUIET REFLECTION

A mirrorlike surface of still, limpid water, undisturbed by splashing spouts, provides an air of tranquility that is most valuable if you need a pond to be a focus for quiet contemplation. The play of light changes throughout the days and seasons, and a smooth surface presents an opportunity to reflect – and so more than double – the beauty of both plants and ornaments.

In this situation, a healthy aquatic environment relies heavily on a careful mixture of plants, including submerged oxygenators and shade-casting, floating-leaved plants (like waterlilies) which will fail to thrive in splashing water.

THE RIGHT PLACE

Before excavating, locate all utilities underground, such as pipes or cables. An ideal site has easy access to electricity (for pumps) and to water (for filling up, as necessary). Good access to the pond and surrounding plantings is also desirable.

Sunny sites are best, but avoid sun traps and provide wind shelter to minimize evaporation. Keep clear of frost pockets and of trees and shrubs, which cast shade and shed potentially polluting leaves.

Decide if you want a clear view of the feature from the house, or if a more secluded location is preferred – for your privacy or for the benefit of wildlife.

SAFETY FIRST

Parents should be aware of the fascination of water for small children and of the dangers it presents. Never allow small children unsupervised access to open areas of water. Converting a pond excavation into a sandbox is one option, but you might also choose a feature without open water, like a bubble fountain or a wall-mounted spout. These are also good choices if the garden is used by those less footsure or of restricted mobility.

If you still want a pond, consider installing a rigid, wire mesh barrier just below the surface, and think about using nonslip surfaces for the pond edges. Don't overlook the dangers of open water to domestic pets and wild animals, like squirrels, who may come to drink. Give them safe access by including a gently sloping beach area or escape ramp.

△ MIRROR, MIRROR
Typha latifolia and water irises create strong, vertical reflections, contrasting here with an attractive pot. Flat paving accentuates the theme of tranquility.

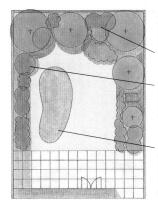

Avoid areas of deep shade, since water plants need high light levels to thrive

Avoid overhanging branches that may clutter water with falling leaves

A sunny site with shelter from wind is ideal – set a pond off center for more dynamic interest

△ FINDING THE PLOT
Take time to observe the movement of sun and shade throughout the day before deciding on the final site. This will avoid mistakes that may be impossible to rectify later.

ALWAYS REMEMBER

WATER AND ELECTRICITY DO NOT MIX

Outdoor electricity at normal voltage is potentially hazardous. For small features, low-voltage equipment, with an indoor transformer to convert power to low voltage, is adequate and safe when used with waterproof connectors that are approved for outdoor use. Larger features may need house electricity; for these, professional advice and installation are essential.

SEE ALSO: Container Ponds, p.207; Installing a Fountain, pp.208–209; Moving Water in Small Spaces, pp.212–213

CONSTRUCTING A WATER FEATURE

WHERE AT ONE TIME impressive water features were the prerogative of wealthy gardeners with ample space, the ready availability of modern liners, durable preformed units, and affordable pumps have brought the pleasures of water gardening within reach of those with more modest plots and pockets. With a modicum of practical skills, even the novice can confidently create an aquatic haven for flora and fauna, which will give many years of enjoyment. The various materials and techniques available are better suited to some purposes than others, so you should ensure at the outset that your choice is capable of meeting your requirements.

FULFILLING YOUR WISH LIST

Your wish list may include a preference for formality or informality, or still or moving water. Consider how important planting is to you and whether wildlife or ornamental fish form part of the plan. Assess your practical skills, your budget, and time for construction and subsequent maintenance.

In terms of availability and ease of construction, there is but little to choose between preformed or flexible liners. Preformed units come in a range of shapes and sizes, but liners are more versatile, especially for irregular forms that vary in depth. Remember that sufficient depth is essential for fish health in extremes of warm or cold weather; different species of fish have different requirements.

If the desired effect is an artful graduation between land and marginal plants, choose a liner. The steep sides of preformed units can be awkward to disguise with planting.

CHOOSING FEATURES FOR THE WATER GARDEN

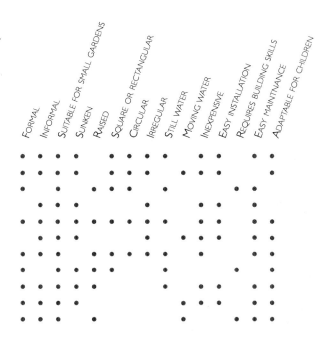

A number of factors influence the choice of water feature and the appropriate means of construction. Most water features demand little in the way of building skills and are well within the capabilities of the novice. It is always best to choose the simplest option to fulfill your needs – if you overstretch your abilities, a poor outcome will become a constant irritation.

	Formal	Informal	Suitable for small gardens	Sunken	Raised	Square or rectangular	Circular	Irregular	Still water	Moving water	Inexpensive	Easy installation	Requires building skills	Easy maintenance	Adaptable for children
SIMPLE POND WITH FLEXIBLE LINER	•	•	•	•		•	•	•	•		•	•		•	•
FLEXIBLE LINER POND AND STREAM	•	•	•	•				•	•	•	•	•		•	
RAISED POND/FLEXIBLE LINER	•		•		•	•	•	•	•		•		•	•	
INDEPENDENT BOG GARDEN		•	•	•				•	•		•	•		•	
RIGID POND UNIT	•	•	•	•		•	•	•	•		•	•		•	
RIGID POND AND STREAM UNIT		•	•	•				•	•	•	•		•	•	
RAISED POOL USING RIGID UNIT	•	•	•		•	•	•		•		•		•	•	
CONCRETE-LINED POOL	•		•	•		•			•			•	•		
CONTAINER WATER FEATURE	•	•	•		•	•			•			•	•	•	
COBBLESTONE FOUNTAIN	•	•	•		•					•	•	•		•	•
WALL-MOUNTED FOUNTAIN	•	•	•		•					•		•	•	•	

◁ **INFINITE VARIETY**
Irregular in form and depth, this flexible-lined pond offers a wealth of planting possibilities. A pebble beach disguises the liner at the shallows and provides a safe exit and drinking place for wildlife.

△ **CUNNING DISGUISE**
This preformed pond unit has been disguised with a clever combination of hard landscaping, container-grown marginal plants, and a luxuriant planting of overhanging moisture-lovers.

SEE ALSO: Buying a Flexible Liner, pp.202–203; Choosing a Preformed Pond, pp.206–207; The Transitional Zone, pp.216–217; The Moisture-Lovers, pp.218–219

USING A PREFORMED POND UNIT

Preformed ponds in brittle plastics and unreal colors have been superseded by a more durable modern range of fiberglass or light-stable plastics in neutral colors. Installation is simple, if the groundwork is done carefully. Even a small unit is heavy when full of water, and it may crack if settlement is excessive after construction.

The perception of scale differs indoors and out, so overestimate the required size when buying. A small pond can become insignificant, especially when the edges are concealed. The edges are more easily disguised by paving than with plants.

STAGES OF CONSTRUCTION

Regardless of size or shape, the same basic techniques apply for installing any preformed pond unit: first, dig a hole slightly larger than the perimeter to make backfilling and soil compression easier, then make sure that the base is absolutely level, free of stones, and is as firm as can be.

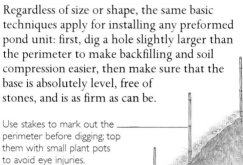

GOOD IDEAS

• Preformed units come in a range of qualities, colors, shapes, sizes, and depths, so shop around to find one to suit your needs.

• To extend planting, choose a unit with marginal shelves. Check that their width is adequate for planting baskets.

• Make sure the depth is adequate if you want to keep fish. Choose small species like common goldfish, which thrive in relatively confined ponds at least 14in (35cm) deep.

Use sand or soil as a backfill between unit and excavation sides; shovel in a little at a time and compress the soil down with a wooden post, consolidating each layer before adding the next

Use stakes to mark out the perimeter before digging; top them with small plant pots to avoid eye injuries.

To give firm support and to avoid punctures when full of water, the unit is cushioned on a layer of sand or finely sifted, stonefree soil or underlay

Soil is excavated to exact depth to accommodate the marginal shelves, if any; expect a little trial and error when contouring the hole for a shelf

Before backfilling, stabilize the unit by filling with about 4in (10cm) of water; continue to fill the pond slowly as you backfill

As the surface of a body of water is always level, when the pond fills, it will be obvious if the unit rim is not level – check constantly with a level at every stage of construction

The rim, which prevents soil from falling into the pond, can be disguised with overhanging plants or slabs; press soil or sand under the rim firmly when backfilling.

INSTALLING A FLEXIBLE POND LINER

There are several types of liner. Poly-ethylene is cheap, but it degrades in sun-light in as little as three to five years. It is far better to invest in more expensive PVC, preferably reinforced with internal nylon net. A good supplier will offer PVC with a ten-year guarantee. Butyl is top of the range in cost and durability; it has superior elasticity, needs minimal folding, and is flexible even when cold. The best grades of butyl have an expected life of 25 to 50 years.

LINING AN EXCAVATION

Even the toughest of liners are vulnerable to puncture, so it is vital that the base is clear of stones or other sharp projections. Try never to walk on a liner at any stage. The tiniest puncture will leak water and may prove impossible to find later.

Smooth curves are easiest to line, and the 20° angle of the sides prevents caving in; for sharp corners, the liner must be pleated carefully

Bricks or stones laid carefully on the margins keep the liner in place during filling – lift them to allow liner movement as the pool fills

The base is flat, firm, and stone free; if the subsoil is very stony, spread a 2in (5cm) layer of sand, tread it down, and rake it smooth

Fill the pool slowly, so the weight of water gradually molds the liner into the contours of the hole

An underlay prolongs the liner's life – use commercial polyester matting, available in rolls of 6ft (2m) width, or improvise with insulation felt or discarded, synthetic domestic carpet

Black or dark brown liners are the least obtrusive

A gently sloping side with a slight rim provides a perfect site for a pebble beach

Allow a 18in (45cm) marginal flap of liner to prevent leakage, and disguise with soil or edging stones

SEE ALSO: Buying a Flexible Liner, pp.202–203; Choosing a Preformed Pool, pp.206–207

BUYING A FLEXIBLE LINER

CALCULATING QUANTITIES for a liner, especially one of irregular shape, often confounds the novice, but the calculation is simple. First, determine the maximum length, width, and depth of the pool. Liner length will be the maximum length plus twice the maximum depth, and liner width will be the maximum width plus twice the maximum depth. Finally, add 18in (45cm) to both length and width to allow for overlap. For circular ponds, substitute the diameter for length and width.

A liner is easier to work with if laid flat in the sun to warm up for half an hour or so, because warmth increases flexibility. Roll it up smoothly before laying.

A SIMPLE POND WITH MARGINAL SHELF

Before excavating, dig a test hole in the center of the site to establish the level of the natural water table. Usually, the water table will not be an issue, but if a liner is laid below the water table or in poorly drained soil, upward pressure of water causes it to balloon up – the "hippo effect." If you do discover poor drainage or a high water table, you may need to improve drainage. Alternatively, avoid the problem by making the pond a semiraised feature, using excavated topsoil to build up the pond edges, which will bring the base above the water table.

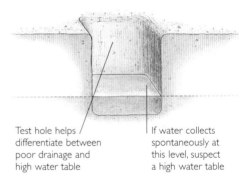

Test hole helps differentiate between poor drainage and high water table

If water collects spontaneously at this level, suspect a high water table

△ DIGGING A TEST HOLE
Dig a hole 18in (45cm) deep and fill it with water. If it doesn't seep away, you have poor drainage or a high water table. Dig down another 18in (45cm); if the hole begins to fill spontaneously, then you have a high water table.

TOOLS AND MATERIALS

- 10–12 pegs, for finding levels
- Club hammer
- Level
- Straightedge
- Shovel and spade
- Rake
- Sand or string, for marking out
- Soft sand or sifted soil for base
- Underlay
- Flexible liner
- Bricks or smooth, rounded stones to hold liner in place during filling

MARKING OUT AND DIGGING

1 LEVELING THE POOL EDGES
Mark the pool outline with sand or string, then position marker pegs at equal intervals around it. With a club hammer, level, and straightedge, use the technique shown on p.206 to ensure that all the pegs are level and the soil around them is horizontal.

2 EXCAVATING THE HOLE
Remove any soil to a depth of 2in (5cm) and retain for edging, if desired. Dig the entire area to 9in (23cm) deep, with the sides slightly sloping outward, then rake the base. Mark the deep zone, leaving at least 12in (30cm) width for a marginal shelf.

3 PREPARING THE DEEP ZONE
Dig the deep zone to a further 15in (38cm). Rake over the base, removing all sharp and large stones, roots, or other projections. Spread a layer of sand or sifted soil, 1in (2.5cm) deep, over the base as an added precaution against punctures.

LAYING THE LINING MATERIAL

1 ROLL OUT THE UNDERLAY
Remove any stones from the sides of the pool, then pat sand into the sides to make them smooth. Drape the underlay over the pool. Working from the center outward, press the underlay firmly into the contours of the hole, with as few creases as possible.

2 LAYING OUT THE LINER
Position the rolled-up liner on one side of the pool and unroll it gently. Don't pull the liner fabric; this will stretch it and make it more vulnerable to puncture. Leave sufficient overlap around the margins and fold in the creases evenly.

3 FILLING WITH WATER
Use bricks to hold the liner in place temporarily. Fill slowly with water. The weight of water will settle the liner into the contours, so make adjustments, if necessary, by pleating creased areas and moving the bricks as the liner becomes taut.

SEE ALSO: Bog Gardens, pp.204–205; Make it Level and True, p.206

TURNING THE CORNER

If a pond is designed with broad, sweeping curves, little adjustment of the liner will be needed, but for more acute curves, careful pleating is necessary, especially around the marginal shelf. In ponds with corners, the liner can be folded and excess tucked in.

Make pleats and folds as generous as possible to avoid overstretching the liner and make as many adjustments as possible before filling with water; its weight makes adjustment very difficult later on.

TRIMMING THE LINER

Once the pool is full of water, the securing bricks can be removed and the excess liner can be trimmed away. Never trim the liner right to the water's edge, but allow an overlap of about 4–6in (10–15cm). This prevents water from seeping behind the liner, which can occur if the water level rises and the pool overflows after heavy rain. It also provides a good base for an edging of hard materials that are to be mortared in place.

◁ **PLEATING**
To accommodate curves, gather the liner to form a series of pleats and hold them top and bottom with bricks until secured by the pressure of water on filling. Although both pleats and folds look unsightly, once compressed by water they become flattened and virtually invisible.

◁ **FOLD AND TUCK**
To make a neat corner, make a diagonal fold in the liner and tuck in the excess with one hand while securing the bottom of the fold with the other. Try to position the fold exactly in the corner for best effect. Hold in place with bricks until secured by the weight of water.

◁ **CUT TO FIT**
Using a pair of sharp scissors, trim away excess liner to leave an edge of 4–6in (10–15cm). Walk carefully around the margins of the pond so that you do not inadvertently kick stones into the water; they may cause punctures if they become lodged under planting baskets.

FINISHING THE EDGES

For hard edging, or if soil is likely to subside beneath grass, install a concrete foundation. Lift the liner overlap and dig out a trench, 6–9in (15–23cm) deep. Roll the liner into the trench, lay a foundation on top, and mortar the edging in place. Keep mortar out of the water; it is toxic to fish and plants. If it does pollute the water, drain the pond and start again.

GOOD IDEAS

• If edging with rocks, try to obtain from a local quarry. Distinctive sorts, like granite or slate, look misplaced when out of habitat.

• Include a stone that slopes into the water as an escape route for frogs and others.

• With hard edges, a slight overhang will cast shadows into the water that disguise the liner and protect it from direct light.

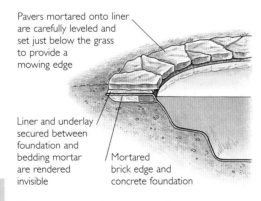

Pavers mortared onto liner are carefully leveled and set just below the grass to provide a mowing edge

Liner and underlay secured between foundation and bedding mortar are rendered invisible

Mortared brick edge and concrete foundation

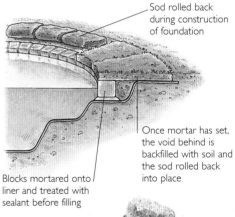

Sod rolled back during construction of foundation

Blocks mortared onto liner and treated with sealant before filling

Once mortar has set, the void behind is backfilled with soil and the sod rolled back into place

FORMAL AND INFORMAL EDGINGS

There is a wealth of edging materials to choose from, ranging from naturalistic sod or rocks to pavers and a wide range of paving slabs. Grass looks natural but becomes muddy under heavy traffic or from paddling domestic pets. Using rocks provides a firm edge with excellent niches to shelter toads and frogs. Hard paving makes an ideal surface for sitting on and enjoying the fruits of your labors.

△ **ON THE BEACH**
For the most natural effect, lay rocks and stones in bands that gradually decrease in size as they get nearer the water. A smooth-pebbled beach is the perfect invitation for birds and small mammals to come to drink, and it is the ideal entry point for amphibians.

PLANES ▷
Rocks like granite have cleavage planes rather than strata. Align the rocks so cleavage planes are broadly parallel for the most natural effect, then mortar them carefully in place.

ROCK STRATA ▷
Sandstones and limestones have strata that look best set in overlapping diagonals, with strata lines running along the sides, rather than the top, to create the impression of an outcrop.

SEE ALSO: On the Edge, p.207; Building a Stream with Waterfalls, p.211

BOG GARDENS

THE BOG GARDEN offers further possibilities for increasing plant diversity in the garden. The typically lush growth of moisture-loving plants provides the perfect frame for open water and a link between land and water that sets the pond in context as well as furnishing a habitat for wildlife. The natural adjunct to a pool, a bog garden can be made as an extension of it or as an independent feature in its own right. The latter has the advantage of safety, since there is no open water, and both types constitute a simple, cost-effective, and water-efficient means of creating the ideal environment for plants that demand constantly moist soil.

EXTENDING THE POSSIBILITIES

The versatility of flexible liners comes clearly to the fore when used to create a range of planting zones to accommodate aquatics, marginals, and moisture-loving plants. The visually seamless transition emulates a naturally damp habitat perfectly, forming a haven for frogs and toads, both voracious consumers of slugs.

TELL ME WHY

WICKS AND WATER LEVELS

If liners extend beyond pool margins to create damp zones, the soil in which moisture lovers are grown must be separated from the body of water. Otherwise, plants will draw water from the pond via the soil, which acts as a wick, resulting in rapid lowering of the pond water level, especially in warm, dry, or windy weather.

PLANTING ZONES

Here, a liner provides continuity across three distinct planting zones, in imitation of a natural aquatic habitat. Plantings in deep and shallow water can be arranged to flow naturally into drifts of moisture-lovers at the margins before reaching dry land.

Separated from the pool by a mortared rock barrier, moisture-loving plants thrive in damp soil, without depleting pool water by the wicking effect (see left). The liner bottom must be perforated

Ridges enclose a shallow zone that can be filled with about 12in (30cm) of soil; marginal plants will luxuriate if unrestricted by a planting basket – the confined soil does not muddy the water in the body of the pool

A deep zone is the vital element for many true aquatics, such as waterlilies and lotuses, and essential if the pool is to be a healthy environment for fish

Pockets of soil contained within the liner are kept moist with a "wick" of sod wedged between rocks. Moisture lovers thrive here, but use only very small soil volumes so they do not greatly deplete the pool water

AN INDEPENDENT BOG GARDEN

For larger and more ambitious bog gardens, an independent feature is the ideal solution. With its own water supply, there is no problem of wicking from a pool and, since the liner is not exposed to sunlight, the cheapest plastic or even old plastic bags can be used as a liner. The greater area provides the possibility of more adventurous massed plantings.

ALWAYS REMEMBER

IT'S A CONSTANT DRAIN!

Waterlogged soil quickly becomes stagnant and sour with the harmful products of anaerobic bacterial decomposition. Few plants thrive in such saturated conditions. Moisture lovers need a constantly replenished supply of water, so the liner must be perforated to allow slow drainage.

Topsoil from excavation is used to refill the hole; if necessary, it can be improved by addition of well-rotted organic matter

The inexpensive plastic liner is perforated at the base to allow slow, steady drainage; the top of the liner is hidden by about 3in (8cm) of soil

BOG GARDEN PROFILE

A bog garden needs to be at least 18in (45cm) deep if it is not to dry out too rapidly. In sunny or windy weather, dense planting reduces the loss of water by transpiration through the leaves. The soil should be of open structure and rich in organic matter so that it is free-draining but moisture-retentive.

Layer of pea gravel prevents soil clogging the perforations in the water supply pipe and liner, aiding drainage. The end of the supply pipe is blocked off

A connector links the perforated water-supply pipe to a hose, which may be coupled to a water barrel or the house supply

SEE ALSO: The Aquatic Environment, pp.214–215; The Transitional Zone, pp. 216–217; The Moisture-lovers, pp.218–219

MAKING A BOG GARDEN

Creating an independent bog garden is simplicity itself. It requires absolutely no building skills and uses materials that are both inexpensive and readily available from any good hardware store. You can reduce costs still further by using plastic bags as the lining material – recycling all those empty potting-mix bags is, after all, a very environmentally friendly option.

For the most realistic appearance, the bog should ideally be sited at a low point in the garden, where water might be expected to accumulate naturally, and its extent should be in scale with its surroundings. If the garden is tiny, a small bog, without a separate irrigation system, is manageable; it can be watered by hand, as necessary. Larger areas are nearly always more visually satisfying, since they have greater potential for varied planting. In this case, a built-in irrigation system really is a labor-saving must: moisture levels must be fairly constant, and hand-watering is tediously time-consuming.

TOOLS AND MATERIALS

- Sand or string for marking out
- Spade
- Rake
- Heavy-duty plastic liner
- Bricks or stones to hold liner in place temporarily
- Garden fork
- Pea gravel
- Rigid plastic pipe, 1in (2.5cm) diameter
- Hacksaw
- Drill
- 2 elbow joints
- Knife or scissors
- Short length of pipe, clip, and a hose connector with male/female lock

CONSTRUCTING AN INDEPENDENT BOG GARDEN USING A FLEXIBLE LINER

1 MARK OUT THE REQUIRED SHAPE
Mark out the shape with string or sand. Dig the hole to a depth of about 24in (60cm) with gently sloping sides so that the soil does not cave in. Store the good excavated topsoil on a spare sheet of plastic nearby, for replacement later. Discard any heavy subsoil. Rake over the base and remove any large or sharp stones.

2 DRAPING THE LINER
Drape the liner over the excavation, and press it into the contours. Hold it firmly in place with bricks or stones so that is does not move when you walk on it. Use a garden fork to make the drainage perforations in the base at 24–39in (60–100cm) intervals. To save expense, you could use smaller overlapping sheets of plastic.

3 ADDING THE GRAVEL LAYER
Spread a 2in (5cm) layer of pea gravel with a rake. Cut a section of pipe the length of the base; drill holes in it at 6in (15cm) intervals, block one end, then lay it on the gravel. Attach it to a second pipe, 24in (60cm) long, with an elbow joint, so that the second pipe rises vertically to ground level. Top with 2in (5cm) layer of gravel.

4 ADDING THE SOIL
Rake gravel level, and shovel in the topsoil without disturbing gravel layer. Before it reaches the top, trim off excess liner and bury edges under 3in (8cm) of soil. Attach an elbow joint to the vertical pipe to make a right-angled turn at ground level. Fit a short length of hose with a clip and attach it to a hose connector.

THE PLANTED BOG GARDEN

Keep the planted garden moist by filling up with fresh water – enough to flood the surface – whenever the surface soil is dry. In hot, sunny weather, the bog may need replenishing often. A rainwater barrel, placed to catch runoff from the house or greenhouse roof, can be fitted with a tap and hose and linked up to the bog garden's irrigation pipe.

While the garden is getting established, weed it regularly, but once the plantings have formed a good cover, any emergent weed seedlings will be deprived of light and unable to grow.

Independent bog gardens can safely be treated with ordinary garden fertilizers, with no danger of nitrogen percolating into a pond to cause algal blooms.

EARLY DAYS ▷
Given such moist, fertile soil, young plants will establish quickly and grow so rapidly that any bare areas of soil will be almost obscured by the end of the first growing season.

SEE ALSO: The Moisture-lovers, pp.218–219

Choosing a Preformed Pond Unit

PREFORMED UNITS can be the ultimate solution for a small-to medium-sized pond – the largest available are about 12ft (3.5m) across. Quick to install and easy to clean, they come in a variety of shapes and materials. The cheapest are plastic, although be aware that the cheapest grades have a short life span, sometimes only two to three years. More costly fiberglass units are long-lasting, lightweight, and durable. Those without marginal shelves are simplest to install and, although square and circular ones are ideal for small formal ponds, they are rather shallow. If you want to stock your pond with fish and a range of plants, choose one with deeper zones and marginal shelves.

Installing a Preformed Unit

The basic requirement when installing a rigid preformed unit is to dig a hole of the exact shape and size so that the unit sits absolutely level in its housing, both across the pond and around its perimeter. The simpler the shape, the easier this will be.

Raised ponds are very simple to make with regularly shaped preformed units of even depth. Those with irregular contours, especially larger models, must have firm support if they are not to distort and fracture when full. With these, the deeper zones at least – and preferably the entire unit – must be sunk into the ground and sit on firm soil.

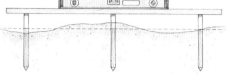

MAKE IT LEVEL AND TRUE △
To obtain level pond edges on uneven ground, use datum, or marker, pegs. Set the first datum point at the ideal level of the pond edge, then use a straightedge and level to align other marker pegs with it. Check levels across the hole and around the perimeter. Cut and fill to correct levels.

Tools and Materials

- Rigid pond unit
- Blocks or bricks to support unit temporarily
- Stakes and string
- Tape measure
- Spade
- Marker pegs
- Level
- Straightedge
- Soft sand or sifted soil
- Rake
- Hose
- Length of wood for backfilling

Good Buys

- Preformed pond units are widely stocked by garden centers, but you may need to search for quality units in neutral colors, so shop around to match your requirements.
- Choose fiberglass for long life; they are also the easiest to repair.
- Make sure marginal shelves are wide enough to hold planting baskets securely.

Installing a Pond Unit with Marginal Shelf

1 MARK OUT THE PERIMETER
Support the unit on bricks and check it is level. Push stakes in vertically around the margin, laying string to mark the edges of the excavation. For symmetrically shaped units, simply invert the pond unit on the soil and mark around it.

2 DIGGING THE HOLE
Measure the depth of the unit from lip to marginal shelf. Excavate the hole to this depth, making it level (see above). Press the unit gently in the hole; the impression made by the deep zone is a guide for further digging.

3 EXCAVATING THE DEEP ZONE
To find the deep zone depth, measure down from a straightedge at several points across the base of the unit. Dig the hole 2in (5cm) deeper, then add a layer of soft sand 2in (5cm) deep. Rake it level and remove any stones.

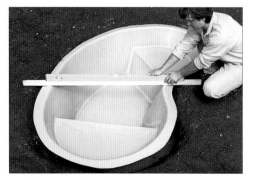

4 MAKING A SNUG FIT
Gently firm the unit into the hole; the deep zone should sit snugly in its hole and the unit must be level. If necessary, remove the unit to adjust further. Do not proceed until unit is level and fully supported.

5 FILLING THE UNIT WITH WATER
Add 4in (10cm) of water to lend stability. Backfill around the sides with sand or sifted soil. Checking levels at each stage, add 2in (5cm) of water at a time, firming down each layer of backfill before adding the next.

SEE ALSO: Constructing a Water Feature, pp.200–201

ON THE EDGE

Preformed pond units are designed with a wide lip for structural strength and to prevent soil from falling into the pond. Unless disguised with edging, the shiny and obtrusive lip forms a very unnatural edge.

Whatever the edging of choice, the lip must be well supported. For a simple sod edge, firmly packing the rim beneath with backfill is sufficient. The sod is then rolled back in place to cover the rim.

For all types of paving edge, however, whether made of slabs or random paving, a foundation is an absolute necessity. A layer of aggregate is adequate for most purposes (see below). Topped with a layer of soft sand to fill any voids, aggregate forms a firm base for a mortar bed and slabs.

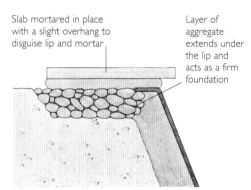

Slab mortared in place with a slight overhang to disguise lip and mortar

Layer of aggregate extends under the lip and acts as a firm foundation

EDGING WITH SLABS △

Excavate a 2½–3in (6–8cm) trench around the perimeter of the pond to the full width of the slabs. Fill the trench with a layer of aggregate, and pack some beneath the lip to support it. Set slabs into place on a bed of mortar, taking care not to allow any mortar to fall into the water. Fill spaces between paving joints with mortar.

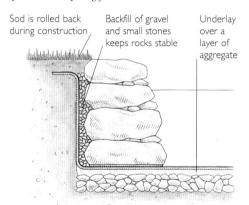

Sod is rolled back during construction

Backfill of gravel and small stones keeps rocks stable

Underlay over a layer of aggregate

△ ROCK WALLS AND SOD EDGES

This technique can be used for simple, almost straight-sided ponds of a single depth, but because of the additional weight, an extra cushioning layer of underlay over a layer of aggregate is recommended. Flat rocks are mortared together and given further stability with a backfill of gravel and wedges of small stones.

CONTAINER PONDS

The diminutive charms of container ponds make water gardening possible even in tiny spaces like roof terraces or balconies. They make a striking focal point on a patio, even in the house or conservatory.

Any watertight container of suitable dimensions can be used (see right), and they will hold a surprising number of plants. Be sure to include oxygenating plants, or consider introducing a small fountain.

Wooden containers must be treated with sealant before use, and all container ponds should be allowed to stand before planting to allow any chlorine to disperse.

ALWAYS REMEMBER

NONE LIKE IT HOT!

Small bodies of water heat up quickly in summer, and they may freeze solid in winter; both extremes will kill plants and fish. Position containers out of direct midday sun, and protect them from winter cold by bringing them indoors in autumn or by emptying them and restocking each spring.

◁ **WATERPROOFING**
Clean thoroughly and paint the inside of the barrel to the rim with a sealant to protect wood and prevent seepage of residues into the water. New barrels will be waterproof; older ones may need a separate liner.

IN GOOD SHAPE △

Glazed earthenware pots are ideal for miniature ponds. Make sure they are watertight, at least 18–24in (45–60cm) wide at the neck, and 15–18in (38–45cm) or more deep. It is risky to leave pots out over winter, even if they are frost-resistant; drain the pots until spring.

Containers hold upright, narrow-leaved sedges and rushes for vertical impact

Free-floating and floating-leaved plants cover the surface

△ BARREL

This barrel holds two or three planting baskets. Narrow-leaved plants give vertical emphasis and take up little space. Create variation in depth by using brick plinths; leave the deep area free for floating plants and a small waterlily.

◁ SUNKEN MINI-POND

Sinking a container reduces temperature fluctuations. Surrounding it with a pebble beach helps keep down weeds and keeps the soil cool and moist for surrounding plants. It also gives the illusion that this tiny pond is much larger than it really is.

SEE ALSO: Finishing off the Edges, p.203; Installing a Fountain, pp.208–209; Submerged Plants, p.214; Planting Water Plants, pp.220–221

INSTALLING A FOUNTAIN

IN THE DAYS BEFORE ELECTRICITY, hydraulic technology relied on gravity, enormous reservoirs, and complex pumping systems. The advent of small, modern, submersible pumps has brought the possibilities of moving water to even the smallest spaces. Not only do fountains lend sound, movement, and sparkle to the garden, they refresh and deionize the air around them with cool humidity and replenish oxygen levels in the water to the benefit of plants and fish. Given due regard to electrical safety, fountain installation is the essence of simplicity; nowadays, excellent fountain kits can be bought off the shelf from any good garden center.

CREATING SIMPLE FOUNTAINS

The mechanics are essentially simple. A fountainhead is connected to an electric pump, which forces water through the head to create the spray. Height varies with pump power and a flow adjuster. Low-voltage pumps give heights up to 4ft (1.2m), and submersible house-voltage pumps up to 7ft (2.2m). For higher jets, a house-voltage surface pump is required.

GOOD IDEAS

• A spray width that is less than half that of the pool will fall entirely within its margins.

• The finer the spray, the more water is lost by evaporation; to minimize losses, use a nozzle that produces a column of water rather than a fine, wide-arching spray.

• Tapwater is fine for replacing water lost to evaporation.

• Place splash-sensitive plants, such as waterlilies, beyond the splash zone.

SIMPLE PUMP INSTALLATION ▽
The simplest type of fountain installation is powered by a low-voltage, submersible pump. A vertical discharge pipe connects the fountainhead to the pump outlet.

Fountainhead emerges directly from outlet of pump, which is fixed to a plinth

Some plants, such as waterlilies, dislike moving water and so need to be placed beyond the immediate splash zone

An overhanging, stone slab edging hides the pump from view

Free-standing fountain head connected to pump outlet with a short length of delivery pipe

◁ **REMOTE PUMP**
In larger ponds, to bring the pump within easy reach for cleaning and maintenance, the pump is best sited near the edge. The fountainhead is fed through a delivery pipe attached to the pump outlet.

Submersible pump mounted on a plinth for stability. The electrical wiring is hidden beneath paving slab

BUBBLE FOUNTAIN ▷
One of the safest ways of bringing the sight and sound of moving water to a small space is to install a bubble fountain. This one is supplied by a single pipe connected to a low-voltage pump hidden in a reservoir beneath the millstone.

SPRAY PATTERNS

Spray patterns are formed by the size and arrangement of holes in the fountain outlet nozzle. Simple nozzles, like those illustrated below, are attached directly to the outlet pipe of the pump.

Spray nozzles for more complex patterns need a special adaptor and may need a more powerful pump, depending on the height and volume of the spray.

◁ **A SINGLE SPRAY**
Elegant in its simplicity, the single spray pattern suits ponds of simple design and is easily accommodated in small pools. The narrower the delivery pipe, the higher the elevation of the spray.

SINGLE-SPRAY NOZZLE

◁ **TWO-TIERED SPRAY**
Two concentric rings of holes in the spray nozzle provide a broader, two-tiered spray. Ideal for larger and more elaborate pools. The splash zone is larger, so in small pools it may disturb plants such as waterlilies.

DOUBLE-SPRAY NOZZLE

BELL-JET NOZZLE

△ **BELL JET SPRAY**
Bell jets produce a shimmering, hemispherical film of water that causes relatively little surface disturbance despite its relatively large splash zone. A Tiffany jet is a bell jet combined with a single-spray nozzle underneath, which gives the effect of a fountain within a fountain.

SEE ALSO: Sound and Movement, p.199; Safety First, p.199

PUMPS AND POWER SUPPLY

For most small water features, a low-voltage pump is safe, adequate, and easy to install. For large features, house power is needed and the hardware must be installed by a professional electrician.

If possible, buy from an aquatic specialist or a garden center with a good aquatic department. They will happily advise; the best manufacturers also have telephone helplines or websites. Be prepared with your answers to the following questions:

■ Will the pump operate a watercourse, fountain, filter, or a combination of these?
■ What is the pool's volume?
■ What type of fountain spray is needed?
■ How high a spray do you want?
■ For water courses, you will also need to know the head height and reservoir pool volume (*see p.210*) and the width of the spillway or stream.

USING HOUSE ELECTRICITY

House electricity is essential for large water courses or fountains in excess of 4ft (1.2m) in height. They are inevitably more costly since all equipment has high safety specifications and installation is a job for the professionals.

Grounded supply switch must be turned off before handling any equipment

Waterproof connectors are essential

Armored, waterproof cable

Circuit breaker is vital for electrical safety outdoors

Plastic conduit is buried 24in (60cm) below ground

Jets taller than 4ft (1.2m) need house electricity to power the submersible pump

A transformer converts house voltage to a low-voltage current and minimizes the risks of electrical shock

USING LOW-VOLTAGE ELECTRICITY

Most small, moving water features, including fountains and cascades, can be driven by a low-voltage pump. Cost advantages are inherent in the scale and specifications of equipment used, in running costs, and, not least, because it is a safe option for do-it-yourself installation.

Small fountains, up to 4ft (1.2m) high, are adequately powered by low-voltage electricity

Submersible pump is kept stable by weight of attached plinth

Waterproof connector above water level also protects from moisture

Plastic conduit provides permanent housing to carry cable safely beneath paving

USING FILTERS

In the quest for crystal-clear water, filters are an important tool. They are fitted pre- or post-pump and may be submersible or located out of the water, depending on design. There are two main types — mechanical or biological — and they are often used in combination. Mechanical filters are simple strainers, usually using spongelike foam to remove suspended particles. Effective as soon as switched on, they may be used intermittently.

Biological filters use colonies of beneficial bacteria to break down the nitrogenous waste of fish and other organisms. They take up to three weeks to take effect and, once switched on, must be kept running; the bacteria need a constant flow of oxygenated water to keep them active.

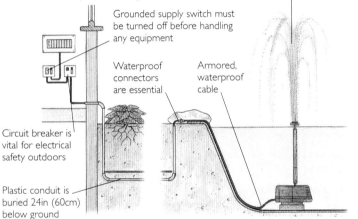

Inlet pipe with spray bar creates a spray of water to keep up oxygen levels for bacterial health

ALL-PURPOSE FILTER ▷
This type of filter is located outside the pond. The inlet spray bar and foam sheets are easily accessible for cleaning. Biofilter media should be cleaned only with pond water or nonchlorinated water.

Water flows downward through layers of open cell foam of increasing density

Biomedia of clay or glass provides large surface area for bacterial colonization

Outlet pipe incorporates overflow so filter is bypassed when blocked

SEE ALSO: Safety First, p.199; Streams and Water Channels, pp.210–211

STREAMS AND WATER CHANNELS

MOST GARDENS CAN ACCOMMODATE a small watercourse as an adjunct to a pool, whether it be a burbling stream, a rocky cascade, or more a formal water canal or rill. The basic requirements are a reservoir pool, a pump of sufficient power to raise the water through a delivery pipe to a header pool, and a sufficient difference in height (known as the head) between the header and the reservoir to ensure that gravity moves the returning water downhill along a totally watertight channel. If no incline exists naturally – and even a small head is adequate – a slope can easily be built up using soil from the excavation of the reservoir pool.

THE ESSENTIAL ELEMENTS

A good specialized supplier will advise on a suitably powered pump for a watercourse, if given the following essential details:

■ **Measure the head** (the height of the header pool above the reservoir pool) and the length and width of the water stream.

■ **Calculate the volume** of the reservoir pool by multiplying maximum depth by width by length. The flow rate per hour must not exceed this volume.

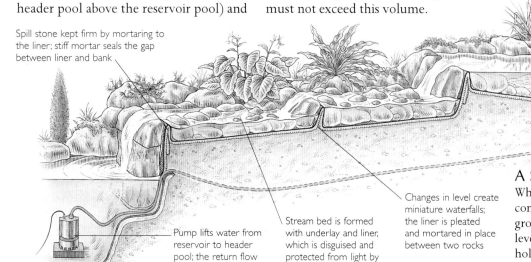

Spill stone kept firm by mortaring to the liner; stiff mortar seals the gap between liner and bank

Backward-sloping header pool retains water should the pump fail: a safety feature for flora and fauna

Delivery pipe buried in trench beside stream and covered with soil, gravel, or small rocks for easy access

Pump lifts water from reservoir to header pool; the return flow is powered by gravity

Stream bed is formed with underlay and liner, which is disguised and protected from light by randomly laid pebbles

Changes in level create miniature waterfalls; the liner is pleated and mortared in place between two rocks

A STREAM IN PROFILE

Whatever the style, a stream, in essence, consists of a channel cut through sloping ground; the channel may traverse changes in level to create waterfalls. The reservoir pool holds a pump and an ample volume of water to circulate via a delivery pipe and header pool.

LINING A WATERCOURSE

Flexible liners come into their own in the creation of watercourses, but to ensure a trouble-free, leakproof channel for both formal and more naturalistic features:

■ **Take care to avoid punctures;** do not walk on the liner or drag it on the ground.

■ **Use an underlay** for added security.

■ **Ensure that the liner overlaps** the channel's sides by a generous margin.

■ **Protect the liner** from direct sunlight.

■ **Start at the bottom** with the reservoir, and work upward to the header pool.

NATURAL ELEMENTS ▷

Water glitters over the rocky cascade and gleams in a smooth sheet over a spill stone into the reservoir pool. A flexible liner forms a waterproof channel and is edged with artfully disposed rocks. Smaller stones of varying size disguise the base while adding sound and sparkle.

△ A SIMPLE WATER CHANNEL

Bringing the gentle murmur of water to the garden, this simple channel is built from natural stone slabs mortared onto a plastic liner. A submersible pump circulates water through an in-pond filter; an ultraviolet filter and small header pool is hidden beneath the horizontal slab.

SEE ALSO: Pumps and Power Supply, p.209; Using Filters, p.209; Moving Water in Small Spaces, pp.212–213

BUILDING A STREAM WITH WATERFALLS

One of the beauties of creating streams with a flexible liner is that you can adapt the basic method to formal and informal style features, with or without waterfalls.

Lightweight butyl rubber or PVC are the most accommodating materials, especially for the beginner. Their flexibility allows them to be folded, tugged, and tweaked carefully into place in irregularly shaped channels. If you want the stream to meander gently along its course, be sure to make the liner wide enough to cover the maximum width with a generous overlap on both sides.

It is not essential that the stream and pond are constructed simultaneously – a watercourse can be added at a later date to complement an existing pond, which will then function as the reservoir pond. This is an ideal solution if you need to spread the costs of materials over more than one season, for example, or if you become bored with, or inherit, an existing pond. As your interest in water gardening grows, as it almost inevitably will, it also allows you to create yet more exciting possibilities for extending the scope of your waterside plantings.

TOOLS AND MATERIALS

- Existing pond with marginal shelf
- Large rocks, for spill stones, foundation stone, and side walls, each weighing 55–110lb (20–50kg)
- Marker pegs and string
- Spade and shovel
- Rake
- Flexible liner and underlay
- Premixed mortar
- Watering can or hose
- Level
- Submersible pump and delivery pipe
- Smaller rocks for hiding liner

STREAM CONSTRUCTION WITH A FLEXIBLE LINER

1 DIG THE HEADER AND STREAM
Mark out and excavate stream bed and backward-sloping header pool, and remove stones. Partly unroll liner, draping one end over existing reservoir pool. Ensure liner covers entire excavation with enough overlap at sides once it is pressed into contours.

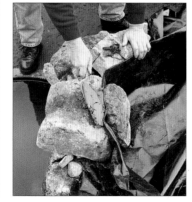

2 LAYING THE FOUNDATION STONE
Place foundation stone on marginal shelf of reservoir pool, butted up hard against liner draped over pool edge. It is easiest if the stone is flat-bottomed; otherwise, the pond must be drained and the stone laid level on a mortar bed on the marginal shelf.

3 SANDWICHING THE STONE
Pack stiff mortar between foundation stone and liner, then roll liner forward over foundation stone, packing gap between liner and soil bank with mortar, too. Sandwiched between two layers of mortar, the foundation stone will be stable and securely supported.

4 SITING THE SPILL STONE
Partly unroll liner to expose foundation stone. Place spill stone on top of, and slightly overlapping, foundation stone. Check flow fall with a hose or watering can. Adjust until satisfactory, then mortar spill stone in place.

5 BUILDING UP THE SIDE WALLS
Mortar first layer of side walls firmly in place on top of liner, then mortar subsequent layers onto previous layer. To prevent spillage, make sure all side wall rocks that flank the spill stone are higher than the spill stone itself.

6 PREVENTING WATER SEEPAGE
Use a can or hose to recheck water flow. To prevent water seepage, pull liner level with top of spill stone, then pleat and mortar liner behind spill stone. Wedge and mortar a second stone behind liner to secure it and protect it from light.

7 FINISHING STREAM AND HEADER
Unroll liner to cover rest of excavation. Build up side walls, arranging large rocks along stream margins and around header pool. Check levels as you work with a level. Mortar a second spill stone in place at header pool outlet.

8 ADDING A SUBMERSIBLE PUMP
Lower submersible pump into reservoir pool and bury delivery pipe along one side of stream. Conceal delivery pipe where it enters header pool with a large, flat stone. Place smaller rocks of random sizes on stream bed to hide liner.

SEE ALSO: Buying a Flexible Liner, pp.202–203

MOVING WATER IN SMALL SPACES

THE PRINCIPLE OF CIRCULATING a relatively small volume of water in a small space is simple and is adaptable to a range of features. It can be used to create a rippling film of water over a millstone, a brimming urn, or a more substantial spout, such as an old-fashioned cast-iron hand pump. All have the great advantage of low maintenance and a small splash zone. Since the recirculating water has little contact with sunlight, algal growth is minimized and potentially pump-blocking debris is excluded, since the reservoir pool is well covered. The largest maintenance job is regular replenishment of water to compensate for losses by evaporation.

A WALL-MOUNTED FOUNTAIN

For patios, courtyards, or conservatories, where space is at a premium, a vertically mounted wall spout is the ideal solution. Wall-mounted spouts range from the traditional stone mask (or a less costly fiberglass facsimile) to metal sculptures in ultra-modern designs. All that is needed is a wall strong enough to take the weight of the spout, a reservoir pool (perhaps an old cistern or brick-built tank), and a circulating pump. The pump is installed in the reservoir or in a chamber to one side of it. If the fall is no more than 4ft (1.2m), a low-voltage model is perfectly adequate.

HOW TO INSTALL A MASK FOUNTAIN OUTLET

1 DRILL HOLES FOR THE WATER PIPES
Drill 2 holes through the wall at a vertical distance apart of no more than 4ft (1.2m). This is easiest with a hammer-action drill fitted with a masonry bit of the same diameter as the copper pipe that will deliver the water. For the best visual effect, the top hole, from which the water emerges, should be just below eye level.

2 CUT COPPER PIPE FOR THE HOLES
Cut 2 lengths of copper pipe to fit the holes: the bottom length 2in (5cm) longer than the width of the wall, the top length 2in (5cm) longer than the width of the wall plus mask, with an angled cut at the outlet end. Thread them into their respective holes. The angled end of the top length of pipe will fit in the mouth of the mask.

△ **ADJUSTING THE WATER FLOW**
Ideally, the water issuing from the spout should fall into the center of the reservoir pool without splashing over its sides. Adjust the flow rate as necessary using the flow adjuster on the pump outlet.

3 CONNECT THE PIPES
At the back of the wall, fit elbow joints to each protruding copper pipe (the top joint turning down and the bottom one up). Attach an 3in (8cm) length of copper pipe to each joint, making push-fit connections watertight with plumbers' tape. Connect top and bottom pipes to one another with flexible hose and clips.

4 FIX THE MASK TO THE WALL
Mix the mortar to a stiff paste. Dampen the back of the mask to ensure good adhesion and apply mortar to the back surface, making sure that you avoid the mask's mouth opening. Spread mortar out evenly, keeping it well clear of the edges so that it does not ooze out from the margins when the mask is pressed into position.

5 CONNECT THE PUMP
Slide the mask over the upper pipe outlet, then press it firmly against the wall. Wipe away spilled mortar. The mortar takes about 36 hours to dry. Use a flexible delivery pipe to connect the pump outlet to the open end of the bottom pipe at the front of the wall, and secure it in place with clips. Site the pump in the reservoir.

SEE ALSO: Sound and Movement, p.199; Safety First, p.199; Pumps and Power Supply, p.209

MAKING A COBBLESTONE FOUNTAIN

The low cost and simple construction makes a cobblestone fountain an ideal project for the novice. It is one of the easiest ways of introducing moving water to the smallest space. To suit larger spaces, the scale can be increased by extending the cobbled area and its surroundings with imaginative planting. For added variety and interest, you can even adjust the cobbled area to suit the spray patterns of different fountain spouts.

CONSTRUCTING THE FOUNTAIN

Sink a trash can into a hole, its rim flush with the ground. Firm soil around the can, and lay a plastic sheet over the prepared area; cut a central hole 2in (5cm) less than the bin's diameter. Introduce the pump, two-thirds fill the can with water, and cover with mesh and stones.

STYLE AND FOCUS ▷
A bubble fountain forms the focal point of this low-maintenance planting design. Plants of strong form are planted through landscaping fabric, which keeps down weeds, and a decorative gravel layer lends a stylish finish.

Plastic sheet catches falling water, channeling it back to the reservoir; ensure sheet extends over entire catchment area and slopes in gently toward the can

Galvanized wire mesh supports the stones, helps keep reservoir free from debris that might block the pump, and ensures a degree of safety for children and animals

Stones of varying size disguise the liner, protect it from light, and keep the outlet pipe upright

Watertight plastic trash can forms the reservoir pool; make sure can is level and secure by backfilling and firming down before filling with water

The low-voltage submersible pump that powers the fountain jet is raised on a plinth to help prevent clogging by debris

ALWAYS REMEMBER

STONES FROM THE BEACH?
In many localities, the removal of sea-washed pebbles and stones from the beach is both illegal and environmentally unacceptable, since it may contribute to erosion of the shore. A range of stones and pebbles suitable for this fountain is available from reputable dealers.

IN ORIENTAL STYLE

Japanese garden makers, the masters of simple but striking design, use natural elements of water, stone, and bamboo in ways that harmonize beautifully with living plants. Their traditional plantings reveal a preference for subtlety, relying more heavily on myriad shades of green and textural contrast than on floristic brilliance. Use the diverse forms of bamboos, grasses, and ferns, perhaps with a seasonal flash of color from evergreen azaleas, to lend unity and harmony.

CONSTRUCTING A TSUKUBAI

The tsukubai is made simply from wood, bamboo, and a stone basin with a depression in the rim to channel outflow directly to the reservoir. A plastic sheet beneath it is all that is needed to direct any seepage to the reservoir.

◁ SHISHI ODOSHI
A hollow bamboo tube is fixed with a pivot, so that the water's weight tips and empties it at regular intervals as it fills. Although now used as an elegant ornament, it functioned originally as a deer-scarer; the bamboo tube would strike a rock to make an intermittent clicking sound.

Mesh to support stones and keep out debris. The water enters at a single point, so a plastic sheet beneath it is unnecessary

Low-voltage submersible pump is set on a brick plinth to avoid blockage by debris; the cable linking the pump to an electrical supply is threaded through a conduit pipe for added safety

Hollowed-out wooden block accommodates bend in delivery pipe; vertical post and outlet are glued into drilled holes in wooden block

Delivery pipe hidden by stones where it exits the reservoir pool — it is then buried below ground, before entering the vertical post made of hollowed-out bamboo

Basin channels outflow through depression in rim

Delivery pipe carries water from pump outlet to water outlet spout

SEE ALSO: Grasses, Bamboos, and Ferns, pp.140–141; Sound and Movement, p.199; Safety First, p.199; Installing a Fountain, pp.208–209

THE AQUATIC ENVIRONMENT

A HEALTHY AQUATIC ENVIRONMENT, which can support fish, newts, tadpoles, and other water creatures, depends on the right balance of various types of plants that perform different functions. To keep water well oxygenated, a pond *must* have a sufficiency of submerged plants. To keep it clear and free from the algae that cause green water, it must include enough plants with floating leaves to cover at least one-third to a half of the water's surface. In any pond, it is only the moisture-loving plants that surround it that are chosen for their beauty alone. In the wild, however, moisture-loving plants mark the beginning of the transition from water to land.

WHAT ARE AQUATICS?

An aquatic plant is any plant that can grow with its roots in water or in saturated soil. The term includes both floating-leaved plants and submerged oxygenators, as well as plants that are grown at the margins. Marginal plants are often those that are native to true bogs, such as marsh marigolds (*Caltha palustris*).

It is important to understand the distinction between true aquatics and moisture-loving plants. Many plants that are recommended for bog gardens or poolside planting are those that thrive in moist, but well-drained, soils. Unlike true aquatics, they are not adapted to function in saturated conditions. For successful plantings, the plants' needs and tolerances must be taken into account.

TELL ME WHY

WHY MAKE THE DISTINCTION?

The roots of true aquatic plants are adapted to allow them to take up dissolved oxygen and nutrients from solution in water. Roots of moisture lovers, many of which also grow in ordinary garden soil, need higher levels of oxygen to function. Without access to the oxygen that is held in the spaces between soil particles, they will succumb to what is, in effect, death by drowning.

FLOATING-LEAVED PLANTS

Floating-leaved plants can be grouped into two basic categories: those that need to root in soil (the muddy bottom or in containers), such as waterlilies (*Nymphaea*), and the free-floating species, such as frogbit (*Hydrocharis morsus-ranae*).

Floating leaves shade out the sunlight that algae need to grow and proliferate. The roots, especially those of free-floating species, take up dissolved nutrients from the water, thus reducing levels available for algal growth. Floating leaves also give invaluable shade and shelter for fish, their fry, and other aquatic wildlife that forms an integral part of the aquatic ecosystem.

△ **YELLOW FLOATING HEART**
Nymphoides peltata *is a deciduous perennial to 24in (60cm) across with heart-shaped, floating leaves. Yellow flowers are held above the water throughout summer; suits depths of 6–18in (15–45cm).*

OTHER RECOMMENDED SPECIES

Aponogeton distachyos, Cape pondweed. Deep water perennial with scented white flowers in summer. *Azolla filiculoides,* Fairy moss. Floating perennial water fern, forming colonies of tiny, soft, pale green leaves that turn red in autumn. Useful for quick cover in new ponds, but may be invasive. *Hydrocharis morsus-ranae,* Frogbit. Perennial floater; has heart-shaped leaves and white blooms in summer. *Nuphar japonica,* Japanese pond lily. Rounded yellow flowers in summer above heart-shaped leaves. *Persicaria amphibia,* Willow grass. Long, narrow, floating leaves and tiny pink flowers in summer. *Stratiotes aloides,* Water soldier. Free-floating rosettes of semievergreen, spiky leaves, like pineapple tops. *Utricularia vulgaris,* Greater bladderwort. Free-floating, bladderlike leaves trap insects; bears pouchlike yellow flowers in summer.

△ **WATER CLOVER**
Marsilea quadrifolia *is a creeping perennial with long, spreading roots. The leaves spread indefinitely across the water's surface in water up to 24in (60cm) deep; in shallower water the leaves will stand above the surface.*

SUBMERGED PLANTS

Submerged plants are the workhorses of the aquatic environment; using the energy of sunlight to produce food, they release oxygen into the water as a byproduct. They help clear water by competing with algae for nutrients and also process fish waste reducing the buildup of toxins.

Most submerged plants are so vigorous and easy to grow that they must be thinned out regularly. If unchecked, the pool and pump become rapidly clogged with growth, and floating-leaved plants fail to thrive against such tough competition. If floating-leaved plants succumb, algae proliferate. It always takes a little while to get the balance right, so be patient.

PLANTS TO PROVIDE OXYGEN

Callitriche hermaphroditica (Water starwort)	*Myriophyllum aquaticum* (Parrot feather)
Ceratophyllum demersum (Hornwort)	*Myriophyllum verticillatum* (Milfoil)
Egeria densa	*Potamogeton crispus* (Curled pondweed)
Lagarosiphon major (Curly water thyme)	

SEE ALSO: The Moisture-lovers, pp.218–219; Planting Water Plants, pp.220–221; Caring for your Pond, pp.222–223; Water Gardens, pp.343, 353

WATERLILIES

There are waterlilies (*Nymphaea*) to suit almost every size, depth, and style of pond. Although those described here are hardy, there are also many tropical species, for warmer climes or for conservatory pools in cold climates. Their exquisite blooms float on, or emerge just above, the water's surface, and their leaves, or pads, provide excellent shade, for clear, healthy water. Fish also appreciate their shelter.

All waterlilies need a sunny, sheltered position and water that is still, or almost so; site them well away from fountain jets or the inlets of cascades and streams. Tropicals need a minimum temperature of 70 F (21 C) to grow and bloom well. All of the waterlilies below are hardy ones unless indiated. Lift, divide, and replant in late spring or early summer to avoid congestion, which reduces flowering. Watch for aphids and other pests.

△ **N. ALBA**
With a spread of 6ft (2m) or more, the white waterlily is a vigorous species suited to a large pond 24–36in (60–90cm) deep. It has dark green pads, 12in (30cm) across, and bears many large, semidouble flowers of creamy white with golden stamens.

△ **N. 'AMERICAN STAR'**
Rounded, light green pads are purplish when young and red beneath. The salmon-pink flowers are star-shaped with golden orange stamens. With a spread of up to 5ft (1.5m), it thrives in depths of 12–18in (30–45cm).

△ **N. 'AURORA'**
This small lily bears flowers that are cream in bud, yellow on opening, and then orange flecked with red. With a spread of about 36in (90cm), less when confined in a barrel, it needs water that is 12–18in (30–45cm) deep. Tropical.

△ **N. 'ESCARBOUCLE'**
Semidouble flowers are borne amid dark green pads; the flowers have white-tipped outer petals surrounding vermilion red inner ones and a boss of golden stamens. It will reach 4–5ft (1.2–1.5m) across, and thrives in depths of 12–24in (30–60cm).

△ **N. 'FULGENS'**
With large blooms of glossy burgundy red, borne from late spring though summer above dark green leaves, this adaptable waterlily is suitable for pools of any size, given a depth of 12–18in (30–45cm). Plants will reach up to 5ft (1.5m) across.

△ **N. 'PYGMAEA HELVOLA'**
With a spread of 24in (60cm) or less, and a need for only 6–9in (15–23cm) of water, this tiny lily is perfect for container pools. The small, semidouble, buttercup yellow flowers are borne freely above neat, oval leaves that are heavily marked with purple.

△ **N. 'GONNÈRE'**
The globe-shaped, fully double flowers are a pristine, pure white and fragrant, borne above pea green pads, which are bronzed when young. It is suitable for any size of pond, spreading to 4ft (1.2m) across, in depths of 12–18in (30–45cm).

△ **N. 'JAMES BRYDON'**
With a spread of 3–4ft (0.9–1.2m), this waterlily needs a depth of 12–18in (30–45cm) and is a favorite for barrels and small to medium ponds. The bronze-green leaves set off double flowers of rich rose-pink to perfection. Tropical.

△ **N. 'CHROMATELLA'**
The soft yellow flowers are borne in abundance above olive green leaves attractively mottled with purple-brown. A reliable performer for pools of any size, it spreads to 5ft (1.5m) across, in depths of 12–18in (30–45cm).

△ **N. 'ROSE AREY'**
Best rooted in a large planting basket or on the pool bottom, this lily reaches 5ft (1.5m) across. It bears semidouble, anise-scented pink flowers, above bronze-green pads that are purple when young. Suits water 14–24in (35–60cm) deep.

△ **N. 'SUNRISE'**
This tropical waterlily needs long, hot summers to bloom well. Semidouble, with long, narrow, bright yellow petals and clear green leaves mottled purple when young, it grows to 5ft (1.5m) across, in a water depth of 14–18in (35–45cm).

△ **N. 'VÉSUVE'**
In water 14–18in (30–45cm) deep, this elegant waterlily will bear its glowing, star-shaped, cherry red blooms over very long periods above large, almost circular, dark green pads. The leaves will cover an area of about 4ft (1.2m).

SEE ALSO: Planting Water Plants, pp.220–221; Caring for your Pond, pp.222–223; More Waterlilies, p.353

THE TRANSITIONAL ZONE

UNDER NATURAL CONDITIONS, marginal plants occupy the shallow waters at a pond's edges. Many also grow with a foot in each camp, thriving equally well in water and saturated or permanently damp soil. This group of plants is invaluable for creating a seamless transition between land and water in informal pools and giving valuable shelter for birds, amphibians, and insects. Marginals are often vigorous and sometimes invasive, but, if necessary, they can be confined in containers and positioned on a marginal shelf. In such a site, they can provide vertical contrast to the strong horizontal lines of more formal pools, breaking up their rigid outlines in pleasing way.

MARGINAL PLANTS

To grow marginals successfully, it is essential to provide them with the depth of water that suits them best; some prefer as little as 1in (2.5cm) of water, others tolerate depths up to 12in (30cm), while many thrive in both wet soil and water. If they are planted in soil on the pond bottom, or in the wet soil margins, their spread into the pond will be limited by their depth tolerances. Since many are vigorous plants, however, their sideways spread can be considerable. If you choose not to use containers, they may need regular thinning and cutting back.

When designing the planting layout, try to match neighboring plants for vigor; the rampant will rapidly outcompete less robust individuals. Large ponds will not be overwhelmed by drifts of marginals, but small ponds will be, so use containers in these cases. Use strongly vertical plants, such as water irises, for emphatic contrasts with horizontal ones that float on the open surface, such as waterlilies.

GOOD IDEAS

• Supplement shade cover at the pool's edges by using those with leaves that spill out across the water, like *Menyanthes trifoliata*.

• To create substantial, but confined, clumps of invasive marginals, use a large planting crate or build isolated planting beds.

• Some invasive species, like *Typha latifolia* (cattail), have hard, pointed roots, which can pierce a pool lining. Confine them to planting crates to protect the liner.

◁ *ORONTIUM AQUATICUM*
Spreading by rhizomes in water up to 12in (30cm) deep, golden club is a deciduous perennial with blue-green leaves, which are silvery beneath. Flowerheads emerge above the water from late spring to midsummer. At 12–18in (30–45cm) tall by 24in (60cm) across, it is ideal for masking pond margins.

◁ *HOUTTUYNIA CORDATA* 'CHAMELEON'
A spreading perennial with heart-shaped, green, pale yellow, and red leaves; its white flowers appear in spring. It is 6–24in (15–60cm) tall and thrives in both damp soil and in water 2in (5cm) deep, so it can spread indefinitely from pond margins to adjacent land. It may be invasive.

△ *ACORUS CALAMUS* 'ARGENTEOSTRIATUS'
The variegated sweet flag has irislike leaves striped cream and green. It thrives in water to 9in (23cm) deep. At 30in (75cm) tall, its strong, vertical lines contrast well with floating-leaved plants.

△ *MENYANTHES TRIFOLIATA*
Thriving in wet soil or in water 6–9in (15–23cm) deep, the bog bean bears dainty, white spring flowers. Although only 9in (23cm) tall, the olive green leaves spill out from the margins across the pool, so that land and water merge seamlessly.

△ *RANUNCULUS LINGUA* 'GRANDIFLORUS'
To 5ft (1.5m) tall, this perennial flowers in early summer. Its rampant growth must be confined to a strong container or it will spread indefinitely. It thrives in 6–9in (15–23cm) of still or moving water.

MENTHA AQUATICA △
Watermint roots in wet soil or in water to 6in (15cm) deep. An excellent soil binder at the margins of a wildlife pool, its rose-pink flowers are attractive to bees. Up to 36in (90cm) tall and wide, it can be invasive, so thin regularly to control it.

SEE ALSO: Planting Water Plants, pp.220–221; Caring for your Pond, pp.222–223; Water Gardens, pp.343, 353

△ *LYSICHITON AMERICANUS*
Emerging in spring, before the glossy, mid- to dark green leaves, the sculptural beauty of the bright yellow spathes is doubled when reflected in still water. Thriving in wet soil or 2in (5cm) of water, the clumps reach 4ft (1.2m) by 30in (75cm) across.

△ *CALTHA PALUSTRIS* 'FLORE PLENO'
In spring, the double-flowered marsh marigold bears waxy, buttercup yellow flowers above dark green, kidney-shaped leaves. Forming clumps 10in (25cm) tall and wide, it thrives in wet soil or very shallow water but tolerates depths of 9in (23cm) for short periods.

△ *PELTANDRA VIRGINICA*
The elegant leaves of the green arrow arum form clumps up to 36in (90cm) tall. It tolerates depths to 8in (20cm), and it makes an excellent soil binder for wet soils. Green flower spathes are borne in early summer, followed by spikes of green berries.

△ *ZANTEDESCHIA AETHIOPICA* 'CROWBOROUGH'
Dark green leaves and pristine summer spathes make this perennial an elegant candidate for a formal pond, growing to 3ft (1m) tall by 24in (60cm) across. At home in wet or dry soil, it is vulnerable to cold in the open garden but is hardier if submerged to 12in (30cm).

OTHER MARGINALS

Acorus gramineus 'Pusillus', Dwarf Japanese rush. Compact, evergreen perennial, to 4in (10cm) tall, with dark green leaves; ideal for containers.
Butomus umbellatus, Flowering rush. Rose-pink flowers in second half of summer and very narrow, olive-green leaves; up to 4ft (1.2m) tall; best in 2–16in (5–40cm) of water in full sun. Open soil or mud is more suitable than containers.
Cyperus longus, Galingale. Upright stems, to 5ft (1.5m) tall, bear terminal tufts of narrow, bright green leaves and red-brown flower spikelets in late summer; grow in depths of 6–12in (15–30cm).
Glyceria maxima var. *variegata*. Sweet grass, Manna grass. Variegated water grass, 32in (80cm) tall, with narrow leaves, boldly striped in cream and green, sometimes flushed pink, and heads of green flowers in summer; grow in water to 6in (15cm) deep.
Pontederia cordata, Pickerel weed. Narrowly heart-shaped leaves and spikes of soft blue flowers in late summer; 30in (75cm) tall, in depths to 6in (15cm).
Saururus cernuus, Lizard's tail, Water dragon. Arching spikes of creamy white, fragrant flowers in summer above narrowly heart-shaped leaves; 9in (23cm) tall, in depths of 4–6in (10–15cm).

WATER IRISES

Invaluable for their exquisite flowers and vertical form, water irises include *I. ensata*, *I. laevigata*, *I. pseudacorus*, *I. versicolor*, *I. virginica*, and their hybrids and cultivars. All need moist or wet soil, but most also thrive in water, 2–4in (5–10cm) deep. Site them in full sun to maximize flowering potential.

△ *IRIS PSEUDACORUS*
Bright yellow flowers emerge from sheaves of sword-shaped blue-green leaves in summer. A vigorous colonizer of wet soils and shallow water, yellow flag makes a good soil binder for the margins of wildlife pools. Reaching up to 6ft (2m) tall, it is best used in larger features.

△ *IRIS LAEVIGATA* 'VARIEGATA'
With soft purple-blue flowers in early summer and fairly broad, white and green variegated leaves to prolong the show, this is an elegant specimen for the margins of a formal pond. It grows to 32in (80cm) tall in either wet soil or water 3–4in (8–10cm) deep.

SEE ALSO: Planting Water Plants, pp.220–221; Caring for your Pond, pp.222–223; Water Gardens, pp.343, 353

THE MOISTURE-LOVERS

THERE IS A HUGE RANGE of plants that positively thrive in damp soils. They include natural inhabitants of moist places, such as seasonally inundated meadows and stream banks, but there are many more that grow in drier soils elsewhere in the garden; given constant moisture and fertile soil, these plants grow with a vigor seldom achieved in open borders, remaining lush in summer heat. In ordinary soil, they may fade rapidly unless shaded – the reason why many border plants are classed as shade-lovers. Although they play no part in the aquatic ecosystem, moisture-lovers shelter wildlife and may prove a valuable food source for nectar-eating insects and seed-eating birds.

PLANTS FOR BOG GARDENS AND POOL FRINGES

When buying moisture-loving plants, be aware that they are often described, and offered for sale, as bog plants. Only true bog natives thrive in saturated soil. All moisture-lovers need drainage and will almost certainly perish in stagnant, waterlogged conditions.

Moisture-lovers form the linking element between water and dry land. Formal ponds may be surrounded by beds or borders and, if the soil is rich in organic matter, it will retain moisture well, so the plants will need additional water only in prolonged dry spells. If soil beds butt up to more informal, lined ponds, they often remain damp naturally, or soil can be kept moist in a specially created bog garden (*see p.204*).

Many moisture-lovers are spreading, so adjacent clumps merge in a naturalistic way. Exploit this growth habit to create luscious designs of contrasting textures, colors, and forms.

OTHER MOISTURE-LOVERS

Astilbe. Clump-forming perennials with divided leaves and plumes of white, pink, lilac, or red flowers in summer.
Filipendula ulmaria, Meadowsweet. Clump-forming perennial with fresh green, divided leaves and heads of creamy flowers in midsummer.
Lobelia cardinalis, Cardinal flower. Perennial with spires of luminous red flowers throughout summer.
Matteuccia struthiopteris, Ostrich fern, Shuttlecock fern. Tall, brilliant green "shuttlecocks" around a central clump of brown, fertile fronds.

△ *TROLLIUS EUROPAEUS*
The globeflower produces glossy, lemon- to mid-yellow flowers in spring above rounded, deeply divided leaves. A compact perennial to 24in (60cm) tall and 18in (45cm) across. It prefers heavy, fertile soils that never dry out, where it will thrive in sun or partial shade.

△ *MIMULUS CARDINALIS*
A creeping perennial with tubular scarlet flowers throughout summer above masses of light green foliage. It reaches 36in (90cm) in height by as much across. If it becomes messy by late summer, cut back to encourage new growth. Grow in moist or dry soil, in sun or light shade.

△ *PERSICARIA BISTORTA* 'SUPERBA'
A vigorous, clump-forming perennial to 36in (90cm) tall, bearing dense, rounded spikes of soft pink flowers, which rise above large, ground-smothering leaves for long periods from early summer. It tolerates dry soil but romps away in moist ones and may be invasive. For sun or partial shade.

◁ *RHEUM PALMATUM* 'ATROSANGUINEUM'
An architectural giant, 6ft (2m) tall, with large, deeply cut leaves, which are red-purple when young. The statuesque plumes of cerise-pink flowers arise in early summer. Best on deep, fertile, moist soils in sun or part shade.

◁ *LIGULARIA PRZEWALSKII*
Dense, dark-stemmed spires of yellow flowers emerge above clumps of deeply cut, lobed leaves in mid- to late summer on this perennial. It needs reliably moist soil, sun, and shelter from wind. Reaches 6ft (2m) in good conditions.

◁ *RODGERSIA PODOPHYLLA*
The jagged, rich green leaves, bronze when young, of this perennial form bold clumps to 5ft (1.5m) tall. Creamy white flower plumes appear from midsummer. Needs reliably moist soil in sun; tolerates drier soils in partial shade.

SEE ALSO: Color, Form, and Texture, pp.128–129; Improving Soil Types, p.142; Bog Gardens, p.p204–205

HOSTAS

With hundreds of species and cultivars to choose from, hostas offer fabulously textured, subtly colored foliage and bear often fragrant, bell-shaped flowers in tall, slender spikes in summer. They thrive in deep, moist, fertile soils. Most prefer some shade, but the variegated ones usually color best in sun. Their luscious leaves are a favorite with slugs and snails, so take steps to protect them (*see p.298*).

OTHER RECOMMENDED HOSTAS

H. 'Birchwood Parky's Gold' has heart-shaped, yellow-green leaves that mature to rich yellow.
H. 'Albomarginata' has pointed, ovate, deep green leaves margined with white.
H. lancifolia has ribbed, narrowly lance-shaped leaves of glossy dark green.
H. undulata var. *univittata* has twisted, undulating, matte olive green leaves with a central zone of creamy white.

△ *H.* 'HADSPEN BLUE'
The mounds of heart-shaped and veined, gray-blue leaves form clumps 10in (25cm) tall by 24in (60cm) wide. In summer, this hosta produces purple-stemmed spires of bell-shaped, mauve-gray flowers.

△ *H. SIEBOLDIANA*
VAR. *ELEGANS*
The bold clumps of large, heart-shaped, deeply wrinkled, gray-blue leaves form mounds 3ft (1m) tall by 4ft (1.2m) wide. In summer, this hosta bears pale lilac-gray flowers in leafy spikes.

△ *H. VENTRICOSA*
'AUREOMARGINATA'
This hosta bears tall spires of purple flowers in late summer above the deeply ribbed, glossy leaves; these are irregularly margined creamy white, and they form clumps 20in (50cm) tall by 3ft (1m) across.

△ *H.* 'FRANCES WILLIAMS'
The blue-green leaves, broadly margined with yellow-green, are deeply puckered; they form clumps 24in (60cm) tall by 3ft (1m) wide. The elegant spikes of gray-white flowers are borne in early summer.

PRIMROSES

There are approximately 400 primrose (*Primula*) species, some of which are native to damp meadows, streamsides, and bogs. They are ideal candidates for waterside plantings. All of them look particularly lovely in informal drifts at the poolside or on streambanks, while those with drumstick-type flowers or candelabra-like tiers of bloom also blend surprisingly well in more formal settings. They are moisture-loving perennials, but they do need some drainage, since they will not tolerate stagnant conditions. A deep, fertile, neutral to acidic soil enriched with organic matter is best, and although most thrive in partial shade, they grow well in sun, provided that the soil never dries out completely. Many will self-seed where conditions suit them, forming extensive colonies with time.

△ *P. BEESIANA*
This species has basal rosettes of long, narrow, fresh green leaves and sturdy, white-mealy stems bearing whorls of red-pink, yellow-eyed flowers in summer. It is 24in (60cm) tall and may remain evergreen, or almost so, in winter, or it will die back to resting buds to reemerge in spring.

△ *P. BULLEYANA*
The basal rosettes of narrow, toothed, semievergreen leaves on this species give rise to stout and long-lasting candelabra-like spires of flowers. Individual flowers are crimson in bud and when newly open, but as they mature they fade to a rich, deep orange. To 24in (60cm) tall.

△ *P. DENTICULATA* VAR. *ALBA*
The drumstick primroses are robust species and may self-seed where conditions are to their liking. The globular heads of small flowers are white in this variety, but the others come in many shades of purple and mauve. Flowers appear from spring to summer. To 18in (45cm) tall.

△ *P. FLORINDAE*
The giant cowslip reaches 4ft (1.2m) in height in good conditions. It is one of the most elegant primroses, with strong, upright stems ending in a cluster of nodding, bell-shaped yellow flowers, which are fragrant and coated with a powdery white meal. The blooms appear in summer.

△ *P. JAPONICA*
'MILLER'S CRIMSON'
The basal leaf rosettes of this primrose give rise to stout stems to 18in (45cm) tall, bearing whorls of dusky crimson flowers from late spring to early summer. The species has flowers of various shades from white to deep red-purple.

△ *P. PROLIFERA*
A vigorous, rosette-forming species producing upright stems to 24in (60cm) tall with whorls of pale to golden yellow, occasionally dull violet flowers in early summer, clothed in a mealy, white powder. They are fragrant, and they look and smell fabulous when planted en masse.

SEE ALSO: Buying Good Plants, pp.146–147; Planting Perennials, p.148; Planting Water Plants, pp.220–221; More Hostas, p.322

PLANTING WATER PLANTS

BY LATE SPRING, garden centers are usually well stocked with aquatic plants, and the weather — and water — is usually warm enough for most of them to establish without check. If planting in containers, use specially formulated aquatic soil mixes or, as second best, unfertilized garden soil. *Never* use ordinary soil mixes, they are too rich and nutrients will leach into the water to feed algae. Unless you choose a fine-mesh container, line it with burlap, so that soil does not fall out before rooting takes place. Always select a container to suit the size of the plant; if too small, growth will be restricted and plants, especially taller marginals, may become top heavy and unstable.

PLANTING TECHNIQUES

Simply place free-floating plants directly onto the surface of the pond. For large pools, bundles of submerged oxygenators can be just dropped in, but in small ponds, as with deep-water and marginal plants, they are more easily managed in containers.

Position containers by hand or, if you have a helper, thread two pieces of rope through the rim and, standing on opposite sides of the pool, use the rope as handles to lower the basket into place.

△ **GOOD HYGIENE**
Before introducing new plants to the pond, rinse them in clean water and inspect them thoroughly. Look for and remove any jelly-like snail eggs and inspect for insects so that you do not introduce any harmful ones, such as great diving beetles, which may attack fish. Remove all dead and rotten material.

A POND DESIGNED FOR PLANTS

The best design for a naturalistic pond includes levels of varying depth to accommodate the differing needs of aquatic and marginal plants. Soil beds or bog gardens butt up to the pool margin, allowing plantings to merge naturally with each other and to disguise the edges.

DEEP-WATER PLANTS ▷
Line the basket and fill three-quarters full with dampened soil or aquatic soil mix. Make a planting hole so that the buds sit 1½in (4cm) below the rim. Add more mix so the plant ends up at the same depth as it was in its original pot. Firm gently so as not to damage new shoots. Top with a ½in (1cm) layer of pea gravel.

◁ **OXYGENATORS**
Line the basket and fill to just below the rim with damp soil mix. Firm lightly and make evenly spaced holes, 2in (5cm) deep. Insert a plant bundle into each and firm in with your fingertips. Top with a ½in (1cm) layer of pea gravel. Trim off excess burlap. A 8in (20cm) basket will hold 5 plant bundles.

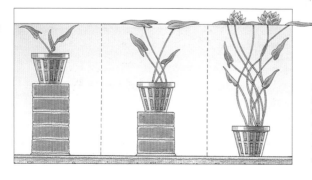

As a watertight barrier prevents water moving into the surrounding soil, beds can be filled with ordinary soil to allow planting of a diverse range of non-moisture-loving plants

THE RIGHT DEPTH ▷
Brick piers make invaluable depth adjusters. Leave permanently in place to bring marginal plants up to their preferred depth. For deep-water plants, remove bricks one by one to lower gradually to the specified depth as new leaves appear and stems elongate.

Brick plinths are used as depth adjusters, either to bring deep-water plants up to their preferred depth, or as temporary measures to allow young deep-water plants to be lowered gradually to the appropriate depth as they grow

An alternative for adjusting planting depths is to incorporate brick planting beds; these are mortared in place onto the liner and filled with aquatic planting soil mix – plants are thus confined but less restricted than in planting baskets

SEE ALSO: Bog Gardens, pp.204–205; The Aquatic Environment, pp.214–215; The Transitional Zone, pp.216–217; The Moisture-lovers, pp.218–219

△ **THE PEA-GRAVEL TOPPING**
Topdressing baskets with a layer of pea gravel or pebbles performs several functions. A ½in (1cm) layer will prevent soil from drifting from the surface and muddying the water. It also prevents disturbance of the soil surface by fish. A 1in (2.5cm) deep layer adds weight and stability for top-heavy marginals and takes up less soil space than bricks or stones set at the bottom of the basket. It is also decorative.

△ **PLANTING IN MOIST OR WET SOIL**
Dig a hole in the soil bed large enough to accommodate the root ball comfortably. Slide the plant gently out of its pot, and place it in the hole so that it is at the same depth as it was in its container. Gently firm the soil around the roots with your fingers, taking care not to compact the soil or to damage any growing points or soft young growth. Thoroughly soak the entire area with water.

BUYING HEALTHY PLANTS

Aquatic plants are sold bare-root or in containers. Containerized plants are useful for instant effects, but in good conditions, smaller and less expensive bare-root ones quickly catch up. It is often worth paying more for larger waterlilies to get flowers in the first year. Make sure that plants are clean, plump, and dense, paying special attention to roots and tubers; they must be fat and sound to nourish the young plant until it is well established and able to make its own food. Keep plants cool and moist at all times, especially when transporting; double bagging will reduce the risk of leakage.

Plant is compact with lots of young leaves; foliage is glossy and dark green with no evidence of pests or diseases

△ **CONTAINERIZED MARGINAL**
Buying containerized plants, here Caltha palustris, *gives them a head start and avoids root disturbance, but make sure the container is large enough to allow for at least one season's growth; otherwise, transfer to a larger pot before introducing to the pond.*

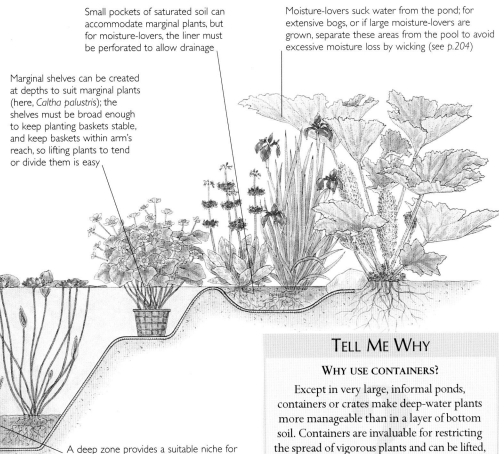

Small pockets of saturated soil can accommodate marginal plants, but for moisture-lovers, the liner must be perforated to allow drainage

Moisture-lovers suck water from the pond; for extensive bogs, or if large moisture-lovers are grown, separate these areas from the pool to avoid excessive moisture loss by wicking (see p.204)

Marginal shelves can be created at depths to suit marginal plants (here, *Caltha palustris*); the shelves must be broad enough to keep planting baskets stable, and keep baskets within arm's reach, so lifting plants to tend or divide them is easy

A deep zone provides a suitable niche for floating-leaved plants, like waterlilies, that thrive in the full depth of water; it may also provide a rooting zone for submerged oxygenators, which need the buoyancy of water to support their soft stems in order to function most efficiently

Tubers are firm and plump with plenty of growth buds; new growth emerging from them is healthy and vigorous

GOOD EXAMPLE

BARE-ROOT PLANTS ▷
Bare-root plants are often sold as offsets, newly divided from their parent plant. If sound and healthy, they grow quickly in good conditions and are less costly than containerized plants. Make sure the root or tuber is plump with plenty of growth buds or young folded leaves emerging from them.

Stems are limp and soggy, and leaves are badly discolored with too few buds or emerging young leaves to replace them

POOR EXAMPLE

TELL ME WHY

WHY USE CONTAINERS?

Except in very large, informal ponds, containers or crates make deep-water plants more manageable than in a layer of bottom soil. Containers are invaluable for restricting the spread of vigorous plants and can be lifted, when necessary, to divide and repot plants as they outgrow their containers. Containerized marginals can be grouped and moved about easily until the desired effect is achieved.

SEE ALSO: The Aquatic Environment, pp.214–215; The Transitional Zone, pp.216–217; The Moisture-lovers, pp.218–219; Caring for your Pond, pp.222–223

CARING FOR YOUR POND

REGULAR POND CARE is essential to maintain a healthy aquatic environment with clear, oxygenated water and thriving plants. Regular renewal of plants, by division in spring, will keep them healthy and trouble-free during summer, allowing them to play their part in controlling algal growth. Algae are the first species to proliferate in spring, and pond water will "green up" temporarily until the ecosystem resumes equilibrium. Try to complete any tasks involving entering the pond in one go to minimize disturbance to the pond and its denizens, and take great care to remove decaying material during the season. Finally, take time to relax, observe, and enjoy!

ROUTINE TASKS

Throughout summer, remove dying foliage and spent flowerheads before they can rot and pollute the water. Maintain the planting balance by thinning submerged and floating plants as necessary. Maintain vigorous growth of waterlilies and other containerized plants by fertilizing in late spring and midsummer with a slow-release, pond-plant fertilizer. These come in tablets or packets, and prevent nutrients from leaking into the water and promoting algae.

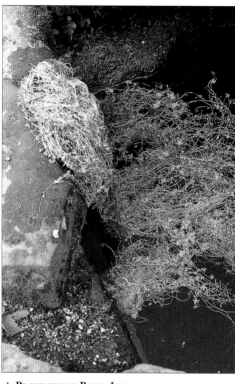

△ **REMOVING BLANKET WEED**
This filamentous algae is an opportunist colonizer that deprives the water of oxygen and chokes other plants. The easiest way to remove it is simply to wind it around a stick; the filaments adhere firmly to the stick and each other.

△ **PROTECTING POND LIFE**
Excess oxygenators should be thinned as necessary by raking them from the surface. They form a niche for insect life and other beneficial creatures; drape thinned weed on the edge for a while, so they can escape back into the water.

△ **REMOVING SURPLUS FLOATING PLANTS**
Surplus floating plants, like duckweed, obscure the water surface, reducing light for submerged plants. Skim off with a piece of wood, held horizontally just below the surface. Dispose of duckweed carefully; it spreads like wildfire.

△ **REMOVING DECAYING LEAVES**
Decaying plant material affects water chemistry, and it may cloud the water and have detrimental effects on other pond life. Cut decaying material away with a sharp knife. If yellowing is excessive, lift and check the plant for disease.

PREPARING FOR WINTER

As the growing season draws to a close, lift tender and half-hardy plants, trim off any dead leaves, and store the plants in containers of damp sand in a frost-free place. Keep covered with a perforated plastic sheet so that air can enter and plants do not dry out. Treat any plantlets needed for propagation in the same way.

Take precautions to protect submerged plants and fish if water freezes over (*see below*). Bog plants and moisture-lovers can be protected from freezing with a thick mulch of clean, dry straw in late autumn.

ALWAYS REMEMBER

DEALING WITH ICE

An ice sheet protects plants beneath it from freezing, but also places pressure on the pond sides as it expands and causes a build-up of noxious gases beneath it. Place floating logs on the surface to absorb expansion. Melt ice gently to allow gases to escape. Never smash ice; shock waves can kill fish.

△ **NETTING PONDS IN AUTUMN**
Leaves falling from surrounding plants fall to the bottom and decompose, forming harmful byproducts. Secure fine-mesh netting with bricks across the top of the pond to prevent this. Remove the netting weekly, gather and compost fallen leaves, and replace the net securely.

SEE ALSO: The Aquatic Environment, pp.214–215

THINNING AND DIVIDING PLANTS

Water plants are propagated in several ways. Some, such as *Eichhornia crassipes*, produce plantlets from the rootstock or on runners, often detaching themselves and sinking to the bottom. They spend winter there as dormant buds, emerging in spring. Others, like waterlilies and irises, have roots, tubers, or rhizomes that must be physically separated. Provided that each division has a portion of root and a few shoots, they can grow independently of the parent plant.

For most water plants, the best time to do this is in late spring to early summer when the water warms up and plants resume active growth. Low water temperatures can cause newly divided plants to rot. When dividing, always discard the older growth in favor of the new; this rejuvenates plants and restores flowering potential, and there may be material left over to increase your own stock or give to friends.

TELL ME WHY

WHY SHOULD PLANTS BE DIVIDED?

Most water plants grow rapidly and, sooner or later, outgrow the site. This can happen in a single season in small ponds, so division is necessary to relieve congestion. Overcrowded plants thrust leaves out of the water instead of floating on it, and flowering will also be impaired. Dividing and replanting only young growth renews productivity and restores pond health.

THINNING OXYGENATING PLANTS

1 SPRING AND AUTUMN
Thin oxygenating plants at the beginning and end of the growing season. Taking great care to avoid contact with the liner, rake out excess oxygenators. Lift out containerized oxygenators, and trim back some stems with a knife.

2 LEAVE SUFFICIENT OXYGENATORS IN PLACE
To fulfill their oxygenating function, it is better to thin little and often, which makes it easier for the planting balance to resume equilibrium. Remember to drape weed on the side before removal, ideally to the compost pile.

REJUVENATING WATERLILIES BY DIVISION

1 LIFT AND DIVIDE THE RHIZOME
Lift the plant and rinse off the soil. Trim off all opened leaves and cut the old, least productive sections of the rhizome away with a knife. Retain the youngest sections with plenty of emerging shoots, and discard the old.

2 REPLANT THE DIVISIONS
Trim long and coarse roots and replant with the crown just below soil level. Top with gravel and lower gradually into the pond. Large plants often yield 2 or more new plants; each division must have at least 2 or 3 growth buds.

DIVIDING OTHER RHIZOMATOUS PLANTS

△ **SEPARATING PLANTLETS AND RUNNERS**
In spring, separate vigorous young plantlets from the parent, either by snapping them off cleanly, as shown here with Eichhornia crassipes, or by severing the connecting runner (creeping stem) with a sharp knife. Floating plants can then simply be returned to the surface of the pool; they quickly generate a root system of their own. If plants are containerized, pot up the young plants in new soil and return to the appropriate depth.

1 LIFT THE PARENT PLANT
Uproot the plant (here, Iris pseudacorus) and rinse the roots clean of soil. Clumps can be pulled or cut apart; separate out vigorous rhizomes, each portion with a number of fibrous roots, shoots, and strong young leaves.

2 TRIMMING THE RHIZOME
Neatly trim the rhizome with a sharp knife, removing any portions that do not have new shoot growth. Trim all topgrowth back to 3–4in (8–10cm) so that when replanted, it will not form a "sail" and be unstable in the wind.

3 REPLANTING THE RHIZOMES
Trim roots so they fit comfortably in the new pot. Replant at the same depth as before; trickle soil around the roots rather than pressing them into a planting hole. Topdress with gravel. Return to the pond with the trimmed topgrowth just above water level.

SEE ALSO: Dividing Perennials, p.163

HERBS IN THE GARDEN AND THEIR USES

CREATING AN HERB GARDEN

HERBS HAVE BEEN PRIZED FOR THOUSANDS of years for their culinary, cosmetic, and curative uses, but many are equally valued for their ornamental qualities. While herbs are rarely showy plants, having pale or small flowers, plenty have handsome foliage, and most are worth growing for their scent alone. Even in a tiny garden, it is worth including a few herbs — whether intermingled in a border, in pots tiered on garden steps, or ranked along a kitchen windowledge; or create your own dedicated herb garden with a collection of favorite herbs, perhaps laid out in a formal, geometric pattern of color-themed beds or in an informal, relaxed group.

PLOTS DEVOTED TO HERBS

Making a dedicated herb garden may sound adventurous, but it can be as simple as you like; in fact, fussy or complicated designs are best avoided. For a formal plot, sketch out your plan on graph paper, then mark it out on the ground with pebbles or string. Low and creeping herbs are just right for formal plots, while shrubby and evergreen herbs, such as various forms of thyme, lavender, sage, and wall germander, provide year-round interest.

In an informal plot, the design comes from the plants themselves, but take care that informality does not slip into chaos, balancing plants of low or creeping habit, such as some thymes and mints, with more sculptural or upright shapes, such as bay or viburnum. There are fewer restrictions than in a formal layout, so include plants of varying heights and tall herbs such as fennel or angelica.

◁ **FORMAL LAYOUT**
Even a small area will accommodate a simple geometric layout. Use low-growing herbs and repeat key plants to give emphasis to the overall design. Add height in the center with a pedestal urn or large pot.

△ **INFORMAL DESIGN**
Herb gardens do not need to be formal, but they should be carefully planned: design your plant compositions as in other border designs, considering echoes and contrasts of texture, form, and shape alongside color.

COLOR THEMING

As well as color from flowers, many herbs have handsomely colored foliage, which is an asset in a formal herb garden or a mixed border. Restricting the color scheme creates a sense of cohesion and harmony and highlights the shape and pattern of the herb-garden layout.

PURPLE-BRONZE
PURPLE BASIL
Ocimum basilicum
'Purple Ruffles'

GOLDEN YELLOW
GOLDEN MARJORAM
Origanum vulgare
'Aureum'

SILVER-GRAY
LAVENDER COTTON
Santolina chamaecyparissus

HERBS FOR COLORFUL LEAVES

GOLDEN YELLOW
Golden lemon balm (*Melissa officinalis* 'Aurea')
Golden marjoram (*Origanum vulgare* 'Aureum')
Golden thyme (*Thymus* × *citriodorus* 'Aureus')
Gold-variegated sage (*Salvia officinalis* 'Icterina')

PURPLE-BRONZE
Bronze fennel (*Foeniculum vulgare* 'Purpureum')
Eau de Cologne mint (*Mentha* × *piperita* f. *citrata*)
Purple basil (*Ocimum basilicum* var. *purpurascens*)
Purple sage (*Salvia officinalis* Purpurascens Group)

SILVER-GRAY
Curry plant (*Helichrysum italicum*)
Lavender (*Lavandula*, many)
Lavender cotton (*Santolina chamaecyparissus*)
Southernwood (*Artemisia abrotanum*)

SEE ALSO: Garden Styles, pp.122–123; Herbs and their Uses, pp.226–227

GROWING HERBS IN MIXED BEDS AND BORDERS

Many herbs are ideal candidates for growing among other plants, in mixed or herbaceous borders, or in a kitchen garden. Include herbs with colored leaves for dense hummocks of color and shape: try purple sage (*Salvia officinalis* Purpurascens Group), blue-gray rue (*Ruta*), or gold-variegated ginger mint (*Mentha × gracilis* 'Variegata'). Some also have colorful flowers that are more than worthy of the border, such as the purple spikes of hyssop (*Hyssopus officinalis*) or the cheerful orange of pot marigolds (*Calendula officinalis*).

Tall herbs such as angelica and evening primrose (*Oenothera biennis*) provide vertical interest. Some herbs such as bay (*Laurus nobilis*) and lemon verbena (*Aloysia triphylla*) may even be trained as standards, adding a focal point at the center of a bed.

In an open border, the play of light on and through foliage can be stimulating visually; watch to see how the light falls, especially at the beginning and end of the day, and site plants such as bronze fennel (*Foeniculum vulgare* 'Purpureum') or red bergamot (*Monarda didyma*), with its blood-red veined leaves, to take advantage of it.

△ **BEAUTIFUL BORAGE**
With its bright blue flowers and buds and stems haloed with fine hairs, borage (Borago officinalis) *is a fine plant for the border. Plant it where the delicate hair-fringed heads will be lit by the sun from behind.*

◁ **BORDER WITH INTERMINGLED HERBS**
Here, green and bronze fennel serve as a link, frothing in waves between the other plants and providing textural mass. Golden hops (Humulus lupulus 'Aureus') *adds a bold splash at the back.*

HERBS IN CONTAINERS

You don't need a grand garden or even a garden at all to grow herbs in containers: a small corner of a patio, balcony, or roof terrace is fine. For the herbs you like to use most often, site a strawberry jar (in which you can also grow mint, thyme, oregano, or marjoram), barrel, or trough where it will be easily accessible.

Make your choices so that the plantings will be decorative as well as useful. Go for plants with colored leaves rather than the plain green; the flavor is often just as good. Try using a bay tree (*Laurus nobilis*) trained as a standard to provide vertical emphasis as a focal point, or a prostrate rosemary (*Rosmarinus officinalis* 'Prostratus') to spread over the edge of a barrel, releasing its scent as you brush past.

Growing herbs in pots allows you to provide varying conditions for a range of plants – separating herbs that enjoy sun and good drainage, for example, from those that prefer shade and moisture. Chervil, chives, parsley, rock hyssop, compact marjoram (*Origanum vulgare* 'Compactum'), and thymes will make good companion plants without the danger of one dominating the others.

◁ **POTTED HERB GARDEN**
A flight of steps hosts a simple group of terracotta pots containing a miniature herb garden, with sages, bay, rosemary, southernwood, and alpine strawberries.

GOOD IDEAS

• If combining different herbs in a single container, make sure you choose those that require the same growing conditions.

• Add height to a collection of containers with a tall pot planted with trailing nasturtiums or a stake tepee covered with climbing golden hops.

• Mint (*Mentha*) is always best grown alone in a pot because it is rampant and invasive.

SEE ALSO: Containers and Raised Beds, pp.166–183; Growing Requirements, p.228; How to Plant up a Strawberry Jar, p.230; Always Remember box, p.231

HERBS AND THEIR USES

HERBS MAY BE ANNUALS, PERENNIALS, shrubs, or even trees, but what defines them as herbs and distinguishes them from other plants is their usefulness. Many herbs – the ones most people are familiar with – are invaluable for cooking, and some possess medicinal properties, which are exploited on a commercial scale as well as being used for home herbal remedies. Others are prized purely for their uplifting scents, whether produced in the garden or captured in an herbal potpourri to perfume the house. Some types of herb provide the basis for home-made cosmetic and beauty preparations, and yet others may be employed for a variety of household uses.

A CULINARY PATCH

Fresh herbs are used in cuisines from all over the world to add an incomparable flavor to an enormous range of dishes. Adding herbs lends more taste to bland dishes and helps to reduce the need for salt in food. Certain herbs seem to be just made to go with particular foods: rosemary with lamb, basil with tomatoes, dill with salmon, coriander with curries.

If you have space, it is worth creating an area specifically for culinary herbs sited as near to the house as possible for ease of harvesting; if your culinary patch is too far away, you may well find you don't pick and use the herbs. Alternatively, you may prefer to include them as part of a kitchen garden, if you have one.

When planning your culinary bed, bear in mind which herbs you use in quantity – for example, you may want to allot more space for chives and parsley if you use them for garnishing as well as flavoring; either of these would make an attractive edging for a culinary patch.

A raised bed is ideal, reducing the need to bend for harvesting, and it is easy to provide the right conditions for your

plants. Alternatively, grow your most-used herbs in containers by the back door.

■ **Flavor comes first** for culinary herbs, but your herb patch can be decorative, too. Include golden, silver, and variegated forms of some herbs for extra color, and site shrubby herbs in key positions to provide structure and shape.

■ **Edible flowers** are an unusual addition to a conventional herb patch. Grow orange and yellow pot marigolds (*Calendula officinalis*) and nasturtiums (*Tropaeolum majus*) for flowers to brighten up a salad.

◁ **DANDY DILL**
The striking form of dill in the border is only one of its attractions – both the leaves and the seeds are used in cooking. Dill is an annual, but it self-seeds easily in the open garden.

BOUQUET GARNI ▷
A bundle of herbs tied together and placed in soups, stews, or casseroles while cooking will lend extra flavor to the dish. This bouquet for flavoring meat consists of rosemary, marjoram, lemon balm, and orange peel.

◁ **CHEERY CHIVES**
As well as providing tasty stems for using in salads or as a garnish, chives give a lift to the front of a summer border with their colorful, globular flowerheads.

HERBS FOR COOKING

If you have even a small sunny space in the garden, it really is worth growing your own herbs for use in the kitchen. As well as the ordinary species, look for other forms that may be more visually attractive, for example those with variegated foliage, especially if growing herbs mixed in the border with other plants or in containers in a prominent position.

Basil (*Ocimum basilicum*)
Bay (*Laurus nobilis*)
Chives (*Allium schoenoprasum*) and try garlic chives (*A. tuberosum*)
Coriander/cilantro (*Coriandrum sativum*)
Dill (*Anethum graveolens*)
Fennel (*Foeniculum vulgare*)
French tarragon (*Artemisia dracunculus*)
Lemon balm (*Melissa officinalis*)
Lovage (*Levisticum officinale*; this is a tall, dramatic plant good for the back of a border)
Marjoram (*Origanum vulgare*)
Mint (*Mentha spicata*, spearmint, is the classic culinary mint, but there are lots to choose from)
Parsley (*Petroselinum crispum*) also try the flat-leaved or continental parsley called 'Italian'
Rosemary (*Rosmarinus officinalis*)
Sage (*Salvia officinalis*)
Thyme (*Thymus vulgare* – lots to choose from)
Winter savory (*Satureja montana*) and try the less hardy summer savory (*S. hortensis*), which has a finer flavor

SEE ALSO: Raised Beds, pp.180–183

AROMATIC HERBS

Culinary herbs usually have delicious fragrances as well as flavors, but there are other herbs that are valued for their scent alone. For example, the curry plant (*Helichrysum italicum*) is not used for making curries – although the leaves are mildly flavored and may be added to rice – but its spicy, curry smell makes a good contrast to other aromatic herbs on a hot day.

Position scented plants by paths, gates, doors, and garden seats, where anyone passing will brush against them and be treated to a wave of scent: use lavender to form miniature hedges on either side of a path, or grow lemon balm in clumps by the front gate so that you can rub the leaves as you enter. For the ultimate in scented relaxation, grow aromatics such as lavender, rosemary, artemisia, and thyme near a hammock.

■ **Create a chamomile lawn**. The non-flowering *Chamaemelum nobile* 'Treneague' is often used (*see p.88*) because this form is naturally low-growing and there are no flowers that would otherwise need to be trimmed off. It is less hard-wearing than grass, so is not suitable for a main lawn.

■ **Remove a paving slab** or a few bricks to create a planting space in a patio for aromatic herbs, so you can rub the leaves between your fingers as you sit outside.

△ SCENT IN THE AIR
*The strongly scented Corsican mint (*Mentha requienii*) forms a low mound or mat; growing it in a container raised above ground will bring the aromas nearer to nose level.*

MEDICINAL, COSMETIC, AND HOUSEHOLD USES

Herbs have been valued for their healing properties for thousands of years, yet it is only relatively recently that Western medicine is once again starting to recognize the benefits that herbs have to offer. In the pharmaceuticals industry, herbal derivatives are used frequently: the principal active constituent of one of the most used drugs in the world – aspirin – is salicylic acid, derived from willow (*Salix*).

For the knowledgeable, the herb garden can be a medicine cabinet containing homemade remedies to treat a number of minor ailments: mint, for example, is renowned for its antiseptic properties, but it is also a mild anesthetic and helps alleviate indigestion – try a cup of peppermint tea after a heavy meal to appreciate its effects.

Some herbs are used to make beauty preparations, such as skin lotions and shampoos. *Aloe vera* is grown commercially for its soothing, anti-inflammatory properties used in skin products. At home, there are many products you can make: infuse rosemary in hot water for a rinse to bring a shine to dark hair.

Many aromatic herbs have uses in the home. Strew artemisia in wardrobes to discourage clothes moths, and mint to

△ HEALING TROUGH
If you don't have space for a herb garden, you can grow herbs just as well in containers and even windowboxes. This trough contains a variety of medicinal plants.

deter mice. Lavender was used to scent linen and is still made into scented sachets.

■ **Tuck the dried leaves** of sweet woodruff (*Galium odoratum*) between sheets and linens to give it the scent of new-mown hay.

■ **Fix the fragrance** of potpourri with some powdered orris root (*Iris* 'Florentina').

■ **Don't suffer sleeplessness**: make a relaxing sleep pillow from muslin stuffed with dried hops and lavender.

ALWAYS REMEMBER

BETTER SAFE THAN SORRY

Don't underestimate the strength of herbs. Seek advice from a qualified herbalist, or consult an authoritative herbal, before trying home herbal remedies. If you are pregnant or breast-feeding, or have reduced immunity, also check with your doctor what it is safe for you to take.

▽ SOOTHING TEA
Fennel and lemon balm may be infused together to produce a delicious and relaxing hot drink.

SEE ALSO: Planting in Gravel, p.63; Alternative Lawns, p.88

PLANTING AND CULTIVATING HERBS

ONE OF THE GREAT JOYS OF HERBS, especially if you prefer relaxing in your garden to toiling in the border, is that many of them are relatively easy plants to cultivate. Certainly, those that are most commonly grown and enjoyed in herb gardens are not very fussy in their requirements and generously reward the gardener with their heady scent and abundance. The best way to give your herbs a good start in life is to know their needs before you plant them. Give them the right conditions in terms of light, soil, and water, and they should thrive. You can even turn these requirements into a virtue – by growing them in an area of gravel, for example.

GROWING REQUIREMENTS

While many herbs require sharp drainage and full sun, others need moisture and a degree of shade. In general, the latter thrive in a richer soil than most Mediterranean species. Many edible herbs come from the Mediterranean "maquis," where they live in dry, poor soil. In nutrient-rich soils, such herbs may have lush, sappy growth and much less flavor, so do not add extra fertilizer. If your soil is very heavy and damp, consider making a raised bed for your herbs, filled with soil mixed with compost and sharp sand.

Check up on their preferred growing conditions when buying plants. The herb itself often provides a clue: those that have silvery, needlelike leaves or tough, leathery foliage, such as lavenders, usually thrive in sunny, well-drained conditions, whereas those with broader, soft green

◁ **MIXED HERBS**
To make life easy, combine herbs that have similar growing requirements; illsutrated here are lavender and chives.

△ **BEEBALM**
*This plant (*Monarda didyma*) tolerates shade and produces bright, edible flowers suitable for salads.*

△ **SWEET WOODRUFF**
*This aromatic herb (*Galium odoratum*) makes a good deciduous groundcover in shade and may be used for medicinal purposes as well as dried in potpourri.*

leaves, such as mints, may tolerate partial shade. Some golden forms, such as golden marjoram (*Origanum vulgare* 'Aureum') may scorch in full sun, so site them where they will be shaded for at least part of the day.

■ **Annuals and biennials** are usually sown as seed directly into the ground. Prepare and rake the soil to form a fine tilth before sowing. Thin the seedlings as necessary. Delay the flowering of biennials (such as parsley) in their second year, after which they die, by continual picking.

■ **The less cold-hardy shrubs,** such as bay or myrtle, are best grown in pots so that you can easily bring them under cover for winter before the first frost.

■ **Prepare the soil** before planting an herb bed by clearing it of perennial weeds.

SHADE-TOLERANT HERBS

Most herbs are sun-lovers, but there are a few that will tolerate or even prefer shady conditions as long as they have moist soil. Prepare the soil for these herbs, and for other moisture-lovers such as angelica, by digging plenty of well-rotted organic matter into the soil (see *pp.142–143*) before planting.

Beebalm
Chervil
Comfrey
French sorrel
Mints (there are numerous mints to choose from, and some are more shade-tolerant than others. The main species used in cooking, *Mentha spicata*, is happy in light shade as long as the soil is kept reasonably moist.)
Parsley
Sweet cicely
Sweet woodruff

SEE ALSO: Clearing Weeds, pp.144–145; Establishing Plants in the Border, pp.148–149; Increasing Border Plants, pp.162–163; Raised Beds, pp.180–183

GRAVEL HERB GARDEN

In a garden, an area of gently sloping gravel provides sharp drainage – ideal for Mediterranean herbs that dislike heavy, damp soil. Plants with silvery leaves, such as lavenders, and those with tiny leaves, such as thymes, are usually fairly drought-tolerant and will thrive in a gravel bed. Compact, bushy, or cushion-forming herbs can often look especially at home in such a setting.

Before laying down gravel, cover the soil with a landscape fabric (see p.145) or plastic sheeting to suppress weeds. You can vary the size of the stones, and include a few well-placed larger rocks as well. The stones act as a mulch, helping to reduce evaporation and so minimize the need for additional watering. A gravel garden can also be established in the well-drained conditions of a raised bed.

HERBS FOR A GRAVEL BED

Any of the following plants should do well if grown in a gravel bed.

Lavender (*Lavandula*)
Lavender cotton (*Santolina chamaecyparissus*)
Rosemary (*Rosmarinus officinalis*)
Rue (*Ruta*)
Sage (*Salvia officinalis*)
Thyme (*Thymus*)
Wormwood (*Artemisia*)

MAKING A GRAVEL HERB AREA

1 POSITIONING
Clear weeds and dig the soil, adding coarse sand for drainage. Bank soil toward the rear to create a gentle slope. Position and bed down any large rocks, angling them so rain will drain onto the plants behind. Set out the plants still in their pots.

2 PLANTING
Plant the larger herbs first, and water well. Use coarse gravel to surround these larger plants. Then plant the smaller herbs: use a trowel to make planting holes, remove the plants from their pots, and plant at the correct depth. Water in.

3 ADDING GRAVEL
Cover the lower, front part of the area with a finer grade of gravel. Use a trowel or your hands to spread it carefully between and around the plants without damaging them. Spread gravel right under the leaves of the plants.

4 DROUGHT-TOLERANT GARDEN
The finished gravel garden provides an attractive, low-maintenance area that should need little watering. In a sunny site, the aromatic oils in the herbs will evaporate and scent the air. The surface layer of gravel will also help conserve moisture in the soil and keep down weeds. Remove any weeds that do appear by hand as soon as you spot them. An alternative is to lay a landscape fabric beneath the gravel and plant through slits.

HERBS FOR CRACKS AND CREVICES

If you have a patio or path made of paving slabs, stones, or bricks, you can grow herbs in the gaps between them. Low-growing, aromatic herbs are the most popular choices because they will not obstruct easy passage and tolerate the treading that releases their delightful scents. Try thymes, creeping savory (*Satureja spicigera*), and chamomile (*Chamaemelum nobile*). Tall subjects like fennel may also self-seed in gaps, but they may be obtrusive here; if so, remove seedlings as soon as you spot them.

It is usual to sow the herbs from seed, but if the gaps are wide enough you could try inserting rooted cuttings or small plants. Scrape out some of the compacted soil,

trickle in a little soil mix, and water well to give the plants a good start.

■ **Plant herbs in your driveway** if it is made of pavers or stones. Site the plants so that they will be mostly avoided by your car's wheels!

■ **If growing chamomile** this way, use the ordinary flowering species and trim off the flowers if you prefer; 'Treneague', which is favored for lawns, is a nonflowering form that cannot be grown from seed.

A SCENTED PATIO ▷
Creeping thymes, such as those shown here, are ideal for the gaps between paving stones — your footsteps will crush the leaves and surround you with fragrance. Bear in mind that, when in flower, thyme is a popular haunt of bees.

SOWING DIRECT ▷
To plant herbs in cracks, it is usually easiest to use seed. Brush soil mix into the crevices between paving, then sow seed directly into them. Keep watered until established.

SEE ALSO: Beds for Drought-tolerant Plants, pp.132–133; Increasing Shrubs, pp.164–165; Raised Beds, pp.180–183

MAKING A CONTAINER HERB GARDEN

Containers can make extremely good homes for a wide range of herbs and offer a practical and attractive solution if you are short of space in the open ground. Any container you intend to use must have adequate drainage holes and a good, well-drained soil mix. Add 1 part coarse sand or perlite, turface, or pumice to 5 parts of soil mix to improve its drainage qualities. Do not take up container space with a layer of broken pots or gravel at the bottom; instead, use a square piece of window screening or wad of straw to cover the drainage hole.

Site a large tub or pot of culinary herbs in a place where you will have easy access to it from the kitchen. Alternatively, you can grow herbs in a trough on the kitchen windowsill. It is a good idea to give larger herbs, such as rosemary or bay, a container all to themselves. Using a strawberry jar, as shown below, is one way to grow a number of herbs in a restricted space.

■ **Grow tender herbs**, such as basil, French tarragon (*Artemisia dracunculus*), or lemon verbena (*Aloysia triphylla*), in pots or containers so that you can put them under cover – in a well-lit place such as a greenhouse – for the winter.

■ **If very short of space,** plant herbs in a hanging basket (*see p.177*). They will need more watering than if grown in a large pot, so choose those such as thyme, sage, and marjoram that are not too thirsty.

GOOD IDEAS

• Herbs in containers look their best if you topdress the soil surface with pebbles, gravel, or even washed shells. A mulch such as this also helps retain moisture.

• If grouping several pots, vary the heights to show them at their best. Use an empty upturned pot as a pedestal if necessary.

• Some shrubby herbs, such as myrtle or lemon verbena, can be grown as a simple "standard," where a length of single, bare stem supports a clipped crown of foliage.

△ **MINIATURE HERB GARDEN**
Place a strawberry jar packed with culinary herbs near the kitchen door for convenience when cooking. This one is planted with alpine strawberries as well as rosemary, savory, marjoram, tarragon, and mint.

HOW TO PLANT UP A STRAWBERRY JAR

1 ADD SOIL MIX
Choose a frost-proof strawberry jar big enough for several plants. Fill it with soil-based or soilless mix up to the first planting hole. Firm the soil mix gently, adding more if required.

2 PLANT IN STAGES
Insert each plant, with its root ball, through one of the holes, starting at the bottom of the pot and working up, filling in with a layer of soil mix after each planting. Firm gently around the root ball.

3 PLANT THE TOP
When you reach the top, plant as normal, firm, and add soil mix until the surface is about ¾in (2cm) below the rim. Water thoroughly and slowly to prevent any mix from being washed away. Top up the soil mix if it sinks.

Chives

Sweet basil

Rosemary

◁ **THE FINISHED RESULT**
A selection of herbs will thrive in a handy, compact container that can be sited to suit you. The rosemary in the top will grow much larger — when that happens, you can remove the chives to give it more space.

Lemon verbena

Curled-leaved parsley

Golden-variegated thyme

Golden-variegated sage

△ **SIDE PLANTING**
Choose herbs growing in small pots. Remove the plant and push the entire root ball through the hole at a comfortable angle.

SEE ALSO: Containers and Raised Beds, pp.166–183; Topiary and Standards, p.173; Herbs in Containers, p.225

Ensuring a Supply for Winter

Some herbs can be lifted from the summer border and brought indoors to overwinter on a bright windowledge or under cover in a greenhouse, conservatory, or enclosed porch. Herbaceous perennials, such as mint, that would be cut back by frost can be lifted as rooted clumps in early autumn and planted up to provide a fresh supply for winter. Chives and garlic chives may be treated similarly (*see right*); they will shoot again from the bulbs given the right conditions of good light and sufficient water. At the end of winter, it is best to discard these "forced" herbs or plant them out in open ground. Do not harvest them until the following year so they have time to reestablish.

■ **Sprigs of evergreen herbs,** such as sage, rosemary, thyme, and winter savory, may also be harvested in winter, but limit your pickings to odd sprigs and leaves. If you cut back stems excessively, this may stimulate growth of new shoots in mild spells, which would then be vulnerable to cold damage.

■ **Provide a supply of home-grown herbs** by preserving your own harvest. They can be air-dried, frozen in ice cubes, or infused in oil or vinegar for use in cooking and salad dressings.

Always Remember

Rampant spreaders such as mint and tansy (*Tanacetum vulgare*) are best planted in a container. If you want to grow them in a border, use a pot or plastic bucket sunk into the ground, with the bottom cut out or holes punched at the base. You should lift the plant and replace its soil mix each spring. Rejuvenate the plant by dividing it and replanting young, vigorous pieces.

Potting up Herbs for Winter Use

1 Dig up a Clump
In early autumn, lift a clump of the chosen herb, complete with roots. Divide the clump into smaller pieces, each with their own root system.

2 Plant a Trough
Carefully plant one of the new divided sections in the end of a small trough filled with standard soil mix, then firm it in.

3 Using Individual Pots
Some divisions may be placed in single pots to grow separately. Plant up each pot as normal, using standard soil mix. Firm and water.

4 Fill the Trough
Add more plants to the trough, remembering to leave enough space between them to grow comfortably.

5 Trimming Chives
Before replanting a clump of chives, cut the stems back evenly to about 6in (15cm) in length.

6 The Finished Trough
Keep the planted trough indoors in a light place, and keep watered. Harvest the herbs as you need them.

Increasing Herbs

A number of herbs may be easily increased by means of division or mound-layering. These simple methods are ideal if you want new plants of a specific form, for example a thyme with silver-variegated foliage that will not come true if sown from seed.

Shrubby plants such as sage, rosemary, thyme, and lavender, which tend to become woody and less vigorous in the center as they age, can be stimulated to produce fresh shoots with new roots by mound-layering. In spring, mound some soil mixed with coarse sand and compost all around the base of the plant, so that only the shoot tips are showing. Replenish the mix after heavy rain. In late summer or early autumn, detach any rooted stems from around the edge of the plant and pot them up or replant them.

Dividing Shrubby and Clump-forming Herbs

1 Lift Plant
In spring or early autumn, insert a fork into the soil well beneath the plant (here, thyme), taking care not to damage any of the roots. By gently moving the fork back and forth, loosen the root ball from the surrounding soil, and lift the plant clear.

2 Trim Foliage
Using pruners, trim back any heavy topgrowth on the sections you want to retain. Always keep some of the foliage intact, however; otherwise, the plant may not be able to regrow. The aim is to create a neat, compact head of foliage.

3 Divide Clump
Now separate the clump into several pieces, using a sharp garden knife, pruners, a hand fork, or your hands, depending on the plant. Keep only the younger, healthier sections, complete with their roots, for replanting. The older pieces should be discarded.

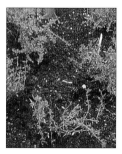

4 Replant
Plant the divided sections where desired, spacing them far enough apart to allow for spread as they grow. Water in and keep the soil moist until the plants are established. Alternatively, they may be potted up singly for growing on in containers.

See also: Increasing Border Plants, pp.162–165; Maintenance, Harvesting, and Preserving, pp.232–233

MAINTENANCE, HARVESTING, AND PRESERVING

ONE OF THE PLEASURES OF HERBS is that they do not, in general, rely on a constant round of watering, pruning, feeding, and mulching in order to thrive – quite the contrary, in fact, since many herbs hail from regions with low rainfall and poor soil. Certain routine tasks will help to keep them in good shape, however, but these are not too taxing. Harvesting your own home-grown herbs is a joy rather than a chore as you handle the aromatic foliage and snip fresh sprigs for cooking or use in the home. Enjoy them freshly picked or capture their scent and flavor for later use by preserving them in various ways – by drying, freezing, or infusing in oil or vinegar.

ROUTINE CARE AND HARVESTING

The maintenance of herbs is generally straightforward and undemanding. Routine care largely consists of cutting back plants in spring and summer to encourage healthy growth, and cleaning up dormant plants in winter. An herb's requirements depend partly on which type of plant it is – whether an annual, perennial, or shrub, for example.

■ **Annuals** (e.g. dill). These flower, set seed, and die all in the same year. You can harvest seed to sow the following season. Dill also self-seeds. Start tender herbs raised annually, such as basil and cilantro, under cover before planting them out. **Biennials** such as parsley survive into a second season and then die.

■ **Perennials** (e.g. beebalm, or *Monarda didyma*, and mint). Regularly picking either leaves or sprigs for use will help keep the plants shapely. Divide perennials periodically (*see p.231*) when the center of the clump has become tired and unproductive. In summer, after rain, apply a mulch around plants that love moisture, both to retain water and improve the soil.

△ **FRESH FROM THE GARDEN**
This home-grown harvest includes bay, rosemary, parsley, basil, and sage, laid in a trug to prevent damage before preserving. Use scissors or pruners to make clean cuts.

■ **Shrubs** (e.g. lavender, rosemary, hyssop, and sage). As with perennials, regular harvesting both maintains a bushy shape and stimulates new growth. Trim off the flowerheads after flowering. Lavender will not regrow if you cut back too hard into old wood; prune in midspring, making sure some green growth remains on each stem. Picking of sprigs should be enough to keep thyme plants in shape.

■ **Do not take too much foliage** from a single plant at any one time. Have several plants of herbs you use in quantity so you can pick here and there from the clumps.

■ **Angelica stems** to be crystallized for cake decoration should be cut while still young and tender, long before flowering.

■ **If picking rue**, wear gloves: for some people, their skin reacts badly after contact with the plant in sunshine.

TELL ME HOW

WHEN AND HOW SHOULD HERBS BE HARVESTED?

Pick herbs for using fresh as you need them. This is the process for most evergreen herbs, but in the case of bay, some cooks prefer the stronger flavor of the dried leaves.

For preserving, harvest herbs on a dry, fine morning after the dew has evaporated but before hot sun has burned off some of the essential oils. The oil content should be at its peak just before the herb comes into flower.

When gathering seed from dill, fennel, or coriander, loosely fasten paper bags over the flowerheads as they start to ripen to make capturing the seed easier.

FLAVOR AT YOUR FINGERTIPS ▷
Growing herbs in pots on a well-lit windowsill ensures they are conveniently at hand whenever you need them. With care, potting up herbs can provide you with a winter supply.

SEE ALSO: Maintaining Border Plants, pp.154–155; Increasing Border Plants, pp.162–163; Routine Care and Maintenance, pp.178–179; Increasing Herbs, p.231

DRYING HERBS

Air-drying is the easiest way of preserving most herbs, although soft-leaved herbs such as mint are better frozen (see box, below right). Spread out sprigs, leaves, flowers, or seedheads in a single layer on a rack and leave in a warm, airy place to dry. Alternatively, tie sprigs or stems in small bunches and hang upside down in a warm, dry – but not too sunny – spot. The drying process should take no more than 48 hours – if the leaves turn black or show any mold, the process has been too slow and the herb should be discarded.

Once completely dry, strip the leaves or the flowers (chamomile flowers, for example, may be infused to make herbal tea) from the stems and discard the stalks. Crush the leaves thoroughly between your hands and store them in airtight dark glass or ceramic containers (they will fade rapidly if kept in clear glass jars). Dried herbs will not keep their flavor indefinitely, so always start fresh the following season with a new batch.

◁ **AIR-DRYING**
Spread out the herbs on a mesh-covered rack, and leave them in a warm place until dry. This should take 1 or 2 days. Alternatively, hang them up in bunches to dry.

It is possible to control, and speed up, the drying process by placing the herbs in a microwave or in an oven heated to a very low temperature – 120–140°F (50–60°C). Microwave-drying should take about 2 or 3 minutes; oven-drying is suitable only for underground plant parts that need lengthy drying, and it may take 2 or 3 hours. The moisture content of herbs varies considerably, so you will need to experiment with timing for best results.

HERBS FOR DRYING

The following list is just a selection of some of the most popular herbs that may be dried successfully. Most are culinary herbs, while some, such as lemon balm and beebalm, are used to make herbal teas. Others, such as southernwood and lavender, are used in the home, in potpourri for example.

Alecost (*Tanacetum balsamita*) L
Bay (*Laurus nobilis*) L
Beebalm (*Monarda didyma*) L F
Chamomile (*Chamaemelum nobile*) F
Chervil (*Anthriscus cerefolium*) L
Cilantro/Coriander (*Coriandrum sativum*) L S
Dill (*Anethum graveolens*) L S
Fennel (*Foeniculum vulgare*) S
Feverfew (*Tanacetum parthenium*) L F
French tarragon (*Artemisia dracunculus*) L
Hyssop (*Hyssopus officinalis*) L
Lavender (*Lavandula angustifolia*) F
Lavender cotton (*Santolina chamaecyparissus*) L F
Lemon balm (*Melissa officinalis*) L
Lemon verbena (*Aloysia triphylla*) L
Lovage (*Levisticum officinale*) L
Marjoram (*Origanum vulgare*) L
Pot marigold (*Calendula officinalis*) F
Sage (*Salvia officinalis*) L
Southernwood (*Artemisia abrotanum*) L
Summer savory (*Satureja hortensis*) L
Sweet woodruff (*Galium odoratum*) L
Thyme (*Thymus vulgaris*) L
Winter savory (*Satureja montana*) L

Key for parts of plants used:
L = leaves or sprigs F = flowers S = seeds

FREEZING TIPS

Many soft-leaved herbs, such as basil and parsley, are better frozen than dried. For short-term storage, pack whole sprigs into plastic bags, label, and freeze until needed. For long-term storage, it is better to blanch the herbs first. Chop the leaves, then dip them in boiling water followed quickly by iced water. Pat them dry, bag, and freeze.

• **Make herb ice cubes**: place single borage flowers or small mint leaves (try ginger mint) in ice-cube trays, add water, and freeze to make decorative ice for drinks. Use this technique also with herbs for cooking. Chop parsley or chives and half-fill an ice tray, filling with water. To use, defrost in a sieve for garnish, or simply add as they are to soups and casseroles during cooking.

△ **FLOWERHEADS**
Pick flowerheads when just opened (shown here, pot marigolds). Spread them on a paper-lined tray. Leave in a warm, dry place.

△ **PICKING PETALS**
With some herbs, only the petals are used. Pluck the petals from the flower centers, and discard the latter. Pot marigold petals are used in potpourri, to flavor and color foods such as rice, and for dye.

OILS AND VINEGARS

One way to preserve the flavor of fresh herbs is to steep them in oil or vinegar, which may then be used for cooking or in salad dressings. This works very well for a number of herbs such as French tarragon, oregano, thyme, and lavender.

■ **To make flavored oil**, fill a clear glass jar with sprigs or leaves of the fresh herb, pour over a good, flavorless oil, such as sunflower, and seal. Leave the jar in a sunny spot for two weeks; shake or stir every day. Strain and bottle, adding a new sprig of the herb as identification. The oil is best stored in a refrigerator.

■ **To make flavored vinegar**, crush the herb or herb mixture and put into a jar, then pour in a good wine or cider vinegar that has been slightly warmed, filling the jar to the brim. Proceed as for flavored oil (*above*). Store in a refrigerator.

■ **For a sweet oil**, such as lavender, use almond oil as the base oil instead. This is usually available from herbalists, since it may also be used for massage.

■ **Preserve basil leaves** by packing them in jars of light olive oil. Make sure they are completely covered with oil, then seal and refrigerate. Use the oil for cooking or in salad dressings, and the leaves in sauces.

▽ **BOTTLED FLAVORS**
Once you have flavored some oil with herbs in a jar, bottle it, add fresh sprigs of the herbs, and seal with a stopper.

SEE ALSO: Herbs and their Uses, pp.226–227

THE EDIBLE GARDEN

PLANNING THE EDIBLE GARDEN

THE FIRST STEP is to consider how much space you want to give over to vegetables and fruit. Growing your crops all in one place in an orderly fashion certainly makes practical sense, in that care and maintenance will be so much easier. However, in small, modern gardens, the traditional kitchen garden plot, separated from the ornamental part of the garden, may not fit the bill. You can, however, grow fruits and vegetables in beds and borders among ornamental plants, and in containers — perhaps not in the same quantity, but enough to ensure a few meals' worth of favorites, fresh from the garden or patio, or even plucked from the windowsill.

WHY GROW EDIBLE PLANTS?

Gardening with ornamental plants is, in a sense, its own reward, and you can choose how much work you want to put into it. Growing fruits and vegetables does commit the gardener to a certain amount of labor but brings tangible, not to mention edible returns. The flavor of home-grown produce is infinitely superior to store-bought. Not only can varieties be selected for inherently better taste; the short interval between harvest and eating means that the fruits of your labors have higher levels of enzymes and vitamins than store-bought. There is the heightened expectancy of waiting for crops to mature in their season, and intense satisfaction to be had from meals made with produce from your own plot. Finally, growing your own allows you the choice of whether to grow organically or not.

GOOD IDEAS

- Don't grow things that nobody in your family really likes — it sounds obvious, but this mistake is surprisingly often made.
- "Maincrop" vegetables are always cheap to buy. Where space is limited, growing more pricey or unusual crops makes sense.
- Growing some crops, such as peas and strawberries, has great appeal for children.

THE TRADITIONAL VEGETABLE PLOT

In a traditional kitchen garden, vegetables and fruits are grown in neat rows or blocks in well-tended plots. That is not to say that flowers must be excluded; the traditional gardener well understands their value in attracting pollinating insects that ensure good crops. And cropping plants, well-grown and orderly, have their own charm, too: this is an edible garden for those who find serenity in predictability, practicality, and productivity. But if you crave more obviously decorative plantings and have only a small garden, you may find this approach eats up too much space.

THE TRADITIONAL KITCHEN GARDEN ▷
Well-ordered and weed-free rows of healthy vegetables are flanked by a band of aromatic, purple-flowered catmint (Nepeta × faassenii) to attract bees and other pollinating insects that ensure good crops.

SEE ALSO: Planning and Practicalities, p.236; Rotating Crops, p.237

COTTAGE GARDEN STYLE

The cottage garden was a place where time, not money, was spent: every inch of space was planted with seed-raised crops and flowers. Although the effect, when well done, is of cheerful chaos, this approach takes quite a lot of upkeep, or the effect will not be one of random profusion, but of a mess. With little space "wasted" on evergreens, garden features, and hard landscaping, this is perhaps the most delightful of styles for those who love to potter in the garden in spring and summer but hibernate indoors in winter.

THE COTTAGE GARDEN ▷
Feathery plumes of fennel flanked by parsnips and straw-berries are interplanted with nectar-rich salvias and roses for cutting. Straw-strewn paths provide clean access and ground space for drying harvested shallots. Tepees and screens support pole beans or other climbers.

THE ORNAMENTAL POTAGER

As pretty as a knot garden or parterre, the potager combines formal beauty with productivity in an exuberant patchwork. Good design and strong permanent plantings are essential to "hold" the look when crops are harvested. The geometric beds must be carefully delineated and paths straight, well built, and attractive; clipped edgings of boxwood and lavender, and, as here, beautifully shaped standard bay trees and roses are key elements.

EXUBERANT POTAGER ▷
Hard-wearing brick paths provide easy access and lend warm, mellow color to a formal geometric framework that delineates highly productive beds. Colorful ribbons of nasturtiums attract hoverflies, whose larvae will feed on aphids, leaving frilly lettuce for their grower to savor.

USING SMALL SPACES

Container-grown crops can range from the utilitarian – peppers in a growing bag, even potatoes in a trash bag – to a tepee of pole beans in a half-barrel planter. Even those with the tiniest of spaces can exploit hanging baskets, pots, and windowboxes with salad greens, bush tomatoes, or chili peppers. Interplant with marjoram, basil, or thyme, and summer salads will always be properly dressed.

◁ URBAN LARDER
Here, lettuce, strawberries, and tomatoes thrive within arm's reach, using the tiniest space in the most productive way.

HANGING GARDEN ▷
Tumbling tomatoes share a hanging basket with French marigolds, grown here as a companion plant.

SEE ALSO: Planting and Cultivating Herbs, pp.228–231; Tender Crops, pp.256–257

PREPARING A VEGETABLE GARDEN

THERE ARE PLENTY of ornamental plants that will cope beautifully with the shady, windy, damp, or stony spots in your garden, but vegetables cannot be given such inferior sites. They need sun, shelter, and fertile, well-drained soil, and thus may command what you consider the "best" part of your yard. If you are not choosing to grow vegetables among ornamental plants or in containers, you still might want to make your vegetable patch as attractive as possible. A system of small beds, edged with flowers and herbs and filled with well-tended, weed-free crops, can be as charming as a purely decorative planting plan.

PLANNING AND PRACTICALITIES

If you are hoping to grow enough to supply your kitchen regularly with fresh produce, plan your patch well in advance with an eye to practicalities. Then, when you begin to sow and plant, you can be sure that all the necessities will be there and working to your advantage. Wind protection such as hedging, fencing, or more utilitarian netting, for example, can create boundaries along which climbing peas and beans could be grown without shading other crops. You will need access to water, ideally from an outside tap and perhaps also from a barrel, and storage space, not just for tools but for all the bits and pieces – such as stakes, row cover, cloches, wire hoops and pegs, peasticks – that the kitchen gardener accumulates. Site a shed or locker carefully so it does not take up or shade good growing space. A compost bin, or ideally two, is a must (see below) unless you are gardening on a

tiny scale. Easy access to a back or side gate, if you have one, means that you can have manure and mulches delivered in bulk; you will need somewhere to pile them. If you are growing on a large scale, a spot reserved for burning makes sense,

△ GENTLE WATERING
Seephose, sometimes called tricklehose, is one of the most useful modern innovations for the kitchen gardener. Not only can it form part of an automatic watering system, but it also delivers water very gently, avoiding any root disturbance to delicate young plants.

provided that local ordinances allow it. Finally, if you become bitten by the self-sufficiency bug, it won't be long before a greenhouse or at least a cold frame appeals to you (see p.240); you might want to earmark a potential site.

GOOD IDEAS

In summer, you may find that even a modest vegetable garden takes you an hour every day to water, and often the only time to do this is in the evenings. If the evenings are quality time for you and your family, then it really makes sense to install a watering system as you design and lay out your vegetable garden. Garden centers and home and garden stores usually offer a range of items such as seephose, timers for taps, and hoses with watering spurs or prongs for containers, and should be able to give advice on combining them. You can then run the hose around beds or pots in a way that minimizes tripping hazards.

MAKING COMPOST

Vegetable growing exhausts the soil and generates lots of garden and kitchen waste. Composting is the perfect solution, reducing clutter and returning the plant material to the soil where it belongs, in a form that lets you continue to garden on soil whose texture and fertility improves year on year.

Constructing your own compost bin or bins is satisfying (see p.283); you may also find that your local government supplies plastic bins at discounted rates as part of its recycling strategy. Compost needs to heat up adequately to be successful; to do this, bins must have a minimum volume of 1–2 cu.yds (cu.m). To make compost,

make a 6in (15cm) deep, basal layer of open, twiggy material, then, ideally add organic waste in successive 6in (15cm) layers. Mix soft, leafy materials with stemmy or shredded twiggy matter in a ratio of 1:2. Alternate layers of organic waste with a shovelful or two of manure; the nitrogen it contains will speed the process. Add water only in prolonged dry spells in summer, and cover in winter to prevent it from freezing solid, if possible. Compost will mature in 2–3 months in summer, but takes longer if left over winter. When it is sweet-smelling and crumbly, use it as a mulch or dig it in.

Most vegetable waste can be composted.

Woody material needs to be shredded first. Add uprooted annual weeds only before they set seed; never put in the roots of perennial weeds. Do not add meat or cooked food (they attract vermin) or pet litter, and never compost diseased or pest-infested plant material.

GRASS CLIPPINGS ▷
Grass clippings are a good source of organic matter in the compost pile but must be added in thin layers or mixed with bulkier fibrous material. In deep layers, they exclude vital air and become slimy.

SEE ALSO: Nourishing your Crops, pp.238–239

TYPES OF BED

If you want to grow your vegetables in a dedicated area, rather than in containers or among ornamental plants, you need to think about the layout that you will use. The traditional vegetable garden, in which big plots contain widely spaced rows of plants to allow easy access between them, takes up lots of space. Moreover, it is not good for the soil's structure, creating bands of trodden, compacted soil where you walk between rows. You can instead make small beds, separated by permanent paths from which all work can be done by stretching over the soil. Provided that you keep soil fertility high (*see overleaf*), you can plant closely in blocks, rather then in conventional rows. This will increase yields, and also allows less space for weeds. The paths could form a formal grid between square or oblong beds; they could cross diagonally to create diamonds and triangles, or cut a circle into segments. Make sure paths are at least 2–2½ ft (60–75cm) wide; kneeling sideways to cultivate is tiring and causes back problems.

Small-bed systems adapt well to "no-dig" and deep bed cultivation – standard practices for organic gardeners, since they increase fertility and moisture retention, aid free drainage, and create an excellent soil structure that helps minimize both nutrient losses and weed germination. Once prepared, they need no further digging; planting is done with a trowel.

Whether you choose this method or more traditional ones, good soil preparation (*see pp. 142–143*) and thorough weed clearance before you plant or sow is essential. Young plants dislike competition and the root disturbance weeding causes, so the longer you can delay the first weeds, the better.

SMALL DEEP BEDS

1 CULTIVATE THE PLOT
Dig over the area of the bed or beds; single digging (see p.143), forking organic matter into the base of the trenches, gives best results. Mound up with topsoil from the surrounding area, improved with more organic matter.

2 PLANTING AND SPACINGS
In each subsequent year, organic matter is applied as a thick surface mulch; there is no need to dig in. Because soil fertility is so much enhanced, plantings can be made at up to four times the density of conventional beds.

PLANTING THROUGH PLASTIC

Black plastic sheet mulches can be used on vegetable beds to suppress weeds and moderate soil temperatures. You can sow seed through holes or long slits in the plastic, but you must watch carefully and if necessary ease the seedlings out. It is easier to use plastic when planting young plants – for example, when setting out plants raised in cell packs – cutting two crosswise slits in the sheet for each. The plastic will exclude rain; laying seephose (*see facing page*) before it is put in place will make watering simple and reliable. Black plastic can also be used for a "no-dig" method of growing potatoes (*see right*).

"NO-DIG" POTATOES

1 "PLANTING"
In a bed prepared as for deep beds, lay seed potatoes on the soil and cover with a 6–8in (15–20cm) layer of well-rotted organic matter. Weed seeds do not germinate, because light is excluded.

2 SHEET MULCH
Cover bed with black plastic; secure by burying in soil. Cut slits for top growth to come through. A sheet mulch prevents potato "greening," a common effect if ripening tubers are exposed to light.

ROTATING CROPS

Crops are rotated to use soil nutrients efficiently and prevent the buildup of soil problems, but do not be daunted by the complex 3-, 4- or even 5-year rotation plans books often prescribe. These were designed for large country-house kitchen gardens, when every crop imaginable had to be grown to provide a choice of fresh produce every day of the year. If you have no interest in growing some vegetable groups – say, onions – do not worry unduly about following a strict rotation plan. It can be simplified.

Crops fall into groups, and whatever you grow, you need to choose something from a different group to follow the next year. Some groups are better planted before or after others. The first of these are the **legumes** – peas and beans. These fix nitrogen in the soil, which will be enjoyed by something next from the **brassica** group: cabbages, broccoli, and some leafy-topped root vegetables including turnips. The more feathery-topped **roots** such as carrots and parsnips, which like poorer soil, usually follow these to give the soil the recommended minimum two-year break before the rotation starts again. You can add another year into the rotation, or substitute any of the above, with one of the following: onions; pumpkins, zucchini and squash; corn; potatoes; or salad greens. The last will thrive after peas and beans, enjoying the nitrogen they leave in the soil, if brassicas are of no interest. They can also be used as interplanting between rows of other crops, or as edging for beds. It's a good idea to sketch your plot in a notebook each year to jog your memory.

TELL ME WHY

HOW DO PEAS AND BEANS FIX NITROGEN?

These crops, together with other related leguminous plants such as clovers, develop small knobby nodules on their roots that enable them to convert nitrogen from the air into nitrates in the soil, in which form it can be used by subsequent plants. This is why you should always dig in the roots of peas and beans, rather than uprooting them with the spent topgrowth.

SEE ALSO: Preparing the Ground, pp.142–143; Clearing Weeds, pp.144–145; Additional Feeding, p.239; Manures and Mulches, p.239

NOURISHING YOUR CROPS

GOOD MANAGEMENT of the soil year after year is the key to productive plants. Different crops need different levels of nutrients such as nitrogen in the soil, so, depending on what you grow, you may need to add specific compounds as well as a general fertilizer. But if your soil does not have good texture, and you do not water when needed, fertilizer will be wasted: there must be air and moisture in soil for plant roots to absorb nutrients, and only well-textured soil holds both simultaneously. If growing crops in containers, fresh soil-based mix every year, with a slow-release general fertilizer, suits most crops – but check that, like tomatoes, they do not need a supplement.

GET TO KNOW YOUR SOIL

Rub soil between your fingers, and you will get to know its texture, whether light or heavy. Unless you are very lucky and have something between the two (the perfect loam) you must improve the texture for crops to do well. The secret is to bulk up the soil with spongy, fibrous organic matter derived from plants and animals. It will make heavy soil give up its water and nutrients more readily to plants, and make light soils hang on to them for longer. Never miss an opportunity to return organic matter to the soil in the vegetable plot – manure, mulches, leafmold, even spent soil mix (if the plants in it were healthy).

Sandy soil feels gritty and will not stick together

△ SANDY SOILS
Light, sandy soils are based on large mineral particles, between which water, and any nutrients dissolved in it, drains through much too quickly (think of a beach as the tide retreats). In estuarine areas, silky-feeling river silt may also be present, helping the soil hang on to moisture.

Clay soils form a more or less malleable ball that holds its shape when pressed

CLAY SOILS △
Clay soils feel sticky, heavy, and cold when wet, and glue together in clods; when these dry out, they become rock-hard. Earthworms are a great ally on clay; they burrow through the clods, threading them with organic matter that they leave in their wake and making them crumble.

SOIL ACIDITY AND ALKALINITY

Most vegetables prefer neutral to slightly acidic soil, measured by pH (*see below and right*). Brassicas are an exception; not only do they like alkaline soil, but it protects them from the disorder clubroot. But for other crops, you will need to neutralize an alkaline (chalky or limy) soil, best done by regularly adding lots of farmyard or stable manure, which is acidic. If you have quite an acidic soil, or even mildly acidic to neutral and want to grow brassicas, you should add lime (*see right*) for success.

TELL ME WHY

WHY IS pH IMPORTANT?

Soil pH affects the solubility of nutrients and hence their availability to plants. Alkaline soils may be deficient in manganese, boron, and phosphates; acidic soils often lack phosphates and may contain harmful levels of aluminum and manganese. Soil pH also influences the incidence of soil-borne pests and diseases; clubroot thrives on acidic soils, potato scab in alkaline ones.

ADDING LIME

For safety, choose a less harsh liming agent such as calcium carbonate over traditional slaked lime. As a gentle way of neutralizing slightly acidic soil, use spent mushroom compost as a mulch; as you will see, it contains crumbs of limy material. Lime soil as well in advance of planting as possible; never less than a month before. Avoid contact with plants. Never apply lime and manure at the same time; they react to let useful nitrogen escape as a gas. If both are needed, apply them in alternate years.

pH TESTING KITS ▷
Soil acidity or alkalinity is measured on the pH scale, which runs from 1 to14: below 7 is acidic, 7 is neutral, and above 7 is alkaline. A simple kit that allows you to test your soil: colors are matched against a chart that will give you a numerical reading.

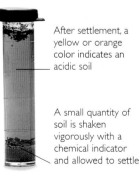

After settlement, a yellow or orange color indicates an acidic soil

A small quantity of soil is shaken vigorously with a chemical indicator and allowed to settle

A brilliant green solution indicates a neutral soil

Dark olive green solution indicates an alkaline soil

◁ LIMING THE SOIL
Choose a still day to apply lime, and wear protective gloves and goggles. Spread on the soil surface with a spade at the manufacturer's recommended rate. Rake, or fork in thoroughly. Do not overlime; you may induce nutrient deficiencies and affect plant growth.

SEE ALSO: Improving Soil Types, p. 142.

MANURE AND MULCHES

Manure is an ideal soil conditioner for the kitchen garden. While relatively low in nutrients (it is after all a waste product) it does wonders for the texture of the soil. There are two main ways of adding it.

The traditional way is to dig it in each autumn; spring is too late for many crops, which dislike or do badly on freshly manured soil. (Potatoes are an exception, and are a boon as a first crop if you have not been able to prepare a vegetable plot before the beginning of the season.) Then, in spring and early summer when the soil is warm and moist, apply an organic mulch – such as compost or leafmold – to the soil around crops to help keep down weeds, conserve soil moisture, and reduce soil temperature fluctuations. Do not use chipped wood or bark unless matured for two years, or it will deplete soil nitrogen. Mulch after watering well, when planting out or when seedlings are at least 2in (5cm) tall. Apply a layer 1–3 in (2.5–7.5cm) deep, avoiding the crowns of the plants.

If you use deep, no-dig beds, you need to dig manure in once, during the initial deep cultivation in autumn. In subsequent years, apply it as a surface mulch in spring; worms and other soil-dwelling organisms will incorporate it during the growing season. Whichever method you use, all manure must be well rotted – otherwise it will scorch your plants. Add at least two 2-gallon (9-liter) buckets for each square yard/meter of soil; unlike fertilizers, you can never apply too much.

△ **ADDING MANURE**
Well-rotted farmyard or stable manure added to the soil is enjoyed by all crops, both fruits and vegetables. When applying it as a mulch, take care not to smother young plants or to let it touch the stems of more mature ones.

ADDITIONAL FERTILIZING

Briefly, plants take three major elements from soil for growth: nitrogen (chemical symbol N) for leaves, phosphorus (P) for fruits and flowers, and potassium (K) for roots. Only the legumes, such as peas, ever put anything back (nitrogen), so the gardener needs to replenish the soil with fertilizers. NPK are not applied pure (nitrogen, for example, is a gas) but in compounds that are more practical to apply or that plants find easier to use, for example nitrates for nitrogen, phosphates for phosphorus, potash for potassium. A general fertilizer, applied in spring (at the recommended rate – more is not better, and can be harmful), will supply balanced amounts of NPK, but some crops need more of one – tomatoes, for example, need plenty of potassium to fruit well. Plants can also be given a boost in spring or early summer with a high-nitrogen fertilizer – no later unless it is a leafy crop, or the leaves will flourish instead of the edible parts. There are other elements needed in smaller quantities: calcium, magnesium, sulfur and, in tiny amounts, the trace elements: iron, manganese, molybdenum, boron. Good soil to which organic matter is regularly added usually contains enough of these. Any deficiency often shows up as specific symptoms (*see pp.296–309*); if you recognize them, you can use specific remedies: borax for boron, or chelated iron compounds.

TEMPORARY COVER

There will inevitably be gaps at times in the vegetable garden, but these are no bad thing, allowing soil to recover. You can also take the opportunity to improve soil, while stopping weeds from colonizing it. Either spread manure over it, then anchor down a sheet of plastic, and let the worms take it in; or, you can grow a living cover crop that will have the same effect. Green manures are increasingly available as seeds and are easy to use (*right*). Be sure to incorporate any green manure before it sets seed, or you may find yourself with a weed problem elsewhere in the garden.

FERTILIZER NUTRIENT CONTENT

While bulky organic fertilizers contain few nutrients weight for weight, they provide vital trace elements, aid good root growth by improving soil structure, and increase water- and nutrient-holding capacities of the soil. Nutrient release by concentrated or slow-release fertilizers is dependent on soil pH, warmth, and moisture.

	% Nitrogen	% Phosphorus	% Potassium
ORGANIC			
ANIMAL MANURE	0.6	0.1	0.5
COMPOST	0.5	0.3	0.8
BONE MEAL	3.5	20	-
FISH, BLOOD, AND BONE	3.5	8	-
HOOF AND HORN	13	-	-
SEAWEED MEAL	2.8	0.2	2.5
MUSHROOM COMPOST	0.7	0.3	0.3
ROCK POTASH	5	8	10
ROCK PHOSPHATE	-	26	12
WOOD ASH	0.1	0.3	1
COCOA SHELLS	3	1	3.2
INORGANIC			
COMMERCIAL (VARIES)			
AMMONIUM NITRATE	35	-	-
TRIPLE SUPERPHOSPHATE	-	42	-
POTASSIUM CHLORIDE	-	-	60
POTASSIUM SULFATE	-	-	49

Never forget: if the soil dries out, plants cannot absorb nutrients. They also respond badly to sporadic watering, making nutrients available in fits and starts. You must water generously and regularly whenever soil is drying out.

△ **USING MUSTARD AS A GREEN MANURE**
Broadcast seeds. A few weeks later, when seedlings are 6–8in (15–20cm) tall, chop them down with a spade and allow to wilt. Dig a series of shallow trenches, scrape green manure into the bottom of each, then refill with soil.

SEE ALSO: Preparing the Ground, pp.142–143; Applying Mulch, p.152; Sowing Annuals and Biennials, p.163

CROP PROTECTION

IF YOU ARE LUCKY enough to garden in a warm climate, crop protection will not be a high priority. Gardeners in colder climates, however, have developed a range of clever techniques to extend their growing season. These range from the totally controlled environment of a greenhouse, which can produce crops year-round with careful management, to improvised cloches for individual plant protection. Cloches and row cover provide a degree of protection from flying pests, both birds and insects; all are invaluable in extending the season by protecting crops directly from adversity or by modifying cold or wet soil conditions before sowing.

CLOCHES, TUNNELS, AND ROW COVER

Simple covers for the soil can extend the growing period at both ends of the growing season. They will warm the soil before sowing and help prevent it from becoming too wet to sow. They shelter fragile young plants in colder climates, aiding good establishment after planting out. Crops that do not need full, bright sun to ripen edible parts (most leafy or root vegetables) can be raised to maturity under row cover where certain pests are particularly troublesome, although when mature they may not need help, freeing up your covers for late-season salad crops.

GOOD IDEAS

• Store-bought cloches are attractive but expensive. Improvise tunnel cloches with row cover and hoops made from heavy-duty wire or reclaimed plastic pipes (e.g. cable ducting pipe). Remember to cover the ends against cold drafts.

• Recycle plastic bottles and use them as individual cloches. Two-liter or larger bottles are the best for this purpose.

• Plastic and glass cloches are impermeable to rainwater. To make watering easier, consider using them with seephose laid alongside plants (*see p.236*).

◁ **COVER TUNNEL**
This tunnel is simply made from wire or plastic hoops and a length of row cover that is pegged or pushed into the soil and tied at each end.

PLASTIC TUNNEL ▷
A corrugated plastic tunnel is held in place by a metal or plastic frame. Here it is open-ended for ventilation, but ends can be blocked off with glass sheets initially.

◁ **FLOATING COVER**
Move the bricks to allow a row cover to "float" up as plants grow; it also protects against flying pests. The fabric allows light and water through.

SINGLE CLOCHE ▷
Cut-off plastic bottles can protect small plants in the early stages of growth.

COLD FRAMES

Cold frames make a useful adjunct to a greenhouse. In small gardens they can function as mini-greenhouses, especially if fitted with soil-warming cables. They are useful for raising hardy seedlings or for hardening off seedlings started off in the greenhouse or on a windowsill. Whether they are fixed or portable, they must have removable or liftable lids for ventilation.

△ **FIXED COLD FRAME**
This fixed frame has sliding lights to permit ventilation; the main drawback of these is that they offer no protection from heavy rain when open. Hinged lights are wedged open for ventilation and still provide protection from rain.

△ **PORTABLE FRAME**
Portable frames have the advantage that they can be placed directly onto the soil in the vegetable plot. They give extra protection to vulnerable crops until established and the weather is warm enough to remove the frame.

SEE ALSO: Looking After the Garden, pp.274–287

GREENHOUSES

A well-managed greenhouse is the ultimate in plant protection. Unheated structures extend the growing period by up to two months; with protection and good light, seeds can be sown earlier. If fitted with a heating system, a greenhouse has potential for year-round cropping.

Site the greenhouse where it is sheltered, but not shaded by buildings or overhanging trees. Easy access to clean water is also essential.

In cool climates with short summers, tender vegetables are more reliably productive under glass. If you have a hard-surfaced floor, crops can be grown in containers and bags. This avoids the main disadvantage of soil borders, especially when growing the same crops year after year: the buildup of soil pests and excessive salt residues from fertilizers. If you need staging for raising seedlings early in the year, many low-growing crops can be grown in containers on top of it. Tall crops, like tomatoes and cucumbers, need more headroom; arrange staging to leave floor space for them.

INSIDE THE GREENHOUSE

An environment controlled to suit plant needs also suits pests and diseases, but enclosure does make them easier to control with biological controls or sprays .

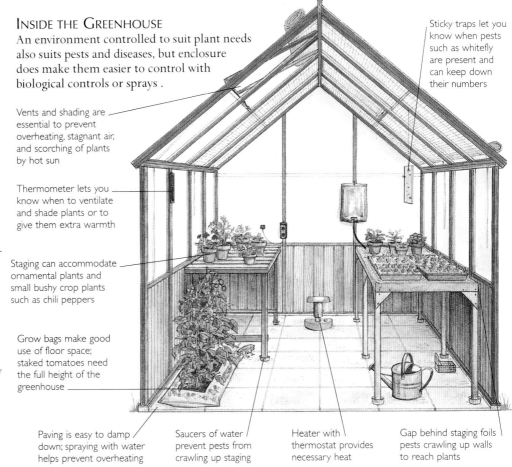

Vents and shading are essential to prevent overheating, stagnant air, and scorching of plants by hot sun

Thermometer lets you know when to ventilate and shade plants or to give them extra warmth

Staging can accommodate ornamental plants and small bushy crop plants such as chili peppers

Grow bags make good use of floor space; staked tomatoes need the full height of the greenhouse

Paving is easy to damp down; spraying with water helps prevent overheating

Saucers of water prevent pests from crawling up staging

Heater with thermostat provides necessary heat

Sticky traps let you know when pests such as whitefly are present and can keep down their numbers

Gap behind staging foils pests crawling up walls to reach plants

PROTECTING AGAINST PROBLEMS

Good garden practice, such as rotating crops and cleaning up debris, can prevent many problems in the vegetable garden, but do not underestimate the value of placing actual, physical barriers between pests and your plants. You must think strategically to erect them to best effect. Vigilance allows pests to be spotted before they do much damage and before they proliferate to epidemic proportions. Preemptive strikes involve calculating which pests are most likely to attack a crop (a wet summer makes some problems more likely than a dry one, for example) and taking preventive measures in the form of traps, barriers, and repellents (*see also p.294*). Organic gardeners often use companion plants that attract pest predators to defend crops.

If these approaches are combined with biological controls, especially effective in greenhouses, and the use of vegetable cultivars that resist specific pests and diseases, the need to use chemicals will be much reduced. If their use is unavoidable, try to spray late in the evening or choose a pest-specific product so that you will leave your allies, the pest predators, unharmed.

△ **PREVENTIVE MEASURES (CARROT RUST FLY)**
A fine-mesh netting screen, 2–3ft (60–90cm) high, makes an effective barrier against rust fly. Adults fly just above ground level; when they meet the barrier, they fly upward, miss the crop, and are carried away by wind.

POSSIBLE PROBLEMS

To read up on problems you may need to anticipate with individual crop plants, consult pp.294–311 on:
Beans: slugs; seedcorn maggot; root aphids; anthracnose; foot and root rots; halo blight; viruses
Beets: birds; cutworms; aphids; fungal leaf spots; boron deficiency
Brassicas: caterpillars; cabbage maggot
Carrots: carrot rust fly; aphids; boron deficiency
Cucumbers: viruses
Eggplant: aphids; caterpillars
Leeks: nematodes; onion maggot; rust; onion white rot
Lettuce: leaf and root aphids; cutworms; slugs; gray mold; mosaic virus; downy mildew; boron deficiency
Onions, shallots, garlic: onion maggot; seedcorn maggot; rots; mildew
Parsnips: celery leafminer (*see leafminers*); root aphids; carrot rust fly; parsnip canker; boron deficiency
Peas: birds; pea moth; pod and leaf spot; mice; pea thrips
Peppers: aphids; caterpillars
Potatoes: cutworm; potato cyst nematode; millipedes; slugs; potato blight; wireworms; scab
Pumpkins, squash, and zucchini: slugs; viruses
Spinach beet, Swiss chard: birds; fungal leaf spots; mildew
Sweet corn: mice; slugs; birds
Tomatoes: viruses; tomato blight; magnesium deficiency; blossom end rot; boron deficiency

Crops grown in the greenhouse may also be prone to: spider mite; mildews; gray mold; aphids; whitefly; mealybugs; thrips

SEE ALSO: Sowing Seeds in Containers, pp.244–245; Tender Crops, pp.256–257

SOWING AND PLANTING OUTDOORS

MOST CROPS THAT YOU CAN raise from seed outdoors are sown *in situ*, where they are to grow. You either trickle the seeds along rows, then thin the young plants, or, with large seeds such as peas and beans, space-sow one seed at every point that you want a plant. If you have germination failures, garden centers usually offer young plants with which to fill in gaps in spring, although there may not be much choice of varieties. Most seeds are sown in spring, not only after any frosts have passed but also after the soil has had time to warm up by a few degrees, and perhaps dry out a little; a row-cover blanket (*see p.240*) can help you get ahead.

BUYING VEGETABLE SEEDS

Because you harvest many vegetables before they flower, seed-saving is not an option, except with peas and beans. However, browsing through varieties in seed catalogs is one of the few jobs in gardening that can be done from a cozy armchair; moreover, when you buy seeds from a reputable source, either mail-order or from a garden center, you also gain the knowledge that they conform to required standards of cleanliness, viability, and purity and have been stored in the requisite cool, dry conditions at least up to point of sale (in garden centers, always check the sell-by date; seeds lose viability with age and if stored in hot conditions).

Always read the packet to check that the seed can be sown outdoors in your locality (*if not, see pp.240–241 for what your options may be*). Follow the instructions on the packet, and take particular note of timings and temperatures for first sowings: most failures in germination occur because seed is sown in ground that is still too cold.

THE RANGE OF SEEDS AVAILABLE

Untreated seeds are cheapest; choose these also if you garden organically and cannot get seed from an organic source. "Primed" seeds germinate quickly if you have missed sowing times; pelleted seeds are easy to handle; and dusted or coated seeds are useful if your seedlings often succumb to pest or disease problems.

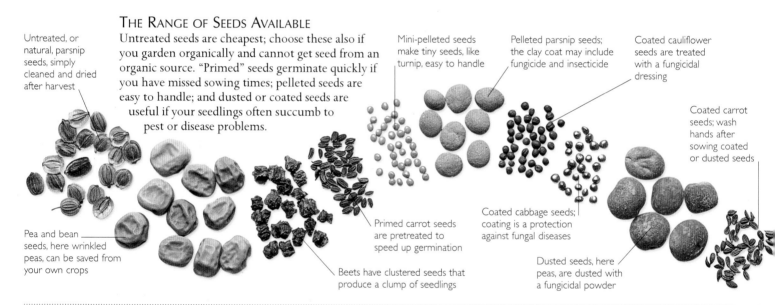

Untreated, or natural, parsnip seeds, simply cleaned and dried after harvest

Pea and bean seeds, here wrinkled peas, can be saved from your own crops

Primed carrot seeds are pretreated to speed up germination

Beets have clustered seeds that produce a clump of seedlings

Mini-pelleted seeds make tiny seeds, like turnip, easy to handle

Pelleted parsnip seeds; the clay coat may include fungicide and insecticide

Coated cauliflower seeds are treated with a fungicidal dressing

Coated carrot seeds; wash hands after sowing coated or dusted seeds

Coated cabbage seeds; coating is a protection against fungal diseases

Dusted seeds, here peas, are dusted with a fungicidal powder

PREPARING THE VEGETABLE PLOT

Seeds need fine, crumbly soil, holding both moisture and oxygen in order to help prepare the seed for germination. If you can, get your initial soil preparations – digging, manuring, and so forth – done in autumn, or at least by early winter. Then (in colder climates) the freeze–thaw action of any frosts will act to your advantage by cracking and breaking up clods still further.

In spring, in preparation for sowing, lightly fork over the soil and clear the plot of any weeds, especially perennial ones, that have germinated over winter; they are easily uprooted completely when still small. Apply a balanced fertilizer; if liming is necessary (*see p.238*), do it at least a month before sowing.

Just before sowing, choose a day when soil is neither excessively wet or bone dry, and rake down the soil to a fine tilth – a loose, crumbly, fine-grained surface. This allows seeds to be sown at a consistent depth. It also ensures that they make close contact with the soil and so can get the moisture needed for growth.

GOOD IDEAS

• Try the stale seedbed technique. Prepare the seedbed a couple of weeks in advance of sowing and allow a crop of weeds to grow. Then hoe off shallowly (or in dry weather, flame-weed), just before sowing. The shallow cultivations bring very few weed seeds up to the light, so vegetable seeds get a head start.

• If you have been using cloches or row cover to warm the soil, remember that they will also have kept off any rain. You may need to water in the seeds (*see opposite*) if the soil has become very dry.

SEE ALSO: Preparing the Ground, pp.142–143; Adding Lime, p.238; Crop Protection, p. 240; Sowing Seeds in Containers, p.244

SOWING IN DRILLS

Even when large seeds are going to be spaced individually, vegetable seeds are usually sown along drills (troughs) of various depths, either in their final site or in a seedbed for transplanting later. Seedbeds are used often for brassicas, which may need a year to grow: you can grow them quite closely when young in a small patch, then plant out when room becomes available after harvesting another crop. Sowing in drills works even if you want vegetables in blocks rather than rows: you just make the drills closer together. Then you can tell exactly what are emerging seedlings, and what are weeds.

In general, the smaller the seed, the shallower the drill should be. Seed packets will indicate the required depth. Where this is quoted as a range, for example, lettuces may be sown at ½–¾in (1–2cm), the shallower depth is used for heavier soils and the deeper for light soils.

Most vegetables are sown in narrow drills; use broad drills for crops like peas, where a broad, dense row is needed, or for early carrots and cut-and-come-again crops that are harvested before maturity; as you harvest some plants, you will create space in which the remainder can grow.

SOWING SEEDS IN A WIDE DRILL

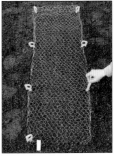

1 MARK OUT
Mark out parallel drills, 6–9in (15–23cm) wide, and to the required depth, using a string line and pegs. Pull a draw hoe steadily toward you; keep the blade at a level depth, applying light, even pressure.

2 SOW SEED
Space-sow large seed at the required spacings given for the individual crop, or trickle small seed, along the base of the drill. Do not sow too thickly, or seedlings will be crowded and may rot or fail to grow well.

3 COVER WITH SOIL
Taking care not to move or dislodge seeds, cover them with soil, either with a draw hoe, a rake, or by drawing soil gently over the seeds with your foot. Water in well using a can or hose fitted with a fine nozzle.

4 PROTECT SEEDS
Protect the seeds from birds or foraging animals such as mice, if necessary, by pegging wire netting down over the row. Remove the netting after germination and before the seedlings are tall enough to grow through the mesh.

SOWING SEEDS IN A NARROW DRILL (MOST VEGETABLE CROPS)

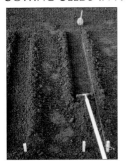

1 MARK OUT
Mark out the row with string line and pegs. Use the corner of a draw hoe or a trowel to draw out a small, even drill of the required depth for the individual seeds.

2 SOW SEED
Space-sow, or trickle seeds thinly and evenly along the bottom of the drill. Cover over with soil carefully to avoid dislodging the seed and water in thoroughly.

WET AND DRY SOIL

If sowing in wet soil is unavoidable, spread sand or vermiculite over the base of the drill before sowing. On deep beds, sow from surrounding paths; otherwise, use a board to protect soil from compaction. Water dry soils before you sow; press seeds lightly into the moist soil before covering.

△ **WET SOIL**
On heavy, slow-draining soils, sprinkle a layer of sand at the base of the drill before sowing. Stand on a board to avoid compaction.

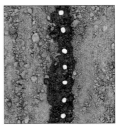

△ **DRY SOIL**
Water the soil in the base of the drill before sowing. Use clean, not rain, water. Sow the seeds and then cover with dry soil.

THINNING AND TRANSPLANTING

You must thin young seedlings to avoid overcrowding. Thin to final spacings in stages to allow for losses. At each stage, aim to leave each seedling just clear of its neighbor. Move crops started in seedbeds, such as leeks or brassicas, as young as possible so that they reestablish quickly.

◁ **THINNING**
When seeds have germinated, thin while still small by pinching them out at the base of the stem between finger and thumb. This avoids disturbing the roots of remaining seedlings.

◁ **TRANSPLANTING**
Lift seedlings gently with as much soil as possible around the roots. Transfer seedlings to a clean plastic bag to avoid moisture loss; carry in a seed tray to avoid damage.

REPLANTING ▷
Replant at required spacing with the lowest leaves just above soil level. Planting too high exposes the stalk, which may not support the weight of the mature vegetable.

Firm the soil in very carefully with a fingertip around the delicate young stalk

SEE ALSO: Protecting against Problems, p.241; Catalog of Vegetables, pp.246–257

SOWING SEEDS IN CONTAINERS

SEEDS NEED TO BE RAISED under cover in pots or trays if temperatures outside are too low for germination. You may want to get ahead with hardy vegetables, especially in a cold spring, or you may want to raise plants that need a longer growing season than your climate offers to germinate *and* grow to ripeness outside, as when growing tomatoes in cool regions. These seedlings would be transplanted outdoors, but you might also want to raise crops to grow in a greenhouse, such as peppers. Whether you have a heated greenhouse or a simple closed case, raising from seed gives you unlimited choice of varieties compared to the range usually on offer as young plants.

SOWING INDOORS OR UNDER GLASS

There is a wide range of containers that are used for sowing seeds under cover.
■ Pots and half-pots are adequate if only small numbers of seedlings are required, for expensive seeds that are sold in small quantities, and for single sowings of large seeds.
■ Trays and half-trays hold enough seedlings for the largest of plots; they are best for crops that tolerate transplanting.
■ Cell packs with individual pockets use less soil mix than trays or pots. Use them to sow directly or to prick out seedlings germinated in trays or pots. Cell-grown seedlings form a compact root ball that allows minimal disturbance on transplanting; it also allows root development to continue if conditions are unsuitable for planting out at the optimum time. Pelleted seeds can be sown singly in packs; others are sown 2–3 per cell and can be "singled," or thinned to the strongest seedling, later.

Once seedlings have germinated, keep them evenly moist but not wet. Place them in good light, but shade from bright sun that may scorch or kill them.

GOOD IDEAS

• When sowing in containers, you nearly always produce more seedlings than you need, leaving spares to swap with gardening friends. If you organize a vegetable swap group, all members can extend their crop range with minimal cost and effort.

• After germination, most seedlings must be kept at a slightly lower temperature in light, well-ventilated, protected conditions. While a kichen windowsill suits germinating seeds, it may get too warm and stuffy for growing seedlings: move them to a cooler room, such a a spare room.

SOWING IN TRAYS

1 PREPARE THE TRAY
Fill the tray with seed soil mix, mounding it up loosely above the rim. Tap the container to remove air pockets and level with a piece of wood. Firm gently so that the surface is about ½in (1cm) below the rim.

2 SOW SEED THINLY
Scatter seed thinly and evenly over the surface and just cover by finely sieving more mix over them. Water in with a nozzle or from below by standing in a tray of clean water until the surface glistens.

3 COVER THE TRAY
Allow soil mix to drain thoroughly and cover tray with a sheet of glass or plastic wrap, or place in a closed case. Remove cover on germination. Keep seedlings in good light; prick out when they have 3–4 leaves.

△ **BROADCAST SOWING IN POTS**
This method is ideal if small numbers of seedlings are needed, or for seeds that germinate erratically. Fill a pot with standard seed soil mix; tap firmly to remove air pockets and firm the surface gently. Scatter seeds thinly and evenly over the surface. Cover seeds to their own depth with finely sieved mix. Water, label and cover with glass, or place in a closed case.

△ **SOWING LARGE SEEDS**
Large seeds, like squash, pumpkins, and cucumbers, are best sown on their sides, one or two seeds to a 2–3½in (5–9cm) pot. On germination, the weaker of the two seedlings will be pinched out. Fill the pot with standard seed soil mix to within 1in (2.5cm) of the rim. Push in the seeds, then cover with about ¾in (2cm) of seed soil mix. Water in, label, and place in a warm spot.

SEE ALSO: Nourishing your Crops, pp.238–239; Greenhouses, p.241

PRICKING OUT

When seedlings have developed their first leaves, they must be "pricked out" to avoid the congestion that leads to damping off (*see p.300*) and weak, leggy growth. Do this as soon as possible; if roots develop sufficiently to become entwined, seedlings are difficult to prick out without damage.

PRICKING OUT SEEDLINGS

1 LIFTING SEEDLINGS
Tap the tray on a hard surface to loosen soil mix. Handle seedlings only by their seed leaves; stems are very vulnerable to damage. Lift individual seedlings with a tool or finger, keeping plenty of soil mix around the roots.

2 TRANSPLANTING SEEDLINGS
Plant seedlings in a tray filled with standard potting mix, or, as here, cells. Make holes in the mix and place one seedling in each cell. Push mix very gently up against the stem; do not press hard.

HARDENING OFF

Vegetable plants that are sown in a warm, protected environment must be hardened off gradually before planting outdoors, or the sharp drop in temperature and humidity will shock them. Ideally, transfer them to a cold frame, gradually opening the lid more over a period of about 7–10 days. Check the weather forecast and, if frost threatens, close the frame and cover with insulation temporarily. Alternatively, place them in a sheltered spot outdoors for increasingly longer periods each day.

TRANSPLANTING POT SOWINGS OUTSIDE

When the roots almost fill the pots, plants are ready for hardening off and transplanting. Before setting pot- or cell-grown plants outdoors, water them thoroughly and set aside to drain. Each plant should then slide easily out of its pot with an entire root ball.

◁ **PLANTING OUT**
Dig a hole with a trowel, large enough for the plant to be set a little deeper than it was in the pot. This ensures that the root ball does not dry out. Firm in and water well.

SOWING IN CELL PACKS

Sowing in cell packs produces high-quality plants that grow well, since they can be planted out with little or no disturbance to the root ball. Seeds can be sown directly into cells, or seedlings can be pricked out into them. If sowing, sow 2–3 seeds in each cell and then thin to the strongest seedling after germination. Alternatively, use the multiblock sowing technique (*see below*).

RAISING SEEDLINGS IN CELL PACKS

1 SOWING SEED
Fill the cells with seed soil mix and make a hole, ¼in (5mm) deep, in each cell. Sow one or two seeds per cell. Cover with sieved mix, label with the variety name and date, and water in with a fine nozzle.

2 PLANTING OUT
Remove each seedling from its cell by pushing the bottom of the cell with your finger. Make a hole to take the root ball. Place the plant in the hole with lowest leaves just above the soil surface. Water in well.

MULTIBLOCK SOWINGS

This method of sowing is useful for leeks, onions, turnips, and beets – with root crops, it is ideal for growing tasty "baby" vegetables. Fill a cell pack with moist soil mix. Sow 3–5 seeds in each cell, cover to their own depth with soil mix, label, and water in. Put the tray in a warm, dry place; seedlings should germinate in 5–7 days.

◁ **PLANTING OUT**
After germination, harden off. When two true leaves have formed, plant out at appropriate spacings.

HARVESTING ▷
Unthinned seedlings grow on to form clusters of small vegetables, here yielding a harvest of baby turnips.

SEE ALSO: Crop Protection, p.240

PEAS AND BEANS

VEGETABLES IN THIS GROUP, often referred to as legumes, are grown for their seedpods. Some are cooked and eaten whole, while others are grown for the seeds that are eaten cooked or raw. Most freeze well, and the seeds of some, such as black-eyed peas, can be shelled and dried. Podded vegetables can be decorative as well as tasty; most have attractive blooms (scarlet runner beans are the perfect cottage garden plant), and climbing types can be trained on tepees or used as screens in the kitchen garden. Remember that most peas and beans leave soil rich in nitrogen, ideal for a brassica crop to follow. After harvest, dig plants into the soil, or lift and compost them.

GREEN BEANS

Green beans are sown from midspring to summer and harvested in summer to early autumn. You can expect about 8lb (4kg) of pods from a 10ft (3m) row, or a sq yd (square meter) block. You can sow seeds outdoors from midspring, buy young plants, or raise your own. There are both dwarf (bushy) and climbing varieties, with pods ranging from pencil-thick to the very fine "filet" types. Pods may be green, green flecked purple, red, purple, or yellow – yellow, wax-pod types have a waxy texture and fine flavor. The unusual-colored beans look striking in the garden; the purple kinds turn green on cooking. Some varieties are especially good for growing for the seeds, not the pods; they are shelled either when immature, for cooking and eating right away (when they are called flageolets), or for drying (such as navy beans).

SITE AND SOIL No special preparations needed; erect supports (*see opposite*) before sowing or planting if growing climbers.

△ **HILLING UP**
Green beans are planted shallowly, so to prevent them from becoming topheavy once they have developed a few leaves, it is a good idea to gently draw a little more soil up around their stems for extra support. Use a draw hoe to draw soil up around the stems almost to the depth of the lowest leaves. This will improve root anchorage.

They grow well in containers in a soil-based mix, but you must water regularly and often.

SOWING AND PLANTING Never sow or plant outdoors until frosts are over. Sow 1½in (4cm) deep, *in situ* or individually in 3in (8cm) pots under glass, hardening off before planting out. Sow every 3 weeks until midsummer for successional crops.

■ The seeds will not germinate at low temperatures, so in a cold spring, either prewarm the soil with cloches or plastic before sowing, or raise seedlings under cover; they need 54°F (12°C) for germination, if using a closed case.

■ You should see seedlings within 2 weeks. If the weather turns cold, cover the soil or young plants with row cover or a cloche.

SPACING Sow or plant dwarf types in staggered rows 9in (23cm) apart each way. Pole beans can grow 10ft (3m) or more tall. Grow in double rows, 2ft (60cm) apart, or on tepees, 6in (15cm) apart.

ROUTINE CARE Hill up the stems of young plants for extra support (*see left*). Mulch well and never allow plants to dry out completely. If conditions are dry during flowering, water very generously, or the flowers will drop off before setting the pods.

HARVESTING Harvest after 7–13 weeks. Pick pods frequently while young and succulent and cook them fresh, or blanch and freeze. If you really cannot cope with a glut, just stop picking; they will stop making new pods while old ones are on the plant. To harvest dry beans, pull up plants when the beans have swelled in the pods, then hang upside down by the roots in a dry frost-free place. Shell beans when dry and store in airtight jars.

GREEN-PODDED
BEANS

PURPLE-PODDED
BEANS

YELLOW-PODDED
BEANS

SEE ALSO: Rotating Crops, p. 237; Sowing in Containers, p. 245; Transplanting Pot Sowings Outside, p. 245; Hoes, p.278

RUNNER BEANS

Runner beans are sown in midspring and harvested from midsummer. Young plants may be available. They may be climbers, about 10ft (3m) tall, or dwarf, bushy plants, about 15in (38cm) tall. You can expect 2lbs (1kg) of pods per plant. They are pretty plants, with pink, red, white, or bicolored flowers; you can grow sweet peas among them for even more decorative appeal. Except in stringless varieties, "strings" along the sides of the pods must be removed before cooking.

SITE AND SOIL Erect supports for climbers before sowing or planting. Runner beans grow best in especially moisture-retentive soil. Make a trench along the row or around a tepee, about a spade's-depth deep, and and fork lots of well-rotted compost into the base for best results: a layer of shredded, soaked newspaper is a traditional alternative. Runner beans grow well in containers in a soil-based mix, but you must water regularly and often.

SOWING AND PLANTING As for green beans, but sow 2in (5cm) deep.

SPACING Sow or plant 6in (15cm) apart.
ROUTINE CARE Mulch the young plants. If conditions are dry as flower buds form (they do so over quite a long period), water generously twice a week. Watch for aphids (*see black bean aphid, p.306*).
HARVESTING Usually ready for picking 13–17 weeks after planting. Pick pods when tender, before the seeds start to swell. Use fresh, or blanch and freeze.

BEAN SUPPORTS

There are several ways to support climbing beans, depending on space. Plants may also be grown on a frame up strings or wire pegged into the ground. Do not use plastic-coated netting, since plants cannot cling to it.

RUNNER BEANS

△ **BEAUTIFUL BEANS**
At maturity, climbing beans disguise their support completely. For more ornamental effects, try combining beans with flowering sweet peas.

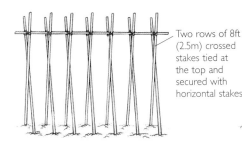

8ft (2.5m) stakes are tied at the top or secured with a commercial plastic tepee support

Two rows of 8ft (2.5m) crossed stakes tied at the top and secured with horizontal stakes

4in (10cm) nylon net stretched on a softwood or recycled wooden pole frame

CROSSED STAKE ROW   **STAKE TEPEE**   **NETTING SUPPORT**

PEAS

Peas are hardier than beans and easier to raise from seed in cool climates. They do not cope with hot summers quite so well. You can start sowing hardy, early peas in late winter (in mild areas, you can even sow in autumn), continuing into spring to harvest from late spring through the summer. There is no need to raise plants under cover. Peas range from 18in (45cm) to over 6ft (2m) tall, and all benefit from the support of twiggy branches known as peasticks. Expect 10lbs (5kg) from a 10ft (3m) row, or a sq. yd (square meter) block.

Shelling peas, including tiny, sweet *petits pois*, are grown for fresh peas extracted from the pod. Snow peas are eaten young, when still flat-podded; round-podded sugar peas are used semi-mature. All can be eaten cooked or raw.

SITE AND SOIL No special preparations. Do not insert peasticks until the plants grow.
SOWING AND PLANTING Sow seeds 1¼in (3cm) deep; 2–3in (5–8cm) apart in blocks,

or, for rows, 2in (5cm) apart in 9in (23cm) wide drills, 24–36in (60–90cm) apart.
■ Early and late sowings are less likely to be affected by pea moth (*see p.306*).
■ Make early spring sowings under a cloche or row cover to speed up germination; if firmly anchored, this should also keep birds and mice from taking the sown peas.
■ For successional crops, sow at 14-day intervals (avoid midsummer in warm areas), or sow early and later-maturing maincrop varieties at the same time.
ROUTINE CARE Cover sowings in open ground with netting to protect from birds. Remove it and erect supports (*see right*) when tendrils develop. Mulch when several leaves have formed to keep roots cool. If the weather is dry during flowering and as pods form, water generously once or twice a week.
HARVESTING Harvest early peas after 11–12 weeks; maincrops after 13–14 weeks. Use fresh, or freeze.

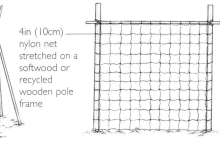

PEAS

SNOW PEAS

SUPPORTING PEAS ▷
When young plants have developed tendrils, push peasticks into the ground as nearly upright as possible, along the outside of the block or row. As peas grow, tendrils wrap around the twigs and draw plants up through them.

SEE ALSO: Crop Protection, p. 240; Sowing Seeds in a Wide Drill, p. 243

BRASSICAS

WITH CAREFUL SELECTION of cultivars that crop at different times, and by including those that store well, the cabbage family (brassicas) can supply you with greens all year round. You might think that they are not particularly inspiring to look at, but crinkled Savoy cabbages and colorful kales take on a beauty of their own when dew-soaked and sparkling. These leafy crops need plenty of nitrogen; plant them after peas and beans if possible, and choose a high-nitrogen rather than a general fertilizer. Most are slow-growing and can be intercropped with greens or, if you want to keep all your brassicas together, turnips and radishes, which also belong in this group.

BROCCOLI AND SPROUTING BROCCOLI

To grow the substantial flowerbud heads sold in the supermarket as broccoli, you need to select varieties carefully; seeds or young plants that you buy labeled "broccoli" may actually be of the much hardier sprouting broccoli, where the leafy shoot tops and small bud clusters are eaten. Broccoli grows fast and is sown in spring for summer eating. Sprouting broccoli grows slowly and is overwintered, to eat from late winter through spring. Like all brassicas, they need a minimum soil pH of 6; add lime (*see p.238*) if needed. Do not grow them on newly manured ground; instead, dress soil before sowing or planting with a high-nitrogen fertilizer.

SOWING AND PLANTING Broccoli may be set back if transplanted; sow it *in situ* in succession from spring to early summer, 2–3 seeds together every 6in (15cm), in rows 12in (30cm) apart, and thin to the strongest seedling. Sow in spring in a seedbed or in cell packs in a cold frame; plant out from early to midsummer, 2ft (60cm) apart each way. Plant them deeply and water well until established.

ROUTINE CARE Grow the first sowings of broccoli under row cover for the earliest, most succulent crops; this will also protect against pests. Do not let plants dry out; water generously as the flowerheads are forming. Broccoli is vulnerable to winter wind damage, so hill up stems and stake tall plants in autumn.

HARVESTING The first and largest flowerheads of broccoli will be ready to cut after 11–12 weeks; if you then feed with a high-nitrogen fertilizer, a second crop of smaller sideshoots will develop. Wash heads well; creepy-crawlies often lurk in the creases. Harvest sprouting broccoli from late winter onward; pick shoots regularly to encourage more.

SPROUTING BROCCOLI

BROCCOLI

KALE

Kale is an easy brassica to grow and also makes a handsome foliage plant: the leaves of different varieties may be blue-green, red, or almost black, and flat (broadleaved) or very curly. It needs the same soil preparation, conditions, and care as broccoli and is a better bet than cabbages for newer kitchen gardens where the soil has not built up very high fertility. It is also less susceptible to clubroot. A very hardy plant, it will crop year-round in favorable regions or during unusually mild winters. Sow in early spring for a cut-and-come again summer crop, and late spring for autumn and winter leaves; you can also eat the flower shoots that develop in spring, rather like sprouting broccoli.

SOWING AND PLANTING For summer crops of young leaves, make spring sowings *in situ*, in rows 6in (15cm) apart. Harvest young plants to thin them out. Sow crops for autumn and winter in a seedbed or in a cold frame, to plant out in midsummer, about 8 weeks later, 30in (75cm) apart each way. Keep as much soil as you can around the roots of young plants as you transplant; cell packs are ideal — they minimize root disturbance. Water them well until established.

HARVESTING Spring-sown crops will be ready after about 7 weeks. If you do not harvest regularly, the leaves tend to coarsen and become less palatable. Pick leaves of autumn and winter crops as needed. The broadleaved varieties are the best to grow for flowering shoots in spring; snap them off when about 4in (10cm) long.

CURLY KALE

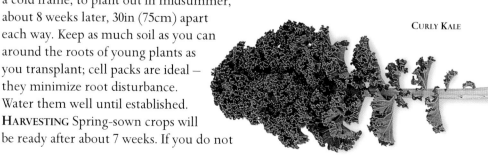

SEE ALSO: Adding Lime, p.238; Fertilizer Nutrient Content, p.239

CABBAGES

Cabbages are vulnerable to a daunting
selection of problems (*see p.306–308*),
which makes it all the more satisfying to
nurture a crop to maturity, the reward
being crops in late winter and early spring,
just when you feel you need the
restorative powers of fresh greens. The
winter and spring cabbages make the best
use of space; although there are varieties
for summer eating, they take up space
you could give to fast-maturing salad
plants. The tight-headed white storing
cabbages are so cheap and ubiquitous in
stores as to be hardly worth growing, but
red cabbage may not always so readily
available. This must be cut by midwinter
(they keep in a cool place) but winter
cabbages, such as Savoy and January King,
and all the spring cabbages are very hardy.
SITE AND SOIL Cabbages need the same soil
conditions and preparation as broccoli (*see
opposite*), but, with spring cabbages, do not
dress the soil with fertilizer before

◁ **COLLARING SEEDLINGS**
*Adult cabbage maggots lay
eggs at the base of the stem.
Placing a brassica collar flat
on the soil around the base
of each seedling helps
prevent this.*

planting; instead, apply it in spring as the
plants start to grow again.
SOWING AND PLANTING Sow in seedbeds or
in cell packs in a cold frame, and
transplant into slightly deeper holes 5–6
weeks later, to 10–12in (25–30cm) apart.
Sow winter cabbage in late spring, and
spring cabbages in late summer; sow
autumn varieties of red cabbage in mid- to
late spring. Growing young plants under a
row cover or collaring them (*above*) should
protect them from cabbage maggot. Water
well until established, and in dry spells.
ROUTINE CARE Keep a very watchful eye
out for potential problems. Hill up
cabbages for stability in winter winds.

RED CABBAGE

SAVOY CABBAGE

TURNIPS

Turnips will grow in light shade, so they
can be grown between leafy crops. Summer
varieties, including the Japanese types, are
sown in spring; they are ready to eat after
about 6 weeks. Other, slower-growing
varieties are sown in summer for eating in
autumn and winter. Sow summer turnips
from midspring at three-week intervals, in
rows 9in (23cm) apart. Thin to 4in (10cm)
apart. They are less hardy than winter
turnips, so early sowings may benefit from
a covering in cold springs; this will also
protect against flea beetles, most
destructive to seedlings in midspring.
Harvest when the roots are the size of a
golfball. Sow turnips for autumn and
winter in mid- to late summer, in rows
12in (30cm) apart. Thin to 6in (15cm)
apart. Maturing in autumn, they
can stay in the soil to be used
when needed until midwinter,
when you should lift and store
them all – or you can leave them
in over winter; although the roots
will become inedible, you can cut the
tops in spring for an early crop of greens.

WHITE TURNIP

RED-TOPPED TURNIP

SUMMER RADISHES

Summer or salad radishes are the simplest
of crops; they take only 3–4 weeks to
grow and are rarely in the soil long
enough for problems to develop, though
you do need to protect against cabbage
maggots; collars are obviously impractical,
but a row cover works well; you can if
necessary keep the cover on until the
radishes are ready, useful if flea beetles are
damaging seedlings. Sow as the soil is
workable in spring, then at 15-day
intervals. Sow ½in (1cm) deep; thin to 1in
(2.5cm). Make rows 6in (15cm) apart, or
tuck them between other, slower-
growing plants. Water well each week, if
conditions are dry.

SUMMER RADISHES

SEE ALSO: Sowing in Narrow Drills, p. 241; Thinning & Transplanting, p. 241; Sowing in Cell Packs, p. 243.

ONIONS AND ROOT VEGETABLES

BOTH OF THESE CROP GROUPS do best in light, well-drained soil. Stony ground is not suitable for them, since the roots will fork or bulbs distort where they meet stones; if you have stony soil, stick to scallions and stubby or round carrot varieties. Many of these earthy stalwarts look good. The feathery foliage of carrots makes charming edging for a bed. Blue-green leeks planted with ruby chard (*see p.255*) is a stunning combination worthy of any border, and a few leeks allowed to flower will rival many an ornamental allium. Because onions need vertical space only, you can interplant them pleasingly with red loose-leaf lettuces or cut-and-come-again salad greens.

ONIONS

Ordinary onions are not especially economical to grow, but unusual types and shallots are well worth giving space to. It is much easier to raise them from sets (small bulbs) than from seed. Onions store well if well ripened and dry.
PREPARATION Do not grow on freshly manured soil. Apply a dressing of balanced fertilizer before planting.
PLANTING Plant onion sets in early spring 4–6in (10–15cm) apart, depending on the size of bulbs you want, in furrows 6–12in (15–30cm) apart, with the tips just above the soil. They may need protecting from birds. Shallot sets can be planted earlier, from midwinter in areas with mild winters. Space them 7in (18cm) apart each way as they form a cluster of bulbs.
ROUTINE CARE Keep weed-free, especially when young. Water only in very dry spells. Watch for onion maggot and rot (*see pp.306–307*).
HARVESTING Choose a dry spell, if possible, in late summer to harvest. Onions must be completely dry before storing, or they

SHALLOT

RED-SKINNED ONION

Thick, or "bull-necked," onions rot readily, so use them first

◁ **STORING ONIONS**
If you cannot dry off pulled onions outdoors, either because of the weather or lack of space, place them carefully in slatted boxes, no more than two layers deep, and keep in a dry, cool, airy place.

will rot or start into growth, so lay them out on dry ground or if necessary under cover (*see above*) for 10–14 days after pulling, with the leaves intact. Either trim the leaves and store the bulbs in nets or slatted boxes, or leave on for stringing.

SCALLIONS

Scallions take 8 weeks or less to mature and are a good choice for intercropping between rows of slower-maturing plants while these are young – including bulb onions. If you sow at intervals from early spring to midsummer, you will have supplies from early summer right through the autumn. For a winter scallion, sow some Welsh onions in spring or summer; they will not be ready until the autumn but they are evergreen and very hardy; you can harvest leaves into winter. Sow both *in situ*, scallions in rows 4in (10cm) apart, or in bands 3in (8cm) wide, 6in (15cm) apart. Sow Welsh onions in rows 12in (30cm) apart and thin to 9in (23cm). They need the same conditions and care as onions.

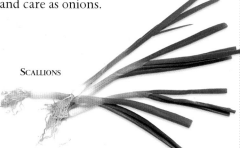

SCALLIONS

GARLIC

Although store-bought garlic makes a cheerful crop for children to grow, for good kitchen supplies you need to buy specially prepared, virus-free cloves from an established nursery or seed firm. They need the same conditions and care as onions and are vulnerable to the same problems. Plant individual cloves in mid-spring – or, if you have light, well-drained soil you can plant in autumn. Place cloves upright at twice their own depth, about 7in (18cm) apart each way. Bulbs for eating fresh should be ready by mid-summer; leave bulbs for storing to swell and ripen until the end of the season. Uproot as the leaves fade, and dry as for onions.

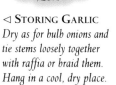

GARLIC

◁ **STORING GARLIC**
Dry as for bulb onions and tie stems loosely together with raffia or braid them. Hang in a cool, dry place.

△ **GARLIC IN CELL PACKS**
To give garlic the longest growing season to ripen, plant in autumn; if your soil is too cold and heavy, you can start the cloves off in cell packs, one clove per cell, in a cold frame. Plant out in spring when they have started to sprout.

SEE ALSO: Adding Lime, p.238; Fertilizer Nutrient Content, p.239; Additional Fertilizing, p.239

LEEKS

Although they can be sown outdoors in any climate, to ensure white stems leeks must be transplanted so that you can set the young plants in much deeper holes. Sow in a seedbed or cold frame or, if space is limited, buy in young plants; set them out in early summer and harvest from early autumn onward; they can stand in the soil through winter to spring. Unlike onions, leeks enjoy ground manured the previous autumn, with a nitrogen-rich fertilizer added before planting.

SOWING AND PLANTING Sow between late winter and spring, ½in (1cm) deep, and transplant when 8in (20cm) tall, spacing them 4–9in (10–23cm) apart.

ROUTINE CARE Keep well watered until established and weed-free at all times. Leeks need no additional water unless dry conditions are prolonged.

LEEKS

△ **TRANSPLANTING**
For white stems, transplant leeks into holes 6–8in (15–20cm) deep, 4–6in (10–15cm) apart. Trim very long leaves. Fill the hole with water so that soil will collect around stems.

△ **TRANSPLANTING CELL-PACK SOWINGS**
Raising leeks in cell packs, with up to 4 seeds per cell, is a simple and convenient technique. When seedlings have 3 leaves, each cell can be planted out in its entirety; thin by pulling baby leeks to give the remainder space to grow.

PARSNIPS

The stumpier varieties of parsnip are best if your soil is the least bit stony. Parsnip canker may be a problem in some areas, so look also for resistant varieties, and lime very acidic soils (*see p.238*), which increase risk of canker. They are sown outside as early as possible, as they have a long growing season, and are ready to lift in autumn; however, except in very harsh winters, you can leave them in for longer, lifting as needed. Frost improves the taste.

SOWING AND PLANTING Parsnip seed loses viability quickly, so always use fresh seed. Sow as soon as the soil is workable in early spring. Prewarming soil with row cover or cloches improves germination, which is notoriously slow. Sow ¾in (2cm) deep, in rows 12in (30cm) apart; thin seedlings to 4–6in (10–15cm) apart.

ROUTINE CARE Keep weed-free, especially when seedlings are growing, and water weekly in dry spells. Do not allow soil to dry out; parsnips tend to split if watered after a prolonged dry spell. Watch for signs of attack by root aphids (*p.309*).

PARSNIP

BEETS

Baby beets are ready 7–8 weeks after sowing outside, or you can leave them to grow larger, even through winter; though the roots become inedible, the leafy tops can be used as winter greens. Beets enjoy the same conditions, soil preparation, and care as carrots; in addition, dress the soil with a nitrogen-rich fertilizer, once before sowing and again in growth.

SOWING AND PLANTING Sow at intervals once the soil reaches 45°F (7°C), either naturally or warmed with a cover. Choose bolt-resistant types for early sowing. Most "seeds" are clusters of 2–3, easy to handle: sow one every 3–4in (8–10cm) and wait to reduce each cluster to one until you can eat the thinnings as baby beets. "Monogerm" seeds make only one plant. Soak seed in warm water for 30 minutes before sowing, ¾in (2cm) deep, in rows 12in (30cm) apart.

△ **HARVESTING BEETS**
Grip the stems firmly and pull gently; the root should lift easily because beets are shallow-rooted. Twist off the leaves and cook the roots with the stalks still attached; the color will bleed from any wound to the root.

CARROTS

Some varieties of carrot are best for eating very young; others improve in flavor as they grow larger, so grow a mixture of these "earlies" and "maincrops." They take about 2 and 3 months respectively before ready to eat, so if you make successional sowings, you can have fresh carrots for several months. Earlies freeze well if blanched. You should lift the last of the maincrops before frost; they will keep in boxes of damp sand in a cool room.

SOWING AND PLANTING Rake soil to a fine tilth and remove any stones. Start to sow earlies *in situ* when the soil reaches 45°F (7°C). Make earlier sowings under row cover or a cloche. Sow maincrops from late spring to early summer. Sow in drills, ½–¾in (1–2cm) deep, in rows 6in (15cm) apart. Try to sow thinly, to minimize thinning, which releases odors that attract carrot rust fly. Thin earlies to 3in (8cm) apart; maincrops to at least 1½in (4cm).

ROUTINE CARE Keep weed-free and water weekly in dry spells. Take precautions against carrot rust fly (*see p.309*) and watch for damage by root and leaf aphids.

CARROTS

SEE ALSO: Sowing Seeds in a Narrow Drill, p.243; Thinning and Transplanting, p.243; Sowing in Cell Packs, p.245

CROPS FOR BLOCK PLANTING

IF YOU ARE USING small beds, you can easily devote an entire block to any of the crops described here. In warm regions, corn and squash are often grown together, the corn shading the squash from scorch, but in cooler areas squash fruits need all the sun they can get. While potatoes are not an attractive crop, rustling, ripening cornstalks are beautiful. Squash plants may look attractive enough to grow with ornamental plants, but their smothering habit and the amount of water they need may not suit companions. They can be trained as climbers, provided that you support fruits individually: letting them trail over sunny banks also looks spectacular.

POTATOES

While there are potato diseases that can, literally, blight a crop (see p.309), these are rare, and usually they are one of the most satisfying crops for the new kitchen gardener. If space is limited, remember that even organic maincrop or "old" potatoes are cheap; concentrate on early varieties ("new" potatoes) or waxy salad potatoes. If, conversely, you have more space than you can manage, maincrops are a useful filler, and growing and harvesting will improve the soil as you turn and manure it, and lift the crop. Potatoes like deep soil rich in organic matter and newly dressed with manure. If your soil is thin, consider the no-dig method (p.237), or you can grow a small crop of new potatoes in a barrel or even a plastic bag.

SOWING AND PLANTING In late winter, you will see potatoes on sale at garden centers: you must use these "seed" potatoes rather than store-bought ones; they are specially produced to make productive, disease-free plants. "Chit" them about 6 weeks before planting (above right). Plant (see above, far right)

FIRST EARLY POTATO

MAINCROP POTATO

Cool, light conditions result in plump, green shoots

△ CHITTING SEED POTATOES
To sprout (chit) seed potatoes, set in a single layer in a box or tray (egg boxes are ideal) with the end of the potato bearing the most eyes upward. Store in a well-lit, airy, frost-free place until sprouts have grown to about ⅜in (2cm) in length. This may take about 6 weeks.

when there is no risk of heavy frost; if the spring is cool, warm the soil with row cover before and after planting. A half-barrel-sized tub or feed sack on end will take three potatoes. Plant with the container half-full of soil mix, then add more to "hill up."

ROUTINE CARE If shoots emerge before risk of frost is over, cover with row cover. Once the foliage is growing well, apply a high-nitrogen fertilizer or liquid feed, and hill up the plants (see right). In dry conditions, water earlies generously every 10–12 days. Delay watering maincrops until tubers are at least marble-sized, then water really generously once. Watch for signs of blight (see p.309), which needs acting on quickly. If plants stop growing, uncover one to check for pests or other problems underground (see pp.308–311).

HARVESTING You can start lifting new potatoes when flowers open. Maincrops should be ready by summer's end, but you can leave them in, lifting as you need them, until midautumn, when you should harvest and store them (see right).

◁ PLANTING POTATOES
Make a drill 3–6in (8–15cm) deep. Place seed potatoes in the bottom, sprouts upward. Cover them carefully with soil. Plant earlies 12in (30cm) apart, with rows 2ft (60cm) apart; maincrops 15in (38cm) apart in rows 2ft 6in (75cm) apart.

△ HILLING UP
When stems are about 9in (23cm) high (or if frost threatens), hill up soil around them with a draw hoe. Hilling up ensures that the potatoes do not grow too near the surface, where light turns them green and unsafe to eat.

△ HARVESTING
In midautumn, cut stem and leaves (the haulm) of maincrop potatoes with a sharp knife, 2in (5cm) above ground. Leave the crop in the ground for two weeks longer before lifting.

△ LIFTING & STORING
Lift potatoes with a fork, digging from the side of the ridge. Allow to dry for a few hours. Store blemish-free potatoes in a light-proof bag; use damaged ones immediately.

SEE ALSO: "No-dig" Potatoes, p.237; Additional Fertilizing, p.239

PUMPKINS AND SQUASH

All of these need similar growing conditions: a warm, sunny site in fertile, well-drained soil that is rich in organic matter and moisture-retentive. Zucchini, ready to eat about 8 weeks after planting, and other summer squash are thin-skinned and need picking and eating a few days after flowering. Zucchini flowers are also edible. Winter squash, a category that includes pumpkins, store well, provided that they have a long, warm growing season to ripen (up to 5 months for pumpkins). Most varieties are sprawling in habit and can be grown upward over sturdy supports; generally, the neatest are zucchini and other summer squash.

SOWING AND PLANTING Sow seeds on edge, 1in (2.5cm) deep (*see p.244*) either *in situ* when risk of frost is over, or under glass in 3in (8cm) pots, at 59–64°F (15–18°C). Set out bush types 3ft (90cm) apart each way and trailing types 4–6ft (1.2–2m) apart.

ROUTINE CARE In cool areas, protect young plants with a cloche or row cover. Mulch after planting. Keep well watered, but do not wet flowers or fruits; seephose is ideal. Apply a tomato fertilizer every two weeks from midsummer on. Watch out for vine borer and wilt.

ZUCCHINI FLOWERS

GREEN ZUCCHINI

YELLOW ZUCCHINI

PUMPKIN

WINTER SQUASH 'Butternut'

SUMMER SQUASH 'Custard White'

GOOD IDEAS

• Use squares of pea and bean netting to make "hammocks" for fruits on plants that are trained up or over supports.

• To store pumpkins, "cure" them first to harden the skins: leave in a dry sunny place for 10 days, or keep at 86°F (30°C) for 4 days.

△ **HARVESTING ZUCCHINI**
For the best flavor, zucchini are best cut when young, succulent, and up to about 4in (10cm) long. Handle fruits carefully to avoid bruising, and cut them away with a sharp knife, leaving about ½in (1cm) of stalk at the top of the fruit. Pick regularly to keep plants productive.

SWEET CORN

In regions with long, warm summers, sweet corn is sown and ripened outdoors with ease, but in cool climates it needs a head start by raising under cover, then planting out and hoping for a good long summer to ripen all the ears. It cannot be grown in a greenhouse. You must grow it in blocks, rather than rows, so that it can be pollinated well by breezes. Expect 1–2 ears per plant; although yields are not high, you can maximize use of space by interplanting with fast-growing greens.

SOWING AND PLANTING In cool areas, to raise your own plants sow seed at 59°F (15°C) in midspring, 1in (2.5cm) deep, in cell packs. Mice may take the seeds in greenhouses. Harden off and plant out, or buy young plants and plant them, when soil temperature reaches 55°F (13°C) and

any risk of frost is long gone. Plant in blocks of at least 9 plants, 12in (30cm) apart each way, to ensure good pollination. Cover with row cover and remove it when plants have five leaves. In warm climates, seed can be sown *in situ* in a block pattern, 3in (8cm) apart, and thinned later; the seeds will need protection from birds.

ROUTINE CARE As with green beans (*see p.246*), give the stems more support by hilling up, to 5in (13cm). If conditions are dry at flowering or when grains are swelling, water generously once a week.

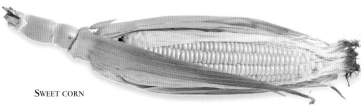

SWEET CORN

△ **TEST FOR RIPENESS**
After tassels turn brown, press a kernel with your thumbnail; if a milky liquid emerges, the ear is ripe; if watery, it is not ready; if doughy, it is overripe.

SEE ALSO: Adding Lime, p.238; Crop Protection, pp.240–241

LETTUCES AND OTHER LEAFY CROPS

ADEQUATE MOISTURE IS THE KEY to producing crisp, succulent salad and leaf crops. All the leafy salad crops thrive in moisture-retentive soils with plentiful organic matter and are ideally suited by deep beds, but you can plant them almost anywhere, in rows between other crops, in pots, as edging, or in patches to fill a potager.

They are not just summer crops: by sowing different types at different times you can have salad leaves all year round. For cooking, although their flavor differs, Swiss chard and spinach beet are often used as substitutes for spinach. They are easier to grow, very decorative, and crop for a much longer period.

LETTUCE

Lettuces grow much better in moderate climates, especially where nights are cool and fresh; in warm climates and hot spells they tend to bolt (flower and set seed), making them taste bitter. There are heat-resistant varieties for warm climates and for growing in high summer; siting summer sowings in partial shade can also help. Lettuces are either hearted (growing in a tight ball) or loose-leaved. Hearted lettuce are harvested once; with loose-leaved varieties, new leaves will sprout after you have cut the first crop (*see below*). Looseleaves are easier to grow if you have difficulty getting Romaine, crisphead, or butterhead lettuces to "heart up"; because harvesting checks their development, they do not bolt. Never grow lettuces in ground manured within the previous year; they will rot at the crown.

SOWING AND PLANTING For a year-round supply, choose a mixture of varieties to sow at 2–3 week intervals between early spring and late summer. Germination is poor at temperatures over 77°F (25°C); avoid overheating by sowing in early evening. In autumn, sow hardy varieties under cover (such as a cloche) for a spring crop. Sow *in situ* or in cell packs, or sow in close rows and transplant thinnings. Later thinnings will probably be big enough to use in salads and garnishes. Transplant at the 5-leaf stage, when soil is moist, with leaf bases just above soil level. Space small varieties at 6in (15cm), larger ones at 12in (30cm). Shade young plants in hot weather until established. Sow cut-and-come-again lettuces thinly in wide bands.

ROUTINE CARE Apply a high-nitrogen granular or liquid fertilizer if plants are not growing well. Water generously in dry conditions; a critical period for hearted types is 7–10 days before maturity. In very hot spells, a row cover or tunnel will shade crops and keep the leaves fresher. Protect autumn and early winter crops with cloches. Watch out for slug and other pest damage, and for rot in wet weather; trimming off leaves that touch the soil can help prevent spread.

HARVESTING Begin harvesting looseleaf lettuces 7 weeks after sowing. Cut leaves fresh as needed; they do not store well. Cut butterheads after 10–11 weeks, Romaine and crispheads after 11–12 weeks; all of these keep well for a few days in the crisper drawer of a refrigerator.

△ **HARVESTING LOOSELEAF LETTUCE**
Looseleaf varieties of lettuce, like baby salad leaves (see opposite), *can be grown as cut-and-come-again crops. When plants are 3–6in (8–15cm) high, cut just above the lowest leaves, leaving 1½in (3cm) of stem; it will soon sprout again. This can be repeated.*

LOOSELEAF LETTUCE
'Lollo Rosso'

BUTTERHEAD LETTUCE

COS LETTUCE

ROMAINE LETTUCE

SEE ALSO: Types of Beds, p.237; Manures and Mulches, p.239

CHICORY AND ENDIVE

Radicchio (red chicory) and curly endive (frisée type) have become so popular that seed and even young plants are readily available. They have much the same requirements as lettuces (*see opposite*) and take 8–12 weeks to mature; you can either pick off leaves or cut the whole head. The older the leaves are, the more bitter they taste, especially in hot weather. Later crops usually taste sweeter than those that mature in high summer, though planting in light shade or with row cover to shade plants, as with lettuces, can help. In cold weather, radicchio becomes crisper and the color intensifies. For pale, sweet leaves at

the center of curly endive, blanch the middles by resting a plate on top of the plants when the leaves are dry for 10 days before harvesting.

SOWING AND PLANTING Sow seed in mid-spring for summer crops, and until mid-summer to crop from autumn into early winter, *in situ*, or in cell packs to transplant after 3–4 weeks. Thin or space to give plants 10–14in (25–35cm) each way, depending on the size of the variety.

ROUTINE CARE Keep well watered, especially in dry spells. Both crops are reasonably trouble free, although slugs may take a fancy to endives.

RED CHICORY (RADICCHIO)

CURLY ENDIVE (BLANCHED)

OTHER SALAD GREENS

Baby leaf crops are easily grown from seed. Some have quite pungent flavors; others are blander. Spinach is much simpler to grow for young leaves than as a mature culinary crop, when it tends either to bolt or be badly pest damaged. Try different leaves to find ones that you like with different sowing and cropping times, so that you have something to pick through the year. Seed mixtures are available. Winter leaves are often the most peppery, and just a few will perk up a salad of store-bought lettuce. These crops thrive in the organic soil of a well-kept vegetable plot but will grow almost anywhere, as well as in containers; on light soils and in hot weather they tend to bolt quite quickly. Follow the instructions on the packet for

each crop. Water regularly, and apply a high-nitrogen feed if plants need a boost. Leaves may be ready in as little as 3 weeks; cropping will continue for as long as you snip off leaves regularly, so that the plants

do not mature. Pick off leaves that develop fungal leaf spots; you may also need to protect from birds. If flea beetles attack arugula, which they love, try sowing some more as far away as possible.

SPINACH

CORN SALAD (MACHE)

ARUGULA

SPINACH BEET AND CHARD

These leaf crops are cooked like spinach, but they tolerate higher temperatures and are less prone to bolting and easier to grow. Spinach beet is also known as perpetual spinach. Red-stemmed chard is a striking crop, good in a border or potager. The broad, white leaf midribs of Swiss chard take longer to cook than the leaves and may be used as a separate vegetable.

SOWING AND PLANTING Sow in spring; sow spinach beet again in mid- to late summer for harvest through winter. Sow *in situ* in rows 15in (38cm) apart for spinach beet,

18in (45cm) apart for chard; thin early to 12in (30cm) apart. Alternatively, sow in cell packs and plant 12in (30cm) apart.

ROUTINE CARE Mulch after planting. Keep well watered and apply a high-nitrogen fertilizer during the growing season if plants are not developing well. Pick off any leaves that develop fungal leaf spots. You may find that birds eat the leaves in winter when other food is scarce.

HARVESTING Begin harvesting after 8–12 weeks; cropping continues for months as long as you pick leaves regularly.

SPINACH BEET

RED-STEMMED CHARD

SEE ALSO: Thinning and Transplanting, p.243; Sowing Seeds in a Narrow Drill, p.243

TENDER CROPS

IN WARM CLIMATES with long summers, these fruiting crops thrive outdoors, but in cool temperate regions, only some tomatoes reliably crop well without protection, and a heated greenhouse or closed case is certainly essential to raise young plants. Whether growing in a greenhouse or, say, on a sunny, sheltered patio, all do well in containers; growing bags are ideal, ensuring that plants grow in fresh, disease-free soil mix each year. If your crops have been healthy, spent soil mix can be added to the compost pile or even used to mulch ornamental plants – not crops, and certainly never potatoes, vulnerable to the same sorts of diseases.

PEPPERS

Small chili pepper bushes make lovely container plants for a patio; in cool areas, you can grow them on under cover until fruits form, bring them out for summer display, then shelter them again once the evenings get cooler. You can in theory do this with larger bell pepper plants, but they are unwieldy to move and stems may snap. Under glass or plastic, peppers grow best at 70°F (21°C); you may need a greenhouse heater until summer.
SOWING AND PLANTING If you cannot give young plants the heat they need at first, wait until late spring to buy them. To raise your own, in late winter or early spring sow seeds ½–¾in (1–2cm) deep, in trays at 65–70°F (18–21°C). Prick out singly into 3in (8cm) pots when 2in (5cm) tall. Before flowers form, plant two to a bag, or singly in 8–10in (20–25cm) pots, or plant out.
ROUTINE CARE Never move plants outside until any danger of frost is long past. Stake plants over 2ft (60cm) tall. Keep well watered, and damp down or mist in the greenhouse to maintain humidity. Feed every two weeks with a balanced fertilizer. In the greenhouse, watch out for spider mites and mildews.

If the last fruits stop ripening as days cool, uproot the plant and hang it upside down, with the fruits still attached, in a warm place; they should color up.

JALAPEÑO PEPPERS

CHILI PEPPERS

BELL PEPPER

CUCUMBERS

Greenhouse cucumbers similar to the ones you may find in supermarkets are demanding and difficult plants. Outdoor cucumbers are much easier to grow and less troubled by pests and diseases than the greenhouse kinds. Modern varieties are not bitter. Some have rough or bristly skin; peel before use. Each plant should yield about 15 fruits, from summer to midautumn.
SOWING AND PLANTING In mid- to late spring, sow 2–3 seeds on edge in 3in (8cm) pots at 68°F (20°C); thin to the strongest. Plant out in early summer, two per growing bag or 18in (45cm) apart in well-manured ground, on a slight mound to prevent rot, under a cloche or row cover.
ROUTINE CARE Pinch out the growing tip after 6 leaves for a bushy plant, and mulch with straw or plastic to keep fruits clean. Train climbing varieties up stakes, or string suspended from a frame. Water when dry; a watering system is ideal to maintain a regular supply. Once fruits develop, feed regularly with tomato fertilizer.

EGGPLANT

In cool climates, a greenhouse heater may be needed for eggplant, especially when young; growth is checked below 68°F (20°C) and ideally they prefer 77–86°F (25–30°C). There are dwarf varieties, ideal to bring out into a sunny spot in summer, but if nights are chilly, it is worth protecting them with a row cover.
SOWING AND PLANTING In late winter or early spring, sow seeds ½–¾in (1–2cm) deep, in trays at 65–70°F (18–21°C). Prick out singly into 3in (8cm) pots when 2in (5cm) tall. When the first flowers form, put dwarf types in 8in (20cm) pots or plant out. Pinch out the tip of the plant when about 15in (38cm) tall.
ROUTINE CARE As for peppers (*see above*),

EGGPLANT

but use a tomato fertilizer rather than a general one. To produce large eggplants, let only 4–6 fruits per plant develop. Watch plants under cover for greenhouse pests and mildews.

△ **HARVESTING EGGPLANTS**
Eggplants are ripe when the entire fruit is colored and the skin is taut and shiny; once it loses its shine, or becomes wrinkled, the flesh will taste bitter. Cut the stalk at least 1in (2.5cm) away from the fruit.

SEE ALSO: Sowing Indoors or under Glass, p.244

TOMATOES

Tomato varieties come in different sizes, shapes, and colors, but their suitability for your climate and their growth habit will have a greater influence on your choice. Bush tomatoes are largely self-supporting, but by far the wider choice of varieties is found among tomatoes with a sprawling habit, grown for convenience as supported single stems. There are tomatoes of both habits that can be grown outdoors without protection in cool-summer climates once plants reach a certain size, but you can virtually double yields, from 4–8lb (2 to 4kg) per plant, under glass.

SITE AND SOIL Before planting tomatoes in open ground, add organic matter and a balanced fertilizer to the soil, since tomatoes are sensitive to nutrient deficiencies. Under glass, use growing bags or 10in (25cm) pots filled with fresh soil mix.

SOWING AND PLANTING Young plants are easy to find in garden centers and markets; if you have a greenhouse, you can buy them early, ensuring the best choice of plants, or grow from seed. Sow seeds ¾in (2cm) deep, in trays or cell packs. Plants to be grown in greenhouses can be started in late winter, sowing at 59–64°F (15–18°C). Outdoor varieties will be ready to harden off and plant out in about 8 weeks, so time sowing of these so that this date will be after any danger of late frosts in your area. Pot on into 3in (8cm) pots at the 2–3 leaf stage and plant once flowers form. A cover over new plants outdoors for the first week or two gets them off to a good start. Plant greenhouse tomatoes three to a growing bag or one to a pot; outdoors, space cordons 18in (45cm) apart; dwarf and bush types 1 and 2ft (30 and 60cm) respectively.

ROUTINE CARE Mulch outdoor plants once the soil is warm. A plastic mulch under bushes will keep low fruits clean; white plastic also reflects the sun, aiding ripening. Never allow plants to dry out completely, or they may develop problems. Regular watering also prevents tough skins, uneven ripening, and split fruits (*see p.304*). A 2-gallon can of water per growing bag per day may be needed in hot spells. After the first cluster of tiny fruits has developed from the flowers, feed weekly with high-potassium tomato fertilizer or an equivalent organic fertilizer. Cordons need support, either with stakes, or with twine suspended from greenhouse rafters. They also need training to form a single, vertical stem (*see below*). Watch out for whitefly (*see p.299*); companion plants of French marigolds may help deter them.

STANDARD TOMATO   PLUM TOMATO

CHERRY TOMATOES

YELLOW TOMATO   STRIPED TOMATO

TRAINING CORDON TOMATOES

1 PINCHING OUT SHOOTS
To train cordon tomatoes upward, tie the main stem loosely to a stake, or to suspended twine, at intervals. Remove all suckers (leafy shoots) that develop where leaves join the main stem, to direct energy into the fruits.

2 PINCHING OUT THE TOP IN COOL REGIONS
By late summer, when 4–6 trusses of fruits have formed, stop more developing by pinching out the top of the plant — there will not be time for them to grow and ripen. Continue to pinch out sideshoots.

GOOD IDEAS

• Where space is limited, dwarf bush and trailing varieties are ideal for 10in (25cm) pots, or even hanging baskets (*see p.177*). The hardier varieties of cherry tomato provide a small but satisfyingly ripe crop and almost never develop blossom end rot.

• In cool climates, in most years the last fruits of the season will not ripen fully: pick green tomatoes and put them on a warm, sunny windowsill; the company of a ripe banana will help them color up and ripen. Alternatively, use them for a relish.

△ **BETTER RIPENING**
In cool climates, outdoor cordons will ripen their last fruits better if detached from their support, laid on a bed of clean straw and given the added warmth of a tunnel cloche. The roots stay in the ground to sustain the plant.

SEE ALSO: Large Seeds, p.244; Sowing in Cell Packs, p. 245

GROWING FRUITS

GROWING YOUR OWN fruit ranks highly in the satisfaction stakes – and most, with attractive blossoms in spring and ripening fruits at harvest, are as ornamental as they are useful. If the garden is large, a separate area can be devoted to fruit cultivation and, if small, some can be grown among ornamentals – a border edging of alpine strawberries, or a grape-shaded pergola. Even a patio has room for a strawberry jar. The main problem with growing fruit decoratively is the need to protect it from birds. Wildlife lovers tend to dislike thread or invisible, fine netting because birds become entangled, but the mesh fabrics that are a safe visual deterrent do look unsightly.

PLANNING A FRUIT GARDEN

The fruits described in these pages are permanent plants – trees, shrubs and perennials – that will be in place for many years. With plenty of space to devote to fruit, you can grow enough to guarantee plentiful supplies for your family and friends: with the soft fruits, you can plant blocks of bush fruits such as blackcurrants (*see p.269*), rows of cane fruits such as raspberries (*see p.270*), and beds of strawberries (*see p.272*). Growing your soft fruits together makes management easier, especially with regard to feeding and watering, wind protection, and pest control (as with fruit cages). In a large garden, you may also have room for several fruit trees: either different fruits, or varieties that crop at different times to give you a long season of cropping and eating. However, with tree fruits you must bear in mind that many varieties need a second tree planted nearby, not necessarily of exactly the same variety, but at least of one that flowers at the same time. This is because many varieties lack the ability to pollinate themselves, the process by which fruit is "set." If space for standard trees is limited, there are ways around this problem (*see below*).

GOOD IDEAS

- A second tree for pollination need not be the same size or shape as the first; consider a dwarf tree or a restricted form such as cordon or espalier (see opposite).
- The second tree need not be in your garden; a neighbor may have a compatible variety.
- Many crabapples will pollinate apple varieties; ask your supplier for advice.
- There are "family" trees that consist of two compatible varieties grafted onto one trunk.

SITE AND CLIMATE

While gardeners in cool climates may envy those in warm countries the range of flowers and tender vegetable crops they can grow with ease, they can console themselves with the fact that many of the most delicious tree and soft fruits thrive only in climates with cold winters and summers that are not long and baking hot. With fruit trees, this need for a cold winter may be expressed as a precise "chilling requirement" – the number of hours below a certain temperature the fruit requires to crop. Gardeners in cool climates can ignore this advice, and instead concentrate on choosing the sunniest, most sheltered areas in which to nurture crops to the peak of ripeness; even to experiment with borderline fruits such as peaches and grapes where obtaining even a small ripe crop generates an enormous sense of achievement.

USE AND BEAUTY ▷
Here, a mature espaliered pear makes a screen to divide one area of the garden from the next and forms a beautiful backdrop to a herbaceous border.

△ **SAFETY IN NUMBERS**
Starwberries grown together in a bed are easy to manage for fertilizing, care, and watering; they can be readily protected with movable cloches.

△ **PERFECT PEACHES**
However desirable you find them, with warm-temperate fruits, like peaches and nectarines, it is important to take account of the limitations of your local climate. Although they need cold winter conditions, they must have plenty of warmth and sunshine to ripen sweet, juicy fruits.

SEE ALSO: Crop Protection, p.240; Bush Fruits, pp.268–269; Cane Fruits, pp.270–271; Strawberries, p.272

FRUIT IN SMALL SPACES

Although you will not obtain the bountiful supplies that typify summer abundance, with careful planning and lateral thinking you can grow fruits in small gardens. Many fruit trees, for example, are sufficiently attractive to be used as specimens in a lawn instead of an ornamental choice, and they certainly have several seasons of interest. You must, however, be aware of pollination needs (*see* Planning a Fruit Garden, *opposite*). For clothing walls, arches, and pergolas, you could consider a grape or perhaps a berry fruit, such as loganberries instead of planting a conventional climber.

If space is very limited, many fruits can be grown in containers. City gardens may be short on space, but they are very often well sheltered; a dwarf peach tree in a pot should produce many juicy fruits for you. Strawberries, both the alpine type and the large-fruited varieties (*see p.272*), are classic choices for container-growing. For more permanent container plants needing less maintenance, blueberry bushes (*see p.269*) are ideal; attractive shrubs, they look splendid in fruit and produce beautiful autumn foliage color.

Always choose large containers with a minimum diameter of 12in (30cm). Use soil-based mixes, place in a sunny site, and water and feed conscientiously.

ALPINE STRAWBERRIES △
Alpine strawberries are ideal for pots on a patio or terrace; they bear a succession of small, sweet fruits all summer. Grow in a soil-based mix, keep well watered, and fertilize regularly. Replace plants after two years.

SIZE AND SHAPE OF FRUIT TREES

Even experienced gardeners are happy to leave the early care of fruit trees to the experts. Specialty nurseries have the resources and expertise to graft fruit trees onto rootstocks that influence their eventual size and to accomplish the early training that can considerably reduce the wait between buying a young tree and obtaining your first crops – not to mention saving you the need to take on the early, trickiest decisions about pruning. For most gardeners, this is well worth the additional expense of buying an older but well-trained young tree.

Fruit trees are grafted onto a variety of rootstocks that make them grow large or small. With some, such as the plum rootstock 'Pixy', you can guess at the intended outcome; with apple rootstocks such as 'M9' or 'M27' you will need guidance to select the appropriate tree. To do so, consider how much space you have available. Standards and half-standards make relatively large trees on tall clear trunks; bush trees grow on a low trunk. The bush form and its variation, the pyramid, have the advantage that they suit a wide range of fruits, and the smaller the tree, the easier picking, spraying and pruning become.

Trees that are grown flat against walls, fences, or post-and-wire supports have great appeal; they take up less space and are both practically useful and undoubtedly ornamental – a row of cordons, for example, makes a beautiful screen when used to divide up the garden. A good nursery will have pretrained fans, espaliers, and cordons of apples, pears, cherries, plums, and peaches. These trained forms need more attention to pruning and tying in than trees and bushes, so think about how much time you are prepared to devote to their upkeep.

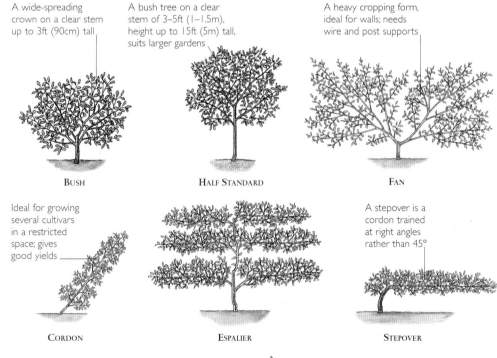

A wide-spreading crown on a clear stem up to 3ft (90cm) tall

A bush tree on a clear stem of 3–5ft (1–1.5m), height up to 15ft (5m) tall, suits larger gardens

A heavy cropping form, ideal for walls; needs wire and post supports

BUSH   **HALF STANDARD**   **FAN**

Ideal for growing several cultivars in a restricted space; gives good yields

A stepover is a cordon trained at right angles rather than 45°

CORDON   **ESPALIER**   **STEPOVER**

SHAPES OF FRUIT TREES

Many fruit trees can be trained in more than one shape; these distinct forms have been developed to suit the fruiting habit of individual fruit trees and gardens of varying size. Every fruit tree needs pruning to some degree; it is essential to become familiar with fruiting habits and growth so that you do not remove the parts that would bear next year's crop.

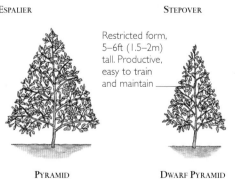

Restricted form, 5–6ft (1.5–2m) tall. Productive, easy to train and maintain

PYRAMID   **DWARF PYRAMID**

SEE ALSO: Containers and Raised Beds, pp.166–183; Pruning Fruit Trees, pp.262–263; Apples and Pears, p. 264–265; Stone Fruits, pp.266–267

PLANTING FRUIT CROPS

PREPARE THE SITE at least two months ahead of planting fruit. Remove all weeds and improve the soil by digging in copious amounts of well-rotted organic matter. If you intend to grow cane fruits such as raspberries and blackberries, or trained forms of tree fruits such as cordons or fans, put supports such as horizontal wiring (*see p.109*) in place before planting. Then, find a supplier that will provide good plants, guaranteed disease-free where regulated certification programs exist. For bush and other soft fruits, apply a balanced fertilizer before planting. Regular mulches of organic matter for all fruits are a must; locating a reliable, convenient supply makes sense.

BUYING GOOD PLANTS

Fruits will be in place for many years, so do not risk buying any old plant. Head instead for the fruit section of a really good garden center, or check out the catalog of a specialized fruit nursery. The range of varieties will be a real eye-opener, and with no Latin names to pronounce or mispronounce, you should feel confident enough to ask for all the advice you need.

ALWAYS REMEMBER

GET AS MUCH ADVICE AS YOU CAN

Size and shape of plants and trees, cropping times, possible pollination needs, suitability to your garden conditions, and susceptibility to problems: make a list of all the questions you want to ask. Local gardening groups may have a specialized interest in growing fruit and are an invaluable source of advice.

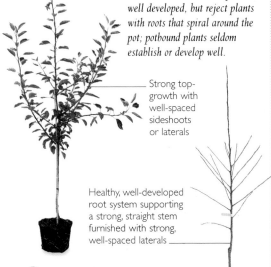

◁ **CONTAINER-GROWN**
Make sure that the root system is well developed, but reject plants with roots that spiral around the pot; potbound plants seldom establish or develop well.

Strong top-growth with well-spaced sideshoots or laterals

Healthy, well-developed root system supporting a strong, straight stem furnished with strong, well-spaced laterals

BARE-ROOT ▷
Make sure that the root system has a good balance of main and fibrous roots and the roots show no signs of having dried out.

PLANTING A FRUIT TREE

Container-grown trees can be planted at any time of year when the soil is not dry, waterlogged, or frozen. Bare-root trees are planted when dormant, from late autumn to early spring; soak the roots well before planting. If conditions are unsuitable, heel in trees (*see p.194*) and keep them watered until conditions improve. The height of the stake depends on the form. Pyramid trees need a tall, permanent stake the same length as the eventual height of the tree. Bushes and standards need short stakes, to just below the lowest branches. These can be single or, better, double – one on either side of the root ball. They can be removed once the tree is established. In lawns, clear a circular area around the tree of grass, or it will compete with the tree.

HOW TO PLANT A BARE-ROOT FRUIT TREE

Drive stake 18in (45cm) into bottom of the hole, so it will be 2ft (60cm) deep after planting

1 DIG OUT THE HOLE
Dig a hole one third wider than the roots. Drive in a stake, 3in (7cm) from the hole's center for pyramids; use one on either side of the roots for standards or bushes. Drive stakes in to at least 2ft (60cm) below ground level.

2 MOUND UP THE BASE
Slightly mound the soil at the base of the hole and place the tree in the center. Check for depth by placing a stake across the hole. The finished soil surface should be level with the soil mark on the tree's stem.

3 PLANT AND FIRM
Adjust the hole's depth, if necessary, then spread roots evenly over the mound. Backfill gradually in layers, firming gently with the ball of your foot so the tree is well anchored and there are no air pockets between the roots.

4 ATTACH TREE TO SUPPORT
Attach a buckle-and-spacer to the top of the stake and then to the tree, with the spacer forming a cushion between stem and stake to prevent chafing (see inset). Adjust as necessary. Protect with a ring of wire netting.

SEE ALSO: Tree Stakes and Ties, p.193; Tree Guards, p.195; Apples and Pears, pp.264–265; Stone Fruits, pp.266–267

PLANTING TRAINED FRUIT TREES

Before planting young cordons, fans, and espaliers, install horizontal wires, tautened with straining bolts, either between 7ft (2.2m) tall concrete posts or fitted with slats and vine eyes, 4–6in (10–15cm) away from a wall or fence. For diagonal supports, attach stakes to the wires at an angle (*right*) and secure the main stems of cordons, or the branches of fans, to them after planting. Make sure when you plant that the graft union – a bulge at the base of the stem – is not covered by soil. Set them 9in (23cm) away from the base of a wall or fence, sloping into the support.

△ **SUPPORTING CORDONS**
Cordons can be trained on a freestanding support of sturdy posts and wires, or on wires set 4–6in (10–15cm) away from a wall or fence to permit adequate air circulation. Space three horizontal wires, 2ft (60cm) apart, with the lowest wire 2½ft (75cm) above ground level.

△ **SUPPORTING STAKE**
Attach a supporting stake at an angle of 45° across the horizontal wires, securing firmly in place with plastic-coated wire.

△ **TIE AT AN ANGLE**
Tie in cordon main stems and fan branches loosely to the stakes with soft twine to keep secure. Avoid the wires chafing the bark.

PLANTING BUSH FRUITS

Bush fruits, like red- and blackcurrants and gooseberries, are planted in the same way as tree fruits but do not need stakes. Autumn planting is best, but they may be planted throughout winter if soil and weather conditions are suitable. If possible, buy plants certified free of disease.

When planting, handle bushes carefully to avoid damaging buds. After planting blackcurrants, cut all stems back (*see p.269*). For redcurrants and gooseberries, in late winter, remove sideshoots growing within 4in (10cm) of soil level, cutting flush to the main stem to create a short trunk. Shorten remaining stems by half, cutting to a strong, outward-facing bud.

HOW TO PLANT BUSH FRUITS

1 DIG OUT THE HOLE
Dig a hole large enough to hold the fully extended roots of the bush and check the depth with a stake laid across the hole. Plant the bush so that the surrounding soil is at the same level as the soil mark on the stem.

2 BACKFILL AND FIRM
Backfill soil gradually in layers, firming each layer gently with the ball of your foot to remove any air pockets around the roots. After planting, level off the soil surface with a rake. In spring, mulch with well-rotted manure.

PLANTING CANE FRUITS

Cane fruits – raspberries, blackberries, and hybrid berries – need permanent support. Post-and-wire is a simple, space-efficient method. For raspberries, use horizontal wires, at 2½, 3, 5¼ft (75cm, 1m, and 1.6m) above ground, strained between two sturdy posts, or stapled to a line of four or five. For blackberries or hybrid berries, use two 8ft (2.5m) posts, with 2ft (60cm) below ground, and four horizontal wires 12in (30cm) apart, the lowest 3ft (90cm) above ground. Plant as for raspberries, between winter and early spring. Space vigorous cultivars 12–15ft (4–5m) part; less vigorous ones, 8ft (2.5m) apart. After planting, cut canes back to 9in (23cm) above ground.

HOW TO PLANT RASPBERRY CANES

1 PLANTING THE CANES
In autumn or early winter, prepare a trench, 2–3in (5–8cm) deep, in well-manured ground. Plant canes 15–18in (38–45cm) apart, in rows 6ft (2m) apart. Spread out roots evenly and backfill the trench with soil.

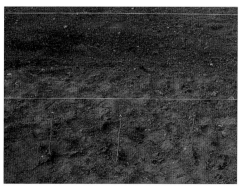

2 PRUNING THE CANES
Gently firm the soil at the base of canes, making sure that they remain vertical. Cut each cane back to a strong bud about 10in (25cm) above ground level. Rake over the soil lightly. Mulch with well-rotted manure in spring.

SEE ALSO: Bush Fruits, pp.268–269; Cane Fruits, pp.270–271

PRUNING FRUIT TREES

THERE ARE THREE primary aims when pruning fruit trees: to influence the direction of shoot growth to create or maintain the desired shape while ensuring structural strength; to maintain a good balance between fruiting wood and growth; and to keep trees healthy by removing dead, diseased, and damaged wood as well as crossing branches, which may rub and wound the bark, and crowded branches that reduce penetration of light and air to the center of the tree. Every pruning cut made should have at least one of these aims in mind. Routine pruning is done during winter dormancy, or sometimes in summer for stone fruits like plums.

ANATOMY OF A FRUIT TREE

Pruning and training fruit trees involves cutting back different types of growth – old and new branches, growth shoots, and fruiting wood. Since pruning aims to influence direction of growth and create a balance between growth and fruiting wood, it is vital to be able to differentiate between buds that will produce fruit and those that make the growth that extends the length of branches and so shapes the tree. New stems emerge only from the slimmer, flatter growth buds and in the same direction as these buds point.
It is also important to know where to make cuts to induce fruit bud formation and how the severity of pruning affects plant response. Removing a short or moderate length from the growing tips of branch leaders induces the production of fruit buds lower down on the same shoot.

THE NAMING OF PARTS
The different types of growth on a fruit tree have been given precise names, so the understanding of pruning techniques is simplified if you are familiar with a few of the simplest terms.

Laterals are sideshoots that grow out from main branches. Sublaterals are sideshoots that grow from laterals

GRAFT UNION ▷
Point at which the fruiting cultivar, or scion, is grafted onto the rootstock; it can be seen as a slight swelling at the base of the trunk.

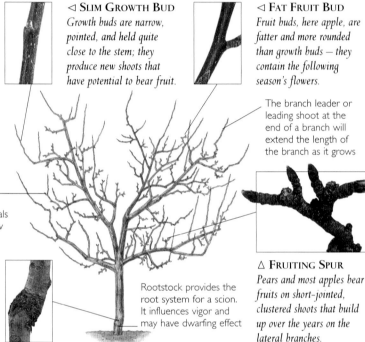

◁ SLIM GROWTH BUD
Growth buds are narrow, pointed, and held quite close to the stem; they produce new shoots that have potential to bear fruit.

◁ FAT FRUIT BUD
Fruit buds, here apple, are fatter and more rounded than growth buds – they contain the following season's flowers.

The branch leader or leading shoot at the end of a branch will extend the length of the branch as it grows

Rootstock provides the root system for a scion. It influences vigor and may have dwarfing effect

△ FRUITING SPUR
Pears and most apples bear fruits on short-jointed, clustered shoots that build up over the years on the lateral branches.

PRUNING WEAK GROWTH

The harder weak growth is pruned, the more vigorous are the shoots that grow out as a result. Prune hard to create a strong new shoot to fill out the shape of the tree or replace an old shoot that no longer crops well. In subsequent years, the pruning of these shoots is moderated to induce them to produce fruit buds.

CUTTING TO A BUD ▷
Approach the stem with pruners from the opposite side of the selected bud and with the narrower, cutting blade nearest to the bud. Make an angled cut about ¼in (5mm) above the bud and sloping away from it.

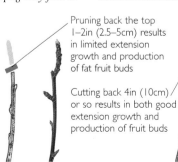

PRUNING WEAK SHOOTS
With light pruning, weak shoots form fruit buds but do not grow much longer. Moderate pruning encourages both growth and fruit bud formation. Hard pruning results in strong growth at the expense of fruit buds.

Pruning back the top 1–2in (2.5–5cm) results in limited extension growth and production of fat fruit buds

Cutting back 4in (10cm) or so results in both good extension growth and production of fruit buds

Hard pruning has encouraged two growth buds to break into growth, resulting in no fruit buds but two strong shoots that may be used to replace old wood

LIGHT PRUNING   **MODERATE PRUNING**   **HARD PRUNING**

ALWAYS REMEMBER

STRIKE A BALANCE
To maintain the size and shape of a fruit tree the rule is to prune weak growth hard and strong growth lightly. Severity of pruning is varied, depending on whether a tree lacks strong new growth, or is growing vigorously but cropping poorly, and on where new growth is needed to replace the old.

SEE ALSO: Pruning Apples and Pears, pp.264–265

PRUNING STRONG GROWTH

Use hard pruning to encourage growth on young trees or, on mature trees, to induce replacement growth for a branch that has been removed because it is unproductive or diseased, or to stimulate production of a shoot to fill in the branch framework.

After hard pruning, a tree's root system has fewer buds to feed, so each bud has great growth potential and produces strong new shoots. Conversely, little or no pruning leaves a smaller ration of food for each bud, so regrowth is limited. If pruning is too light, however, there is a risk of producing too many small fruits, which exhausts the tree at the expense of new growth that could bear future crops. Balance is the order of the day.

PRUNING STRONG SHOOTS

Tip-pruning vigorous shoots (that is, cutting out the growing tip) or leaving them unpruned produces moderate extension growth and several fruit buds. Pruning strong shoots moderately induces branching but reduces the number of fruit buds formed, while pruning strong shoots hard results in yet more vigorous growth at the expense of fruit buds.

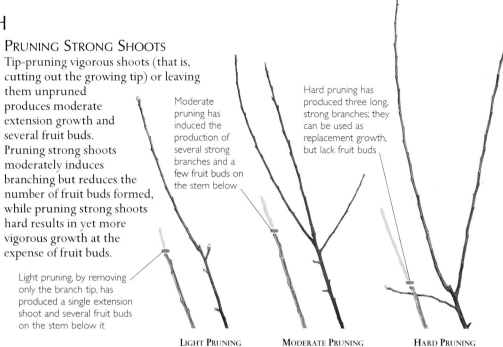

Light pruning, by removing only the branch tip, has produced a single extension shoot and several fruit buds on the stem below it

Moderate pruning has induced the production of several strong branches and a few fruit buds on the stem below

Hard pruning has produced three long, strong branches; they can be used as replacement growth, but lack fruit buds

LIGHT PRUNING   **MODERATE PRUNING**   **HARD PRUNING**

SPUR-PRUNING AND THINNING IN WINTER

Spur-pruning is practiced only on pears and spur-bearing apples; it accentuates their natural habit. It is not used for other tree fruits or for tip-bearing apples (ask your supplier for advice about these varieties). It consists of shortening laterals to stimulate fruiting sideshoots. Growth from these is shortened in turn, producing a system of spurs. Branch leaders are pruned to encourage the production of further laterals. After some years, as spur systems become congested, they are thinned by removing the oldest, most complicated growth.

SPUR-PRUNING

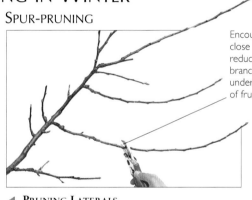

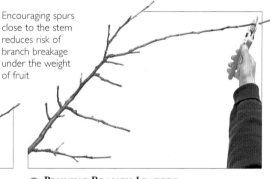

Encouraging spurs close to the stem reduces risk of branch breakage under the weight of fruit

1 PRUNING LATERALS
Pruning laterals stimulates spur formation close to their bases. Using an angled cut, cut long laterals back to 5–6 buds and reduce weak laterals to 2–3 buds.

2 PRUNING BRANCH LEADERS
Cutting to a bud, prune branch leaders by a quarter to a third of the previous season's growth. If they are very vigorous, just prune out the tip.

SUMMER PRUNING

Plum and cherry trees are pruned in summer in areas where winter pruning leaves them vulnerable to silver leaf disease (*see p.297*). Pruning does not follow a system, as with spur-bearing apples and pears, but simply thins growth as necessary to ensure that the sun ripens the fruits well. You must also summer-prune all tree fruits, including apples and pears, that are grown in special trained forms, such as fans, espaliers and cordons. By cutting back the long, leafy shoots that develop, especially those that grow outward from the wall or support, you will retain the shape of the tree, concentrate its energies and the available sunlight on ripening the fruits already present, and encourage the development of next year's flower buds. All new shoots 6–9in (15–22cm) long are shortened to 2in (5cm) as the lowest third of their bases become woody. Shoots develop during early summer, and as regrowth from early pruning cuts is also shortened to ¾in (2cm), pruning may extend over 2–3 weeks or more. Remember that your principal aim is to maintain the form, allowing sunlight to reach ripening fruits.

If laterals are allowed to grow unrestricted, they spoil the trained form and shade ripening fruits

△ **BEFORE**
New laterals have grown on this espalier and are maturing from the base up. If not shortened, the trained form will be lost.

△ **AFTER**
The form is visibly restored, and more sun will reach ripening fruits. Summer pruning cuts also stimulate future fruit buds.

SEE ALSO: Stone Fruits, pp.266–267; Bush Fruits, pp.268–269

APPLES AND PEARS

THE BEST PLANTING time for apples and pears is during dormancy. Apples can be planted in autumn or late winter; late winter plantings may need additional watering in the first growing season until established. Pears are best planted in autumn, when the soil is still warm, or at the latest by early winter. They often come into growth very early in spring, so autumn planting allows good root establishment before growth emerges. In hot, dry summers, especially in the early years, watering will usually be needed. Applying a mulch of well-rotted manure or compost helps retain moisture and reduces risks of trace-element deficiencies.

PEARS

Pears thrive in similar conditions to apples, but they need more consistent warmth to crop well. Pears can be trained as cordons, fans, espaliers, and in free-standing forms. The dwarf pyramid, the most compact, should be planted 4ft (1.2m) apart on the rootstock 'Quince C', and 5ft (1.5m) apart on 'Quince A'.

Fully grown pear trees can be very decorative, with their beautiful blossoms, silvery foliage, gnarled bark, and attractive fruits. They can be grown as ornamental trees and will produce an adequate crop with very little pruning. But for reliable heavy crops, the pyramid, a variation on the bush form, is recommended, kept in shape by regular pruning. To train a dwarf pyramid, start with a two-year-old tree with wide-angled lateral branches. In the first summer, prune new growth on all laterals to 5–6 leaves; cut sublaterals back to 3 leaves. The next winter, prune the leading shoot to leave 10in (25cm) of new growth; cut to a bud on the opposite side to the previous pruning. Each subsequent year, prune the leader to buds on alternate sides. When the tree reaches the required height, cut back the leader in late spring to one bud on new growth.

Mulch trees annually in early spring and feed as for apples. To supply adequate nitrogen, dress with ammonium nitrate at a rate of up to 1oz/sq yd (35g/sq m). After natural fruit drop in midsummer, thin fruit to leave one per cluster if the crop is heavy, or two if cropping is light. Pears are grouped into early, mid-, and late season cultivars. Timing of picking is most important, especially for late cultivars. If left on the tree too long, the centers turn brown. Fruit is ripe when it parts easily from the tree if gently lifted and twisted. Pick early cultivars just before fully ripe, and later cultivars when fully mature.

Pears are affected by caterpillars (*see p.298*), fireblight (*p.301*), scab (*p.304*), and brown rot (*p.304*).

ALWAYS REMEMBER

ENSURING GOOD CROPS

Provision for good pollination must be made by planting two cultivars. Some need two pollinators, so check with the supplier before buying. Pears flower in mid- to late spring and early blossoms may be damaged by frost, so choose a warm, sheltered site to provide some protection.

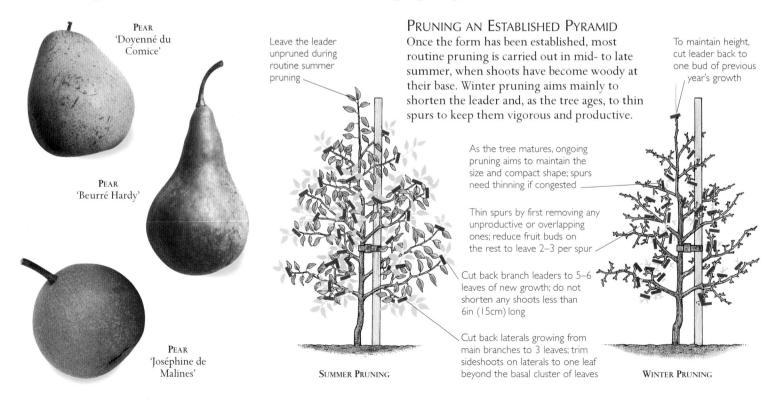

PEAR 'Doyenné du Comice'

PEAR 'Beurré Hardy'

PEAR 'Joséphine de Malines'

Leave the leader unpruned during routine summer pruning

SUMMER PRUNING

PRUNING AN ESTABLISHED PYRAMID

Once the form has been established, most routine pruning is carried out in mid- to late summer, when shoots have become woody at their base. Winter pruning aims mainly to shorten the leader and, as the tree ages, to thin spurs to keep them vigorous and productive.

As the tree matures, ongoing pruning aims to maintain the size and compact shape; spurs need thinning if congested

Thin spurs by first removing any unproductive or overlapping ones; reduce fruit buds on the rest to leave 2–3 per spur

Cut back branch leaders to 5–6 leaves of new growth; do not shorten any shoots less than 6in (15cm) long

Cut back laterals growing from main branches to 3 leaves; trim sideshoots on laterals to one leaf beyond the basal cluster of leaves

To maintain height, cut leader back to one bud of previous year's growth

WINTER PRUNING

SEE ALSO: Size and Shape of Fruit Trees, p.259; Planting a Fruit Tree, p.260

APPLES

Apples grow well in most moderately fertile, well-drained soils. They need a sunny, sheltered site and a compatible pollinator for consistent cropping; seek advice on pollinators when buying. The many apples available, both cooking and eating varieties, cover a ripening period from midsummer to late winter; some can be kept in storage until midspring. If summers are cool and short, choose early ripening cultivars, and, if late frosts are likely, choose late-flowering types so that blossoms are not damaged.

The choice of rootstock depends on the tree size required and the soil type. A wide range is available, from super-dwarfing to standard size and adaptable to heavy and alkaline soils. If soil is poor, a more vigorous rootstock can compensate; ask your supplier for specific advice. Apples can be trained as cordons, fans, espaliers, and in a range of free-standing forms. A half-standard, with a clear trunk, makes a beautiful ornamental tree and will crop quite well with only essential pruning (removing dead or diseased branches, for example), but for reliable heavy crops, bush trees cannot be beaten. The bush is a compact form; plant 6ft (2m) apart on dwarfing rootstocks, and 11–18ft (3.5–5.5m) apart on a more standard-sized rootstock. Mulch annually in early spring. As trees reach flowering size, apply 3–4oz/sq yd (105–140g/sq m) of balanced fertilizer each spring. If growth is poor, use ammonium nitrate at a rate of 1oz/sq yd (35g/sq m). In early summer, thin by removing the central fruit in each cluster and again in midsummer to leave one good fruit per cluster. Apples may be affected by codling moth caterpillars (see p.298), spider mite (p.301), scab (p.304), brown rot (p.304), canker (p.300), and mildew (p.296).

DESSERT APPLE
'George Cave'

COOKING APPLE
'Bramley'

PRUNING AN APPLE BUSH

The aim is to create an open-centered bush with 8–10 main branches that radiate evenly from the top of a trunk, 2–2½ft (60–75cm) tall. Begin with a two-year-old tree with at least 3–4 strong, well-placed laterals. After the basic shape has been formed, pruning spur-bearing and tip-bearing apples differs; check the fruiting habit of your variety before pruning. To dictate the direction of growth, always prune to a bud that points in the intended direction.

PRUNING AT PLANTING ▷
Cut back the leader to just above 3–4 strong laterals. Cut laterals back by two-thirds of the length to upward-facing buds on horizontal shoots, to outward-facing buds on upright ones.

8–10 strong laterals are chosen to form the main branch framework

These 3–4 strong laterals form the base of the framework for the mature tree

△ **YEAR 2, WINTER**
Shorten laterals chosen to form main branches by half and all others to 4–5 buds. Remove shoots that are badly placed or crossing and any that make narrow V-angles with the stem.

Vary the severity of pruning depending on the vigor of growth

△ **YEAR 3, WINTER, SPUR-BEARERS**
Shorten branch leaders by one-quarter of the previous year's growth. Prune strong laterals to 4–6 buds, and weak ones to 2–3 buds. Cut out badly placed shoots completely.

Tip-bearers produce fruit buds at the ends of laterals, so they are not pruned; remove them if badly placed

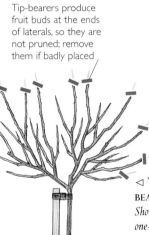

◁ **YEAR 3, TIP-BEARERS**
Shorten branch leaders by one-quarter of the previous year's growth and leave all laterals unpruned unless badly placed or crossing.

◁ **MATURE SPUR-BEARER**
Shorten weak branch leaders by a half and strong ones by no more than a quarter of their length. Prune other new shoots to 4–6 buds, the latter on stronger growth. Thin or remove old, crowded spur systems.

◁ **TIP-BEARERS**
When mature, cut back some of oldest, fruited wood to a young shoot or basal bud to promote replacement growth. Tip-prune branch leaders.

SEE ALSO: Pruning Fruit Trees, pp.262–263

STONE FRUITS

PLUMS, CHERRIES, AND PEACHES are tree fruits known as stone fruits, because of their single hard kernel. They do not produce fruiting spurs, and so pruning techniques differ to accommodate their fruiting habit. Unless they are grown in a special, trained form (most commonly a fan, which suits their growth and fruiting habit), they do not need a regular regime of pruning once established; you just need to use common sense to take out old, unproductive branches as necessary. If you live in an area prone to silver leaf (see p. 297), unless you need to remove a damaged or diseased branch, stone fruits should be pruned in spring and summer, not winter.

PLUMS

Grow plums, gages, and damsons in moderately fertile, well-drained soil and a sunny, sheltered site; all flower early in spring, so for good fruit set they need a site as frost-free as possible. In cool areas choose damsons and traditional, hardy varieties of plum; even if your summer does not produce fully ripe fruits, they can be used for cooking. In mild areas, or on a sunny, sheltered wall, try dessert types. Many plums are self-fertile, while others need a pollinator.

Plums can be trained as bushes, pyramids, or fans. The bush is a fairly compact form; it needs little pruning once established. 'Pixy' (dwarfing), or 'St Julien A' rootstocks make small- to medium-sized trees. Plant 12ft (4m) apart, in late autumn (no later than midwinter), since trees come into growth early. Mulch annually in early spring, and, when trees reach flowering size, apply a balanced and a high-nitrogen fertilizer, as for pears. In summer, after natural fruit drop, thin remaining fruit to 3–4in (7–10cm) apart to yield better-quality fruit and reduce the risk of branch breakage.

Plums may be affected by birds (see p.307), caterpillars (p.298), canker (p.300), and brown rot (p.304).

PLUM
'Marjorie's
Seedling'

PLUM
'Coe's Golden
Drop'

PLUM
'Victoria'

DAMSON
'Merryweather'

GREENGAGE
'Cambridge Gage'

△ PLUM IN FRUIT
Trees in the plum group do not fruit on spur wood but at the base of year-old wood and all along two-year-old and older wood. Pruning must take account of this habit.

PRUNING A PLUM BUSH

Aim to produce a clear trunk of at least 2½ft (75cm). Once established, in early summer prune weak, dead, damaged, crossing, or unproductive growth back to its point of origin or to a replacement shoot.

Cut lateral branches to outward-facing buds, or to upward-facing buds on horizontal shoots

Shorten sublaterals by half, cutting back to a bud facing in a direction that will produce a balanced, open-centered crown

To keep the crown open and well balanced, remove any overly vigorous new shoots that develop and any that cross the center or rub against main branches

With naturally spreading cultivars, make cuts to upward-facing buds or shoots. Horizontal branches will droop and may break under the weight of fruit

◁ YEAR 1, EARLY SPRING
Shorten 3–4 well-spaced laterals by two-thirds. Cut the leader back to the highest of the selected laterals, about 3ft (90cm) above ground. Shorten low laterals to 2 buds; pinch out subsequent growth to 2 leaves throughout the season.

◁ YEAR 2, EARLY SPRING
On each lateral, shorten 2–3 strong sublaterals by half. Remove completely any weak, badly placed, or narrow-angled shoots. Remove low laterals that were pruned and pinched back the previous year. If further low shoots emerge, rub them off.

◁ YEAR 3
Delay pruning until spring or early summer. Prune branch leaders that are weak or growing horizontally by a quarter, cutting to a bud facing in a direction where new growth will fill in the branch framework.

SEE ALSO: Planting Fruit Crops, pp.260–261; Pruning Fruit Trees, pp.262–263

CHERRIES

Sour cherries will produce a culinary crop even in cold areas; in mild regions, or if you have a sunny, sheltered site, sweet cherries can be grown, although birds will fight you for them. Grow cherries in moderately fertile, well-drained soil and a sheltered site; sour cherries tolerate light shade. Most sour cherries and a few sweet cherries are self-fertile; both are most usually grafted onto a semivigorous rootstock, on which a bush-trained tree will reach 12ft (4m) tall. In most gardens, there is seldom room for two trees of this size (to meet pollination needs) so select the self-fertile sweet cherry 'Stella' and the sour cherry 'Morello'.

Cherries are commonly trained as bushes or fans. Sweet cherries fruit at the base of year-old shoots and all along older wood; they make excellent bushes, pruned and trained as for plums. Sour cherries fruit on the previous year's growth, so the aim of pruning is remove some fruited wood each year to make way for year-old wood. Mulch in early spring, also applying ammonium nitrate at 1oz/sq yd (35g/sq m) to sour cherries, but only to sweet cherries if growth is poor. Irrigate well in dry conditions. Fruit thinning is seldom necessary. Cherries may be affected by birds (*see p.307*), caterpillars (*p.298*), canker (*p.300*), and brown rot (*p.304*).

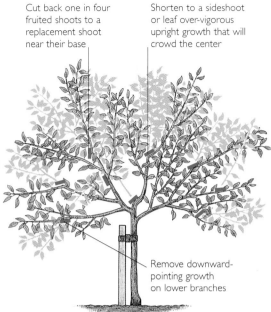

Cut back one in four fruited shoots to a replacement shoot near their base

Shorten to a sideshoot or leaf over-vigorous upright growth that will crowd the center

Remove downward-pointing growth on lower branches

PRUNING A SOUR CHERRY BUSH
Formative pruning is as for a plum bush, in spring. Sour cherries fruit on young growth produced the previous year. Once established, do the main pruning after fruiting. On older trees, also cut back one or two branches annually in spring to encourage new growth.

SWEET CHERRIES

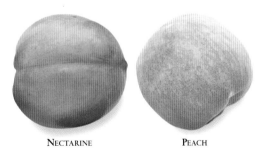

SOUR CHERRIES

PEACHES AND NECTARINES

Peaches and nectarines do best in areas with dry, sunny summers. Plant them in late winter in a deep, fertile, acidic soil for best results. They are usually trained into bush form. Most are self-fertile. Peaches and nectarines do not ripen well in cool-summer climates unless given a favored spot; here they are best fan-trained and need a 15ft (5m) wide wall. If you have a suitable wall, the easiest option is to buy a partially trained fan and plant it in early winter. It will have two laterals, trained at an angle. Each of these needs two well-spaced shoots on the upper side and one below; tie in to stakes lashed to wires as

NECTARINE   PEACH

they grow to form "ribs." Form new ribs by pruning main arms back by a third in early spring to produce laterals that are tied in during summer. Pinch out all unwanted shoots to one leaf. Both sideshoots and developing fruitlets need thinning on established fans. Leave one sideshoot on each flowering shoot below the flowers; pinch out the rest to one leaf. Tip- prune this sideshoot when it reaches 18in (45cm) long and, after fruiting, cut each fruited shoot back to a replacement sideshoot. Peaches are affected by peach leaf curl (*see p.297*), root knot nematodes (*p.309*), and canker (*p.300*).

THINNING SHOOTS

1 BEFORE THINNING
If all the closely grouped shoots on this branch grow out, they will overcrowd the branch, produce small, poor quality fruits, and shade them from the sun.

2 AFTER THINNING
Pinch out excess sideshoots at their point of origin to leave the remaining shoots at 4–6in (10–15cm) spacings.

THINNING FRUIT ▷
When the thinned fruits reach the size of walnuts, and some fruitlets have been shed naturally, they are thinned again to one every 6–9in (15–22cm) of branch. Loosely wrap ripening fruits in muslin to protect from birds.

BUSH FRUITS

THESE ARE COOL-CLIMATE FRUITS, impossible to grow in hot countries; all tolerate some part-day shade. It makes sense to grow gooseberry and currant bushes together. It makes it more convenient to give them all the well-rotted manure they love each spring, and also to enclose them with netting that will protect buds and fruits from birds.

Blueberries need very different conditions. If your soil has the acidity they need, you will almost certainly have limed the kitchen garden for other crops, and they will not grow there. Grow these attractive shrubs either in ornamental beds or in containers, which is also the solution if your soil is not acidic.

GOOSEBERRIES

Gooseberries need cool summers; where summers are hot, site in light shade. They need shelter; the young shoots are quite brittle. Dig in well-rotted manure well before planting, and buy plants certified disease-free. Plant 4–5ft (1.2–1.5m) apart, in autumn or winter, then in late winter, prune by cutting back main stems by half; remove low shoots to form a short trunk, 6in (15cm) tall. Next winter, prune new shoots by half to an outward-facing bud. Prune shoots growing in- or downward to one bud. Once established, gooseberries do not need regular pruning, although if the bush is widely spreading you should cut off any very low branches. As the bush ages, fruits will get smaller and become more difficult to harvest amid crowded, spiny shoots, at which point you can take out an entire old branch or two (*see below*). Every spring, mulch with well-rotted manure and apply balanced fertilizer and 1oz (35g) of potassium sulfate per bush. Pick off leaves showing signs of mildew or leaf spot. Pick off caterpillars, probably sawfly larvae (*see p.298*); even if these get out of hand and strip bushes of leaves, the fruits should still be harvestable.

WHITE GOOSEBERRIES

RED GOOSEBERRIES

◁ **PRUNING A GOOSEBERRY**
In late winter, remove oldest branches and shoots that cross the center to prevent overcrowding and maintain an open center. The pruned bush should have a crown of evenly spaced shoots pointing upward or outward (depending on how the variety grows).

Remove all low-growing shoots to maintain a short trunk that keeps fruits clean by reducing soil splash

Three-year-old wood is darker brown with fruiting spurs. Older wood gradually becomes less fruitful

Second year wood bears fruit and is smooth and gray-brown

The newest, current season's growth has pale, yellow-green bark; fruit buds are not formed until the second year

◁ **FRUITING SHOOTS**
Fruit-laden branches on gooseberries take three years to form. In the first year a shoot grows, in the second it bears fruits, and in the third the wood darkens and begins to send out new sideshoots of its own to fruit the following year.

REDCURRANTS

Redcurrants grow and fruit in a very similar way to gooseberries (although they are not spiny). They tend to make taller, more upright bushes. The key difference is that the fruits need more sun to ripen, so you must prune them a little each year to let the light in.

Dig plenty of well-rotted manure into the soil before planting. In autumn or winter, buy young plants from a reliable supplier; there is no certification program for redcurrants that guarantees they are virus-free. Plant 4–5ft (1.2–1.5m) apart. Over the next two years, shape young bushes as for gooseberries (*see above*). When established, prune after fruiting or in autumn or winter; trim the tips from all of the main, leading branches, cutting to a bud, and cut back all of the sideshoots to one bud from the branch. Every spring, mulch with well-rotted manure and apply balanced fertilizer and 1oz (35g) of potassium sulfate per bush. Water in dry weather as the fruits develop, but not as they ripen; this causes skins to split. Be watchful for caterpillars, and pick off any leaves with spots or mildew.

REDCURRANTS

SEE ALSO: Applying Lime, p.238

BLACKCURRANTS

Although they are related to redcurrants, blackcurrants grow and fruit in quite a different way. Whereas redcurrants grow as a bush with a definite single trunk, blackcurrants send up shoots in a thicket from ground level. Once fully grown, they must be pruned each year to thin this thicket of growth, or the fruits will be shaded and smothered. Blackcurrants fruit best on wood made the previous season, so it is the oldest stems that need to be removed. You can expect crops two years after planting, modest at first but later around 10lb (5kg) per plant.

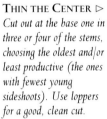
BLACKCURRANTS

Before planting, dig plenty of well-rotted manure into the soil. Always buy bushes from a reputable supplier that guarantees virus-free stock. Plant them more deeply than when in their containers, 4–5ft (1.2–1.5m) apart, in autumn or winter.

Cut all the stems back to about 3in (8cm) from the soil, cutting to a bud; it sounds drastic, but will result in much better growth. In the next two winters, remove only any weak or downward-pointing shoots. From then on, prune each year before late winter as below. Every spring, mulch with well-rotted manure and apply a balanced fertilizer, and also 1oz/35g of potassium sulfate per bush. Water in dry weather but not as fruits ripen; this causes skins to split. There are usually few problems, although birds and squirrels can strip a plant overnight.

PRUNING A BLACKCURRANT ▷
Once the bush is established, pruning each winter consists of removing some stems close to the ground, and cutting other side branches back to where they join main stems. Concentrate on removing old wood, branches that sweep the ground, and those that cross the center, crowding the bush.

THIN THE CENTER ▷
Cut out at the base one in three or four of the stems, choosing the oldest and/or least productive (the ones with fewest young sideshoots). Use loppers for a good, clean cut.

◁ BRANCH TOO LOW
Cut back any branches that spread out over the ground; when laden with fruit they will brush the soil and the fruits will get dirty or be eaten by mice and other creatures.

BLUEBERRIES

Related to ornamental *Vaccinium* and to several wild swamp- or bog-dwelling shrubs, blueberries thrive only in moist, ideally peaty, acidic soil. While their wilder relatives are mostly low-growing, the most desirable blueberries to grow are the highbush varieties, which make well-shaped, medium-sized shrubs, attractive in their own right; if you have suitable soil, they look good among rhododendrons and heathers, although you may lose fruits to birds this way. If you do not have acidic soil, you can mimic the conditions blueberries enjoy by using an acidic soil mix in a container; it must be a good-sized pot, and you must water regularly to ensure the soil mix never dries out (you must use lime-free water; rainwater is ideal). Container growing makes it easy to throw bird netting over the bushes. Each spring,

mulch them with well-rotted manure, or work a little bonemeal into the soil mix. Blueberries do not need regular pruning, but they tolerate it in winter if they grow too large or very congested. In the right conditions, blueberries are remarkably trouble-free; lime-induced chlorosis (*see general leaf-yellowing, p.296*) is the most common complaint.

BLUEBERRIES

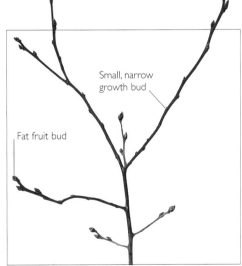
Small, narrow growth bud

Fat fruit bud

◁ BLUEBERRY CROP
Blueberries ripen over a long season, so while you may need to pick over the bushes several times, there is not the problem of gluts, as with some other fruits.

△ WHAT TO PRUNE
Mature blueberries benefit from judicious pruning in winter. Fruit buds are quite distinctive, helping you identify the least productive branches for removal.

SEE ALSO: Containers and Raised Beds, pp.166–183

CANE FRUITS

RASPBERRIES, BLACKBERRIES, and hybrid berries are temperate climate crops, growing best where summers are not scorching and moisture is plentiful. They are susceptible to virus diseases, so buy stock certified free of disease, and do not plant where cane fruits have grown before. They need slightly acidic soil, around pH 6; if higher than pH 7, they may suffer from yellowing of the leaves at the margins and between the veins (see p.296). If this does occur, spray with liquid seaweed or treat with a chelated form of iron and manganese. Equip yourself with a pair of thick gloves for pruning and training raspberries and prickly varieties of blackberry.

RASPBERRIES

Raspberries grow as long, slender stems (canes) that, for the best crops, are cut down after they have fruited once. They need fanning out and tying in to a support system in a sunny, sheltered site to allow the fruits to ripen; they also need protection from birds. With summer-fruiting varieties, canes grow in one year and crop the next, in high summer; they are then cut out and the new young canes that have grown that year are tied in in their place (see below). With autumn-fruiting varieties, canes grow and fruit in the same season, cropping from late summer on, after which they are all cut down. Do not allow summer raspberries to crop in their first year (pinch out any flowers that appear); autumn-fruiters crop well the first year after planting. Before planting (see p.261), erect supports

RASPBERRIES

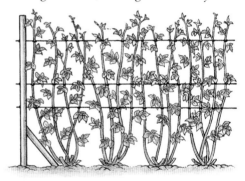

△ **SUPPORTS FOR RASPBERRIES**
Install post and wire supports (top picture) as described on p.261. An easy alternative method is to guide canes between posts and nylon string (shown viewed from the top, above). Loop nylon string 18in (45cm) above ground between two 6ft (2m) posts; with a second loop at 4ft (1.2m). Add connecting ties at intervals between the parallel strings to prevent canes from slumping or being blown about.

△ **FIRST SEASON AFTER PLANTING**
In spring, new canes will grow in a cluster from ground level around the original single stem. Space them out evenly and tie them in to their supports as they grow upward. In midsummer, remove the old, original cane by cutting it back to its base.

and prepare an area at least 3ft (90cm) wide for the rows, digging in plenty of well-rotted manure or compost; raspberries need fertile, moist, but well-drained soil. Every spring, mulch ideally with well-rotted manure or with leafmold (do not bury the canes), and apply a balanced fertilizer to the soil at least 2ft (60cm) on either side of the row, at 3–4oz per yd (100–140g per meter). Keep weed-free and well watered. To keep the plants manageable, remove canes that emerge from the soil more than 9in (22cm) from the main row. Each year, after fruiting, prune back the canes after you have picked the last fruits, and tie in the new ones as they grow. Watch out for signs of raspberry fruitworm (see p.305), gray mold (p.305), and viruses (p.305).

PRUNING AND TRAINING SUMMER-FRUITING RASPBERRIES

1 AFTER FRUITING
Cut out all of the fruited canes at the base immediately after harvesting. Leave the new, pale-stemmed canes that have not borne fruit.

2 SPACING CANES
Tie in or space out the new canes to the supporting wires at 4in (10cm) apart. Here, continuous lacing with twine is used, but you can tie them in indidually; use figure-eight knots so that the canes do not chafe against the wires.

3 TIP-PRUNING
At the end of the growing season, loop over the tips of canes that are taller than the wires, then tie them into the top wire to stop them thrashing about in winter winds. In spring, before growth begins, tip-prune all canes to a healthy bud about 6in (15cm) above the top wire.

SEE ALSO: Planting Cane Fruits, p.261

BLACKBERRIES AND HYBRID BERRIES

Blackberries and their hybrids, such as loganberries, boysenberries, and tayberries, fruit in late summer on long, slender stems (canes) produced the previous year. Thornless cultivars are less vigorous than prickly ones but are easier, or at least more comfortable, to train and harvest. They need the same growing conditions as raspberries, so prepare the site and maintain them in the same way. Provide support wires, spaced 12in (30cm) apart, as described on p.261.

Plant during winter. If the weather or soil conditions are very cold and wet, delay planting until late winter or early spring. Some varieties are more susceptible to cold damage than others and may be killed in very cold areas; seek advice from a local supplier. Training methods vary (*see below*), but all aim to separate the current year's fruiting canes from newly developing ones that will fruit in the following year. As the fruits develop, they will need protection from birds. After cropping, cut out the fruited canes at ground level. Retain the new canes that have developed during the current season and tie them in to the support. Remove any that are weak or damaged at the base. In early spring, tip-prune any canes that show dieback as a result of cold damage. Harvest regularly, leaving in the central core of the fruits.

Blackberries and hybrid berries may be affected by raspberry fruitworm (*see p.305*), gray mold (*p.305*), and viruses (*p.305*).

CULTIVATED BLACKBERRIES

TAYBERRIES

LOGANBERRIES

Cut back to 4–5in (10–13cm) from the ground

△ **PRUNING, SPRING AFTER PLANTING**
Blackberries and hybrid berries, like raspberries, are usually bought as a single stem (cane), planted in late winter or early spring. Once you see new shoots growing strongly from ground level around the original plant, the old stem can be cut back.

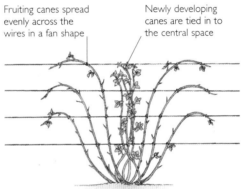

Fruiting canes spread evenly across the wires in a fan shape

Newly developing canes are tied in to the central space

△ **FAN-TRAINING METHOD**
This is an ideal method for less vigorous cultivars and suits those with more rigid canes. The fruiting canes are splayed out and tied in across the fan on either side of the center. New canes are tied into the central space as they grow and lowered and tied into place after fruited canes are cut out.

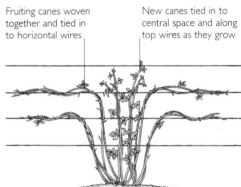

Fruiting canes woven together and tied in to horizontal wires

New canes tied in to central space and along top wires as they grow

△ **ROPE-TRAINING METHOD**
This is a good method for vigorous cultivars with many flexible canes. Fruiting canes are twisted loosely together and tied along the lower wires; new canes up the middle and, if necessary, along the top. When fruited canes are cut out, the new ones are divided between the lower wires.

△ **TYING IN NEW SHOOTS**
Use soft twine and make a figure-eight knot to secure the cane firmly to the wire (this is easiest with thornless cultivars, like 'Oregon Thornless'). Space the canes evenly across the support so that each cane receives its share of sunlight and good air circulation is maintained.

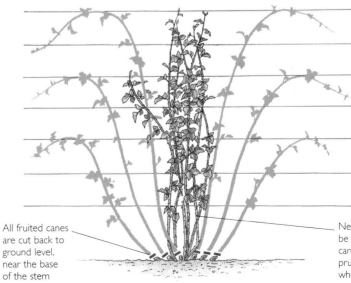

All fruited canes are cut back to ground level, near the base of the stem

Newly developed canes can be bundled gently and carefully together during pruning and spaced out when pruning is complete

◁ **PRUNING AFTER FRUITING**
Once established, annual pruning is done immediately after harvest. Here, new canes have been tied in a central bundle to separate new from old. Cut all fruited canes out at the base. Tie new canes securely to horizontal wires according to the system used. Continue tying in as the canes grow during the season.

SEE ALSO: Ways of Supporting Plants, pp.108–109; Planting Cane Fruits, p.261

OTHER FRUITS

A STRAWBERRY BED ranks highly among the delights of summer, although for healthy, heavy crops it requires a certain amount of care and attention. If you are not committed to a full-scale kitchen garden, a few plants can be grown attractively in containers, however, and alpine strawberry plants will grow happily in the front of a border and look good, too. Rhubarb is also a handsome perennial, although since it needs regular manuring you might not want to give it too prominent a site; beside the compost pile is traditional. Grapevines score highly on looks, too, which is a bonus in cooler climates, where heavy, ripe crops are not assured outdoors.

STRAWBERRIES

There are three types of strawberry: summer-fruiting, which bear over 2–3 weeks in summer; everbearing, which crop in summer and again in autumn, and alpine varieties, which bear a long succession of small, piquant fruits. These are often grown as ornamentals and make attractive edging, but the heavier-cropping varieties are best grown and cared for all together in a strawberry patch or container; the specially made urn-shaped jars with planting pockets make lovely patio ornaments.

Buy plants that are certified virus-free in late summer and early autumn, to bear the next summer. They should bear well for four years or more. Grow in a warm, sunny site in fertile, preferably slightly acidic, moist but well-drained, well-manured soil, or good-quality soil-based mix. In beds, plant 18in (45cm) apart in slightly raised rows 30in (75cm) apart, with the base of the central crown at soil level. On sandy or alkaline soils, apply a balanced fertilizer before planting.

Keep weed-free and well watered. Protect flowers from frost with row cover; lift it in the day for pollination. Protect fruits from birds and from contact with the soil, to guard against rot and slug damage. Remove runners, the creeping stems on which young plantlets develop; they take energy from the fruits. This runnering habit is useful, however, for raising your own plants (right), easy to do and ideal to propagate a variety that grows well for you.

Harvest frequently when fully ripe, complete with stalks. After harvest, clear away surplus runners, weeds, straw and old foliage. Apply a balanced fertilizer.

EARLY-FRUITING STRAWBERRIES

ALPINE STRAWBERRIES

△ **USING PLASTIC MULCH**
Planting through crosswise slits in a black-plastic mulch reduces weeding, retains soil moisture, and encourages early cropping by warming the soil; it also helps keep fruit clean.

△ **REMOVING RUNNERS**
Remove excess runners by pinching them out carefully close to the parent plant. If left in place, they divert the plant's energy away from ripening fruits and reduce yields.

△ **KEEPING FRUIT CLEAN**
Laying straw is the traditional way of keeping fruits clean; woven mats may also be used. Pack a thick layer of straw beneath plants when in flower or when fruits are forming.

RAISING YOUR OWN STRAWBERRY PLANTS

1 PLANT VIRUS-FREE PLANTS
Plant some virus-free plants each year for new stock. Remove all flowers. As runners form, spread them out evenly around the parent; let them root into the ground, or pin them down into small pots sunk into the ground.

2 SEVER THE ROOTED RUNNERS
Once the runners have rooted and are making new growth, lift the plantlet or the pot carefully and sever the runner from the parent plant. Transplant to well-prepared soil, or move them into larger pots for planting out later.

SEE ALSO: Rotating Crops, p.237; Nourishing your Crops, pp.238–239

RHUBARB

Rhubarb is a trouble-free, very hardy perennial that may be productive in good conditions for twenty years. It is a temperate climate crop and does not thrive in warm conditions. Rhubarb grows in a wide range of soils, provided they are fertile and well drained. Dormant plants, known as crowns or sets, are available to buy usually in autumn.

RHUBARB

Before planting, prepare the soil by digging in copious amounts of well-rotted manure or compost. Plant crowns in autumn or spring, 2½–3ft (75–90cm) apart. Mulch plants heavily each year in autumn or early spring. Apply 1½–2oz (45–55g) of a high-nitrogen fertilizer per plant at first, increasing to 4oz (110g) when mature. Water thoroughly in dry weather. Remove any flowering stems. Divide plants (*above right*) when they become very crowded.

For forced stems, more tender and ready for harvest about three weeks earlier than

unforced stems, cover dormant crowns with a 4in (10cm) layer of clean, dry straw in late winter, then cover with a forcing pot or a 18in (45cm) deep bucket. Watch out for signs of crown rot (*see p.304*); rhubarb may also be affected by honey fungus (*p.301*).

DIVIDING RHUBARB

1 LIFT OR EXPOSE THE CROWN
Once the leaves have died back in autumn, lift or expose the crown. Cut through the crown with a spade, taking care not to damage buds. Ensure that there is at least one good growth bud on each section.

2 REPLANT THE SECTIONS
Prepare the soil by digging in manure. Replant the sections 2½–3ft (75–90cm) apart, with the crown bud just above the soil. Firm in gently, water in, and rake the soil level around the plant.

◁ **HARVESTING RHUBARB**
Harvest stems in spring and early summer. Grasp the stem firmly and twist slightly while pulling upward and outward. Do not harvest (or harvest only very lightly) in the first year so plants establish well. Once established, harvest until early to midsummer, then stop.

GRAPES

In warm winemaking regions, grapes are grown on open supports of posts and wires so that air can circulate around them. However, in colder areas a sunny, sheltered wall – equipped with horizontal wires every 12in (30cm) – will help the fruits ripen. Even so, in a poor summer the crop may not be up to much, but the beauty of the vine is some compensation. Buy a young vine (most likely a two- or three-year vertical stem) in late autumn to early winter, and plant against the wall as for any climber (*see p.110*). This central

stem, once it reaches the top wire, is kept cut back to that height. The aim is to allow horizontal side branches to grow out every year, tying them into the wires. After they have borne fruit, they are cut back hard to the central stem (*see below*), which will become increasingly gnarled. Water whenever dry, reducing as fruits ripen. Apply tomato fertilizer every 2–3 weeks once shoots develop; stop as fruits start to ripen. Prune in summer (*see below*). Grapes may be affected by mildew (*see p.296*) and gray mold, as on strawberries (*p.305*).

WHITE MUSCAT GRAPES

BLACK GRAPES

Tie leader to the horizontal in midwinter, and retie to the vertical as buds break in spring

SUMMER-PRUNING ▷
Once all the sideshoots are tied in, summer-pruning aims to control vigorous leafy growth, concentrating energy into a few, choice bunches of grapes. Prune side branches without fruit bunches to 5–6 leaves, and ones with fruits to 2 leaves beyond the last bunch. If there are lots of fruit clusters, thin them to one every 12in (30cm). Pinch back sideshoots to one leaf.

WINTER-PRUNING ▷
In midwinter, prune all the side branches back to one bud if the bud looks strong, or two buds if not. Where the central stem is becoming very gnarled and congested, use a pruning saw to saw off the oldest sections. Cut back the central stem to a bud just below the top wire. Untie it and bend to the horizontal to encourage shoots to break evenly lower down.

SEE ALSO: Ways of Supporting Plants, pp.108–109; Preparing the Ground, pp.142–143; Preparing a Vegetable Garden, pp.236–237

LOOKING AFTER THE GARDEN

MAKING THE MOST OF YOUR GARDEN

WHEN YOUR GARDEN IS ESTABLISHED, you will want to keep it looking as good as possible. To do this, you will need some basic tools and other items of equipment, as well as somewhere to store them. A garden shed is the obvious answer, if you have room, but there are other choices. Sheds and storage areas can be attractively integrated into the garden design. Maintaining a garden produces a lot of waste material, but there are a number of ways of recycling this to produce organic matter for feeding your plants and soil. If you intend to propagate from your own plants or grow some tender ones, protection in the form of cold frames or a greenhouse will be necessary.

STORING TOOLS

You will soon start to acquire a variety of implements useful in the garden, whatever its size. If your garden already has a shed, no doubt you will make use of this for storage. If not, consider all the options before purchasing one.

In small gardens, there may not be room for a shed, so think about whether the tools could be stored in the garage, inside the house or conservatory, or in some sort of weatherproof storage chest outside. An important consideration is whether you can gain quick and easy access to an item when it is required. If you decide on a shed, there are several shapes and sizes to choose from; your choice will largely be dependent on whether you need room for large items, such as lawnmowers and bicycles, as well as for smaller tools.

A NEAT SHED ▷
Not only will your tools and equipment be easier to find if neatly stored inside a shed, but it will also be a safer place. Large tools with handles may be hung up on nails or hooks, as shown here, and smaller ones placed on shelves or in labeled boxes or drawers.

△ **AN INTEGRAL FEATURE**
A shed need not be purely functional but can be seen as a feature in its own right, chosen to blend in with the style of the surrounding garden. Climbing plants may later be enticed to grow up the sides of the shed, softening its outline and providing seasonal color. Access to the shed should always be kept free, however, so that its contents may be easily reached and moved to other areas.

◁ **COMMERCIAL STORAGE RACK**
For extra neatness and safety, attach a metal hanging rack to the inside wall of your shed; it is dangerous to leave rakes and forks lying around or entwined with wires and other tools.

SEE ALSO: Storage Areas, pp.276–277; Tools and Equipment, pp.278–281

RECYCLING WASTE

Gardens create a lot of waste in the form of grass and hedge clippings, prunings, and fallen autumn leaves. Because this is all organic matter, it is a shame to throw it away. Instead, it may be recycled in a compost pile or wormery, together with suitable kitchen scraps, to make a rich, fertile compost that can be dug into the soil to improve it. Leafmold can also be spread around plants as a nutritious mulch and soil improver. The waste must be allowed to rot thoroughly before it is ready for use. Although this process can take some time, depending on the time of year and the material, it is usually worth the effort. If you have room, it is a good idea to have two compost piles: one to be used, after rotting, and the other to be filled up. In this way, you should have a continuous supply of compost, saving you money.

HOMEMADE PILE ▷
Although you can buy commercial compost boxes or frames, it is possible, as shown here, to contain a compost pile with any suitable materials that you have handy, such as old fence panels, wooden posts, and chicken wire.

PROTECTING PLANTS

In warm climates, gardeners do not need to worry about providing cold protection for their plants, but in colder areas this can be quite a problem if you wish to grow tender or exotic species or to create your own stock of new plants from seeds or cuttings. There are many fully hardy plants that will withstand low winter temperatures, and these will not require any protection. Half-hardy or frost-tender plants, however, will need to be grown under glass for at least some of the time.

The simplest way to provide some protection is to use a cold frame, which is suitable for small numbers of plants. You will need a greenhouse if you have a large number to protect or you wish to create a display. Greenhouses can also be heated to a specific temperature to accommodate the needs of particular plants.

◁ **BLENDING IN**
This simple wooden greenhouse forms an integral and decorative garden feature in its own right, as well as providing a protective environment for young and tender plants.

▽ **GROWING EXOTICS**
A greenhouse is the best place to grow a collection of exotic plants that require special growing conditions, particularly if some or all of them are frost-tender. This show of carnivorous plants includes some pitcher plants; they digest insects that have fallen into a pool of liquid inside the pitcher.

A FINE SHOW ▷
Sections of a greenhouse may be used to produce a spectacular display of flowering plants that require frost-free, dry, or other particular conditions in order to thrive.

SEE ALSO: Making Compost, p.236; Greenhouses, p.241; Compost, pp.282–283; Cold Frames and Greenhouses, pp.284–287

STORAGE AREAS

YOU WILL NEED TO FIND AN AREA, somewhere in the garden, house, or garage, that can be used for storing all the tools and items of equipment required for maintaining the garden. Whether this turns out to be a small corner of the garage or a large, custom-built shed depends on your budget and space limitations. Whatever you choose, however, the storage area must be waterproof and readily accessible when you are working outside, and ideally it should blend in harmoniously with the style of its surroundings. Small items may be stored invisibly inside bench seats, and a potentially obtrusive shed may be painted or festooned with colorful climbers.

TOOL STORAGE

For many small gardens or courtyards, a shed would be inappropriate. In these cases, simple storage for hand tools is sufficient. Set aside an area in the house, conservatory, or garage for a tool chest or shelf. If you have no suitable area indoors, use a watertight chest outside.

Some box-style benches for interior or exterior use have good-sized storage compartments under the seat for keeping tools and equipment completely out of

sight. Ideally, place the bench against a wall near the back door. The seat lifts up to reveal a generous area for storing trowels, forks, footwear, gloves, pots, trays, and other items. When the day's tasks are completed, close the lid and sit back to enjoy the results of your labors.

◁ **UNDER-BENCH STORAGE**
This pine bench combines practicality with style, and it can be stained in a color that suits your garden.

SHEDS: TYPES AND USES

Some sheds have an apex roof, which is like an inverted "V"; others have a pent, or sloping, roof; concrete sheds may have a flat roof. If you intend to install a work-bench along one side of the shed, an apex roof is preferable because it will give you more headroom when working. Choose a thick roofing felt.

Sheds may be made of fiberglass, rust-resistant metal, concrete, or wood. The first three are durable but not as attractive as wood. Cedar is long-lasting but costly; softwoods are cheaper, but make sure that the wood has been pressure treated.

■ **Eaves** should overhang the sides and ends by at least 2in (5cm).

■ **Wooden cladding** should fit closely, with no daylight visible through the boards from inside the shed.

■ **Gutters** are not a standard item, but they are easy to attach yourself.

BUYING A WOODEN SHED ▷
Compare a selection of erected sheds before making a decision on which is right for you. Check that the shed is the correct size, that it will be suitable for your intended use, and that it is well constructed from good-quality wood.

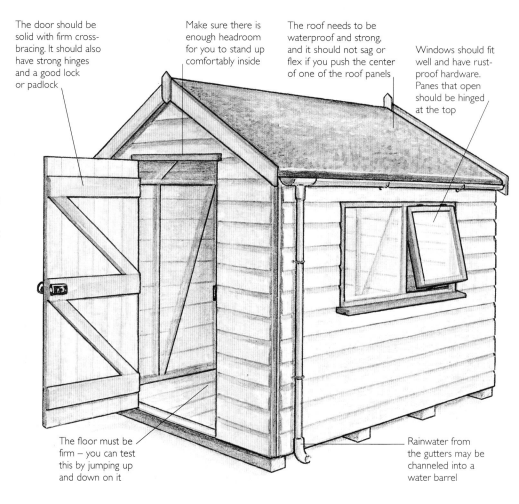

The door should be solid with firm cross-bracing. It should also have strong hinges and a good lock or padlock

Make sure there is enough headroom for you to stand up comfortably inside

The roof needs to be waterproof and strong, and it should not sag or flex if you push the center of one of the roof panels

Windows should fit well and have rust-proof hardware. Panes that open should be hinged at the top

The floor must be firm – you can test this by jumping up and down on it

Rainwater from the gutters may be channeled into a water barrel

SEE ALSO: Storing Tools, p.274; Tools and Equipment, pp.278–281

SITING THE SHED

In a large garden, you will probably have the luxury of a choice of sites for the shed and will be able to find a spot that is both practical and unobtrusive. Remember that you may need to be able to get a wheelbarrow, lawnmower, or other large item in and out of the shed with as much ease as possible, so a path or other hard surface outside the door is preferable to grass. Ideally, you should be able to open the doors and windows to their full extent.

In small gardens, you may find your options restricted to a position either next to the house or at the end of the garden. If the shed is likely to dominate the eye, try to lessen its impact by camouflaging it with plants or painting it in a color that blends in with the general design.

INTEGRATING A SHED INTO THE GARDEN ▷
Various methods may be employed to disguise the shed in order to reduce its visual dominance. In this small garden, where the shed could have become an unattractive eyesore, it has been softened with paint and clever use of climbers.

This shed has been painted with a mixture of wood preservative and colored paint, and draped with climbing plants

Flowers in other parts of the garden echo the color of the shed to help integrate it into the design

There should always be easy access to the shed – a path will also help avoid undue wear on the lawn

Shrubs and containers on the patio by the house serve to divert the eye away from the shed

---

ALWAYS REMEMBER

Large sheds and greenhouses should be erected on a concrete base. Dig a trench, 10in (25cm) deep, to match the dimensions of the building. Place a 6in (15cm) layer of stone in the bottom, and cover it with a 4in (10cm) layer of concrete. Smaller sheds may be laid on a moistureproof material or on pressure-treated wooden beams.

USING THE SHED

Most people use the shed for storage of anything from garden spades and forks to bicycles and outdoor toys. It is vital to use the available space as efficiently as you can. The addition of shelves, boxes, and hooks will make storage of items simpler and neater. Keep frequently used items, such as trowels and pruners, within easy reach near the front of the shed, and keep little-used or bulky items at the back.

If you intend to work in the shed, for example when propagating plants or doing a bit of carpentry, you will need to construct a workbench along one side, preferably in a position where most natural light is available. In a shed with a pent roof, where the window is on the higher side, it is a good idea to put the bench beneath the window and store your tools on the lower side. Some items may be placed beneath the workbench as long as they do not impede your movements.

However you use your shed, you will save time, money, and effort if you take proper care of it. Check regularly that no leaks have developed that could cause metal tools to rust, and re-treat wooden sheds with preservative as necessary.

GOOD IDEAS

• Keep all chemical fertilizers and pesticides well out of children's reach, and preferably under lock and key.

• Line a wooden shed with waterproof building paper (this can be obtained from a builder's store) to reduce the risk of moisture penetration.

• Install an electric light in the shed if you intend to work there regularly during non-daylight hours.

• Always lock or padlock the shed at night to guard against theft.

SEE ALSO: Laying Concrete, pp.60–61; Storing Tools, p.274; Tools and Equipment, pp.278–281

TOOLS AND EQUIPMENT

MANY OF THE ROUTINE TASKS required to keep the garden looking attractive are made easier if you have the right tools or equipment for the job. For small gardens, the basics of fork, spade, trowel, hoe, pruners, and a watering can may be enough, but for larger areas you will probably also need shears, long-handled pruners, a rake, a hose, a wheelbarrow, and sundry items like gloves, stakes, and plant ties. If you intend to raise your own plants, you will find a range of pots, trays, and labels invaluable. Tools should be of good quality and well maintained.

HOES

These are ideal for weeding and aerating the soil, and some types may also be used to create seed drills. The versatile Dutch hoe is designed to be pushed back and forth through the soil surface, with the blade parallel to the ground; other types of hoe should be drawn through the soil. The handle should be long enough for you to work in a near-upright position without back strain.

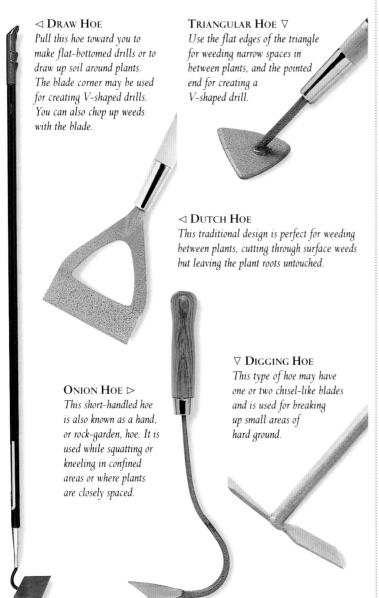

◁ **DRAW HOE**
Pull this hoe toward you to make flat-bottomed drills or to draw up soil around plants. The blade corner may be used for creating V-shaped drills. You can also chop up weeds with the blade.

TRIANGULAR HOE ▽
Use the flat edges of the triangle for weeding narrow spaces in between plants, and the pointed end for creating a V-shaped drill.

◁ **DUTCH HOE**
This traditional design is perfect for weeding between plants, cutting through surface weeds but leaving the plant roots untouched.

▽ **DIGGING HOE**
This type of hoe may have one or two chisel-like blades and is used for breaking up small areas of hard ground.

ONION HOE ▷
This short-handled hoe is also known as a hand, or rock-garden, hoe. It is used while squatting or kneeling in confined areas or where plants are closely spaced.

FORKS AND SPADES

Spades and forks are both essential in general cultivation. Forks are better for lifting root crops and moving manure or compost; spades are necessary for digging areas of soil and making planting holes. Trowels and hand forks are ideal for use in confined areas.

△ **DIGGING SPADE**
The plastic handle, or hilt, and the tread on top of the blade provide extra comfort, and the coated blade is easily cleaned.

△ **GARDEN FORK**
The pronged head and neck are formed from a single piece of metal for strength. The wooden shaft fits into a long socket in the neck, and the handle is plastic.

NARROW BLADE

WIDE BLADE

HAND FORK △
Hand forks are useful for lifting small plants and for loosening the soil when weeding. A fork may be better than a trowel if you are planting in heavy soils, since a fork will not compact the soil.

TROWELS △
Use a wide-bladed trowel for digging holes to plant small plants or bulbs, and when working in containers or raised beds. Narrow blades are good for use in extremely confined areas such as rock gardens.

HANDLE DESIGNS ▷
Handles come in various shapes. Y-type hilts are weaker than D-type ones because they are formed by splitting the shaft wood, but may be more comfortable for large hands.

D-TYPE HILT　　**Y-TYPE HILT**

SEE ALSO: Preparing the Ground, pp.142–143; Sowing in Drills, p.243; Storing Tools, p.274; Looking After Tools, p.281; Weeds in the Garden, pp.288–289

RAKES

There are two main types of rake: general garden rakes and lawn rakes. Garden rakes are used for leveling and breaking up the soil surface before planting. Lawn rakes are used to remove leaves and other debris that may have fallen on the grass, and to scarify the lawn in autumn.

TOOLS FOR CUTTING AND PRUNING

A general-purpose garden knife will be invaluable for taking cuttings, harvesting certain vegetables, cutting string, and some light pruning tasks. Heavier pruning will require pruners, long-handled or tree pruners, or a pruning saw. Shears are useful for clipping bushes and hedges.

For any cutting or pruning tasks in the garden, it is essential that you use the correct tool for the job and that the blades are as clean and sharp as possible. Wipe the blades of cutting tools after every use with an oily rag or steel wool to remove any sap that may have dried on. Then lightly oil the blades. From time to time, tighten the blade tension of garden shears in order to achieve a better finish.

To sharpen pruning tools, remove any blades that are badly blunted or damaged and either regrind or replace them.

GARDEN RAKE ▷
This has a strong, one-piece metal rake head with short, wide, rounded teeth that are well suited to routine tasks such as soil preparation, ground clearing, and general garden cleanup.

◁ SPRING-TINED LAWN RAKE
The light head has long, flexible, rounded wire tines that are perfect for removing leaves, moss, and other debris from a lawn. The action of vigorous raking should also improve aeration.

FLAT-TINED LAWN RAKE ▽
For raking leaves and other loose material from the lawn, this has long, flat, plastic or metal tines and a light head, which will not damage any young grass shoots.

BYPASS PRUNERS ▷
These are used for pruning stems up to about ½in (1cm) thick and for soft shoots of any thickness. They employ a scissorlike action.

GARDEN KNIFE △
You will need a general-purpose knife for all cutting tasks except heavy pruning.

△ BOW SAW
This can cut through thick branches quickly but is too large for use in a fairly confined space.

LONG-HANDLED BYPASS PRUNERS ◁
These allow you to prune stems that are high up or too thick for pruners.

GENERAL-PURPOSE PRUNING SAW

CURVED SAW

△ PRUNING SAWS
Small-bladed saws like these are ideal for pruning in awkward places. Blades may be straight or curved.

◁ TREE PRUNER
Use this to cut branches to 1in (2.5cm) thick that would otherwise be out of reach. Lower the hook over the branch.

◁ HEDGE SHEARS
These have centrally balanced, straight blades, one with a notch to hold a thick shoot during cutting.

SEE ALSO: Choosing a Mower, pp.82–83; Scarifying, p.85; Making Pruning Cuts, p.156; Storing Tools, p.274; Looking After Tools, p.281

WATERING EQUIPMENT

Some plants will grow quite happily in the garden requiring no water other than that supplied by rainfall, but new plants will need watering until they are established, especially in dry areas. Plants grown in pots or containers, and those in the greenhouse, will need a regular water supply.

The simplest method is to use a plastic or metal watering can, usually with a perforated nozzle, also called a rose, on the end of the spout. Fill the can from a water barrel, from an outside faucet, if you have one, or from the kitchen faucet. For large gardens, you will need a hose, for which an outside faucet is probably essential. Hoses may be rigid or flat when empty; the latter takes up less space on a reel when not in use.

Sprayers are useful for mist-spraying plants and for applying pesticides and fertilizers. Sprinklers are an option for lawns and large borders. Always check whether there are any restrictions on the use of hoses or sprinklers in your area.

WHICH NOZZLE?

• Use a fine nozzle for seeds and seedlings, because the gentle spray will neither damage them nor wash the soil mix away.

• For more established plants, a coarse-spray nozzle delivers water more quickly.

• Brass nozzles are more expensive than plastic ones, but they last longer, and they tend to give a finer spray.

• A watering-can dribble bar is more accurate than a nozzle for applying weedkiller.

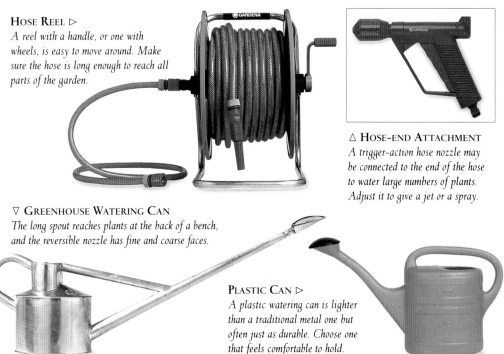

HOSE REEL ▷
A reel with a handle, or one with wheels, is easy to move around. Make sure the hose is long enough to reach all parts of the garden.

△ **HOSE-END ATTACHMENT**
A trigger-action hose nozzle may be connected to the end of the hose to water large numbers of plants. Adjust it to give a jet or a spray.

KNAPSACK SPRAYER ▷
When mist-spraying large areas of plants, use a knapsack sprayer that sits neatly on your back. The spray is pumped up by the lever.

▽ **GREENHOUSE WATERING CAN**
The long spout reaches plants at the back of a bench, and the reversible nozzle has fine and coarse faces.

PLASTIC CAN ▷
A plastic watering can is lighter than a traditional metal one but often just as durable. Choose one that feels comfortable to hold.

WATER BARREL ▷
To gather and store rainwater from a house or greenhouse roof, install a barrel in a suitable place. The barrel should have a tap and a lid, which keeps out debris. You may need to raise the barrel on bricks to allow a watering can to fit beneath the tap.

WHEELBARROWS

There are times in the garden when you need to move bulky or heavy plants, soil, compost, or other material from one place to another. The least time-consuming and back-breaking way to do this is to put it in a wheelbarrow. These may be made of metal or plastic, and although plastic is lighter and therefore easier to push, metal is more durable.

Never overload a barrow or cart, and distribute the contents so that the greatest weight is at the front. This will make pushing or pulling much easier. Check the inflation of the tires regularly.

△ **TRADITIONAL WHEELBARROW**
This type of barrow has a single, solid wheel and a shallow bin that is deeper at the front in order to allow more weight to be carried. Galvanized metal is more expensive than plastic, and it should last well before any rust appears.

△ **GARDEN CART**
A cart such as this one enables you to transport a remarkable amount of material with surprisingly little effort. Be careful not to overload the front of the cart (over the tires) excessively, or the cart may flip up and spill.

SEE ALSO: Watering a Lawn, p.84; Watering Techniques, p.152; Storing Tools, p.274; Chemicals for Weed Control, p.290

OTHER USEFUL ITEMS

What other items you will need will depend on how you use your garden. If you have a greenhouse and intend to use it for raising plants, then pots, saucers, trays, cell packs, and labels will be essential. In the open garden, plant stakes and ties, carriers, gloves, and sieves may all make life easier. For sowing and planting, widgers and dibbers come in handy; a dibber is a pencil-shaped tool used for making planting holes, and a widger is a narrow spatula for lifting seedlings.

POTS AND PANS ▷

Plant containers come in all shapes and sizes. The larger, ornamental ones are excellent for growing specimen plants and may be moved around the garden. Smaller pots and shallow pans are ideal for cuttings and young plants. Pots and pans are made of clay or plastic. Clay is porous, so the soil mix tends to dry out more quickly.

◁ TRAYS AND CELL PACKS

These are useful for individual seeds and cuttings. A rigid outer tray holds a single-use flexible pack consisting of plastic cells, which are filled with soil mix. Seedlings and young plants may be separated with minimal damage to the roots.

PLANT STAKES ▷

Some perennials may need support, in the form of stakes, to grow their best. Ring stakes are best for clump-forming plants, and link stakes are suitable for tall ones.

RING STAKE

LINK STAKE

WOODEN TRUG

△ WIRE-MESH SIEVE

Garden sieves are used for separating out stones and other coarse material from soil or soil mix before sowing or planting. Wire mesh is more long-lasting than plastic.

△ COTTON-FABRIC GARDENING GLOVES

Fabric or leather gloves will protect your hands against thorns as well as keeping them clean. Some have vinyl grips for extra protection and comfort.

CARRIERS ▷

A trug is handy for carrying flowers or fruit. Plastic sheets and bags are ideal for moving light but bulky waste, such as hedge clippings. Bags should have strong handles.

CARRYING SHEET AND BAG

Bamboo stake

Rose stake

Green bamboo stake

Split stake

LOOKING AFTER TOOLS

• Clean off any soil, grass clippings, or other garden material immediately after use.

• After cleaning, wipe all metal parts with an oily rag to prevent rust from developing.

• Store neatly in a dry place, such as a garden shed. Remember that you should never leave tools out in the rain.

• Regularly remove and sharpen the blades of pruning and cutting tools.

• Tools that will not be used over winter should be especially well oiled before storing them.

PLANT TIES △

Use plastic ties to secure plants to their supports. The tie should not constrict the stem.

LABELS AND MARKERS △

There is a wide variety of labels and markers available for garden use. They should be durable, weather-resistant, and large enough to contain all relevant information.

PLANT SUPPORTS ▷

Standard roses require sturdy stakes. Bamboo or split wooden stakes are fine for other single-stemmed plants.

SEE ALSO: Ways of Supporting Plants, pp.108–109; Supporting and Staking, p.154; Sowing Seed in Pots, p.162; Storing Tools, p.274

COMPOST

CREATING YOUR OWN compost is an excellent way of recycling garden and kitchen waste and returning it as organic matter to enrich the soil. This improves aeration and aids the retention of moisture and nutrients. You will need to be patient; composting can be a slow process.

The presence of worms in the waste, however, accelerates decomposition and creates an even better product. Dead leaves that have fallen onto the lawn or borders can also be recycled either by turning them into leafmold or by adding them to the compost pile.

THE COMPOST PILE

To create a successful compost pile, you must put in a mixture of "wet" material, such as grass clippings or other soft, leafy material, and "dry" material, like shredded paper, bark, or straw. Add any vegetable waste, but *never* add meat or cooked foods (it attracts rats), perennial weeds, or woody stems (unless shredded). Also add manure, but not from cats and dogs. The pile must reach a high temperature for bacteria to thrive; for this to happen, the pile must be at least 1 cubic yard (1 cubic meter) in volume. It takes up three months to mature in summer, longer at lower temperatures. Turning the pile helps speed up the process. Use the compost only when extremely well rotted – it should be dark, crumbly, and sweet-smelling.

◁ LAYERS
Start with a thick layer of twiggy material, then build up the pile in 4– 6in (10–15cm) layers. Add a little manure on top of each layer.

USING A WORMERY

Earthworms of several kinds are of great benefit in the garden, because they quickly break down organic matter through their digestive systems. They can be introduced into a cold compost pile or kept in a commercial wormery. The worms work upward from the bottom of the pile, and a wormery is designed to take advantage of this by allowing you to remove the bottom layer of finished compost. The worms will feed on most vegetable matter from the kitchen or garden, as long as you do not overload the bin. They prefer warm temperatures and so go dormant in winter.

GOOD IDEAS

• Place the wormery in a sunny, sheltered part of the garden – the optimum temperature for the worms is 68–75°F (20–24°C).

• Remember to mix together the different types of waste to be added.

• Never add more than a few inches (centimeters) of waste material at any one time.

• Wait for the worms to digest one layer before adding the next.

• Add small amounts of animal manure or partially rotted compost on top of each new layer. Manure may be added on its own.

LEAFMOLD

Leaves take even longer than other waste vegetable matter to decompose, because the process involved is different – they are broken down by fungi rather than by bacteria. It is best, therefore, to keep them in a separate pile. When they do rot down, after about a year or more, the resulting leafmold is well worth the wait. It can be used as a mulch or to improve the soil, but is also good enough to use as a seed or potting mix.

Find a little-used corner of the garden where there is plenty of light and the pile can be left undisturbed. Make a simple container out of wire and stakes (*see below*). Place fallen leaves in the container, and firm them down each time. Add a little water in hot, dry periods.

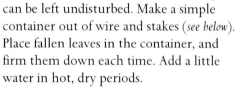

1 ATTACHING THE CHICKEN WIRE
You will need 4 wooden stakes, driven 12in (30cm) into the ground, and a length of chicken wire. If your cage is to be next to a fence or wall, first staple the wire to 2 of the stakes with a hammer. Otherwise, attach the wire after inserting the stakes.

2 COMPLETING THE WIRE CAGE
Attach the 2 cut ends of the chicken wire firmly to the last stake by hammering in staples. It is a good idea to wear gloves at this stage to avoid cutting your hands on the sharp edges.

3 THE FINISHED CONTAINER
The leafmould cage should be square and reasonably low and broad to allow for easy access to the middle. You will need to be able to compact the leaves after putting them in, either by treading on them or by firming with a rake, broom, or other suitable tool.

SEE ALSO: Applying Mulch, p.152; Making Compost, p.236; Recycling Waste, p.275

MAKING A COMPOST BIN

You can make garden compost in a free-standing pile, but a container of some sort will keep the compost neat and moist throughout. Premade plastic or slatted-wood containers are sufficient for only small amounts of compost. Larger containers may be constructed at home from various recycled materials, such as posts and wire, bricks, wood, or plastic fruit barrels, but bricks should be used only if the pile will never be moved.

It is quite simple to make your own wooden compost bin (*see right and below*). The sliding front panels make removal of the well-rotted compost much easier. If you have space, consider having two bins going, using the second when the first is full.

TOOLS AND MATERIALS

- 4 × 3ft (1m) lengths of 2×4in (5×10cm) wood for uprights
- 19 × 3ft (1m) boards of wood for sides
- Strong nails
- Wooden spacer, ½in (1cm) wide
- 4 × 30in (75cm) slats
- 2 small bits of wood
- 5 × 30in (75cm) lengths of wood for front panels
- Wood preservative
- Thick nylon string

THE FINISHED BIN, READY FOR USE

CONSTRUCTING THE FRAME

1 MAKING THE SIDES
Put 2 of the uprights on the ground, 30in (75cm) apart, and lying parallel to each other. Using 4 nails per board, nail 1 of the side boards securely into position, 3in (8cm) from the bottom of each of the uprights.

2 COMPLETING A SIDE
Nail 5 more side boards to the uprights, using the wooden spacer to keep them ½in (1cm) apart. They should be parallel to each other and at right angles to the uprights. Repeat for the opposite side.

3 MAKING THE BACK
Stand the 2 sides parallel to each other, 30in (75cm) apart and at right angles to a wall. Nail 2 strips of wood across the top of each of the opposite uprights to keep them stable. Attach 6 side boards to the back.

4 PREPARING THE FRONT
Remove the stabilizing strips, and turn the bin around so that the back is flush against the wall. Nail just 1 side board across the front of the uprights, 3in (8cm) up from the bottom.

5 ATTACHING SLATS
Place 2 slats on the side edge of each of the front uprights, making sure that the front panels can easily slide between them. Attach the slats with nails, then nail a small bit of wood across the bottom of each slat, which will keep the panels in place.

6 FITTING THE FRONT PANELS
Try sliding each of the front panels in between the slats to make sure that they fit well. If necessary, cut them down to the required length.

7 PAINTING THE BIN
Coat the entire bin, including all the cut edges and the front panels, with a water-based wood preservative, and then leave it until completely dry.

8 FINISHING THE BIN
Slide all the front panels into position. Finally, tie a length of thick nylon string or rope across the top of the container so that the sides will not start to bulge out when the bin is filled with compost.

SEE ALSO: Recycling Waste, p.275

COLD FRAMES AND GREENHOUSES

IN COLDER CLIMATES, where there is severe cold, only fully hardy plants will survive in the open garden. You can still grow marginal and frost-tender ones, however, if you provide them with some form of protection. This means growing them under glass, either in a cold frame or in a greenhouse. For certain tender plants, such as ones that originate in the tropics, you will need to maintain a minimum level of heat and humidity in the greenhouse. Cold frames and greenhouses are also ideal for raising cuttings, seedlings, and young plants.

USING COLD FRAMES

Cold frames can be used throughout the year to grow a wide range of crops. In spring, they are useful for hardening off plants raised in a greenhouse, and in winter they protect winter-flowering plants, autumn-sown hardy annual seeds, and alpine plants that are susceptible to wet weather. The framework is made of wood or metal and it is fitted with glass or clear plastic at the top and sometimes also the sides. The top panels, called lights, should be hinged, sliding, or removable to give easy access.

GOOD IDEAS

• To be practical, a cold frame should be at least 48×24in (120cm×60cm), but you can use whatever space you have.

• For plants in pots or tall vegetable seedlings, raise the frame temporarily on loose bricks to increase its height.

◁ INEXPENSIVE, LIGHTWEIGHT COLD FRAME
The clear plastic panels at the top of this cold frame slide back to provide extra light and ventilation for plants during the day when they need less protection. The aluminum struts make it relatively long-lasting.

◁ WOODEN FRAME
Traditional wooden frames retain heat well. Before planting directly in the frame, cover the base with a thick layer of drainage material, such as broken pots or coarse gravel. Then add a 6in (15cm) layer of good garden soil or compost. Plants may also be grown in the frame in individual pots or in trays.

△ SLIDING LIGHTS
Lights that slide open to allow air to enter and circulate inside the frame are not as vulnerable as hinged lights to sudden gusts of wind, but heavy rain will get inside.

△ HINGED LIGHTS
These may be held open on warm, sunny days to provide ventilation but may not stand up to a gust of wind. To harden plants off, eventually remove the lights completely.

WHY A GREENHOUSE?

If you have the room and the money, do not be afraid to invest in a greenhouse – it will give you an all-weather place for carrying out routine tasks and will vastly increase the variety of plants you are able to grow. An unheated greenhouse will help extend the growing season of hardy and marginal plants, but a heated one allows a far greater range of plants to be grown, including frost-tender species, and provides a suitable environment for raising plants. The greenhouse can also form an attractive garden feature.

◁ RAISING YOUR OWN NEW PLANTS
Using the greenhouse to propagate from your own garden plants, or to raise new plants from seed, will not only save you money in the long run but will also give you a great deal of pleasure and satisfaction.

SEE ALSO: Protecting Plants, p.275; Crop Protection, pp.240–241

CHOOSING A GREENHOUSE

A great variety of shapes and sizes of greenhouses are available, from conventional span or lean-to greenhouses to specialized houses for certain types of plant, such as alpines, or decorative shapes, such as domes or polygons. To decide on the best type of greenhouse for your garden, think about how you intend to use it.

■ A traditional span (*see below right*) or Dutch light greenhouse is best for functional purposes, such as growing border plants or propagation. A Dutch light has sloping sides and allows in maximum sunlight.

■ For displaying tropical or semitropical plants, an attractively shaped greenhouse, perhaps with room for central staging, will form an eye-catching feature.

■ A lean-to greenhouse (*see below*) is ideal for conserving heat and creating a "garden room" next to the house.

■ Alpine houses are designed specifically for protecting alpine plants from winter rain – they are minimally heated to prevent freezing temperatures.

△ METAL FRAME
Aluminum alloy frames are light but very sturdy. They also require very little maintenance.

△ WOODEN FRAME
For the more traditional look, a durable hardwood such as cedar is a good, low-maintenance option.

POINTS TO LOOK FOR

There are so many different types of greenhouse to choose from that it is advisable to have a good idea of what you are looking for before you go to buy one. The most important considerations are rigidity, access, height, and ventilation. The greenhouse should have a firm base and a rigid structure to withstand strong winds. Doors should be at least 24in (60cm) wide. The height at the eaves should be at least 4½ft (1.35m). Roof ventilators are often inadequate as supplied; the total ventilation area should equal one-sixth of the floor area.

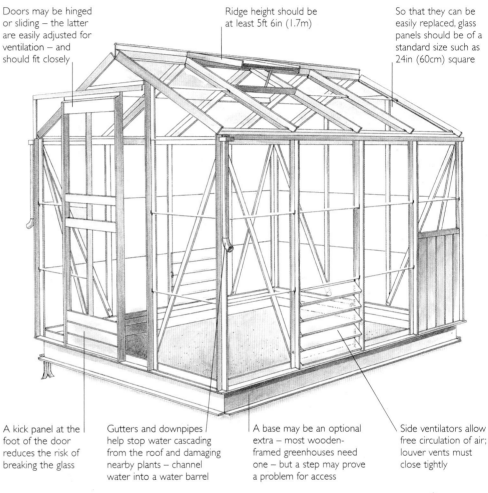

Doors may be hinged or sliding – the latter are easily adjusted for ventilation – and should fit closely

Ridge height should be at least 5ft 6in (1.7m)

So that they can be easily replaced, glass panels should be of a standard size such as 24in (60cm) square

A kick panel at the foot of the door reduces the risk of breaking the glass

Gutters and downpipes help stop water cascading from the roof and damaging nearby plants – channel water into a water barrel

A base may be an optional extra – most wooden-framed greenhouses need one – but a step may prove a problem for access

Side ventilators allow free circulation of air; louver vents must close tightly

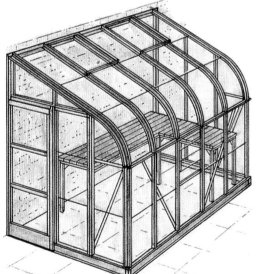

◁ LEAN-TO GREENHOUSE
Where space is limited, or a mainly decorative showhouse is preferred, a lean-to greenhouse is an excellent choice. Some resemble conservatories, and they may be used as a garden room. It is cheaper and easier to provide power and water supplies for a lean-to because it is nearer the house, and the house wall may help to conserve heat and provide extra insulation.

TRADITIONAL SPAN GREENHOUSE ▷
This freestanding greenhouse has vertical sides and a span roof, giving ample growing space as well as headroom. A traditional span greenhouse is ideal for growing border plants and raising seedlings, providing good use of space for relatively little cost.

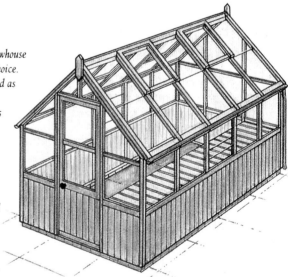

SEE ALSO: Greenhouses, p.241; Protecting Plants, p.275

ERECTING A GREENHOUSE

Before you erect a greenhouse, take some time to choose the right spot. A free-standing greenhouse should be sited in an open position where it will receive good light but is sheltered from strong winds. If there is no natural protection, you can construct a windbreak. Which way your greenhouse should face depends on its use. If it is intended mostly for summer displays, its longer axis should run north to south. For raising young plants in spring or overwintering tender species, an east-to-west orientation of the longer axis provides reasonable light for much of the day.

The greenhouse should be erected on solid foundations, such as brick or concrete built in advance to the correct dimensions, as for a shed (*see p.277*).

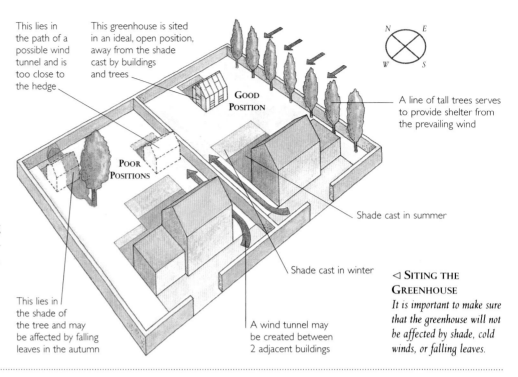

This lies in the path of a possible wind tunnel and is too close to the hedge

This greenhouse is sited in an ideal, open position, away from the shade cast by buildings and trees

GOOD POSITION

POOR POSITIONS

A line of tall trees serves to provide shelter from the prevailing wind

Shade cast in summer

Shade cast in winter

This lies in the shade of the tree and may be affected by falling leaves in the autumn

A wind tunnel may be created between 2 adjacent buildings

◁ **SITING THE GREENHOUSE**
It is important to make sure that the greenhouse will not be affected by shade, cold winds, or falling leaves.

CONTROLLING THE ENVIRONMENT

Your greenhouse represents an oasis in the garden – a place where you are in control of the environment. Instead of choosing plants to suit the conditions available, you can now alter the conditions to suit the plants you want to grow.

It is vital to achieve a balance in the conditions, however. Insulation to retain heat and keep out drafts must be considered together with the need for thorough ventilation. Additional humidity may be a requirement of the plants, and this is provided either by a special humidifier or by damping down the paths with water from a can or hose. For a heated greenhouse, choose an efficient and reliable, economic heater. In summer, shading (*see opposite*) is essential to prevent overheating. In low light conditions, a growing lamp (*see below*) may be necessary.

TELL ME WHY

WHY HEAT THE GREENHOUSE?

Heat in the greenhouse gives you more options for growing different and exciting plants than either an unheated greenhouse or a cold frame. Such plants include tender ones that cannot survive winter in cold climates. It also provides ideal conditions to create new plants from seeds and cuttings early in the season.

GROWING LAMP ▷
This supplies additional light to stimulate or improve plant growth when light levels are low. It should be secured directly over the plants, if possible.

△ **COLD ALARM**
If you have tender plants, a cold alarm is a useful safeguard against a power failure or heater breakdown. The bell will alert you to near-freezing temperatures.

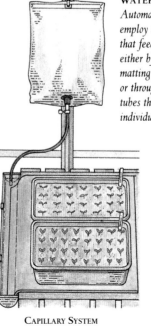

WATERING SYSTEMS
Automatic irrigation systems employ an overhead reservoir that feeds water to plants either by means of capillary matting underneath the plants or through small-bore trickle tubes that supply water to individual pots.

CAPILLARY SYSTEM

TRICKLE SYSTEM

SEE ALSO: Laying Concrete, pp.60–61; Protecting Plants, p.275; Siting the Shed, p.277; Choosing a Greenhouse, p.285

USING THE GREENHOUSE

When you start to use the greenhouse, you will soon discover the need for good organization within it. The various elements required for creating the right environment must all be correctly positioned and accessible. You will need some benches, known as staging, to work on. To maximize the space available for pots and plants, you may also need shelves or hanging-basket brackets. Shade-loving plants can be placed beneath the staging.

◁ FIXED STAGING
Permanent staging may be supplied with the greenhouse. This should be fitted during initial construction.

◁ FREESTANDING STAGING
These benches are movable and therefore allow for greater flexibility within the greenhouse.

◁ SLATTED STAGING
Attractive wooden slats allow more air to circulate around the plants, but they are not suitable for a capillary watering system.

A NEAT LAYOUT ▷
The greenhouse will be easier to work in if all the elements are sensibly and neatly organized. This well-planned layout for a lean-to greenhouse makes best possible use of a limited amount of space.

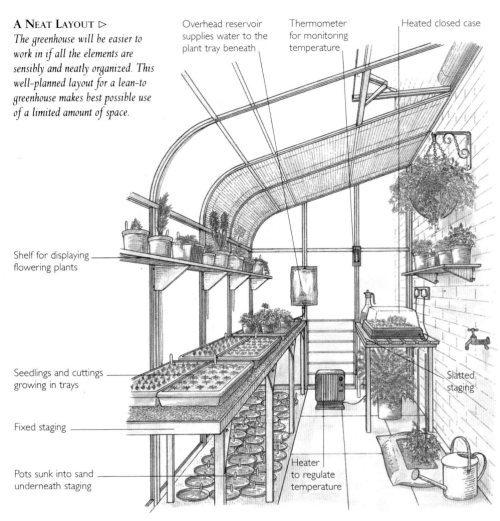

Overhead reservoir supplies water to the plant tray beneath

Thermometer for monitoring temperature

Heated closed case

Shelf for displaying flowering plants

Seedlings and cuttings growing in trays

Fixed staging

Pots sunk into sand underneath staging

Slatted staging

Heater to regulate temperature

SHADING AND VENTILATION

In summer, when the sun is strong, you will need to provide some shading in your greenhouse in the form of roller blinds, a shading wash, or plastic mesh. Remember not to block out too much light, however, because this will inhibit plant growth. Remove the shading in late summer.

Good air circulation, even in winter, is vital, so make sure the greenhouse is fitted with vents. Hinged roof vents should open wide, to an angle of about 45°, to allow maximum airflow while preventing gusts of wind from entering. They should also be staggered, or air will simply blow across. Louver vents allow air in at just above ground level. Fit automatic vent openers to at least some of the hinged or louver vents. A mechanically driven fan ventilation system is another option.

△ SHADING
A shading wash should be applied to the outside of the greenhouse at the beginning of the sunny season. This prevents the temperature from rising too high, without greatly reducing light. Wash off in late summer.

△ FLEXIBLE MESH
Plastic mesh netting can be cut to size and used for shading greenhouse plants.

△ AUTOVENT OPENER
This automatically opens a vent when the temperature rises above a certain level.

△ HINGED VENTS
These are normally fitted in the roof. They should open widely and securely.

△ ROLLER BLINDS
Durable blinds provide a versatile way of shading the greenhouse.

△ LOUVER VENTS
These are fitted in the side just above ground level to improve internal air flow.

SEE ALSO: Increasing Border Plants, pp.162–163; Protecting Plants, p.275; Choosing a Greenhouse, p.285

DEALING WITH WEEDS AND PLANT PROBLEMS

WEEDS IN THE GARDEN

THERE ARE PEOPLE who actually enjoy weeding, but many find it a dull garden chore. Weeds must be dealt with, however, if the plants that you do want in your garden are to thrive and stay healthy. There are a number of ways to prevent and control garden weeds, which fall into two basic categories: annual and perennial weeds.

Annual weeds are opportunists, seeding themselves into any welcoming gap among ornamental plantings. If they are removed before they flower, they cannot perpetuate themselves. Perennial weeds are much more insidious, persisting in the soil all year and coming up not only around but among the roots of ornamental plants.

WHAT IS A WEED?

A weed is not so much "a plant in the wrong place," it is a plant growing where it is not wanted. Traditionally, wild plants and flowers were viewed as weeds, while cultivated garden varieties were prized, but the range of plants that we grow, and reasons why we grow them, is much wider today, and many native wild plants are now valued. For some gardeners, the term "weed" is reserved for plants that can be invasive, so even cultivated plants can become weeds or be weedy – an ajuga planted as a groundcover that runs riot, for example, or a maple that self-seeds to the point of nuisance.

WHY WEED?

Even the most informal meadow planting of wildflowers needs careful management if weeds are not to overtake it. Weeds are most often fast growing and invasive, competing with cultivated plants for food, water, light, and air, usually emerging as the victors. Plants crowded by weeds will grow small and weak and will not flower or crop as freely as they should; they will also be more vulnerable to pests and diseases, for which weeds may act as hosts. Clear the ground before you plant. Even though it will not eliminate annual weed seeds, it is just as important as controlling any weeds that subsequently appear.

TELL ME WHY

WHY ARE WEEDS SO PROLIFIC?

Many weeds are foreign invaders that are perfectly suited to the disturbed, open soil of many gardens. Others are equally well-adapted native plants. They have developed survival strategies for even rare extremes of climate, such as drought, as they affect their natural habitat. This is why they flourish and swiftly regenerate in the most challenging conditions.

△ *ALCHEMILLA MOLLIS*
Lady's mantle is a classic example of a garden plant that is both useful and attractive, yet it can get out of hand if its abundant self-sown seedlings are not controlled.

◁ FORMAL BORDER
Weeds will spoil the look of a carefully planted border and guzzle soil moisture; close planting will minimize areas of free soil space that they can colonize.

△ WANTED "WEEDS"
Impoverished soil and regular mowing allow wildflowers to flourish among grass in this less manicured area of the garden.

SEE ALSO: Lawns with Added Interest, p.75; Controlling Weeds, p.87; Naturalistic Effects, p.89

USEFUL WEEDS

As managed meadows and field edges disappear from the farmed landscape, the gardener has an opportunity to restore the balance in favor of local wildlife by introducing some less controlled areas into the garden. Ivy, for example, should be allowed to grow bushy and fruit; if it is kept cropped close to a wall, it loses almost all of its value as a food source and nesting site for birds. Some annual wildflowers have great ornamental charm as well as being beneficial to wildlife, and they are easily prevented from seeding too profusely. Moreover, many insects have marked preferences for native food plants. Retain a clump of "weeds" in an out-of-the-way spot where they can be left alone and undisturbed; the weedy patch may actually lure harmful garden creatures, such as voracious butterfly and moth caterpillars, away from more valuable plants, minimizing damage.

ENGLISH IVY ▷
Ordinary forms of garden plants, such as ivy, are often preferred by local birdlife over more unusual cultivated varieties.

◁ **FIELD POPPY**
Soil cultivation in some areas is likely to bring poppy seeds to the surface to sprout; keep them not only for their looks but also to attract hoverflies and insect-eating birds.

SOIL IMPROVER ▷
Some weeds, such as this black medick and clover species, actually enrich garden soil by adding nitrogen through their roots. These plants can be dug in and are frequently used as a green manure (see The Edible Garden, p.239).

PREVENTING WEEDS

One of the key factors in preventing weed growth is really effective ground clearance before planting. The subsequent growth of weeds will then be much easier to control by hand weeding, and the need for chemical weedkillers will be greatly reduced or completely unnecessary.

Organic gardeners set great store by preventive measures. The guiding principle behind most preventive measures is light deprivation; without light, the weeds are simply unable to grow. You can exclude light from the soil surface by mulching either with organic materials applied in a really chunky layer, or with a thick dressing of gravel, or with sheet mulches (*see below*). Sheet mulches have the added advantage of keeping new weed seeds from entering the soil.

Close planting, especially with ground-hugging plants, also creates a dark canopy over the soil. A fast-growing groundcover can be a real boon in a new garden, particularly in problem areas, but do ensure that the plant you choose as a groundcover will not become a weed itself. Plants such as *Vinca major*, the greater periwinkle, can metamorphose from solution to problem very rapidly. Clump-forming perennials are more manageable in a mixed planting; planted close, they can always be lifted and divided. Herbaceous kinds are especially valuable where spring bulbs are planted, because their foliage will grow to cover the bare patches left as bulb leaves die down.

TOOLS OF THE TRADE

Applying chemical weedkiller requires a certain amount of paraphernalia (*see p.290*), but for hand weeding a good, strong hand fork that will not bend is the most useful tool; if you loosen the soil before pulling up a weed, you are much less likely to leave the roots behind. There are special tools for weeding lawns and paving, but an old kitchen knife is just as effective. Sheet mulches for suppressing weeds are now very widely available.

△ **TRUSTY FRIEND**
Invest in a quality hand fork for years of service. Those with a separate hasp and handle are usually strongest; wood is warm and comfortable to hold.

SHEET MULCH ▷
This porous material may also be referred to as landscape fabric, geotextile, or planting membrane. It is usually bought as a roll in a range of widths.

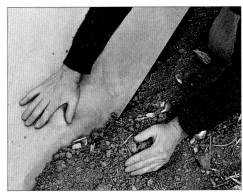

SEE ALSO: Groundcovers, p.75; Preparing the Soil, p.78; Groundcover Plants, p. 88

DEALING WITH WEEDS

HOW YOU CONTROL WEEDS is determined by whether or not you wish to use chemical weedkillers. Often, the use of weedkillers can be avoided only by putting in long hours of clearing weeds by hand, but there are alternatives if you are willing to make certain compromises. There is no doubt that chemical weedkillers save time and work, and they are sometimes the only practical way of turning around really badly neglected patches of land. For effective control, you must also match the methods you use to the type of weeds you are contending with, whether annual or perennial, so learning to recognize common weeds is time well spent.

CHEMICALS FOR WEED CONTROL

There are a great many weedkillers on the market, and they work in different ways. You must decide exactly what you want a weedkiller to do and then select an appropriate product.

Preemergent weedkillers prevent seeds from germinating. They are useful where you will not be sowing seeds of desirable plants, such as lawns or established beds.

Contact weedkillers destroy any plant material that they touch and are often used on paths and paving. They will kill annual weeds completely but kill only the topgrowth of perennial weeds. Contact weedkillers do not affect the soil.

Systemic weedkillers are sprayed or dabbed onto plants and are absorbed by the plant and taken down into the roots, where they kill the plant. They are sometimes called translocated weedkillers because they are transported through the plant. Systemic weedkillers eradicate both annual and perennial weeds, although more than one application may be needed for the latter. These weedkillers do not affect nearby plants provided that the chemical does not touch them during application, and they do not persist in a harmful way in the soil.

Soil-acting weedkillers are absorbed by plant roots, then they move up the plant to kill it. They are also known as residual weedkillers and are useful for clearing infested ground, but they can remain active in the soil for many months, so you will need to wait out the manufacturer's stated time lapse before you can plant.

Selective weedkillers usually kill broadleaved plants, but not grasses. They are used in lawns mainly and are also called broadleaved weedkillers.

APPLYING CHEMICALS

Methods of application vary according to the size of the problem. In a small garden, especially for isolated weeds in beds, lawns, or paths, spot or touch applicators, or small, premixed sprays are ideal. For a larger area, unless you are using a soil-acting granular product, you will probably need to mix up quantities of dilute chemical, and safety here is paramount. A watering can with fine nozzle or spray bar is not an ideal dispenser except on gravel, driveways, unplanted ground, or lawns, since you will not be able to control the amount or direction of the flow well enough. A pump-action sprayer with wand is a good investment, especially in larger gardens; it makes it much easier to direct the weedkiller where you want it. Accurate spraying is essential when you are killing weeds among garden plants; any drifting or splashing will damage and can kill the plants. A useful tip is to cover desirable plants carefully with supermarket plastic bags or trash bags while you spray; wear gloves when removing the bags, and dispose of them safely. Then wash your hands.

SAFETY FIRST

The corrosive and toxic potential of any garden chemical means that it must be used with extreme care.

■ Choose the right product for the job, reading all labeling before you buy.

■ Follow the manufacturer's instructions carefully, especially for rates for dilution, which must be strictly followed.

■ Keep chemical equipment completely separate, rinsing thoroughly after use.

■ Wash your hands after use.

■ Always dispose of unused diluted weedkiller; read labels carefully before you buy. Never pour diluted or undiluted weedkiller down drains – if you have old products to get rid of, take them to an approved regulated dumpsite. Spray very small amounts left over on an out-of-the-way patch of vacant ground.

■ Keep products in their original containers, out of reach of children and animals, preferably in a locked overhead cupboard. Tape labels on if necessary to keep instructions intact and readable. Try to keep the attached booklets.

△ **SAFETY WITH CHEMICALS**
A cool, dark cupboard keeps products in good condition, slows moldering and fading of labels, and can be locked to keep them safe from children. Give it a good cleaning periodically, so that you do not keep obsolete chemicals.

<table>
<tr><td>

ALWAYS REMEMBER

NEVER SPRAY ON A WINDY DAY

Always spray in calm, still weather; otherwise, you risk spray drifting onto neighboring valued plants and onto any beneficial insects hovering nearby. Spray may also be blown over your clothing and face. Always check the instructions for accidental skin contact before you start mixing and spraying, so you know what to do should an accident occur.
</td></tr>
</table>

SEE ALSO: Controlling Weeds, p.87; Using the Shed, p.277

ALTERNATIVES TO CHEMICALS

There is much more scope for controlling annual weeds without using chemicals than perennial weeds. Annuals can be dug into the soil, rather than dug out, and they are easily removed by hand or hoe. They can also be smothered or burned off.

Annual weeds grow, flower, set seed, and die within one year. Although they do not persist, their seeds arrive continuously, either on the wind or borne by birds and animals. They are fast-growing, and several generations may appear in one growing season; in a mild winter, autumn-germinated weeds, especially chickweed, may survive to create a year-round nuisance. They appear most often on regularly cultivated land, such as vegetable plots, where the soil is regularly turned over to expose more seeds. Although chemicals can be used to clear infested areas, annual weeds are just as easily dug or rototilled into the ground, provided that they have not set seed (if so, they should be dug out and destroyed). Established plantings can usually be kept weed-free by hoeing and hand pulling, but the difficulty arises among juvenile or seedling plants: annual weeds are faster-growing and will smother them. Instead of repeatedly hoeing rows of young crops, some vegetable gardeners put down plastic or carpet to smother and prevent weeds, planting through it as for a sheet mulch. This works well as long as provision is made for watering; plastic and synthetic-backed carpet may keep rain off the soil, but they also keep moisture in, so ensure the ground is wet before the mulch is laid. Where annual flowers are grown from seed, it can be difficult to tell them from weed seedlings; sowing in rows rather than broadcasting helps.

On patios, paths, and gravel, where hand weeding is awkward, a small garden flamethrower is an ideal tool for burning off annual weeds, with one exception: it must not be used if the hard landscaping is laid over plastic or landscape fabric.

ALWAYS REMEMBER

CATCH WEEDS BEFORE THEY SEED

If you don't have the time or aren't in the mood for a proper weeding session, you can still help control weeds by nipping off their topgrowth or flowering heads before they set seed and multiply. Repeated removal of topgrowth will weaken perennial weeds considerably. If you get into this habit, you can save yourself a great deal of work in the future.

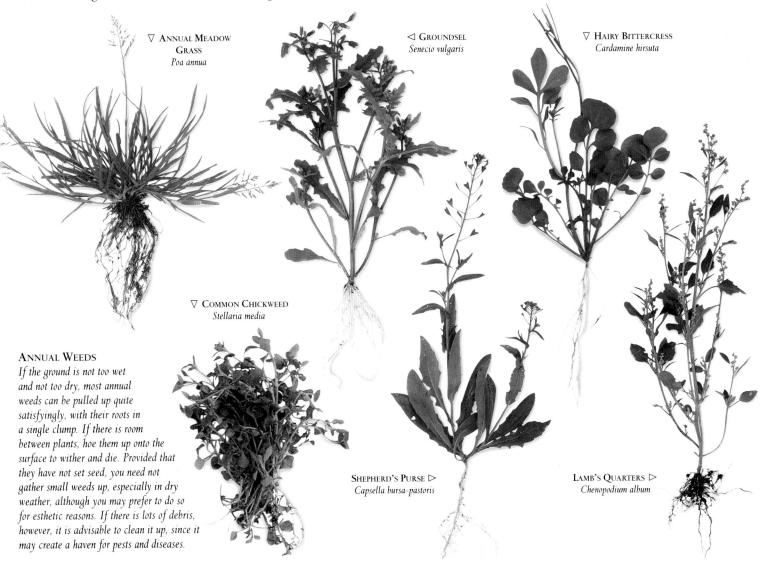

▽ ANNUAL MEADOW
GRASS
Poa annua

◁ GROUNDSEL
Senecio vulgaris

▽ HAIRY BITTERCRESS
Cardamine hirsuta

▽ COMMON CHICKWEED
Stellaria media

ANNUAL WEEDS
If the ground is not too wet and not too dry, most annual weeds can be pulled up quite satisfyingly, with their roots in a single clump. If there is room between plants, hoe them up onto the surface to wither and die. Provided that they have not set seed, you need not gather small weeds up, especially in dry weather, although you may prefer to do so for esthetic reasons. If there is lots of debris, however, it is advisable to clean it up, since it may create a haven for pests and diseases.

SHEPHERD'S PURSE ▷
Capsella bursa-pastoris

LAMB'S QUARTERS ▷
Chenopodium album

SEE ALSO: Controlling Weeds, p.87; Perennial Weeds, pp.292–293; Sowing in Drills, p.243

PERENNIAL WEEDS

Some perennial weeds are imported garden plants that have run wild, like Japanese knotweed, while others are native plants of field and woodland that really relish the good soil and relative lack of competition they find in a garden. If you are prepared to put in the time, and the soil is free of weeds before you plant, then odd perennial weeds can be removed immediately or kept weak by persistent hand pulling, so that they never really get a grip. Alternatively, a dab-on systemic weedkiller, which kills only the weed and will not last in the soil, is a real boon. Infestations of perennial weeds are, however, a more serious problem.

DEALING WITH OVERGROWN PERENNIAL WEEDS

If you inherit or decide to tackle a patch of ground infested with perennial weeds, getting rid of them takes time and planning. Moreover, it is nearly impossible to eliminate perennial weeds growing strongly in and around plants by hand. On herbaceous (leafy) weeds, you can carefully apply a systemic weedkiller (glyphosate is the most popular). On weeds with extensive root systems, repeat applications may be needed. The best time to apply glyphosate is when the weeds are growing strongly, but check labels for timing as well. Leave enough time for the weedkiller to do its job; if you lift wilting weeds too early, you run the risk that the chemical will not have traveled down to the root tips.

If the infestation is so bad that there are more weeds than ornamental plants, it is better to lift the ornamentals and treat the whole area, especially if woody weeds, such as brambles and tree seedlings, have taken hold. For these, a soil-acting weedkiller is

△ LESSER CELANDINE
Ranunculus ficaria

▽ QUACKGRASS
Elymus repens

◁ HEDGE BINDWEED
Calystegia sepium

HORSETAIL ▷
Equisetum arvense

◁ PERENNIAL
STINGING NETTLE
Urtica dioica

△ FIELD BINDWEED
Convolvulus arvensis

◁ GOUTWEED
Aegopodium podagraria

SEE ALSO: Controlling Weeds, p.87; Weeds in the Garden, pp.288–289; Dealing with Weeds, pp.290–291

needed. Do not replant any ornamental without hosing its roots thoroughly to check that no weed root or shoot fragments are present.

Clearing ground infested with perennial weeds without the use of chemicals is a challenge. Every scrap of weed root must be forked out by hand; rototillers are no good because they simply chop roots and can produce many new weeds. The alternative, if you are prepared to wait at least a year before you can use that part of the garden, is to totally smother the soil with an impenetrable material such as black plastic sheeting, old carpet, or a thick layer of newspapers or cardboard weighted down with bricks. Be prepared also to sink plastic barriers at least 18in (45cm) deep into the soil at the garden boundaries if you know that weeds like goutweed are spreading from a neighboring area. Grassing over is another long-term remedy for very persistent weeds such as horsetail, but you must keep the grass closely mown for several years.

TELL ME WHY

WHY CAN'T YOU KILL WEEDS IN WINTER?

Many perennial weeds are evergreen, and while the snowless times during winter may seem the ideal time to apply weedkiller, treatment will not be effective. Although the plants are in leaf, they are not growing (or growing only very sluggishly) and systemic weedkillers will not be transported around their systems to do their work.

△ JAPANESE KNOTWEED
Polygonum cuspidatum

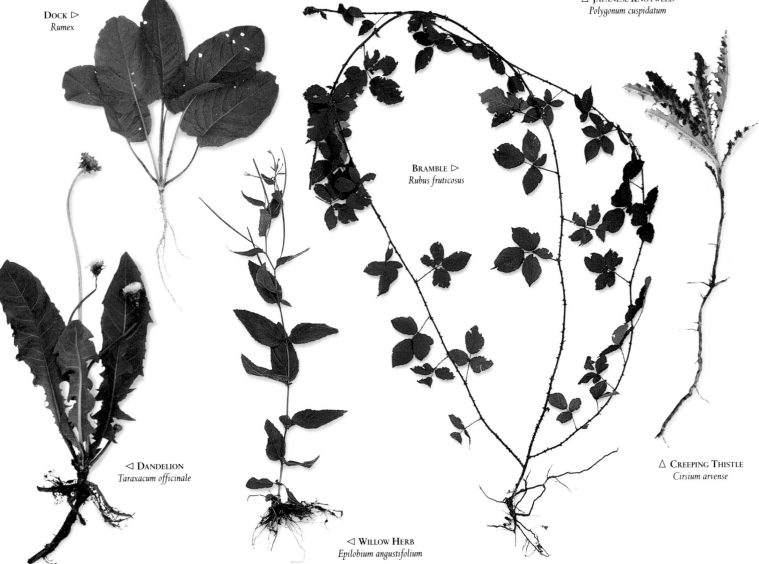

DOCK ▷
Rumex

BRAMBLE ▷
Rubus fruticosus

◁ DANDELION
Taraxacum officinale

△ CREEPING THISTLE
Cirsium arvense

◁ WILLOW HERB
Epilobium angustifolium

SEE ALSO: Controlling Lawn Weeds, p.87; Weeds in the Garden, pp.288–289; Dealing with Weeds, pp.290–291; Manure and Mulches, p239

DEALING WITH PESTS AND DISEASES

PREVENTION IS ALWAYS better than cure where plant pests and diseases are concerned. Good gardening that results in strong, healthy plants makes them less vulnerable to attack. Even before planting, check plants when you buy for telltale signs such as eaten leaves, fungal growth, or old stem damage that does not seem to have healed, and you will not bring problems into your garden. Plant with care and, at first, water regularly to help plants establish well and quickly gain in strength. Maintain good soil fertility and keep plants weed-free to give them the best chance of absorbing the water and nutrients they need in order to stay healthy and shrug off problems.

INTEGRATED PEST MANAGEMENT (IPM)

Integrated pest management refers to a state of mind as much as to a practical approach. Gardeners who practice it do not automatically resort to chemicals: they try every trick they can: choosing resistant varieties; preventing pests from landing on plants, or luring them elsewhere; picking off diseased or infested growth so that problems cannot spread; "quarantining" affected areas, washing tools, boots, and even wheelbarrow wheels to contain disease – and accepting that it's just not worth growing some plants that seem to attract trouble. Good diagnosis is crucial: the same symptoms can signal a pest or a disease or even an easily curable disorder, such as a simple mineral deficiency in the soil. Accurate diagnosis can save you time and worry and of course can save your plants.

ALWAYS REMEMBER

IS INTERVENTION REALLY NECESSARY?
Always assess how bad a problem is before reaching for a spray. Has it really reached the stage where it is harming the plant? Just like us, healthy plants can often recover from minor ailments without help – and overuse of chemicals can build resistance in the organisms they are meant to combat.

USING TRAPS, BARRIERS, AND REPELLENTS

Organic gardeners in particular work hard to prevent pests from getting near plants. They even deploy garden waste creatively: clearing debris from around plants removes places for pests and disease-causing organisms to lurk and provides material for the compost pile; prickly prunings will keep cats off seedbeds; and stones can be piled up to create a "snake hotel." In the kitchen garden especially, protective barriers (see p.241) will keep off birds, deer, and rabbits and create "no-fly zones" for winged insect pests such as carrot rust fly. Pests can also be confused or repelled by strong-smelling companion plants such as rue, catmint, or garlic. Sticky bands stop pests from climbing up trees and pots; saucers of water under greenhouse bench legs foil sowbugs and ants. Traps can be used full-time to control pests such as slugs and snails (see p.298), or at particular times of the year when certain pests attack – the traps are watched so that, at the first sign of the pest, a biological or chemical control can be used swiftly and effectively.

◁ EARWIG TRAP
Earwigs damaging flowers will climb a stake to sleep in an inverted pot filled with straw. You can kill the earwigs you catch or simply move them to a place where they can do no harm.

WASP CONTROL ▷
Yellowjackets and other stinging insects also attack ripe fruit. Protect crops and remove a real hazard to children and pets with a beer trap; the paper lid has a wasp-sized hole in it.

BIOLOGICAL CONTROLS

These are still a relatively new way to control a number of specific pests and, indirectly, the diseases that they spread. They are tiny living organisms that you buy by mail order and introduce onto your plants or into the soil. They may spread a disease among the pests, or they may be tiny predators or types of parasite that need their host only for a certain stage in their development and therefore have no compunction about killing it. One reason that we have not taken this type of biological warfare wholesale into the garden is that most of these creatures need the warmth of high summer or a greenhouse; many die or go dormant in cold weather that leaves pests unharmed.

The key to using biological controls effectively is to choose the right one (if there is one) for your problem, and to follow the instructions for use to the letter. These are living things that simply will not survive incorrect treatment or application or an unsuitable environment. Moreover, they are quite expensive compared to garden chemicals, so getting it wrong is a waste not only of time and effort but also of money.

SEE ALSO: Protecting against Problems, p.241

NATURAL PEST PREDATORS

Without aphids there would be no ladybugs to eat them; without slugs, toads would have less reason to visit our gardens; without caterpillars, we would miss the beauty of butterflies and moths. A garden kept obsessively weed- and pest-free would soon lose its appeal to so much of the wildlife that not only entertains but also helps the gardener, leaving crops unpollinated and plants exposed, with no protecting army of pest predators when problems do arrive. Plant colorful flowers to attract bees, butterflies, and (valuable for pest control) lacewing and hoverfly larvae. A patch of weeds confined in a corner can become a residence for creatures that might otherwise attack favorite plants. Above all, never harm ground beetles, frogs, toads, or snakes, which gobble up pests, or earthworms, which recycle garden debris where disease could breed.

△ GARDEN FRIENDS
Spiders are good garden news — indeed, anything largish and fast-moving is often a pest predator, rather than a slow grazer of plants. Millipedes (p.311), not to be confused with the helpful centipede, are an exception. The hoverfly looks like a bee for its own protection, but it will not sting.

GARDEN SPIDER   **HOVERFLY**   **CENTIPEDE**

△ LADYBUG LARVA
Immature ladybugs may be the ugly ducklings of the garden, but it is in fact at this stage, rather than as the more appealing adults, that they do their best work for the gardener, feeding voraciously on aphids.

CHEMICAL CONTROLS

Very few specific chemical controls are mentioned by name in the pages that follow. This is because the availability of chemicals changes all the time, with some being removed by governmental agencies for health and ecological reasons, and new ones appearing on the market every year. Consult local experts for advice. Never use a general insecticide when something that is specific to the pest is available, so that you protect beneficial garden insects. Some fungicides are better not only for certain diseases than others, but also for certain plants, so again, read labels carefully. Above all, be sure that whatever you use on fruits and vegetables is specifically recommended for that purpose and that you will be able to observe the product's recommended safe harvest date after applying any chemical.

HOW CHEMICALS WORK

Most insecticides work either directly on the pest itself, on contact or because the pest eats a poisoned bait, or indirectly by making the plant poisonous to the pest, so that when it feeds on the plant, it dies. Fungicides are similarly either contact in action, killing growth on surfaces and preventing spore germination, or systemic, traveling around the plant to eliminate infection.

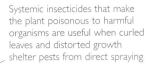

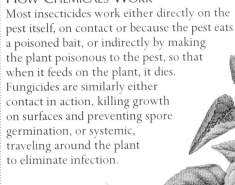

Systemic insecticides that make the plant poisonous to harmful organisms are useful when curled leaves and distorted growth shelter pests from direct spraying

Contact sprays control pests and also harmful pathogens (fungi and bacteria) on leaves and stems

Thorough spraying must include the underside of leaves, where pests often congregate

Dusts can be used on foliage and are also convenient to apply along seed rows

Soil-acting chemicals diluted to form a root drench must be applied liberally to soak well into the ground

Pests underground will not be affected by systemic insecticides applied to foliage; a soil treatment is necessary

Poisoned baits, unnaturally colored to stop them from appealing to birds and pets, are used in the control of slugs, ants, and rodents

CHEMICALS AND SAFETY

You must be safety conscious when using any garden chemical, and you are legally obliged to obey the statutory part of the pesticide label. Some common-sense rules appear on page 290 and above. If you are concerned about the general safety of chemicals, remember that some remedies are considered "natural" and are used by many organic gardeners. For example: insecticidal soap, excellent for aphid control; pyrethrum, derived from a chrysanthemum relative; and rotenone. The two last are nonselective and will harm beneficial creatures.

△ USING SPRAYS SAFELY
Wear rubber gloves so that you can apply sprays thoroughly. Spray at dusk to avoid harm to beneficial flying insects. Never use any type of chemical on plants in ponds, or you will destroy a delicate ecological balance.

SEE ALSO: Safety First, p.290

DISCOLORED AND SPOILED LEAVES

SOME LEAF MARKINGS are caused by diseases and nutrient deficiencies. Weaker fungal diseases are likely to cause real damage only to a plant that is already not growing well – because it is growing in unsuitable conditions, has not been well cared for, or is suffering from some other plant problem. Improved care and remedying any other disorder, disease, or pest that is weakening the plant may be necessary. Many leaf problems can be controlled by catching the problem early, picking off the affected foliage to prevent its spread. Never compost diseased or infested material picked or pruned off plants; instead, destroy it – either burn it (if legal) or discard it.

LEAF MARKINGS, DISCOLORATION, AND DISTORTION

BACTERIAL LEAF SPOT

Black or brown spots, circular or angular, without the dark dots of a fungus (*as in* Fungal Leaf Spot, *shown below*) but often with a yellow halo around the spot, may signal a bacterial infection. These are difficult to control.
■ Pick off all affected leaves and destroy them, and do not water the plant from overhead; splashing may spread the infection. If the plant is not strong enough to recover and is lost, uproot and destroy it. Soil treatments are not effective.

GENERAL LEAF YELLOWING (CHLOROSIS)

Deficiencies of some minerals, including boron and magnesium, have distinctive symptoms, but where a plant is otherwise well cared for, leaf yellowing may be due to a lack of nitrogen, phosphorus, or iron, the last especially when plants that like acidic conditions grow on alkaline soil; this is called lime-induced chlorosis.
■ Apply a general, balanced fertilizer or, if you want to be more precise, use a soil-test kit. If you suspect yellowing is due to alkaline soil, products such as chelated iron will probably be useful.

MILDEW

There are two basic types of mildew, both producing white fungal growth on leaf surfaces, often accompanied by general yellowing and distortion at shoot tips. Powdery mildew is floury, while downy mildew produces fuzzy, grayish or mauve fungal growth, usually beneath leaves.
■ Pick off and destroy affected leaves. Your choice of fungicide may depend on the plant, so check product labeling. Dry but humid weather encourages powdery mildew; water affected plants regularly, but not from overhead. Damp weather and still air encourage downy mildew; ensure plants are not overcrowded, and remove weeds and debris promptly.

FUNGAL LEAF SPOT

Gray or brown circles that gradually join together, sometimes covered in raised, dark dots, often indicate a fungal infection that may have spread from rotting leaves or debris left around the plant.
■ If infection is light, pick off and dispose of affected leaves as soon as seen. In severe cases, choice of fungicide depends on the plant; read labels or ask for advice.

GALL MITES

These tiny creatures secrete substances that cause the plant to make thickened or abnormal growth, often seen as raised, discolored, or felted spots or patches on leaves. Blistering and curled leaf edges are also signs, as are swollen, distorted buds. They mainly appear on woody-stemmed plants and usually do no harm, however bad the infestation. You can pick off leaves on small plants that are lightly affected.

SPIDER MITE

Leaves turning a dull green with a fine, pale mottling are the first sign of infestation by this greenhouse pest; later, leaves turn yellowish white, and the silk webbing spun by the mites will be visible. Seen through a hand lens, in summer, they will be yellowish green, with two dark blotches behind the head, usually with spherical eggs nearby; the mites turn red in autumn and winter.
■ Several insecticides, including soaps, are effective if thoroughly applied several times. There is also a biological control that works well, but it will be killed by insecticides, so these must not be used

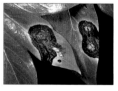

△ FUNGAL LEAF SPOT

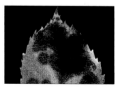

△ ROSE BLACKSPOT

◁ RUST ON ROSE LEAF

Leaf tissue between rust spots usually remains green at first

△ CUCUMBER MOSAIC VIRUS ON SQUASH LEAF

Floury white growth on upper leaf surface

△ POWDERY MILDEW

SEE ALSO: Thrips (silvery leaves), p.299; Bean Halo Blight, p.306; White Blister (on brassicas), p.307

with it. Spider mites thrive in warm, dry, still air, so ventilate greenhouses and mist plants regularly with water.

LEAF CURL

Poplars, peach trees, and to a lesser extent any *Prunus* may develop leaf curl, in which leaves become distorted, puckering and blistering and curling up. These leaves drop, to be followed by a flush of usually healthy foliage. This is a fungal disease that large, healthy trees often tolerate, although it is disfiguring (watering regularly helps, as new, healthy leaves appear); but if it attacks cropping trees year after year, they will lose vigor.
■ A copper-based fungicide applied in autumn before leaf fall, then several times in winter, should eliminate the fungus. Covering trees from midwinter to spring with plastic shelters (most practical on wall-trained trees) prevents spores from taking hold and gives effective control.

LEAFHOPPERS

These sap-feeders cause coarse, pale leaf-mottling, which gradually weakens the plant as green chlorophyll is lost. They are common on blackberries, salvias, mints, phlomis, plums, roses, and beech, and can be seen jumping when disturbed.
■ Most products recommended for aphid control will deal with severe infestations.

LEAFMINERS

The larvae of several insects tunnel in leaves, producing meandering lines or blotches that usually turn white or beige. Celery leafminer, which also attacks parsley, gives the crop a bitter taste.
■ Trees and shrubs such as hollies and lilacs can usually withstand attack, and clipping privet or beech hedges removes the problem. On perennials and crops, pick off affected leaves. For severe infestations, applying a pesticide nay be the only effective control.

MAGNESIUM DEFICIENCY

Pale mottling between leaf veins is caused by a lack of magnesium in the soil.
■ Apply Epsom salts to soil – or there are fast-acting products applied to the leaves.

ROSE BLACKSPOT

Purplish black spots or blotches on rose leaves, usually with general leaf yellowing, indicate blackspot, a very persistent fungal infection. Pick off leaves or even prune out whole stems that show the signs, and burn or discard them.
■ There are several products for treatment of bad or stubborn cases; you may need to spray more than once. If blackspot is a problem every year, check catalogs for roses that show some resistance.

RUSTS

Rusts are fungal infections, encouraged by moisture and characterized by orange to brown pustules, streaks, or blotches.
■ Remove affected leaves and improve air circulation around the plant and between its stems by reducing overcrowding or removing debris. Plants often recover; if not, spray with a suitable fungicide. Do not overuse high-nitrogen fertilizers such as chicken manure. Mallows and willowherbs are notorious rust-carriers, so if rust is a problem, do not grow these, and remove promptly any that appear as weeds. *See also* Leek Rust, *p.306.*

SCORCH

Both hot, dry weather and frost can give leaves a scorched, withered appearance, as can spraying with contact weedkiller.
■ There is no treatment but to cut back affected stems to healthy leaves, and take adequate precautions in future. If there has been no severe weather, occasionally a scorched appearance may be the result of potassium deficiency; try a soil test (*see p.238*). *See also* Fireblight, *p.301.*

SILVER LEAF

Not often encountered, plum and cherry trees are the most vulnerable to this fungal disease, which produces a silver sheen on the leaves. Affected branches show brown staining down the center. It enters via wounds in cold, damp weather, which is why plums and cherries in silver leaf-prone areas should be pruned only in summer, so that the wounds can heal well before the fungus fruits. It is a serious, untreatable disease, and only mildly affected, strong trees may recover.
■ Cut back affected stems until clean wood is reached, wash tools, then make another cut 6in (15cm) farther down; this may work, but is no guarantee that the tree will be saved. Destroy prunings.

VIRUSES

Streaks, flecks, mottling, and marbling patterns on leaves are common signs of virus infections, which also cause stunting and distortion of plants, and streaking on flower petals (*see p.303*). Cucumber mosaic virus is one of the most common causing leaf markings; it can affect many plants, including pumpkins and squash.
■ There is no treatment for viruses, which can severely damage plants and spread rapidly via handling, feeding pests, soil-dwelling nematodes, and even weeds. Swift control is vital. Uproot and destroy affected plants and weeds around them, washing hands and tools thoroughly afterward. Do not replant the same plant on the same site. Look for virus-resistant cultivars and plants certified as virus-free. Control aphids and leafhoppers, which spread viruses, and weeds.

△ PEACH LEAF CURL

△ SPIDER MITE   △ MAGNESIUM DEFICIENCY   △ VIRUS ON PETUNIA LEAF   △ APHIDS

SEE ALSO: Aphids (distortion at shoot tips), p.299; Psyllids and Suckers, p.299; Wilts, p.301

PESTS EATING AND INFESTING LEAVES

HOLES IN LEAVES are usually, but not always, the result of attack by pests. Inspect the plant, looking especially under leaves, and you will often detect the culprit or culprits. Sometimes infestation by small creatures is the most noticeable aspect of the problem, particularly when the insects excrete sticky substances or spin webbing. If you see no insects, look at holes carefully, especially if you have not scrutinized plants lately. A brown ring of dead tissue round the hole, particularly if the leaf is spotted or blotched, probably means that a diseased spot has fallen away, a phenomenon known as shothole; the problem may not be a pest (see Leaf Markings, p.296).

HOLES IN LEAVES

CATERPILLARS
The larval stages of moths and butterflies always have three pairs of forelegs and two to five pairs of clasping back legs, known as prolegs. Some are leaf miners (*see p.297*), and others live underground (*see p.310*), but most exist and feed on leaf surfaces, some within silk webbing.
■ Light infestations can be picked off by hand, both the insects and any silk nests (wear gloves if the caterpillars are hairy; some can cause rashes); on trees and shrubs, entire shoots can be pruned out. In bad cases, spray with an insecticide. The biological control *Bacillus thuringiensis* can also be effective. Sticky bands around the trunks of fruit trees in autumn will prevent wingless female moths (such as gypsy moths) from climbing up them to lay eggs. (*See also p.307.*)

FLEA BEETLES
These small, shiny beetles may be black with yellow stripes, metallic blue, or yellowish brown. They graze on the leaf surface, so the holes they make may not go all the way through the leaf; the thin tissue that remains will turn brown and crispy. They can kill young plants.
■ Use row cover on young plants.

LEAF-CUTTING BEES
Almost circular holes cut from the edges of rose, wisteria, and epimedium leaves in particular are the work of leaf-cutting bees – valuable pollinators. Only one bee will be at work, making her nest. The damage can normally be tolerated.

RABBITS
Foliage, soft shoots, and bark all appeal to rabbits, but persistent defoliation of herbaceous plants and leafy crops gives gardeners the most grief.
■ Barriers of wire netting, with a mesh no wider than 1in (2.5cm), need to be at least 4ft (1.2m) tall and buried at least 1ft (30cm) underground. These may be concealable around garden boundaries and acceptable around kitchen plots but are intrusive around beds and individual plants. Bark guards will protect individual trees, but rabbitproofing the entire garden is the best, if laborious, solution.

SAWFLY LARVAE
Sawfly larvae can be distinguished from caterpillars in having more than five pairs of prolegs (*see left*). They are capable of completely defoliating a plant. Columbines, pines, Solomon's seal, and gooseberry and currant bushes are vulnerable.
■ Pick off by hand or use a suitable pesticide; some are organic and are safe to use on fruit.

SLUGS AND SNAILS
The most likely cause of leaf damage in damp conditions, slugs and snails come out at night to feed voraciously on foliage.
■ Some slug pellets are nowadays claimed to be safe for pets, but many gardeners still prefer not to use them; some products are less toxic. Traps are very effective: try a hollowed-out grapefruit half or potato or a jar of beer or milk sunk into the ground. Slugs are less likely to cross certain surfaces: a layer of ashes, pine needles, or bran around plants can protect them, and there are commercial copper strips to wrap around containers. Hand-picking snails by flashlight can control populations, but slugs can be elusive. There is a biological control for slugs underground (*see p.309*).

WATERLILY LEAF BEETLES
Both adults and larvae graze dark strips out of waterlily leaves, and the damage attracts fungal rots. The adult beetles feed on flowers. Because of the danger to pond life, chemical controls cannot be used.
■ Pick off by hand, or remove badly infested leaves. If this is impractical, a strong jet of water may dislodge enough beetles to control the situation.

△ CATERPILLAR DAMAGE

Lots of tiny holes grazed out of the leaf surface

◁ SLUG DAMAGE

◁ FLEA BEETLE DAMAGE

SEE ALSO: Brassicas, pp.248–49; Codling Moth, p.304; Pea and Bean Weevils, p.306; Birds, p.307

Insects on Leaves

Aphids

Aphids (*see also Flowers, p.302*), which come in many colors, may attack almost any plant. They cause a loss of vigor and distort growth at shoot tips, where they gather to suck sap. They can also spread viruses via their mouthparts.

■ A strong spray of water can dislodge them and control light infestations. Many products kill aphids, but use a biological control, if possible, to leave beneficial insects unharmed. Organic insecticides include rotenone and pyrethrum (both nonselective) and insecticidal soap. Encourage natural predators by growing a varied selection of plants. Some crops can be raised under protective row cover (*see p.240*). Dormant oil in winter kills overwintering eggs on fruit trees.

Lily Leaf Beetles

These very distinctive red beetles may be seen on lilies and fritillaries; both the adults and their larvae devour plants. Pick off the beetles and their grubs, orange-red and covered in black excrement, and destroy. Several effective sprays are available.

Scale Insects

These slightly domed creatures may infest leaves and stems (*see p.301*), feeding on sap under a waxy shell, usually brown or grayish white, which protects them from spraying. They can be removed from smooth leaves and stems with a damp cloth but on some plants are difficult to dislodge. The most effective time to use a suitable spray is when they are newly hatched nymphs, in early to midsummer on garden plants but throughout the year under glass, where treatment may have to be repeated several times.

■ Several pesticides are usually suitable, although insecticidal soap is better against scales on indoor plants. Remember to spray the undersides of leaves thoroughly. Dormant oil on fruit trees kills overwintering scales.

Thrips

A silvery leaf sheen may be the first visible sign of thrips, but on closer inspection the insects will be seen: 1/16in (2mm) long, often with black bodies, some with white spots, giving a banded appearance. Their wings, usually folded, have hairy fringes. When immature they are creamy yellow. Thrips spread viruses and should be controlled.

■ Many products will control them: read labels to see what is best for the plant. Pyrethrum is an organic option.

Psyllids and Suckers

Certain plants are prey to these sap-feeding insects, which cause distorted foliage at shoot tips. When immature they look squashed flat from the side; the adults resemble winged aphids. They may cause concern on apple, pear, boxwood, or bay. Clipping mature shaped plants will eliminate the pests, but on plants that are still maturing it will stunt growth.

■ Apple trees may be protected by dormant oil in winter; on already affected apples and other plants, a pesticide is needed.

Black Vine Weevil (Adult)

A characteristic notching around the edges of leaves is caused by this weevil. The beetles emerge after dark and can be found by flashlight. Adults graze on foliage without harming the plant unduly; the larvae, however (*see p.311*), do enormous damage below ground to roots and corms, particularly to plants growing in containers.

■ Always pick off and destroy vine weevils, and make sure you do not bring the pest into the garden on purchased plants. Smearing a band of a commercial "sticky stuff" around the outside of plant pots will prevent the adults from climbing up into them. There are both chemical and biological controls for the larvae in the soil.

Whiteflies

These sap-feeding, white-winged insects fly up from under leaves when the plant is disturbed. Their nymphs (immature stage) are flat and scalelike; they also coat the plant in honeydew, sticky excrement, which often attracts sooty molds.

■ Pyrethrum and insecticidal soap as well as a number of pesticides can be used on whiteflies; it is important to spray well under the leaves if they are to be effective. Plantings of French marigolds seem to deter whiteflies, for reasons that are unclear: possibly the pest dislikes the smell. The *Encarsia* biological control works in greenhouses from midspring to mid-autumn, applied when the adults are seen on yellow sticky traps.

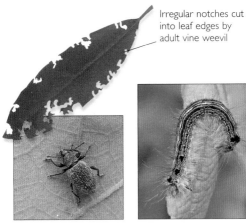

Irregular notches cut into leaf edges by adult vine weevil

△ Vine Weevil Damage   △ Moth Caterpillar

Bright red beetles are appealing but will ruin plants

Lily Leaf Beetles ▷

△ Hemispherical Scale

△ Black Bean Aphids

See also: Leafhoppers, p.297; Cabbage Whitefly, p.306

STEMS

Stems contain the vessels that transport water and nutrients around a plant, so damage or blockage is likely to result in secondary problems above or below the problem. Stems, particularly woody ones, also form the plant's skeleton, and their failing will cause structural weakness. In the case of trees, this can pose a considerable safety risk. Always check ties on trees and wall-trained woody plants and loosen them if necessary to prevent chafing wounds, a key entry point for diseases. If you discover or inherit serious problems with large trees, particularly near buildings, seek the advice of a qualified arborist.

DISEASES

BLACKLEG OF CUTTINGS

Cuttings that rot rather than root are usually the victims of poor or unhygienic growing conditions.
■ Prevent as for damping off (*below*). You can, when taking cuttings, use a rooting powder that incorporates a fungicide.

CANKER

There are a number of cankers; one of the most serious for gardeners affects fruit trees. Canker usually causes raised or sunken, rough bark, sometimes splitting and oozing; the branch may also swell. It often enters via wounds. If it encircles stems, growth above dies, so the lower down a tree it is, the more dangerous.
■ Infected branches must be removed, in winter for apples, pears, and broadleaved ornamental trees, in summer for stone fruits (particularly plums and cherries) and conifers. Cut back to clean wood, and try to improve general growing conditions. Sprays for apples against scab and mildew give some protection from canker. Stone fruit trees can be protected with a copper-based spray. On large branches or trunks, pare early cases out to clean wood, but do not endanger the tree's stability. Make all pruning cuts cleanly. Canker-resistant fruit trees may be available.

CORAL SPOT

This fungus colonizes dead wood, but infection will spread into the rest of the plant. There is no chemical control.
■ Prune out wood showing the coral-red pustules (*see below*), cutting well back into healthy wood. Always prune out and get rid of any dead or dying wood promptly so that coral spot cannot take hold.

DAMPING OFF

Seedlings that collapse and blacken (*see below*) are prey to a fungal stem rot that will quickly spread through a batch or tray, usually because growing conditions are less than ideal. Waterlogged soil mix, overcrowding, dirty equipment or water, and stagnant air all encourage the disease.
■ When sowing, use new or scrubbed trays or pots, clean water, and new, sterile soil mix rather than unsterilized mix or garden soil. Sow thinly and evenly, thin seedlings when necessary, and ensure good light and air circulation. Soil mix can be drenched with a fungicide before sowing.

DIEBACK

A major cause of dieback in woody plants is badly placed pruning cuts, leaving stubs that die; this then spreads down the stem. Dieback on unpruned plants, which may start at shoot tips, bases, or even halfway down, can be a result of poor root growth caused by lack of water or poor planting, leaving roots unable to penetrate soil. Dieback can also signal fungal diseases such as wilts (*see facing page*), and anthracnose, especially if dark, sunken blotches form on stems.
■ Prune out affected growth completely and destroy it. Try to improve the care given to the plant.

△ APPLE AND PEAR CANKER

△ HONEY FUNGUS

△ CORAL SPOT

△ DIEBACK FROM PRUNING CUT

△ DAMPING OFF IN SEEDLINGS

SEE ALSO: Anthracnose, p.306; Crown Rot, Foot and Root Rots, p.308

FIREBLIGHT

So called because affected branches look as if a bonfire has been lit beneath them, this serious disease affects apple, pear, cotoneaster, and related trees and shrubs, usually at flowering time. The stems develop sunken dark patches, often oozing; if you cut into the inner bark, rusty red discoloration can be seen.
■ Prune back all affected branches until you reach clean wood; disinfect pruning tools, then cut back a further 6in (15cm). Carefully clean tools again. If the plant is small or badly affected, it is safer to remove it.

HONEY FUNGUS (ARMILLARIA ROOT ROT)

Any woody plant that gradually fails for no apparent reason should be checked for honey fungus, a very serious parasite that spreads below ground and is extremely difficult to eradicate from gardens. The trunk bases or the roots of infected plants develop a creamy white layer of fungal growth between the bark and the wood, with a mushroom smell. Black, branching rootlike structures grow into the soil, and honey-colored toadstools may appear on the surface or on tree trunks.
■ Infected plants must be uprooted and destroyed, digging up all of the root system where possible. A local nursery should be able to advise on a replacement that is resistant to the fungus, but there are few plants that are unaffected.

WILTS

Wilting of foliage followed by dieback of stems is caused by fungi that block the plant's vascular system, and it is not treatable. Wilt often affects only part of the plant, helping to distinguish it from drought; plants also do not perk up after watering.
■ With clematis and peonies, which are both vulnerable to wilt, cut affected stems out to ground level or below; the plant may reshoot from the base. Otherwise, uproot and destroy affected plants and the soil around their roots. Do not plant the same kind of plant on the same site again.

PESTS ON STEMS

SPITTLEBUGS

White froth around a stem or occasionally coating a flower is a protective substance sheltering the nymphal stage of spittlebugs, yellowish green insects that suck sap. Although unsightly they are temporary and rarely numerous enough to need control; you can pick them off if you like, or remove the affected shoot.

DEER

Deer will eat almost any part of almost any plant, and the males also rub bark off trees with their antlers.
■ Deer are rarely put off for long by commercial repellents. Save these to use on new plants, to which these inquisitive creatures are usually drawn; the temporary respite they can provide may be enough to allow a plant to get established. Look around your locality to see which plants seem to be left untouched, and consider planting these in your garden. Only complete enclosure with a barrier at least 6ft (2m) high will keep deer out.

FRUIT TREE SPIDER MITE

A different mite from the greenhouse pest, this lives on apple and plum trees, laying overwintering eggs in crevices under branches, in such numbers that the bark has a reddish hue.

■ Fruit tree spider mites do not usually need controlling, but if, in summer, leaves turn dull, with masses of mites clustered beneath them, use a chemical control.

MEALYBUGS

Greenhouse plants, especially cacti and succulents, may be infested with these soft-bodied, gray or pinkish white insects, in leaf axils and other crevices, secreting a white, fluffy wax and excreting sticky honeydew over the plant.
■ There is a biological control, effective only during warm weather; at other times, use a suitable spray or insecticidal soap.

SCALE INSECTS

Although scale insects commonly infest leaves (see p.299), there are types that congregate on stems, sucking sap under the protection of their waxy shells. Oystershell is one of the most common on garden plants: oyster-shaped, gray-brown domed objects that cover the stems of, particularly, apples, euonymus, cotoneasters, and boxwood. Heavy infestations cause plants to lose vigor.
■ Dormant oil in winter can protect fruit trees and shrubs or, on infested plants, use a pesticide in early summer.

△ OYSTERSHELL SCALE

DEER DAMAGE ▷

△ MEALYBUGS

△ SPITTLEBUG

Deer are not deterred even by thorny plants such as roses

SEE ALSO: Spider Mite, p.296

FLOWER PROBLEMS

DAMAGE TO FLOWERS can spoil a display you have been waiting for all year; it can also devastate a crop in embryo. Damage may occur to the open flowers or to buds. It is the stage of development when plants are most susceptible to adverse conditions, especially when they flower early and frosts are late, so careful placement and protection of early-flowering plants is important. Lack of flowers can be a result of damage to buds or may be because the plant is not well tended, or because weeds are competing for nutrients. High-potassium fertilizers, such as rose and tomato fertilizers, are generally applied to boost flowering performance.

DAMAGE TO FLOWERS AND BUDS

APHIDS

Aphids may attack many flowers: roses, dahlias, honeysuckle, begonias, waterlilies, and chrysanthemums, to name a few.
■ For controls, see p.299. A jet of water is useful to dislodge aphids from waterlilies, since chemicals cannot be used in ponds.

BIRDS

Although they are a nuisance when they take or damage unprotected fruit, birds can cause much more annoying damage if they eat flowers or flower buds. Targets include primroses and crocuses; birds can take all flower buds from fruit trees, resulting in no fruit at all. Forsythia buds are also sometimes taken, appealing to birds at a time when food is scarce. Fruit bushes and trained forms are relatively easy to net at flowering times. Where netting is impractical or its looks would spoil the effect of the flowers, old cassette or video tape, stretched so that it hums in the wind, can be effective. Repellent sprays do not work very well.

BLINDNESS

When bulbs produce healthy leaves but no flower buds, or dry buds that contain few if any petals, they are usually in need of more care; they may be lacking nutrients or water (see also Dry Buds, facing page), especially if clumps are crowded, or their leaves may have been cut down too early after flowering the previous year, preventing the bulb from building up its reserves. Blind shoots are also common on roses: a shoot appears perfectly normal but never develops flower buds at the tip.
■ Divide congested clumps of bulbs and replant in improved soil. Water them in dry spells. Let the leaves die down naturally, and do not tie them up. Prune blind rose shoots to a leaf farther down and facing outward: a new flowering sideshoot should then develop.

BLOSSOM WILT

Flower clusters on *Malus* and *Prunus*, both ornamental and fruiting, and occasionally amelanchiers, wither but remain on the tree, so the fungal infection responsible spreads to adjacent leaves. Pinprick-sized pustules appear, and there may be dieback.
■ Spraying with a copper-based fungicide before flowering should help; if it is too late, prune out and destroy affected flower clusters to contain the infection.

DRY BUDS AND BUD DROP

Buds that form but fall before opening, or that wither and crisp before opening, are usually the result of dry weather when buds are forming, which can be as early as the summer of the previous year. Plants in containers are especially vulnerable.
■ Always water plants during periods of drought; mulching also lessens the risk of soil drying out completely.

EARWIGS

Ragged holes in flower petals, especially of clematis, dahlias, and chrysanthemums, may be the work of earwigs. Because they feed at night, you may need to do a flashlight inspection to confirm it.
■ Although you can use chemical sprays, earwigs are easy to trap, since they like to

△ ROSE APHIDS

△ POLLEN BEETLE

△ GRAY MOLD

Spots of discoloration, sometimes edged with a dark ring, appear on petals

△ FROST DAMAGE

SEE ALSO: Spider Mite, p.296; Spittlebug, p.301; Wilts, p.301

hide in warm, cozy places. Hang a flowerpot stuffed with straw upside down on a stake near plants (*see p.294*) and the earwigs should crawl up the stake and into the pot. Check daily, then destroy them or move them elsewhere.

FROST AND WIND DAMAGE

Both frost and harsh, cold, drying winds can harm buds and flowers. As frost thaws the petals become flaccid, while desiccating winds produce crispy damage. Plants receiving early morning sun after night frosts are especially vulnerable.
■ Site early-flowering and slightly tender plants carefully. A row-cover blanket can protect plants. Mesh fencing and hedges are better at lessening cold winds than solid barriers. See also Scorch, p.297.

GRAY MOLD

On flower petals, this fungal infection, also called botrytis, produces "ghost spots" – white or buff flecks – which may gradually destroy flowers without any of the more familiar grayish white, fluffy growth (*see p.305*). The spores spread rapidly by rain or water splash and can persist in the soil or in dead plant matter.
■ It is important to remove and destroy infected growth quickly, cutting well back into healthy growth, and to clear up debris on and around the plant. Several fungicides will control bad cases.

JAPANESE BEETLE

These colorful beetles are famous for their ability to devastate a rose garden, but they

△ EARWIG DAMAGE

damage other plants, including grape and linden foliage and peaches. Their populations go through cycles, with some years seeing very few adults and other years seeing an explosion of beetles.
■ Small numbers can be picked off and dropped into soapy water or crushed, but larger numbers require more effort. Traps can capture many of them.

PLANT BUGS

These long-legged green insects may be responsible for flowers opening unevenly and for small holes in the leaves at shoot tips, because they secrete toxic saliva into the plant as they suck its sap, damaging the tissue. Fuchsias, chrysanthemums, and dahlias, as well as several popular shrubs, including buddleias, hydrangeas, forsythia, and caryopteris, are most susceptible.
■ Hand pick, or spray.

POLLEN BEETLES

These small, shiny, bronze or green-black beetles often migrate into gardens from crops to feed in flowers. They cause no damage to plants and should be tolerated. They are, however, a nuisance if brought into the house on cut flowers: leave these in a shed or garage for a few hours, and the beetles will desert them.

PROLIFERATION AND FASCIATION

A weirdly shaped, congested flower on a perfectly healthy plant may be due to either of these conditions. With fasciation, stems and leaves may also be distorted; with proliferation, buds develop within buds to produce a double- or even triple-decker flower. Both are harmless and fascinating when they occur at random; when they appear all over a plant year after year, the cause may be a virus, so the plant should be removed.

RHODODENDRON BUD BLAST

Rhododendrons are prone to dry bud (*see above left*), but this infection covers the buds in tiny black fungal growths. It is spread by rhododendron leafhopper.
■ Difficult to control, but you may contain it by picking off affected buds.

ROSE BALLING

Rose buds swell and appear to be about to open fully, but then petals wither and get moldy. Usually only some flowers are affected. The cause is believed to be rain followed by hot sun which, shining through water droplets, leaves a scorched outer layer of petals that prevents opening.
■ It cannot be treated or prevented, but do not water roses from above when the sun is strong. Pick off affected flowers so that molds do not spread onto healthy buds or cause dieback (*see p.300*). If all the buds on a shoot are affected, prune back to a healthy leaf to encourage another shoot to grow.

VIRUSES

Viruses that affect flowers may cause a distinctive flecking or streaking of the petals, pale on dark colors and brightly colored on pale backgrounds. Known as "color-breaking," it can be attractive, but the virus will spread and do harm.
■ Since there is no cure, the plant should be destroyed (*see also p.297*).

WESTERN FLOWER THRIPS

This type of thrips (*see also p.299*) is drawn to greenhouse, house, and conservatory plants, such as gloxinias, streptocarpus, African violets, and geraniums, causing pale flecking in flower petals initially, then gradual deterioration of the blooms and plants. Thrips also spread viruses.
■ There is a biological control that works well if the infestation is not too heavy. Sprays are less effective, since the thrips hide in buds or folded leaves. Inspect plants upon purchase to make sure that you do not introduce these pests.

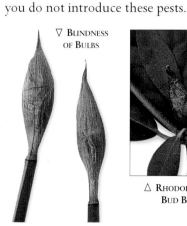

▽ BLINDNESS OF BULBS

△ RHODODENDRON BUD BLAST

SEE ALSO: Gall Mites, p.296; Scorch, p.297; Thrips, p.299; Psyllids, p.299; Premature Bolting, p.307

FRUIT AND FRUITING VEGETABLES

DAMAGE TO FRUITLETS and to ripening fruits takes away the whole *raison d'être* of some plants. Make sure you identify the real cause of the problem: rots often enter only because there is damage to fruit skins through crack or scab, for example, and earwigs are often blamed when they colonize fruits via holes made by wasps. Many pests are drawn by the high sugar content of ripening fruit, so traps and lures can be very effective. Tomatoes have their own specific problems, but when grown under glass they and other crops also become prey to greenhouse pests, attracted not only by the plants but also by the warm, sheltered conditions.

TREE FRUITS

BITTER PIT

A disorder of apples that causes brown speckling on the skin and through the flesh of the fruit, tainting the flavor. It is caused by calcium deficiency, either because it is lacking in the soil or because the soil is dry and the tree cannot extract it. (A deficiency of boron causes the same symptoms in pears; *see p.308.*)
■ Mulching and regular watering help prevent bitter pit, and you can spray developing fruits with a calcium nitrate solution to overcome it. This chemical can damage some varieties, so read instructions carefully.

BROWN ROT

This fungal rot develops distinctive rings of white pustules (*see below*) that rupture to spread spores onto other fruits.
■ Pick off and destroy affected fruits promptly. If the whole fruit has been affected and remains on the tree, looking mummified, prune out the spur it is attached to as well. Bird pecks and wasp damage most commonly cause the wounds through which the fungus enters, so control measures for these pests will help limit brown rot.

CODLING MOTH

The caterpillars of this moth are the pest that causes maggotty apples. A very characteristic sign is their crumby excreta around the eye end of apples; the damage inside (*see below*) can be considerable.
■ You must act before caterpillars bore into the fruits; use a pheromone trap to detect when the adult moths are about and laying eggs, then use an insecticide, following the timing instructions. On isolated apple trees, the trap itself may catch enough moths to limit damage.

PEAR MIDGE

Blackened pear fruitlets are a sign that this small fly's whitish orange larvae are feeding within. Entire crops can be lost.
■ Trees can be sprayed at white bud stage (just before flowers open); the non-chemical alternative is to pick off affected fruitlets to prevent the larvae from pupating in the soil when the fruits drop, resulting in fewer flies the next year.

SCAB

Apples, crabapples, and pears (*see below left*) can develop scabby patches which, if extensive, can deform and crack the fruits, creating entry points for rots. The leaves also show gray-brown patches.
■ Dispose of fallen leaves, and prune out and destroy scabby shoots, to prevent the fungus from overwintering. Spray with a fungicide. There are resistant varieties.

SPLITTING OF FRUITS

Splits in apples and pears usually callus over and can be tolerated, but in other fruits with soft flesh and thin skins, such as plums, grapes, and tomatoes, splits can ruin them. The cause is uneven watering; a lot of water after a dry spell causes a growth spurt that can rupture the fruits.
■ Keep trees regularly watered, and mulch soil around them when moist to reduce drying out.

WASPS

Wasps damage ripe fruits, leaving holes prey to secondary problems, such as rots and invasion by earwigs.
■ If you have only a few, choice fruits (for example, on a peach fan) you can enclose them in muslin bags. To make a wasp trap, fill a jar with beer, or coat it inside with syrup or jam. Make a paper lid and pierce a wasp-sized hole in it, then hang it from a branch (*see p.294*). If you can locate the nest, there are chemical preparations to deal with it, but keep in mind that wasps are beneficial predators.

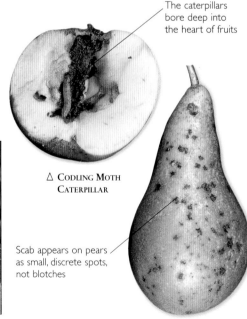

The caterpillars bore deep into the heart of fruits

△ CODLING MOTH CATERPILLAR

Scab appears on pears as small, discrete spots, not blotches

△ BROWN ROT

△ PEAR SCAB

SEE ALSO: Canker, p.300; Birds, p.302

BERRIES AND CURRANTS

GOOSEBERRY MILDEW
An infection causing whitish gray fungal growth and, in bad cases, distorted shoot tips. Infected fruits turn brown on cooking but are still edible.
■ Crowding and soft growth encourage it, so prune well and do not overfeed bushes with nitrogen. Some varieties show some resistance. Prune out affected branches and use a fungicidal spray.

GRAY MOLD ON STRAWBERRIES
Fuzzy gray growth on softening fruit (*see below*) is a fungal infection encouraged by moisture, often entering wounds made by other pests. It persists in the soil.
■ Keep fruits clean and dry on straw (*see p.272*) and clean up plants regularly. Do not water from above. A fungicidal spray at flowering time protects them. Destroy affected fruits promptly.

RASPBERRY FRUITWORM
Dried-up patches at the stalk end of raspberries, blackberries, and hybrid berries are the work of beetle larvae.
■ Spray with rotenone when beetle larvae are newly hatched; exact timing varies with the type of fruit.

Another berry and currant problem: sawfly larvae (eaten gooseberry leaves), p.298

Dried-up area around the stalk caused by feeding larvae

△ RASPBERRY FRUITWORM DAMAGE

△ GRAY MOLD

TOMATOES, PEPPERS, SQUASH, AND CUCUMBERS

BLOSSOM END ROT
Tomatoes and peppers may be affected by this disorder, in which dark patches appear at the base of developing fruits; these gradually sink and rot (*see below right*). The cause is not a disease, but dry soil around the roots that prevents the plant taking up the mineral calcium.
■ Regular watering is the key to saving the rest of the crop (discard affected fruits) and preventing the deficiency from recurring. Plants growing in small containers are more vulnerable, as the soil or soil mix will dry out more quickly. Small-fruited tomatoes are less prone to this deficiency.

TOMATO BLIGHT
Brown patches develop on leaves, which dry and curl; stems may blacken. Fruits develop brown discoloration and shrink (*see below left*), then rot. Uproot and destroy affected plants, and check any potato crops nearby; this is the same fungal infection as potato blight (*see p.309*).
■ Several fungicides can be used for preventive spraying on both crops; copper-based mixtures, acceptable to some organic gardeners, can be used on tomatoes.

UNEVEN RIPENING OF TOMATOES
Unripe patches on tomatoes fall into two categories. A regular ring of green, leathery tissue around the stalk end of the fruit is a condition called greenback, to which some varieties are genetically prone, while others are not. The exact cause is not known.

■ Adequate shading of fruits from hot sun, good greenhouse ventilation, and ensuring plants get enough potassium and phosphorus help prevent greenback. General uneven patches of unripeness on tomatoes are a symptom of inadequate care, probably a deficiency of potassium worsened by inadequate or uneven watering and high temperatures; the same preventive measures as for greenback can be used.

VIRUSES
All these crops are vulnerable (*see also pp.297 and 303*), especially to mosaic viruses, which cause mottled leaves and sometimes curled or distorted, stunted foliage.
■ There is no cure; infected plants should be destroyed immediately, and all other remaining plants at the end of the season. Many varieties show good resistance, so seek them out on the seed racks or at the nursery or garden center. Control aphids and other sap-feeding pests, because they spread viruses. Some viruses are transmitted by handling.

Other tomato, pepper, squash, and cucumber problems include: gray mold (zucchini are especially prone), see left; fruit splitting (tomatoes), see facing page.

Affected areas of flesh start to sink

Tomato skin turns leathery as fruits ripen

△ TOMATO BLIGHT

△ BLOSSOM END ROT

VEGETABLES

EVEN IF YOU ARE not averse to using chemical controls on ornamental plants, you may think twice about applying them to crops. There is no direct safety risk in any of the formulations available to gardeners, if used correctly, but many of us worry about chemical residues in the foods that we eat. Traps, barriers, lures, biological controls, resistant varieties, garden hygiene, crop rotation, and encouraging pest predators form the armory of the organic kitchen gardener. Remember that if you use chemicals they may also kill beneficial insects – valuable for pest control and pollination – as well as pests. Spraying in late evening may cause less harm.

PEAS AND BEANS

BEAN AND PEA WEEVILS
These insects eat U-shaped notches out of leaf edges but do not invade pods, so rarely do real harm. There are chemical controls.

BEAN ANTHRACNOSE
This fungal disease in beans causes long, sunken, brown stem marks, reddening leaf veins followed by leaf withering, and reddish brown spots. Sometimes, in wet weather, pink slime appears on pods.
■ Remove and destroy plants. Some varieties have some resistance.

BEAN HALO BLIGHT
A bacterial leaf spot (see also p.296) causing small, angular markings that develop a yellow halo; the leaf also soon yellows. Pods develop gray, sodden-looking patches.
■ Pick off affected leaves, and do not water plants from above. Destroy affected plants at the end of the season. Some varieties show a degree of resistance.

BEAN APHID
Heavy infestations spoil a number of crops.

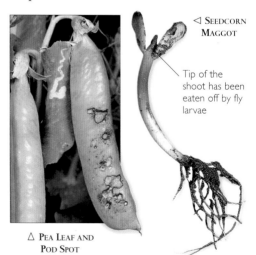

◁ SEEDCORN MAGGOT

Tip of the shoot has been eaten off by fly larvae

△ PEA LEAF AND POD SPOT

■ In early stages, hosing off and spraying with organic insecticides can control it. If you must use a chemical on bad cases, try to use insecticide soap first.

PEA LEAF AND POD SPOT
Fungal infections cause brown or yellow, often sunken spots on leaves, stems, and pods, covered in pinprick-sized, dark fruiting bodies. They can persist in the soil.
■ Be scrupulous when clearing up diseased plant material after cropping, and plant next year's peas on a fresh site.

PEA MOTH
The moth lays its eggs on pea flowers.The caterpillars, white with a brown head, live in pods and feed on the peas.
■ Varieties that flower before early summer and from late summer onward will avoid the problem. You can also start spraying a week into flowering to kill newly hatched larvae.

SEEDCORN MAGGOT
Bean seedlings may be eaten by the white, legless maggots of this fly; look for ragged leaves and stems, and branching because shoots have lost their tips. Plants that survive do crop, often later than expected.
■ To prevent attack, sow in pots or trays, waiting to transplant until soil is warm and not too wet; apply manure in autumn, not spring, because when fresh it attracts the flies; and treat seed holes for direct sowing with insecticide dust.

Other pea and bean problems include: thrips (silvery pea pods – bad infestations may need spraying), p.299; rust (dark brown pustules under bean leaves), p.297

LEAF VEGETABLES

BORON DEFICIENCY
A lack of this element produces leaf distortion and hollow stems in brassicas.
■ See p.308 for treatment.

CABBAGE MAGGOT
All brassicas, related root crops, and flowers including stocks and wallflowers may have their roots eaten by these maggots. Mature plants usually tolerate the damage, but young plants are killed.
■ Dust transplants with an insecticide or protect them under row cover or by fitting collars around them (see p.249).

CABBAGE WHITEFLY
White, winged insects cluster under leaves, flying up when the plants are disturbed; flat, oval, scalelike nymphs (see newly hatched nymphs opposite) also occur on the undersides of leaves. Leaves become sticky with their excrement – honeydew –

ONION FAMILY

LEEK RUST
Bright orange pustules on leeks indicate a rust (see p.297) that may affect only outer leaves; the crop can often still be eaten.
■ Destroy affected leaves and all plant debris at harvest. Grow next year's leeks on a fresh site. Choose resistant cultivars, space leeks widely, and do not overapply high-nitrogen fertilizers, which produce soft, vulnerable leaves. Do not grow leeks after legumes, when soil is nitrogen-rich.

ONION MAGGOT
The maggots of a fly related to seedcorn maggot (see left) feed on seedling roots of onions, leeks, shallots, and garlic, causing

SEE ALSO: Viruses, pp.297 and 305; Birds, p.302; Foot and Root Rots, p.308; Root Aphids, p.309

and this in turn attracts sooty molds.
■ Light infestations can be tolerated, but if leaves are being spoiled, spray with insecticidal soap or a chemical control. Several treatments at weekly intervals may be necessary.

CATERPILLARS

The cabbage looper and cabbage butterfly in particular are drawn to all brassicas to lay their eggs, and the feeding larvae (caterpillars) can ruin a crop.
■ Pyrethrum or the biological control *Bacillus thuringiensis* are organic alternatives to the many chemical controls available. Crops can be protected by row cover.

CABBAGE APHIDS

These whitish gray aphids congregate under leaves, causing yellow patches above, and also cluster on shoot tips, distorting growth.
■ Insecticidal soap or a blast of water from a hose should control them if caught early, but badly infested plants, especially young ones, may need a chemical control.

BRASSICA WIRE STEM

Yellow mottling of leaves and stunting, especially of seedlings, can indicate a soil deficiency of the element molybdenum.
■ Molybdenum can be added in various preparations. Wire stem is common on

acidic soils, which can be limed to counteract it.

BIRDS

In winter when food is scarce, birds may strip brassica leaves to the midribs.
■ Netting is the best solution; scaring devices work only for a limited period.

PREMATURE FLOWERING (BOLTING)

Flowering and setting seed too early may be a response to cold, wet springs or dry summers and cannot be predicted or prevented. Early varieties are more likely to bolt. Looseleaf lettuces resist it better than hearted ones. Spinach beet and chard are less prone to bolting than spinach.

WHITE BLISTER

This fungal infection causes white pustules to erupt on brassica leaves, mostly underneath, while the upper side develops sunken yellow pits. The pustules are sometimes arranged in concentric circles. It is encouraged by damp, humid weather and cannot be controlled.
■ Pull off and destroy affected leaves; uproot and destroy badly infected plants. Some varieties resist white blister well.

Other leaf vegetable problems include: clubroot, p.308; flea beetles, p.298

▽ CABBAGE CATERPILLARS

Cabbage looper/ caterpillar, which may be yellowish-brown or green, like the caterpillar lying curled above it

△ WHITEFLY NYMPHS

△ CABBAGE APHIDS

---

the young plants to collapse; a second generation in late summer bores into bulbs.
■ Onions that have been grown from sets rather than seeds stand up better to this pest. There is no cure for an infestation: lift and destroy affected bulbs and the soil around them. Growing plants under row cover will keep the egg-laying females away.

ONION ROTS

A number of fungal infections cause rots in onions, either growing or in storage.
■ Downy mildew (*see p.296*) can be treated, but white rot (*see right*) is untreatable, so

affected plants must be destroyed together with the soil around them. Following infection, do not grow onions on the same site again for at least eight years. Neck rot may affect onions late in the season as leaves die down and usually spreads into bulbs in storage. Sets or seeds bought from unreliable sources may bring in this infection with them. Dusting with fungicide on planting helps avoid neck rot; the heavy use of high-nitrogen fertilizers encourages it. Some varieties show resistance to all these fungal ailments.

Other onion family problems include: nematodes, p.309; seedcorn maggot, facing page

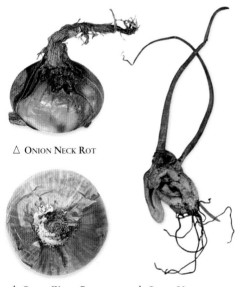

△ ONION NECK ROT

△ ONION WHITE ROT

△ ONION NEMATODE

SEE ALSO: Adding Lime, p.238; Storing Onions, p.250

PROBLEMS AT AND BELOW SOIL LEVEL

PROBLEMS AT THE BASE of a plant are serious and need to be identified quickly. Sometimes there is no cure, but at least you may be able to contain the problem and protect other plants nearby. Because root damage is invisible, problems are usually noticed only when the topgrowth becomes affected, so they can easily be misdiagnosed.

Often the only answer is to dig up the plant and clear the soil from the roots so that you can have a good look at them. This will set back the plant's growth, if not damage it. Root crops cannot be replanted successfully once lifted. However, by sacrificing a few plants you may gain information that will help you save the rest of the crop.

DISEASES AND DISORDERS

BORON DEFICIENCY
Root vegetables are affected by a lack of this mineral (*see also p.306*), showing rough areas, splitting, and, when cut across, a condition called brown heart, with brown tissue usually in concentric rings (carrots may turn gray). Radishes may not discolor, but the flesh becomes woody.
■ You can add borax before sowing or planting; it is worth doing this every year where vegetables are being grown on dry, light soils or on soil that has been limed. Organic matter neutralizes alkaline soil, but do not use spent mushroom compost, since this often contains large amounts of lime.

CLUBROOT
Brassicas (cabbage family) are especially vulnerable to infection by this soil-dwelling mold, which makes roots swell and stunts topgrowth. Stocks and wallflowers may also be affected. It is very difficult to eradicate and is easily spread on boots, tools, and wheelbarrows. It prefers acidic and waterlogged soils.
■ Lift and destroy plants promptly before they rupture to release more spores into the soil; rinse off boots and tools. If you must grow brassicas on previously infected soil, lime it and improve drainage if necessary. Choose well-grown young plants or raise your own, and dip roots into a suitable fungicide before planting. There are clubroot-resistant varieties of most crops. Crop rotation is critical in coping with clubroot.

CROWN ROTS, FOOT AND ROOT ROTS
A variety of fungal infections, including those responsible for wilts (*see p.301*), attack the bases of herbaceous plants, usually causing blackening and collapse; roots usually rot, too. Among the worst rots are phytophthora. When seedlings are affected the condition is known as damping off (*see p.300*). Rhubarb flowering stems nearly always rot as they die down, infecting the crown. Parsnips and carrots are vulnerable to violet root rot, which wraps roots in mauve strands of fungal growth. Didymella is a basal stem rot that attacks tomatoes and sometimes eggplants, causing black-brown sunken patches, usually accompanied by the growth of white roots from the stem above soil level; eventually older leaves yellow, and the fruits rot, too.
■ You must remove infected stems promptly, cutting out any affected tissue at the base of the plants and the soil around it. If badly affected, the plant is usually lost; dispose of it and the soil around the roots to try to eliminate the fungus. Destroy affected crops and grow something different on the site next year. Do not let debris build up around the base of plants; it will attract fungal growth. Do not reuse old soil mix, for example from pots, and replace soil in greenhouse borders every few years. Remove rhubarb flowering stems before they flower. Buy vegetable seeds precoated with fungicide. Do not use fresh manure around lettuces or other leafy crops.

IRREGULAR WATERING
Watering in fits and starts produces growth spurts and lulls that distort root crops, causing cracks that offer entry points for infection. Always water

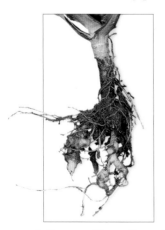

△ CLUBROOT (YOUNG CABBAGE)

△ POTATO SCAB

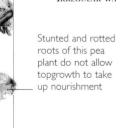

△ FOOT AND ROOT ROT

IRREGULAR WATERING ▷

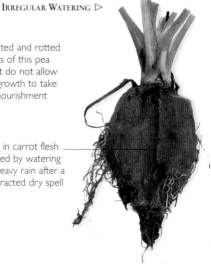

Stunted and rotted roots of this pea plant do not allow topgrowth to take up nourishment

Split in carrot flesh caused by watering or heavy rain after a protracted dry spell

SEE ALSO: Adding Lime, p.238; Soil and Bulbs, pp.310–311

regularly. Work bulky organic matter into light soil to aid water retention between waterings; mulching also helps.

POTATO BLIGHT

The same organism that causes tomato blight (*see p.305*) also causes this fungal disease of potatoes, encouraged by wet, warm, humid weather and readily spread by rain splash. The leaves develop brown patches in damp weather, usually with white fluffy growth around the edges, then wither; infection in the stems may cause the topgrowth (haulm) to collapse. The blight will eventually affect the tubers, causing them to develop sunken, dark patches with discoloration of the flesh, which often deteriorates into slime.
■ Copper-based sprays for foliage include Bordeaux mixture; apply when infection is seen, or before if conditions are favorable to blight (warm, damp summers), or a "Blight Infection Period" is announced by local media. If you do not want to spray, remove and destroy affected haulms, then lift potatoes a couple of weeks later, because, in the early stages, the crop may still be harvestable. Hilling up well protects the tubers. Many varieties have some resistance.

POTATO SCAB

These raised, roughened scabby patches on potato skins usually leave the flesh within edible. Scab is caused by a fungus that is common on light, sandy soils that dry out easily, especially if they have been limed or were once grassed over.
■ Working in organic matter and regular watering helps prevent scab, and several varieties resist it well.

SOUTHERN BLIGHT

■ Many plants develop watersoaked and discolored stem spots near the soil line. Often, the spots darken and encircle the stem, causing the entire plant to die. A white mass of webbing may spread out over the soil.
■ Make sure the soil is well drained, and thin overcrowded plants. Grow resistant varieties, and rotate crops.

PESTS

CARROT RUST FLY

The slender, creamy white maggots of this fly bore into the roots of carrots and also occasionally parsnips, celery, and parsley. There are chemical controls and other strategies to foil the egg-laying females.
■ Carrots sown late and harvested early will miss two egg-laying periods. Plants can also be protected with a blanket of row cover or with a barrier 24in (60cm) high around the carrot plot (*see p.241*); the flies fly low and will not fly up and over the barrier. Remove carrot thinnings promptly, because the smell of the crushed foliage attracts the flies. Some varieties show a degree of resistance.

POTATO CYST NEMATODES

A pest that infests and blocks potato roots, preventing water and nutrient uptake. Typically, a small group of plants begins to yellow and die, but the infection soon spreads. You may be able to see on roots the small white or yellow spheres in which eggs are laid. There is no cure.
■ Destroy affected plants and their soil. There are, however, many resistant varieties. Crop rotation is crucial to prevent buildup of nematodes but will not clear badly infected sites; do not grow potatoes or tomatoes on the site for eight years.

ROOT APHIDS

Plants that are not growing well and are prone to wilting may be infested around the roots with these creamy or bluish green sap-feeding aphids. There are different types on different plants.

■ All can be controlled with a variety of insecticides, diluted to spray strength and watered into the soil. Rotate crops to prevent any one type building up. Lettuces are particularly prone to attack, but there are resistant varieties.

ROOT KNOT NEMATODES

These are microscopic creatures, sometimes called root knot eelworms, that disrupt the intake of water and nutrients so that plants lack vigor and have poor leaf color. They are mainly a greenhouse pest but are also found in light sandy soils. They cause knobby swellings on plant roots, not to be confused with the nodules on pea and bean roots that fix nitrogen in the soil.
■ There is no effective chemical control. Destroy affected plants with the soil in which they were growing.

SLUGS

Slugs in the soil may eat root crops and are particularly drawn to potatoes.
■ Traps are less effective against slugs underground (*see p.298*), but there is a biological control that can be watered in to provide some control. Regular cultivation – hoeing, for example – will also bring the eggs to the surface, where they will dry up. They are caramel-colored and spherical, like very small peas. So are some slow-release pelleted fertilizers, often added to pot plants: the two are easily confused, causing panic in plant purchasers, but slug eggs can be squashed between your fingers.

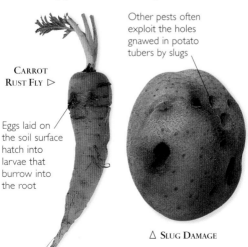

CARROT RUST FLY ▷

Eggs laid on the soil surface hatch into larvae that burrow into the root

Other pests often exploit the holes gnawed in potato tubers by slugs

△ SLUG DAMAGE

△ ROOT APHIDS

SEE ALSO: Adding Lime, p.238; Soil and Bulbs, p.310–311

SOIL AND BULBS

THERE ARE SOME PESTS that, if infesting the soil, may cause concern even when, like ants and sowbugs, they are merely a disruptive presence rather than a threat to plant roots. In the kitchen garden, crop rotation is critical in preventing the buildup of any pest or disease that affects a particular plant or group of plants; this applies to the problems detailed on pp.308–309 as well as to some of the soil-based pests described here. Soil-dwelling pests are difficult to eradicate because they can migrate unseen from an area that has become inhospitable. Many are larvae (immature stages), and some controls rely on preventing adult pests from laying eggs near plants.

PESTS VISIBLE IN THE SOIL

ANTS

Ants need controlling only if they become a real nuisance. They do not eat plant material, but they can mine in and around plant roots to form their nests; the soil disruption can prevent the plants from thriving, especially if they are young. Ants also "farm" aphids for their honeydew, fighting off aphid predators to protect their stock. Eliminating individual ants is no good; you must treat the nest.
■ There are many preparations on the market for ants. Organic gardeners may use pyrethrum, although this may harm other insects.

BLACK VINE WEEVIL LARVAE

Adult black vine weevils, which are distinctive beetles (see p.299), nibble foliage – but this is harmless to plants compared with the damage the larvae can do underground to roots. They are often first seen only once the root ball of a purchased plant is removed from the container, as fat white grubs with brown heads (see facing page, below). If you find one, destroy it and rinse the roots off thoroughly to expose any more. Inspect all other plants purchased from the same source. (The root balls of container-grown plants are likely to contain pellets of slow-release fertilizer that are sometimes mistaken for vine weevil larvae. If in doubt, squeeze between your fingers – larvae will readily squash.) Once black vine weevils have been introduced to the garden they are difficult to control. In open ground they may not damage any one particular plant too badly, but in containers they can be devastating, and any plant that is faring poorly for no apparent reason should be lifted out of its pot and the roots inspected.
■ Some insecticides applied as a drench or purchased premixed in soil mix give good control of the grubs. There are also biological controls that are effective in containers and on confined areas of warm, light but moist soil. Always destroy adult weevils – each is female and can lay many hundreds of eggs in the soil in summer.

CUTWORMS

Cutworms cause the same sort of damage as wireworms (see facing page), eating through the stems of seedlings just below soil level or into root vegetables, but they also emerge above ground at night to eat foliage. However, they look very different and are the larvae of a number of moths. Often they are present only in ones and twos, so if you can find the culprit in the soil and squash it, you may solve the problem.
■ Placing collars around seedlings can deter them. Dust planting holes and rows with an insecticide, as for wireworms, to protect against the young larvae, but older cutworms resist chemical controls.

FUNGUS GNATS

Tiny but active flies run over the soil surface of potted plants and fly up when disturbed. Their larvae live in the soil and eat mostly decaying organic matter, but they sometimes eat and damage roots or the bases of cuttings.
■ Damage is usually insignificant. Large numbers of flies can be controlled with soil drenches.

LEATHERJACKETS

These are usually a minor lawn pest, causing yellow-brown patches where they eat through the grass stems below ground. The larvae of the crane fly, which lays its eggs in late summer, they are grayish brown, tubular, up to 1¾in (4.5cm) long, with no obvious head.
■ Treatment is as for white grubs (see left). You can also bring leatherjackets to the surface and pick them off by covering areas of grass with black plastic overnight, or after heavy rain or a good watering.

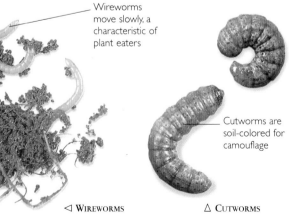

Wireworms move slowly, a characteristic of plant eaters

◁ WIREWORMS

Cutworms are soil-colored for camouflage

△ CUTWORMS

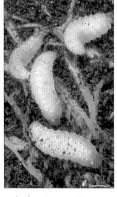

△ VINE WEEVIL LARVAE

SEE ALSO: Problems At and Below Soil Level, pp.308–309

MILLIPEDES

Millipedes feed mainly on decaying matter on the soil, but they sometimes damage seedlings and are a particular nuisance when they attack strawberry fruits.
■ Lifting strawberry fruits up onto straw helps protect them, and dusting seedling rows may also deter millipedes. If you find them in potatoes, they are not the real culprits: they get in through holes made by slugs, so if you deal with these, you should solve the problem. Millipedes have two pairs of legs on each segment of their bodies; do not confuse them with centipedes (see p.295), which have only one pair. Centipedes are valuable predators.

SLIME MOLDS

These funguslike organisms look like slime on plants and soil until they reach the spore stage, when they form into masses or individual dots of spores.
■ Damage is usually only cosmetic. Wash slime molds off with water.

SOWBUGS

Sowbugs (sometimes referred to as pillbugs) do no real harm to plants, except possibly to seedlings in confined areas where populations can build up, since their activities can disturb soil.
■ If sowbugs become troublesome in greenhouses, a thorough cleaning, removing any debris or other matter that provides them with hiding places, should encourage them to move elsewhere. Saucers of water under greenhouse staging legs will prevent them from climbing up and onto benches.

White grubs curl into distinctive C-shape

△ WHITE GRUBS

SPRINGTAILS

Lively, tiny, whitish insects appear to bounce around on the soil surface of potted plants, especially when disturbed by watering. They feed on decaying plant matter, including peat in soil mixes.
■ They normally cause little or no harm and so do not require control.

WHITE GRUBS

White grubs curl into a C-shape when exposed, which helps identify them (see facing page, below). The larvae of various beetles, they have three pairs of legs at the front of their bodies. They eat roots, making plants wilt suddenly. In flower beds, if you identify the problem swiftly, you may be able to dig up all the grubs and squash them; there may not be very many. However, populations commonly build up in lawns unseen, causing widespread yellow patches. Pecking or digging in lawns by birds and skunks, which relish the grubs, is usually confirmation of their presence.
■ Good cultivation of the grass will make the turf more vigorous and more tolerant of pest damage. There are some chemical and biological controls available for dealing with pests in lawns.

WIREWORMS

These click beetle larvae are especially common where planting areas were once grassed over, and the problem usually subsides after a few years if the soil is kept cultivated. They feed on any roots, but the chief damage they cause is to seedlings as they eat through the stems below ground, and to root crops, into which they tunnel. They are orange-brown segmented creatures (see facing page, below), up to 1in (2.5cm) long, with three pairs of legs at the front end.
■ If you identify wireworms in your soil, avoid growing potatoes and carrots in it for a few years if possible; if not, growing early varieties and lifting crops as soon as they are mature should prevent too much damage. Seedlings can be protected by dusting planting rows.

BULBS AND CORMS

NARCISSUS BULB FLY

A relative of horseflies, the larvae eat out the center of narcissus (daffodil) and amaryllis bulbs (see below).
■ It cannot be treated with chemicals, but you can protect valuable spring bulbs after flowering by mounding soil around their bases and laying row cover to prevent the flies from laying eggs at the base of the plant. Leave the protection in place until midsummer. Bulbs planted in shade or windy sites may be less vulnerable.

NEMATODES

Some nematodes feed on roots (see p.309) but some attack bulbs of daffodils and also onions, producing stunted growth; when daffodil bulbs are cut across, brown rings can be seen. There is no treatment.
■ Always buy onion sets and daffodil bulbs from reputable suppliers. Crop rotation should eliminate an infestation of onion nematode. Narcissus nematode is difficult to eradicate and can ruin naturalized daffodil plantings, but there is no effective option other than to lift and destroy any bulbs suspected of infestation.

MICE AND OTHER RODENTS

Crocus corms are a favorite food of mice, as are pea, bean, and sweet corn seeds, which mice can locate even before they have had a chance to germinate. Nibbled green shoot tips on the ground where crocuses and crops are growing is the more common scenario, however.
■ There are several types of humane trap if you do not prefer to use the traditional variety, but a mouse can find its way back over distances of up to a mile, so disposal may become a chore. Press soil down firmly over crocus corms to make it more difficult for mice to locate them. Chicken wire over the soil can deter them, but it must have a fine mesh.

Core of bulb is eaten away and destroyed by bulb fly larvae

△ NARCISSUS BULB FLY

SEE ALSO: Problems At and Below Soil Level, pp.308–309

PART THREE

WHAT LOOKS GOOD WHEN

GOOD YEAR-ROUND 1

STRUCTURE PLANTS

SASA VEITCHII
Z6–10 ↕ 3–6ft (1–2m) ↔ indefinite
This bamboo has strongly upright stems with white-margined leaves. It is useful for very shady areas, but keep it in a container in the ground to restrict its spread.

SAMBUCUS NIGRA 'GUINCHO PURPLE'
Z6–8 ↕ 20ft (6m)
This dark-leaved elder is a fast-growing deciduous shrub. The broad, flat clusters of white flowers in early summer develop into glossy round fruit. Effective for structure in a wild garden.

BETULA PENDULA 'TRISTIS'
Z2–7 ↕ 80ft (25m) ↔ 30ft (10m)
Silver birches are graceful trees with unusual peeling bark, yellow-brown catkins in spring, and pretty foliage colors in autumn. On 'Tristis', the peeling bark remains white underneath.

BERBERIS THUNBERGII 'RED PILLAR'
Z5–8 ↕↔ 5ft (1.5m)
This deciduous, densely leaved shrub makes an excellent hedge with attractive red-purple foliage. The shape opens out as the shrub matures. For better autumn color, grow in a sunny spot.

COTINUS COGGYGRIA 'NOTCUTT'S VARIETY'
Z5–8 ↕↔ 15ft (5m)
This smoke bush is a dense deciduous shrub with fuzzy-looking, purple-pink flowers in summer, which give the plant a distinctive texture. Red-purple leaves provide good color contrasts.

CRYPTOMERIA JAPONICA
Z6–9 ↕ to 80ft (25m) ↔ to 20ft (6m)
The Japanese cedar grows into a tall, conical tree, valued for its red bark and decorative cones. It tolerates a variety of garden conditions and requires little pruning to keep in shape.

PHORMIUM 'BRONZE BABY'
Z9–10 ↕↔ 24–32in (60–80cm)
Good in a coastal garden or in large pots, New Zealand flaxes form a focal point with their evergreen, blade-like leaves. 'Bronze Baby' is a dwarf variety with rigidly upright, bronze-colored leaves.

FATSIA JAPONICA
Z8–10 ‡↔ 5–12ft (1.5–4m)
This evergreen shrub suits a container or mixed border in a sheltered courtyard or town garden. It is loved for its large, shiny leaves and autumn flowers. Brings structure to a shady corner.

ACER NEGUNDO 'FLAMINGO'
Z5–8 ‡ 50ft (15m) ↔ 30ft (10m)
This fairly fast-growing, deciduous maple tree produces large, multicolored leaves in spring. It loves a sunny position and can be kept small by regular pruning.

AUCUBA JAPONICA 'CROTONIFOLIA'
Z6–10 ‡↔ 10ft (3m)
This tough evergreen shrub is ideal for all kinds of difficult sites, such as full shade, polluted areas, and places exposed to sea winds. 'Crotonifolia' produces red berries in autumn.

PRUNUS PENDULA 'PENDULA RUBRA'
Z6–8 ‡↔ 25ft (8m)
This pretty cherry tree has a weeping habit. It comes into its own in spring, when dark pink flowers emerge on the slim branches before the leaves. The deciduous leaves turn yellow in autumn.

MALUS 'RED SENTINEL'
Z5–8 ‡↔ 22ft (7m)
One of the crabapples, grown as much for its fragrant flowers as the long-lasting autumn fruits, which mature to glossy dark red. An excellent specimen tree for smaller gardens.

MORE CRABAPPLES

MALUS BACCATA VAR. MANDSCHURICA **Z3-7**
Rounded tree; scented blossoms in spring

M. FLORIBUNDA **Z4-8**
Popular and reliable crabapple; pink spring flowers

M. HUPEHENSIS **Z5-8**
Vigorous; fragrant white flowers in spring

M. 'JOHN DOWNIE' **Z5-8**
Edible crabapples in autumn; white spring blossoms

M. 'PROFUSION' **Z4-8**
Purple-pink spring blossoms

M. 'PROFESSOR SPRENGER' **Z5-8**
White spring blossoms

M. SARGENTII **Z4-8**
Long-lasting, dark red autumn fruit

M. × ZUMI 'GOLDEN HORNET' **Z5-8**
Small yellow crabapples persist into winter; large, pink-flushed white flowers in late spring

GOOD YEAR-ROUND 2

MORE STRUCTURE PLANTS

LIGUSTRUM OBTUSIFOLIUM
Z3–7 ↕ 10ft (3m) ↔ 12ft (4m)

Most familiar as a hedge, privet can also be grown as a spreading shrub. Its flowers, which can have an unpleasant scent, are followed by round black berries in autumn. Good for alkaline soil.

YUCCA GLORIOSA
Z7–10 ↕↔ 6ft (2m)

With its dagger-shaped evergreen leaves, this yucca makes an excellent architectural plant in the ground or in a large pot basking in full sun. Its flowers appear from late summer to autumn.

SKIMMIA JAPONICA 'BRONZE KNIGHT'
Z7–9 ↕↔ to 20ft (6m)

Ideal in a shrub border, this evergreen bears dark red buds in winter and glossy leaves all year round. It prefers shade but tolerates most conditions and needs little attention.

COTONEASTER FRIGIDUS 'CORNUBIA'
Z7–8 ↕↔ 20ft (6m)

This vigorous, semievergreen shrub makes a good hedge, bearing white summer flowers that develop into masses of red berries. Some leaves turn bronze in winter. Cut back hard to rejuvenate.

TAXUS BACCATA 'REPENS AUREA'
Z7–8 ↕↔ 3–5ft (1–1.5m)

Yews are tolerant of difficult growing conditions, including dry soils and polluted areas. This cultivar has gold-bordered leaves, yellow shoots, and red fruits in autumn. A good hedge or specimen.

ACER PALMATUM VAR. DISSECTUM
DISSECTUM ATROPURPUREUM GROUP
Z6–8 ↕ 6ft (2m) ↔ 10ft (3m)

These Japanese maples are small, round, deciduous shrubs with red-purple, finely dissected leaves, turning gold in autumn. Shade from strong sun.

PYRACANTHA 'MOHAVE'
Z6–9 ↕ 12ft (4m) ↔ 15ft (5m)
Often called firethorn for its showy, long-lasting, bright red berries, this vigorous, spiny shrub can be grown either in a border or on its own. Easy to grow, it is a good barrier hedge for warding off intruders.

SORBUS SARGENTIANA
Z5–7 ↕↔ 30ft (10m)
The pretty ornamental leaves and flowers of this mountain ash make it an asset in any small garden. It is an upright tree, that tolerates pollution and likes to grow in moist but well-drained soil.

CRATAEGUS LACINIATA
Z6–8 ↕↔ 20ft (6m)
Hawthorns are good specimen trees tolerant of most situations, including exposed and coastal sites. This species bears bunches of late spring flowers, followed by round, orange-red berries.

ILEX AQUIFOLIUM 'PYRAMIDALIS AUREOMARGINATA'
Z7–9 ↕ 20ft (6m) ↔ 15ft (5m)
Best in a sunny spot, this holly makes a shrub or small tree with green leaves bordered with gold. Plenty of bright red berries appear in autumn.

MORE HOLLIES

I. AQUIFOLIUM **Z7-9**
English holly; suitable for hedging
I. × ATTENUATA **Z6-9**
Topel holly; good in SE US. Several varieties.
I. CORNUTA 'BURFORDII' **Z7-9**
Rounded shrub; plenty of red berries in autumn
I. CRENATA 'CONVEXA' **Z5-7**
Dense, broad shrub; black berries in autumn
I. GLABRA **Z5-9**
Inkberry holly. Tolerant shrub, 'Compacta' is more rounded and better clothed at the base.
I. × MESERVEAE BLUE PRINCESS **Z5-9**
Dark greenish blue leaves
I. opaca **Z5-9**
American holly; many varieties have been introduced. Good as a specimen or large hedge

PYRUS SALICIFOLIA 'PENDULA'
Z5–9 ↕ 15ft (5m) ↔ 12ft (4m)
This weeping pear almost has the look of a small willow, with its slim, gray-green leaves and gracefully hanging branches. It tolerates pollution and is good on its own on a small garden lawn.

SEMIARUNDINARIA FASTUOSA
Z6–9 ↕ to 22ft (7m) ↔ 6ft (2m) or more
This tall, upright bamboo is ideal for providing height in a display, in a woodland garden, or on its own. The young stems in particular have purple-brown stripes. It may be invasive.

CORDYLINE AUSTRALIS 'VARIEGATA'
Z10–11 ↕ 10–30ft (3–10m) ↔ 3–12ft (1–4m)
This New Zealand cabbage palm is a dramatic plant with cream streaks on its long, spiky leaves. Excellent in a courtyard or cool conservatory. Bring it inside for winter where not hardy.

LONG FLOWERING SEASON

SUN	SUN OR SHADE

CERASTIUM TOMENTOSUM
Z3–7 ↕ 2–3in (5–8cm) ↔ indefinite
This plant, known as snow-in-summer, is rather
useful in dry, sunny sites, such as on a garden wall,
in a rock garden, or as a groundcover. The flowers
appear in profusion from late spring.

ANTHEMIS 'GRALLAGH GOLD'
Z3–7 ↕↔ 24–36in (60–90cm)
Golden marguerites are excellent in a mixed border,
flowering over a long summer season, and they last
well when cut. Cut this cultivar back hard after
flowering to preserve vigor for the following year.

CAMPANULA CARPATICA
'BRESSINGHAM WHITE'
Z4–7 ↕ to 6in (15cm) ↔ to 24in (60cm)
This bellflower is a low-growing, spreading plant
with large flowers from summer to autumn. It is
useful on a sunny bank or wall.

AJUGA REPTANS 'BRAUNHERZ'
Z3–9 ↕ 6in (15cm) ↔ 24–36in (60–90cm)
Bugle is an evergreen perennial valued as a
colorful and easy groundcover for shaded areas.
It will tolerate most soils as long as they are moist.
The flowers appear in spring and summer.

ALCHEMILLA MOLLIS
Z4–7 ↕ 24in (60cm) ↔ 30in (75cm)
Good as a groundcover, lady's mantle also makes
an appealing cut flower. It is useful for shade, but it
self-seeds freely and may take over. It flowers over
a long summer season.

VINCA MINOR 'ARGENTEOVARIEGATA'
Z4–9 ↕ 10–20cm (4–8in) ↔ indefinite
This periwinkle flowers best in sun from midspring
to autumn amid cream-margined leaves. Useful
groundcover, but cut it back in early spring to
prevent it from taking over. Tolerates partial shade.

PERSICARIA AMPLEXICAULIS 'FIRETAIL'
Z5–8 ‡↔ to 4ft (1.2m)
Knotweed likes moist soil and would be ideally placed in a bog garden. Its flowers emerge on tall stalks from clumps of leaves in summer and early autumn. Suitable for full sun or partial shade.

PHYGELIUS × RECTUS 'MOONRAKER'
Z8–9 ‡↔ to 5ft (1.5m)
This upright, evergreen shrub flowers over a long period in summer and into autumn. The shrub may spread widely by its suckering shoots. It is usually grown as a tender perennial in cold areas.

TIARELLA WHERRYI
Z5–9 ‡ to 8in (20cm) ↔ to 6in (15cm)
Generally, tiarellas prefer moist, shady conditions, although they tolerate a range of soils. This species is slow growing with flowers emerging from spring. Good groundcover under trees and shrubs.

GERANIUM MACRORRHIZUM
'BEVAN'S VARIETY'
Z4–8 ‡ 20in (50cm) ↔ 24in (60cm)
Useful groundcover for shade, this geranium has small flowers and scented leaves that color in autumn. Good for a woodland or wild garden.

MORE GERANIUMS

G. 'ANN FOLKARD' **Z5-9**
Continuous magenta flowers from midsummer to autumn

G. CLARKEI 'KASHMIR WHITE' **Z5-8**
Large, white, pink-veined flowers throughout summer

G. HIMALAYENSE **Z4-7**
Blue flowers until autumn, most profuse in early summer

G. NODOSUM **Z4-8**
Useful for groundcover in dry shade; purplish pink flowers from late spring to autumn

G. × OXONIANUM 'WARGRAVE PINK' **Z4-8**
Vigorous; bright salmon-pink flowers from spring to autumn

G. PSILOSTEMON **Z5-8**
Brilliant magenta flowers throughout summer

G. SANGUINEUM 'ALBUM' **Z4-8**
Pure white flowers all through summer

G. SANGUINEUM VAR. STRIATUM **Z4-8**
Compact; pink flowers in profusion throughout summer

SYMPHYTUM 'GOLDSMITH'
Z5–9 ‡↔ 24in (60cm)
Comfrey is a good groundcover plant for a shady area, with variegated leaves. Nodding, pale blue, cream, or pink flowers appear in spring from red buds. It can be grown under shrubs.

EUPHORBIA PALUSTRIS
Z5–8 ‡↔ 36in (90cm)
A robust perennial with slim leaves that turn yellow and orange in autumn. The plant likes a sunny spot with reliably moist soil; it is good beside water. Cut back in spring to keep it compact.

NEPETA 'SIX HILLS GIANT'
Z4–8 ‡ to 36in (90cm) ↔ 24in (60cm)
Masses of flower spikes are borne throughout summer on this vigorous plant, commonly known as catmint because the scent attracts cats. Nepetas are ideal for mixed herbaceous borders.

LAMIUM ORVALA
Z4–8 ‡ to 24in (60cm) ↔ 12in (30cm)
The toothed leaves of this clump-forming deadnettle make an effective foil for the flower spikes, which appear from late spring into summer. Good as a groundcover.

ALL-SEASON FOLIAGE INTEREST 1

VERTICAL INTEREST

BEDS AND BORDERS

HUMULUS LUPULUS 'AUREUS'
Z4–8 ‡↔ 20ft (6m)

This vigorous, twining climber is a bright gold-leaved version of the hops used in brewing. The small summer flowers are are overshadowed by the large leaves, which color best in full sun.

HEDERA HELIX 'ANNE MARIE'
Z5–10 ‡↔ 4ft (1.2m)

This self-clinging climbing ivy is valued for its gray-green, cream-edged foliage. It is less hardy than others, so it is best grown against a sheltered, sunny wall. It does not need support.

ACTINIDIA KOLOMIKTA
Z5–10 ‡↔ 15ft (5m) or more

This twining climber bears scented white flowers in early summer. The deciduous, dark green leaves are purple-tinged on young plants, maturing to white and pink. Grow against a wall or through a tree.

ASPLENIUM SCOLOPENDRIUM CRISPUM GROUP
Z6–8 ‡ 18–28in (45–70cm) ↔ 24in (60cm)

This group of evergreen ferns is best in a moist, shaded spot, such as a woodland garden. The long leaves are strongly crinkled, which gives them a striking appearance in a border of mixed foliage.

MORE FERNS

ADIANTUM PEDATUM **Z3-8**
Deciduous, fishbonelike fronds on wiry stalks

ASPLENIUM TRICHOMANES **Z5-8**
Slender, black-stalked evergreen fronds with neatly paired divisions; a delicate-looking, but tough little fern

DRYOPTERIS AFFINIS **Z6-8**
Bright green, deeply divided, semievergreen fronds; forms a shuttlecock-like shape; tolerates alkaline soil

POLYPODIUM CAMBRICUM **Z6-8**
Fronds remain fresh and green until late winter

POLYSTICHUM SETIFERUM DIVISILOBUM GROUP **Z6-9**
Finely divided, rich green fronds; for well-drained soil

WOODSIA POLYSTICHOIDES **Z4-8**
Deeply divided, pale green fronds; forms small clumps, ideal for walls or rock crevices

ELAEAGNUS × EBBINGEI 'GILT EDGE'
Z7–10 ‡↔ 12ft (4m)

A popular, rounded or spreading evergreen shrub that grows well in exposed sites. The insignificant autumn flowers are followed by berries. Full sun is best, and the plant tolerates quite dry soil.

ARTEMISIA 'POWIS CASTLE'
Z7–9 ‡ 24in (60cm) ↔ 36in (90cm)

The feathery foliage of this shrubby perennial makes an excellent backdrop in a herbaceous border. Take cuttings in autumn, just in case outdoor plants die during a severe winter.

RHEUM PALMATUM 'BOWLES' CRIMSON'
Z5–9 ‡ to 8ft (2.5m) ↔ to 6ft (1.8m)

This ornamental rhubarb has large, imposing leaves, and the dark red flowers appear in early summer. It is best near water or in a woodland garden, needing deep, moist soil.

CYNARA CARDUNCULUS
Z7–9 ↕ 5ft (1.5m) ↔ 4ft (1.2m)
The cardoon is a tall, elegant, thistlelike perennial, which creates an imposing presence in a mixed border. The autumn flowerheads are purple and make good cut flowers either living or dried.

ATRIPLEX HORTENSIS VAR. *RUBRA*
Annual ↕ 4ft (1.2m) ↔ 12in (30cm)
A spinachlike annual grown for its blood red or purple-red foliage, very effective used as a contrast color in a summer border, especially against gray and silver. The flowering spikes are dark red.

FOENICULUM VULGARE 'PURPUREUM'
Z4–9 ↕ 6ft (1.8m) ↔ 18in (45cm)
A slender-stemmed perennial, this fennel has finely cut, anise-flavored, bronze-purple foliage. Flat heads of tiny yellow flowers appear in summer. Grow in well-drained soil in full sun.

MELISSA OFFICINALIS 'AUREA'
Z3–7 ↕ 24–48in (60–120cm) ↔ 12–18in (30–45cm)
This drought-tolerant perennial is known as lemon balm from the smell of the crushed leaves. The leaves are splashed with yellow. Cut back in early summer to promote new growth.

STACHYS BYZANTINA 'SILVER CARPET'
Z4–8 ↕ 18in (45cm) ↔ 24in (60cm)
This nonflowering foliage plant has rosettes of silvery gray, thick and wrinkled leaves. It may be susceptible to mildew. Grow in a sunny part of the garden; also ideal as hedging or groundcover.

ALL-SEASON FOLIAGE INTEREST 2

MORE BEDS AND BORDERS

BRACHYGLOTTIS 'SUNSHINE'
Z9–10 ↕ 5ft (1.5m) ↔ 6ft (2m)
This spreading bush has white-hairy evergreen foliage with scalloped edges. Bright yellow, daisy-like blooms appear against this background from summer to autumn. Good for coastal sites.

HOSTA 'GOLDEN TIARA'
Z3–8 ↕ 12in (30cm) ↔ 20in (50cm)
Hostas are suited to moist, shady sites, like woodland or bog gardens, but the attractive foliage needs protecting from slugs and snails. Spikes of deep purple flowers appear on this cultivar in summer.

MORE HOSTAS Z3-8

H. 'BLUE ANGEL'
Bluish gray leaves, 16in (40cm) long; white flowers

H. 'CRISPULA'
Deep green leaves irregularly margined with white

H. 'FORTUNEI AUREOMARGINATA'
Deeply veined leaves with yellow margins

H. 'FRANCEE'
Very puckered, blue-green leaves with green-yellow margins

H. 'GOLD STANDARD'
Green-yellow leaves; lavender-blue flowers in summer

H. PLANTAGINEA VAR. GRANDIFLORA
Wavy leaves; fragrant flowers in late summer

H. 'SUM AND SUBSTANCE'
Yellow-green to yellow leaves; for sun or partial shade

H. VENUSTA
Dark green leaves; violet flowers in summer and autumn

H. 'ZOUNDS'
Thick golden leaves

GUNNERA MANICATA
Z7–10 ↕ 8ft (2.5m) ↔ 10–12ft (3–4m)
This large perennial is grown for its immense and spreading leaves, up to 2m (6 ft) across. It is splendid at the side of a pond or stream, needing moist soil and plenty of room.

BALLOTA PSEUDODICTAMNUS
Z7–9 ↕ 18in (45cm) ↔ 24in (60cm)
An evergreen shrub with yellowish, gray-green leaves that will tolerate the driest of soils, and it flowers in late spring. It makes a good groundcover in a border; cut it back in spring to keep it bushy.

ORIGANUM VULGARE 'AUREUM'
Z5–9 ↕ 12–36in (30–90cm) ↔ to 12in (30cm)
Golden marjoram forms dense, low-growing pads of aromatic yellow leaves. Pink flowers emerge in clusters in late summer. It makes a decorative addition to an herb garden.

CAREX ELATA 'AUREA'
Z5–9 ↕ to 28in (70cm) ↔ 18in (45cm)
This splendid perennial tufted sedge forms a clump of arching, grasslike leaves. Flowers emerge in late spring, but the plant is usually valued for its rich yellow foliage. Grow in sun or partial shade.

PACHYSANDRA PROCUMBENS
Z6–9 ↕ 8in (20cm) ↔ indefinite
Grown mainly for its luxuriant, textured foliage, this semievergreen perennial is an attractive groundcover plant, ideal for a shaded part of the garden. Cut back each year to keep it neat.

CONTAINERS

SALVIA OFFICINALIS 'TRICOLOR'
Z5–8 ‡ to 32in (80cm) ↔ 3ft (1m)
A decorative version of the herb sage with gray-green, aromatic leaves with cream and pink to purple shading. The color is most noticeable in a sunny site. Lilac-blue flowers appear in midsummer.

SEMPERVIVUM TECTORUM
Z4–8 ‡ 6in (15cm) ↔ 20in (50cm)
The rosettes of this common hen and chicks form evergreen mats of spine-tipped leaves. These rosettes die after producing red-purple flowers, but new rosettes follow. Good for containers.

HEDERA HELIX 'SPETCHLEY'
Z5–10 ‡↔ 6in (15cm)
This ivy is very compact. It has very small, dark green leaves and looks effective as a houseplant or in a mixed container. It is also useful as an evergreen groundcover.

OSMUNDA REGALIS
Z4–9 ‡ 6ft (2m) ↔ 12ft (4m)
The deciduous royal fern is suited to damp soil. The bright green fronds – up to 3ft (1m) long – are joined by distinctive, tassel-tipped brown fronds in summer. Keep moist at all times.

AEONIUM 'ZWARTKOP'
min. 50°F (10°C) ‡↔ to 6ft (2m)
Dramatic rosettes of fleshy leaves spring from base shoots on this succulent plant. In late spring, yellow flowers emerge from the centers of the rosettes. Grow in a pot and bring indoors over winter.

LYSIMACHIA NUMMULARIA 'AUREA'
Z4–8 ‡ to 2in (5cm) ↔ indefinite
Also known as golden creeping Jenny or golden moneywort, this yellow-leaved evergreen is very vigorous and forms carpets of foliage. Bright yellow, cup-shaped flowers appear in summer.

HELICHRYSUM PETIOLARE 'LIMELIGHT'
Z10–11 ‡ to 20in (50cm) ↔ 6ft (2m) or more
Excellent in a hanging basket or container, the bright lime green leaves of this shrub make an effective foil against deep colors, such as violet or dark blue. Often grown as an annual.

SENECIO CINERARIA 'SILVER DUST'
Z8–10 ‡↔ 12in (30cm)
Lacy, white-gray felted leaves are the main feature of this evergreen shrub. Yellow flowerheads are produced in the second year if the plant survives the winter. Good for a warm, sunny corner.

WINTER TO EARLY SPRING 1

WALLS	BEDS AND BORDERS

JASMINUM NUDIFLORUM
Z6–9 ↕↔ 10ft (3m)
Useful for splashes of winter color, this deciduous winter jasmine bears its small flowers in winter and spring. It can be trained against a wall, even a north-facing one, and cut back after flowering.

CLEMATIS ARMANDII
Z7–9 ↕ 10–15ft (3–5m) ↔ 6–10ft (2–3m)
This vigorous evergreen climber keeps its glossy green leaves through winter and, once established, flowers abundantly in spring. Provide shelter by growing against a sunny wall. Pruning Group 1.

GARRYA ELLIPTICA
Z8–10 ↕↔ 12ft (4m)
This evergreen shrub comes into its own in winter, when tassel-like, long gray catkins appear. Plants are either male or female; the catkins are more showy on males. Very good against a wall.

ERANTHIS HYEMALIS
Z4–9 ↕ 2–3in (5–8cm) ↔ 2in (5cm)
Winter aconites prefer a damp woodland site, so to ensure winter flowering do not let the soil dry out in summer. Once established, aconites can form a carpet of bloom under deciduous trees.

SALIX ACUTIFOLIA 'BLUE STREAK'
Z5–8 ↕ 30ft (10m) ↔ 40ft (12m)
This slender, arching willow is grown for its colorful winter shoots. Cut it back hard every few years to ensure good color and to keep the plant small.

LONICERA × PURPUSII 'WINTER BEAUTY'
Z7–9 ↕ 6ft (2m) ↔ 8ft (2.5m)
This honeysuckle forms a shrub and may be deciduous or semievergreen. The very fragrant flowers, white with yellow anthers, are produced throughout winter and early spring.

CORNUS MAS
Z5–8 ↕↔ 15ft (5m)
The Cornelian cherry is a deciduous shrub or small tree that flowers in winter and early spring. In autumn, the dark green leaves turn red-purple. Grow at the back of a border; it tolerates most sites.

MORE CORNUS

C. ALBA 'AUREA' **Z2-8**
Dark red winter shoots; yellow leaves

C. ALBA 'ELEGANTISSIMA' **Z2-8**
Red winter shoots; gray-green leaves with uneven white margins

C. ALBA 'SPAETHII' **Z2-8**
Red winter shoots; yellow-margined leaves

C. MAS 'AUREA' **Z5-8**
Yellow flowers in late winter; leaves yellow when young, maturing to green

C. MAS 'VARIEGATA' **Z5-8**
Compact shrub; abundant yellow flowers in late winter followed by red fruits; white-margined leaves

C. STOLONIFERA 'FLAVIRAMEA' **Z2-8**
Vigorous shrub; yellow-green winter shoots; white flowers in late spring; leaves redden in autumn

BERGENIA × SCHMIDTII
Z4–8 ↕ 12in (30cm) ↔ 24in (60cm)
This vigorous perennial forms rosettes of leathery leaves and bears its flowers in late winter. Good groundcover for moist soil in partial shade; the plant may attract slugs and snails.

CYCLAMEN COUM F. *ALBISSIMUM*
Z5–9 ↕ 2–3in (5–8cm) ↔ 4in (10cm)
This perennial thrives in a well-drained, partly shaded site. White flowers with dark carmine-red throats appear on slender stems above heart-shaped, silver-patterned leaves in winter and early spring.

VIBURNUM × BODNANTENSE 'DAWN'
Z7–8 ↕ 10ft (3m) ↔ 6ft (2m)
From late autumn to spring, clusters of fragrant, dark pink flowers that mature to pinkish white are borne on the bare branches of this deciduous shrub. The young leaves are bronze, later green.

SARCOCOCCA HOOKERIANA VAR. *DIGYNA* 'PURPLE STEM'
Z6–9 ↕ 5ft (1.5m) ↔ 6ft (2m)
An undemanding shrub with very fragrant, pink-tinged, white winter flowers followed by black berries. The young shoots are dark purple-pink.

MAHONIA AQUIFOLIUM
Z6–9 ↕ 3ft (1m) ↔ 5ft (1.5m)
The Oregon grape is a robust and versatile shrub and will tolerate a variety of sites. It is grown for its spiny, glossy evergreen foliage, which turns red-purple in winter. Yellow flowers follow in spring.

WINTER TO EARLY SPRING 2

MORE BEDS AND BORDERS | ACIDIC SOIL

CORNUS SANGUINEA 'WINTER BEAUTY'
Z5–7 ↕ 10ft (3m) ↔ 8ft (2.5m)
This cultivar of the bloodtwig dogwood is an
upright shrub with bright young shoots, giving
much-needed color in winter. Cut back hard
every spring for good winter color.

GALANTHUS 'ATKINSII'
Z3–9 ↕ 8in (20cm) ↔ 3in (8cm)
This snowdrop bears its nodding white flowers
on slim stems in late winter and early spring.
Naturalize under trees, under shrubs in a mixed
border, or in a lawn.

ERICA CARNEA 'SPRINGWOOD WHITE'
Z5–7 ↕ 8–10in (20–25cm) ↔ to 22in (55cm)
A scented evergreen with needlelike leaves, this
heather forms a low, spreading shrub. The white,
bell-like flowers appear in late winter and continue
into spring. Vigorous and reliable.

HAMAMELIS × INTERMEDIA 'JELENA'
Z5–9 ↕↔ 12ft (4m)
This deciduous witch hazel bears spiderlike
clusters of flowers on its bare branches in early
and midwinter. The foliage turns to orange and
red in autumn. Tolerates alkaline soil.

HELLEBORUS ARGUTIFOLIUS
Z6–9 ↕ to 4ft (1.2m) ↔ 36in (90cm)
This perennial is most effective when grouped
in light shade in rich soil. Unusual, bright green
flowers emerge on strong stems from among the
leathery leaves in late winter and early spring.

CHIMONANTHUS PRAECOX 'GRANDIFLORUS'
Z7–9 ↕ 12ft (4m) ↔ 10ft (3m)
Wintersweet is a spreading, slow-growing shrub
grown for its waxy, fragrant winter flowers, which
appear on the bare branches before the leaves. Needs
full sun and rich soil; prune only to limit size.

PIERIS JAPONICA 'FIRECREST'
Z6–8 ↕ 12ft (4m) ↔ 6ft (2m)
The new leaves on this evergreen shrub are bright
red, maturing to dark green; they may be damaged
by frost. The loose clusters of flowers appear at the
tips of the shoots in late winter and spring.

CONTAINERS

NARCISSUS 'GRAND SOLEIL D'OR'
Z8–9 ‡ 18in (45cm)
Gold-petaled, orange-centered flowers are borne
in clusters on single stems on this early spring-
flowering bulb. For an indoor display, plant the
bulbs in early autumn. Very effective in drifts.

VIOLA FAMA SERIES
Z4–8 ‡ 6–9in (16–23cm) ↔ 9–12in (23–30cm)
This series of winter pansies is excellent for a long
flowering season in winter and spring, and they
come in a wide range of colors. Also good as
bedding; deadhead to prolong flowering.

BRASSICA OLERACEA
Annual ‡↔ to 18in (45cm)
Ornamental cabbages are suitable for either
containers or mixed bedding displays. They
are grown annually from seed for their rounded,
loose heads of variously colored foliage.

CAMELLIA 'FRANCIE L'
Z8 ‡ 15ft (5m) ↔ 20ft (6m)
This camellia suits either a site against a wall or a
container. Its large, semidouble blooms appear
from late winter to spring. Although it is a robust
grower, the buds may be damaged by late frosts.

IRIS 'J. S. DIJT'
Z5–8 ‡ 4–6in (10–15cm)
Many irises have a brief flowering period, but this
one lasts well. Its fragrant flowers appear in late
winter and early spring from clumps of narrow
leaves. Needs well-drained soil.

PRIMULA JOKER SERIES
Z6–8 ‡ 3–4in (8–10cm) ↔ 8in (20cm)
These colorful primroses all have creamy yellow
centers, but the petals come in blue, red, pink,
yellow, or bicolored. Fertilize when in flower.
Also good as temporary houseplants.

MID-SPRING 1

WALLS	BEDS AND BORDERS IN SUN OR PARTIAL SHADE

CHAENOMELES × SUPERBA 'NICOLINE'
Z5–9 ↕ 5ft (1.5m) ↔ 6ft (2m)

The flowering quince produces an abundance of vivid scarlet flowers on its spiny branches from early spring. Train against a wall or grow on a bank. A sunny site improves flowering.

CLEMATIS ALPINA 'FRANCES RIVIS'
Z6–9 ↕ 6–10ft (2–3m) ↔ 5ft (1.5m)

This delicate, spring-flowering clematis also bears fuzzy seedheads in late summer. A sunny, sheltered site with well-drained soil suits this climber best. Pruning Group 1.

MORE CLEMATIS

C. ALPINA 'PINK FLAMINGO' **Z6-9**
Freely produces semi-double, pale pink flowers from spring to early summer. Pruning Group 1

C. ARMANDII 'APPLE BLOSSOM' **Z7-9**
Pinkish white spring flowers. Pruning Group 1

C. CIRRHOSA **Z7-9**
Evergreen clematis; cream flowers from late winter; seedheads follow. Pruning Group 1

C. MACROPETALA 'MARKHAM'S PINK' **Z6-9**
Sugar pink flowers from spring to early summer; silver seedheads follow. Pruning Group 1

C. MONTANA F. GRANDIFLORA **Z6-9**
Very vigorous, ideal for covering a large, featureless wall; big, white spring flowers in abundance. Pruning Group 1

C. MONTANA 'ELIZABETH' **Z6-9**
Scented, pale pink flowers in spring. Pruning Group 1

C. MONTANA 'TETRAROSE' **Z6-9**
Satiny pink flowers in spring. Pruning Group 1

MAGNOLIA × SOULANGEANA 'LENNEI ALBA'
Z5–9 ↕↔ 20ft (6m)

This magnolia gives a magnificent display of goblet-shaped, fragrant flowers in mid- and late spring. It tolerates heavy clay soils and also makes a good specimen tree on a lawn.

MUSCARI ARMENIACUM 'BLUE SPIKE'
Z4–8 ↕ 8in (20cm) ↔ 2in (5cm)

This bulbous perennial is also known as grape hyacinth. It is a vigorous plant that spreads easily, so it may need to be kept in check. The dense flower spikes are borne in spring amid fleshy leaves.

CAMELLIA JAPONICA 'COQUETTII'
Z7–8 ↕ 28ft (9m) ↔ 25ft (8m)

In spring, this slow-growing shrub bears a profusion of lovely deep red flowers on downward-sweeping branches. An elegant addition to a border or woodland garden; it also looks effective in a container.

CHIONODOXA FORBESII 'PINK GIANT'
Z3–9 ↕ 4–8in (10–20cm) ↔ 1¼ in (3cm)

This slug-resistant, bulbous perennial bears pretty pink, star-shaped flowers in early spring from clumps of upright leaves. Under deciduous shrubs or trees, this perennial should naturalize freely.

CROCUS TOMMASINIANUS
Z3–8 ↕ 3–4in (8–10cm) ↔ 1in (2.5cm)

This bulbous perennial bears small, slender-petalled flowers from late winter to spring. Grow in drifts under trees or at the front of a border. It self-seeds in suitable conditions.

SALIX HELVETICA
Z5–8 ↕ 24in (60cm) ↔ 16in (40cm)
The Swiss willow is a graceful tree with slim, gray-green leaves. In early spring, silver-gray catkins appear from little golden yellow buds. Suitable for a shrub border; dislikes poor, alkaline soil.

MORE WILLOWS

SALIX BABYLONICA 'TORTUOSA' **Z6–9**
Fast-growing; yellow-green catkins in spring; curiously twisted shoots give structural interest in winter

S. CAPREA 'KILMARNOCK' **Z6–8**
Weeping habit; good for small gardens; gray spring catkins

S. DAPHNOIDES **Z5–9**
Silky gray catkins in spring; purple young shoots

S. ELAEAGNOS **Z4–7**
Slender green catkins in spring; gray shoots turn red-yellow

S. EXIGUA **Z5–8**
Grows well on sandy soils; gray-yellow catkins in spring

S. GRACILISTYLA 'MELANOSTACHYS' **Z5–8**
Bushy shrub; black catkins with red anthers in spring

S. HASTATA 'WEHRHAHNII' **Z5–8**
Shrubby growth; silvery gray catkins in spring

S. PURPUREA 'NANA' **Z4–7**
Compact, suitable for a hedge; silvery green spring catkins

CHOISYA 'AZTEC PEARL'
Z9–10 ↕↔ 8ft (2.5m)
Choisyas are grown for their evergreen leaves and star-shaped spring flowers. Excellent and easy to care for in a shrub border. The flowers may reappear in autumn.

OSMANTHUS × BURKWOODII
Z7–9 ↕↔ 10ft (3m)
This dense, rounded evergreen shrub also works well as a hedge and can be trained into different shapes. The tubular white flowers are fragrant and appear in mid- and late spring.

KERRIA JAPONICA 'PLENIFLORA'
Z4–9 ↕↔ 10ft (3m)
This shrub is especially vigorous with double yellow flowers in mid- to late spring. Easy to grow, although the long green shoots may need a little support. Also suitable for a woodland garden.

FRITILLARIA MELEAGRIS
Z3–8 ↕ to 12in (30cm) ↔ 2–3in (5–8cm)
The broadly bell-shaped, spring to early summer flowers of this bulb are purple, pinkish purple, or even white. Like crocuses, fritillaries look good in drifts and can be naturalized in grass.

MIDSPRING 2

MORE BEDS AND BORDERS IN SUN OR PARTIAL SHADE

BEDS AND BORDERS IN SHADE

FORSYTHIA × INTERMEDIA 'ARNOLD GIANT'
Z6–9 ↕↔ 5ft (1.5m)
This shrub is grown for its deep yellow spring flowers, which appear in early and midspring before the leaves. Like other forsythias, this cultivar can also be grown as a hedge.

ERYSIMUM ALLIONII
Z3–7 ↕ 20–24in (50–60cm) ↔ to 12in (30cm)
This bright orange wallflower with a curiously spicy scent is ideal for the front of a sunny border or a raised bed. The spring flowers are produced in the second year. A short-lived perennial.

DORONICUM ORIENTALE 'FRÜHLINGSPRACHT'
Z5–8 ↕ to 16in (40cm) ↔ 36in (90cm)
Sometimes labeled 'Spring Beauty', this yellow double daisy makes a bright splash of color in a border. It flowers from midspring, bearing blooms on slender stems, and it is also good for cutting.

TULIPA 'KEES NELIS'
Z4–8 10–16in (25–40cm)
The single flowers of this spring-flowering tulip are blood red with lighter, orange-yellow margins. As well as being an effective bedding plant, it is also good as a cut flower. Attractive in groups.

MORE TULIPS Z4–8

T. 'ANCILLA'
Soft pink spring flowers with red throats

T. CLUSIANA VAR. *CHRYSANTHA*
Clusters of yellow flowers from early spring

T. 'KEIZERSKROON'
Broadly yellow-margined scarlet flowers in midspring

T. LINIFOLIA
Slender habit; bowl-shaped red flowers in early spring

T. 'PRINSES IRENE'
Unusual, orange and purple flowers in midspring

T. TARDA
Clusters of yellow spring flowers with white petal tips

T. TURKESTANICA
Clusters of up to 12 star-shaped, white spring flowers

T. 'ZAMPA'
Primrose yellow spring flowers with bronze and green bases; leaves marked dark bluish maroon

ANEMONE BLANDA 'WHITE SPLENDOUR'
Z4–8 ↕↔ 6in (15cm)
The tubers of this spreading perennial produce prettily toothed leaves and large, open, white spring flowers, pink-tinged beneath. It should naturalize well and form large clumps quickly.

EPIMEDIUM × VERSICOLOR 'SULPHUREUM'
Z5–9 ↕ 12in (30cm) ↔ 3ft (1m)
This perennial tolerates fairly dry soils, forming clumps of divided evergreen leaves with dark yellow flowers in mid- and late spring. Also good as a groundcover.

ERYTHRONIUM DENS-CANIS

Z3–9 ‡ 4–6in (10–15cm) ↔ 4in (10cm)

The dog's-tooth violet is a bulbous perennial also good under deciduous trees or in a rock garden. The white, pink, or lilac spring flowers have backward-curving petals. Keep stored bulbs slightly damp.

BRUNNERA MACROPHYLLA 'DAWSON'S WHITE'

Z3–7 ‡ 18in (45cm) ↔ 24in (60cm)

Useful as a groundcover in a woodland garden or shady border, this perennial is grown for its white-margined foliage and bright blue spring flowers, which are very similar to forget-me-nots.

PULMONARIA SACCHARATA

Z4–8 ‡ 12in (30cm) ↔ 24in (60cm)

This lungwort bears red-violet or violet flowers from late winter to late spring on a background of white-spotted leaves. One of the earliest perennials to flower, it is also attractive to bees.

PRIMULA VULGARIS SUBSP. *SIBTHORPII*

Z4–8 ‡ 8in (20cm) ↔ 14in (35cm)

The spring flowers on this yellow-centered primrose vary from rose-pink or purple to red or white. Good at the front of a border or under trees and shrubs.

OMPHALODES CAPPADOCICA 'CHERRY INGRAM'

Z6–8 ‡ to 10in (25cm) ↔ to 16in (40cm)

This perennial is similar to the forget-me-not, bearing deep blue flowers from clumps of evergreen leaves. Grow in a woodland garden or use as a groundcover in a shady border.

RIBES SANGUINEUM 'BROCKLEBANKII'

Z6–8 ‡↔ 4ft (1.2m)

This yellow-leaved version of the flowering currant is a thornless, deciduous shrub, which bears pale pink, tubular flowers in spring, followed by black berries. The leaves pale slightly in summer.

SCILLA SIBERICA

Z5–8 ‡ 4–8in (10–20cm) ↔ 2in (5cm)

This pretty woodland plant is grown for its bowl-shaped, deep blue spring flowers. Grow under trees or shrubs, or naturalize in grass. There is no need to water these once they have finished flowering.

HYACINTHOIDES HISPANICA

Z4–9 ‡ 16in (40cm) ↔ 4in (10cm)

The Spanish bluebell is a vigorous bulbous perennial that suits woodland gardens or sites under tall shrubs. The bell-shaped flowers emerge from among the strap-shaped leaves in spring.

MIDSPRING 3

ACIDIC SOIL

CONTAINERS

RHODODENDRON 'BEETHOVEN'
Z6–9 ↕↔ 4½ft (1.3m)
This spring-flowering evergreen dwarf azalea is a suitable shrub for a site with dappled shade. The showy flowers have a deep mauve mark inside each petal; they may be damaged by late frosts.

ARABIS CAUCASICA 'VARIEGATA'
Z4–8 ↕ 6in (15cm) ↔ 20in (50cm) or more
The fragrant spring flowers of this perennial emerge against green leaves with striking, pale yellow margins. Also grows well in a rock garden or as a groundcover; needs sunny, well drained soil.

RHODODENDRON 'IROHAYAMA'
Z7–9 ↕↔ 24in (60cm)
This compact, evergreen dwarf azalea has small leaves and small clusters of funnel-shaped, lilac-edged white flowers in spring. It likes a sunny spot and is also effective in a massed planting.

RHODODENDRON 'CÉCILE'
Z5–8 ↕↔ 7ft (2.2m)
Large, trumpet-shaped flowers are borne on this vigorous deciduous azalea in mid- and late spring, the buds opening into dense clusters of salmon-pink blooms. A large shrub; needs plenty of space.

BELLIS PERENNIS TASSO SERIES
Z4–8 ↕↔ 2–8in (5–20cm)
A cultivar of the English daisy with double, quill-petaled flowers in pink, white, or red. It is often grown as spring bedding, but it grows easily in containers in full sun or partial shade.

MORE RHODODENDRONS

R. 'HINOMAYO' **Z7-9**
Dense, dwarf evergreen azalea; pink flowers in midspring

R. LUTEUM **Z6-9**
Large deciduous azalea; scented yellow flowers into summer

R. 'MAY DAY' **Z7-9**
Low-growing evergreen; scarlet flowers in midspring

R. 'MRS G.W. LEAK' **Z7-9**
Good large shrub for clay; pink spring flowers

R. 'NARCISSIFLORA' **Z5-8**
Compact; scented yellow flowers; leaves bronze in autumn

R. 'STRAWBERRY ICE' **Z5-8**
Medium shrub for full sun; pale pink flowers in spring

R. 'SUSAN' **Z6-9**
Vigorous, compact, pollution-tolerant shrub; mauve, mid-spring flowers fade to white

R. YAKUSHIMANUM **Z5-9**
Popular, medium-sized evergreen; pink spring flowers

NARCISSUS 'EMPRESS OF IRELAND'
Z3–9 ↕ 16in (40cm)
One of the largest trumpet daffodils, 'Empress of Ireland' has creamy white spring flowers, with a single trumpet on each stem. It also makes an effective display in a shrub border.

HYACINTHUS ORIENTALIS 'BLUE JACKET'
Z5–9 ↕ 8–12in (20–30cm) ↔ 3in (8cm)
Hyacinths are excellent for spring color, whether grown in pots or used in bedding displays, and they are easy to look after. The waxy, fragrant blooms of 'Blue Jacket' are intense navy to purple-blue.

WATER GARDENS

PRIMULA PULVERULENTA 'BARTLEY STRAIN'
Z4–8 ‡ to 3ft (1m) ↔ 24in (60cm)
A candelabra primrose with whorls of tubular, shell pink flowers with red eyes on upright stems until early summer. It prefers a permanently moist, shady spot, ideally in a bog garden or by a stream.

PRIMULA PROLIFERA
Z4–8 ‡↔ 24in (60cm)
The spring blooms of this candelabra primrose vary from creamy white to golden yellow. The basal leaves form a rosette. Grow in a bog or woodland garden, as long as the soil is permanently moist.

HOUTTUYNIA CORDATA 'CHAMELEON'
Z6–11 ‡ to 6–12in (15–30cm) or more ↔ indefinite
Use this as part of a damp border or at the side of a pond. 'Chameleon' is grown for its bright, variegated leaves, which are colored green, pale yellow, and red. It can be invasive.

CALTHA PALUSTRIS
Z3–7 ‡ 4–16in (10–40cm) ↔ 18in (45cm)
Calthas, also known as marsh marigolds, are best grown at the edge of water, although they can survive in a border if kept very moist. This species has waxy yellow, buttercup-like flowers.

LYSICHITON CAMTSCHATCENSIS
Z7–9 ‡↔ 30in (75cm)
The white skunk cabbage is a marginal aquatic perennial grown for its glossy green leaves and striking, usually pointed white spathes that appear from early spring and have a musky scent.

LATE SPRING TO EARLY SUMMER 1

WALLS IN SUN

WALLS IN SUN OR PARTIAL SHAD

CALLISTEMON VIMINALIS 'ROSE OPAL'
Z10–11 ↕ 5–6ft (1.5–2m) ↔ 5–12ft (1.5–4m)
This shrub is known as a bottlebrush because of its brushlike flower spikes in late spring, which are made up of numerous tiny flowers with long stamens. Grow against a warm, sunny wall.

ABUTILON VITIFOLIUM VAR. *ALBUM*
Z8–9 ↕ 15ft (5m) ↔ 8ft (2.5m)
A fast-growing deciduous shrub suited to a sunny, sheltered, well-drained site. It produces showy white flowers on long stalks in early summer. Prune in late winter or early spring.

FREMONTODENDRON 'PACIFIC SUNSET'
Z9–10 ↕↔ 6ft (2m)
A good evergreen shrub for the back of a sheltered border as well as a sunny wall, with large, saucer-shaped yellow flowers over a long period from early summer. The shoots and leaves may irritate skin.

WISTERIA SINENSIS 'ALBA'
Z5–8 ↕ 28ft (9m) or more
Chinese wisteria is a vigorous climber that will twine itself around a supporting framework or into a tree. Very long fronds of fragrant white flowers appear in late spring and early summer.

SOLANUM CRISPUM 'GLASNEVIN'
Z9–10 ↕ 20ft (6m)
Vigorous and scrambling, this climber is ideal for rapid cover of a wall or shed. Decorative blue-purple flowers appear from early summer until autumn, followed by yellowish white fruits.

JASMINUM HUMILE
Z7–9 ↕ 8ft (2.5m), sometimes to 12ft (4m) ↔ 10ft (3m)
Usually (but not always) fragrant, this jasmine forms a bushy shrub and is valued for its delicate yellow flowers and bright green leaves. Prune in autumn, once flowering has finished.

ROSA 'MME GRÉGOIRE STAECHELIN'
Z5–9 ↕ to 20ft (6m) ↔ 12ft (4m)
A vigorous, arching climbing rose with a good covering of dark green leaves, forming a backdrop for the fully double, red-flushed pink roses in early summer. Large, round red hips follow.

MORE ROSES

R. BANKSIAE **Z8-9**
Thornless climber, best if protected from frost; clusters of violet-scented, double white flowers in late spring

R. BANKSIAE 'LUTEA' **Z8-9**
Thornless climber that needs a sheltered wall; double yellow flowers in late spring

R. 'CITY OF YORK' **Z5-9**
Climber; clusters of scented, semidouble, creamy white flowers in early summer

R. 'HANDEL' **Z5-9**
Repeat-blooming climber with stunning raspberry-edged white blooms

R. 'MAIGOLD' **Z5-9**
Strong climber; scented, bronze-yellow, early summer flowers, may bloom again in autumn

R. XANTHINA 'CANARY BIRD' **Z5-9**
Arching shrub; musk-scented, single yellow flowers in late spring, may bloom again later in season

LATHYRUS GRANDIFLORUS
Z6–9 ‡ 5ft (1.5m)
The everlasting pea will, if supported, climb up
a wall or through shrubs and small trees. From
early summer, pink-purple and red, pealike
flowers emerge in a showy display.

CLEMATIS 'WILLIAM KENNETT'
Z5–9 ‡ 6–10ft (2–3m) ↔ 3ft (1m)
In early summer, this deciduous climber bears
large, single, pale lavender-blue flowers with dark
red anthers. They appear on the previous year's
growth. Pruning Group 2.

LONICERA JAPONICA 'HALLIANA'
Z4–10 ‡ 30ft (10m)
This delightful twining climber is a very vigorous
Japanese honeysuckle, bearing fragrant, pure white
flowers from late spring to late summer, which
mature to dark yellow. Blue-black berries follow.

AKEBIA QUINATA
Z5–9 ‡ 30ft (10m)
The pretty leaves, which tinge purple in winter,
make the chocolate vine an attractive climber
even without its spring flowers, which are brown-
purple and vanilla-scented. It is very vigorous.

HYDRANGEA PETIOLARIS
Z4–9 ‡ 50ft (15m)
The climbing hydrangea clings to a framework by
means of aerial roots. The flowers emerge from
early summer and the leaves yellow in autumn.
Slow to establish, but worth the wait.

LATE SPRING TO EARLY SUMMER 2

BEDS AND BORDERS HOT AND DRY

HELIANTHEMUM 'FIRE DRAGON'
Z6–8 ‡ 8–12in (20–30cm) ↔ 12in (30cm)
This spreading, sun-loving shrub is ideally suited
to a rock garden or raised bed. The bright flowers
of this sun rose are carried over a long period from
late spring to midsummer. Easily grown.

LOBULARIA MARITIMA 'LITTLE DORRIT'
Annual ‡ to 4in (10cm) ↔ 8–12in (20–30cm)
Most cultivars of sweet alyssum are useful bedding
plants from early summer on. They grow well
just about anywhere, including crevices between
paving stones. This one has white flowers.

ARMERIA MARITIMA 'VINDICTIVE'
Z3–9 ‡ to 8in (20cm) ↔ to 12in (30cm)
This cultivar of sea thrift has profuse rose pink
flowerheads from late spring to summer and stiff,
upright stems. It forms clumps and prefers a dry
and sunny, open site; a rock garden is good.

CYTISUS 'PORLOCK'
Z6–9 ‡↔ 10ft (3m)
This broom is a vigorous, semievergreen shrub.
The late spring, pealike flowers are very fragrant,
and they are followed by downy seedpods.
Tolerates all but very alkaline soil.

LINUM NARBONENSE
Z7–9 (borderline) ‡ 30–60cm (12–24in) ↔ 45cm (18in)
The saucer-shaped flowers of this Mediterranean
perennial are borne continuously in the first half
of summer. It prefers full sun and needs protection
from winter moisture. Ideal for a rock garden.

CISTUS × *CYPRIUS*
Z8–10 ‡↔ 3ft (1m)
This shrub bears small clusters of white flowers
from early summer. Each bloom lasts only a day,
but they are soon replaced. It is unsuitable for very
alkaline soil but is easily grown in a container.

IRIS 'SILVERADO'
Z3–9 ‡ to 3ft (1m)
The large, beautifully ruffled flowers of this tall
bearded iris are a pretty pale silver-blue and appear
in midspring. The broad leaves appear in a fan
shape. For a mixed or herbaceous border.

MORE IRISES

I. BUCHARICA **Z5-9**
Fast-growing; up to six golden yellow to white flowers per
stem in mid- and late spring

I. INTERMEDIATE BEARDED VARIETIES **Z3-9**
Shorter and earlier blooming than the tall beardeds.
Come in a wide color range.

I. FOETIDISSIMA **Z7-9**
Dull purple flowers in early summer followed by attractive
seed capsules for autumn display

I. GRAMINEA **Z6-9**
Plum-scented, rich purple-violet flowers borne among the
bright green leaves in late spring and early summer

I. INNOMINATA **Z7-9**
Beardless, Pacific Coast iris; early summer flowers range
from bright yellow to cream, and purple to pale blue

I. PALLIDA 'VARIEGATA' **Z5-9**
Large and scented, soft blue flowers in late spring and
early summer; bright green leaves with yellow stripes

BEDS AND BORDERS IN SUN OR PARTIAL SHADE

CEANOTHUS 'CONCHA'
Z9–10 ↕↔ 10ft (3m)

In late spring, the reddish purple buds of this evergreen shrub open to a profusion of dark blue flowers. Most ceanothus cultivars grow to twice their normal height when trained against a wall.

ERYSIMUM 'JOHN CODRINGTON'
Z5–8 ↕ 10in (25cm) ↔ 12in (30cm)

This evergreen perennial wallflower adds color to any border or raised bed in full sun with its late spring flowers. Also good against a wall; trim after flowering.

DIANTHUS 'PIKE'S PINK'
Z5–8 ↕ 6in (15cm) ↔ 8in (20cm)

An alpine pink for the rock garden, raised bed with good drainage, or border edge. The double, pale pink flowers are clove-scented and bloom from early summer.

POTENTILLA 'WILLIAM ROLLISON'
Z5–8 ↕ to 18in (45cm) ↔ 24in (60cm)

Potentilla flowers provide good color over a long season. This clump-forming perennial produces its flowers from early to late summer. It is useful for late color in a mixed border.

EXOCHORDA GIRALDII VAR. WILSONII
Z6–9 ↕↔ 10ft (3m)

This pretty flowering shrub needs a well-drained site, but it is otherwise very easy to look after. New leaves are pinkish green, maturing to pale green. A profusion of white flowers in late spring.

ROSA 'CHARLES DE MILLS'
Z3–9 ↕↔ 1.2m (4ft) or more

This dense and arching old garden rose has midgreen foliage and can be grown as a hedge. Pink buds appear in early summer, opening to fully double, fragrant, mulberry-colored flowers.

LABURNUM × WATERERI 'VOSSII'
Z6–8 ↕↔ 8m (25ft)

A spreading tree grown for its hanging chains of flowers, that bloom in late spring. Unsuitable for a family garden: all parts are toxic if eaten.

MORE ROSES

R. 'BLANC DOUBLE DE COUBERT' **Z3–9**
Dense, spreading habit; semidouble, fragrant white flowers with yellow stamens from early summer to autumn

R. 'BUFF BEAUTY' **Z6–9**
Rounded habit; large clusters of lightly fragrant, fully double apricot flowers from early summer

R. 'CONSTANCE SPRY' **Z4–9**
Arching habit that will climb if supported; fully double, myrrh-scented pink flowers from early summer

R. GLAUCA **Z2–8**
Vigorous species; single, reddish pink flowers with gold stamens from early summer; red hips in autumn

R. 'GRAHAM THOMAS' **Z5–9**
Arching habit; fully double, fragrant yellow flowers continue from early summer until autumn

R. 'WILLIAM LOBB' **Z4–9**
Arching, prickly stems may need support; double, scented, purple to lavender-gray flowers from early summer

LATE SPRING TO EARLY SUMMER 3

MORE BEDS AND BORDERS IN SUN OR PARTIAL SHADE

WEIGELA 'LOOYMANSII AUREA'
Z5–9 ‡↔ 5ft (1.5m)
This slow-growing, spreading deciduous shrub for partial shade has flowers that appear in late spring and early summer. Useful at the back of a border; trim to size, but do not cut into old wood.

CENTAUREA CYANUS
Annual ‡ 8–32in (20–80cm) ↔ 6in (15cm)
An upright annual, the cornflower has dark blue flowerheads from late spring to midsummer, which are attractive to bees and butterflies. Grow in well-drained soil in full sun.

THALICTRUM AQUILEGIIFOLIUM
Z5–9 ‡ to 3ft (1m) ↔ 18in (45cm)
Suited to a wild or woodland garden, this upright perennial produces fluffy clusters of flowers with bright purple-pink stamens in early summer. Take care not to damage dormant plants in spring.

COREOPSIS GRANDIFLORA 'SUNRAY'
Z4–9 ‡ 20–30in (50–75cm) ↔ 18in (45cm)
The double, deep yellow flowers of this annual will brighten up a sunny border display. Borne on long stalks, the flowerheads attract bees. Coreopsis flowers are splendid for cutting.

SALVIA × SYLVESTRIS 'BLAUHÜGEL'
Z5–9 ‡ 20in (50cm) ↔ 18in (45cm)
This perennial forms clumps of wrinkled, scalloped leaves. Tall stems of bright blue flowers emerge in early summer, which provide brilliant color for a bedding display.

PAEONIA
'DUCHESSE DE NEMOURS'
Z3–8 ‡↔ 28–32in (70–80cm)
This herbaceous peony is grown for its large and fragrant, early summer flowers. Stake the flowers for support, and do not move once established.

CAMASSIA LEICHTLINII
Z4–10 ‡ 24–54in (60–130cm) ↔ 4in (10cm)
A bulb to grow in a wildflower meadow or border. Star-shaped, creamy white flowers appear in late spring; as they fade, the flower segments twist together. Avoid waterlogged soil.

SYRINGA VULGARIS 'MRS. EDWARD HARDING'
Z4–8 ‡↔ 22ft (7m)
Large sprays of double, fragrant, purple-red flowers appear in late spring and early summer on this shrubby lilac tree for a sunny site. Grow in a shrub border or on its own; needs light pruning only.

DELPHINIUM 'BLUE BEES'
Z3–7 ↕ 5½ft (1.7m) ↔ to 30in (75cm)
Delphiniums are the classic cottage garden perennial. The tall, wiry flower stems will need staking if exposed to wind. Cut down to ground level in autumn. Blooms appear in early to late summer.

ROSA 'JUST JOEY'
Z5-9 ↕ 30in (75cm) ↔ 28in (70cm)
A hybrid tea bush rose of open, branching habit. Rounded, fully double, fragrant, copper-pink flowers with wavy-margined petals are borne from early summer until autumn.

MORE ROSES Z5-9

R. 'INTRIGUE'
Compact floribunda with dark red double flowers from early summer to autumn

R. 'PRINCESSE DE MONACO'
Vigorous hybrid tea; fragrant white flowers from early summer to autumn

R. 'REMEMBER ME'
Hybrid tea; wide sprays of copper-orange flowers from early summer to autumn; glossy leaves

R. 'TROPICANA'
Hybrid tea; rounded, fully double, lightly scented, pale amber-colored flowers from early summer to autumn

R. 'QUEEN ELIZABETH'
Vigorous grandiflora with rounded, double pink flowers on long stems from early summer to autumn

R. 'VALENCIA'
Hybrid tea with an open habit; fragrant, double, amber-yellow flowers from early summer to autumn

PHILADELPHUS 'VIRGINAL'
Z5–8 ↕ 10ft (3m) or more ↔ 8ft (2.5m)
The mockorange is a popular shrub with strongly orangeblossom-scented flowers in early summer. Establishes easily in a shrub border or woodland garden, and it makes a good screen.

DEUTZIA GRACILIS
Z5–8 ↕↔ 3ft (1m)
A bushy shrub with bright green leaves for a shrub border or as a specimen plant. Many fragrant, star-shaped white flowers are produced from spring to early summer. It is happiest in a sunny site.

ANCHUSA AZUREA 'LODDON ROYALIST'
Z3–8 ↕ 36in (90cm) ↔ 24in (60cm)
The deep blue flowers of this sturdy perennial appear in early summer. It should not need staking, but deadhead it after the first flush of flowers to promote further flowering.

LATE SPRING TO EARLY SUMMER 4

| MORE BEDS AND BORDERS IN SUN OR PARTIAL SHADE | SHADE |

SPIRAEA 'ARGUTA'
Z5–8 ↕↔ 8ft (2.5m)

Also known as bridal wreath because of the foamy, white spring flowers, this slender, arching shrub makes a dense, rounded bush. It prefers a site in full sun. Prune after flowering.

ALLIUM HOLLANDICUM 'PURPLE SENSATION'
Z4–10 ↕ 3ft (1m) ↔ 3in (7cm)

This bulb, an ornamental member of the onion family, does well in sun and gives impact in a border. Large, round heads made up of many star-shaped flowers appear in early summer.

LUZULA NIVEA
Z4–9 ↕ to 24in (60cm) ↔ 18in (45cm)

The snowy woodrush is a grasslike evergreen perennial that is good as a groundcover in shady or damp areas. Clusters of shiny, brownish white flowers are produced from early summer.

NIGELLA DAMASCENA 'PERSIAN JEWELS'
Annual ↕ to 16in (40cm) ↔ to 9in (23cm)

The showy summer flowers of this slender-stemmed annual are followed by green seedpods that can be dried for flower arrangements. Grow love-in-a-mist at the front of a border.

GLADIOLUS CALLIANTHUS
Z8–10 ↕ 28–39in (70–100cm) ↔ 2in (5cm)

In summer, this perennial bears loose spikes of very fragrant flowers that arch gracefully on long, slim tubes and are suitable for cutting. Plant in groups for best effect.

KOLKWITZIA AMABILIS 'PINK CLOUD'
Z5–9 ↕ 10ft (3m) ↔ 12ft (4m)

This cultivar of the beauty bush produces masses of bell-shaped pink blooms from late spring. Each flower has a yellow-flushed throat. It is a deciduous shrub, suitable for a sunny border.

TROLLIUS PUMILUS
Z5–8 ↕ to 12in (30cm) ↔ to 8in (20cm)

This yellow-flowered perennial has pretty, glossy, toothed basal leaves and cup-shaped, late spring flowers, similar to buttercups. Moist, heavy soil is best, such as a bog garden.

MYOSOTIS SYLVATICA 'VICTORIA ROSE'
Z5–9 ↕ to 10in (25cm) ↔ to 6in (15cm)

A vaariety of the common forget-me-not with large, bright pink flowers in spring to early summer. Vigorous and upright, this is a useful biennial for spring bedding. Protect from slugs.

SMILACINA RACEMOSA
Z4–9 ↕ to 36in (90cm) ↔ 24in (60cm)
A good perennial for a shady border or woodland garden that bears creamy white, sometimes green-tinged flowerheads in mid- and late spring. The leaves turn yellow in autumn.

DICENTRA SPECTABILIS
Z4–9 ↕ to 4ft (1.2m) ↔ 12in (45cm)
Known as bleeding heart or dutchman's breeches for the unusual shape of the hanging flowers from late spring, this perennial is ideal for woodland, tolerating some sun if the soil stays moist.

DIGITALIS PURPUREA EXCELSIOR HYBRIDS
Z4–8 ↕ 3–6ft (1–2m) ↕ 24in (60cm)
These are pastel-colored variants of the common foxglove with early summer spikes of creamy yellow, white, purple, or pink flowers. They make excellent cut flowers. Grow from seed each season.

CONVALLARIA MAJALIS
Z2–7 ↕ 9in (23cm) ↔ 12in (30cm)
Lily-of-the-valley is a perennial with arching clusters of bell-shaped, strongly scented, waxy white flowers in late spring. It makes a good groundcover in a damp and shady border.

POLEMONIUM CAERULEUM
Z4–8 ↕ 12–36in (30–90cm) ↔ 12in (30cm)
Jacob's ladder is a perennial grown for its early summer flowers. It grows well in grass and prefers moist but well-drained soil. Deadhead regularly to promote flowering.

POLYGONATUM × HYBRIDUM
Z6–9 ↕ to 5ft (1.5m) ↔ 12in (30cm)
Common Solomon's seal is a perennial for moist soil in full or partial shade. Its leaves turn yellow in autumn, and its greenish white flowers hang from arching stems in late spring. Black berries follow.

AQUILEGIA 'MAGPIE'
Z3–9 ↕ 24in (60cm) ↔ 18in (45cm)
An unmistakable perennial with attractive, fern-like foliage and striking, black-purple to white flowers in late spring. Easy to grow in light shade, or in sun if the soil remains moist.

LATE SPRING TO EARLY SUMMER 5

CONTAINERS

PETUNIA 'PURPLE WAVE'
Annual ↕ 18in (45cm) ↔ 12–36in (30–90cm)
A good plant for a hanging basket, 'Purple Wave'
has bright magenta flowers and spreads easily.
It is susceptible to rain damage, so grow it in a
sheltered spot. Also suitable as a groundcover.

MORE PETUNIAS ALL ANNUAL

P. CARPET SERIES
Single, widely trumpet-shaped flowers in white and shades
of pink, red, purple, and yellow

P. DADDY SERIES
Large, heavily veined flowers in pastel to deep pink,
purple, or lavender-blue

P. MIRAGE SERIES
Flowers in white or shades of blue, pink, red, or purple, some
with veining or bands on petals; tolerant of wet weather

P. SUPERCASCADE SERIES
Free-flowering over a long period; large flowers in white,
blue, pink, and red

P. SURFINIA SERIES
Large white, pink, magenta, red, lavender-blue, or blue flowers;
vigorous and weather-resistant; ideal for hanging baskets

P. ULTRA SERIES
Large, star-patterned flowers in shades of blue, pink, and
red; weather resistant

LOBELIA CASCADE SERIES
Annual ↕ 4–9in (10–23cm) ↔ 4–6in (10–15cm)
This trailing perennial is excellent as part of a
mixed container or hanging basket. It needs little
attention, and the long-lasting summer flowers
come in shades of red, purple, blue, pink, and white.

NEMESIA STRUMOSA 'KLM'
Annual ↕ 7–12in (18–30cm) ↔ 4–6in (10–16cm)
The contrasting, two-lipped flowers of this
nemesia are blue and white with yellow throats.
It is colorful in summer bedding as well as in
a container. They make good cut flowers.

IMPATIENS SUPER ELFIN GROUP
Annual ↕ to 10in (25cm) ↔ to 24in (60cm)
Impatiens give long-lasting summer color for
containers, and these annual cultivars come in a
variety of colors, including pastels and various
shades of purple, orange, pink, and red.

MATTHIOLA INCANA CINDERELLA SERIES
Z7–8 ↕ 8–10in (20–25cm) ↔ to 10in (25cm)
Better known as stocks, these useful spring and
summer bedding plants bear double flowers and
come in a range of colors including red, blue,
pink, purple, and white.

DIANTHUS IDEAL SERIES 'CHERRY PICOTEE'
Annual ↕ 8–14in (20–35cm) ↔ 9in (23cm)
This brightly colored pink has, from early
summer, scarlet flowers with contrasting white
fringes;,an effect known as "picotee." Deadhead
this annual or biennial to encourage flowering.

WATER GARDENS

APONOGETON DISTACHYOS
Z9–11 ↔ 4ft (1.2m)
The scented, small white flowers of this aquatic perennial are held above the bright green, floating leaves in spring and autumn. Grow in soil at the bottom of a pond in sun.

DARMERA PELTATA
Z5–9 ↕ to 6ft (2m) ↔ 3ft (1m) or more
The large, round leaves of this clump-forming perennial emerge after the late spring flowers, which are borne in umbrella-like clusters. Grow in moist or boggy soil in sun or partial shade.

HYDROCHARIS MORSUS-RANAE
Z6–11 ↔ indefinite
Frogbit is rather like a small waterlily and has flat, floating or submerged leaves. From early summer, three-petaled, papery white flowers appear. Best in shallow water in full sun.

CALLA PALUSTRIS
Z4–8 ↕ 10in (25cm) ↔ 24in (60cm)
The bog arum is a good plant for softening the edges of a pond. It has glossy dark green leaves and showy, white-spathed flower clusters in summer. Dull red berries appear in autumn.

RANUNCULUS LINGUA 'GRANDIFLORUS'
Z4–9 ↕ 5ft (1.5m) ↔ indefinite
Greater spearwort has big, golden yellow, buttercup-like flowers from early summer. Grow at a pond or stream margin; the very vigorous perennial growth must be contained in a strong container.

ORONTIUM AQUATICUM
Z6–11 ↕ 12–18in (30–45cm) ↔ 24–30in (60–75cm)
Grow golden club in deep wet soil at a pond edge, giving it room to spread. The leaves look best if grown in sun. Bright yellow, pencil-like spadices stand above the water from late spring.

VERONICA BECCABUNGA
Z5–11 ↕ 4in (10cm) ↔ indefinite
This evergreen aquatic perennial has fleshy leaves and creeping, fleshy stems. The blue flowers appear in late spring on upright stems. Grow in full sun in wet soil or at a pond or stream margin.

ZANTEDESCHIA ELLIOTTIANA
min. 50°F (10°C) ↕ 24–36in (60–90cm) ↔ 8in (20cm)
This calla lily bears golden yellow flowers on tall stems from early summer. The heart-shaped, dark green, upright leaves are covered in translucent white spots. Grow in full sun at a pool margin.

HIGH SUMMER 1

WALLS IN SUN

PASSIFLORA CAERULEA 'CONSTANCE ELLIOT'
Z6–9 ↕ 30ft (10m) or more
This white form of the blue passionflower is a fast-growing climber with slender stems, dark green foliage, and fragrant white flowers from summer into autumn. Good on a sheltered wall or trellis.

RHODOCHITON ATROSANGUINEUS
min 45°F (7°C) ↕ to 10ft (3m) or more
Both foliage and flowers are attractive on this slim-stemmed climber; the leaves are heart-shaped and the flowers appear in summer. Grow as an annual in cold climates. Also good for pergolas.

TROPAEOLUM SPECIOSUM
Z8–10 ↕ to 10ft (3m) or more
The flame nasturtium is a slender perennial climber with spurred, bright red flowers from summer to autumn; blue berries follow. Try to keep the roots and lower stems in shade.

IPOMOEA PURPUREA
Annual ↕ 6–10ft (2–3m)
The common morning glory is a twining climber with showy trumpets of purple-blue, magenta, or white flowers in summer. Grow as an annual in warmth and sun.

THUNBERGIA ALATA
Annual ↕ to 2.5m (8ft)
This climber is known as black-eyed Susan vine because of the dark centers on the flowers, which appear profusely from summer to autumn. Often grown as an annual; it can be trained up an obelisk.

TRACHELOSPERMUM JASMINOIDES
Z9–10 ↕ 28ft (9m)
A woody evergreen climber, star jasmine has dark green leaves, that turn bronze-red in autumn. The foliage is very glossy – a good foil to the pure white, very fragrant summer flowers.

LATHYRUS ODORATUS BIJOU GROUP
Annual ↕↔ to 18in (45cm)
This cultivar of sweet pea is a quite bushy annual climber with pink, blue, red, or white, gently fragrant summer flowers. They are good for cutting, which encourages further flowering.

ECCREMOCARPUS SCABER ANGEL HYBRIDS
Z10–11 ↕ 10–15ft (3–5m)
This colorful group of Chilean glory flowers are fast-growing evergreen climbers. The lopsided flowers appear for a long season and are red, pink, orange, or yellow. Provide support.

WALLS IN PARTIAL SHADE

ROSA 'SEAGULL'
Z5–9 ↕ to 20ft (6m) ↔ 12ft (4m)
This rambling rose sports a profusion of yellow-centered white flowers in summer on arching shoots. Its rampant growth can also be trained over pergolas, fences, or into a tree.

CLEMATIS 'HAGLEY HYBRID'
Z4–9 ↕ 6ft (2m) ↔ 3ft (1m)
This vigorous climber produces quite large summer flowers in shades of pink and mauve on the current year's shoots. It tolerates a sunny site, although the flowers will fade. Pruning Group 3.

MORE CLEMATIS Z4-9

C. 'DR. RUPPEL'
Large pink summer flowers. Pruning Group 2

C. 'JACKMANNII'
Dark purple flowers from midsummer. Pruning Group 3

C. 'NELLY MOSER'
Pinkish mauve summer flowers. Pruning Group 3

C. 'NIOBE'
Deep red flowers in summer. Pruning Group 2

C. 'ROUGE CARDINAL'
Grow in full sun; crimson-velvet flowers in midsummer. Pruning Group 3

C. 'ROYALTY'
Purple-mauve flowers from midsummer are initially semi-double, later single. Pruning Group 2

C. 'STAR OF INDIA'
Large, purple-blue midsummer flowers. Pruning Group 3

FALLOPIA BALDSCHUANICA
Z5–9 ↕ 40ft (12m)
This twining deciduous climber is a useful plant for quick cover. It is very vigorous and is sometimes known as the "mile-a-minute" plant. Sprays of pinkish white flowers appear in summer to autumn.

JASMINUM OFFICINALE
'ARGENTEOVARIEGATUM'
Z9–10 ↕ 12m (40ft)
This vigorous climber bears clusters of very fragrant white flowers from summer to early autumn. It twines over any support, including shrubs or trees.

BEDS AND BORDERS HOT/DRY

LAVANDULA ANGUSTIFOLIA 'LODDON PINK'
Z5–8 ↕ 18in (45cm) ↔ 24in (60cm)
This compact cultivar of lavender is a bushy shrub with dense spikes of fragrant, soft pink flowers from midsummer. Sometimes dried for pot-pourri. It can be clipped to make formal edging.

THYMUS SERPYLLUM 'ANNIE HALL'
Z4–9 ↕ 10in (25cm) ↔ 18in (45cm)
A fragrant, low-growing, trailing evergreen herb that can also be planted in crevices in walls or between paving stones, releasing its scent when walked on. The flowers appear in summer.

JOVIBARBA HIRTA
Z5–8 ↕ 6in (15cm) ↔ to 12in (30cm)
This flowering succulent with rosettes of often red-tinted leaves is easy to grow and is suitable for a rock garden, wall, or trough. The open clusters of pale yellowish brown flowers appear in summer.

HIGH SUMMER 2

MORE BEDS AND BORDERS HOT AND DRY

DICTAMNUS ALBUS
Z3–8 ↕ 16–36in (40–90cm) ↔ 24in (60cm)
Gas plant forms clumps of leathery, lemon-scented leaves and long stems of five-petaled flowers in early summer. A suitable perennial for a dry and sunny, well-drained border.

ACANTHUS HIRSUTUS
Z8–10 ↕ 6–14in (15–35cm) ↔ 12in (30cm)
An excellent structure plant with spikes of pale yellow or greenish white flowers from late spring to midsummer and clumps of dark green leaves. Cut back to ground level after flowering.

CLARKIA PULCHELLA DOUBLE MIXED
Annual ↕ 12in (30cm) ↔ 8in (20cm)
These annuals carry white, violet, or rose-pink double flowers that are good for cutting on slender stems throughout summer. Grow in well-drained soil in full sun.

LAVATERA 'BREDON SPRINGS'
Z8–10 ↕↔ 6ft (2m)
Excellent for lasting summer color, this vigorous mallow bears showy, mauve-flushed pink flowers over a long flowering season. Grow against a sunny wall where marginally hardy.

OSTEOSPERMUM 'WHIRLIGIG PINK'
Z10–11 ↕↔ 24in (60cm)
This perennial is grown for its daisylike flowers, which have pinched petal ends. It flourishes from late spring to autumn in any sheltered, sunny site; protect in winter or grow as an annual.

PHLOMIS ITALICA
Z9–10 ↕ 12in (30cm) ↔ 24in (60cm)
This upright, evergreen shrub bears hooded, lilac-pink midsummer flowers above woolly gray leaves, similar to the herb sage. Phlomis needs full sun to thrive and is most effective when planted in groups.

BEDS AND BORDERS IN SUN OR PARTIAL SHADE

LIMONIUM LATIFOLIUM
Z4–9 ↕ 24in (60cm) or more ↔ 18in (45cm)
The sea lavender is a perennial with branched, wiry stems bearing spikes of flowers in the second half of summer. Tolerant of coastal conditions and poor, sandy, or rocky soils. Also useful in a gravel garden.

VERBENA BONARIENSIS
Z7–11 ↕ to 6ft (2m) ↔ 18in (45cm)
The tall, slim, branching stems of this perennial support crowded clusters of tiny, fragrant, lilac-purple flowers from midsummer into autumn. In dry, alkaline soil, the plant will self-seed.

INDIGOFERA POTANINII
Z6–9 ↕ 6ft (2m) ↔ 8ft (2.5m)
This spreading shrub is grown for its elegant, gray-green leaves and small, pealike pink flowers. The flowers last through summer into early autumn. Grow in moist but well-drained soil.

GENISTA TINCTORIA
Z2–8 ↕ 24–36in (60–90cm) ↔ 3ft (1m)
Dyer's greenweed is an upright, deciduous shrub with sprays of golden yellow flowers in spring and summer. Grow in light, well-drained soil in full sun, and protect from excessive winter moisture..

ERYNGIUM GIGANTEUM
Z5–8 ↕ 36in (90cm) ↔ 12in (30cm)
A striking structural plant with spiny stem leaves and branching summer flowerheads that are good for cutting and drying. Protect from winter moisture; it is popular with slugs.

POTENTILLA FRUTICOSA 'GOLDFINGER'
Z3–7 ↕ 3ft (1m) ↔ 5ft (1.5m)
This compact and bushy, deciduous shrub flowers over a long period, producing a good display of large flowers from late spring to midautumn. A useful, easy-care plant.

VERBASCUM CHAIXII F. ALBUM
Z5–9 ↕ 36in (90cm) ↔ 18in (45cm)
Tall stems carry white flowers from midsummer on this perennial. Excellent toward the back of a mixed border; best in poor, dry soil, or in a gravel garden. The stems need support if the soil is rich.

HYDRANGEA MACROPHYLLA 'BLUE BONNET'
Z6–9 ↕ 6ft (2m) ↔ 8ft (2.5m)
This deciduous shrub bears rounded, ball-shaped flowerheads from midsummer. The flowers are either blue or pink depending on soil acidity; the more acidic the soil, the more pronounced the blue.

HIGH SUMMER 3

MORE BEDS AND BORDERS IN SUN OR PARTIAL SHADE

PENSTEMON DIGITALIS 'HUSKER RED'
Z2–8 ↕ 20–30in (50–75cm) ↔ 12in (30cm)
The striking maroon-red young leaves on this perennial are in contrast to the pink-tinted white flowers, which appear from early to late summer. Cut back in spring to keep compact.

SCABIOSA 'BUTTERFLY BLUE'
Z3–8 ↕↔ 16in (40cm)
Scabiosas are good perennials for attracting bees and butterflies; great for a cottage garden. The lavender-blue flowerheads appear in mid- and late summer. Good as a cut flower.

GYPSOPHILA ELEGANS 'ROSEA'
Annual ↕ to 60cm (24in) ↔ 30cm (12in)
The delicate, star-shaped, pale pink flowers of this annual are borne in summer on tall and slender, branching stems. It looks good in a mixed border and is also useful as a cut flower.

LOBELIA SPECIOSA 'FAN SCARLET'
Z3–8 ↕ 20–24in (50–60cm) ↔ 9in (to 23cm)
The vivid scarlet flower spikes of this perennial lobelia add a bright splash of color to a summer border. The narrow-petaled flowers are borne from summer to autumn. Prefers moist soil.

BUDDLEJA DAVIDII 'HARLEQUIN'
Z6–9 ↕ 10ft (3m) ↔ 15ft (5m)
This deciduous, fast-growing shrub flowers over a long season from summer to autumn. It is known as butterfly bush because the flowers attract them in abundance. This cultivar has variegated leaves.

ALCEA ROSEA
Z3–9 ↕ 5–8ft (1.5–2.5m) ↔ to 24in (60cm)
The hollyhock is an upright perennial grown for summer structure, producing tall, slender flower spikes, which often need staking for support. It is often seen as part of a cottage garden display.

ROSA 'ABRAHAM DARBY'
Z5–9 ↕↔ 5ft (1.5m)
This vigorous shrub rose grows into a bushy shape. It has large, deep green leaves and double, scented, apricot-pink flowers from summer to autumn. Grow in a mixed border or with other shrub roses.

MORE ROSES

R. 'DUBLIN BAY' **Z5-9**
Fragrant climber, which can be pruned to form a shrub; bright red flowers from summer to autumn

R. 'MARGARET MERRIL' **Z5-9**
Floribunda; fragrant pale pink to white flowers

R. X ODORATA 'MUTABILIS' **Z7-9**
Shrubby but can also be grown as a climber; fragrant pink summer flowers on reddish purple stems

R. 'ROSERAIE DE L'HAŸ' **Z4-9**
Vigorous, dense growth; strongly scented, double, rich purple-red flowers from summer to autumn

R. 'ROYAL WILLIAM' **Z5-9**
Hybrid tea; fragrant deep crimson flowers borne singly or in open clusters from summer to autumn

R. 'SILVER JUBILEE' **Z5-9**
Hybrid tea; rose-pink double flowers

R. 'WARM WISHES' **Z5-9**
Peach-pink, scented blooms throughout summer

ASTRANTIA MAJOR 'HADSPEN BLOOD'
Z4–7 ↕ 12–36in (30–90cm) ↔ 18in (45cm)
The toothed and deeply cut green leaves of this
perennial form a background for the rising stems
of ruby red flowers in summer. The flowerheads
can be dried for indoor arrangements.

PHLOX PANICULATA 'STARFIRE'
Z4–8 ↕ 36in (90cm) ↔ 24–39in (60–100cm)
This bright and showy perennial phlox carries
scented, deep crimson-red flowers from summer
to autumn. It will need regular watering and
feeding if grown in a very sunny spot.

ALSTROEMERIA AUREA
Z7–10 ↕ 3ft (1m) ↔ 18in (45cm)
Left alone, alstroemerias spread to great effect in a
border, flowering in summer. Also suitable for
containers and as cut flowers. Give slightly moist
soil and winter protection where marginally hardy.

TROPAEOLUM MAJUS 'EMPRESS OF INDIA'
Annual ↕ to 12in (30cm) ↔ to 18in (45cm)
Over a long flowering season from summer to
autumn, this dwarf annual nasturtium bears many
velvety flowers. Both the flowers and leaves are
edible, adding color to salads.

MONARDA 'PRÄRIENACHT'
Z4–8 ↕ 36in (90cm) ↔ 18in (45cm)
Beebalms are excellent aromatic perennials for a
summer border, bearing tall stems of long-lasting,
colorful flowers that attract bees. They are prone
to mildew if not kept watered.

COSMOS SULPHUREUS LADYBIRD SERIES
Annual ↕ 12–16in (30–40cm) ↔ 8in (20cm)
A reliable plant for a border or a container with
bright summer flowers. Deadhead regularly to
encourage repeat flowering, but leave some
flowers if it is to self-seed.

HIGH SUMMER 4

MORE BEDS AND BORDERS IN SUN OR PARTIAL SHADE		SHADE

HEMEROCALLIS 'STAFFORD'
Z3–10 ↕ 28in (70cm) ↔ 12in (30cm)
This daylily bears star-shaped scarlet flowers in
midsummer instead of the more familiar yellow.
A showy perennial for impact in a mixed border.
Grow in well-drained soil.

OENOTHERA PERENNIS
Z5–8 ↕↔ 8in (20cm) or more
A clump-forming perennial, known as sundrops,
grown for its funnel-shaped yellow flowers in
summer. The plant is quite tough and tolerates
stony soil.

NICOTIANA 'HAVANA APPLE BLOSSOM'
Annual ↕ 12–14in (30–35cm) ↔ 12–16in (30–40cm)
Nicotianas are excellent as summer bedding
annuals, the flowers remaining open in sun or
shade. This cultivar is quite compact, and it is
best positioned at the front of a border.

BAPTISIA AUSTRALIS
Z3–9 ↕ 5ft (1.5m) ↔ 24in (60cm)
A dry, sunny bank is a suitable site for this upright
perennial. In summer, dark blue, pealike flowers
appear, followed by large pods. The flowers are
often flecked white or cream.

VERONICA SPICATA SUBSP. *INCANA*

FILIPENDULA PALMATA 'RUBRA'
Z3–9 ↕ 4ft (1.2m) ↔ 24in (60cm)
Feathery clusters of red-pink flowers appear on
single stems in midsummer from the clumps
of divided leaves. This perennial prefers moist
conditions and thrives in a woodland garden.

LYCHNIS CHALCEDONICA
Z4–8 ↕ 3–4ft (0.9–1.2m) ↔ 12in (30cm)
Grow this stiff perennial in moist, fertile soil, and
deadhead for extended displays of its star-shaped
scarlet flowers in summer. Suitable for a mixed
border, but requires support. It self-seeds freely.

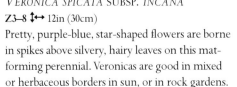

VERONICA SPICATA SUBSP. *INCANA*
Z3–8 ↕↔ 12in (30cm)
Pretty, purple-blue, star-shaped flowers are borne
in spikes above silvery, hairy leaves on this mat-
forming perennial. Veronicas are good in mixed
or herbaceous borders in sun, or in rock gardens.

LIGULARIA 'THE ROCKET'
Z4–8 ↕ 6ft (1.8m) ↔ 3ft (1m)
This tall perennial produces long, slim stems with
masses of yellow flowerheads in early and late
summer. It needs moist growing conditions, such
as a shady border or bog garden.

CONTAINERS

ARGYRANTHEMUM GRACILE 'CHELSEA GIRL'
Z10–11 ↕↔ 60cm (24in)
In frost-free areas, marguerites flower almost continuously and make excellent perennials for beds or containers. The daisylike flowers of 'Chelsea Girl' are white with yellow centers.

BIDENS FERULIFOLIA 'GOLDEN GODDESS'
Z8–10 ↕ to 12in (30cm) ↔ indefinite
The spreading, trailing habit of this perennial suits a hanging basket or container, where the stems can trail over the sides. Daisylike yellow flowerheads are produced from midsummer to autumn.

CIMICIFUGA SIMPLEX ATROPURPUREA GROUP
Z4–8 ↕ 3–4ft (1–1.2m) ↔ 24in (60cm)
These clump-forming perennials produce tall or arching stems of bottlebrush flowers until autumn. They need moist conditions and benefit from shelter or support from strong winds.

DIASCIA 'SALMON SUPREME'
Z8–9 ↕ 6in (15cm) ↔ to 20in (50cm)
A reliable container perennial with pretty pale apricot flowers over a long season from summer to autumn. Place in full sun, and promote flowering by regular feeding and removal of fading flowers.

HEUCHERA 'FIREFLY'
Z4–8 ↕ 30in (75cm) ↔ 12in (30cm)
An excellent foliage plant with clumps of dark green leaves. In early summer, fragrant red flowers, which attract bees, appear on tall stems. Use as a groundcover or in a mixed border.

LANTANA CAMARA 'RADIATION'
min 50°F (10°C) ↕↔ 3–6ft (1–2m)
Lantanas are popular shrubs for containers because of their showy, long-lasting flower clusters that appear from late spring to late autumn. Many other color combinations are available.

LILIUM 'STAR GAZER'
Z4–8 ↕ 3–5ft (1–1.5m)
This vigorous and easy-to-grow, sun-loving lily is good in a container and also makes an excellent cut flower. The star-shaped, unscented red flowers with white petal margins appear in midsummer.

HIGH SUMMER 5

MORE CONTAINERS

FELICIA AMELLOIDES 'READ'S WHITE'
min 37°F (3°C) ↕↔ 12–24in (30–60cm)
Felicias are grown for their long-lasting, daisylike
blue flowers from summer to autumn. This white-
flowered form becomes quite bushy if the growing
tips are pinched out regularly.

BEGONIA NON STOP SERIES
min 50°F (10°C) ↕↔ 12in (30cm)
The double flowers of these tuberous begonias
come in many bright colors, making them
excellent plants for a long-lasting summer display.
They need good light, but not direct sun.

AGAPANTHUS 'BLUE GIANT'
Z8–10 ↕ 4ft (1.2m) ↔ 24in (60cm)
The striking flowerheads of this perennial appear
from midsummer, emerging on long stems from
clumps of strap-shaped leaves. The flowers are
suitable for cutting. Mulch for protection.

VERBENA × HYBRIDA 'NOVALIS'
Annual ↕ to 10in (25cm) ↔ 12–20in (30–50cm)
This bushy perennial bears flowers from summer
to autumn in rose-pink, deep blue, and scarlet. It
suits containers in sunny sites and can also be used
as edging.

DIMORPHOTHECA PLUVIALIS
Annual ↕ to 16in (40cm) ↔ 6–12in (15–30cm)
An attractive, upright annual with white summer
flowerheads that close in dull weather – they need
full sun. They have violet-brown centers and are
deep violet-blue below. Deadhead regularly.

FUCHSIA 'PRESIDENT MARGARET SLATER'
Z8–10 ↕ 12–18in (30–45cm) ↔ 18–30in (45–75cm)
This pretty fuchsia bears flowers throughout
summer and autumn. It is a good trailing shrub
for a hanging basket. Keep moist and avoid full sun;
provide protection where marginally hardy.

PLATYCODON GRANDIFLORUS
Z4–9 ↕ to 24in (60cm) ↔ 12in (30cm)
In the second half of summer, clusters of balloon-
like buds open up to bell-shaped flowers on the
perennial balloon flower. Good for cutting; grow
in a container or at the front of a border.

HELIOTROPIUM ARBORESCENS 'MARINE'
Z11 ↕ to 18in (45cm) ↔ 12–18in (30–45cm)
Heliotropes are short-lived shrubs grown for their
sweetly scented, slightly flattened flowerheads in
summer. This cultivar is quite compact. An
excellent container or summer bedding plant.

WATER GARDENS

NUPHAR LUTEA

Z6–11 ↔ 6ft (2m)

This aquatic bears bright yellow, almost ball-shaped flowers in summer above spreading, leathery, floating leaves. It is also known as the yellow pond lily. The scent of the flowers can be unpleasant.

NYMPHAEA 'JAMES BRYDON'

Tropical ↔ 3–4ft (0.9–1.2m)

Rounded, bronze-green leaves form a backdrop to the bright rose-pink summer flowers of this waterlily. Grow in undisturbed water in sun and feed with aquatic fertilizer when in growth.

MORE WATERLILIES

NYMPHAEA 'BLUE BEAUTY'
Star-shaped, fragrant, midblue summer flowers; wavy-margined leaves. Tropical

N. CAROLINANA 'NIVEA'
Star-shaped, fragrant, ivory-white flowers with yellow stamens; pale green leaves. Hardy

N. 'FROEBELII'
Cupped, then star-shaped, burgundy-red flowers with orange-red stamens; pale green leaves. Hardy

N. 'GLADSTONEANA'
Star-shaped white flowers in summer; rounded, wavy-margined, dark green leaves. Tropical

N. ODORATA 'SULPHUREA GRANDIFLORA'
Very large, star-shaped, bright rich yellow flowers held slightly above water; marbled, dark green leaves. Hardy

N. TETRAGONA 'HELVOLA'
Slightly fragrant, vivid yellow flowers; heavily mottled, purple-marked leaves. Hardy

RODGERSIA PINNATA 'SUPERBA'

Z5–8 ↕ to 4ft (1.2m) ↔ 30in (75cm)

Grow this perennial near water at a woodland margin or in a bog garden. It has glossy dark green leaves that are purplish bronze when young. The mid- to late summer flowers are bright pink.

BUTOMUS UMBELLATUS

Z5–11 ↕ to 5ft (1.5m) ↔ 18in (45cm)

A decorative perennial with delicate, fragrant flowers from midsummer. Grow in full sun in shallow water at a pond margin or in a bog garden. The leaves emerge bronze-purple as they expand.

SAGITTARIA LATIFOLIA

Z5–11 ↕ 18–36in (45–90cm) ↔ 36in (90cm)

An excellent plant for the margin of a wildlife pond; the tubers attract waterfowl. The flowers are borne in summer. Trim back spreading growth in late summer.

MIMULUS LUTEUS

Z7–9 ↕ 12in (30cm) ↔ to 24in (60cm)

The yellow monkey flower is a vigorous, spreading perennial, which self seeds freely. It suits a damp border or a bog garden, but it can be grown in water to 3in (7cm) deep.

GLYCERIA MAXIMA VAR. VARIEGATA

Z5–9 ↕ 32in (80cm) ↔ indefinite

This vigorous, aquatic grass is grown for its foliage, which is striped cream, green, and white. It spreads easily in water up to 6in (15cm) deep, making it good for cover in a large pond.

LATE SUMMER TO EARLY AUTUMN 1

WALLS IN SUN

WALLS IN SHADE

MAGNOLIA GRANDIFLORA 'GOLIATH'
Z7–9 ↕ 20–60ft (6–18m) ↔ to 50ft (15m)
A particularly striking evergreen magnolia with blooms up to 12in (30cm) across from late summer and broad, slightly twisted leaves. The tree can be trained against a warm wall; it tolerates dry soil.

CAMPSIS × *TAGLIABUANA* 'MME. GALEN'
Z5–9 ↕ 30ft (10m) or more
This woody climber is vigorous with long stems of leaflets and trumpet-shaped, orange-red flowers that appear from late summer to autumn. It may take two or three years to establish.

CLEMATIS 'PAUL FARGES'
Z4–9 ↕ 21–28ft (7–9m) ↔ 10ft (3m)
This vigorous deciduous climber carries a profusion of small flowers from midsummer to autumn. They appear on the current year's shoots. Pruning Group 3.

MORE CLEMATIS

C. 'ALBA LUXURIANS' **Z5-9**
Small white flowers from midsummer. Pruning Group 3

C. 'BILL MACKENZIE' **Z6-9**
Lanternlike yellow flowers in abundance from midsummer. Pruning Group 3

C. 'ETOILE VIOLETTE' **Z5-9**
Small and nodding, violet-purple flowers until late autumn. Pruning Group 3

C. FLAMMULA **Z7-9**
Star-shaped white flowers into autumn. Pruning Group 3

C. 'PERLE D'AZUR' **Z4-9**
Azure blue blooms from midsummer. Pruning Group 3

C. 'POLISH SPIRIT' **Z5-9**
Deep purple-blue flowers from midsummer. Pruning Group 3

C. REHDERIANA **Z6-9**
Scented yellow flowers until late autumn. Pruning Group 3

C. VITICELLA 'PURPUREA PLENA ELEGANS' **Z5-9**
Purplish mauve flowers to late autumn. Pruning Group 3

LAPAGERIA ROSEA VAR. *ALBIFLORA*
Z10–11 ↕ 15ft (5m)
Grown for its showy, elongated flowers that appear from summer to late autumn, this evergreen twining climber usually grow best against a sheltered wall.

CELASTRUS ORBICULATUS
Z4–8 ↕ 46ft (14m)
Train this deciduous climber up a wall, fence, pergola, or into a tree. Plant males with females so the small, green summer flowers are followed by yellow fruits that split to reveal orange seeds.

BERBERIDOPSIS CORALLINA
Z8–9 ↕ 15ft (5m)
This woody evergreen climber blooms from summer to early autumn, some flowers hanging and others in clusters. Let it twine through a support in partial shade.

BEDS AND BORDERS HOT AND DRY

ECHINOPS RITRO
Z3–9 ‡ to 24in (60cm) ↔ 18in (45cm)
Globe thistles are easy to look after and grow in almost any soil. This perennial species has round, metallic blue flowerheads in late summer. They are suitable for cutting and drying.

PEROVSKIA 'BLUE SPIRE'
Z6–9 ‡ 4ft (1.2m) ↔ 3ft (1m)
Tall, gray-white stems support a profusion of flowers in late summer and early autumn on this shrub. Grow in a mixed border; cut back hard in spring to promote flowering and compactness.

ZAUSCHNERIA CALIFORNICA 'DUBLIN'
Z8–10 ‡ to 10in (25cm) ↔ to 12in (30cm)
Also known as the California fuchsia, this deciduous perennial bears bright red, funnel-shaped flowers over a long season from late summer. Excellent for late season color.

SEDUM SPECTABILE 'ICEBERG'
Z4–9 ‡↔ to 24in (60cm)
In early autumn, this fleshy-leaved perennial bears flat flowerheads of white flowers. Grow at the front of a mixed border or in a rock garden; it is attractive to beneficial insects. It tolerates light shade.

CROCOSMIA 'BRESSINGHAM BLAZE'
Z6–9 ‡ 30–36in (75–90cm) ↔ 3in (8cm)
The spikes of brilliant orange-red, funnel-shaped flowers of this perennial make a hot splash of color at the edge of a mixed border. It flowers in late summer and is excellent for cutting.

TAMARIX RAMOSISSIMA 'PINK CASCADE'
Z3–8 ‡↔ 15ft (5m)
This graceful shrub has arching, red-brown shoots and rich pink flowers on new growth in late summer and early autumn. Particularly good for an exposed coastal garden.

LATE SUMMER TO EARLY AUTUMN 2

BEDS AND BORDERS HOT/DRY | BEDS AND BORDERS IN SUN OR PARTIAL SHADE

GAILLARDIA PULCHELLA 'RED PLUME'
Annual ↕↔ 12in (30cm)
From summer to autumn, double flowerheads are borne on this upright annual. Gaillardias have a long flowering period, and they are also good for cutting. Deadhead regularly.

ECHINACEA PURPUREA
Z3–9 ↕ to 5ft (1.5m) ↔ 18in (45cm)
Also known as coneflower for the distinctive, cone-shaped center of the daisylike flowerhead, this perennial flowers from midsummer. It is very popular for mixed or herbaceous borders.

TRADESCANTIA × ANDERSONIANA 'KARMINGLUT'
Z5–9 ↕↔ 16–24in (40–60cm)
From summer to autumn, carmine-red flowers appear on this perennial amid the tufts of leaves. Cut back after flowering to encourage more blooms.

GAURA LINDHEIMERI
Z6–9 ↕ to 5ft (1.5m) ↔ 36in (90cm)
This graceful, bushy, clump-forming perennial has slender stems and star-shaped flowers that open from late spring to early autumn. It is unsuitable for very dry soils.

RUDBECKIA HIRTA 'BECKY MIXED'
Z3–7 ↕ to 10in (25cm) ↔ 12–18in (30–45cm)
This dwarf rudbeckia is usually grown as an annual in borders or summer beds. Its abundant summer to early autumn, daisylike flowers are good for cutting.

CARYOPTERIS × CLANDONENSIS 'WORCESTER GOLD'
Z6–9 ↕ 3ft (1m) ↔ 5ft (1.5m)
This deciduous shrub has warm yellow leaves and aromatic, lavender-blue flowers in late summer and early autumn. Thrives in heat.

GALTONIA VIRIDIFLORA
Z8–10 ↕ to 3ft (1m) ↔ 4in (10cm)
This bulbous perennial with broad and very long, lance-shaped leaves bears compact clusters of flowers in late summer. Best in a sunny border; it makes a good cut flower.

CERATOSTIGMA WILLMOTTIANUM
Z6–9 ↕ 3ft (1m) ↔ 5ft (1.5m)
This spreading and deciduous shrub is grown for its pretty blue flowers and for its autumn leaf color. Best in a sunny, sheltered spot; good as a groundcover in a mixed border.

LEYCESTERIA FORMOSA
Z9–10 ↕↔ 6ft (2m)
The Himalayan honeysuckle is a thicket-forming shrub with bamboolike young shoots. Flowers appear in summer and early autumn, followed by purple-red berries. Prune hard in spring.

ASTER AMELLUS 'VEILCHENKÖNIGIN'
Z5–8 ↕ 12–24in (30–60cm) ↔ 18in (45cm)
Asters can be found for most garden sites, and this violet-purple cultivar (also sold as 'Violet Queen') prefers a well-drained, open, and sunny position. In late autumn, after flowering, cut back and mulch.

MORE ASTERS

A. × *FRIKARTII* 'MÖNCH' **Z5–8**
Tolerant of air pollution; long-lasting, lavender-blue flowerheads with yellow-orange centers from late summer

A. LATERIFLORUS 'HORIZONTALIS' **Z4-8**
Widely spreading branches; pink-tinged white flowerheads with darker pink centers from midsummer to midautumn

A. 'LITTLE CARLOW' **Z5-8**
Large clusters of violet-blue flowerheads with yellow centers in early autumn; excellent for cutting and drying

A. NOVAE-ANGLIAE 'ANDENKEN AN ALMA PÖTSCHKE' **Z4-8**
Vigorous, strong-stemmed growth; sprays of bright salmon-pink flowerheads with yellow centers from late summer

A. NOVAE-ANGLIAE 'PURPLE DOME' **Z4-8**
Deep purple flowers on compact plants.

A. NOVI-BELGII 'LITTLE PINK BEAUTY' **Z4-8**
Semidouble, soft pink flowerheads from late summer

A. TATARICUS **Z3-8**
Large clusters of lavender-blue flowers. To 8 ft (2.5m)

HELIANTHUS DECAPETALUS
'TRIOMPHE DE GAND'
Z5–9 ↕ to 6ft (2m) ↔ 4ft (1.2m)
This perennial cultivar of the classic sunflower has large flowerheads. Provide plenty of sun, and support the stems to prevent them from breaking.

HEBE 'PURPLE QUEEN'
Z9–10 ↕↔ 5ft (1.5m)
Hebes are versatile evergreen shrubs grown for their foliage and flowers. This cultivar has large, late summer flowers and dark green leaves. Suitable for a container.

ANEMONE × *HYBRIDA* 'SEPTEMBER CHARM'
Z4–8 ↕ 24–36in (60–90cm) ↔ 16in (40cm)
In mid- to late summer, this upright perennial bears branched stems of flowers. Grow in moist, fertile soil, adding a mulch in spring and late autumn in colder areas. A popular cottage garden flower.

LATE SUMMER TO EARLY AUTUMN 3

MORE BEDS AND BORDERS IN SUN OR PARTIAL SHADE

NERINE BOWDENII 'MARK FENWICK'
Z8–10 ↕ 18in (45cm) ↔ 3in (8cm)
This bulbous perennial carries open clusters of pink autumn flowers on top of upright, dark green stalks. Plant bulbs in early spring in well-drained soil in sun. Water freely during active growth.

PHYSALIS ALKEKENGI
Z5–8 ↕ 24–30in (60–75cm) ↔ 36in (90cm) or more
Chinese lantern is a vigorous, spreading perennial with bell-shaped flowers from midsummer. Grown for its papery, lanternlike red calyces surrounding the fruits. Suitable for cutting and drying.

HELENIUM 'BUTTERPAT'
Z4–8 ↕ 36in (90cm) ↔ 24in (60cm)
This upright perennial has bright, rich yellow flowerheads from midsummer with yellow-brown centers. They are attractive to bees and are suitable for cutting. A colorful addition to a flower border.

SOLIDAGO 'GOLDENMOSA'
Z5–9 ↕ to 30in (75cm) ↔ 18in (45cm)
Called goldenrod for its tall, bright yellow flowerheads from late summer to autumn, this bushy perennial is suitable for natural gardens, because the flowers attract bees and butterflies.

ACONITUM CARMICHAELII 'ARENDSII'
Z3–7 ↕ to 4ft (1.2m) ↔ 12in (30cm)
Monkshood is a good upright perennial with rich blue flowers, borne in autumn, which are suitable for cutting. Ideal for a woodland garden or mixed border; it may need staking.

ANGELICA GIGAS
Z4–9 ↕ 3–6ft (1–2m) ↔ 4ft (1.2m)
This short-lived perennial is grown for its striking flowers, which are carried on tall stems and appear in late summer and early autumn. Grow in full or partial shade. This is not the edible angelica.

PHYSOSTEGIA VIRGINIANA 'VIVID'
Z4–8 ↕ 12–24in (30–60cm) ↔ 12in (30cm)
The obedient plant is named for its unusual flowers, which remain in the new position if moved. This cultivar is a clump-forming perennial that flowers from midsummer; suitable for cutting.

HIBISCUS SYRIACUS 'DIANA'
Z5–9 ↕ 10ft (3m) ↔ 6ft (2m)
This reliable deciduous shrub bears particularly large flowers, to 5in (12cm) across, from late summer to midautumn. It needs a hot summer to flower well.

BEDS AND BORDERS IN SHADE | CONTAINERS

LIRIOPE MUSCARI
Z6–10 ‡12in (30cm) ↔ 18in (45cm)
An evergreen perennial with long, pointed leaves. It flowers in autumn, producing bright purple flowers, followed by black berries. It makes a good groundcover and is tolerant of dry sites.

FUCHSIA MAGELLANICA
Z6–9 ‡to 10ft (3m) ↔ 6–10ft (2–3m)
This upright, shrubby fuchsia produces red and purple flowers with long red tubes throughout summer. It will grow in a variety of sites; partial shade is best, and do not let the soil get too dry.

GENTIANA ASCLEPIADEA
Z6–9 ‡24–36in (60–90cm) ↔ 18in (45cm)
The willow gentian looks effective grown with shade-loving ferns and grasses. It is a clump-forming perennial with trumpet-shaped blue flowers in the second half of summer.

SCENTED GERANIUMS 36°F (2°C)

PELARGONIUM 'AROMA'
Small, sweet-smelling, gray-green leaves; white flowers

P. 'ATOMIC SNOWFLAKE'
Large, yellow-variegated leaves with a lemon scent

P. 'ATTAR OF ROSES'
Rose-scented leaves; clusters of mauve summer flowers

P. 'CLORINDA'
Cedar-scented, lobed leaves; clusters of rose-pink flowers

P. CRISPUM 'VARIEGATUM'
Cream-margined, lemon-scented leaves; pale mauve summer flowers

P. 'FAIR ELLEN'
Deeply lobed, very spicy leaves; purple-pink flowers

P. 'FILICIFOLIUM'
Fernlike leaves with a balsam scent; pale mauve flowers

P. 'FRAGRANS'
Pine-scented, gray-green foliage; white summer flowers

P. 'LADY PLYMOUTH'
Eucalyptus-scented, silver-margined leaves; lavender-pink summer flowers

P. 'MABEL GREY'
Strongly lemon-scented leaves; purple summer flowers

P. 'OLD SPICE'
Spicy-scented leaves; white flowers throughout summer

P. 'PRINCE OF ORANGE'
Small, orange-scented leaves; clusters of mauve flowers

P. 'ROYAL OAK'
Spicy-scented leaves shaped like oak leaves; clusters of mauve flowers in summer

P. TOMENTOSUM
Peppermint-scented leaves; white flowers; trailing stems

CEANOTHUS × PALLIDUS 'PERLE ROSE'
Z8–10 ↔ 1.5m (5ft)
A pink form of a traditionally blue-flowered shrub. It is bushy and deciduous, and it flowers from midsummer to autumn. Grow in a shrub border or against a sunny wall. Prune annually.

HYDRANGEA PANICULATA 'UNIQUE'
Z4–8 ‡10–22ft (3–7m) ↔ 8ft (2.5m)
This vigorous shrub bears large conical heads of white flowers, which can be dried for indoor display, in late summer and early autumn. This large shrub is best on its own or in a large border.

PELARGONIUM 'GRAVEOLENS'
min 36°F (2°C) ‡24in (45–60cm) ‡16in (20–40cm)
The leaves of this scented geranium have a strong lemony aroma, and pale mauve flowers appear in summer. Good in a border.

AUTUMN TO WINTER 1

WALLS	BEDS AND BORDERS

COTONEASTER HORIZONTALIS

Z5–7 ↕ 3ft (1m) ↔ 5ft (1.5m)

A rigid shrub that will grow flat against a sunny wall or strong fence in a fishbone pattern. Bees visit the tiny spring flowers, and the autumn berries are eaten by birds. The leaves turn red before they fall.

CLEMATIS TANGUTICA

Z6–9 ↕ 12–20ft (5–6m) ↔ 6–10ft (2–3m)

A twining climber with beautiful, bell-shaped yellow flowers from midsummer to autumn. Its seedheads persist among ghostly gray stems into winter. Provide support. Pruning Group 3.

PARTHENOCISSUS QUINQUEFOLIA

Z3–9 ↕ to 50ft (15m) or more

The Virginia creeper is best on large, featureless walls where it climbs without support. Its leaves turn a brilliant red in autumn. Do not let the vigorous growth interfere with gutters.

VIBURNUM OPULUS 'XANTHOCARPUM'

Z4–8 ↕ 15ft (5m) ↔ 12ft (4m)

This yellow-berried guelder rose is a deciduous shrub with lacecaplike heads of white flowers in summer. The leaves redden before they fall. Allow plenty of room.

CALLICARPA DICHOTOMA

Z6–8 ↕↔ 4ft (1.2m)

This dense deciduous shrub bears extraordinary purple berries that follow the pale pink summer flowers. The fruits are not attractive to most birds, so they usually persist long after the leaves fall.

GAULTHERIA PROCUMBENS

Z3–8 ↕ 6in (15cm) ↔ to 3ft (1m) or more

A creeping evergreen shrub for groundcover, with leathery leaves gradually turning red as the days grow colder. The pinkish white summer flowers are followed by berries. Unsuitable for alkaline soil.

RUBUS COCKBURNIANUS

Z5–9 ↕↔ 8ft (2.5m)

This ornamental bramble is deciduous and has red stems with a white coating. The summer flowers are deep purple, and the fruits are inedible. Cut back hard in spring for good winter stem color.

COLCHICUM 'WATERLILY'

Z4–9 ↕ 5in (12cm) ↔ 4in (10cm)

This autumn crocus looks good if the bulblike corms are planted in drifts under deciduous trees. The unusual, feathery double flowers are lilac-pink. Also suitable for a container.

IRIS UNGUICULARIS 'MARY BARNARD'
Z7–9 ↕ 12in (30cm)
A low-growing evergreen perennial with fragrant, almost stemless flowers during mild spells in winter. It soon forms clumps in a sunny, sheltered spot. Avoid slug-infested areas.

CHRYSANTHEMUM 'SALMON FAIRIE'
Annual ↕ 12–24in (30–60cm) ↔ to 24in (60cm)
A beautiful florists' chrysanthemum with pompon-shaped, salmon-pink flowerheads, 1⅝in (4cm) across, in late autumn. Apply a balanced liquid fertilizer weekly for the best display.

CHRYSANTHEMUMS

Chrysanthemums are considered THE flower of autumn in much of North America. Although there are some species and varieties that are reliably perennial, most of the showy chrysanthemums are not very cold-hardy and require extra care to grow them successfully. In fact, many people simply buy new plants every autumn to replace the previous season's plants, which failed to survive winter's cold and moisture.

Enthusiasts grow spectacular chrysanthemums for exhibition from cuttings started in spring, either from plants overwintered in a cold frame or similar area, or from rooted cuttings bought from specialist nurseries. They follow set schedules for fertilizing and cutting back to produce perfect blooms at the right time for shows.

Ask a neighbor for local advice on growing chrysanthemums in your area.

FOTHERGILLA GARDENII
Z5–9 ↕↔ 3ft (1m)
The witch alder is a dense, bushy shrub with spikes of fragrant white flowers in early spring. It dislikes alkaline soil. Particularly good for its vibrant autumn color.

RUSCUS ACULEATUS
Z7–9 ↕ 30in (75cm) ↔ 3ft (1m)
Planted in groups, butcher's broom makes a spiny, subshrubby evergreen groundcover that thrives in dry shade. Vivid red berries appear on female plants from autumn to winter.

CORNUS 'EDDIE'S WHITE WONDER'
Z5–8 ↕ 20ft (6m) ↔ 15ft (5m)
Beautiful most of the year, this small and spreading deciduous tree has orange, red, and purple foliage in autumn and inconspicuous flowers surrounded by creamy bracts in spring. Needs a sunny site.

AUTUMN TO WINTER 2

MORE BEDS AND BORDERS

BERGENIA 'BALLAWLEY'

Z3–8 ↕ 24in (60cm) ↔ 18–24in (45–60cm)
Good for colorful late-season groundcover: the
leaves of this perennial turn bronze-purple in
winter. Crimson flowers appear in mid- and late
spring. A sheltered site is preferable.

SYMPHORICARPOS × DOORENBOSII
'WHITE HEDGE'

Z4–7 ↕ 5ft (1.5m) ↔ indefinite
This snowberry is a useful deciduous shrub for
most areas. Good for a city garden; it tolerates
pollution. Also used for informal hedging.

CROCUS SPECIOSUS 'OXONIAN'

Z3–8 ↕ 4–6in (10–15cm) ↔ 2in (5cm)
Plant drifts of this crocus in late summer for
a beautiful display of autumn flowers, which are
violet-mauve with dark violet bases. It prefers
sunny, well-drained soil that is not too rich.

MAHONIA × MEDIA 'BUCKLAND'

Z8–9 ↕ to 15ft (5m) ↔ to 12ft (4m)
This evergreen shrub is grown for its spiky foliage
and fragrant, bright yellow flowers on arching
stems from late autumn to late winter. A showy
shrub, it makes a good barrier.

MORE ROSES FOR HIPS

R. 'FRAU DAGMAR HARTOPP' **Z2-9**
*Small shrub; large and single, pink summer flowers; huge,
tomato red hips in autumn*

R. MOYESII **Z4-9**
*Tall, arching rose; scarlet or pink flowers in summer; large,
flagon-shaped hips in autumn*

R. GLAUCA **Z2-8**
Rather large shrub, unique reddish/gray foliage, red hips

R. PIMPINELLIFOLIA **Z3-9**
*Spreading, prickly shrub; white, early summer flowers;
round, purplish black hips in autumn*

R. ROXBURGHII **Z6-9**
Stiffly growing shrub; unusual, spiny autumn fruit

R. 'SCHARLACHGLUT' **Z4-9**
Can be trained as a climber; scarlet autumn hips

R. 'SCHNEEZWERG' **Z2-9**
*Dense bush; flat, scented white flowers from summer to
autumn; tomato-shaped, orange-red hips follow*

ROSA RUGOSA

Z2-9 ↕↔ 3–8ft (1–2.5m)
The Japanese rose has very prickly stems and makes
a useful barrier hedge. It is grown for its fat, glossy
red hips from autumn into winter. Purple-red
flowers and "quilted" foliage precede the display.

ACIDIC SOIL

EUONYMUS OXYPHYLLUS
Z6–9 ↕ 8ft (2.5m) or more ↔ 8ft (2.5m)
Glowing autumn leaf color distinguishes this
deciduous small tree from the well-known
evergreen kinds. It useful in a shrub border or
for impact on its own.

MORE EUONYMUS

E. ALATUS **Z4-9**
*Dark green leaves turn brilliant red in autumn; spherical,
reddish purple fruit appear in autumn; deciduous shrub*

E. BUNGEANUS **Z5-8**
*Pale green foliage turns to yellow and pink in autumn;
yellow-white winter fruit; graceful deciduous shrub*

E. EUROPAEUS 'RED CASCADE' **Z4-7**
*Foliage turns red in autumn; red fruit in autumn and
winter, deciduous shrub with conical shape*

E. FORTUNEI 'EMERALD 'N' GOLD' **Z5-9**
*Bright green leaves with broad, bright yellow margins,
tinged pink in winter; compact, evergreen shrub*

E. FORTUNEI 'SILVER QUEEN' **Z5-9**
*White-margined, dark green leaves, margins tinged pink
in winter; bushy and upright evergreen shrub*

E. KIAUTSCHOVICUS **Z6-8**
*An open, spreading evergreen to 10ft (3m) with interesting
pink fruit that split open to reveal orange seeds*

DISANTHUS CERCIDIFOLIUS
Z5–8 ↕↔ 10ft (3m)
This rounded deciduous shrub is grown for its
autumn leaf color, which turns to yellows,
oranges, reds, and purples – all displayed at
once. Plant alone for maximum impact.

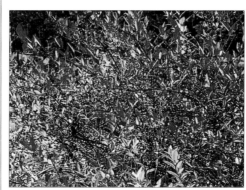

VACCINIUM ANGUSTIFOLIUM
VAR. *LAEVIFOLIUM*
Z2–8 ↕↔ 4–24in (10–60cm)
The lowbush blueberry is a spreading, deciduous
shrub with white spring flowers. It is grown for its
blue-black, edible berries. Good autumn color.

CALLUNA VULGARIS 'ANNEMARIE'
Z5–7 ↕ 20in (50cm) ↔ 24in (60cm)
From midsummer to late autumn, this heather
forms long spikes of flowers that are good for
cutting. Cut back in spring to encourage
production of the next season's flowers.

PART FOUR

WHAT
TO DO
WHEN

HOW TO USE THIS SECTION

All gardens, even low-maintenance ones, require some care throughout the year to keep them looking their best and the plants healthy and thriving. When you think about jobs to be done, remember that they are opportunities to go into the garden and enjoy it, rather than chores.

Working among the plants in your garden will bring you close to them and allow you to appreciate the textures of foliage, the flourish of a tiny flower, the chattering song of birds in the hedge, or a sweet perfume floating on the air. Whether weeding a border or planting a tree, take time to stop and look about you at the fruits of your labors and at how the garden changes through the seasons.

WHAT NEEDS TO BE DONE WHEN?

To enable you decide easily what needs to be done in the garden and at what time of year, this section consists of listings largely distilled from previous chapters in the book. Individual, one-time projects are suggested on the facing page. The season-by-season listings in the rest of this chapter serve as brief reminders of routine tasks that you might need to carry out during the gardening year. Use the Index to Seasons (*see right*) to find a season and the appropriate task list.

KEEPING CLIMBERS TO SIZE

■ **If a climber outgrows** its allotted space on the house, or any other, wall, spring is the time to cut it down to size.

■ **Cut back overly long shoots** with pruners, cutting just above an upward- or downward-facing bud.

■ **For a natural look,** trim the shoots to irregular lengths within the desired outline of the plant.

CUTTING BACK IVY

USING THE SEASONAL LISTINGS

Most seasons are split into month-long slots, for example "Early spring," "Mid-spring," and "Late spring," because the timing of garden tasks depends on the growing conditions, not the calendar month. There is also a category for tasks such as cleaning tools that are not dependent on the season ("Anytime").

■ Within the seasons, the tasks are further divided into columns for different areas of the garden, for example "Herbs" or "Beds and Borders," to remind you which areas of the garden are likely to need your attention.

■ Within quieter seasons such as winter, there may be no listing covering some areas of the garden, if there is little to do at that time of year.

■ Possible tasks are allocated to the part-season or season in which it is best to carry them out. Some tasks may be carried out in more than one season, so they appear wherever relevant.

■ To enable you to prioritize work in the garden, essential tasks are highlighted at the top of each column. These include activities that may cause problems later if not done at the recommended time, such as watering new lawns, and others that can be done only at the indicated time, for example taking cuttings.

■ Bear in mind however that the listings *should be taken only as a guide*, not as rules to be followed slavishly. If you live in a warm climate or the weather is unusually mild, you may be able to start some tasks earlier and finish later; if in a cold region, you may need to delay them. Every garden is unique: its site (sheltered or exposed) and soil type (wet, dry, heavy, or light) affect the rate at which plants grow and the time when various activities are best carried out.

ADDITIONAL INFORMATION

■ Cross-references lead you from the listing to more detailed information on how to carry out the task in appropriate chapters of the book.

■ The listing also features tips boxes with additional information (*see example, left*), ideas, or lists of relevant plants.

GARDEN PROJECTS FOR ALMOST ANY TIME OF THE YEAR

As well as tasks that are dependent on the seasons or on the plants in the garden (*see following pages*), there are other, usually one-time, projects that affect the garden's permanent structure (*see below*) to be done at any time, as long as the soil is not sodden or frozen. Some may be necessary to keep the garden looking neat and functioning efficiently, such as laying paths or erecting a tool shed, but most are projects to be undertaken as and when you wish to enhance your own enjoyment of the garden.

Projects involving construction or major changes to the garden layout may involve more effort than routine tasks but can have a great impact in the garden and be very rewarding.

Before embarking on a project, it pays to spend a little time in planning – consider how the new feature will fit into the garden layout, if you have all the materials and tools you need, delivery times of materials, how much time the job will take, if you need any help, and if any plants need to be prepared in advance.

PATHS AND PAVING
■ **Lay a patio** (*see pp.56–59*) to provide a link between the house and garden and a space for outdoor living.

■ **Use concrete or gravel** to create a path, driveway, or area of hard surfacing (*see pp.60–63*). For a softer look, introduce planting pockets (*see p.63 and p.72*) with tough, low-growing herbs or grasses, or alpine plants.

■ **Install decking** to provide a patio, sitting area, or walkway (*see pp.64–65*). Leave it in natural tones to weather and blend in with the garden or paint it in bright colors for an original, contemporary look.

■ **Make or renew a path** with hard surfacing, such as brick or random paving, or soft materials, such as bark chips (*see pp.66–67*).

■ **Build some steps** to create a point of interest or to link different levels of the garden (*see pp.68–69*).

■ **Extend the possibilities** of the garden by installing lighting (*see pp.70–71*), to allow use of it at night and to highlight the hidden beauty of favorite plants.

■ **Jazz up the patio** by introducing plants in containers, a water feature, barbecue, or patio furniture (*see pp.72–73*).

POINTED CEMENT PAVING SLABS

BOUNDARIES AND DIVISIONS
■ **Erect fencing** such as wood panels (*see p.94*) and picket fencing (*see p.95*) to enclose or divide up the garden. Paint it with wood preservative in natural tones or in bright colors for a contemporary look.

■ **Put up a trellis** to support plants (*see p.95*) and enable them to clothe walls and buildings or as a divider between areas of the garden.

■ **Create an arch** to entice the eye along a path – assemble a premade one (*see p.99*) or build your own.

■ **Build a pergola** on which to grow climbers for a charming shady retreat. You can assemble the pergola from a kit (*see p.101*). Alternatively, construct a simple one out of plain lumber or from rustic poles, or employ someone to build it for you.

BEDS AND BORDERS
■ **Create a gravel bed** to provide ideal growing conditions for alpine and drought-tolerant plants as well as an attractive feature in the garden (*see p.132*). You could also plant it with herbs (*see p.229*).

■ **Mark out a new border** to increase the space for planting (*see p.145*).

CONTAINERS AND RAISED BEDS
■ **Brighten up windows** – set brackets in the wall so that you can add a splash of color or touch of greenery with a windowbox (*see p.166*).

■ **Make a windowbox** or planter out of wood – a good way of obtaining unique containers while saving money (*see p.171*).

■ **Build a raised bed** with bricks or wooden railroad ties (*see p.181*). You can fill them with plants that need special soil conditions, such as acidic-soil lovers like azaleas and heathers, or that are small and better appreciated at close hand, such as alpine plants.

■ **Customize your containers:** paint or decorate them (*see pp.169–170*), or age new terracotta and stone planters to give them a weathered look (*see p.171*).

WATER GARDENING
■ **Build a pond,** using a preformed pond unit (*see p.201 and p.206*) or a flexible pond liner (*see pp.201–203*). It will form a focal point in the garden, attract wildlife, and increase the range of plants you can grow; if it is big enough, you can also keep a few fish.

■ **Introduce the sound** of running water by installing a fountain – in a pool or a pond (*see pp.208–209*), on a wall or in a ground-level feature (*see pp.212–213*). For a unique feature, try recycling an old sink, watering can, or piece of scrap metal as a base for the fountain.

BARREL POOL

■ **Make a bog garden** (*see pp.204–205*) as a specialized planting area or to complement and entend an existing water feature.

■ **Prepare containers** such as wooden barrels or earthenware pots for use as small ornamental ponds (*see p.207*).

THE HERB GARDEN
■ **Create an herb garden** as a decorative feature in a formal or an informal style (*see p.224*), or a simple culinary patch near the house to supply the kitchen (*see p.226*).

THE EDIBLE GARDEN
■ **Plan a vegetable plot,** fruit bed, or ornamental potager, taking account of sowing and cropping times, yields, and soil needs (*see pp.234–237*), for a year-round harvest. Then mark out and prepare the beds, at least a month before sowing or planting them.

GARDEN STRUCTURES
■ **Erect a tool shed** (*see p.276*), garden shed (*see pp.276–277*), or greenhouse (*see p.286*). If you want to grow tender plants in a cool or cold climate or to raise your own plants, a greenhouse can be invaluable.

■ **Make a compost bin** (*see p.283*), create a leafmold bin, or set up a wormery (*see p.282*). You can use these to recycle garden waste into homemade compost, thereby enriching your soil and saving money.

EARLY SPRING

LAWNS	BOUNDARIES AND DIVISIONS

ESSENTIAL TASKS

- **Control moss in lawns** if necessary (*see p.87*).

- **Cut meadow grass** before flowering plants are too far into growth (*see p.89*).

- **Sow seeds in containers** of herbs and similar plants to create a nongrass lawn (*see p.88 and p.162*).

SOWING AND PLANTING

- **Lay sod for a new lawn** (*see p.77 and pp.80–81*) as soon as the weather permits, so that the grass has time to establish before summer. Keep well watered.

- **Prepare the soil and site** (*see p.78*) for spring sowings of grass seed.

- **Plant plugs or sprigs** for a new lawn in warm climates (*see p.81*). Keep well watered.

- **Plant divided sections** of herbs (*see p.231*) to create a nongrass lawn (*see p.88*).

ROUTINE CARE

- **Begin mowing established** lawns as soon as weather permits, at appropriate intervals for the lawn type (*see p.82*); set the mowing height to maximum.

- **Neaten lawn edges** by recutting them (*see p.83*).

- **Trim nongrass lawns** to remove dead or straggly growth (*see p.88*).

ESSENTIAL TASKS

- **Plant bare-root** climbing roses against walls, fences, or trees (*see p.110*) before they start into growth.

- **Prune Groups 2 and 3 clematis** (*see p.114*).

PLANTING

- **Plant shrubs** against walls, fences, or trees (*see p.110*). Train stems into formative shapes (*see p.113*).

- **Plant clematis** against walls, fences, or trees; tie stems into desired shape (*see p.111*).

- **Plant hedges** (*see p.120*).

ROUTINE CARE

- **Feed and mulch climbers** and wall shrubs. Use a general-purpose fertilizer, according to the manufacturer's instructions. Climbing roses are hungry feeders and do well if given specialized rose fertilizer.

- **Feed and mulch evergreen** hedges to prepare them for renovation pruning in midspring (*see p.121*).

PRUNING AND TRAINING

- **Prune established** climbers and wall shrubs that flower on the current season's shoots (*see pp.112–113*). These include bignonias, trumpet vines (*Campsis*), the Chilean bellflower (*Lapageria*), *Solanum crispum*, and stephanotis among climbers; abutilons, forsythias, lavateras, perovskias, and *Spiraea japonica* among shrubs.

- **Renovate evergreen climbers** if needed, before they start into growth (*see p.115*).

- **Prune hedges,** if they include plants such as *Fuchsia magellanica* and *Lonicera nitida* (*see chart, p.117, and p.121*).

KEEPING CLIMBERS TO SIZE

- **Climbers growing up house walls** can cause damage if allowed to grow into gutters and window frames or under roof slates and tiles.

- **If a climber outgrows** its allotted space on the house, or any other, wall, spring is the time to cut it down to size.

- **Cut back overly long shoots** with pruners, cutting just above an upward- or downward-facing bud.

- **For a natural look,** trim the shoots to irregular lengths, within the desired outline of the plant.

CUTTING BACK IVY

BEDS AND BORDERS

ESSENTIAL TASKS

■ **Cut back tender grasses** and bamboos to the ground, before they start into growth but after the frosts have abated.

■ **Water newly planted** plants regularly, if the weather is dry (*see p.152*).

■ **Pruning established** deciduous shrubs that flower on the current season's growth (*see p.158*).

■ **Finish pruning roses,** including hybrid tea roses, and China, Bourbon, and Portland old roses (*see p.161*).

PLANTING

■ **Plant hardy perennials** (*see p.148*), grasses (*see p.140*), and shrubs, except containerized ones (*see p.150*). Buy good, healthy plants (*see pp.146–147*) for the best results. Give shrubs an initial prune after planting (*see p.151*) and stake if necessary (*see p.150*).

■ **Plant bare-root roses** (*see p.151*). Buy good, healthy plants (*see p.147*) for the best results. Give the roses an initial prune before or after planting (*see p.151*).

■ **Prepare light, sandy soils** for planting by forking in well-rotted organic matter to help the soil hold moisture (*see p.142*).

ROUTINE CARE

■ **Feed plants in gravel beds**, if they have not grown well in the previous season (*see p.133*).

■ **Neaten gravel beds:** renew the top-dressing and remove any dead or damaged shoots from the plants (*see p.133*).

■ **Deadhead** spring-flowering plants, such as camellias (*see p.158*), bulbs, and alpine plants, as soon as the flowers fade. Leave the foliage on bulbs to die down naturally.

■ **Feed and mulch roses** after pruning. A specialized rose fertilizer is best.

■ **Mulch beds and borders**, if not done in autumn (*see pp.152–153*).

■ **Apply slow-release** fertilizer before the plants have begun to grow (*see p.153*).

PRUNING AND TRAINING

■ **Carry out initial pruning** for shape (*see p.157*) and restorative (*see p.159*) pruning of deciduous shrubs.

■ **Prune** hydrangea hybrids and shrubs with canelike stems that flower in summer, such as Himalayan honeysuckle (*Leycestera formosa*) and *Kerria japonica* (*see p.159*).

■ **Prune dogwoods** (*Cornus*) grown for winter stems and shrubs such as *Cotinus* grown for bright young foliage (*see p.159*).

RAISING YOUR OWN PLANTS

■ **Sow seed outdoors** (*see p.149 and p.163*) of hardy annuals.

■ **Sow seed indoors** of tender and half-hardy annuals and of perennials (*see p.162*).

■ **Divide perennials** (*see p.163*).

■ **Take softwood cuttings** from shrubs (*see p.165*).

■ **Layer shrubs** (*see p.165*).

CONTAINERS AND RAISED BEDS

ESSENTIAL TASKS

■ **Water containers** if needed – check regularly (*see p.178*), even if it has been wet.

■ **Pinch-prune** plants such as coleus, chrysanthemums, and fuchsias in containers (*see p.173 and box, p.381*).

PLANTING

■ **Plant in containers** (*see p.176*): shrubs, roses, hardy perennials, hardy annuals and biennials, summer-flowering bulbs, and spring-flowering alpines.

■ **Cut back invasive** or vigorous plants in raised beds.

ROUTINE CARE

■ **Feed or renew** soil mix of any established raised beds, then topdress or mulch (*see p.183*). Replace any exhausted or diseased plants.

■ **Repot or top-dress** permanently planted climbers, shrubs, bulbs, and alpines in containers, except spring-flowering ones. Root-prune if needed (*see p.179*).

PRIMROSE

EARLY SPRING

ORNAMENTAL TREES	WATER GARDENING	HERBS

ESSENTIAL TASKS

■ **Finish coppicing and pollarding** trees (*see p.197*).

PLANTING

■ **Prepare the soil** (*see p.192 and pp.142–143*) for midspring plantings of container-grown, bare-root, or evergreen balled-and-burlapped trees.

■ **Plant bare-root** deciduous trees (*see p.194*). When filling in the planting hole, make sure there are no air pockets in between the roots by gently shaking the stem up and down.

ROUTINE CARE

■ **Topdress or repot** trees in containers before they start into growth. To top-dress, replace the top 2in (5cm) of soil mix mixed with slow-release fertilizer. Water well, and mulch with gravel or bark chips.

■ **Watch out for suckers** and watershoots growing from tree trunks or roots and remove them before they get too big and spoil the tree (*see p.197*).

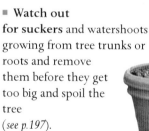

TOPIARY

ROUTINE CARE

■ **Thin oxygenating plants** to clear out old growth in preparation for the growing season (*see p.223*).

CLEANING WATER PUMPS

■ **Why do I need to clean the pump?** All pumps have filters to stop debris from the pond entering the pump. If the filter becomes silted up, the water flow will be impeded and the pump may be overloaded and break down.

■ **When does a pump need cleaning?** It depends on the model. Follow the manufacturer's advice – some models need to be cleaned up to once a week in summer. It is also advisable to get pumps serviced once a year.

■ **How do I clean a pump?** Always disconnect the pump from the electric supply first. Lift out the pump and detach the filter, or strainer; sluice reusable filters with clean water and replace disposable filters.

ESSENTIAL TASKS

■ **Prepare the soil** (*see p.228*) for spring plantings of moisture-loving herbs.

ROUTINE CARE

■ **Lift invasive herbs** planted in sunken containers (*see p.231*), divide, and repot in fresh soil, soil mix, or a mixture of both.

■ **Cut off old growth** on perennial herbs, in cool climates.

■ **Discard or plant out** herbs that were potted up for winter use (*see p.231*).

■ **Top-dress or repot** perennial herbs grown in containers. To topdress, replace the top 1–2in (2.5–5cm) of soil mix. Water well, and mulch with gravel or coarse sand.

PRUNING AND TRAINING

■ **Cut back shrubby herbs** hard to encourage bushy new shoots.

RAISING YOUR OWN PLANTS

■ **Sow seed outdoors** (*see p.149 and p.163*) of hardy annual herbs, such as chervil, cilantro, and dill.

■ **Sow seed indoors** (*see p.162*) of tender and half-hardy annual herbs, such as basil.

■ **Rejuvenate sprawly shrubby** herbs by mound layering (*see p.231*).

■ **Divide large shrubby** or clump-forming herbs (*see p.231*), if not done in early autumn.

THE EDIBLE GARDEN

ESSENTIAL TASKS

■ **Water newly planted vegetables** and fruit crops if needed (*see box, p.236*).

■ **Dig in green manures** that were sown in the previous autumn (*see p.239*).

■ **Finish sprouting seed potatoes** to prepare them for planting (*see p.252*).

■ **Plant early seed potatoes** (*see p.252*).

■ **Finish planting bare-root fruit trees** and cane fruits (*see pp.260–261*).

■ **Protect newly planted or sown** crops from frosts in cool climates under cloches, row cover, or, with strawberry plants, sheets of newspaper.

SOWING AND PLANTING

■ **Sow seed of vegetables indoors** in containers (*see p.244*), such as:
Broccoli (*see p.248*)
Eggplant, chilies, and peppers (*see p.256*)
Greenhouse tomatoes (*see p.257*)
Lettuce (*see p.255*), in a cold frame
Sprouting broccoli (*see p.248*), in a cold frame.

■ **Sow hardy vegetable seed outdoors** (*see p.242*), under cloches in cold areas, such as:
Beets (*see p.251*)
Broccoli (*see p.248*)
Bulb and spring onions (*see p.250*)
Early carrots (*see p.251*)

Lettuce (*see p.255*)
Hardy peas, under netting to deter birds and mice (*see p.247*)
Leeks (*see p.251*)
Parsnips (*see p.251*)
Salad leaves (*see p.255*)
Scallions (*see p.250*)
Spinach beet and Swiss chard (*see p.255*)
Sprouting broccoli (*see p.248*)
Summer kale (*see p.248*)
Summer radishes (*see p.249*)

■ **Sow seed of green manures** to cover empty soil temporarily during the growing season (*see p.239*).

■ **Protect vegetables outdoors** from frosts, if necessary, under cloches (*see p.240*).

■ **Plant onion and shallot sets** (*see p.250*).

■ **Plant rhubarb** (*see p.273*).

ROUTINE CARE

■ **Feed vegetable beds** (*see p.239*), and fork over and weed the soil in preparation for planting or sowing.

■ **Warm the soil** in cooler regions by placing cloches (*see p.240*) or row cover over it, to prepare it for sowing.

■ **Feed fruit trees**, bush and cane fruits, strawberries, and rhubarb (*see pp.264–273*).

■ **Erect supports** (*see p.247*) for peas and climbing beans.

PRUNING AND TRAINING

■ **Prune young plum** (*see p.266*) and sour cherry trees (*see p.267*), once the buds have opened.

■ **Prune off the cane tips** of summer-fruiting raspberries, blackberries, and hybrid berries, before growth begins (*see p.270*).

■ **Re-tie leaders of grapevines** as the buds appear (*see p.273*).

HARVESTING

■ **Pick winter vegetables**, such as:
Beets (*see p.251*)
Broccoli (*see p.248*)
Kale flower shoots (*see p.248*)
Leeks (*see p.251*)
Parsnips (*see p.251*)
Spinach beet (*see p.255*)
Sprouting broccoli (*see p.248*)
Turnip tops (*see p.249*)
Winter cabbages (*see p.249*)
Winter lettuce (*see p.255*).

GREEN MANURES

Sow these in empty patches of soil to protect the soil from drying out and to lock nutrients into the soil. Choose fast-growing types in spring and summer that are dug in before they flower and hardy types to occupy beds over winter.

SPRING-SOWN
Alfalfa
Annual ryegrass
Buckwheat
Crimson clover (also autumn)
Red clover (also autumn)
Soybeans
Sweet clover
White clover

AUTUMN-SOWN
Alsike clover
Hairy vetch
Winter rye

MIDSPRING

LAWNS

BOUNDARIES AND DIVISIONS

ESSENTIAL TASKS

■ **Water new lawns** (*see p.84*) regularly in dry weather, so that they establish properly.

■ **Sow seed for a new lawn** (*see p.77 and p.79*) on prepared, moist ground, so that the grass has time to establish before summer. Keep the plot well watered.

SOWING GRASS SEED WITH A NEAT EDGE

SOWING AND PLANTING

■ **Plant plugs or sprigs** for a new lawn in warm climates (*see p.81*).

■ **Prepare the soil and site** (*see p.78*) for late-spring planting of seedlings to create a nongrass lawn.

ROUTINE CARE

■ **Mow established lawns** at appropriate intervals for the lawn type (*see p.82*); set the mowing height to maximum. Trim the edges (*see p.83*).

■ **Repair damaged patches** in lawns (*see p.86*) and reseed or resod if necessary.

LIVING TAPESTRY

If the lawn area is not used frequently, consider making it more decorative by planting it with different, low-growing plants to form a tapestry of contrasting textures and colors.

■ **Mark out the planting area** with a simple pattern: a checkerboard grid is easy to plant and very effective. You could also try stripes or swirls, but avoid anything complex – it will look fussy. Then plant with small plants as for a nongrass lawn (*see p.88*).

■ **Good plant choices** are baby's tears (*Soleirolia soleirolii*), thymes, *Dichondra micrantha*, and green and black cultivars of the grassy perennial, *Ophiopogon planiscapus*. Make sure that you choose plants that grow at roughly the same rate for a balanced effect.

■ **Use paving or wooden slabs** in a checkerboard pattern, alternating with squares of chamomile, herbs, or a even a meadow mixture, for a more durable nongrass lawn.

PLANTING

■ **Plant shrubs or climbers,** including clematis, against walls, fences, or trees (*see pp.110–111*). Train stems into the desired shape (*see p.113*). Plant hedges (*see p.120*).

PRUNING AND TRAINING

■ **Prune evergreen climbers** and wall shrubs (*see pp.112–113*), after frosts are over.

■ **Renovate evergreen climbers** (*see p.115*) and hedges, if necessary (*see p.121*). Fertilize and mulch them afterward.

■ **Prune evergreen flowering hedges** of *Garrya elliptica*, lavender, and pyracantha (*see chart, p.117, and p.121*).

RAISE A NEW CLIMBER

■ **Many climbers root readily** from their stems to produce a new plant, if given the opportunity. Some even have aerial roots, such as ivies (*see p.108*).

■ **The best time to start** a new plant is in midspring or autumn.

■ **Choose a long, low stem** and peg onto the soil (layering). Scraping the stem where it touches the soil helps it root. Bury 6in (15cm) of the stem. Keep it watered until new shoots appear; usually about a year. Dig up the stem, detach from the plant, and pot up.

LAYERING A CLIMBING HYDRANGEA SHOOT

BEDS AND BORDERS

ESSENTIAL TASKS

- **Water newly planted** plants regularly, if the weather is dry (*see p.152*).

- **Finish initial pruning** for shape (*see p.157*) and restorative (*see p.159*) pruning of deciduous shrubs before they start into growth.

- **Finish pruning** hydrangea hybrids (*see p.159*).

PLANTING

- **Plant hardy perennials** (*see p.148*), summer-flowering bulbs (*see p.149*), grasses (*see p.140*), and evergreen and container-grown shrubs (*see p.150*). Buy good, healthy plants (*see pp.146–147*) for the best results. Give shrubs an initial prune after planting (*see p.151*) and stake if necessary (*see p.150*).

ROUTINE CARE

- **Fertilize plants in gravel beds**, if they have not grown well in the previous season (*see p.133*).

- **Neaten gravel beds**: renew the gravel and remove any dead or damaged shoots from the plants (*see p.133*).

- **Thin perennials** that form clumps, while they are still small, to guarantee bigger and better flowers later in the season (*see p.154*).

- **Deadhead** spring-flowering plants, such as camellias (*see p.158*), bulbs, and alpine plants, as soon as the flowers fade. Allow the foliage on bulbs to die down naturally.

- **Mulch beds and borders**, if not done in autumn (*see pp.152–153*).

- **Apply slow-release fertilizer** before the plants have begun to grow away (*see p.153*).

- **Stake perennials and biennials** that might flop over when fully grown (*see p.154*).

PRUNING AND TRAINING

- **Prune evergreen shrubs**, both newly planted (*see p.157*) and established (*see p.158*) shrubs. Wait until all danger of frost is passed to minimize damage to new shoots.

CAMELLIA JAPONICA 'ALEXANDER HUNTER'

- **Prune shrubs** with canelike stems that flower in summer, such as Himalayan honeysuckle (*Leycesteria formosa*) (*see p.159*).

- **Trim lavender bushes** to prevent them from becoming straggly and sparse (*see p.155*).

RAISING YOUR OWN PLANTS

- **Sow seed outdoors** (*see p.149 and p.163*) of hardy annuals.

- **Take softwood cuttings** from shrubs (*see p.165*).

- **Layer shrubs** (*see p.165*).

CONTAINERS AND RAISED BEDS

ESSENTIAL TASKS

- **Pinch-prune** plants such as coleus, fuchsias, and chrysanthemums in containers (*see p.173 and box, p.381*).

- **Water containers** when necessary – check them regularly (*see p.178*), even if it has been wet.

PLANTING

- **Plant in containers** (*see p.176*) climbers, shrubs, roses, hardy perennials, hardy annuals and biennials, summer-flowering bulbs, and succulents.

ROUTINE CARE

- **Deadhead** regularly (*see p.178*) and keep plants well shaped by removing any tired, diseased, or straggly foliage.

- **Repot or top-dress** permanently planted climbers, shrubs, and alpines in containers, unless they are spring-flowering ones. Root-prune if needed (*see p.179*).

- **Feed or renew soil mix** of any established raised beds and top-dress or mulch (*see p.183*). Replace any exhausted or diseased plants.

- **Regularly weed** raised beds.

- **Discard or plant out** bulbs that have been grown in containers.

PRUNING AND TRAINING

- **Regularly clip** established topiary and standard plants (*see p.178*).

- **Prune woody plants** in raised beds once risk of frost is past (*see p.156–161*).

- **Trim lavender bushes** to prevent them from becoming straggly and sparse (*see p.155*).

MIDSPRING

ORNAMENTAL TREES	WATER GARDENING	HERBS

ORNAMENTAL TREES

PLANTING

- **Prepare the soil** (*see p.192 and pp.142–143*) for late-spring plantings of container-grown, hardy evergreen bare-root, or evergreen balled-and-burlapped trees.

- **Plant balled-and-burlapped evergreen** trees (*see p.195*).

ROUTINE CARE

- **If you use inorganic fertilizers,** now is the time to feed established trees with a liquid or granular one (*see p.197*).

- **Check tree ties** and stakes (*see p.193*) and remove or loosen them as necessary to avoid their chafing and damaging the tree bark.

BALLED-AND-BURLAPPED
LEYLAND CYPRESS

- **Check tree guards** (*see p.195*) are still in place.

- **Watch out for suckers** and water shoots growing from tree trunks or roots, and remove them before they get too big and spoil the tree (*see p.197*).

WATER GARDENING

ESSENTIAL TASKS

- **Divide overcrowded plants,** except waterlilies, soon after they start into growth, to rejuvenate them (*see p.223*). Mature plants can be increased by division.

DIVISIONS OF JAPANESE RUSH
(*ACORUS GRAMINEUS*)

PLANTING

- **Plant** (*see pp.220–221*) most water garden plants, except those that require a very warm water temperature.

ROUTINE CARE

- **Thin oxygenating plants** to clear out old growth in preparation for the growing season (*see p.223*).

HERBS

ESSENTIAL TASKS

- **Transplant seedlings** of biennial herbs such as angelica and caraway (*see p.149*) to their final positions.

- **Prune lavender** (*see p.232*) once all danger of frosts is past.

PLANTING

- **Plant container-grown** perennial or shrubby herbs in beds, in paving, or in pots and hanging baskets (*see pp.228–231*).

- **Plant rooted cuttings** or small plants in between paving (*see p.229*).

- **Plant divided sections** of herbs (*see p.231*) to create a nongrass lawn (*see p.88*).

ROUTINE CARE

- **Lift invasive herbs** planted in sunken containers (*see p.231*), divide, and repot in fresh soil, soil mix, or a mixture of both.

RAISING YOUR OWN PLANTS

- **Sow seed outdoors** (*see p.149 and p.163*) of hardy annual herbs.

- **Rejuvenate tired shrubby** herbs by mound layering (*see p.231*).

THE EDIBLE GARDEN

New Herbs from Old

There are several fairly easy ways of growing your own herbs (*see below*). All annuals and biennials, and in cool climates many tender perennials, must be raised from seed.

DIVISION
Chives, fennel, French tarragon, horseradish, lemon balm, lovage, mint, oregano, sorrel, thyme.

MOUND LAYERING
Artemisia, lavender cotton, lavender, rosemary, sage, thyme, winter savory.

CUTTINGS
Hyssop, lemon balm, mint, oregano, rosemary, sage, thyme.

VARIEGATED SAGE
(*SALVIA OFFICINALIS* 'TRICOLOR')

SEED
Angelica, basil, borage, caraway, chervil, cilantro, coriander, dill, hyssop, parsley, sweet marjoram.

Essential Tasks
- **Water newly planted vegetables** and fruit crops if needed (*see box, p.236*).

- **Plant early seed potatoes** (*see p.252*).

Sowing and Planting
- **Sow seed of green manures** to cover empty soil temporarily during the growing season (*see p.239*).

- **Plant container-grown** vegetables. If necessary, protect the plants from frosts under cloches or fleece (*see p.240*).

- **Sow seed of vegetables indoors** in containers (*see p.244*), such as:
Chicory and endive (*see p.255*)
Lettuce (*see p.255*)
Runner beans (*see p.247*)
Sprouting broccoli (*see p.248*)
Pumpkins and squashes (*see p.253*)
Tomatoes (*see p.257*).

- **Sow hardy vegetables outdoors** (*see p.242*), under cloches in cold areas, such as:
Beets (*see p.251*)
Broccoli (*see p.248*)
Early carrots (*see p.251*)
Hardy lettuce (*see p.255*)
Leeks (*see p.251*)
Parsnips (*see p.251*)
Peas, under netting to keep off birds and mice (*see p.247*)
Red cabbage (*see p.249*)
Salad leaves (*see p.255*)
Scallions (*see p.250*)
Summer radishes (*see p.249*)
Spinach beet and Swiss chard (*see p.255*)
Sprouting broccoli (*see p.248*)
Summer turnips, under cloches (*see p.249*).

- **Plant out garlic cloves** or plants started earlier in cell packs (*see p.250*).

- **Plant rhubarb** (*see p.273*).

Routine Care
- **Feed vegetable beds** (*see p.239*) and fork over and weed the soil in preparation for planting or sowing.

- **Dig in green manures** that were sown in the previous autumn or in early spring (*see p.239*).

- **Warm the soil** in cooler regions by placing cloches (*see p.240*) or row cover over it, to prepare it for sowing.

- **Mulch vegetables and fruit** crops, while the soil is warm and moist (*see p.239*).

- **Erect supports** (*see p.247*) for peas and climbing beans. Support young peas by sticking peasticks – strong, twiggy stems left over from pruning – into the ground around them (*see p.246*).

- **Fertilize bush fruits** (*see pp.268–269*).

- **Check ties and stakes** (*see p.193*) on fruit trees and remove or loosen them as necessary to avoid them chafing and damaging the bark.

Pruning and Training
- **Thin out sideshoots** on peach trees (*see p.267*).

- **Cut back blackberry** and hybrid berry canes after winter planting (*see p.271*).

Harvesting
- **Pick winter and early vegetables,** such as:
Broccoli (*see p.248*)
Leeks (*see p.251*)
Spinach beet (*see p.255*)
Spring cabbages (*see p.249*)
Scallions (*see p.250*)
Sprouting broccoli (*see p.248*)
Winter lettuce (*see p.255*).

- **Pick early fruit crops, such as:**
Forced rhubarb (*see p.173*).

LATE SPRING

LAWNS	BOUNDARIES AND DIVISIONS	BEDS AND BORDERS

ESSENTIAL TASKS
- **Water new lawns** (*see p.84*) regularly in dry weather, so that they establish properly.

SOWING AND PLANTING
- **Plant plugs or sprigs** for a new lawn in warm climates (*see p.81*).

- **Plant out seedlings** for a nongrass lawn (*see p.88*).

ROUTINE CARE
- **Begin mowing new grass** once it is 2in (5cm) tall (*see p.79, p.80, and p.82*). Set the mower to maximum height.

- **Mow established** lawns at appropriate intervals for the lawn type (*see p.82*); set the mowing height to maximum. Trim the edges (*see p.83*).

- **Apply lawn fertilizer** to grass lawns (*see p.84*) or general fertilizer to nongrass lawns (*see p.88*).

ESSENTIAL TASKS
- **Keep an eye out for pests** and diseases such as aphids and blackspot, and take steps to prevent them from taking hold (*see p.111*).

PLANTING
- **Plant shrubs or climbers**, including clematis, against walls, fences, or trees (*see pp.110–111*). Train stems into the desired shape, for example a fan (*see p.113*).

- **Plant hedges** (*see p.120*).

ROUTINE CARE
- **Deadhead plants** to prolong flowering.

PRUNING AND TRAINING
- **Train climbers** (*see pp.108–109*) and roses (*see p.115*) into supports as they grow. Check old ties.

- **Thin overgrown Group 1 clematis** (*see p.114*).

- **Prune hedges,** if they include plants such as boxwood, *Forsythia* x *intermedia*, and Leyland cypress (*see chart, p.117, and p.121*).

- **Prune recently planted hawthorn** and privet shrubs into shape (*see p.120*).

BEATING APHIDS

LADYBUG LARVA

- **Squash aphids** by gently running your fingers up and down infested stems.

- **Wash them off** with a strong spray from the hose, or spray with a solution of insecticidal soap.

- **Only use pesticides** that allow the aphid predators like ladybug larvae to do their work.

ESSENTIAL TASKS
- **Finish planting** summer-flowering bulbs (*see p.149*), container-grown and all evergreen shrubs (*see p.150*), and grasses (*see p.140*). Buy healthy plants (*see pp.146–147*) for the best results. Give shrubs an initial prune after planting (*see p.151*) and stake them if necessary (*see p.150*).

- **Finish mulching** beds and borders, if not done in autumn (*see pp.152–153*), onto moist soil; water it beforehand if necessary.

- **Water new and established** plants as necessary (*see p.152*).

- **Stake perennials and biennials** that might flop over when fully grown, before they become too big to stake without spoiling their appearance (*see p.154*).

STAKE AND TWINE SUPPORT

- **Finish pruning shrubs with canelike** stems that flower in spring, such as Himalayan honeysuckle (*Leycesteria formosa*) (*see p.159*).

- **Finish thinning perennials** that form clumps, while they are still small, to guarantee bigger and better flowers later in the season (*see p.154*).

- **Sow seed outdoors** (*see p.149 and p.163*) of hardy, half-hardy, and tender annuals for flowers in mid- to late summer.

PLANTING

- **Plant perennials** (*see p.148*). Buy good, healthy plants (*see p.146*) for the best results.

- **Plant out plug plants** (seedlings with sturdy root balls that are available mail-order or from plant centers) of hardy annuals and biennials for an early show of flower in the garden.

ROUTINE CARE

- **Neaten gravel beds**: renew the top-dressing and remove any dead or damaged shoots from the plants (*see p.133*).

- **Deadhead** bulbs, perennials (*see p.155*), alpine plants, and flowering shrubs, such as rhododendrons (*see p.158*), as soon as the flowers fade. Allow the foliage on bulbs to die down naturally.

- **Lift tulips,** once their leaves are yellow and faded, and store in a warm, dry place in a paper (not plastic) bag over summer, or discard them.

- **Fertilize plants in gravel beds**, if they have not grown well in the previous season (*see p.133*).

- **Give extra fertilizer** to any plants that need a boost, if necessary (*see p.153*).

- **Nip off the shoot tips** ("stop") of flowering sideshoots of those perennials that produce them, such as dahlias, chrysanthemums, and some asters, to increase the number of flowers (*see p.154*).

PRUNING AND TRAINING

- **Prune established** deciduous shrubs that flower on the previous year's growth (*see p.158*).

- **Prune evergreen shrubs**, both new (*see p.157*) and established (*see p.158*) plants, once all danger of frost is passed.

PRUNING LAVENDER COTTON (*SANTOLINA*)

RAISING YOUR OWN PLANTS

- **Plant out seedlings** of tender annuals that were sown earlier in the year.

- **Sow seed of biennials** in rows in a spare patch of soil or seedbed (*see p.149*).

- **Take softwood cuttings** from shrubs and perennials; take greenwood cuttings from shrubs (*see p.165 and p.381*).

- **Layer shrubs** (*see p.165*).

CONTAINERS AND RAISED BEDS

ESSENTIAL TASKS

- **Water containers** when necessary – check them regularly (*see p.178*), even if it has been wet.

- **Finish repotting or** topdressing permanently planted climbers, shrubs, and alpines in containers, unless they are spring-flowering ones. Root-prune if needed (*see p.179*).

- **Finish feeding or renewing** soil mix of any established raised beds and topdress or mulch (*see p.183*). Replace any exhausted or diseased plants.

- **Pinch-prune** plants such as coleus, fuchsias, and chrysanthemums in containers (*see p.173 and box, p.381*).

- **Finish pruning woody** plants in raised beds once all risk of frost has passed (*see p.196*).

PLANTING

- **Plant in containers** (*see p.176*) climbers, shrubs, roses, perennials, hardy annuals and biennials, and cacti and succulents.

ROUTINE CARE

- **Regularly deadhead** and keep plants well shaped by removing any tired, diseased, or straggly foliage (*see p.178*).

- **Weed raised beds** regularly.

- **Lift and divide** perennials in raised beds, keeping new healthy growth and discarding old, tired parts (*see p.155*).

- **Discard or plant out** bulbs that have been grown in containers.

PRUNING AND TRAINING

- **Clip established** topiary and standards regularly (*see p.178*).

LATE SPRING

ORNAMENTAL TREES

ESSENTIAL TASKS
- **Water if needed**, especially trees planted in the last 2–3 years. A couple of bucketfuls of water every so often is better than frequent but light watering (*see p.197*).

PLANTING
- **Plant** container-grown, evergreen bare-root, or evergreen balled-and-burlapped trees.

ROUTINE CARE
- **In cold or cool climates**, move tender trees, such as citrus, in containers (*see p.195*) from their winter shelters into the open garden for the summer.

- **Mulch** around trees with organic material such as bark chips (*see p.197*).

FLOWERING CHERRY
PRUNUS 'KANZAN'

- **Check tree ties** and stakes (*see p.193*) and remove or loosen them as necessary to avoid chafing and damaging the bark.

- **Check tree guards** (*see p.195*) are still in place.

- **Watch out for suckers** and water shoots growing from tree trunks or roots and remove them before they get too big and spoil the tree (*see p.197*).

WATER GARDENING

ESSENTIAL TASKS
- **Divide overcrowded plants**, including waterlilies, soon after they start into growth, to rejuvenate them (*see p.223*). Mature plants can also be divided to yield several new plants.

DIVIDING JAPANESE RUSH (*ACORUS CALAMUS*)

PLANTING
- **Plant** (*see pp.220–221*) all water garden plants.

ROUTINE CARE
- **Thin oxygenating plants** to clear out old growth in preparation for the growing season (*see p.223*).

- **Give the first fertilizing** of the season to waterlilies and other container-grown plants (*see p.222*).

- **Cut back or thin out** (by division, *see p.223*) overcrowded or straggly marginal plants.

- **Clean out neglected ponds** if necessary. Siphon off most of the water; remove container-grown plants; move floating plants and fish to holding containers. Scoop out the mud, clean the liner and make any necessary repairs, then replant and refill the pond.

HERBS

ESSENTIAL TASKS
- **Finish sowing seed outdoors** (*see p.149 and p.163*) of hardy annual herbs.

- **Sow seed outdoors** (*see p.149 and p.163*) of half-hardy and tender annual herbs.

PLANTING
- **Prepare the soil** (*see p.228 and pp.142–143*) for summer plantings of moisture-loving herbs.

- **Plant container-grown** perennial or shrubby herbs in beds, in paving, or in pots and hanging baskets (*see pp.228–231*).

- **Plant** rooted cuttings or small plants in between paving (*see p.229*).

- **Plant divided sections** of herbs (*see p.231*) to create a nongrass lawn (*see p.88*).

ROUTINE CARE
- **Move tender herbs in containers** from their winter shelters into the garden (*see p.195*) for the summer.

- **Water herbs** in containers.

RAISING YOUR OWN PLANTS
- **Rejuvenate tired shrubby** herbs by mound layering (*see p.231*).

- **Plant out seedlings** of tender annual herbs that were sown earlier in the year.

- **Sow seed of biennial herbs,** such as angelica and caraway, in rows in a spare patch of soil or seedbed (*see p.149*).

HARVESTING
- **Cut angelica stems** for crystallizing (*see p.232*).

THE EDIBLE GARDEN

ESSENTIAL TASKS

- **Water newly planted vegetables** and fruit crops if needed (*see box, p.236*).

- **Protect your carrot crop** against the carrot rust fly by erecting a barrier around the plot (*see p.241*) before the first generation of flies begins to lay eggs.

- **Plant maincrop seed potatoes** (*see p.252*).

- **Finish planting out garlic** started earlier in cell packs (*see p.250*).

- **Hill up early potato plants** to stop the tubers from going green (*see p.252*).

- **Thin peach fruitlets** under glass to obtain good-sized fruits later (*see p.267*).

SOWING AND PLANTING

- **Sow green manures** to cover empty soil temporarily during the growing season (*see p.239*).

- **Sow seed of vegetables indoors** in containers (*see p.244*), such as:
Autumn and winter kale (*see p.248*)
Sprouting broccoli (*see p.248*).

- **Sow seed of vegetables outdoors** (*see p.242*), such as:
Autumn and winter kale (*see p.248*)
Beets (*see p.251*)
Broccoli (*see p.248*)
Chicory and endive (*see p.255*)
Green beans (*see p.246*)
Leeks (*see p.251*)
Lettuce (*see p.255*)
Maincrop carrots (*see p.251*)
Peas, under netting to keep off birds and mice (*see p.247*)
Pumpkins and squashes (*see p.253*)
Red cabbage (*see p.249*)
Runner beans (*see p.247*).
Salad leaves (*see p.255*)
Scallions (*see p.250*)
Spinach beet and Swiss chard (*see p.255*)
Sprouting broccoli (*see p.248*)

Summer radishes (*see p.249*)
Summer turnips (*see p.249*)

Sweet corn (*see p.253*)
Winter cabbages for using fresh (*see p.249*).

- **Plant out young plants of:**
Eggplant, chilies, and peppers (*see p.256*)
Rhubarb (*see p.273*).
Runner beans (*see p.247*).
Tomatoes (*see p.257*).

ROUTINE CARE

- **Feed vegetable beds** (*see p.239*) and fork over and weed the soil in preparation for planting or sowing.

- **Dig in green manures** that were sown in the previous autumn, or earlier in spring (*see p.239*).

- **Mulch vegetables and fruit** crops, while the soil is warm and moist (*see p.239*).

- **Fertilize bush fruits** (*see pp.268–269*).

- **Remove flowers from strawberry** plants that were planted late (*see p.272*).

GREENHOUSE SHADING

- **The greenhouse in summer** can get very hot: plants can wilt or be scorched.

- **As soon as the weather** warms up, shade the greenhouse.

- **Greenhouses can be shaded** with a wash, roller blinds, or plastic mesh.

- **A greenhouse wash** is cheap, but it must be cleaned off again in late summer, when the light levels fall.

PRUNING AND TRAINING

- **Cut back pear tree leaders** (*see p.264*).

- **Cut back older sour cherry** trees to encourage new fruiting branches (*see p.267*).

- **Tie in fruit canes** of blackberries and hybrid berries (*see p.271*) and of raspberries (*see p.270*) to supports.

HARVESTING

- **Pick winter and early vegetables,** such as:
Broccoli (*see p.248*)
Leeks (*see p.251*)
Salad leaves (*see p.255*)
Spinach beet (*see p.255*)
Spring cabbages (*see p.249*)
Scallions (*see p.250*)
Sprouting broccoli (*see p.248*)
Summer radishes (*see p.249*)
Winter lettuce (*see p.255*).

- **Pick early fruit crops, such as:**
Forced rhubarb (*see p.273*).

STICKY TRAPS

- **What insects do they catch?** Whitefly, thrips, and fungas gnats.

- **How do they work?** The bright color attracts the insects and they stick to the nondrying glue.

HANGING UP A STICKY TRAP

EARLY SUMMER

LAWNS	BOUNDARIES AND DIVISIONS	BEDS AND BORDERS

LAWNS

ESSENTIAL TASKS
- **Water new lawns** (*see p.84*) regularly in dry weather, so that they establish properly.

SOWING AND PLANTING
- **Plant plugs or sprigs** for a new lawn in warm climates (*see p.81*).

ROUTINE CARE
- **Mow lawns** at appropriate intervals for the lawn type (*see p.82*); the mowing height may be reduced. Trim the edges (*see p.83*).

- **Apply lawn fertilizer,** if not done in late spring (*see p.84*).

- **Look out for weeds** and keep under control (*see p.87*).

- **Mow spring-flowering meadows** once the flowers have safely set seed for the next generation.

BOUNDARIES AND DIVISIONS

ESSENTIAL TASKS
- **Keep an eye out for pests** and diseases such as aphids and blackspot, and take steps to prevent their taking hold (*see p.111*).

- **Prune climbers and wall shrubs** that flower on the previous year's shoots, immediately after flowering (*see pp.112–113*).

- **Water if needed,** especially recently planted or young plants.

- **Prune climbing roses** immediately after flowering (*see p.115*).

ROUTINE CARE
- **Deadhead** plants, as needed, to prolong flowering, unless you want seeds later.

PRUNING AND TRAINING
- **Train climbers** (*see pp.108–109*) and roses (*see p.115*) into supports. Cut out any dead or diseased shoots and check ties.

TYING IN A CLEMATIS

- **Thin overgrown Group 1 clematis;** prune Group 3 clematis (*see p.114*).

- **Prune hedges,** if they include plants like *Berberis* x *stenophylla* (*see chart, p.117, and p.121*).

BEDS AND BORDERS

ESSENTIAL TASKS
- **Water new and established** plants as necessary (*see p.152*).

- **Give extra fertilizer** to any plants that need a boost, if necessary (*see p.153*).

- **Finish stopping perennials** that produce flowering sideshoots to increase the number of flowers (*see p.154*).

- **Finish sowing seed outdoors** (*see p.149 and p.163*) of half-hardy and tender annuals.

- **Stake perennials and biennials** that might flop over when fully grown, before they become too big to stake without spoiling their appearance (*see p.154*).

PLANTING
- **Plant autumn-flowering bulbs** (*see p.149*). Buy good, healthy bulbs (*see p.146*) for the best results.

- **Plant out plug plants** (available mail-order or from plant centers) of hardy annuals and biennials.

ROUTINE CARE
- **Lift tulips,** once their leaves are yellow and faded, and store in a warm, dry place over summer or discard them.

- **Deadhead** bulbs, perennials (*see p.155*), annuals and biennials, alpine plants, roses, and flowering shrubs, such as rhododendrons (*see p.158*), as soon as the flowers fade. Allow the foliage on bulbs to die down naturally.

PRUNING AND TRAINING
- **Prune deciduous shrubs** that flower on the previous year's growth (*see p.158*).

RAISING YOUR OWN PLANTS
- **Sow seed of biennials** in rows in a spare patch of soil or seedbed (*see p.149*).

CONTAINERS AND RAISED BEDS

- **Gather seed** of early-flowering perennials as they ripen (*see p.155*) and sow (*see p.162*) immediately for the best results.

- **Divide spring-flowering** perennials (*see p.163*) once the flowers fade.

- **Take softwood cuttings** from shrubs (*see p.165*), greenwood cuttings from shrubs, and softwood cuttings from perennials.

CUTTINGS OF PERENNIALS

- **When do I take cuttings?** As soon as the plant produces suitable shoots.

- **What are the best shoots?** Look for strong, healthy shoots from this season's growth, with closely spaced leaves, that are still soft and pliable (softwood).

KEEPING CUTTINGS MOIST

- **How do I take a cutting?** Choose the top 3–5in (8–13cm) of a stem, and cut it off just below a leaf joint.

- **How do I prepare a cutting?** Trim off all but the top 2 or 3 leaves; don't leave any snags. Insert the cuttings in pots of soil mix, and treat in the same way as shrubby cuttings (*see p.165*).

ESSENTIAL TASKS

- **Water containers** regularly – check them daily (*see p.178*).

- **Water** raised beds if necessary (*see p.183*).

- **Pinch-prune** plants such as coleus, fuchsias, and chrysanthemums in containers (*see p.173 and box, below*).

PINCH-PRUNING

- **Why do you do it?** To train shrubby plants into standard plants (with a single stem and round, treelike canopy) or simple shapes, or to make them bushy.

- **When do you do it?** From when the plant starts into growth until 2 months before flowers are needed or, if the plant is grown for its foliage, until the end of the growing season.

- **How do you do it?** Use your forefinger and thumb to nip off soft new shoot tips repeatedly to shape the plant and encourage it to produce dense, bushy growth.

- **What shapes can you make?** Try a standard, ball, cone, pillar, fan, or poodle – several balls, one above the other.

- **Will the plant flower?** The flowers should all open at the same time, 6–8 weeks after the last pinch-prune.

PLANTING

- **Plant in containers** hardy deciduous climbers, roses, perennials, annuals and biennials, summer-flowering alpines, and cacti and succulents.

ROUTINE CARE

- **Fertilize containers** 6–8 weeks after planting (*see p.178*) at regular intervals, if a slow-release fertilizer was not used. Foliar or liquid kinds are most convenient.

- **Regularly deadhead** and keep plants well shaped by removing any tired, diseased, or straggly foliage (*see p.178*).

- **Weed raised beds** regularly.

- **Lift early spring-flowering** bulbs once the leaves die down to store over summer. Clean off the bulbs; lay on a tray to dry; and store in a paper (not plastic) bag.

PRUNING AND TRAINING

- **Clip established** topiary and standards regularly (*see p.178*).

- **Tie in climbing plants** to supports (stakes or a trellis) as they grow (*see pp.108–109*). Support tall annuals or perennials in pots before they become top-heavy and floppy; string twined around some stakes is ideal. As the plants grow, they will hide the stakes.

SUPPORTING SALPIGLOSSIS

EARLY SUMMER

ORNAMENTAL TREES	WATER GARDENING	HERBS

ORNAMENTAL TREES

ESSENTIAL TASKS

■ **Water if needed,** especially trees planted in the last 2–3 years. A couple of bucketfuls of water every so often is better than frequent but light watering (*see p.197*).

GALVANIZED STEEL WATERING CAN

ROUTINE CARE

■ **Watch out for suckers** and water shoots growing from tree trunks or roots, and remove them before they get too big and spoil the tree (*see p.197*).

PRUNING AND TRAINING

■ **Prune deciduous trees** that flower in spring if necessary (*see p.196*).

WATER GARDENING

ESSENTIAL TASKS

■ **Divide overcrowded plants** soon after they start into growth, to rejuvenate them (*see p.223*). Mature plants can also be divided to yield several new plants.

■ **Remove blanketweed** at regular intervals (*see p.222*).

■ **Thin floaters,** oxygenators, and duckweed at regular intervals (*see p.222*).

PLANTING

■ **Plant** (*see pp.220–221*) all water garden plants.

ROUTINE CARE

■ **Regularly remove** spent flowers and dying foliage to avoid polluting the water (*see p.222*).

KEEPING A POND HEALTHY

■ **Remove spent flowers** and dying foliage promptly before they rot and foul the water.

■ **Control choking algae,** such as blanketweed, by removing it at regular intervals throughout the summer.

■ **If the water level falls** in hot weather, fish and plants can suffer from lack of oxygen. Keep the pond filled up with a slowly trickling hose.

■ **If the plants cover** more than half the surface, thin or cut them back to let sunlight penetrate the water below.

■ **Remember to clean pumps** as often as recommended by the manufacturer: a clogged filter may stop the pump from working effectively.

■ **Don't overfeed fish** – uneaten fish food will decompose, foul the water, and encourage algae.

HERBS

ESSENTIAL TASKS

■ **Water and feed** herbs in containers.

■ **Finish sowing seed outdoors** (*p.149 and p.163*) of half-hardy and tender annual herbs.

PLANTING

■ **Plant container-grown** herbs in beds, in paving, or in containers (*see pp.228–231*).

■ **Plant** rooted cuttings or small plants in between paving (*see p.229*).

ROUTINE CARE

■ **Pick and deadhead** plants regularly.

■ **Mulch moisture-loving** herbs with bulky organic matter, after rain or a thorough watering.

RAISING YOUR OWN PLANTS

■ **Sow successive** batches of regularly used herbs such as basil and parsley (*see p.243*) outdoors every 2–4 weeks.

■ **Sow seed of biennials** in rows in a spare patch of soil or seedbed (*see p.149*).

HARVESTING

■ **Pick sprigs and flowers** as they mature for drying, freezing, or infusing (*see p.233*).

MINT

■ **Cut angelica stems** for crystallizing (*see p.232*).

THE EDIBLE GARDEN

ESSENTIAL TASKS

■ **Water crops** as needed outdoors and water any in bags, containers, or in greenhouses regularly, so they grow strongly and consistently (*see box, p.236*).

■ **Damp down the greenhouse floor** and increase ventilation in hot weather to help prevent the crops from overheating and deter spider mite (*see p.296*).

■ **Finish mulching around crops** – water the soil well beforehand (*see p.236*).

MULCHING WITH WELL-ROTTED MANURE

■ **Regularly fertilize vegetables** in containers and bags, and of greenhouse crops, according to their needs.

■ **Hill up potato plants** to prevent the tubers from going green (*see p.252*).

■ **Thin fruits on apple and plum trees** (*see p.265*) and on peach trees (*see p.267*).

■ **Summer-prune grapevines** (*see p.273*) regularly, to avoid tangled shoots. Tie in to supports.

SOWING AND PLANTING

■ **Sow green manures** to cover empty soil temporarily during the growing season (*see p.239*).

■ **Sow summer vegetables outdoors** (*see p.142*) in successive batches for a prolonged harvest, as well as seed of winter vegetables, such as:

Beets (*see p.251*)
Broccoli (*see p.248*)
Chicory and endive (*see p.255*)
Green beans (*see p.246*)
Lettuce, in cool of evening (*see p.255*)
Maincrop carrots (*see p.251*)
Runner beans (*see p.247*)
Peas, under netting to keep off birds and mice (*see p.247*)
Pumpkins and squashes (*see p.253*)
Salad leaves (*see p.255*)
Scallions (*see p.250*)
Summer radishes (*see p.249*).

■ **Plant out** winter brassicas, container-grown vegetables, and tender vegetables.

■ **Plant out young plants of:**
Eggplant, chilies, and peppers (*see p.256*)
Kale (*see p.248*)
Leeks (*see p.251*)
Lettuce (*see p.255*)
Sprouting broccoli (*see p.248*)
Tomatoes (*see p.257*).

ROUTINE CARE

■ **Mulch vegetables and fruit** crops, once the soil is warm and moist (*see p.239*).

■ **Water the compost pile** in dry weather to keep it moist and active.

■ **Dig in green manures** that were sown earlier, before they flower (*see p.239*).

■ **Give a boost to vegetables** with a high-nitrogen fertilizer if needed (*see p.239*).

■ **Pinch out tomato sideshoots** (*see p.252*) to keep cordon plants growing tall and upright and make it easier to pick off the fruits. Tie the stems into stakes.

■ **Pinch off flowers** of first-year summer-fruiting raspberries to give the plant time and energy to establish (*see p.270*).

■ **Net strawberries** to protect the ripening fruits from pests (*see p.272*). Remove surplus runners from plants. Place straw beneath fruits to keep them clean.

PRUNING AND TRAINING

■ **Summer-prune** formally trained stone-fruit trees (*see p.263*).

■ **Prune newly planted pear** trees (*see p.264*).

■ **Tie in raspberry canes** to supports and cut back weaker canes (*see p.270*).

■ **Tie in fruit canes** of blackberries and hybrid berries to supports (*see p.271*).

RAISING YOUR OWN PLANTS

■ **Root strawberry runners** of selected plants (*see p.272*).

HARVESTING

■ **Pick vegetables, such as:**
Beets (*see p.251*)
Early carrots (*see p.251*)
Early potatoes (*see p.252*)
Lettuce (*see p.255*)
Peas (*see p.247*)
Salad leaves (*see p.255*)
Scallions (*see p.250*)
Spinach beet and Swiss chard (*see p.255*)
Summer kale (*see p.248*)
Summer radishes (*see p.249*)
Summer turnips (*see p.249*).

■ **Pick early fruit crops, such as:**
Gooseberries from thinning, for cooking (*see p.268*)
Rhubarb (*see p.273*)
Strawberries (*see p.272*).

MIDSUMMER

LAWNS	BOUNDARIES AND DIVISIONS	BEDS AND BORDERS

LAWNS

ESSENTIAL TASKS
■ **Water new lawns** (*see p.84*) regularly in dry weather, so that they establish properly.

ROUTINE CARE
■ **Mow lawns** at appropriate intervals for the lawn type (*see p.82*); the mowing height may be reduced. Trim the edges (*see p.83*).

■ **After spring-flowering** bulbs (*see p.82*) have died down, make the first mowing of long grass.

■ **Look out for weeds** and keep under control (*see p.87*).

DIGGING OUT PERENNIAL WEEDS

BOUNDARIES AND DIVISIONS

ESSENTIAL TASKS
■ **Water if needed,** especially recently planted or young plants.

■ **Keep an eye out for pests** and diseases such as aphids and blackspot, and take steps to stop their taking hold (*see p.111*).

■ **Prune established** climbers and wall shrubs that flower on the previous year's shoots, immediately after flowering (*see pp.112–113*).

■ **Prune climbing roses** immediately after flowering (*see p.115*).

ROUTINE CARE
■ **Deadhead** plants, as necessary, to prolong flowering, unless you want seeds later.

■ **Feed climbing** roses; specialized rose fertilizer is easiest.

PRUNING AND TRAINING
■ **Train climbers** (*see pp.108–109*) and roses (*see p.115*) into supports as they grow. Cut out any dead or diseased shoots and check ties.

■ **Prune formal hedges,** if they include plants such as *Berberis thunbergii*, hornbeam, and yew (*see chart, p.117, and p.121*).

BEDS AND BORDERS

ESSENTIAL TASKS
■ **Water new and established** plants as necessary (*see p.152*).

■ **Finish lifting tulips,** once their leaves are yellow and faded, and store in a warm, dry place over summer, or discard them.

■ **Finish planting** autumn-flowering bulbs (*see p.149*). Buy good, healthy bulbs (*see p.146*) for the best results.

■ **Feed and mulch** roses. A specialized rose fertilizer is best.

FLORIBUNDA ROSE, *ROSA* 'PLAYBOY'

■ **Finish taking greenwood cuttings** from shrubs (*see p.165*).

ROUTINE CARE
■ **Deadhead** bulbs, perennials (*see p.155*), annuals and biennials, alpine plants, roses, and flowering shrubs as soon as the flowers fade. Let bulb foliage die down naturally.

PRUNING AND TRAINING
■ **Prune established deciduous** shrubs that flower on the previous year's growth (*see p.158*).

■ **Prune most old garden roses** once they have flowered (*see p.161*).

RAISING YOUR OWN PLANTS
■ **Sow seed of biennials** in rows in a spare patch of soil or seedbed (*see p.149*).

CONTAINERS AND RAISED BEDS

- **Gather the seed** of early-flowering perennials (*see p.155*), and of annuals and biennials, as they ripen. Sow seed of the perennials immediately (*see p.162*) and store that of annuals and biennials for an autumn or spring sowing (*see pp.162–163*).

- **Divide perennials that** flower in early summer (*see p.163*), once the flowers fade.

- **Take semiripe cuttings** from shrubs (*see p.164*).

- **Take softwood cuttings** from perennials (*see p.165 and p.381*).

WATERING TIPS

- **Watering is best done** in early morning and evening (to allow the foliage to dry before nightfall to reduce the possibility of disease).

- **Try to water thoroughly** or not at all – water one part of the garden thoroughly rather than giving the whole garden a brief soaking, which may cause roots to grow up to the surface and be more subject to drought.

- **Apply a thick mulch** to keep soil moist, but make sure that the soil is thoroughly moist first.

- **If there is a water shortage,** concentrate on watering newly planted plants and containers.

ESSENTIAL TASKS

- **Water containers** regularly – check them daily (*see p.178*).

- **Water raised beds** if necessary (*see p.183*).

- **Pinch-prune** plants such as coleus in containers (*see p.173 and box, p.381*).

PLANTING

- **Plant in containers** (*see p.176*) hardy deciduous climbers, perennials, annuals and biennials, autumn-flowering bulbs, and alpines.

ROUTINE CARE

- **Regularly deadhead** and keep plants well shaped by removing any tired, diseased, or straggly foliage (*see p.178*).

- **Weed raised beds** regularly.

- **Fertilize containers** from 6–8 weeks after planting (*see p.178*) at regular intervals, if a slow-release fertilizer was not used. Foliar and liquid kinds are most convenient.

- **Lift spring-flowering** bulbs once the foliage has died down and store over summer. Clean off the bulbs; lay on a tray to dry; and store in a paper (not plastic) bag.

PRUNING AND TRAINING

- **Clip established** topiary and standards regularly (*see p.178*).

- **Tie in climbing plants** to supports (stakes or a trellis) as they grow (*see pp.108–109*).

RESCUING A DRIED-OUT CONTAINER

- **Soak the container** in a large bowl of water to rewet the soil mix.

- **Once the surface** of the soil mix is moist, take out the container and place in a shady spot until the plants recover.

- **Nip off any withered** flowers or leaves before putting the container back in position.

RESOAKING A DRIED-OUT BASKET

MIDSUMMER

ORNAMENTAL TREES	WATER GARDENING	HERBS

ORNAMENTAL TREES

ESSENTIAL TASKS

▪ **Prune espaliered flowering cherries,** peaches, plums, and apricots (*Prunus*), if necessary (*see p.196*).

▪ **Water if needed,** especially trees planted in the last 2–3 years. A couple of bucketfuls of water every so often is better than frequent but light watering (*see p.197*).

ROUTINE CARE

▪ **Watch out for suckers** and water shoots growing from tree trunks or roots and remove them before they get too big and spoil the tree (*see p.197*).

HARVESTING

▪ **Gather any edible nuts** and fruits when ripe (*see p.197*).

WATER GARDENING

ESSENTIAL TASKS

▪ **Regularly remove** spent flowers and dying foliage to avoid fouling the water (*see p.222*).

▪ **Remove blanketweed** at regular intervals (*see p.222*).

▪ **Thin floaters,** oxygenators, and duckweed at regular intervals (*see p.222*).

PLANTING

▪ **Plant** (*see pp.220–221*) oxygenating, marginal, and bog plants, and deep-water plants.

ROUTINE CARE

▪ **Feed waterlilies** and other plants in containers (*see p.222*).

HERBS

ESSENTIAL TASKS

▪ **Water and feed** herbs in containers.

HERBS IN TIERED CONTAINERS

▪ **Gather seed** from annual and biennials as soon as it is ripe. Clean the seed and store in paper packets in a cool, dry, dark place.

▪ **Finish sowing** seed of biennial herbs, such as angelica and caraway, in rows in a spare patch of soil or seedbed (*see p.149*).

ROUTINE CARE

▪ **Pick and deadhead** plants regularly.

RAISING YOUR OWN PLANTS

▪ **Take cuttings** from perennial and biennial herbs (*see box, p.381*).

▪ **Sow successive batches** of regularly used herbs such as basil and parsley (*see p.243*) outdoors every 2–4 weeks.

HARVESTING

▪ **Pick sprigs and flowers** as they mature for drying, freezing, or infusing (*see p.233*).

THE EDIBLE GARDEN

ESSENTIAL TASKS

■ **Water crops** as needed outdoors and water any in bags, containers, or in greenhouses regularly, so they grow strongly and consistently (*see box, p.236*).

■ **Damp down the greenhouse floor** and increase ventilation in hot weather to help prevent the crops from overheating and deter spider mite (*see p.296*).

■ **Regularly fertilize vegetables** in containers and bags, and of greenhouse crops, according to their needs.

■ **Shade young salad plants** (*see p.255*) in hot weather.

■ **Thin pear and apple fruits** (*see p.264*).

■ **Summer-prune grapevines** (*see p.273*), to avoid tangled shoots. Tie into supports.

SOWING AND PLANTING

■ **Sow green manures** to cover empty soil temporarily in the growing season (*see p.239*).

■ **Sow summer vegetables outdoors** (*see p.142*) in successive batches for a prolonged harvest, and winter vegetables, such as:
Beets (*see p.251*)
Carrots (*see p.251*)
Chicory and endive (*see p.255*)
Lettuce, in cool of evening (*see p.255*)
Peas, under netting to keep off birds and mice (*see p.247*)
Salad leaves (*see p.255*)
Scallions (*see p.250*)
Sweet corn (*see p.253*)
Spinach beet (*see p.255*)
Summer radish (*see p.249*)
Winter turnips (*see p.249*).

■ **Plant out** winter brassicas, container-grown vegetables, and tender vegetables.

■ **Plant out young plants of:**
Autumn and winter kale (*see p.248*)
Leeks (*see p.251*)
Lettuce (*see p.255*)
Sprouting broccoli (*see p.248*)
Winter cabbages for storing (*see p.249*).

ROUTINE CARE

■ **Water the compost pile** in dry weather to keep it moist and active.

■ **Dig in green manures** that were sown earlier, before they flower (*see p.239*).

■ **Give a boost to vegetables** with a high-nitrogen fertilizer, if needed (*see p.239*).

■ **Remove surplus runners** from strawberry plants (*see p.272*). Place straw beneath fruits to keep them clean. Neaten plants that have finished fruiting.

■ **Gather up and discard** rotten fruit that has fallen from fruit trees and bushes to reduce the spread of diseases.

PRUNING AND TRAINING

■ **Summer-prune** formally trained stone-fruit trees (*see p.263*).

■ **Cut out original raspberry canes** of new plants (*see p.270*).

■ **Tie in fruit canes** of blackberries and hybrid berries to supports (*see p.271*).

PRUNING A
PLUM TREE
(*PRUNUS*)

■ **Prune pyramid pear trees** (*see p.264*).

■ **Pinch out tomato sideshoots** (*see p.252*) to keep cordon plants growing tall and upright and make it easier to pick off the fruits. Tie the stems into stakes.

RAISING YOUR OWN PLANTS

■ **Root strawberry runners** on selected plants (*see p.272*).

HARVESTING

■ **Pick vegetables, such as:**
Beets (*see p.251*)
Broccoli (*see p.248*)
Chicory and endive (*see p.255*)
Early carrots (*see p.251*)
Early potatoes (*see p.252*)
Garlic (*see p.250*)
Green beans (*see p.246*)
Leeks (*see p.251*)
Lettuce (*see p.255*)
Peas (*see p.247*)
Pumpkins and squashes (*see p.253*)
Runner beans (*see p.247*)
Salad leaves (*see p.255*)
Scallions (*see p.250*)
Shallots (*see p.250*)
Spinach beet and Swiss chard (*see p.255*)
Summer cabbages (*see p.249*)
Summer kale (*see p.248*)
Summer radishes (*see p.249*)
Summer turnips (*see p.249*)
Sweet corn (*see p.253*).

■ **Pick fruit crops, such as:**
Blackcurrants (*see p.269*)
Blueberries (*see p.269*)
Dessert gooseberries (*see p.268*)
Sweet cherries (*see p.267*)
Peaches (*see p.267*)
Redcurrants (*see p.268*)
Rhubarb (*see p.273*)
Summer-fruiting raspberries (*see p.270*)
Strawberries (*see p.272*).

LATE SUMMER

LAWNS	BOUNDARIES AND DIVISIONS	BEDS AND BORDERS

ESSENTIAL TASKS

■ **Water new lawns** (*see p.84*) regularly in dry weather, so that they establish properly.

SOWING AND PLANTING

■ **Prepare the soil and site** (*see p.78*) for autumn sowings of grass seed or laying of sod.

■ **Prepare the soil and site** (*see p.78*) for autumn planting of a nongrass lawn.

ROUTINE CARE

■ **Mow lawns** at appropriate intervals for the lawn type (*see p.82*); the mowing height may be reduced. Trim the edges (*see p.83*).

■ **Apply autumn fertilizer** formulated for lawns (*see p.84*).

■ **Look out for weeds** and keep under control (*see p.87*).

■ **Trim nongrass lawns** to remove dead or straggly growth (*see p.88*), if not done in early spring.

ESSENTIAL TASKS

■ **Water if needed,** especially recently planted or young plants.

■ **Keep an eye out for pests** and diseases such as aphids and blackspot and take steps to prevent their taking hold (*see p.111*).

■ **Prune established** climbers and wall shrubs that flower on the previous year's growth, immediately after flowering (*see pp.112–113*).

■ **Prune climbing roses** immediately after flowering (*see p.115*).

ROUTINE CARE

■ **Deadhead** plants as needed to prolong flowering, unless you want seeds later.

CLEMATIS 'ROUGE CARDINAL'

PRUNING AND TRAINING

■ **Train climbers** (*see pp.108–109*) and roses (*see p.115*) into supports as they grow. Cut out any dead or diseased shoots and check ties are not too tight.

■ **Summer-prune** established wisterias (*see p.111*).

■ **Prune formal hedges,** if they include plants such as beech, hornbeam, and holly (*see chart, p.117, and p.121*).

■ **Prune hawthorn and privet** shrubs that were planted last winter into a good shape (*see p.120*).

ESSENTIAL TASKS

■ **Water new and established** plants as necessary (*see p.152*).

PLANTING

■ **Begin to plant** spring-flowering bulbs (*see p.149*), including tulips (*see p.137*). Buy good, healthy bulbs (*see p.146*).

■ **Prepare the soil** in beds or borders – except on light, sandy soil – to improve their condition and ready them for planting (*see pp.142–143*) or improve a patch of soil (*see p.150*).

ROUTINE CARE

■ **Deadhead** bulbs, perennials (*see p.155*), annuals and biennials, alpine plants, roses, and flowering shrubs as soon as the flowers fade. Leave the foliage on bulbs to die down naturally.

PRUNING AND TRAINING

■ **Prune established deciduous** shrubs that flower on the previous year's growth (*see p.158*).

RAISING YOUR OWN PLANTS

■ **Gather seed** of summer-flowering perennials (*see p.155*), and annuals and biennials, as they ripen. Store them for an autumn or spring sowing (*see pp.162–163*).

■ **Take semiripe cuttings** from shrubs (*see p.164*).

■ **Take softwood cuttings** from perennials (*see p.165 and p.381*).

CONTAINERS AND RAISED BEDS

ORNAMENTAL TREES

LILIES FROM BULBILS

■ **What are bulbils?** Some lilies, such as *Lilium lancifolium* (Tiger lily) and some Asiatic lilies, form what look like small dark berries at the bases of their leaves. They provide an easy, if somewhat slow, way of growing new lilies.

■ **How do I gather them?** If the bulbils are ripe, they should come away easily.

■ **How do I grow them?** Treat them like large perennial seeds, and sow them in pots (*see p.162*) or trays.

■ **When do I plant them out?** Plant out the entire pot of "seedlings" in the following autumn.

GATHERING LILY BULBILS

CACTI AND SUCCULENTS IN METAL CONTAINERS

ESSENTIAL TASKS

■ **Water containers** regularly – check them daily (*see p.178*).

■ **Liven up summer containers** by replacing a few spent plants with late-flowerers such as asters, Japanese anemones, and pansies.

■ **Water raised beds** if necessary (*see p.183*).

■ **Pinch-prune** plants such as coleus in containers (*see p.173 and box, p.381*).

PLANTING

■ **Plant in containers** (*see p.176*) hardy deciduous climbers and autumn-flowering alpines.

ROUTINE CARE

■ **Fertilize containers** from 6–8 weeks after planting (*see p.178*) at regular intervals, if a slow-release fertilizer was not used. Foliar and liquid kinds are most convenient.

■ **Regularly deadhead** and keep plants well shaped by removing any tired, diseased, or straggly foliage (*see p.178*).

■ **Weed raised beds** regularly.

PRUNING AND TRAINING

■ **Give a last trim to** established topiary and standards (*see p.178*).

■ **Tie in climbing plants** to supports (stakes or a trellis) as they grow (*see pp.108–109*).

ESSENTIAL TASKS

■ **Water if needed**, especially trees planted in the last 2–3 years. A couple of bucketfuls every so often is better than frequent but light watering (*see p.197*).

ROUTINE CARE

■ **Watch out for suckers** and water shoots growing from tree trunks or roots, and remove them before they get too big and spoil the tree (*see p.197*).

PRUNING AND TRAINING

■ **Prune evergreen trees** if necessary (*see p.196*). Don't cut back conifer shoots too far; most will not regenerate from old wood.

HARVESTING

■ **Gather any edible nuts** and fruits when ripe (*see p.197*).

LATE SUMMER

WATER GARDENING	HERBS

ESSENTIAL TASKS

■ **Finish planting** (*see pp.220–221*) deep-water plants.

WATERLILY (*NYMPHAEA* 'FIRECREST')

ROUTINE CARE

■ **Remove the last of** the spent flowers, dying foliage, blanketweed, floaters, and duckweed, to avoid fouling the water (*see p.222*).

■ **Thin oxygenating plants** at regular intervals (*see p.222*).

ESSENTIAL TASKS

■ **Water and feed** herbs in containers.

■ **Gather seed** from annual and biennial herbs as soon as it is ripe. Clean the seed and store in paper packets in a cool, dry, dark place.

■ **Finish taking cuttings** from perennial and biennial herbs (*see box, p.381*).

PLANTING

■ **Take rooted shoots** from mound-layered herbs (*see p.231*) and repot or replant them or plant in crevices in paving (*see p.229*).

ROUTINE CARE

■ **Pick and deadhead** plants regularly.

HARVESTING

■ **Pick sprigs and flowers** as they mature for drying, freezing, or infusing (*see p.233*).

KEEPING HERBS TRIM

■ **Pick leaves or sprigs** regularly throughout the growing season of all herbs to keep the plants neat and vigorous.

■ **Deadhead any herbs** grown for their foliage to encourage plenty of strong, new shoots.

■ **Removing flowerheads** of shrubby herbs as soon as they fade prevents the plants from wasting energy on seed production.

■ **Watch out for** plain green shoots on variegated herbs; if they are not removed, the entire plant can revert to plain green.

■ **Second-year biennial** herbs will last longer if regularly picked and deadheaded.

GREEK BASIL

THE EDIBLE GARDEN

ESSENTIAL TASKS

■ **Water crops** as needed outdoors and water any in bags, containers, or in greenhouses regularly, to keep them growing strongly and consistently (*see box, p.236*).

■ **Damp down the greenhouse floor** and increase ventilation to prevent overheating and to deter spider mite (*see p.296*).

■ **Remove shading wash** from the greenhouse, if you have used one. Don't leave it on into autumn, because the light levels will be too low for healthy growth.

■ **Regularly fertilize vegetables** in containers and bags, and of greenhouse crops, according to their needs.

■ **Shade young salad plants** (*see p.255*) growing outdoors in hot weather.

■ **Finish pruning new pear trees** and established pear pyramids (*see p.264*).

■ **Finish summer-pruning** of formally trained stone-fruit trees (*see p.263*); summer-prune formally trained apple trees (*see p.263*).

■ **Prune established sour cherry** trees after fruiting (*see p.267*).

■ **Finish summer-pruning grapevines** (*see p.273*) regularly, to avoid tangled shoots. Tie into supports.

SOWING AND PLANTING

■ **Sow green manures** to cover empty soil temporarily during the growing season (*see p.239*).

■ **Sow summer vegetables outdoors** (*see p.142*) in successive batches for a prolonged harvest, as well as seed of winter vegetables, such as:
Bulb onions and scallions (*see p.250*)
Salad leaves (*see p.255*)
Spinach beet (*see p.255*)
Spring cabbage (*see p.249*)
Summer radishes (*see p.249*)
Winter turnips (*see p.249*).

■ **Plant out** winter brassicas and container-grown and tender vegetables.

■ **Plant strawberry plants** (*see p.272*). Apply a fertilizer to sandy or alkaline soils before planting.

ROUTINE CARE

■ **Dig in green manures** that were sown earlier, before they flower (*see p.239*).

■ **Water the compost pile** in dry weather to keep it moist and active.

■ **Give a boost to vegetables** with a high-nitrogen fertilizer if needed (*see p.239*).

LAYERS OF COMPOST IN THE BIN

■ **Pinch out tops of cordon tomatoes** (*see p.252*) to encourage the last fruits to ripen.

■ **Clean up** strawberry plants that have finished fruiting (*see p.272*).

■ **Gather up and discard** rotten fruit that has fallen from fruit trees and bushes, to reduce the spread of diseases.

PRUNING AND TRAINING

■ **Cut back summer-fruiting** raspberry canes after fruiting, and tie in strongest canes to supports (*see p.270*).

RAISING YOUR OWN PLANTS

■ **Root strawberry runners** of selected plants (*see p.272*).

HARVESTING

■ **Pick vegetables, such as:**
Beets (*see p.251*)
Bulb onions (*see p.250*)
Broccoli (*see p.248*)
Chicory and endive (*see p.255*)
Eggplant, chilies, and peppers (*see p.256*)
Garlic (*see p.250*)
Green beans (*see p.246*)
Lettuce (*see p.255*)
Maincrop carrots (*see p.251*)
Maincrop potatoes (*see p.252*)
Peas (*see p.247*)
Pumpkins and squashes (*see p.253*)
Runner beans (*see p.247*)
Salad leaves (*see p.255*)
Scallions (*see p.250*)
Shallots (*see p.250*)
Spinach beet and Swiss chard (*see p.255*)
Summer radish (*see p.249*)
Sweet corn (*see p.253*)
Tomatoes (*see p.257*).

■ **Pick fruit crops, such as:**
Apples (*see p.265*)
Blackberries and hybrid berries (*see p.271*)
Raspberries (*see p.270*)
Peaches (*see p.267*)
Plums (*see p.266*)
Strawberries (*see p.272*).

EARLY AUTUMN

LAWNS	BOUNDARIES AND DIVISIONS	BEDS AND BORDERS

ESSENTIAL TASKS

■ **Plant rooted shoots** of mounded herbs (*see p.231*) to create a nongrass lawn (*see p.88*).

SOWING AND PLANTING

■ **Lay sod for a new lawn** (*see p.77 and pp.80–81*), if not done in spring, once the weather cools.

■ **Sow seed for a new lawn** (*see p.77 and p.79*), if not done in spring, if the soil is moist.

■ **Plant bulbs in grass** to flower in spring (*see p.89*) as soon as the bulbs are available.

ROUTINE CARE

■ **Mow lawns** at appropriate intervals for the lawn type (*see p.82*); set the mowing height appropriately. Trim the edges (*see p.83*).

■ **Scarify, aerate, and topdress** grass lawns to keep them in condition (*see p.85*).

■ **Apply autumn fertilizer** formulated for lawns, if not done in late summer (*see p.84*).

PLANTING

■ **Plant shrubs or climbers** against walls, fences, or trees (*see p.110*), including clematis (*see p.111*). Train stems into the desired shape, for example a fan (*see p.111 and p.113*).

■ **Plant hedges** with container-grown trees and shrubs (*see p.120*).

ROUTINE CARE

■ **Deadhead** plants to prolong flowering.

PRUNING AND TRAINING

■ **Check supports for climbers,** wall shrubs, and roses and renew them if necessary; finish tying in any stray shoots; check old ties (*see pp.108–109*).

■ **Prune climbing roses** once flowering is finished (*see p.115*).

■ **Prune evergreen hedges,** such as Lawson cypress, *Lonicera nitida*, and *Thuja plicata* (*see chart, p.117, and p.121*).

CHECKING PLANT TIES

■ **Why must ties be checked?** As the stem grows and thickens, old ties bite into the bark and cause wounds that may girdle and kill the stem, allow disease to enter, or weaken the stem so that it snaps in the wind. Check ties when pruning, and at least twice a year.

STEM DAMAGED BY OVERLY TIGHT TIE

ESSENTIAL TASKS

■ **Water new and established** plants as necessary (*see p.152*).

■ **Divide peonies** (*see p.135*) before the soil gets too cold. Use a knife to cut the fleshy roots into sections, each with 2 or 3 buds. Try to avoid bruising the soft roots. Dust the cuts with fungicide, and replant the pieces with the buds just below the surface.

■ **Finish taking semiripe cuttings** from shrubs (*see p.164*).

■ **Finish taking softwood cuttings** from perennials (*see p.165 and p.381*).

PLANTING

■ **Plant spring-flowering bulbs** (*see p.149*), including tulips, daffodils, and lilies (*see p.137*). Buy healthy bulbs (*see p.146*) for good results.

■ **Prepare the soil** in borders – except on light, sandy soils – to condition them and ready them for planting (*see pp.142–143*) or improve a patch of soil (*see p.150*).

■ **Plant perennials** (*see p.148*) and balled-and-burlapped and container-grown shrubs (*see p.150*). Buy good, healthy plants (*see p.146*) for best results. Give shrubs an initial prune after planting (*see p.151*) and stake if needed (*see p.150*).

ROUTINE CARE

■ **Deadhead** late-flowering plants, particularly perennials (*see p.155*) and annuals and biennials.

■ **Mulch beds and borders,** if not done in spring (*see pp.152–153*). Make sure that the soil is moist; water it beforehand if needed.

■ **Cut down** perennials to clear away dying, messy growth, except in cold regions (*see p.155*). Clear away dead and dying annuals and biennials.

■ **Lift begonia, dahlia, and gladioli** rootstocks to store over winter (*see p.397*).

CONTAINERS AND RAISED BEDS

ASTER

PRUNING AND TRAINING
■ **Cut back** tall rose bushes to prevent winter winds from rocking the bush and working loose the roots (*see p.160*).

RAISING YOUR OWN PLANTS
■ **Transplant biennial seedlings** to their final flowering position (*see p.149*).

■ **Gather seed** of summer-flowering perennials (*see p.155*), and annuals and biennials, as they ripen. Store them for autumn or spring sowing (*see pp.162–163*).

■ **Sow seed outdoors** (*see p.149 and p.163*) of hardy annuals for an early show next year.

■ **Divide perennials** (*see p.163*), except in regions with cold winters.

■ **Plant out rooted shrub cuttings** taken the previous year from shrubs (*see p.164*), whether hardwood or semiripe, or grow them on in pots.

ESSENTIAL TASKS
■ **Water containers** as necessary – check them regularly (*see p.178*).

■ **Give final fertilizer** to plants in containers before the end of the season (*see p.178*) if slow-release fertilizer was not used.

■ **Pinch-prune** plants such as coleus in containers (*see p.173 and box, p.381*).

PLANTING
■ **Plant in containers** (*see p.176*) hardy climbers, shrubs, and spring-flowering bulbs for next year.

■ **Plant containers for winter** with small conifers, evergreen shrubs and climbers, and spring-flowering bulbs. Add winter-flowering pansies for bright color.

ROUTINE CARE
■ **Regularly deadhead** to prolong the display and keep plants well-shaped by removing any tired, diseased, or straggly foliage (*see p.178*).

■ **Repot or topdress** spring-flowering climbers and alpines in containers; root-prune if necessary (*see p.179*).

■ **Give raised beds** a final weeding.

■ **Lift and divide perennials** in raised beds, keeping new healthy growth and discarding old, tired parts (*see p.155*), if not done in spring.

PRUNING AND TRAINING
■ **Tie in climbers** to supports such as stakes or a trellis (*see pp.108–109*).

RAISING YOUR OWN PLANTS
■ **Sow seeds of hardy annuals** in pots, trays, or cell packs (*see p.162*) to grow on for planting out next spring.

■ **Layer shrubs** (*see p.165*).

STORING SEEDS

■ **Make sure the seeds are dry** before storing them; otherwise, they may rot and die. If gathering them, choose a sunny day and lay the seeds on a tray in a warm, airy place to dry.

■ **Clean the seeds** by sorting them from the chaff – sift the seeds in a sieve.

■ **Place the seeds in paper bags** – black photographic film containers are good alternatives. Remember to label them with the plant name and the date.

■ **Store the seeds** in a cool, dry, dark place, or the bottom of a refrigerator, for up to a year.

STORING SEEDS IN FILM
CONTAINERS

EARLY AUTUMN

ORNAMENTAL TREES	WATER GARDENING	HERBS

PLANTING

- **Prepare the soil** (*see p.192 and pp.142–143*) for midautumn plantings of container-grown, bare-root, or, balled-and-burlapped trees.

FORKING IN ORGANIC MATTER

ROUTINE CARE

- **Watch out for suckers** and water shoots growing from tree trunks or roots and remove them before they get too big and spoil the tree (*see p.197*).

- **Gather up fallen fruit,** leaves, and other debris that has fallen from trees and place on the compost heap. Discard any rotten fruit to reduce disease spread.

HARVESTING

- **Gather any edible nuts** and fruits when ripe (*see p.197*).

ESSENTIAL TASKS

- **Net ponds to catch** falling leaves and gather up the leaves regularly (*see p.222*).

SILVER MAPLE LEAVES
(*ACER SACCHARINUM*)

ROUTINE CARE

- **Rejuvenate marginals** and bog plants by dividing them, if not done in spring (*see p.223*).

- **Thin oxygenating plants,** removing excess growth and debris that might rot over winter (*see p.223*).

ESSENTIAL TASKS

- **Take rooted shoots** from mound-layered herbs (*see p.231*) and repot or replant them or plant in crevices (*see p.229*).

ROUTINE CARE

- **Pot up for winter use** herbs such as chives or mint (*see p.231*).

RAISING YOUR OWN PLANTS

- **Plant out seedlings of biennial** herbs into their final positions (*see p.149*).

- **Sow seeds** (*see p.149 and p.163*) outdoors of hardy annual herbs, for an early spurt of growth the next year.

- **Divide large shrubby** or clump-forming herbs after flowering (*see p.231*), if not done in early spring.

THE EDIBLE GARDEN

ESSENTIAL TASKS

■ **Water crops** as needed outdoors and water any in bags, containers, or in greenhouses regularly, so they grow strongly and consistently (*see box, p.236*).

SOWING AND PLANTING

■ **Dig over vegetable beds** (*see p.239 and pp.143–143*) to enrich and condition the soil.

■ **Sow green manures** to cover empty soil through winter and dig in ones that were sown earlier, before they flower (*see p.239*).

■ **Plant out garlic cloves** or plants raised in cell packs in well-drained soil (*see p.255*).

■ **Sow vegetable seed indoors**, such as:
Winter lettuce (*see p.255*)
Salad leaves, such as rocket
Spinach beet (*see p.255*)
Summer radish (*see p.249*).

■ **Sow hardy vegetable seed outdoors**, such as:
Salad leaves (*see p.255*)
Summer radishes (*see p.249*)
Winter lettuce, under cloches (*see p.255*).

■ **Plant bush and cane fruits** and container-grown fruit trees (*see pp.260–261*).

■ **Plant strawberry** plants (*see p.272*) and rhubarb (*see p.273*).

ROUTINE CARE

■ **Lay outdoor cordon tomatoes** down on beds of straw or pick them and put on a windowsill, to ripen more quickly (*see p.257*).

■ **Hill up winter cabbages** (*see p.249*) and sprouting broccoli (*see p.248*) and remove any rotting leaves. Stake tall broccoli.

■ **Clean up strawberry plants** that have finished fruiting (*see p.272*).

■ **Mulch rhubarb**, if not done in early spring (*see p.273*).

■ **Gather up and discard** rotten fruit that have fallen from fruit trees and bushes, to reduce the spread of disease.

■ **Check ties and stakes** (*see p.193*) on fruit trees and remove or loosen them as needed to avoid them damaging the bark.

PRUNING AND TRAINING

■ **Cut back blackcurrants** on planting (*see p.261*) to above soil level.

■ **Prune established redcurrants** (*p.268*).

■ **Cut back summer-fruiting** raspberry canes, after fruiting, and tie in strongest new canes to supports (*see p.270*). Do the same with blackberries and hybrid berries (*see p.271*).

RAISING YOUR OWN PLANTS

■ **Split mature rhubarb** plants into new sets (*see p.273*), once the leaves die down.

HARVESTING

■ **Pick vegetables, such as:**
Beets (*see p.251*)
Broccoli (*see p.248*)
Bulb onions (*see p.250*)
Chicory and endive (*see p.255*)
Eggplant, chilies, and peppers (*see p.256*)
Green beans (*see p.246*)
Kale (*see p.248*)
Leeks (*see p.251*)
Lettuce (*see p.255*)
Maincrop carrots (*see p.251*)
Maincrop potatoes (*see p.252*)
Peas (*see p.247*)
Pumpkins and squashes (*see p.253*)
Runner beans (*see p.247*)
Salad leaves (*see p.255*)
Scallions (*see p.257*)
Spinach beet and Swiss chard (*see p.255*)
Summer radishes (*see p.249*)
Sweet corn (*see p.253*)
Tomatoes (*see p.257*).

■ **Pick fruit crops, such as:**
Apples (*see p.265*)
Autumn-fruiting raspberries (*see p.270*)
Pears (*see p.264*)
Perpetual-fruiting and alpine strawberries (*see p.272*)
Plums (*see p.266*).

HARVESTING VEGETABLES

■ **Root vegetables:** leave in the ground or layer in boxes of slightly moist sand.

■ **Peas and beans:** hang uprooted plants, such as dried beans and peas, upside down to dry; then shell and store the beans in airtight jars.

■ **Pumpkins and squash:** cure, or ripen, by leaving them in a warm, dry place that is exposed to the sun, such as the greenhouse bench, for a few weeks.

■ **Cabbages and onions:** hang up in net bags, or place on wooden slats or in boxes in a cool, dry, frost-free place.

STORING ONIONS

MIDAUTUMN

LAWNS	BOUNDARIES AND DIVISIONS	BEDS AND BORDERS

ESSENTIAL TASKS

■ **Plant bulbs** in grass to flower in spring (*see p.89*) as soon as the bulbs are available.

SOWING AND PLANTING

■ **Lay sod for a new lawn** (*see p.77 and pp.80–81*), if not done in spring.

ROUTINE CARE

■ **Mow lawns** at appropriate intervals for the lawn type (*see p.82*); set the mowing height appropriately. Trim the edges (*see p.83*).

■ **Clear dead leaves** from the lawn by sweeping or raking them; compost the leaves for leafmold in a chicken-wire cage or in a pile.

■ **Repair damaged patches** in lawns (*see p.86*) and reseed or resod if necessary.

WORM BINS

Here are a few tips for keeping the worms in your bin happy.

■ **Some worms hate acidity:** don't put in much citrus fruit at one time, and add a little dried calcium now and again to keep the mix alkaline.

■ **If the compost looks soggy,** add a layer of shredded newspaper.

■ **Remember to tap off the liquid** that collects at the bottom of the worm bin regularly – before it drowns the compost and the worms. It makes a good fertilizer when diluted in water.

■ **Wrap the worm bin** in some insulating material for the winter (*see p.282*) or bring them into a protected place.

PLANTING

■ **Plant shrubs or climbers** against walls, fences, or trees (*see p.110*). Train stems into the desired shape (*see p.111 and p.113*).

BOSTON IVY
(*PARTHENOCISSUS TRICUSPIDATA* 'VEITCHII')

■ **Plant clematis** against walls, fences, or trees; train stems into shape (*see p.111*).

■ **Plant hedges** with container-grown trees and shrubs (*see p.120*).

PRUNING AND TRAINING

■ **Prune climbing roses** once flowering is finished (*see p.115*).

■ **Cut back Group 3 clematis** plants that are outgrowing their bounds (*see p.114*).

■ **Prune flowering hedges,** such as *Cotoneaster lacteus*, escallonia, and hawthorn (*see chart, p.117, and p.121*).

PLANTING

■ **Plant spring-flowering bulbs** (*see p.149*), including tulips and daffodils (*see p.137*). Buy healthy bulbs (*see p.146*) for good results.

■ **Prepare the soil** in beds or borders – except on light, sandy soils – to improve their condition and ready them for planting (*see pp.142–143*) or improve a patch of soil (*see p.150*).

■ **Plant perennials** (*see p.148*) and balled-and-burlapped and container-grown shrubs, (*see p.150*). Buy good, healthy plants (*see pp.146–147*) for the best results. Give shrubs an initial pruning after planting (*see p.151*) and stake if needed (*see p.150*). Water the roots of each plant well before planting – soak the pot in a bucket for about an hour.

WATERING A
HEUCHERA
BEFORE
PLANTING

ROUTINE CARE

■ **Deadhead** late-flowering plants, particularly perennials (*see p.155*).

■ **Mulch** beds and borders, if not done in spring (*see pp.152–153*).

■ **Renew topdressing** or mulch on established gravel beds (*see p.133*).

■ **Lift begonia, dahlia, and gladioli** to store over winter. Trim back the foliage and clean off excess soil and any dead or dying material; leave on a tray to dry for a few weeks; then pack loosely, roots downward, in vermiculite or coir; keep in a dry, frostfree place. Don't forget to label them!

- **Cut down perennials** to clear away dying, messy growth, except in cold regions (*see p.155*). Clear away dead and dying annuals and biennials.

- **Cut back grasses** and bamboos to the ground, unless they are tender plants or decorative in winter. Store cut bamboo stems for use as garden stakes next year.

PRUNING AND TRAINING
- **Carry out initial pruning** for shape (*see p.157*) or restorative pruning (*see p.159*) of deciduous shrubs.

- **Cut back** tall rose bushes to prevent winter winds from rocking the bush and working loose the roots (*see p.160*).

RAISING YOUR OWN PLANTS
- **Plant out seedlings of biennials** to their final flowering position (*see p.149*).

- **Gather seed** of late-flowering perennials (*see p.155*) as they ripen. Sow immediately or store them for sowing next year (*see pp.162–163*).

- **Sow seed outdoors** (*see p.149 and p.163*) of hardy annuals for an early show of flower next year.

- **Divide perennials** (*see p.163*), except in regions with cold winters.

- **Layer shrubs** (*see p.165*).

CONTAINERS AND RAISED BEDS

ESSENTIAL TASKS
- **Water containers** as necessary – check them regularly (*see p.178*).

PLANTING
- **Plant containers for winter** with small conifers, evergreen shrubs and climbers, and spring-flowering bulbs. Add winter-flowering pansies for bright color.

WINTER PLANTING OF JUNIPER AND WINTERGREEN

ROUTINE CARE
- **Deadhead** and remove any tired, diseased, or straggly foliage (*see p.178*) to keep the plants well shaped.

- **Repot or topdress** spring-flowering climbers and alpines in containers; root-prune if necessary (*see p.179*).

- **Renew mulch** on established raised beds (*see p.183*).

- **Lift and divide** perennials in raised beds, keeping new healthy growth and discarding old, tired parts (*see p.155*), if not done in spring.

- **Protect marginal plants** in containers (*see p.179*) and marginal plants in raised beds (*see p.183*) against winter cold, if necessary.

- **Lift summer-flowering bulbs** once the foliage has died down and store over winter. Clean off the bulbs; lay on a tray to dry; and store in a paper (not plastic) bag.

ORNAMENTAL TREES

ESSENTIAL TASKS
- **Check tree ties** and stakes (*see p.193*) and remove or loosen them as necessary to avoid chafing and damaging the bark.

PLANTING
- **Prepare the soil** (*see p.192 and pp.142–143*) for late-autumn plantings of container-grown trees.

- **Plant evergreen** balled-and-burlapped trees (*see p.195*), except in cold regions.

ROUTINE CARE
- **Mulch established trees** with a 2–3in (5–8cm) layer of well-rotted manure or compost. Keep the mulch away from the trunk. Mulch 10–12ft (3–4m) out, or to the edge of the canopy of a young tree.

- **Make sure tree guards** (*see p.195*) are still in place.

- **Watch out for suckers** and water shoots growing from tree trunks or roots and remove them before they get too big and spoil the tree (*see p.197*).

- **Move tender trees** in containers under cover for the winter in cool or cold climates before the first frosts.

- **Gather up fallen fruit,** leaves, and other debris that has fallen from trees and place on the compost pile. Discard any rotten fruit, to stop diseases spreading.

HARVESTING
- **Gather any edible nuts** and fruits when ripe (*see p.197*).

MIDAUTUMN

WATER GARDENING	THE EDIBLE GARDEN

ESSENTIAL TASKS

■ **Gather fallen leaves** regularly from netting over ponds (*see p.222*).

■ **Protect container ponds** (*see p.207*) from winter cold by bringing them under cover or sinking them into the soil.

■ **Lift tender** plants in cold climates for storage overwinter (*see p.222*) before the first frost.

ROUTINE CARE

■ **Thin oxygenating plants,** removing excess growth and debris that might rot over winter (*see p.223*).

■ **Cut back or thin out** (by division, *see p.223*) overcrowded or straggly marginal plants and clear out any rotting material from the water.

RAISING YOUR OWN HERBS

■ **Plant out seedlings of biennial** herbs to their final positions (*see p.149*).

■ **Sow seed outdoors** (*see p.149 and p.163*) of hardy annual herbs, for an early spurt of growth next year. In cold regions, protect the seedlings over winter with cloches or row cover.

ESSENTIAL TASKS

■ **Cover tender crops** and root vegetables in the ground (*see p.89*) to protect them over winter in cold climates.

SOWING AND PLANTING

■ **Plant out garlic cloves** or plants raised in packs in well-drained soil (*see p.255*).

■ **Sow green manures** to cover empty soil through the winter (*see p.239*).

■ **Dig over vegetable beds** (*see p.239 and pp.143–143*) to enrich and condition the soil.

DIGGING OVER A DEEP BED

■ **Sow hardy, overwintering vegetables** (*see p.242*) outdoors under cover, such as:
Salad leaves (*see p.255*)
Summer radish (*see p.249*)
Winter lettuce (*see p.257*).

■ **Plant bush and cane fruits** and container-grown fruit trees (*see pp.260–261*), except plums.

■ **Plant rhubarb** (*see p.273*).

ROUTINE CARE

■ **Gather up and discard** rotten fruit that have fallen from fruit trees and bushes, to prevent diseases from spreading.

■ **Check ties and stakes** (*see p.193*) on fruit trees and remove or loosen them as needed to avoid their damaging the bark.

■ **Clean up strawberry plants** that have finished fruiting (*see p.272*).

■ **Mulch rhubarb,** if not done in early spring (*see p.273*).

PRUNING AND TRAINING

■ **Cut back blackcurrants** on planting (*see p.261*) to one strong bud on each stem.

■ **Prune established redcurrants** (*see p.268*).

RAISING YOUR OWN PLANTS

■ **Split mature rhubarb** plants to obtain several new sets (*see p.273*), once the leaves die down.

HARVESTING

■ **Pick vegetables, such as:**
Autumn kale (*see p.248*)
Beets (*see p.251*)
Bulb onions (*see p.250*)
Chicory and endive (*see p.255*)
Early peas (*see p.247*)
Eggplant, chilies, and peppers (*see p.256*)
Leeks (*see p.251*)
Lettuce (*see p.255*)
Maincrop carrots (*see p.251*)
Maincrop potatoes (*see p.252*)
Parsnips (*see p.251*)
Red cabbages (*see p.249*)
Salad leaves (*see p.255*)
Scallions (*see p.250*)
Spinach beet and Swiss chard (*see p.255*)
Tomatoes (*see p.257*)
Winter turnips (*see p.249*).

■ **Pick fruit crops, such as:**
Apples (*see p.265*)
Autumn-fruiting raspberries (*see p.270*)
Pears (*see p.264*).

■ **Cut down haulms (topgrowth)** of maincrop potato plants two weeks before lifting the crop (*see p.252*).

LATE AUTUMN

LAWNS

ESSENTIAL TASKS
- **Mow lawns for the last time** before the onset of winter; set the mowing height to maximum (*see p.82*). Trim the edges (*see p.83*).

SOWING AND PLANTING
- **Lay sod for a new lawn** (*see p.77 and pp.80–81*), if not done in spring.

- **Finish planting bulbs** in grass to flower in spring (*see p.89*) as soon as the bulbs are available.

ROUTINE CARE
- **Clear dead leaves** from the lawn by sweeping or raking them; compost the leaves for leafmold in a wire netting bin.

- **Cut summer-flowering meadows** once flowering plants have safely set seed for next year (*see p.89*).

BOUNDARIES AND DIVISIONS

ESSENTIAL TASKS
- **Feed and mulch deciduous** hedges to prepare them for renovation pruning in midwinter (*see p.121*).

PLANTING
- **Plant shrubs or climbers** against walls, fences, or trees (*see p.110*), including clematis (*see p.111*). Train stems into the desired shape, for example a fan (*see p.111 and p.113*).

PLANTING A CLEMATIS BY A WALL

- **Plant bare-root** climbing roses against walls, fences, or trees (*see p.110*).

- **Plant hedges** (*see p.120*).

PRUNING AND TRAINING
- **Prune climbing roses** once flowering is finished (*see p.115*).

- **Cut back Group 3 clematis** plants that are outgrowing their bounds (*see p.114*).

- **Prune hedges,** if they include plants such as boxwood and *Cotoneaster lacteus* (*see chart, p.117, and p.121*).

BEDS AND BORDERS

ESSENTIAL TASKS
- **Finish planting bulbs** that flower in spring (*see p.149*), including tulips and daffodils (*see p.137*). Buy healthy bulbs (*see p.146*) for good results.

- **Finish mulching** beds and borders, if not done in spring (*see pp.152–153*), before the ground becomes too cold.

- **Finish planting out biennial** seedlings to their final flowering positions (*see p.149*).

- **Finish sowing seed outdoors** (*see p.149 and p.163*) of hardy annuals, for an early show of flower next year. In cold regions, protect the seedlings over winter with cloches or row cover.

PLANTING
- **Prepare the soil** in beds or borders – except on light, sandy soil – to improve their condition and ready them for planting up (*see pp.142–143*) or improve a patch of soil (*see p.150*).

- **Plant perennials** (*see p.148*) and shrubs, except containerized and evergreen ones (*see p.150*). Buy good, healthy plants (*see pp.146–147*) for the best results. Give shrubs an initial pruning after planting (*see p.151*) and stake if necessary (*see p.150*).

- **Plant bare-root roses** (*see p.151*), except in cold regions. Buy good, healthy plants (*see p.147*) for the best results. Give the roses an initial pruning after planting (*see p.151*).

ROUTINE CARE
- **Cut back grasses** and bamboos to the ground, unless they are tender plants or decorative in winter. Store cut bamboo canes to use as garden stakes next year.

- **Cut down perennials** to clear away dying, messy growth, except in cold regions (*see p.155*). Clear away dead and dying annuals and biennials.

(*Continued next page.*)

LATE AUTUMN

| BEDS AND BORDERS (CONT.) | CONTAINERS AND RAISED BEDS | ORNAMENTAL TREES |

PRUNING AND TRAINING

■ **Carry out initial pruning** for shape (*see p.157*) and restorative (*see p.159*) pruning of deciduous shrubs.

■ **Cut back** tall rose bushes to prevent winter winds from rocking the bush and working loose the roots (*see p.160*).

RAISING YOUR OWN PLANTS

■ **Gather seed** of late-flowering perennials (*see p.155*) as they ripen. Sow immediately or store for sowing next year (*see pp.162–163*).

■ **Divide perennials** (*see p.163*), except in regions with cold winters.

■ **Take hardwood shrub cuttings** (*p.164*).

■ **Layer shrubs** (*see p.165*).

TAKING ROOT CUTTINGS

Some perennials are easy to propagate from pieces of their fleshy roots. Try taking root cuttings at this time of year from Oriental poppies, sea hollies (*Eryngium*), and verbascums.

■ **Dig up a healthy plant** and gently wash the soil off the roots. Look for roots of average thickness and cut them off close to the plant. Take no more than a third of the roots; replant the plant.

■ **Cut up the roots** into pieces 3in (8cm) long. So you know which way up the cuttings should be, cut a slant at the downward tip and straight across at the top end of each piece.

■ **Fill a pot with cuttings soil mix,** then insert the cuttings vertically, so that the straight top is level with the surface. Top with coarse sand and label.

■ **Keep in a sheltered** place and keep just moist until new shoots and roots appear in spring. Grow on and plant out in autumn to flower the following year.

ESSENTIAL TASKS

■ **Water containers** as necessary – check them regularly (*see p.178*).

■ **Check that terracotta or ceramic** containers of hardy plants are raised on bricks or "feet" (*see p.169*). Group the containers together in a sheltered spot. Begin bringing in tender plants.

■ **Protect tender plants** in containers (*see p.179*) and tender plants in raised beds (*see p.183*) against winter cold, if necessary.

INSULATING A CONTAINER WITH BURLAP

■ **Shield alpines** in raised beds from winter wet (*see p.183*).

ROUTINE CARE

■ **Lift and divide perennials** in raised beds, keeping new healthy growth and discarding old, tired parts (*see p.155*), if not done in spring.

■ **Lift summer-flowering** bulbs once the foliage has died down and store over winter. Clean off the bulbs, lay on a tray to dry, and store in a paper (not plastic) bag.

ESSENTIAL TASKS

■ **Move tender trees** in containers under cover for the winter in cold regions.

ROUTINE CARE

■ **Watch out for suckers** and water shoots growing from tree trunks or roots and remove them before they get too big and spoil the tree (*see p.197*).

■ **Gather up fallen fruit,** leaves, and other debris that has fallen from trees and place on the compost pile. Destroy any rotten fruit to prevent diseases from spreading.

PLANTING

■ **Prepare the soil** (*see p.192 and pp.142–143*) for winter plantings of container-grown, hardy deciduous bare-root, or deciduous balled-and-burlapped trees.

■ **Plant bare-root trees** (*see p.194*) of hardy deciduous species, except in cold regions. When filling in the planting hole, make sure there are no air pockets in between the roots by gently shaking the stem up and down.

HARVESTING

■ **Gather any edible nuts** and fruits when ripe (*see p.197*).

WATER GARDENING	HERBS	THE EDIBLE GARDEN

ESSENTIAL TASKS

■ **Protect container ponds** (*see p.207*) from winter cold by emptying them, bringing them inside, or sinking them into the soil.

■ **Mulch bog plants and** moisture-loving marginals (*see p.222*) to insulate them against severe cold, which could kill them.

■ **Clear leaves** from netting over ponds (*see p.222*).

ROUTINE CARE

■ **Thin oxygenating plants,** removing excess growth and debris that might rot over winter (*see p.223*).

■ **Cut back or thin out** (by division, *see p.223*) any overcrowded or straggly marginal plants and clear out any rotting material from the water.

END-OF-SEASON CLEANUP

■ **Clean and oil tools** before putting them away for the winter (*see p.281*) to prevent rusting.

■ **Clean empty containers** to get rid of any disease or pests that could infect fresh soil mix or plants. Scrub the pots and trays thoroughly with horticultural disinfectant or household bleach.

SCRUBBING POTS WITH DETERGENT

ESSENTIAL TASKS

■ **Move tender or half-hardy** herbs in containers under cover (*see p.230*) for the winter in cool climates before the first frost.

■ **Finish planting out biennial** herb seedlings to their final positions (*see p.149*).

■ **Finish sowing seed outdoors** (*see p.149 and p.163*) of hardy annual herbs, for an early spurt of growth next year. In cold regions, protect the seedlings over winter with cloches or row cover.

ROUTINE CARE

■ **Cut off old growth** on perennial herbs, in mild climates.

■ **Remove dead leaves** or other debris from low-growing evergreens to avoid fungal rot attacking them.

ESSENTIAL TASKS

■ **Cover tender crops** and root vegetables in the ground to protect them over winter in cold climates.

SOWING AND PLANTING

■ **Dig over vegetable beds** (*see p.239 and pp.143–143*) to condition the soil.

■ **Sow green manures** to overwinter (*p.239*).

■ **Sow hardy vegetables outdoors,** such as: Hardy peas, under netting (*see p.247*).

■ **Plant out garlic cloves** or plants raised in cell packs in well-drained soil (*see p.255*).

■ **Plant bare-root fruit** trees (*see pp.261–261*), bush and cane fruits and container-grown fruit trees (*see pp.260–261*), and grapevines in early winter (*see p.273*).

ROUTINE CARE

■ **Mulch rhubarb,** if not done in early spring (*see p.273*).

■ **Gather up and discard** fallen rotten fruit and nuts to prevent diseases from spreading.

PRUNING AND TRAINING

■ **Cut back blackcurrants** on planting (*see p.261*). Prune redcurrants (*see p.268*).

■ **Tie in cane tips of** summer-fruiting raspberries to avoid winter damage (*see p.270*).

HARVESTING

■ **Pick vegetables, such as:** Cabbages (*see p.249*); chicory and endive (*see p.255*); early peas (*see p.247*); kale (*see p.248*); leeks (*see p.251*); lettuce (*see p.255*); maincrop potatoes (*see p.252*); parsnips (*see p.251*); salad leaves (*see p.255*); spinach beet and Swiss chard (*see p.255*); scallions (*see p.257*); summer radishes (*see p.249*); winter turnip (*see p.249*).

■ **Pick fruit crops, such as:** Apples (*see p.265*).

EARLY TO MIDWINTER

BOUNDARIES AND DIVISIONS	BEDS AND BORDERS	ORNAMENTAL TREES

ESSENTIAL TASKS

■ **Finish planting bare-root** roses against walls, fences, or trees (*see p.110*) before it becomes too cold.

PLANTING

■ **Plant hedges** (*see p.120*).

PRUNING AND TRAINING

■ **Renovate deciduous climbers** and hedges, if necessary (*see p.115 and p.121*).

■ **Prune established** vines and wall shrubs that are grown for foliage (*see pp.112–113*).

ELAEAGNUS PUNGENS '*MACULATA*'

■ **Winter-prune wisteria** in midwinter (*see p.111*).

■ **Prune flowering hedges** of *Cotoneaster* or hawthorn (*see chart, p.117, and p.121*).

■ **Prune young hawthorn and privet** shrubs into a good shape (*see p.120*).

ESSENTIAL TASKS

■ **Finish planting bare-root roses** (*see p.151*), except in cold regions, in early winter. Buy good, healthy plants (*see p.147*) for the best results. Give the roses an initial pruning after planting (*see p.151*).

PLANTING

■ **Plant containerized shrubs** and container-grown ones (*see p.150*). Buy good, healthy plants (*see p.147*) for the best results. Give the shrubs an initial pruning after planting (*see p.151*) and stake if necessary (*see p.150*).

ROUTINE CARE

■ **Cut back grasses** and bamboos to the ground by early winter, unless they are tender plants or decorative in winter. Store cut bamboo canes for use as garden stakes next year.

■ **On light, sandy soils,** spread a thick 3–5in (8–13cm) layer of well-rotted organic material over the surface, and leave until early spring to dig in.

PRUNING AND TRAINING

■ **Carry out initial pruning** for shape (*see p.157*) and restorative (*see p.159*) pruning of deciduous shrubs.

RAISING YOUR OWN PLANTS

■ **Divide perennials** (*see p.163*), except in regions with cold winters.

■ **Take hardwood cuttings** from shrubs (*see p.164*).

ESSENTIAL TASKS

■ **Prevent snow damage** to conifer branches by brushing it off immediately or tying the plant with twine or panty hose to preserve its shape.

■ **Formative prune** young trees for shape (*see p.196*).

HOLLY (*ILEX* X *ALTACLERENSIS*)

PLANTING

■ **Plant hardy bare-root** trees (*see p.194*), except in cold regions.

■ **Plant balled-and-burlapped deciduous** trees (*see p.195*). When filling in the planting hole, make sure there are no air pockets in between the roots by gently shaking the stem up and down.

WATER GARDENING

ESSENTIAL TASKS
■ **In very cold weather,** don't forget to protect pond surfaces from freezing over (*see p.222*), especially if you have fish. If you cannot prevent the pond from freezing, take steps to protect marginally hardy and tender plants, and consider keeping the fish under cover during winter.

THE EDIBLE GARDEN

ESSENTIAL TASKS
■ **Finish planting grapevines** in early winter and prune for shape (*see p.273*).

■ **Winter-prune grapevines** (*see p.273*) when sap bleeds less readily.

SOWING AND PLANTING
■ **Sow seed of hardy vegetables** indoors (*see p.244*) in midwinter.

■ **Plant fruit trees,** except pears, and cane fruits (*see pp.260–261*). Tie in cordons to supports (*see p.261*).

■ **Plant bush fruits,** if soil and weather are suitable (*see p.261*).

■ **Plant rhubarb** (*see p.273*).

■ **Plant shallot sets** (*see p.250*).

ROUTINE CARE
■ **Cover the compost pile** or bin with old carpet or plastic sheeting to protect it over winter.

PRUNING AND TRAINING
■ **Cut back blackcurrants** on planting (*see p.261*); prune established blackcurrants and redcurrants (*see p.268*).

■ **Winter-prune fruit trees,** such as apples and pears (*see pp.262–265*).

■ **Cut back blackberry** and hybrid berry canes after planting (*see p.271*). Thin blueberries, if needed (*see p.269*).

HARVESTING
■ **Pick winter vegetables,** such as:
Beet tops (*see p.251*)
Chicory and endive (*see p.255*)
Leeks (*see p.251*)
Parsnips (*see p.251*)
Red cabbage (*see p.249*)
Salad leaves (*see p.255*)
Spinach beet and Swiss chard (*see p.255*)
Winter cabbages (*see p.249*)
Winter kale (*see p.248*)
Winter lettuce (*see p.255*)
Winter turnips (*see p.249*).

PLANNING FOR NEXT YEAR

■ **While away the long evenings** of winter by ordering seed catalogs and making up a list of crops to purchase for sowing in the new year.

■ **Plan the vegetable plot** for next year, and consider how much room each crop will need and how long it will occupy the soil, in order to work out how many seeds to buy.

■ **If you have gathered** your own seeds, plan to sow them a little more thickly than purchased seeds.

LARGE SEEDS

FLAT SEEDS

FINE SEEDS

LATE WINTER

LAWNS	BOUNDARIES AND DIVISIONS	BEDS AND BORDERS

SOWING AND PLANTING

- **Prepare the soil and site** (*see p.78*) before in early spring laying sod or planting divided herbs for a nongrass lawn, or, in warm climates, for plantings of plugs or sprigs.

ROUTINE CARE

- **Clean and service lawnmowers** and other equipment.

DOGS IN THE GARDEN

- **Avoid yellow patches** developing on the lawn where a dog urinates by throwing a bucket of water over the spot immediately afterward, if possible.

- **Protect tree trunks** from the attentions of a dog by surrounding the base with a prickly collar of straw.

ESSENTIAL TASKS

- **Finish pruning established** vines and wall shrubs that are grown for foliage (*see pp.112–113*).

ENGLISH IVY (*HEDERA HELIX* 'GOLDHEART')

- **Winter-prune** flowering quince (*p.113*).

PLANTING

- **Plant hedges** (*see p.120*).

PRUNING AND TRAINING

- **Prune established climbers** and wall shrubs that flower on the current season's shoots (*see pp.112–113*).

- **Thin overgrown Group 1 clematis;** prune Groups 2 and 3 clematis (*see p.114*).

- **Renovate deciduous climbers** (*p.115*).

- **Check supports** and renew them if necessary (*see p.109 and p.115*).

- **Prune flowering hedges,** such as *Cotoneaster* and hawthorn (*see chart, p.117, and p.121*).

ESSENTIAL TASKS

- **Finish planting** containerized and container-grown shrubs (*see p.150*). Give shrubs an initial pruning after planting (*see p.151*) and stake if needed (*see p.150*).

ROUTINE CARE

- **Cut back hardy grasses** and bamboos that have been left over winter to the ground, before they start into growth.

- **On light, sandy soils,** spread a thick 3–5in (8–13cm) layer of well-rotted organic material; leave until early spring to dig in.

PRUNING AND TRAINING

- **Prune deciduous shrubs** for initial shape (*see p.157*) and for restoration (*p.159*).

- **Prune established deciduous** shrubs that flower on new shoots (*see p.158*).

- **Prune bush roses,** including hybrid teas, floribundas, and miniature, repeat-flowering roses, and China, Bourbon, and Portland old roses (*see p.161*).

RAISING YOUR OWN PLANTS

- **Sow seed indoors** of tender and half-hardy annuals and of perennials (*see p.162*).

WINTER ACONITE (*ERANTHIS HYEMALIS*)

ORNAMENTAL TREES

ESSENTIAL TASKS
- **Finish planting balled-and-burlapped** trees of deciduous species (*see p.195*).

- **Prevent snow damage** to conifer branches by brushing it off immediately or tying the plant with twine or panty hose to preserve its shape.

PLANTING
- **Prepare the soil** (*see p.192 and pp.142–143*) for early spring plantings of container-grown or hardy deciduous bare-root trees.

- **Plant bare-root trees** (*see p.194*) of hardy deciduous species, except in cold regions, when conditions are good. When filling in the planting hole, make sure there are no air pockets in between the roots by gently shaking the stem up and down.

PRUNING AND TRAINING
- **Prune deciduous trees** that flower in late summer – except cherries, plums, peaches, and apricots (*Prunus*) – if necessary (*see p.196*).

- **Coppice and pollard** trees (*see p.197*).

THE EDIBLE GARDEN

ESSENTIAL TASKS
- **Sprout early seed potatoes** to prepare them for planting (*see p.252*).

- **Finish planting bush fruits** (*see p.261*), if soil condition and weather are favorable.

- **Plant peach trees** (*see p.260*).

- **Finish winter-pruning fruit trees** (*see pp.262–265*), such as pears and apples.

- **Force rhubarb into growth** for an earlier spring crop (*see p.273*).

SOWING VEGETABLE SEED

SOWING AND PLANTING
- **Sow seed of tender vegetables** in containers indoors (*see p.244*), such as: Eggplant, chilies, and peppers (*see p.256*) Greenhouse tomatoes (*see p.257*).

- **Sow hardy vegetable seed outdoors** (*see p.242*), under cloches in cold areas, such as: Leeks (*see p.251*).

- **Plant fruit trees** and cane fruits (*see pp.260–261*), except pears and plums.

- **Plant rhubarb** (*see p.273*).

ROUTINE CARE
- **Warm the soil** in cooler regions by placing cloches (*see p.240*) or row cover over it, to prepare it for sowing.

PRUNING AND TRAINING
- **Cut back blackcurrants** on planting (*see p.261*).

- **Prune redcurrants** and gooseberries (*see p.261 and p.268*).

- **Cut down autumn-fruiting** raspberry canes (*see p.270*).

HARVESTING
- **Pick winter vegetables,** such as:
Beet tops (*see p.251*)
Broccoli (*see p.248*)
Leeks (*see p.251*)
Parsnips (*see p.251*)
Spinach beet and Swiss chard (*see p.255*)
Sprouting broccoli (*see p.248*)
Winter cabbages (*see p.249*)
Winter kale (*see p.248*)
Winter lettuce (*see p.255*).

ANYTIME

| KEEPING THE GARDEN HEALTHY | LAWNS | BOUNDARIES AND DIVISIONS |

- **Keep plants well watered** so they do not suffer a check in growth. Use discretion – a thorough soaking for plants that need it (herbaceous, newly planted, and container-grown plants) is more effective than a light spray over the entire garden (*see p.280*).

- **Fertilize appropriately** to keep plants healthy and resistant to pests and diseases.

- **Watch for signs of pests or disease** in the garden. If you take prompt action (*see pp.294–311*), the problem will be easier to control. Bear in mind that not all insects are pests (*see box, below*).

GARDEN SNAIL

- **Weed cultivated areas regularly** to avoid weeds competing with garden plants for moisture and nutrients (*see pp.288–293*). Cover a fallow area of soil with a mulch (*see pp.152–153*) or sow it with a green manure (*see p.239 and p.371*) so the area does not become a seedbed for weeds that can spread to other parts of the garden.

FRIENDLY INSECTS

- **Why are they useful?** Some insects in the garden prey on other insects that attack garden plants; they also help pollinate the plants and so increase the amount of flowers and fruits.

- **What are they?** Friendly insects include bees, hoverflies, lacewings, and ladybugs, both larvae and adults.

- **How can I encourage them?** Leave some areas of wood litter for the insects to shelter in. Avoid using pesticides, or choose one that is environmentally friendly and apply it at dusk, when the beneficial insects are less active.

SOWING AND PLANTING

- **Plan a lawn,** considering the site, shape, and suitable type of grass (*see pp.76–77*). If necessary, install a drain (*see p.79*).

ROUTINE CARE

- **Level out humps** and hollows in grass lawns (*see p.87*), except in times of severe cold or drought.

PLANTING

- **Plant container-grown** climbing roses against walls, fences, or trees (*see p.110*), except in periods of severe cold or drought.

- **Prevent bamboo from spreading** by making an underground barrier (*see p.118*).

- **Plant climbers** to clothe an arch (*see p.99*) or pergola.

PRUNING AND TRAINING

- **Prune out any dead,** diseased, or damaged wood, and reverted shoots on variegated plants (*see p.112*), whenever necessary.

- **Prune hedges** grown for their fruits and berries immediately after the display has finished (*see p.117 and p.119*).

PRESERVING WOOD

- **What good does this do?** Applying preservative to wood every 3–4 years prolongs its life; if not treated, most softwoods rot in a few years, especially where they are in contact with the soil.

- **When should it be done?** Any time of year, but autumn and winter are good times because structures such as fencing, trellises, arches, and pergolas are easier to reach after plants die down for the winter.

- **Should the wood be prepared?** Before applying preservative, make sure the wood is free of loose dirt and debris and that it is thoroughly dry.

PAINTING A TRELLIS
WITH PRESERVATIVE

BEDS AND BORDERS

PLANTING

▪ **Mark out a new border** (*see p.145*), and prepare the soil well (*see pp.142–145*) before planting it. If needed, the border could be planted with container-grown plants soon after, but many plants are best planted in certain seasons (*see pp.369–405*).

▪ **Plant container-grown** shrubs (*see p.150*) and roses (*see p.151*), except in drought, severely cold, or waterlogged conditions. Buy good, healthy plants (*see p.147*) for the best results. Give the plants an initial pruning after planting (*see p.151*), if necessary, and stake if necessary (*see p.150*).

ROUTINE CARE

▪ **Keep weeds under control** by clearing soil of them before planting (*see pp.144–145*), and regularly weeding established beds and borders (*see p.152*).

▪ **Get rid of rose suckers** as soon as they appear (*see p.160*).

REMOVING A ROSE SUCKER

PRUNING AND TRAINING

▪ **Remove all-green** shoots from variegated plants as soon as they appear (*see p.157*).

CONTAINERS AND RAISED BEDS

PLANTING

▪ **Plant raised bed walls** with alpine plants (*see p.183*), except in times of drought or severe cold and wet.

ROUTINE CARE

▪ **Prepare wooden containers** by treating them with preservative (*see p.169*).

WATERING CONTAINERS

▪ **In hot weather,** the soil mix in containers dries out and plants wilt very quickly; water twice daily if necessary, in the morning and evening.

▪ **In cold weather,** keep containers on the dry side, but they may still need watering in mild spells.

▪ **Water thoroughly,** soaking the soil mix until water runs out of the base of the container.

ORNAMENTAL TREES

PLANTING

▪ **Plant container-grown** trees (*see p.194*), except in drought, severely cold, or waterlogged conditions.

ROUTINE CARE

▪ **Mulch if needed** with organic material such as bark chips, whenever the soil is moist.

▪ **Keep weeds under control** around trees (*see p.197*) so they do not compete with the tree roots for nutrients and moisture.

ANYTIME

HERBS	THE EDIBLE GARDEN	GENERAL MAINTENANCE

PLANTING

- **Plant container-grown** perennial or shrubby herbs in beds, pots, or hanging baskets (*see pp.228–231*), except in drought, frosty, or waterlogged conditions.

ROSEMARY

- **Make a gravel garden** in which to plant herbs (*see p.229*) or build raised beds.

PLANTING

- **Lime the soil** if necessary (*see p.238*) at least one month before planting any vegetables.

- **Prepare the soil** at least two months before planting any fruit (*see p.260*).

- **Plant container-grown fruit** trees (*see p.260*), except when the ground is frozen, dry, or waterlogged.

ROUTINE CARE

- **Remove weeds** regularly to stop competition with the crops (*see pp.288–293*).

STRUCTURES

- **Re-treat wooden sheds** and cold frames with preservative, and make any repairs as necessary.

- **Keep greenhouse glass clean** so that plants within receive the maximum light.

RUST-FREE TOOLS

- **Garden tools** will function better and last longer if regularly cleaned and oiled (*see p.279*).

- **Clean small tools** by rubbing them with an oily cloth or with a handful of oily sand.

- **Clean large tools** by plunging them several times into a bucket of oily sand.

PLUNGING A
FORK INTO
OILED SAND

GLOSSARY

Acidic (of soil) With a pH value of less than 7. See also *alkaline* and *neutral*.

Alkaline (of soil) With a pH value greater than 7. See also *acidic* and *neutral*.

Annual Plant that grows, flowers, sets seed, and dies in a single growing season.

Biennial Plant that produces leafy growth in the first year after germination then flowers, sets seed, and dies in the second. See also *annual* and *perennial*.

Blind Of a shoot that fails to produce a flower.

Bolt To produce flowers and set seed prematurely.

Brassica Member of the cabbage *family*.

Broadcast To scatter fertilizer or seed over the ground rather than in *drills*.

Cloche Small, generally portable structure made of clear plastic, glass, or horticultural row cover on a supporting framework. Used to warm the soil and/or protect crops in open ground.

Closed case (also called propagator) Structure that provides a protected environment for raising seeds and rooting cuttings.

Cold frame Boxlike structure made from brick, metal, wood, or plastic, with a hinged or removable glass or clear plastic lid. Used to protect seeds, seedlings, and other plants from excessive cold.

Compost *Organic* material formed by the decomposition of plants or other organic matter. Used as a soil improver or mulch.

Cultivar (abbr. cv.) Variant of a *species* selected or artificially bred for a special characteristic, such as its flower or foliage form or color (for example *Helianthus atrorubens* 'Monarch').

Deadhead To remove faded flowers or flowerheads to prevent self-seeding.

Division Method of increasing plants by dividing them into pieces, each with its own roots and growing point.

Dormancy Pause in active plant growth, usually in winter.

Drill Straight furrow in soil used for sowing seeds or transplanting seedlings.

Family Group of several *genera* that share some common characteristics. For example, *Bellis* and *Helianthus* both belong to the daisy family, Asteraceae.

Forma (abbr. f.), **Subspecies** (abbr. ssp. or subsp.), **Varietas** (abbr. var.) Naturally occurring variants of a *species*. For example, *Helianthus debilis* subsp. *cucumerifolius* is a shorter variant of the species *Helianthus debilis*, and also has larger flowerheads.

Frost pocket Area of ground, often a hollow or beside a solid structure, in which cold air accumulates and where frosts may be severe and/or prolonged.

Genus (pl. genera) Group of related plant *species* linked by several common characteristics (for example *Helianthus*); the rank of plant classification between species and *family*.

Graft To join artificially one plant part to another. See also *rootstock* and *scion*.

Harden off Gradually to acclimatize plants that have been raised in a protected environment to outdoor growing conditions.

Hardy Of a plant that is able to withstand a wide range of climatic conditions, including cold, year-round. See also *tender*.

Herbaceous Nonwoody plant with topgrowth that dies back at the end of the growing season.

Hill up To draw up soil around the base of a plant to encourage its stems to produce roots, to blanch the stems, or to reduce wind rock.

Humus Chemically complex, gel-like residue of decayed *organic* matter in soil.

Hybrid Offspring of two genetically distinct plant parents. Indicated by the symbol "×" in the Latin name (for example, *Helianthus × multiflorus*).

Mulch Material applied to the soil surface to suppress weeds, conserve moisture, or insulate roots. Can also be used to add *organic* matter to the soil.

Neutral (of soil) With a pH of 7; neither *acidic* nor *alkaline*.

Nursery bed Soil bed for germinating seeds or growing on young plants until transferred to their permanent site.

Organic (1) Of carbon-based matter of natural plant or animal origin. (2) Of cultivation without the use of synthetic or nonorganic materials.

Perennial Plant that lives for three or more seasons. Is usually applied to herbaceous plants, even though the term in fact also includes woody perennials (shrubs and trees).

pH Measure of acidity or alkalinity on a scale of 1–14. See also *acidic*, *alkaline*, and *neutral*.

Pinch out To remove the growing tip on a plant to stimulate growth of sideshoots lower down the stem, or the formation of flowerbuds.

Prick out To transfer young seedlings from their germination site into a pot or *nursery bed*.

Rootstock (1) Root system of a plant. (2) Plant that provides the root system for a *grafted* plant.

Sheet mulch Sheet of artificial material, for example landscape fabric or plastic, used as a *mulch*.

Soil mix (also called potting medium, potting mix) Mix of soil, sand, peat substitute (or peat), and nutrients in varying proportions. Used for growing container-grown plants. Soilless mixes are usually made of peat (or substitute) and nutrients; they contain no soil.

Species Group of plants that breed naturally to produce offspring with similar characteristics (for example, *Helianthus debilis*); the rank of plant classification between *genus* and *forma*, *subspecies*, and *varietas*.

Subsoil Layer of soil that is less fertile and of poorer texture and structure than the *topsoil* above it.

Subspecies (abbr. ssp. or subsp.) See *forma*.

Sucker Shoot arising from a plant's roots or underground stem, or from the *rootstock* of a *grafted* plant.

Systemic Of a pesticide or fungicide that is absorbed throughout a plant when put on its foliage or planting site.

Tender Of a plant that is vulnerable to frost and cold damage. See also *hardy*.

Topdress To apply *compost*, decorative dressing (for example, sand or pebbles) fertilizer, or fresh soil, to the soil surface around a plant or on a lawn.

Topsoil Topmost, usually most fertile, layer of soil. See also *subsoil*.

Varietas (abbr. var.) See *forma*.

INDEX

ACKNOWLEDGMENTS

Publisher's Acknowledgments
Dorling Kindersley would like to thank all staff at the RHS, in particular Susanne Mitchell, Barbara Haynes, and Karen Wilson at Vincent Square, and staff at the RHS Garden Wisley. Grateful thanks also to the following people for their invaluable contributions to this book: Lee Griffiths and Mary-Clare Jerram for their support and faith in the book production team. Jane Simmonds, Lin Hawthorne, and Pamela Brown for developing the original synopsis; Louise Abbott, Lynn Bresler, Pamela Brown, Alison Copland, Annelise Evans, and Lesley Riley for expert and patient editorial help; Frances Hutchison and Ray Rogers for commenting on the picture selection; Louise Abbott, Murdo Culver, Stephen Josland, and Wesley Richards for organizing and helping with new photography; Murdo Culver, Ursula Dawson, Clive Hayball, Wesley Richards, and Alison Shackleton for additional design assistance; Richard Dabb for help with sourcing pictures from the Dorling Kindersley picture library; Andrea Hill for additional DTP assistance; Barry Prescott for help with administration. David Joyce (contributor, Part One) and the publisher wish to thank Andrew Lawson for the material that provided the basis for the garden illustrated and described on pages 52–53.

Special thanks to Connie M. Robinson for editorial help.

Commissioned Photography
Peter Anderson

Illustrations
Gill Tomblin, pages 50, 51, 52; Karen Gavin, lighting illustrations p. 71

Agency Picture Credits
The publisher would like to thank the following for their kind permission to reproduce their photographs:

(Key: a=above; c=center; b=below; l=left; r=right; t=top)
Heather Angel: 302br; **A-z Botanical Collection:** 301bcr; **Jonathan Buckley:** 31cr; **Linda Burgess:** 43br; **Neil Campbell-sharp:** 232br; **Eric Crichton Photos:** 74c, 89tr, 95bl, 184bc, 224bl; **Emap Active:** 35tr, 35bc, 70cl; **Derek Fell:** 26tl; **Garden Picture Library:** Ann Kelley 183cl; Brian Carter 36tr, 75cra, 180bl; Brigitte Thomas 74bc; Chris Burrows 87bcr; Clay Perry 8-9; Clive Nichols 312-313; Eric Crichton 19bl, 24tc; Gary Rogers 28br, 36tc, 180c; Gil Hanly 122bl; Howard Rice 82bl, 92br, 98c, 139bcl, 280crb; Jacqui Hurst 81bl; Jane Legate 81clb; Janet Sorrell 54-55; Jerry Pavia 29tl; John Baker 24bc, 28bc; John Glover 1c, 88bc, 228c, 274bl; John Miller 35tc; JS Sira 11tr, 75bl, 362br; Juliette Wade 34tc, 75tc, 174bl, 364-365; Lamontagne 37bc; Marie O'Hara 32bl; Marijke Heuff 30bc; Mayer/Le Scanff 106tr; Mel Watson 37tr; Michael Howes 17b; Rex Butcher 29bl; Ron Sutherland 12tr, 22bl, 24br, 33bc, 65br; Rowan Isaac 25bc; Stephen Jury 189bc; Steven Wooster 23b, 31bc, 36bl, 172cr; Tommy Candler 30bl; **The Garden Magazine:** Tim Sandell 299bcl, 310bl, 311br; **John Glover:** 18-19, 21br, 26bc, 27br, 32tr, 32bc, 33tr, 34tr, 36bc, 37tl, 37tc, 48bc, 76br, 88bl, 97c, 100bl, 275c; Bosvigo 968 30tc; **Greenworld Pictures Inc.:** Mick Hales 18bl; **Jerry Harpur:** 11tl, 11bc, 12bl, 14cl, 14c, 15bl, 19br, 21bc, 24tr, 26tc, 31bl, 34bl, 35bl, 41br, 44c, 48crb, 61br, 96br, 100bc, 184cr; Design: Edwina Von Gal 41bl; Designer: Christopher Masson 13tr; Designer: Simon Fraser 46c; Designer: Wesley & Susan Dixon 10bl, 75cr; Diana Ross, London 2, 48tr; Neil Diboll, Wisconsin 42bc; P. Hickman, Thames Ditton 76bl; The Priory, Hatfield Peverel, Essex 40tc; **Holt Studios International:** Nigel Cattlin 295bl, 296clb, 296bl, 296bcr, 297bcl, 297bcr, 297bcrr, 299br, 299bcl, 300br, 302bcl, 304bl, 304bcl, 304bcr, 305bl, 305br, 306bl, 307c, 308bl, 308bcl, 308bcr, 310bcr; **Anne Hyde:** 13br, 26tr, 31tl, 39tl, 39bl, 46bl; **The Interior Archive:** Herbert YPMA 28tr; **Andrew Lawson:** 11bc, 20bl, 20-21, 25tc, 25tr, 25br, 27tr, 29tc, 31tc, 31tr, 41tl, 41bc, 43tr, 49tc, 49c, 50tr, 50br, 51tr, 52tr, 52cla, 52clb, 52bl, 52br, 53tl, 53cl, 53bl, 76clb, 181bc, 195c; Designer: Lynden Miller 29cra; Designer: Penelope Hobhouse 37br, 47cl; Designer: Ryl Nowell, Wilderness Farm 27bl; Designer: Sir Miles Warren 30tr; York Gate, Leeds 26bl; **Marianne Majerus:** 19tr, 30tl; Design: Lesley Rosser 32br; Designer: Jon Baillie 10bl; **Clive Nichols:** 27tl, 36br, 38tr, 38br, 63bc, 73cr; Andrew & Karla Newell 33tl, 72cr; Anthony Noel 2; Bassibones Farm, Bucks 41tc, 75br; Chenies Manor, Bucks 38bl, 42tr; Clive & Jane Nichols 13bl, 16-17; Designer: Anthony Noel 27bc, 43bc; Designer: Elisabeth Woodhouse 41tr; Designer: Jill Billington 43tl, 47bc; Designer: Keeyla Meadows 11bl; Designer: Sarah Hammond 44bl; Designer: Vic Shanley 24bl; Garden & Security lighting 71cr; Hilary Macpherson 74br; Lambeth Horticultural Society 33bl; Little Coopers, Hampshire 33br; Parnham House, Dorset 40bc; Paula Rainey Crofts 34br; The Anchorage, Kent 40br; The Priory, Kemerton, Worcs 22c; White Windows, Hampshire 81cr; **Oxford Scientific Films:** Colin Milkins 292cl; **RHS Wisley:** 307crb; A.J. Halstead 307br; J. Maynard 301abc; K.M. Harris 306bcl; P. Becker 307cr, 310bcl; **Derek St Romaine:** 34bc, 37bl; **Scotts of Stow:** 274bc, 276ac; **J S Sira:** 180br; **Elizabeth Whiting & Associates:** 16bl, 17tl, 28tc, 28bl, 29bc, 29br, 30br, 31br, 35tl; **Jo Whitworth:** 176br; **Steve Wooster:** 25tl, 26br, 27tc, 32tc, 33tc, 38bc, 40tr, 90bl, 103tr, 103cr, 186bc, 187tc, 189tr, 190c; Designer: Anthony Paul 10c; Designer: Piet Oudolf 12c; Hannah Deschar Gallery 13c.

Jacket: Jerry Harpur: back acr.

Hardiness zones

This map, derived from the map prepared by the United States Department of Agriculture, is based on average annual minimum temperatures recorded throughout North America from 1974 to 1986. The larger, more detailed map is available from the USDA and many cooperative county extension services.

Hardiness zones ranges are given for all plants in Part 3 of this book, except tender plants (those plants generally unable to survive temperatures below 41°F/5°C) and annuals (including some perennials commonly grown as annuals). Many subtropical plants that tolerate temperatures slightly below freezing are indicated as being hardy in Zones 10–11.

Generally speaking, the term "hardiness" refers to the ability of a plant to withstand an average minimum temperature. However, although useful as an indicator of a plant's dependability in a given area, a hardiness zone range is not the only indicator of the possible success of a plant. Many factors, including soil type and fertility, soil moisture and drainage, humidity, and exposure to sun and wind, determine a plant's growth and success or failure in its environment.

All hardiness zone ranges presented in this book are intended as approximate guides and should not be considered definitive.

RANGE OF AVERAGE ANNUAL MINIMUM TEMPERATURE

°F	ZONES	°C
BELOW -50°	1	BELOW -46°
-50° TO -40°	2	-46° TO -40°
-40° TO -30°	3	-40° TO -34°
-30° TO -20°	4	-34° TO -29°
-20° TO -10°	5	-29° TO -23°
-10° TO 0°	6	-23° TO -18°
0° TO 10°	7	-18° TO -12°
10° TO 20°	8	-12° TO -7°
20° TO 30°	9	-7° TO -1°
30° TO 40°	10	-1° TO 4°
ABOVE 40°	11	ABOVE 4°

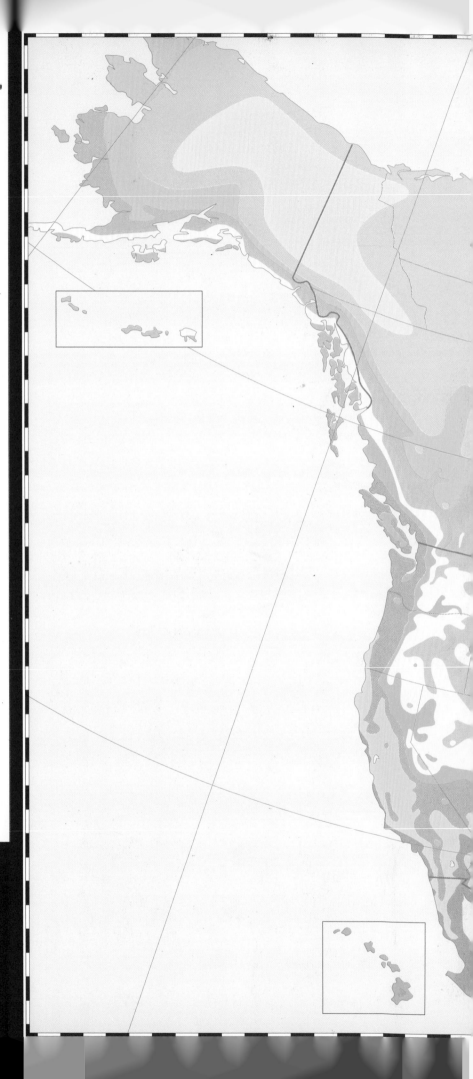